THE WORLD OF WORK

PRENTICE-HALL SOCIOLOGY SERIES
Herbert Blumer, Editor

THE World OF Work

Industrial Society and Human Relations

ROBERT DUBIN

Englewood Cliffs, N. J.
PRENTICE-HALL, INC.

LIBRARY OF CONGRESS
CATALOG CARD NUMBER: 58–9615

Second printing, March, 1959

PRINTED IN THE UNITED STATES OF AMERICA
96825

The following organizations have graciously consented to the reproduction of the illustrations appearing on the pages listed.

Amalgamated Clothing Workers of America: 17, 319; Creole Petroleum Corporation: 6, 8, 9, 19, 81, 202, 213; Crompton & Knowles Corporation: 174; Ford Motor Company: 10. 11, 15, 19, 27, 41, 45, 77, 106, 107, 127, 175, 182, 185, 186, 193, 194, 200, 212, 225, 292. 346, 379, 394; Gilbert Davis: 12, 20, 37, 94, 101, 183, 215, 221, 229, 237, 242, 257, 264; Hewlett-Packard Company: 15, 22, 106, 293, 301, 307; International Association of Machinists, AFL-CIO: 318; Pacific Telephone and Telegraph Company (D. W. Bond, photographer): 18, 20, 23, 34, 37, 61, 68, 100, 105, 110, 178, 204, 241, 274, 278, 283, 289, 292, 329, 374, 378; Santa Fe Railway: 173; Sequoia Wire Company: 13; Standard Oil Company of New Jersey: 7, 9, 21, 46, 57, 71, 147, 153, 161, 170, 191, 198, 215, 244, 250, 255, 283, 328, 335, 341, 351, 364, 385; United Automobile Workers Union: 16, 17,23, 314:Varian Associates:15,19,31,102,184, 254, 336, 390.

Dedicated with deepest affection
to Dr. Elisabeth Ruch Dubin
whose intellectual companionship
is exceeded only by her wifely devotion

PREFACE

This book concerns American industry and commerce. It is based on the conviction that knowledge comprises facts, and ideas about how the facts relate to one another. The facts we call empirical knowledge; the ideas we call theoretical knowledge. Knowledge is not complete without both. I have given prominence to ideas about work in our society because I think in the analysis of this important aspect of social behavior we have been singularly naive about the theory we have used. At the same time, I have sought diligently all the facts I could accumulate from studies and observations of working behavior, to maximize the practical knowledge about which the theory makes sense.

This entire volume is devoted to what people do while they are working, and the reasons for their behavior. The world of work is given more extensive coverage, and intensive analysis, than in any comparable volume. I have purposely minimized the treatment of union-management relations in this book in order to be able to include the scope and depth of materials covered. This does not mean I consider union and company relations unimportant. The opposite is true. In my opinion, industrial relations are so crucial for the economy that their analysis has been reserved for a companion volume, Robert Dubin, *Working Union-Management Relations* (Englewood Cliffs, N. J.: Prentice-Hall, Inc., 1958). The two volumes together analyze the major facets of American industrial society. They share a common theoretical framework, and can be read in sequence or independently.

A supplementary bibliography is included at the end of the volume. It should prove useful, in addition to the chapter citations, as a guide to the extensive literature in this field.

This book should prove valuable as an attempt to make systematic sense out of work in our industrial world. The balance of fact and theory is useful to those interested in understanding this complex world for the knowledge it brings, and the value of its future application.

To men and women doing the work of our society—management and workers, specialists and line executives, union officials and government functionaries dealing with industry and commerce—this book should prove helpful for its organizing ideas about working behavior. Most of you have vast practical knowledge. I hope this volume helps make sense of the fund of facts you have, by organizing your information through meaningful ideas, mapping it into understandable patterns.

To my professional colleagues who are also devoting lifetimes to studying people at work, I offer this book as a challenge. There are ideas contained herein for which our factual knowledge is incomplete; there are some facts not included because they do not make sense in any theoretical scheme. This book, I hope, will prove useful in stimulating future research so that subsequent editions may be vastly improved by the feedback of your studies and theoretical contributions. My obvious present debt to you is indicated in the citation of your works.

It is a great satisfaction to acknowledge contributions people and organizations have made to this volume. Many business executives, union leaders, workers, and students of work have shared their knowledge unstintingly to answer and illuminate queries about working in the contemporary United States. Professor Theodore Caplow, University of Minnesota, has generously read the majority of chapters. Professor William Kornhauser, University of California, also read several chapters and improved their content by his comments. Professor Herbert Blumer, University of California, has read the entire manuscript, bringing to bear on it his superior critical evaluations, tempered by his own considerable knowledge of American industry.

A year as Fellow at the Center for Advanced Study in the Behavioral Sciences permanently indebted me to the Ford Foundation, its sponsor, and to Director Ralph Tyler and his staff, who "facilitated" its operations. The bliss of uninterrupted work with only self-chosen breaks can never be duplicated in any other kind of environment. Most important, however, was the full measure of devotion to intellectual exchange by the Center's Fellows. A number of them cheerfully accepted the task of reading chapters of this book in their areas of professional interest. It owes much to their criticism and suggestions, so thank you, Professor Kingsley Davis, University of California; Professor Harold Guetzkow, Northwestern University; Dr. A. H. Halsey, University of Birmingham, England; and Professor John Thibaut, University of North Carolina—all Center colleagues, who especially made the years 1956–57 memorable.

Others, of course, have made writing this book easier. Dean Austin Grimshaw, School of Business Administration, University of Washington, made excellent secretarial services available during two summers' teaching there. Mrs. Eugene W. Dils typed the entire manuscript, giving it professional editorial attention in the process. Orville A. Collver and Peter Johnson did detailed work as assistants, and Milton Bregman executed the charts with imagination. Samuel L. Johnson prepared the index.

A sensitive and knowledgeable editing of the manuscript was important in improving readability; a task done with distinction by David Vanderburgh of Prentice-Hall, Inc. His colleague, W. W. Worcester, designed an elegant format and expedited production.

Acknowledgement is made of the courtesy of the following publishers and journal in granting permission to reprint statistical materials from their copyrighted works: Harper & Brothers, King's Crown Press of Columbia University Press, *Manchester Guardian,* Social Science Research Council, Twentieth Century Fund, and John Wiley and Sons.

A number of companies, unions, and individuals have generously made photographs available. Photograph credits are listed on the copyright page.

It is difficult to sum up two decades of indebtedness to my wife, together with her actual work on the manuscript as critical reader and commentator. The dedication of this book recognizes, but scarcely rewards her many contributions.

It has been fun writing this book, and I have learned a great deal while doing it. I hope it is just as informative and as much fun to read.

ROBERT DUBIN

CONTENTS

PART I WORK IN MODERN SOCIETY

PART II ORGANIZATION OF WORK

PART III WORKING POPULATION

PART IV GETTING WORK DONE

15. [illegible] (cont.)

16. Work Groups and Work, [illegible]

17. [illegible]

PART V. MANAGEMENT OF WORK ORGANIZATIONS

18. Communication [illegible] Work, [illegible]

19. [illegible]

20. [illegible]

21. [illegible]

Part I

WORK IN MODERN SOCIETY

Chapter 1

WORLD OF WORK

The historic dream of mankind is of a utopia where human work is moderate or unnecessary. The real facts of life are that almost all adults work, everywhere in the world. Work is a central fact of our lives. This book is all about work in urban-industrial United States.

Industrial work is carried out in organizations. The business firms of commerce and industry are complex, permanent organizations whose operations display some characteristic features that are the consequence of organization. Continuous production of goods and services for mass markets requires organization to secure, and keep together, materials, machines, and men.

There are other factors leading to permanent work organizations. We need only mention some at this point. For many productive activities, considerable investment in plant, material, and equipment is necessary. The investment in capital equipment and materials often exceeds the resources of single individuals, but a corporate group is capable of raising money to finance these expenditures.

Another factor requiring continuous organization of work activities is the division of labor into specialized tasks and functions. In order that the janitor, lathe operator, accountant, salesman, purchasing agent, production control manager, engineer, and file clerk can all perform their several duties in unison, it is necessary for the tasks to be organized systematically with respect to each other. This can best be done through formal organization—tying the individual jobs together and coordinating their activities.

Continuity of output is a consequence of the fulfillment of all specialized tasks involved in production at the required time, and in the required quantities. This means that work activities must be at least partially independent of the individual workers involved. Were this not so, the whole productive enterprise might grind to a temporary halt with the absence of one or several persons from their work stations. In order, therefore, to achieve continuity of output, it is necessary to organize the total productive activity so that rapid substitution can be made of one worker by another when this is necessitated by illness, quitting or dismissal. An organization is capable of handling problems of staffing. A collection of independent craftsmen working together might be very much less efficient in handling such problems, particularly those of staff turnover.

Work *organizations* exist because an organizing system is necessary to meet the conditions of modern work. Indeed, one of the great social inventions of the industrial revolution was the modern business organization. We do not often think of inventiveness being displayed in the area of social arrangements. It is notably true that major inventions have, indeed, been made in the social structuring of work relationships.

One of the themes of this book is the social inventiveness of man. New ways of working together and new systems of social relationships have been, and are still being, invented. These social inventions incorporated in business, productive, and service organizations of our society are just as important to output and efficiency as machines, materials, and industrial processes.

WORK IN INDUSTRY

We are concerned with behavior of people at work. It is clear, however, that work has a variety of meanings. Our first task is to indicate the special meaning assigned to work in this volume.

WORK

By work we mean continuous employment, in the production of goods and services, for remuneration. This definition has three elements: (A) that work is continuous; (B) that it results in production of goods and services; and (C) that the work is performed for pay. These three elements in the definition of work are necessary to differentiate work behavior from other kinds of human activities.

CONTINUITY OF WORK

It is necessary to limit attention to work that is continuous. This means that the work is carried out regularly over a period of time. The importance of emphasizing continuity of work lies in two basic facts.

The production of goods and services almost universally requires continuous effort. Without continuity of effort, goods or services produced are either trivial, or immaterial to the total output of a society.

In addition, emphasis on continuity of work has significance for the context of work, and for the life history of workers. When work is performed continuously, it tends to take place in a permanent organization. In our society we call this a business firm. We therefore deal exclusively with work as it takes place in some kind of business firm.

From the standpoint of the life history of the individual, the significant work he performs is done continuously by him. We describe a major segment of everyone's career by the kind of work performed. We point to a man's profession or occupation as an important characteristic of his total life history. We even discover that social standing is intimately associated with the continuous work that he performs in the society. We certainly become aware of the fact that a major share of waking hours is devoted to work performed on a continuous basis.

It should be clear, then, why it is that only work carried on continuously over a significant period of time will be considered as our central subject matter.

PRODUCTION OF GOODS AND SERVICES

Production of goods and services as part of our definition of work is important to differentiate it from other human efforts. There are many daily activities involving expenditures of human energy. Human energy is expended on recreational activities; personal care including eating, washing, and dressing; affectional relations as among people in families; and physical activities like walking, driving, and talking. In a physiological sense, an expenditure of energy is defined as work. In a sociological sense, only those expenditures of human energy producing goods or services are defined as work.

PAY

A third element in the definition of work is that the work is performed for pay. This special limitation imposed on the definition of work confines our attention to a modern exchange economy.

A very brief consideration of modern urban industrial life reveals that many human activities meet the first two criteria but do not meet the third, namely that activities are carried on for pay. The most general example is the housewife. Her housework is continuous (many believe much too continuous!) and results in producing goods like food, clothing, and household adornments, or services like cooking, cleaning, and child-rearing. The housewife does not get paid directly for these services. Indeed, it would clearly not fit the marriage institution for her services to be valued in money or paid for on a per-hour basis. The housewife falls outside the subject matter of our field. However, if the same services are performed by someone working for pay, then the activity falls within our definition of work. This distinction is neither artificial nor troublesome. We would study the housewife as a significant part of the family institution. We study the housemaid as a part of the market economy. Both may perform identical services, but the contexts in which the services are carried out are markedly different. The context is that of family functions on the one hand, and industrial or economic employment on the other.

In summary, then, our subject matter is work continuously performed, in the production of goods and services, for which the worker receives pay.

This book is about work in commerce and industry. It is believed that many of the conclusions reached also apply to other kinds of formal organizations, like government bureaus and voluntary associations. Some of the generalizations may also be relevant to work in independent professions, and among the self-employed.

MANAGEMENT

Management of business firms is a group process. Group thinking, collective responsibility, and shared decisions are central features of operating management.

Higher level managers get together regularly to coordinate departmental activities they direct. Top managers are constantly exposed to appraisal, criticism, and reward from management colleagues in these conferences.

Technical brains are often "plugged into" the organization through *ad hoc* conferences with operating people. Technical specialists learn about operating problems and apply their knowledge in suggesting appropriate solutions.

Even among management's staff specialists interaction is frequent. Informally, problems are discussed, advice sought, and approval expected in "bulling" with older, more mature colleagues.

Talking is an important behavior of management men (and the few women who rise to management ranks). They talk a lot to each other. This is above and beyond the interaction involved in innovating for subordinates, and directing, controlling, and coordinating their activities.

Meeting of top level department managers in a large corporation. Group thinking to coordinate diverse activities is a prominent feature of these meetings, held weekly, or more often.

Operating plans are worked out by technical specialists and operating department officials, at special conferences held only as required.

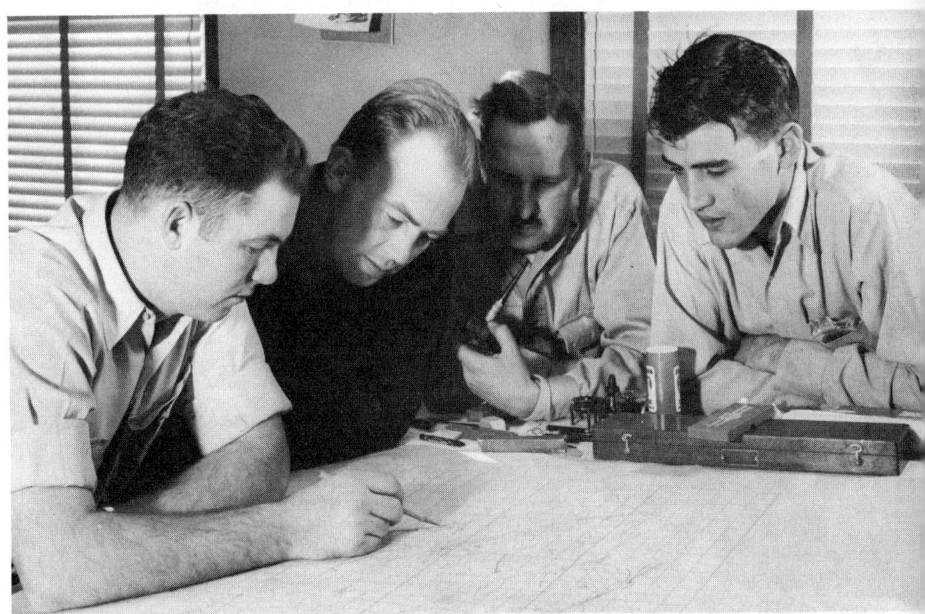

Geologists, important technical men in oilwell drilling, work out a special problem. Such conferences are not regularly scheduled, but occur frequently among management staff experts to share knowledge, and secure colleague approval for difficult decisions.

INDUSTRY AROUND US

Three large classes of industry are not housed in offices and factories. Transportation systems cover the surface of the earth with ribbons of highways and steel rails, and extended invisibly through water and air, to carry goods and people from here to there. Nature's raw materials are made ready for processing by logging, mining, and fishing (not forgetting agriculture, which lies outside the scope of this book). Buildings to house people and their work have to be constructed, as do the changes man makes in the face of nature to suit his own needs and conveniences.

Many men work out-of-doors at hard, sometimes dangerous, and usually weatherbeaten jobs. Wherever possible their work is lightened by using power-driven equipment—cranes, saws, concrete mixers. The brawny men of industry are largely to be found in outdoor work.

Transhipping steel from a railroad flat car to the hold of a ship. Most industrial products travel first as raw materials and then as finished goods.

Felling a Ponderosa pine tree with an electric chain saw powered by a diesel tractor. Mechanization has even taken to the woods.

Pouring reinforced concrete pilings. Big construction requires large equipment, sometimes dwarfing the men who work with it.

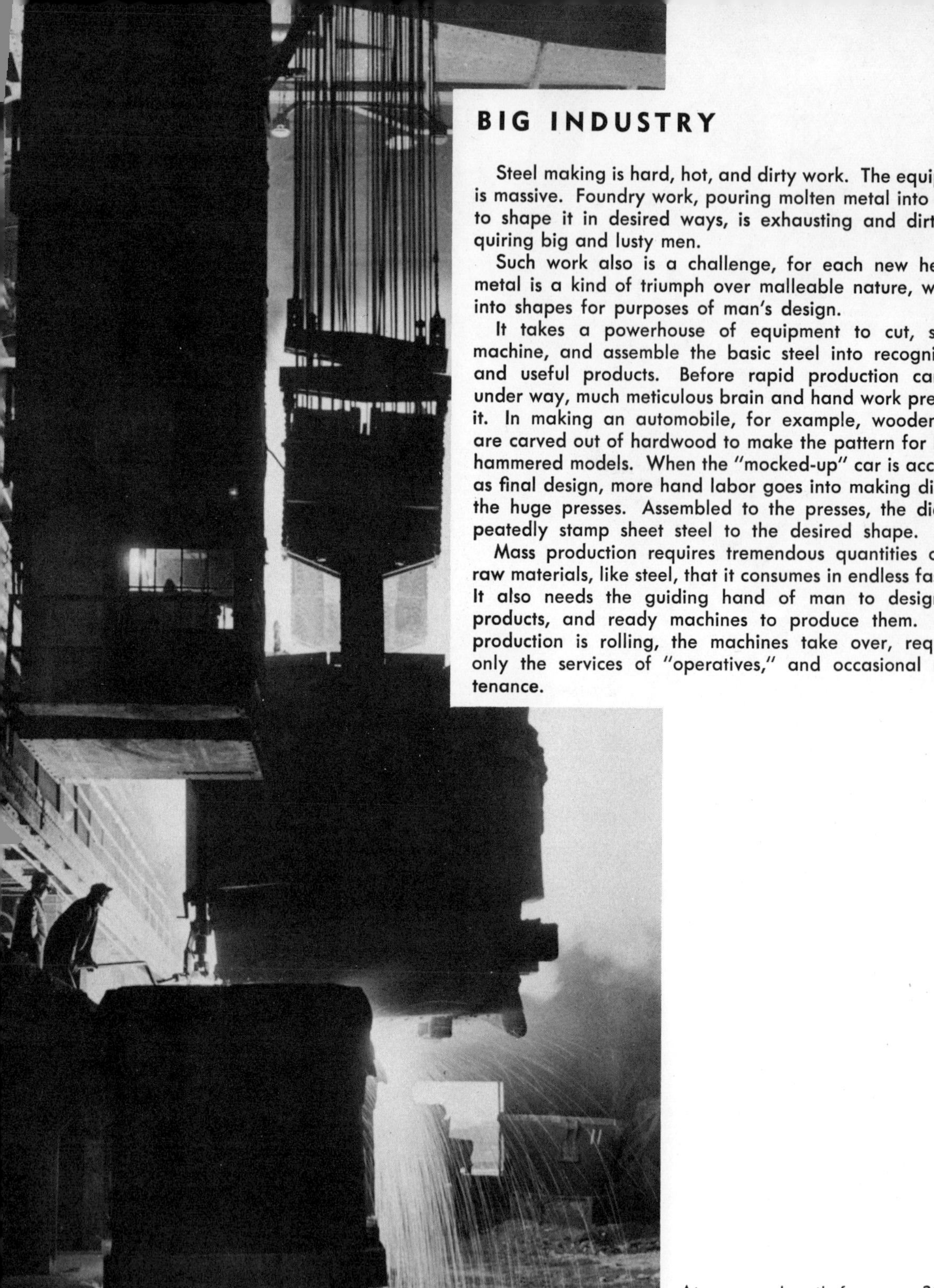

BIG INDUSTRY

Steel making is hard, hot, and dirty work. The equipment is massive. Foundry work, pouring molten metal into molds to shape it in desired ways, is exhausting and dirty, requiring big and lusty men.

Such work also is a challenge, for each new heat of metal is a kind of triumph over malleable nature, worked into shapes for purposes of man's design.

It takes a powerhouse of equipment to cut, shape, machine, and assemble the basic steel into recognizable and useful products. Before rapid production can get under way, much meticulous brain and hand work precedes it. In making an automobile, for example, wooden dies are carved out of hardwood to make the pattern for hand-hammered models. When the "mocked-up" car is accepted as final design, more hand labor goes into making dies for the huge presses. Assembled to the presses, the dies repeatedly stamp sheet steel to the desired shape.

Mass production requires tremendous quantities of the raw materials, like steel, that it consumes in endless fashion. It also needs the guiding hand of man to design the products, and ready machines to produce them. Once production is rolling, the machines take over, requiring only the services of "operatives," and occasional maintenance.

At an open-hearth furnace a 200-ton ladle hanging from an overhead crane pours hot steel into an ingot mold. A single operator controls the flow of molten steel from ladle to mold.

Hot metal, just tapped from the furnace, is poured, by hand, to make a casting of a tractor transmission housing.

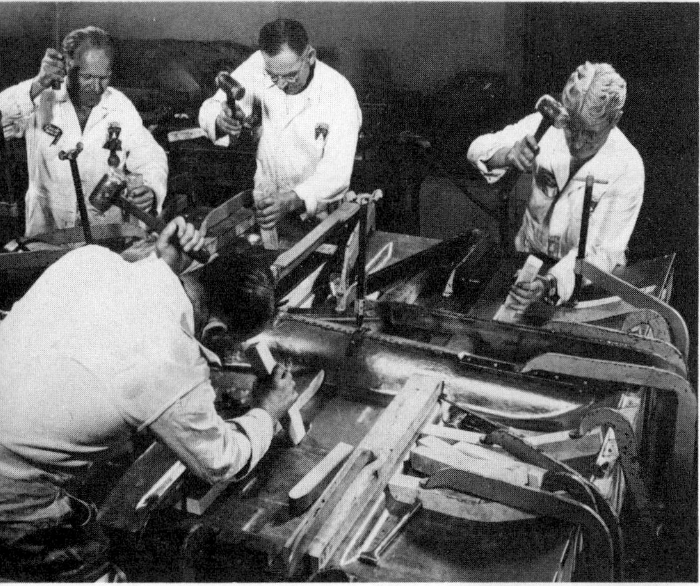

Skilled workers are hammering sheet metal into shape on a wooden form. In this way, the prototype automobile, for next year's production model, is manufactured by expert hands.

When the prototype automobile design is finally accepted for a production model, dies are made to stamp body parts. This huge press, with a single stroke, shapes a flat sheet of steel into a quarter panel for the rear half of the car's side.

MECHANIZATION AND FLOW

Two outstanding characteristics of industrial production are mechanization of tasks and continuous flow of work in process.

Mechanization replaces human energy with powered equipment. The latest triumph of the machine is automation. Through automation the brain of the human operator is replaced by an electronic brain that acts in its stead as a sensing and order-giving center.

Mechanization means more output. Materials flow rapidly from one work station to the next. So do subassemblies and partially finished products. Products flow through machines in continuous streams. They move on endless chains and moving belt lines between work stations, each worker doing his small task to the rhythm of the moving line.

Machines mean more output and more motion. Industrial production is dynamic and dramatic.

Setting printing type by hand was mechanized by the introduction of the Linotype machine. Operated like a typewriter, the machine sets and casts an entire line of type at one time. The operator still must possess brains and dexterity. Mechanization has multiplied speed.

Putting insulating coating on electrical wire. Bare wire unreels through lower chamber where it is given a plastic cover, passing to upper cylinder to dry. Operator is top-paid production worker. He inspects moving wire and adjusts machine for coating thickness, concentricity, and surface texture.

Sub-assembly line continuously carrying parts to the final assembly of an automobile transmission.

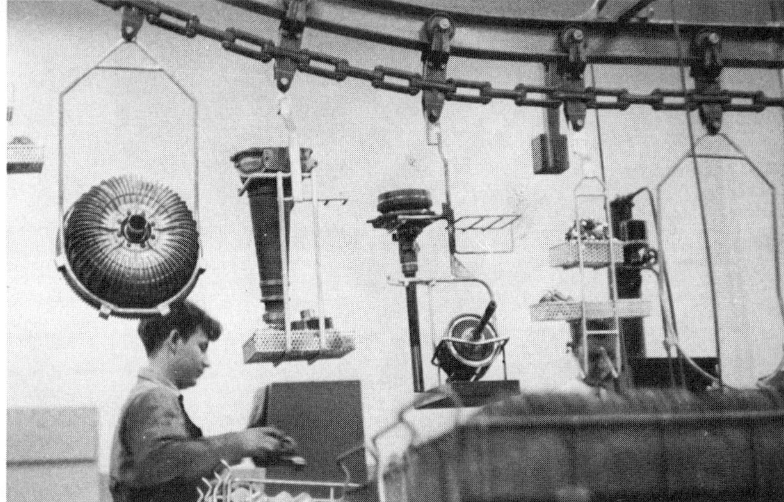

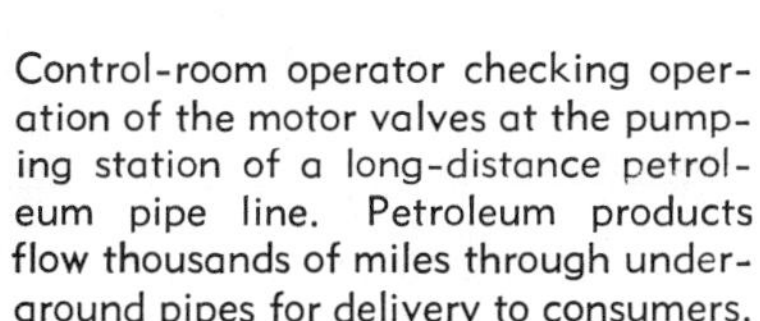

Control-room operator checking operation of the motor valves at the pumping station of a long-distance petroleum pipe line. Petroleum products flow thousands of miles through underground pipes for delivery to consumers.

A 13-inch-swing lathe, standard machine tool equipment, operated by a skilled mechanic who can make an item from blueprint instructions.

MAKE AND ASSEMBLE

Characteristically individual parts are made repetitively by single workers or work groups. Making each part and performing each operation are standardized procedures, so that high proficiency can be developed through constant repetition.

The dramatic part of manufacturing is the final assembly of parts into a finished product. Sometimes small parts are put into intricate equipment, as in electronics products. This work is painstaking, requiring high and continuous attention. Big items like automobiles build rapidly into recognizable entities on the final assembly line.

Industrial production begins with small units of manufacture, and then puts them all together in the assembled finished product.

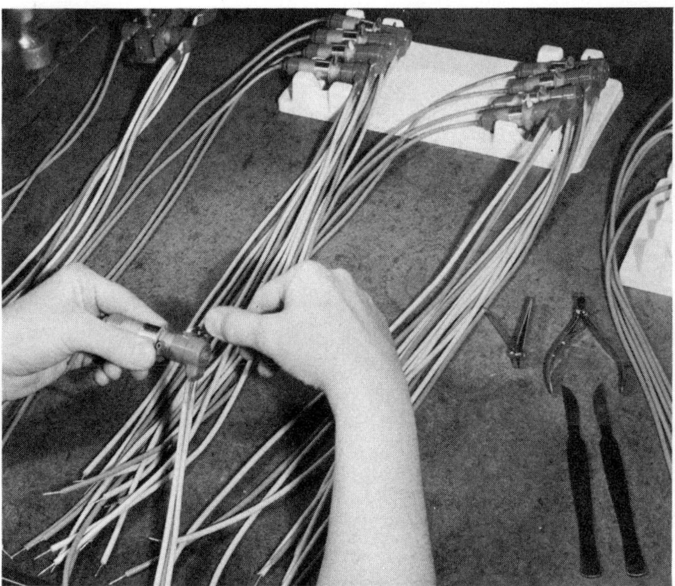

Final adjustment and stripping wire leads in making Klystron electronic tubes. Some hand work still has not been economically replaced by machines.

Assembling electronic test equipment —intricate work requiring care and patience.

Automobile final assembly line—classic example of line production methods. Requires high coordination among teams of workers to add more to the partially assembled cars moving past their work stations.

IN UNION THERE IS STRENGTH

The individual worker, confronting a large company as his employer, may feel helpless and impotent to voice his grievances. In labor unions he finds the strength of mass support.

Unions have lost much of the drama attendant on gaining a foothold in industry. Even strikes now tend to be drab affairs, with desultory picketing of plant gates. Conferences, meetings, thinking, scheming, and planning are more characteristic daily behaviors in labor unions.

Unions exist to bargain collectively with employers. The symbol of success is a union contract, preferably a "good" one.

The relations between companies and unions are analyzed in a companion volume, Robert Dubin, *Working Union–Management Relations: The Sociology of Industrial Relations* (Englewood Cliffs, N. J.: Prentice-Hall, Inc., 1958).

The men and women who work are the labor force—statistics in a mass, until they organize into a labor union and have a program and leadership.

Strikes may be pretty bleak, lacking even the excitement of a barrier of human pickets barring the plant gates to strikebreakers and "loyal" workers.

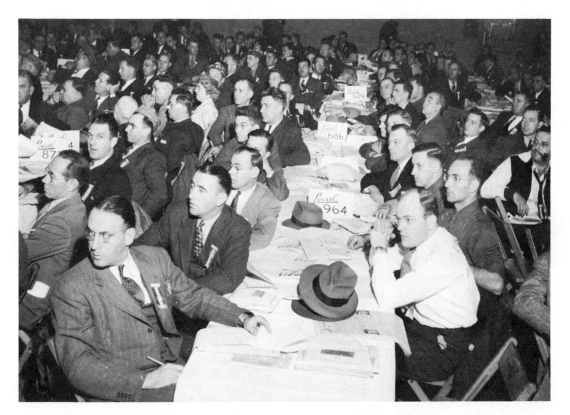

A recent conference of the United Automobile Workers, representing all the local unions in the General Motors Corporation, to plan collective bargaining strategy.

The union contract is the goal. An employer signing a contract with the Amalgamated Clothing Workers Union, flanked by the top union officials, with union shop committeemen and company officials standing in the background.

A stock room where small parts are kept on inventory, released by the stock clerk as required in production.

INDIRECT LABOR

The men behind production lines do a lot of work that may not "show" in the finished products of industry. Materials and parts have to be banked up ahead of the time they are used in production. New equipment has to be installed, or old equipment repaired and maintained. At almost every step in any precision manufacturing process, controls and inspection insure that a minimum of defects will move to the next stage of production. Increasingly, industry is doing its own innovating through research laboratories and development work.

Many people working behind the scenes are highly essential to output.

Installing central office equipment in the telephone company. Highly skilled men make thousands of connections to make the equipment operative.

Process inspection in oil refining. These men are doing routine inspection of samples taken from the continuous refining process.

A single operator with a fork lift truck can handle heavy and bulky materials in and out of storage. Moving materials and products around is a big job in industry.

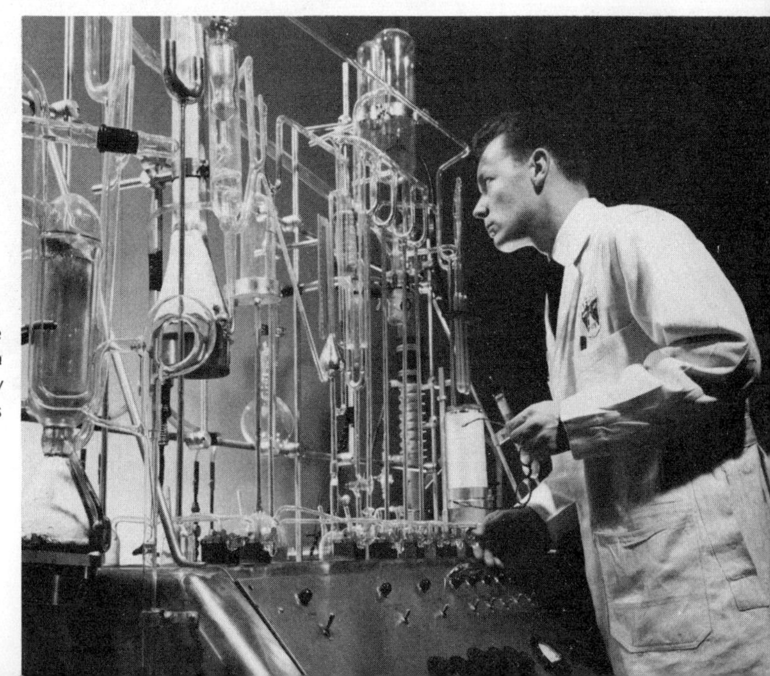

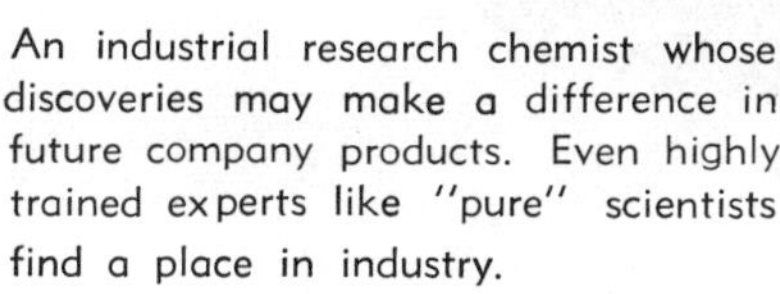

An industrial research chemist whose discoveries may make a difference in future company products. Even highly trained experts like "pure" scientists find a place in industry.

A department composed entirely of women doing light assembly work on electronic devices.

Assembling and packing paper novelties in a small industrial plant.

WOMEN AT WORK

Women in large numbers have left dish mop and dust pan to work in commerce and industry. They have been welcomed to factory jobs where their hands can do dexterous work, or where they can fill jobs of minimum skill at minimum wages. Females have pushed men out of office work and dominate sales and service occupations.

Women prefer office work where they give up least of the feminine touch in surroundings, dress, and discipline. Besides, eligible bachelors abound in offices, and daily contact can often lead to permanent alliances.

The big, future opportunity for working women is mass movement into management ranks. This is almost exclusively for the future, since few women have been able to become managers—many more marry them!

Manual switchboard operators in a central telephone exchange, a typical service occupation.

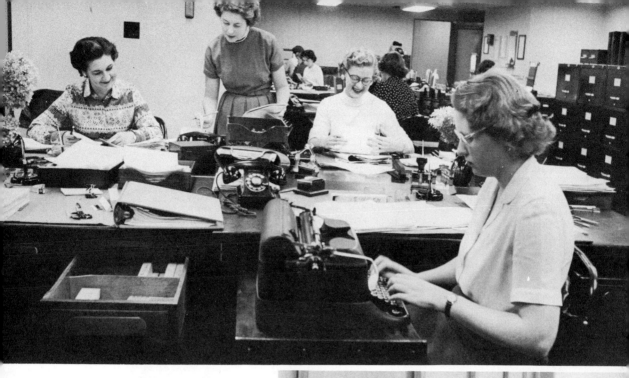

Typical office work with its characteristic typewriter, file cabinets, and telephones. Self pacing rather than machine pacing, or quotas, guides work output.

Office work can be interesting, and so can the people who work there.

FAREWELL

It is usually a ceremonial, and sometimes a solemn, occasion to leave work for newer pastures. Whether the occasion be marriage or retirement, informal and formal recognition comes to the departing colleague.

Inevitably, people working together come to know each other as personalities, friends, and peers. Turn back now and re-examine the pictures in this chapter. The normal working environment contains other people close at hand. The human relations among people at work are necessary to get work done, and inevitable because human beings are sociable.

These pictures of people working are the introduction to the study of work in our industrial society. It is the task of this book to analyze the major features of the world of work.

The wedding bells toll, and fellow workers speed the bride-to-be on her happy way with an informal party in the shop.

tirement brings deserved recognition for a job well done, and good wishes for the years later maturity. Above, the company honors a woman for her long and faithful service a reception. Not to be outdone by management, some unions (below) salute their nbers whose days in the shop are over.

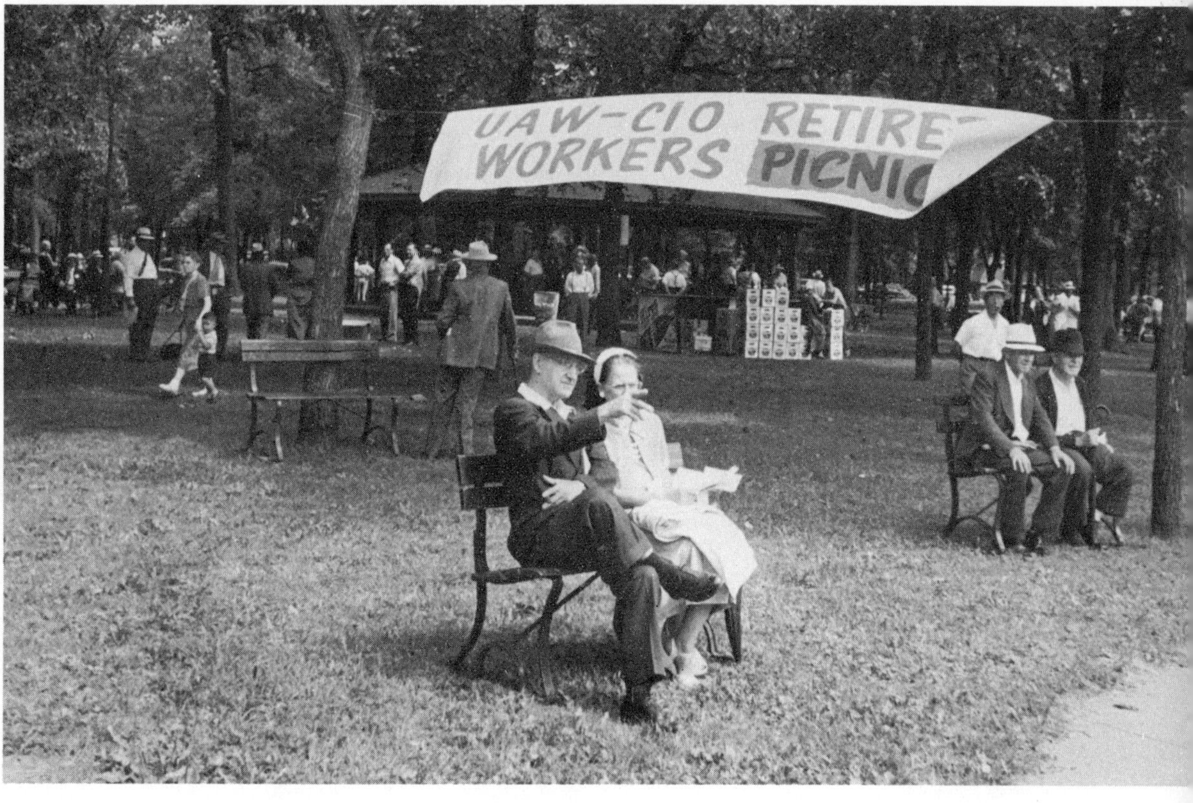

Part II

ORGANIZATION OF WORK

An automobile designer giving instructions to the foreman of the experimental shop about construction of a hand-made model of a new automobile. Designer and foreman each perform distinctive functions separately from each other, but only the sum of their separate functions make the final product possible; this is a power relationship of dependency. The designer is giving instructions or orders to the foreman, an authority relationship. Can you tell by the way they dress what their relative status is in the organization?

Chapter **2**

HUMAN RELATIONS

Work is typically carried out in organizations. The purpose of this chapter is to examine the basic human relations of work organizations.

The human interactions of work organizations will be examined first as basic types of human relations. This entire chapter is devoted to the analysis of power relations, authority relations, and status relations, as the three basic types of human relations of work.

The next five chapters continue the analysis of the general characteristics of all work organizations. The present chapter, and the following five, contain the fundamentals of a theory of work organizations.

BASIC HUMAN RELATIONS

By basic human relations we mean the established types of human interaction that are independent of the personalities of the people involved. How can we classify human interaction patterns that are independent of personality? This is the problem to which we first turn our attention.

We will start by establishing three important limits on the discussion. In the first place, we will limit attention to the basic human relations *in* organizations. There is no difficulty in recognizing that two people in love are not interacting in an organization framework; that parents and children interact in a very special kind of organization called the family; and that people crushed together in a crowded subway car are interacting in still another type of human aggregation called a crowd. In focusing attention on interaction in organizations we want to discover the persistent patterns of human relations that serve to relate and integrate the working positions of the organization regardless of who occupies these positions.

A second restriction on our discussion of basic human relations is that they must have real consequences for action. These human relationships must be visible in the actual action of people. This restriction is important because it eliminates from our analysis any concern about non-objective modes of interaction. If an observer cannot see actual behavior that constitutes ongoing interaction, or see the positions that are related by the interaction, then serious question can be raised whether the actors themselves are aware that a human relationship exists.[1]

The third and obvious restriction is that we limit attention to patterned interaction among human beings. This seems like a self evident requirement in viewing *human* relations. It is particularly important, since we will draw a distinction between human relations and human behavior systems. Human relations are patterned interactions among human beings who occupy established positions with respect to one another. Behavior systems, on the other hand, are systems of patterned action of any person with respect to his environment. This environment will, of course, consist largely of other people, but it will also include non-human objects. Thus, a worker interacts with his machine in a highly predictable fashion; that is, in a behavior system that we will call the technological behavior system.

We can put the distinction between human relations and behavior systems in another way. From the standpoint of human relations, we see the total organization and all its participating members systematically related—we are looking at human interaction as a total social system. From the standpoint of behavior systems, we see each participating person interacting with his total organization environment—we are looking at human interaction from the position of the person's own behavior. The human relations approach gives us an understanding of the total social system called the work organization. The behavior system approach provides the basis for understanding the actions of any given member of the work organization. The behavior systems of work are analyzed in Chapter 4.

The three types of basic human relations in organizations are: power relations, authority relations, and status relations. We will examine each in turn.

POWER RELATIONS

The most general observation about any work organization is that everyone in it has something to do. Each member has some activity or task that he regularly performs in doing the work of the organization. We say that every member of the organization has functions to perform.

POWER RELATIONS DEFINED

Since every member of the work organization has at least one function in it, we can ask immediately, How are these functions interrelated? How do various single functions add up to produce the organization's services or products?

Our first approximate answer is to suggest that each function performed is *dependent* on the performance of other functions, if the product or service is to be forthcoming. We now have to examine further what we mean by *dependent.* Some functions or tasks cannot be performed until others are carried out ahead of them. Some functions and tasks have to be carried out at the same time. It seems clear that there is some kind of network, organizing and interrelating the separate functional tasks of a work organization. It is in this network, holding and binding together the separate functions of a work organization, that we find the location of power relations.

Before defining power it is necessary to define function.

A *function* is the observable consequence of an act or operation in its environment.

The late Professor Louis Wirth of the University of Chicago was fond of making the following observation about a function: "If there is a difference, it makes a difference." That puts very succinctly the meaning of a function. Where there are observable consequences in the environment of an act or operation, we can say it is functional in that environment. We can add, further, that the particular function of the act or operation is to produce the environmental consequence.[2]

We can now define power. Power is the necessity that a given function has in a work organization.

This definition tells us that all functions are not of equal necessity to the organization. Some functions, like that of executive decision, are so essential to the organization that it would shortly cease to operate if executive decisions were not forthcoming. Other functions, like that of personnel counsellor, may be dispensed with for long periods of time without affecting the continuity of the organization's operations.

We started out to define power relations. We can now do this.

Power relations are the relations among organization members that correlate their separate functions according to the necessity these functions have for the organization.

Power relations serve to tie organization members to each other by organizing systems of functional interdependence. In these terms it now makes sense to talk about the power of the staff engineer, of the janitor, of the vice president and of his secretary. Each has power but in different amounts, because each performs functions that have different degrees of necessity for the organization. The staff engineer has specialized knowledge and training as an engineer. The engineer cannot give a command to the line organization, but he is often able to have the last word in engineering matters because of the high value placed on engineering knowledge applied to production problems. The janitor, too, has power in the organization, even though small in amount. In emptying waste baskets and sweeping floors, the janitor is performing functions that are essential to the esthetic sensibilities, and the operating efficiency, of others. The vice president is powerful because in his hands lies responsibility for coordinating many activities of divisions and departments. His coordinating function is highly essential in keeping the divisions and departments working together. Finally his secretary, though moderately paid, and with a relatively minor title, may wield considerable power because she controls access of organization members to her boss. Her power rests in her function of screening contacts with the vice president. Department heads, men of much higher pay and title, may solicit the secretary's favorable attention in order to open channels more readily to their mutual boss.

Power relations organize human interaction in terms of the interrelated functions performed by members of the organization. In the next chapter we will examine the power structures that result from power relations. For the present we are only concerned with power relations as the action counterpart of functional interdependence.

It should be noted that power relations do not depend on happy agreement among those interacting. Every individual is a participant in a power relationship whether he likes it or not so long as he is performing a function that brings him into a direct relationship with someone else. A department head may find "buttering up" the v.p.'s secretary personally repugnant but nevertheless does it in order to have ready access to the vice president. Men in a steel storage yard may have an active hatred for the overhead crane operator who moves the heavy pieces of steel around the yard with the crane, but can and must interact with him in keeping the storage yard in order.

The human relationships that we call power relations are an orderly and organized set of integrated functions. Bases for establishing the integrated functions may vary widely. Most commonly, functional interdependence and power relations are the result of a technological division of labor. There are also other divisions of labor that are grounded in tradition (e.g., the Congressional sergeants-at-arms); in sex differences (the female secretary but the male company secretary); in age differences (the office boy); in prestige (the personal advisor or confidant of a chief executive); in competence (the trouble shooter); in education (college degrees required for accountancy, engineering, and other specialized business jobs); and in character (the trusted lieutenant).

Power relations are systematic in character, non-consensual for the participant, and varied as to the basis for the underlying division of labor. Power itself varies in amount according to the necessity of a given function in a work organization. Power relations may therefore involve relations among people having unequal amounts of power. Power relations may also involve contests for organizational power in the struggle between two people or two cliques to perform a given set of functions. Power relations are a fundamental process in collective bargaining where the union constantly presses management to share decisions about functions affecting employee welfare.

AMOUNT OF POWER: ESSENTIALITY

One way of measuring the amount of power is to determine the essentiality of a given function or set of functions for the organization. Highly essential functions have relatively high power. Less essential functions have relatively low power.

The essentiality of a function determines one important facet of the power of a person. This essentially in turn rests on:

A. Whether the work organization can continue operating without the function being performed,

B. Whether the person can continue to be a productive member of the work organization without carrying out his assigned functions.

Both of these criteria of essentiality of functions require empirical verification in each instance studied. That is, we cannot state categorically that a function found to be highly essential in, let us say, The General Motors Corporation, will have the same measure of essentiality in the Studebaker Corporation, even though both produce automobiles as their major product. We would have to study the functions of a person in each organization to determine their respective essentiality. We may find they rank about the same in each company. We may, however, find that they have different rankings in the two organizations. Therefore, the power relations flowing from the performance of what seem to be identical functions may be different in the two organizations.

It follows that the amount of power a person holds, measured in terms of the essentiality of his functions, is a unique product of the organization in which he operates. This is an important generalization, particularly when we analyze the effects of a person transferring from one work organization to another. Suppose he takes a job in a new company, bearing the same title as the job he left. In his power relations in the new work organization, he will be inclined to operate in the patterns learned at his previous place of employment. These patterns of power relations may not fit the new organization. Trouble can result. Either the man himself will have to develop the power relations that fit the new organization, or the organization will accept the new man's redefinition of his power position and be modified accordingly. In the first case, the new employee is re-educated. In the second case, his new employing organization has its power structure modified. In either instance, a significant readjustment by the new employee takes place with respect to the power relations of the new organization.

AMOUNT OF POWER: EXCLUSIVENESS

Another facet of the amount of power in power relations is exclusiveness of responsibil-

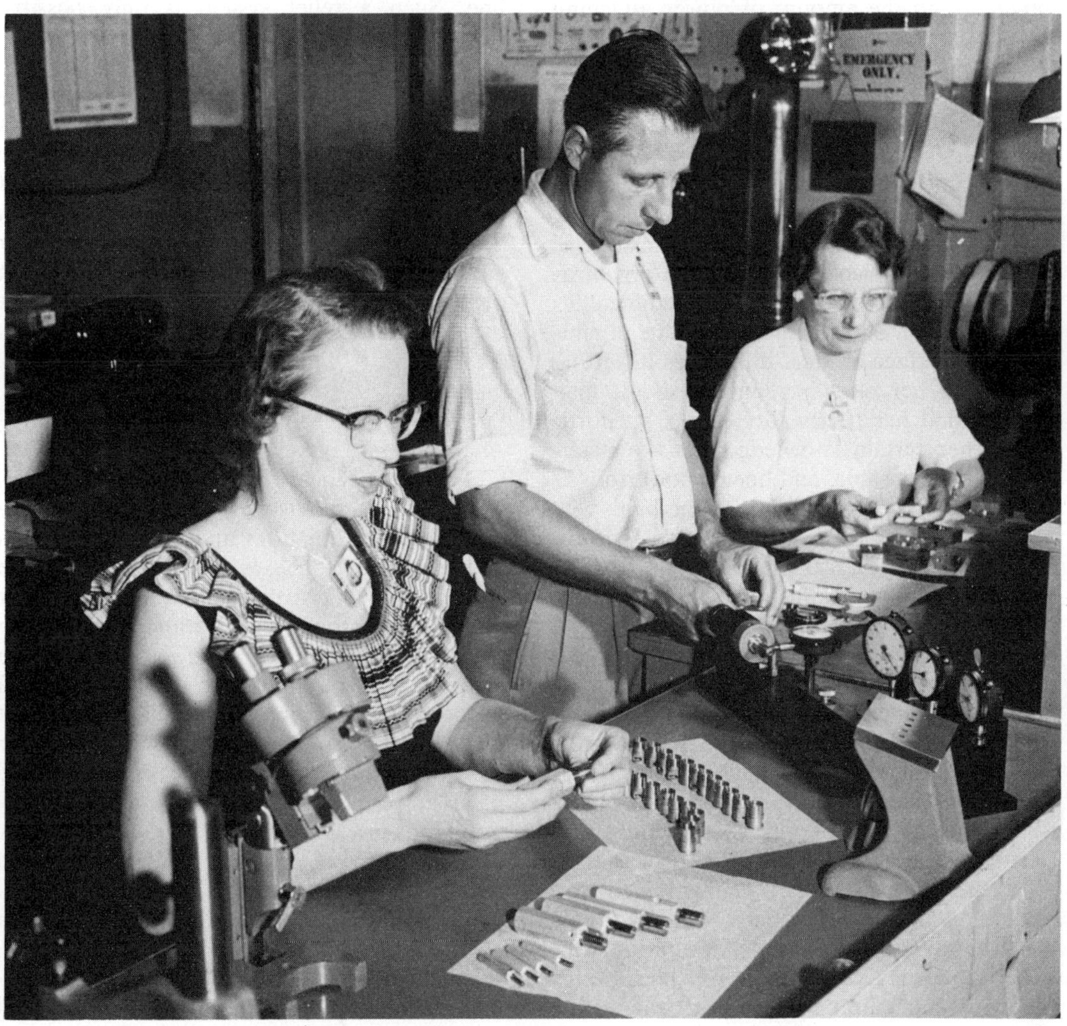

How essential a function is, and the exclusiveness with which it is performed, determine the power of each working person. Here, a chief inspector checks gages for accuracy before turning them over to two process inspectors for their use in inspecting materials. The chief inspector has more power than the process inspectors. The accuracy of their work depends on his skill in setting gages, a task he alone performs.

ity for performing a given function. Where a function is performed by a single person, the amount of power attaching to the performance of the function will tend to be relatively high. Where several, or many, people perform the same function, the amount of power attaching to it is relatively low.

The impact of numbers upon the amount of power rests upon the possibility of rapid substitution of a replacement for a missing, or absent, member of a work organization. In general, where one person performs a function, substituting for him may be more difficult than where several are performing the function. The "indispensable man" of an organization is most often the person who exclusively performs a function and for whom there is no ready replacement.

Two examples will make clear the relationship between exclusiveness in performing a function, and the amount of power attaching to it. It is not uncommon in small organizations for a single girl to be in charge of the filing system. Her particular methods of filing may be individualistic to the point where no other person can find anything in the files. At the same time, she can put her finger immediately on any paper needed. This file clerk has relatively high power, and typically has an amount of indispensability to the organization that far exceeds the technical difficulties of her position. She may be kept in the organization in the face of great difficulties in getting along with her on a personal basis. It may even be that her personality quirks are fortified by her certain knowledge that she is relatively indispensable, and hence, powerful!

The second example pictures the bank wiring room of the Hawthorne Works, Western Electric Company, celebrated in the studies of Elton Mayo and his associates.[3] In the unit studied, there were nine wiremen wiring a complicated set of terminals together, and three soldermen who soldered the connections after the wiremen completed the wiring. Each solderman performed the same functions as all others; each wireman did exactly what every other one did. Within each group there was a high degree of interchangeability and substitutability. Furthermore, there was even an exchange of jobs between wiremen and soldermen although the company did not officially approve this practice. Any one man of either group had very little power because his functions could be performed at a moment's notice by others of equal competence. This is true, in general, in production line operations where there is rapid replacement of any missing worker. Some continuous line operations are even organized so that individual workers can be relieved temporarily by a roving relief man who can substitute on all the tasks in the line. Such a relief system is only possible where the power attaching to the tasks is relatively low.

The exclusiveness with which a function is performed by itself seldom fully determines the amount of power held by a person. The essentiality of the function likewise does not fully establish the amount of power. When we take essentiality and exclusiveness together we have the two major facets of the amount of power in power relations found in work organizations.

POWER RELATIONS SUMMARIZED

The importance of this operational definition, of the amount of power as measured by essentiality of functions and the exclusiveness of their performance, is great. It provides the student of work organizations with a major tool for analyzing organization behavior. In the past, the concept of power has been so abstract as to be difficult to use for analytical purposes.[4] It is common to talk glibly about power, but the analysis quickly founders for lack of concrete ways of measuring it.[5] We have suggested two important ways of measuring power. With these tools we can now deal with power relations as a central and objective aspect of the human relations of work organizations. We will show in the next chapter how power relations are structured. We will also show how power structures relate to, and are articulated with, authority and status structures.

We can now summarize power relations in work organizations in the diagram, Chart 2.1.

This diagram contains all the essential features of the elements composing power relations. It presents the visual counterpart of the preceding discussion.

AUTHORITY RELATIONS

Another very broad observation we can make about work organizations is that they are composed of people who give orders, and people who execute orders. Commands and orders are the most frequent subject of formal communication in getting work done. Indeed, a major share of the paper work of every work organization consists of communications, issuing orders, and responding to them. Furthermore, every member knows who his boss is, and knows who looks to him as boss. Authority is a basic feature of work life.

CHART 2.1

POWER RELATIONS ARE A CONSEQUENCE OF FUNCTIONAL INTERDEPENDENCE

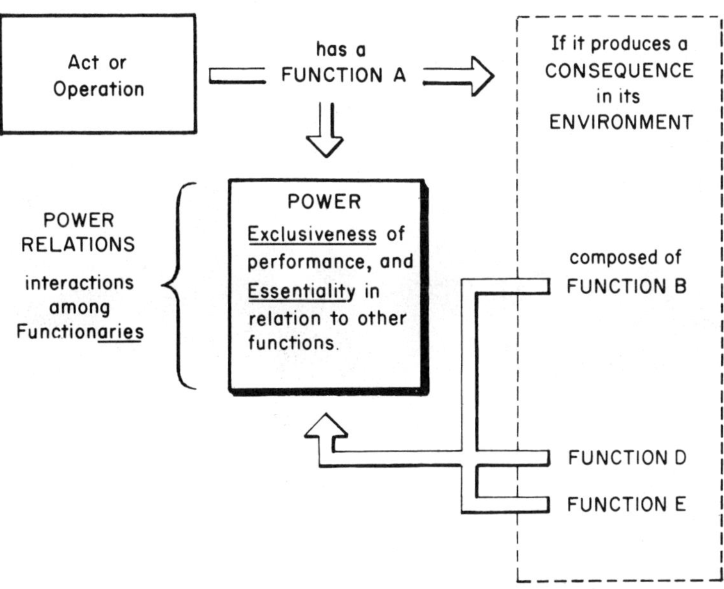

AUTHORITY RELATIONS DEFINED

With bosses a standard part of the work environment, and with ordering a major feature of getting work done, we have the question of how to define and describe this pervasive characteristic of work organizations. What do we mean by a boss? What do we mean by giving orders?

These two questions are obviously related. We know it is a boss who gives orders. When a man is acting like a boss he is usually giving orders. What is there about the behavior of a boss, and our response to him, that is embodied in a fundamental type of human relation?

We are here concerned with authority relations. The boss is an authority, and his orders involve others in an authority relationship with him.

An *authority relation* is one person's making decisions that guide the actions of another person.[6]

An authority relationship occurs when one person makes and transmits decisions, expecting that they will be accepted by another person. The other person, in turn, expects such decisions and determines his resulting conduct according to the decision made for him.

In analytical terms, an authority relation exists where there are alternatives for action in a given situation. Faced with these alternatives, a person may make his own decision and thus act without reference to another decision maker. But if the other decision maker does make the choice for him, then an authority relation comes into existence.

It should be apparent, then, that there are many situations in which there is a temporary authority relation that terminates with the decision establishing the choice for action among alternatives presented. Such situations occur frequently in work organizations. Temporary authority relations, even though occurring often at work, are not the primary authority relations with which we are concerned.

Permanent authority relations involve a continuing double expectation. The decision maker expects that, in all the defined work situations of behavior choice, he and only he will designate the proper choice, and that it will be accepted by those carrying out the action. The recipient of the decision expects to have the choice made for him and to execute it once it is made. In Simon's words, "he holds in abeyance his own critical faculties for

This supervising telephone operator exercises authority over the switchboard operators. She takes over and makes decisions when a switchboard operator has a difficult situation not covered by standing orders, and therefore requires an on-the-spot decision. It is also characteristic of authority holders that they are physically separated from subordinates, often do not work like them, and frequently can exercise visual control over them.

choosing between alternatives and uses the formal criterion of the receipt of a command or signal as his basis for choice."[7] The decision maker expects to make the decision and the recipient of the decision expects to carry it out. This is the essence of a permanent authority relation.

We will not here examine the structure of authority relations, although it is immediately apparent that it involves, in most instances, a superior-subordinate relationship. The discussion of this will be taken up in Chapter 3.

LEGITIMACY OF AUTHORITY

When authority is a permanent relationship we have the analytical problems of determining why it becomes established and how it is maintained.

Why is authority established? The answer lies basically in the continuing need of work organizations to face situations in which choices are possible. When choices are possible in getting work done, decisions are necessary to resolve the alternatives in favor of one. In the extreme case, failure to make the deciding choice may halt work completely. In less extreme situations, a random basis for choice, or conflicting choices, will at least impair the efficiency with which work is accomplished. The continuing existence of choices for action and the need for deciding among them are the basic reasons for specializing the decision making operation in an authority holder.

How is authority maintained? The first impulse is to suggest that some sort of punishment will befall anyone who disobeys an order or command. The work organization can fire the disobedient worker. Or he may be bawled out, suspended temporarily from work, denied promotion, or denied some privilege. These are some of the methods of force used to maintain authority.

It would not be realistic, however, to limit our analysis to force as the buttress of authority. There are other influences operating in the work organization that help to maintain authority relations.[8]

Pressure to conform in authority relations

can be a product of the disapproval of fellow workers. Insubordination can be embarrassing because fellow workers may not approve of "kicking the boss in the teeth." People immersed in an organization have a sense of propriety about the exercise of authority and response to it. This sense of propriety can be described as a "zone of acceptance" of authority, to use Simon's phrase. When a person rejects his place in an authority relation his behavior may fall outside this zone of acceptance and he will lose the sympathy of his fellow workers because of it.

At a more abstract level, the authority relations of a work organization are grounded in some going view of their legitimacy. This sense of legitimacy may rest on a belief in the need for order that results from the exercise of authority. It may also rest on a belief that the exercise of authority has some legal justification—that the decision maker is simply fulfilling his legal right in issuing orders. Finally, this sense of legitimacy may be grounded in a moral belief. For example, the decision maker may be viewed as having a moral obligation to his employer, or to the company stockholders, to exercise authority in keeping the work organization going. Whatever the ascribed basis for their legitimacy, permanent authority relations are always viewed by those involved as being legitimate for the work situation. This sense of legitimacy is important in maintaining authority relations.[9]

Authority relations may also be maintained through shared belief in the purposes of the work organization. Where purposes are viewed as important, the member of the work organization is willing to obey commands because he realizes that the resulting coordination contributes to the realization of the organization purposes. This may not be nearly as important in maintaining authority relations in large scale organizations as in smaller ones. In the large organizations the purposes often seem remote to the vast majority of members. In smaller organizations there may be a much broader sharing of a sense of purpose between the decision makers and their associates. This same sharing of purpose may also be achieved in large scale organizations at the department or production unit level.

Finally, there may be simple unwillingness to incur responsibility for decision, leading to accepting decisions made by others. This is a common circumstance that lends support to authority relations. Indeed, we will show that there is a substantial body of workers in American industry today who have very little interest in their work organizations. For this group, refusal of responsibility for decisions is the simplest response to authority relations, thereby tending to support and maintain these relations.

AUTHORITY RELATIONS SUMMARIZED

Authority relations occur when alternatives for action in work organizations require decision to select an appropriate course of action. When this decision making is vested permanently in a person or position, responsibility for decision is authority. When authority positions are established, others must forego decision making responsibility. When we find a decision maker and those who execute decisions, we have an authority relation.

Authority relations are maintained over a period of time by punishing insubordination, by the pressure of fellow workers to conform to authoritative decisions, by a belief in the legitimacy of the exercise of authority, by a shared belief in the purposes of the work organization, and by simple unwillingness to accept responsibility for making decisions.

The accompanying diagram presents the main features of authority relations.

CHART 2.2

AUTHORITY RELATIONS INVOLVE DECISION MAKING FOR OTHERS

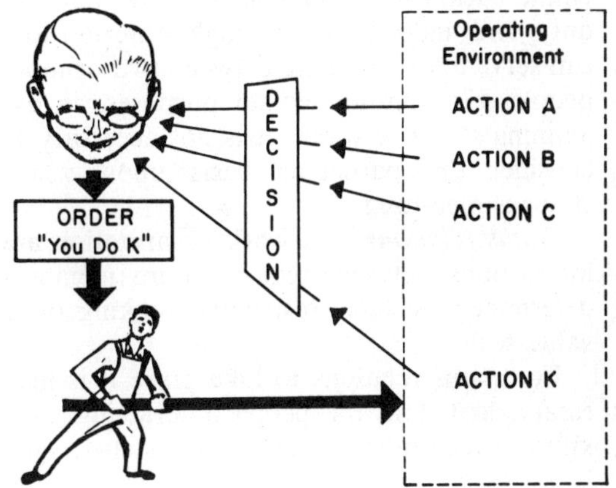

STATUS RELATIONS

The third major way of looking at organization behavior is in terms of the universal phenomenon of ranking people from high to low on some common basis. Some workers are respected as high class craftsmen, while others are ordinary in their skill and ability. Executives appear to rank higher than workers. Union officers are likely to rank higher than union members. Engineers have a higher standing than office boys. Secretaries have a higher standing than stenographers, and both stand at a higher level than file clerks.

This characteristic ranking of people is a pervasive feature of all work organizations. It also gives rise to one of the basic types of human relations in organizations, since the rankings have consequences for the kinds of interactions that take place among people.

STATUS RELATIONS DEFINED

Each member of a work organization has one or more positions, or ranks, that place him with respect to all other people in the organization. As a consequence of everyone's having a rank, the ways they act toward each other are determined in some measure by their respective ranks.

Work status can be defined as the rank occupied by a work organization member on some scale of value.

This scale may have a variety of bases. It may be grounded in competence, education, importance, appearance, manners, racial or ethnic background, religion, skill, devotion to duty, and, indeed, in any single criterion that can serve to differentiate between two or more people. For our immediate purposes, in examining status relations, it is not necessary to consider the particular basis upon which status is measured.

Status relations in a work organization are interactions between two or more members determined by their respective ranking on a value scale.[10]

For status relations to take place it is necessary, first, that the people interacting must know each other's respective status; and second, that this knowledge of the statuses of the interacting persons actually affects their behavior toward each other.

The interacting persons must have some cues for recognizing each other's status. These cues are typically highly visible aspects of a person's behavior, appearance, or place in the work organization. Every person in the work organization has indelibly imprinted upon him, or his work place, the marks of his particular status. These marks are the recognition signals by which others react to him in status relations.

The interactions that take place once status positions are recognized are of a particular sort. These interactions consist of reacting toward the other person as a superior, an equal, or an inferior. From these reaction patterns, two basic types of status relations are derived.

Status relations are identical for each person in the interaction only when they see each other as equals. When people see each other as equals their behavior has special characteristics. They have a feeling of ease in each other's company. The subjects they talk about represent common experiences, and shared judgments and evaluations. They can become argumentative and disagree with each other, believing each has an equal right to his own opinions. They can give and take advice and criticism without feeling imposed upon, or coerced. In short, they interact with each other as colleagues or peers.

The second general type of status relation is that of superior with inferior. This kind of relationship is markedly different from status relations between equals. There is likely to be considerable restraint in the emotional quality of the interaction. The superior member has the initiative throughout the interaction. The inferior member ordinarily has to play a subservient role. The superior member typically has the initiative with regard to the subject matter of the interaction. He can define what they will talk about and largely how they will talk about it. The superior member will tend to guard himself against any expressions, or behaviors, that are likely to reduce the distance between himself and the inferior member. The inferior member, on his part, is equally constrained not to behave in ways that will move him up too close to the superior member. The superior attempts to maintain his position by employing all the human devices to keep the inferior in his place.

These two basic patterns of interaction in status relations produce two very distinctive types of human relations. When equals interact they tend to forge bonds that further unite them. When unequals interact they tend to create, and maintain, barriers that keep them distinctly apart.

MARKS OF STATUS

In work organizations the most obvious marks of status are titles attached to occupations. These titles are partly descriptive of the work done. They are equally descriptive of the implicit or explicit status attaching to the occupations. A machinist II and a machinist I do slightly different things. They also have distinctly different status with respect to each other. The typist, stenographer, and secretary share many job tasks. Their differential titles represent minor job differences, but major status differences. The secretary of a department head, and the secretary to the president, may have the same title, but differ vastly in status.

Two clerks working in widely different settings. The girl at the left is an office clerk. The girl at the right is working right on the factory floor as a shop clerk. Does the contrast in setting in which almost identical kinds of work is done make a difference in status between the office and shop clerk?

Both kinds of status relations have their group counterparts in work organizations. The superior-subordinate type of relationship is built into the formal organization. The peer or colleague type of relationship is built into informal groups. These two basically different modes of grouping people are universal in work organizations. In our further analysis we will see how important these two kinds of status relations are in understanding working behavior.

Another mark of status typically found in work organizations is the rate of pay. Pay is usually calculated to represent task differences among jobs. It is also calculated to represent differences in quality of job performance. Having taken these aspects of the job into account, the amount of pay has a residual status value that can distinguish among people's status in terms of dollars and cents.

Seniority may be an important status-conferring aspect of work organizations. The person of long seniority may rank materially above an equally competent but recent company employee. This senior member may enjoy special privileges that result from his higher status.

Rights and privileges are important marks of status at work. The right to go to work and leave without ringing a time clock is a mark of high status. The right to determine hours of work, and even the days on which work will be performed, is a mark of even higher status. The right to take a coffee break at your own convenience is a mark of higher status than the requirement to take coffee at a particular time. There is almost an inexhaustible range of rights and privileges that define relative status in work organizations.

Clothing and insignia are other marks of status. The white collar worker is marked by his dress, and is readily distinguished from the plant worker in his overalls or coveralls. The Brooks Brothers suit may mark the executive off from the male clerical staff. The uniform of the plant guard distinguishes him from all other members of the organization. It requires no further elaboration to indicate that dress is an important mark of working status.

Work place location may be another mark of working status. Locations close to the boss may have higher status than those more removed. Locations on upper floors are a literal translation of superior status. Working beside an outside window may rank above locations along an inside wall. A private secretary may enjoy an office of her own, but typists may work in a shared room. The boss will typically have a less accessible location than the receptionist.

Still another mark of status is the degree of privacy in a work location. Generally, the more private the work space, the higher the status of its occupant.

The quality and quantity of furnishings in a work space may constitute still another mark of status. Degree of cleanliness, adequacy of ventilation, level of illumination, amount of noise, and countless other features of the individual location constitute an almost inexhaustible list of ways for marking differential status.

There is no wonder that immediately upon entering a work organization a stranger can readily place most of its members in their status positions. He has countless cues by which he can judge their status. For every member of the organization, cues are even greater in number by which he is able to observe and know the finer status distinctions that place everyone in relation to everyone else. The status symbols surrounding work are the badges for labeling workers. It takes only common observation to note these badges, and to understand the statuses they symbolize.

STATUS RELATIONS SUMMARIZED

We can summarize status relations as defining two fundamental types of human interaction. The first is the interaction among equals. The second is the interaction among persons of unequal status. These two types of human relations are quite different from each other. Both are to be found in work organizations.

We can now summarize status relations in work organizations in the following diagrams.

CHART 2.3

PERCEIVING MARKS OF STATUS IS FOLLOWED BY STATUS RELATIONS

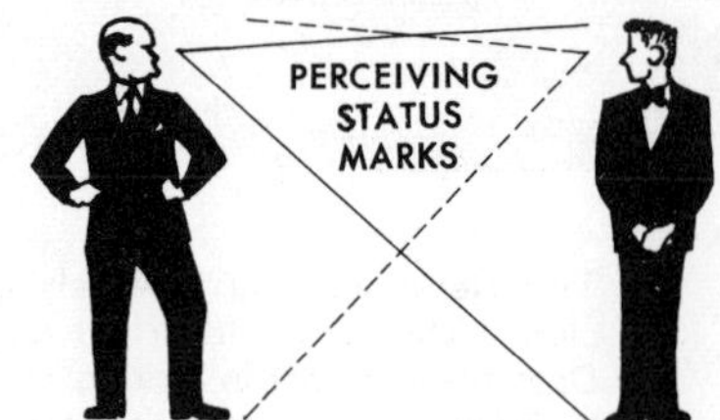

PEERS SUPERIOR-SUBORDINATE

POWER, AUTHORITY, STATUS

Power, authority, and status relations are the three fundamental ways by which people are oriented to each other at work. These are the processes of human interaction while working.

Interactions *among people* working can be analyzed through the power, authority, and status relations that govern their modes of behavior towards each other. Most of the time all three types of human relationships operate simultaneously when people interact at work. For analytical purposes we have treated separately each basic type of human relationship of work. Obviously, in any real situation, we would have to discover the particular ways in which all the basic human relations are exhibited.

In Chapter 3 we will proceed immediately to show how the three fundamental human relationships are organized into permanent systems of interaction. We are now prepared to understand the *structures* of human relations, knowing the *processes* involved, and the range of possible types.

NOTES FOR CHAPTER 2

[1] It is not the intention to question here the fact that the psychic life of a person may be filled with thought, fantasy, and imaginary objects. We are not concerned with personality or its components. We are not focusing on the vast and complicated inner processes of mental activity. Our problem is to discover the processes of *interaction* and their structuring at work.

[2] Functionalism in behavioral science has a long intellectual history. Robert K. Merton presents an excellent summary of its history and makes brilliant contributions to its analysis in "Manifest and Latent Functions," Chapter 1 in his *Social Theory and Social Structure* (Glencoe: The Free Press, 1949), pp. 21-81. Radcliffe-Brown has written, for example, "The function of any recurrent activity such as the punishment of a crime, or a funeral ceremony, is the part it plays in the social life as a whole and therefore the contribution it makes to the maintenance of the structural continuity." A. R. Radcliffe-Brown, "On the Concept of Function in Social Science," *American Anthropologist,* 37:395-96 (1935).

Malinowski suggests a similar formulation of functional theory when he states that the theory "aims at the explanation of anthropological facts at all levels of development by their function, by the part which they play within the integral system of culture, by the manner in which they are related to each other within the system. . . ." B. Malinowski, "Anthropology," *Encyclopaedia Britannica,* First Supplementary Volume (London and New York: The Encyclopaedia Britannica Co., 1926), pp. 132-33.

[3] F. J. Roethlisberger and W. J. Dickson. *Management and the Worker* (Cambridge: Harvard University Press, 1939). The bank wiring room is described on pages 392-395.

[4] The specific application of the concept of power to the kinds of problems here dealt with was made in its most enduring form by Max Weber, *Theory of Social and Economic Organization* (New York: Oxford University Press, 1947). H. Goldhammer and E. Shils, "Types of Power and Status," *American Journal of Sociology,* 45:171-178 (September, 1939), following Weber's analysis, see power as "the extent to which [the power holder] influences the behavior of others in accordance with his own intentions." It becomes impossible to differentiate this view of power from the concept of authority, except to say that authority is legitimate power. Furthermore, there is no objective way of determining a person's intentions—we have to take his word as to what they "actually" were in a given case. Inasmuch as social interaction involves adjustments in one's own intentions as well as others' behavior, even a thoroughly sincere person would have difficulty in distinguishing initial and modified intentions, and initial and modified behavior. Finally, the mature personality rarely permits himself serious intentions as to the behavior of others unless he is fairly confident of being able to carry them out through his influence; by Goldhammer's and Shils' definition, then, any well-adjusted person possesses unlimited power.

[5] Robert Bierstedt, "An Analysis of Social Power," *American Sociological Review,* 15:730-736 (December, 1950), treats power as "latent force" and, therefore, something that is beyond measurement. He considers authority as institutionalized power, a formulation not unlike that of Goldhammer and Shils, *op. cit.*

[6] This follows Herbert Simon, *Administrative Behavior* (New York: Macmillan Co., 1947). p. 125. See also a more recent restatement by Simon in "Authority," Chapter 7 in C. M. Arensberg, *et al.* (eds.), *Research in Industrial Human Relations* (New York: Harper & Bros., 1957, Publication No. 17, Industrial Relations Research Association, pp. 103-115.

NOTES FOR CHAPTER 2 (CONT.)

[7] Simon, *Administrative Behavior,* p. 125.

[8] The following discussion of the factors sustaining authority in the organization is similar to Simon's treatment, in *Administrative Behavior.*

[9] Note that legitimacy of the exercise of authority is only one basis on which authority relations are sustained. This differs sharply from the idea that authority is legitimate power, or even the idea that authority is institutionalized power.

[10] The classic treatment of status in work organizations is by C. I. Barnard, "Functions and Pathologies of Status Systems in Formal Organizations," in W. F. Whyte (ed.), *Industry and Society* (New York: McGraw-Hill, 1946). See also, E. C. Hughes, "Dilemmas and Contradictions of Status," *American Journal of Sociology,* 50:353-359 (March, 1945); Kingsley Davis, "A Conceptual Analysis of Stratification," *American Sociological Review,* 7:309-321 (June, 1942); and also Davis' *Human Society* (New York: Macmillan, 1949), Chapter 4, "The Organization of Statuses."

The structures of work organizations are planned. The engineers are designing a production layout showing location of operations, and work flow. Theoretically speaking, they are concerned with integrating the separate parts of the power structure, putting together the elements of the division of labor.

Chapter **3**

STRUCTURES OF ORGANIZATION

It is necessary to know the structures of work organizations to understand the human behaviors that occur in them. In this chapter we will be examining some of the more important structural features of work organizations. Special emphasis will be placed on authority structures, power structures, and status structures.

You will remember that the basic human relations as set forth in the previous chapter are authority relations, power relations, and status relations. In this chapter, we are concerned with discovering how these basic types of human relations in work organizations come to be organized and structured.

We are using here a simple view of structure. The dictionary defines a structure as a combination of related parts; as the arrangement and organic union of parts in a body or object; as the formation or organization of anything; or as the specific mode or way in which anything is put together.

We are concerned with the way in which the basic human relations of work organizations are put together as a combination of related parts. We are concerned with the persistence of these human relationships in enduring patterns of interaction. In short, we are concerned with the structure of basic human relations of work organizations.[1]

AUTHORITY STRUCTURES

The authority structure of an organization is a product of the distribution of decision making opportunities or rights affecting the behavior of other members. Some members of the organization make decisions frequently, while others have only infrequent decisions to make, or none at all. There are a few members of the organization who make its critical and important decisions. Other people in the organization may make routine decisions either frequently or infrequently. There are differences among individuals in the frequency with which they make decisions affecting the organization, and in the importance of such decisions.

AUTHORITY AND CRITICAL DECISIONS

Work organizations typically have a concentration of authority at the top. Authority tends to be centered in the hands of the chief operating executives of the business firm. These executives make the most important decisions. In descending order from the principal executives are successively less authoritative officials in whose hands lie decisions of decreasing importance.

Within the firm there is a clear-cut structure with respect to the ways in which decisions will affect its operations. At the top, the most difficult decisions are made, and, as one moves downward in the organization, decisions become less critical. The foreman of a group of workers makes much less critical decisions than does the shop superintendent, who in turn is less likely to be involved in critical decisions than the superintendent in charge of manufacturing. The vice president in charge of operations may have far greater responsibility for decision making, and ultimately the president or the board of directors may possess the last word on organization decisions.[2]

AUTHORITY AND FREQUENT DECISIONS

Measured by the frequency of decision, the structure of authority is not always precise. There may be many routine decisions constantly being made by individuals at all levels of organization. Conversely, the number of critical decisions may be relatively few. Top operating officials of the organization may not make as many decisions as individuals routinely deciding issues on a day-in day-out basis. A foreman may be expected to examine constantly the rate of output of his department, deciding when workers need to be urged to greater effort. The foreman's decisions may occur every hour, or even more frequently. Over the period of a day, he may make a number of decisions affecting his department's output and the quality of the product. At the same time, the president of the company may not make a significant decision for a number of days. Therefore, measured by frequency of decisions alone, there is no direct clue as to the nature of the authority structure of the organization.

Frequent working decisions are often based on standardization of choices among which decisions are made. For a foreman who is concerned with directing his workers in setting speeds and feeds of machine tools, it is perfectly possible to establish fixed standards by which he can arrive at this judgment. There is really nothing problematic about the way in which he makes the decision, or the point at which he decides speeds and feeds need changing. He can be given a set of instructions laying down specifically the conditions under which he decides one way or the other. Standardizing choices is what makes decisions routine. It is a characteristic of modern, rational work organizations to incorporate as much as possible of decision making into fixed routines.

The more routine a decision, the greater is the possibility of having it done frequently, and having it performed by a relatively unskilled member of the organization. In large scale organizations, making routines out of decisions has been central in delegating fixed and known responsibilities. The foreman can, in fact, be made responsible for the speeds at which machines operate in his department. The limits of this responsibility are readily fixed if the decisions are routine enough that he can both comprehend and apply them.

Whole departments of large corporations are devoted entirely to the development of standard methods by which routine decisions can be made. These are often called standards or methods departments. The products of such departments are standard (or standing) operating procedures for carrying out specific tasks and jobs. Responsibility is established clearly in the standards for job operations, and is placed squarely upon the shoulders of the job holders.

Although routine decisions are likely to be made with greater frequency than critical and important decisions, it does not follow that important decisions are always relatively rare. There may be periods in the history of an organization when it is undergoing rapid change, and when important decisions may be made daily and hourly. At other times and under other circumstances, the organization may make relatively few changes or adjustments to its operating environment, and critical decisions may be infrequent or even absent for long periods. The situation may be likened to that of an army in garrison contrasted with an army under battle conditions. The garrison army may well operate with few, if any, command decisions being made at the top levels of the organization. Under battle conditions, however, there may be a constant flow of tactical and strategic decisions determining the hourly course of battle, and its final outcome.

In general, responsibility for decision making, when measured in terms of the significance of the decision, forms a hierarchy with positions of greatest importance at the top, and positions of the least importance at the bottom. When decision making functions are measured in terms of frequency of decisions no clear-cut structure appears. Critical and important decisions may be made either frequently or infrequently, depending on the conditions under which the firm is operating. Routine decisions are likely to be made frequently, but even these may diminish in number as automation replaces the decision making function of machine operators and machine tenders.

AUTHORITY IN THE LARGE CORPORATION

There is an interesting problem in the modern corporation in distinguishing the authority of operating management, the board of directors, and the stockholders. It is probably generally true that operating management is only indirectly responsive to the stockholders as an authority group within the corporation. The evidence that exists for this general statement suggests that operating management is largely able to control the stockholder group in ways that perpetuate management's continued direction of the firm.[3]

There have been widely publicized fights in recent years for control of firms by groups seeking to wrest operating management from incumbents. The most spectacular of these fights was the one in which Robert R. Young obtained control of the New York Central Railroad System. Very shortly thereafter, in 1954, Louis Wolfson attempted a similar move on Montgomery Ward and Company, but his efforts were unsuccessful, and Sewell Avery was able to retain control of that organization. Institutional investors and stockholders—a large and often controlling segment in corporate ownerships—tend to support the incumbent management group.

Individual stockholders are likely to have such minority share holdings that singly they are relatively impotent in affecting the course of active management of the firm. Reading minutes of stockholders' meetings of corporations that publish them, like the Standard Oil Company of New Jersey, gives clear evidence that the stockholders are engaging essentially in ceremonial approval of present management, rather than significantly affecting decision making within management.

For all practical purposes, we can view the modern corporation in the United States as having the pinnacle of its authority structure in the board of directors and in the upper reaches of operating management.[4] Authority is concentrated at this point and is diffused downward in the organization, diminishing rapidly as it reaches lower levels of the organization.

It is notable, for example, that in plans for decentralizing large corporations, decision making responsibility usually remains concentrated close to the top.[5] Thus, in the General Motors Corporation, the world's largest, decentralization stops abruptly at the divisional level. The Buick, Chevrolet, and Oldsmobile divisions, along with many others, constitute units to which authority is delegated. Within each of these divisions, however, authority remains concentrated at the top, and each division exhibits the same pyramid of maximum authority at the top and minimum authority at the bottom.[6]

FLOW OF AUTHORITY

The general direction of order-giving in an organization is from the top downward. Much less frequently is there order-giving from one job holder to another at the same level. Most infrequently do orders originate at a lower level, affecting people in a higher position.

Let us illustrate the three directions of order-giving before proceeding to their analysis. The direction of an order from a higher to a lower level is illustrated when the production manager asserts that output ought to go up about three per cent in the next day. Whether the production manager makes this a suggestion or says, "You are directed to increase output three per cent," the net effect is the same. His subordinates must react to this command or order, modifying production in a serious attempt to increase it by three per cent. Similarly, if the president of the firm declares that it might be a good idea to have the sales report compiled for the previous three weeks, this declaration constitutes a directive to his subordinates to provide the report. Order giving from a higher to a lower level is the most common case of authority and its exercise.

The flow of commands and orders between jobs at the same level is a somewhat less common, though clearly recognized circumstance. Thus, when the hooker directs the crane operator to hoist away after a load has been secured to the crane hook, the hooker is clearly issuing a command to the crane operator. In another instance, a foreman of an operating department may call upon the maintenance department to repair a broken machine tool. The maintenance department cannot initiate its action until a request comes from the operating department. In this instance, although the operating department requests maintenance on its vital machine tool, it is, in effect, ordering that the machine tool be maintained.

The third kind of order-giving situation in which orders flow from a lower to a higher level is the most uncommon of the three types of authority. A good example is the instance of the gate guard who is responsible for determining that everyone entering the plant gate is authorized to do so. He may demand credentials even of the president before passing him through the gate. In other circumstances where there may be danger involved in an operation, the operator may often be given full responsibility for determining who shall be permitted in the area of the operation, at what times, and under what circumstances. Even his superiors in the organization may require his permission before entering the dangerous area.

It is a characteristic of the exercise of authority that it flows only in one direction in a given situation. The direction of order-giving remains stable for each situation. It is also usually true that there will not be orders affecting a situation coming simultaneously from different directions.

Where there is the possibility of conflict, so that orders may come from several directions to a person filling a job, he is under pressure to resolve the conflict in favor of one.[7] It is not necessarily certain that the order coming from above will always be given preference to that coming from someone at the same level. It is clear, however, that situations of conflicting orders are likely to be resolved rapidly by the individual affected. Should he fail personally to find a satisfactory basis for a choice, he may seek clarification from somebody sufficiently in authority to declare the precedence that one order takes over all others conflicting with it. Conflict of authority is thus resolved either informally by the order receiver or formally by a higher decision declaring the priority of one of the conflicting orders.

Plant manager making his daily rounds talking shop with one of his department managers. The plant manager, at Ford's Cleveland engine plant, wears a characteristic badge of production-oriented top managers—his street hat. The authority relationship is clearly expressed in the gestures and postures of the two men.

An order is a declaration that action should take place. Where conflicts in orders exist, the action cannot move forward. It is precisely this block to action that is the most important force leading to the resolution of the conflict between orders. Blocked action becomes immediately clear to the individual whose action has been stopped, and to those who observe the situation. The moment this is recognized, there is considerable pressure to remove the block, permitting action to move forward.

The flow of orders from higher to lower levels is the most significant aspect of the authority structure from the standpoint of organization. Top authorities are responsible for most changes in the organization. Most situations of uncertainty are resolved by orders originating at the top of the organization.[8]

Business organizations, like modern military organizations, place great dependence on chain of command and the general downward flow of orders in the authority structure. Indeed, the chain of command is one of the major factors in designing the structure of an organization.

SPAN OF AUTHORITY

Where one man gives orders to a number of subordinates, the problem of how many subordinates can be efficiently directed becomes an important one. Span of authority is used to describe the limiting number of subordinates who can be adequately supervised.

The most obvious limit on the span of authority is the amount of time the authority holder has to distribute among his subordinates. If, for example, an average of 30 minutes per day is to be spent directing each subordinate, then a man working eight hours would have 16 people as a limit to his span of authority. As the amount of time per person supervised decreases, the number included within the span of authority can increase. Conversely, as the amount of time spent in directing each person increases, the span of authority must decrease. Measured on the time dimension alone, this relationship is obvious.

A secondary influence on the time spent in exercising authority is the homogeneity or diversity of the activities directed. If activities are relatively homogeneous, the amount of time an authority holder spends in acquainting himself with each will be lessened, and his span of authority may be large. If the authority holder has to direct radically different activities he may need more time to acquaint himself with each one. His span of authority may correspondingly have to be narrow. Within a department or division of an organization, where tasks are relatively homogeneous, we would expect the span of authority to be broad. Where the authority holder has to direct a number of departments or divisions, the span of authority would be narrow.[9]

be a horizontal flow of orders regulating the stages through which the product passes. The need for such regulation is a consequence of the need for coordinating and keeping in proper phase the steps in a technological division of labor. It is clear that even this lengthy list of steps does not begin to include all those possible. We have, for example, excluded the accounting and bookkeeping operation accompanying each step.

It is characteristic of the horizontal flow of authority that it has the general function of initiating and stopping coordinated activities. It does not have the function proper to downward flow of authority—that of directing the kind of activity to be undertaken. We can visualize the horizontal flow of authority as traffic signals regulating the flow of work among different activities that must be coordinated for the total enterprise to be effective. The horizontal flow of authority is found in any situation in which it is necessary to coordinate activities following closely upon each other.[10]

The horizontal flow of authority is characteristically between equals. Here are three men of the Comptroller's department of a large corporation meeting together to work out a problem in coordination of their work. In general demeanor and appearance they convey the spirit of equality among them.

AUTHORITY STRUCTURES AND POWER RELATIONS

The flow of horizontal authority in an organization is a product of its technological division of labor. In particular it exhibits the step-by-step connection between stages of a technological process. The horizontal authority structure tells us essentially the order in which steps in a technology are carried out.

For example, an ordered series of steps are followed from the original design of a product, through experimental model construction; testing in use; modification and redesign; acceptance for production; purchase of materials and equipment for manufacture; manufacture and assembly; and distribution. Between each of these general steps there will

INVERSE FLOW OF AUTHORITY

The exercise of authority from lower to higher ranks takes place in highly restricted situations, characterized by repetitive and limited activities having an element of danger, secrecy, or other mark of exclusiveness surrounding them.

The plant protection guard is the classic example of a low ranking person with large amounts of authority. His task is highly repetitive, protecting against unwanted and unwarranted intruders, with authority over all possible persons passing through the plant gates. Product designers, working on plans kept secret until the products are placed on the market, may be given authority to exclude all but a select group from viewing the design in the process of development. A workman who operates an exclusive process, not shared with competitors, may be given authority to exclude almost everyone from viewing the process, and becoming familiar with it. The secretary to a department executive may refuse to open his correspondence files to a superior executive from another division on the grounds that these files are confidential and for use only within the parent division of which the department is a part. Such exercise of authority through refusal to follow an order is justified on the grounds that the order from the "foreign" executive must come down through proper channels.

Exercise of authority from lower to higher levels has the primary function of excluding unauthorized persons from a given situation. While the authority may be universal, applying indiscriminately to all possible persons, it is highly restricted and limited to the specified and clearly established reason for exclusion. These are the two basic characteristics of the upward or inverse flow of authority.

AUTHORITY STRUCTURES SUMMARIZED

The authority structures of an organization have three separate dimensions. Downward flow of authority gives direction to actual operations, including the choice of purposes and goals for the operations, and their particular characteristics. Horizontal flow of authority coordinates steps in a technological division of labor. Inverse, or upward flow of authority is limited to situations where protection against hazards or unwarranted disclosure is necessary.

From the standpoint of their effects on human relations in the organization, the three different kinds of authority have different consequences. Downward flow of authority is what we usually mean when we talk about the authoritarian character of an organization. Subordinates are directed, ordered, or commanded to do things in fulfilling their jobs in the organization. When we commonly talk about a person having authority, we point to the fact that he is in a position superior to others, to whom he can issue orders.

We cannot, however, ignore the horizontal flow of authority that comprises the signals by which coordination is achieved through order-giving, requesting, or initiating behavior. This coordination is central to the efficient technological division of labor. Indeed, complex technology would break down without this coordination. There are many signals moving directly between equal levels of the organization that display authority as a coordinating mechanism. We are less likely to be aware of the horizontal flow of authority, although it has important consequences for human relations. In instances of breakdown or obstruction in the flow of horizontal authority, the finely balanced technological division of labor may prove less efficient than planned.

Least important, although still an obvious third dimension of authority structures, is inverse authority that goes from lower to higher levels. This kind of authority is functional, but only under a limited set of circumstances.

POWER STRUCTURES

Power structures of an organization are a product of the division of labor within it. Some tasks, jobs, and functions are performed by only one or several persons, while others are carried out by large numbers of people. Some functions are highly essential to the organization, others less so. Having established these kinds of differences in the previous chapter, we now want to find out how this division of labor hangs together—what keeps special tasks and operations coordinated and integrated with each other. We want to get at the structures that give unity to the separate parts composing the division of labor.

TECHNOLOGICAL DIVISION OF LABOR

The complexity of work in modern organizations leads inevitably to a technological division of labor. This division of labor is the consequence of diverse tasks being performed to fulfill the total purposes of the organization.[11]

There are two fundamental conditions leading to technological division of labor within work organizations. *First* there must be a high volume of demand for a particular function, service, or job. *Second* the specialized work must have a unity about it such that it may be performed as a separate task.

A given function is not assigned to a distinct department, division, or unit of an organization until it requires the full-time attention of a single individual or staff. When this volume of specialized activity is reached, the special activity is likely to be made a standard job, and another unit is established in the technological division of labor.

The second requirement leading to special jobs is that the work have enough unity about it that a single individual or staff may comprehend the function as a coherent task. Then the individual performing it can understand the requirements of his task and undertake them with at least minimum competence and efficiency.

When these two conditions are met there is theoretically no limit on the extent of division of labor. In smaller business organizations, there may be simple divisions according to the functions of producing, selling, and purchasing raw materials. As the volume of activity increases, the broad functions may be further subdivided. Departments may grow up dealing with phases of production. A production control department may arise, having this as its primary function. An inspection department may be created to control quality of output. Similarly, a maintenance department may be established, along with an engineering department and a tool designing department.

Each one of the smaller work units may continue to subdivide. For example, the maintenance department may have an electricians' gang, a machinists' gang, a millwrights' gang, and a plumbers' gang. Even these smaller units may be further sub-divided as the volume of specialized services requires; the electricians' gang may be split between plant electricians and electronics maintenance men. These examples should be sufficient to indicate the nature of the sub-dividing process by which the technological division of labor is continually elaborated.

SPECIALIZATION AND INTEGRATION

Once a job, task, or function is specialized, its performance includes the exercise of power in the organization. Power is the effect that the kind of performance, or failure to perform, has on the rest of the work organization.

We can now view the power structures of work organizations as having two fundamental, and opposed, dimensions.

Specialization of tasks, functions, and jobs tends to pull the organization apart. It makes of the work organization a collection of individual operations. Each time specialization is pushed one step further, a division is created between the specialty and other parts of the organization. Specialization tends toward disunity, toward difficulty in coordination. Specialization has a centrifugal influence on organization; it fractures the central unity of work processes.

At the same time specialization creates automatic dependence. A task, job, or function can be specialized only if it fits together with other specialisms to make some kind of whole. A specialized job operating in isolation produces nothing useful. A man drilling holes for bolts is performing a meaningless task unless the hole is tapped with threads, another bored piece is placed on the first, and a bolt is inserted in the holes to hold the two pieces together. The unit of output is the joined pieces of metal. The hole drilling operation is necessarily dependent on succeeding operations to make it meaningful and useful.

The dependence resulting from specialization leads to unity, to coordination. Dependence has a centripetal influence on organization; it gives rise to unity of work processes.[12]

The power structures of work organizations are composed, then, of jobs, tasks, and functions that are specialized in their performance and joined together in networks of interdependence. In analyzing power structures we are concerned with (A) how task differentiation takes place, and its consequences; and (B) how bonds of dependence are maintained among related tasks. We will examine these two general problems in the succeeding paragraphs.

TASK SPECIALIZATION

Specialized tasks develop for several reasons.

The most general reason for task specialization is the complexity of cooperative activity. The complex nature of the final product of cooperative activity may have an important impact on the number of specialized activities needed for it. Thus a primitive group of fishermen in a longboat requires at least the division of labor into oarsmen or paddlers, helmsman, lookout, and spearmen who spear the fish when sighted and approached. An alternate organization would find each individual in the canoe prepared to undertake every task as he perceived the need for it in the unfolding fishing situation. Inevitably under such circumstances, several people would attempt to do the same thing and get in each other's way. Somebody else might fail, at a crucial point, to do a required thing, making the difference between success or failure in catching fish.

Where several separate and distinguishable tasks have to be performed simultaneously, the need for division of labor will also necessarily arise. Furthermore, where the timing of the ongoing activity may be crucial to the outcome, it becomes even more important that the work be divided and specialized among several participants.

A third factor producing task specialization is the criticalness of the outcome. There are some kinds of activities which may be repeated until the desired result is achieved. Under these circumstances a great deal of inefficiency may be accepted in getting the task accomplished. On the other hand, there may be critical situations in which the group involved may have only one chance to achieve the desired result. The all-or-none outcome of the task demands high competence in all its phases. Where several people are involved in the critical task, each will tend to specialize to improve competence of performance, thus guarding the critical outcome against unnecessary failure.

On a hunt in which primitive tribesmen are stalking game, the coordination of beaters and hunters must be paramount. A failure at any point may permit the game to escape. In such an instance the outcome is all important. There is no margin for error or lack of coordination that would destroy the hunting pattern. Under these circumstances we are likely to get significant division of labor according to the tasks the members of the hunting group perform.

Besides differentiation of tasks in a group of people working together simultaneously, there are, of course, other kinds. Differentiation in tasks may take place where two different jobs have to be performed in different locations at the same time. It may also occur where the same general job may be carried out with different kinds of materials. Differentiation is also possible where the same kind of job can be performed with different technologies.

We can analyze tasks in work organizations in terms of four general questions: (A) what is done; (B) how it is done; (C) why it is done; (D) where it is done. These four aspects of the task give us a basis for determining the nature of the functional specialization that we find in all modern organizations.[13]

TASK: WHAT IS DONE

What people do in providing useful services and labor differs among them. The evidence of our senses tells us that there is something different between the work of a herdsman and that of a farmer. We can also observe that a pot maker does something different than a candlestick maker. We can look at a watchmaker and a watchman at work and know that their respective jobs are different.

Distinctive occupations are given separate titles in the languages of all peoples. Descriptive titles usually indicate the working behavior in the occupation. Such titles are illustrated in the following list: truck driver, saleslady, sewing machine operator, cylinder borer, coil winder, and steno-typist. Occupational descriptions may also emphasize the product of the occupation, as in this list: doughnut maker, supervisor, receptionist, core maker, foundry moulder, stock clerk, and instrument maker.

We have continued to designate occupations by what is done or what is produced. The *Dictionary of Occupational Titles,* by no means a complete listing of all occupations, contains more than fifty thousand job titles found in American industry.[14] Modern work organizations contain a wide variety of tasks to be performed and, therefore, a wide variety of different kinds of job designations.

One of the organization consequences of job differentiation is the tendency to place similar jobs in the same department. There may be conflicts between keeping similar jobs together in a department, and maintaining an adequate, progressive flow of work from one task to another. Dissimilar tasks are often grouped together because they represent successive stages in the progression of work towards the finished product. What is more typical, however, is to have the work pass from one specialized department to another as dissimilar tasks are performed. Thus, a customer order may go to the special design department for engineering design. The working drawings may go to the purchasing department to guide procurement of materials and any special tools required. From that point, the delivery of the materials and tools from the receiving department will be made to the production floors. On the production floors, the order is then fitted into the existing production schedule. When the proper tools and materials are on hand, and when the production schedule calls for it, the various production departments will handle the order. Upon completion of production, the shipping department will take over and see that the order is delivered to the customer. This does not include all the steps possible—billing operations, credit operations, and similar paper work have been left out of this picture.

Separate tasks are kept in special departments and under specialized supervision where there is continuous repetition of these tasks. Where tasks are repeated regularly, it is considered more desirable and efficient to segregate them into specialized departments. Thus, production scheduling is a continuous operation in the preceding example. People who specialize in production scheduling will handle all orders of the company. They will do this continuously. Therefore it is possible to separate and specialize the production scheduling operation.

It would be conceivable to have one person perform all working tasks. However, it is more efficient to have specialists perform the individual tasks because they are continually demanded operations.

TASK: HOW IT IS DONE

How a task is done focuses attention upon behavior while fulfilling the task. We shift attention away from the product being worked on to the activities necessary for doing the work.

Operations can be done in different ways that result in almost identical products. For example, we can hand-carve decorations in furniture, or do it with machines that rout out designs with similar results. In both instances, the end product is a carved piece of wood, containing a decorative design, to be used on a piece of furniture. The man who does hand-carving is considered a fine craftsman, with a high degree of skill. Of lesser skill is the man operating a routing machine cutting the design with a mechanically directed cutting head following a pre-determined pattern which the operator does not design or control. We would distinguish between a craftsman woodworker, on the one hand, and what we would probably call a routing machine operator on the other.

The basis of distinction in this example lies in the difference in the way an almost identical outcome is accomplished. This type of distinction is particularly important in considering the impact of technology on job changes. Jobs are defined differently as their technology changes.

Changing technology affects tasks as the machines, equipment, and methods are changed. Not all tasks are as obviously different as in the illustration of wood carving. Some job differences are much more subtle, and sometimes only very small. They may involve the difference, let us say, between working on a four spindle screw machine or a six spindle screw machine. The operations of four and six spindle machines are very similar, but the operators of these machines can carry separate titles because of the relatively minor differences in what they do in performing their jobs. This difference might even be emphasized by paying distinctive rates for the two jobs.

One of the most heavily weighted aspects of job differentiation is how the job is done. In job evaluation and job description, for example, this is usually given more total weight than any other factor. The interest in motion analysis that has grown up in conjunction with the job description and job evaluation centers on finding common units for analyzing how tasks are accomplished. These are typically units of bodily movement.[15]

TASK: WHY IT IS DONE

Why a task is done is another basis on which identical tasks can be differentiated from each other. This factor is important in contrasting legitimate with illegitimate occupations. For example, an individual who paints automobiles in a regular body shop has a task which is legitimate. However, should the same individual be employed by a ring of auto thieves for rapid painting of stolen cars to minimize their quick identification, we would probably conclude that while the technological aspects of the illegal painting are the same as the legal, the purpose of painting stolen cars is illegitimate.

The distinction between legitimate and illegitimate jobs is not the only one for which the purpose of the task is important. A laboratory technician who is doing routine chemical analyses of on-going processes would probably have a different view of himself if he were doing identical chemical analyses in a research setting. To take another example, the machinist employed in the experimental shop of an automobile company where new models are first developed, although he performs operations identical to those of the machinist in the production shop, is set apart from the latter and considered to be performing a distinct task. We can multiply these examples in all fields of organization behavior. The central point to be remembered, however, is that the purpose or goal of a task can be extremely important in differentiating it from other tasks. This holds even though there is an identical technology and an identical method of operation involved in the two tasks.

The goal of a task as one of its distinctive characteristics is an important incentive for individuals to do good work. The clear recognition that an otherwise humdrum task has significant goals may make it exceedingly important to the job holder.

TASK: WHERE IT IS DONE

Another aspect of a task is the location at which it is performed. There are statuses attached to special locations within the organization. For example, a shop clerk may do exactly the same thing as a clerk in the accounting department. Yet, the shop clerk may be located in the production shop while the accounting clerk may be in the office section of the establishment. The office location may have slightly higher status. Accordingly, there may be pressure toward recognizing the accounting clerk as being different from the production clerk. The way in which the jobs are performed and what is turned out may be undervalued in placing emphasis on where the tasks are performed.

Identical or almost identical tasks may be considered different by their incumbents if they are performed in different places. In the field of administration, for instance, being a member of the central staff of a far-flung organization, may rate higher than being a member of a local plant staff, even though the jobs performed are identical.

Task differentiation based on status location plays an important role as an incentive in modern organizations. A hierarchy of identical jobs can become a career line, if each step up the career ladder is the same job having a different locale. Promotions are then to different places, rather than to different tasks. Such locational changes may also have higher status confirmed by an increase in pay. The private secretary of a vice president, for example, who becomes the president's secretary, may continue to perform identical tasks, but receive a handsome increase in salary because of the status move.

Task specialization is based on what is done in a job, how it is done, why it is done, and where it is carried out. What is done in a task is important in assigning the task to a department of the work organization. How a task is done is important in following out the consequences of technology for work, and in evaluating pay levels through job evaluation. Why a task is carried out is significant as a test of its legitimacy and as an incentive for workers who are convinced of the importance of their work. Finally, where a task is physically or organizationally located may provide status rewards that are important as incentives for working.

POWER STRUCTURES AND DEPENDENCE

A consequence of the technological division of labor is the mutual dependence of specialties. As tasks and functions are specialized, there is need for their coordination and integration in order to perform the whole operation of which they are parts.

Whiting Williams pointed out in the 'twenties, after working with industrial workers, that whether a man was a lowly coal passer in the hold of a ship, or a highly trained tool and die maker working on intricate dies, he tended to justify his importance as an indispensable link in the production process.[16] The coal passer would declare the ship could not run if he did not fire the boilers. The die maker would, with similar pride, point out that the quality of the produce was entirely dependent on the precision of the die he made. Both men, of course, were right, calling attention to the necessity of each link in a chain of technological dependence.

The bond of dependence is one of the most important consequences of the technological division of labor. Merely being a part of the production chain serves to call attention to one important basis for attachment to the job and company. This may be quite independent of any positive or negative feelings about management of the company, working conditions offered, or working associates found on the job.

The technological division of labor and the resulting structure of functional interdependence among separate and distinct jobs constitute an important human tie between individual workers and the organizations of which they are members. This simple fact is often overlooked in management programs designed to "sell companies" to their employees.

The dependence of specialized tasks upon each other modifies the distribution of power in work sequences. The very fact that most jobs are not independent places restraints on their occupants, limiting arbitrary action and arbitrary use of power.

The range of action open to someone in a dependent position is limited by the range of acceptance of those with whom he is linked. This is the secret of self-discipline in work groups. Fellow workers in a dependent work team establish their range of acceptance for task performance for every member.[17] No single member of the team can use the power of his job or task to exceed the limits of fellow worker range of acceptance. An attempt to do so will call forth sanctions and punitive action by fellow workers.

The work organization similarly can control arbitrary use of power by a job holder, by clearly specifying what is done, how it is done, why it is done, and where it is done. The job holder has these given him; they constitute affirmative definitions of his task, and equally specific prohibitions against doing what is not concretely defined as part of the task. When the job holder fails to recognize the prohibited areas of action surrounding his task he is quickly corrected. He may be accused of "exceeding his responsibility." He may be charged with "empire building" in trying to take over someone else's functions. He may even be fired for not doing his job as it is laid out for him.

The informal work team and the formal work organization both use dependence among tasks as a major limit on abuse of power residing in the task. Task dependence is one of the central bonds uniting the power structures of work organizations. Dependence is the cement that holds together the specialized tasks into unified and coherent work processes.

POWER STRUCTURES AND STATUS

One of the important consequences of the technological division of labor is the attachment that people develop for the technical characteristics of their jobs. This leads to contentions that special knowledge is required to fill the job. In the case of union organization established on a craft basis, there is emphasis on the distintive features of the craft, and a desire to retain them as the hallmark of the craftsman. Similarly in other specialties like those of personnel, process engineering or any other technical functions, there is constant clamor on the part of the specialists to "professionalize" their areas. They want to assert their possession of specialized skills and protect them from encroachment.

Whether it be through the labor union channel or through a professional organization, the functional specialists of industry organize to protect themselves and establish standards for the recognition of future specialists entering the field. In recognized professions like engineering, this has reached the point where the profession exercises important jurisdiction over training schools and colleges, as well as jurisdiction over certification, through state examinations, of future practitioners. In trades like plumbing and electrical wiring, the control of apprenticeship leading to craftsman status, as well as participation in state certification, are important goals of craft unions.

The technological division of labor produces a myriad of specialists. Task specialists seek recognition for the independence and significance of their specialties.[18]

The functional division of labor on technological grounds determines the occupational structure of industry, and of society. Occupational structure comes to have an evaluative or normative dimension.[19] Specialists rate themselves, and establish conditions for becoming and remaining a specialist. They are equally concerned with where their specialization ranks in relation to others. The assignment of status to an occupational group is at least partly based on the technological function performed by that group. If the function is difficult or complex, the group performing it is likely to be highly rated. If the function is simple and routine, the group is likely to have a lower rating.

From the standpoint of human relations, the technological division of labor contributes to establishing status differences among technical functions. Tasks are ranked in the power structures of work organizations. Status differences based on task factors are established. For job holders, their jobs have "standing."

POWER STRUCTURES SUMMARIZED

Every job has a sphere of influence in the work organization; that is, every job has an effect on the performance of some other jobs. Tasks are combined in dependent structures, each contributing something to the total product.

These structures of dependent tasks are the power structures of work organizations. Chart 3.1 shows a power structure. The tasks are shown as interacting with each other to get work done.

A power structure has permanence. It continues through time to exhibit the same patterns of dependence among specialized tasks. The behavior of workers is tied, in part, to the power structures in which they operate. These behaviors are standardized by the power relations among job holders. We can, therefore, see power structures as permanent features of work organizations, binding specialized tasks into coherent and productive units.

We can complicate our view of power structures by noting that each separate power structure is in turn connected to others. Chart 3.2 presents this. It will be noted, first, that not all tasks within a given power structure connect with other power structures. This connection is maintained only through one or several jobs. The connecting jobs are generally more powerful than those that do not serve as bridges between power structures.

CHART 3.1

A POWER STRUCTURE CONSISTING OF SIMPLE DEPENDENT JOBS WITHIN A DEPARTMENT

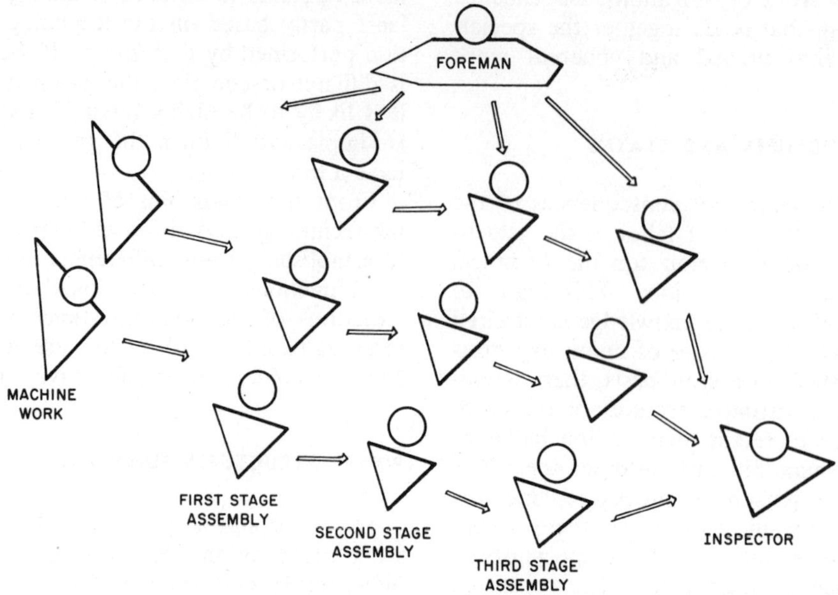

FOREMAN

MACHINE WORK

FIRST STAGE ASSEMBLY

SECOND STAGE ASSEMBLY

THIRD STAGE ASSEMBLY

INSPECTOR

A second observation about linked power structures is that they permit us to locate points in work organization structures at which authority and power coincide. A first approximation would be to suggest that the bridging jobs are ones that also involve the exercise of authority. It is through such jobs that horizontal authority flows. It is also through these tasks that vertical authority flows into the individual power structures. We will examine these points in Chapter 5. At this stage we want to become sensitive to the fact that our step by step analysis of work organization structures is beginning to add up to a total view of working behavior.

We started this section by noting that work organizations tend to disunity through task specialization. We later noted that dependence maintained connections among specialized functions. To this structuring of special tasks into systematic production units we have given the name, power structures.

STATUS STRUCTURES

In Chapter 2 we analyzed the general phenomenon of ranking and rating people in discussing status relations. We now ask the question, Are there relatively permanent systems of ranking that characterize work organizations?

Such stable ranking systems do exist. We call them status structures. Each task and job fits into one or more status structures.[20]

FUNCTIONS OF STATUS STRUCTURES

Status structures have the primary function of providing incentives for effective membership in work organizations. For the individual member, his organization status or rating confirms his present standing relative to other members. Status fixes a person's qualitative standing compared with others. Status ranking gives satisfaction to the individual because it provides him with a perch from which he can view those who are equal to him, and those who are of lower rank. The incentive value of this aspect of status is simple. The human personality needs to be reinforced constantly in its acceptance of a *present* standing in a social structure. Status ranking that is similarly valued by both the person and those around him reinforces his self esteem.[21]

CHART 3.2

A DEPARTMENTAL POWER STRUCTURE LINKED THROUGH TWO KEY PEOPLE TO OTHER POWER STRUCTURES

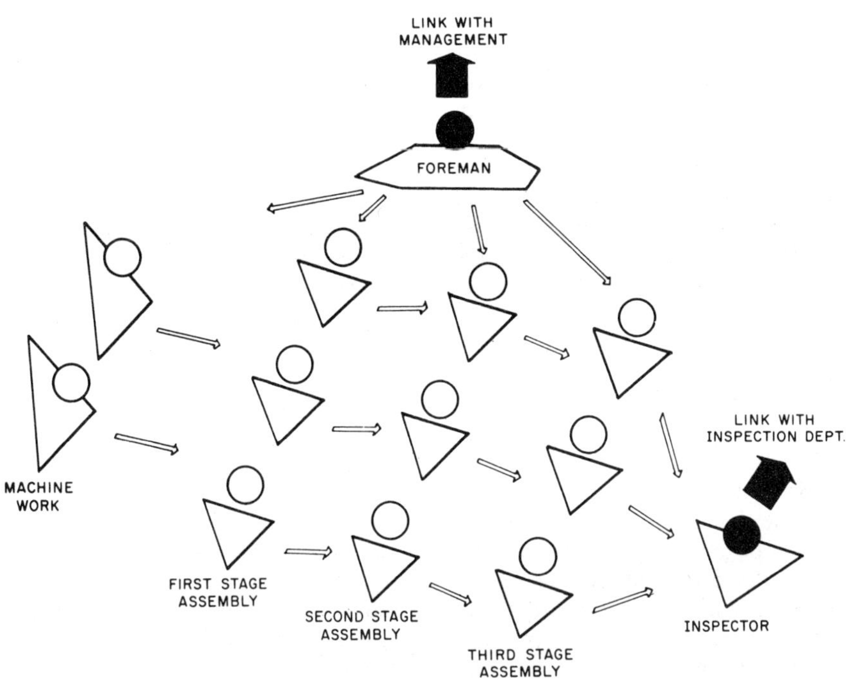

Status structures also provide incentives for advancement. A status structure includes many ranks, ordered from low to high in related series. For any given rank there is usually a higher series of rankings to which movement is possible for the individual.[22] Upward mobility in the work organization is signaled by a move to higher status rank. The structure of status ranks provides the vista for viewing future progress through the organization. In this sense, by pointing to the future standings attainable, the status structure reinforces a person's desire for advancement.

It is noteworthy that the functions of status structures are different from the functions of authority and power structures. Authority and power structures are operating features of work organizations. They are necessary in getting work done. Authority structures are the frameworks for order giving and order receiving. Power structures are the frameworks for task specialization and task integration. Both of these have to do with actual behavior in getting work accomplished. On the other hand, status structures are rewarding, not operating, features of work organizations. They function to provide members with visible satisfactions to keep them performing adequately at work, and to spur them on to advancement.[23]

FEATURES OF STATUS STRUCTURES

There are two major features of status structures that need to be analyzed here: the generality of evaluating criteria for a given work organization; and the differential application of particular status symbols.

By generality of evaluating criteria we mean that each organization has certain commonly valued attributes shared throughout its membership. Every member is expected to exhibit these valued characteristics. For example, in the army, bravery is a commonly valued attribute of military men. In a sales organization, aggressiveness is a shared value; in a university, intellectual capacity; in a chorus line, beauty; in the medical profession, diagnostic or surgical skill.

Some evaluating criteria are held within more limited areas of the organization—production jobs, executive positions, and so on. These valuing standards apply to everyone within a limited area. The executive may be valued for his decisiveness, but the engineer may be equally valued for his deliberate thoughtfulness. Members of the inspection department may be valued for their literal adherence to inspection standards; but product designers may be encouraged by the high value placed upon their originality and departure from present standards.

By differential application of particular status symbols we mean that from one limited area of the organization to another the same valuing standards may have different meanings. For example, length of service, and task competence, may be general valuing standards throughout the work organization. For executives as a group, length of service may be viewed as one basis upon which competence is developed; the executive tasks are so complex that it takes a long time to develop competence in them. For production workers, on the other hand, length of service may have the essential meaning that the employee is a loyal member of the organization because he has remained with it so long. A production worker's task may be learned to a high level of competence in a relatively short time; beyond that period of time his continued service with the organization is viewed, not as furthering his competence, but as a measure of his loyalty. Thus standards of valuing bearing the same name may actually have different meanings in different parts of the organization.

TYPES OF STATUS STRUCTURES

We have indicated in the last chapter that there is no theoretical limit to the valuing standards that constitute the bases of status structures. This is always one of the surprising discoveries that newcomers make when they join a work organization, and become familiar with its unique valuing standards. The surprise consists in discovering that unlikely things have differentiating significance in sorting people out, and valuing them as organization members.

Barnard has suggested five general types of status structures as characteristic of work organizations.[24] We will present these briefly with the understanding that there are many possible variations within each type.[25]

The first type of status structure is based on ceremonies of induction and appointment to a new job. These ceremonies may be formal or informal. They signalize for the person his achievement of the new ranking and constitute a public recognition for all members of the organization to observe that the new rank has been achieved. A very simple kind of ceremony is the personal congratulations of a high executive on a promotion. Another simple public act of recognition is published announcement in an organization news letter or magazine of the changed ranking. For apprentices who achieve craftsman status there may be a much more elaborate ceremony including a banquet, presentation of certificates, and general public congratulation.

The status structure of ceremony varies with different levels of the organization. In general, the change in status at the higher levels of the organization will often entail more complex ceremony than at lower levels. On the other hand, a critical change in status, like that from apprentice to craftsman, may be signalized by high ceremony even though the change takes place between two relatively low levels of the organization.

A second general status structure is based on visible marks of status like badges, uniforms, and insignia. One of the most common features of work organizations is the distinguishing value of clothing to signalize status. Individual occupations and trades have their characteristic work clothing. There are noticeable differences in dress and appearances between office and factory workers. Executives can often be distinguished by the cut of their clothes. Personal possessions can be insignia of status, like the car used to drive to work, the quality of brief cases (or dispatch cases for "top" executives) used to carry work papers, and the like.

External marks of status may be formally required by company policy. Thus, uniforms, badges, safety or other special work clothes, office and work place furnishings may be provided or required by the organization. Personal marks of status, on the other hand, are chosen by the individual to display his own ideas about "living up" to his status. Formal and personal external marks of differential status are highly visible on even casual inspection of any group of people at work.

A view of one section of the producing coordination department of Standard Oil Company of New Jersey shows a top executive consulting with a staff expert. Note the window washer at the rear of the room. Does the marked difference in dress reveal the status gradations in the three levels of the organization represented by these people?

A third general status structure is built around titles and names for tasks and jobs. These titles are both formal, as actual job titles, and informal, as the talking designation of a job. A person may be an assistant to the vice president, but he may also be called the v.p.'s "flunkey." The formal and informal titles together tell us a good deal about the assistant's organizational status. In general, it is not always safe to take the formal job title as the single indicator of status rank without inquiry into the informal designation as well.

A fourth general status structure is based on emoluments, perquisites, and privileges. These features of jobs have status valuations in addition to any material value that may be attached to them as compensation for working. Many kinds of job features fall into this category including private offices, use of company cars, having private secretaries or even pretty secretaries, ringing time clocks, using general or restricted wash rooms, having oak or walnut desks, and so on. All such job features set forth the organization status system, which is thoroughly understood by its members, and fairly easily sensed by an outside observer.

The fifth general status structure that Barnard suggests is grounded in the limitations and restrictions surrounding behavior of job holders. He points out that a status ranking not only entitles the holder to behave in accordance with his position, but it also tends to prohibit his behaving like those of lower status.[26] For example, higher status people are not free to go to places frequented by those of lower status (e.g., the saloon or tavern hard by the plant gates), or do things that lower status people may do (like shoot craps during lunch periods), or even use language that is the privilege of lower status organization members. These behavior restrictions work in both directions on the status ladder. It is always considered presumptuous for a lower status person to imitate the behavior of higher status people. In general, members of work organizations understand well the limitations on behavior in their organization. Nevertheless this kind of status structure is never made explicit and is understood only through participation in the life of the organization.

It should be emphasized, again, that these are five general types of status structures. Each work organization has its special variants of these types unique to it.

STRUCTURE OF JOB DIFFERENTIALS

We can consider in greater detail one important work status structure. It represents the general type based on emoluments, perquisites, and privileges, called the structure of job differentials. The structure of job differentials is one of the more important short-run incentive devices used in organizations.

The structure of job differentials is the small but clearly recognized differences that distinguish stages of the same task or job. These differences are usually signalized by differential pay. They may also be denoted by slight modifications in job title, and added perquisites and privileges.

It is common, for example, in industry to designate a job rate range for specific job titles. Thus, the job title, machine operator A, may carry the rate range of $1.60 to $1.73. The meaning of this rate range is clear. Typically, the newcomer to the classification is paid $1.60 per hour. After a trial period in which, among other things, his competence to fill the job is demonstrated, he may then be advanced to a wage of $1.63 per hour. This may come in a matter of weeks or several months. From that point on the individual is considered eligible for merit increases. These merit increases are rationalized on the basis of the increasing skill and competence that the worker develops from continuous performance of his job. After a fairly lengthy period of time ranging up to several years, the worker may have his rate of pay established at the top of the rate range, namely, $1.73.

It is clear that this worker is performing the same task throughout his learning period, the period of increasing proficiency, and the period when he is finally given the top pay for the job classification. Job differentials within a specific job classification are based on the assumption that proficiency and skill develop with practice in the occupation.

The structure of job differentials for factory jobs, for common clerical jobs, or generally for what are called the manual skills and occupations, tends to be relatively narrow for each job classification. It is common to have a 10 to 20 cent rate range for factory jobs.

At higher points in the occupational heirarchy, the structure of job differentials will increase. For engineers, for example, there may be as much as a 20% range between the lowest and the highest paid individual in a given job classification. At the level of principal executives of the firm, this range may increase still more.

The structure of job differentials within a given classification of jobs is designed to establish rational differences, between individuals performing the same job, as a basis for differentially rewarding them according to ability. The senior person by virtue of his length of service, and presumed increased proficiency that comes with long practice, is supposed to be rewarded more than the newcomer to the occupation, who is assumed to have many things to learn before his proficiency is established at its maximum level.

The distinction between bottom and top job performances, however, is often either very subtle or more apparent than real. For many kinds of jobs the learning period is so short that if all the wages were tied directly to the learning curve, individuals new to the occupation would be able to move to the top rate within a week or two. On the other hand, there are some occupations where skill is largely a matter of practice and experience. In such occupations it could well take a number of years for individuals to learn, through practice, the subtle skills involved in becoming a craftsman in the occupation.

It is precisely for these reasons that job differentials are one of the very short range incentive features of organizations. It is presumed that the individual newly entered into a job classification will, through his efforts, seek to earn the top rating. He strives to learn the job in order that his rewards will reach top level.[27]

The structure of job differentials distinguishes the relative standing of two people, each of whom is similarly classified by occupation. Job differentials serve to provide minor marks of status distinctions in the industrial organization. Unlike the technological division of labor which distinguishes groups of different occupations, the structure of job differentials provides status rewards for occupants of the same job classification.

HUMAN RELATIONS AND ORGANIZATION STRUCTURE

It is generally true that if we know where a person stands in the power, authority, and status structures of an organization, we have an excellent picture of how that member fits into it. We will not be able to describe fully all his working human relationships, but we will be able to locate the points of his contacts and interactions with others. However, it requires detailed analysis to comprehend the ways in which the structures of human relations are woven together in a particular organization. In some respects, this constitutes one of the major tasks of the remainder of this volume.

NOTES FOR CHAPTER 3

[1] The subject of organization structure is a standard one treated in all textbooks on organization and management. See, as an example of a good analysis, E. H. Anderson and G. T. Schwenning, *The Science of Production Organization* (New York: John Wiley & Sons, 1938), Chapter 4, "Organization Structure." Chester I. Barnard, *Organization and Management* (Cambridge: Harvard University Press, 1948), in Chapter 5, "Concepts of Organization," sets forth a view of organization in which the social system of the firm includes customers as part of the organization. There is obviously an important systematic relationship between customers and a business firm, and in this sense the human relationship is organized. However, when viewed from the standpoint of the internal state of affairs of a business organization, the firm-customer relationship lies in a different social system.

[2]The analysis of authority structure follows some of the leads suggested by Herbert Simon, *Administrative Behavior* (New York: The Macmillan Company, 1947). For example, on authority and "the last word" see pp. 129-130. See also Chester I. Barnard, *The Functions of the Executive* (Cambridge: Harvard University Press, 1938), Chapter 7, "The Theory of Authority," which contains a thoughtful and penetrating analysis of authority.

[3] For example, Peter F. Drucker, "The Employee Society," *American Journal of Sociology* 58: 358-363 (January, 1953) makes the general point that all members of management with the exception of the owner-manager, as well as workers, are employees. Nevertheless, management does succeed in retaining effective control of business decisions without sharing it with the nominal owners, the stockholders.

[4] For an excellent study of the functions of the board of directors, see J. C. Baker, *Directors and Their Functions: A Preliminary Study* (Boston: Harvard University Graduate School of Business Administration, 1945).

[5] A series of papers on centralization vs. decentralization is contained in H. J. Kruisinga (ed.) *The Balance between Centralization and Decentralization* (Leiden, Netherlands: H. E. Stenfert Kroese, 1954). A more specific study dealing with decision making and industrial relations is: Helen Baker and R. R. France, *Centralization and Decentralization in Industrial Relations* (Princeton: Princeton University Press, 1954).

[6] Peter F. Drucker in *Concept of the Corporation* (New York: John Day, 1946) has given us an excellent sociological analysis of the General Motors organization. He points out that the pull between centralization and decentralization is ultimately resolved in favor of what he calls an industrial federation, with each federated unit (operating divisions of the company) having centralization of internal authority.

[7] Cf. Simon, *Administrative Behavior,* Chapter 2, where the problem of unity of command is considered in general as a problem of subordinates resolving conflicting orders, and pp. 140 ff., where the problem of conflicting orders is dealt with specifically.

[8] A detailed study of planned changes in authority structure and in participation in decision making clearly shows that the primary flow of authority is from the top down, even when efforts are made to increase the amount of horizontal flow of authority. See Elliott Jacques, *The Changing Culture of a Factory* (London: Tavistock Publications, 1951). Gresham M. Sykes, "The Structure of Authority," *Public Opinion Quarterly* 17:146-150 (Spring, 1953) criticizes a general over-emphasis on the analysis of the downward flow of authority, and suggests some modifications that would be compatible with those discussed here.

[9] Span of authority is a generally accepted concept used by organization analysts. See for example W. H. Newman, *Administrative Action: The Techniques of Organization and Management* (Englewood Cliffs, N. J.: Prentice-Hall, Inc., 1951).

[10] This should be distinguished from conflicts arising in the horizontal flow of authority between staff and line departments. The staff-line conflicts center on innovation in the organization. The horizontal flow of authority is concerned with maintaining balance among existing elements in the flow of work. See Melville Dalton, "Conflict Between Staff and Line Managerial Officers," *American Sociological Review* 15:342-351 (June, 1950), for the analysis of conflict over innovating. See E. Wight Bakke, *Bonds of Organization: An Appraisal of Corporate Human Relations* (New York: Harper & Brothers, 1950) who gives detailed charts and tabular descriptions of the work flow, including the horizontal flow of orders, involved in processing a customer request for a telephone installation, through the departments of the telephone company.

[11] The classic sociological treatment of industrial division of labor is Emile Durkheim's *On the Division of Labor in Society,* translated from the French by George Simpson (New York: the Macmillan Company, 1933; first published in Paris in 1893). Observation of division of labor and its analysis traces back to the Greek philosophers. Adam Smith, *The Wealth of Nations* (1776), was much impressed with technological division of labor, and used the example of common pin manufacture to suggest the reasons for specialization and division of labor.

[12] Cf. Durkheim, *On the Division of Labor in Society,* pp. 371-373.

[13] The elements of tasks analyzed here correspond to major elements in standard job analyses. We have emphasized the human relations aspects of these task elements, while the usual job descriptions focus on the activity aspects of task elements. See for example John F. Mee (ed.), *Personnel Handbook* (New York: Ronald Press, 1951), for a concise explanation of job analysis.

[14] U. S. Department of Labor, *Dictionary of Occupational Titles,* rev. ed. (Washington: Govern-

NOTES FOR CHAPTER 3 (CONT.)

ment Printing Office, 1949).

[15] Frederick W. Taylor, the "father" of scientific management, was very much concerned with developing the "one best way" of performing specific tasks. In attempting to solve this problem, he chose bodily movements as the common feature of tasks, and attempted to standardize bodily activity on the simplest, and least work demanding, movements necessary to accomplish a given task. His successes laid the foundation for a new discipline called motion study, concerned with rationalizing bodily movements in work. See Taylor's *The Principles of Scientific Management* (New York: Harper & Brothers, 1911) for the best comprehensive treatment of his position. Taylor's *Shop Management* (New York: Harper & Brothers, 1911) contains many case examples of the application of his principles of scientific management. Taylor was a leading exponent of specialization in management, and his influence has been widely felt in the design of management organizations.

[16] Whiting Williams, *Mainsprings of Men* (New York: Charles Scribner's Sons, 1925), pp. 58-63. Williams used the colorful phrase "social handles of the pay cup" to describe the sense of personal worth that a worker feels.

[17] Barnard, *The Functions of the Executive*. pp. 168-169, describes what he calls the "zone of indifference" in a subordinate's response to authority acts. The zone of indifference is the area in which there is unquestioned acceptance of authority. In the same sense, we are here suggesting that there is a zone of indifference for the task performance of fellow workers, where there is unquestioned acceptance of performance.

[18] There are a number of studies dealing with broad classes of organization specialists and the problems of their power in the organization. See for example Thorstein Veblen, *The Engineers and the Price System* (New York: The Viking Press, 1921), and James Burnham, *The Managerial Revolution* (New York: John Day, 1941). Part of identifying the independence and significance of a specialty is to assert its power in the operation of the organization. There is a tendency to equate power with functional essentiality, and to protect the exclusiveness of the functions performed by controlling entry of new people into the specialty.

[19] See Alex Inkeles and Peter H. Rossi, "National Comparisons of Occupational Prestige," *American Journal of Sociology* 61:329-339 (January, 1956), where six countries with widely different cultures were contrasted according to the ranking of occupations within them. High correlations were found, which the authors attribute to the universal features of the industrial system and the centralized national state. Variations in occupational standings occurred principally among agricultural and service occupations. See also E. J. Redmon, "Class Stratification in Industry: Its Social Implications," *Sociology and Social Research*, 33:212-217 (January-February, 1949).

[20] M. B. Sherif, Jack White, and O. J. Harvey, "Status in Experimentally Produced Groups," *American Journal of Sociology* 60:370-379 (January, 1955), have shown that when experimental group members are given an unstructured task for which they are sufficiently motivated, their estimates of each others' performance are influenced by the status each occupies in the group hierarchy. This study confirms the rapidity with which status ranking develops, even in experimentally formed groups.

[21] See Talcott Parsons, "An Analytical Approach to the Theory of Social Stratification," *American Journal of Sociology* 45:841-862 (May, 1940), where emphasis is placed on the general sharing of the criteria for assignment of status to individuals.

[22] See P. K. Hatt, "Occupation and Social Stratification," *American Journal of Sociology,* 55:533-543 (May, 1950), where the fact is stressed that there is no single ranking scale for all occupations, and that the socially meaningful rankings are usually made within major functional groups, rather than between them.

[23] Chester I. Barnard, "Functions and Pathologies of Status Systems in Formal Organizations," in W. F. Whyte (ed.), *Industry and Society* (New York: McGraw-Hill Book Co., 1946), points to the double side of the incentive coin when he asserts (p. 78) that "the resistance to loss of status is in general stronger than the desire to achieve higher status." This essay is the best single analysis of status in work organizations.

[24] *Ibid.*

[25] Specific examples of status systems in work organizations are contained in: Katherine Archibald, "Status Orientations Among Shipyard Workers," in R. Bendix and S. M. Lipset (eds.) *Class, Status and Power* (Glencoe: The Free Press, 1953); Orvis Collins, "Ethnic Behavior in Industry: Sponsorship and Rejection in a New England Factory," *American Journal of Sociology,* 51:293-298 (January, 1946); Julie Meyer, "Hierarchy and Stratification of the Shop," *Social Research* 14:168-190 (June, 1947); R. R. Meyers, "Myth and Status Systems in Industry," *Social Forces,* 26:331-337 (March, 1948); and David Rodnick, "Status Values Among Railroadmen," *Social Forces,* 20:89-96 (October, 1941).

[26] See G. C. Homans, "Status Among Clerical Workers," *Human Organization* 12:5-10 (Spring, 1953), where ledger clerks, who considered their status to be higher than cash posters, complained that they were being demeaned by being asked to do cash poster's work.

[27] T. N. Whitehead, *Leadership in a Free Society* (Cambridge: Harvard University Press, 1937), *passim,* has observed that methods of income payment have symbolic significance independent of the amount. F. J. Roethlisberger and W. J. Dickson, *Management and the Worker* (Cambridge: Harvard University Press, 1939, *passim,* have also reported that wages are sometimes viewed by workers as being meaningful in terms of competitive status in the organization.

The easiest behavior system to observe is the technological one. A highly skilled technician checking the wiring at a central telephone exchange, repeats many of the same tests when checking trouble reports. His tasks determine a great deal of his actual working behavior.

Chapter 4

BEHAVIOR SYSTEMS

In this chapter we will examine the behavior systems within which each member of a work organization carries out his daily round of tasks.

We analyzed power relations, authority relations, and status relations in Chapter 2 as fundamental types of human relations, and discovered how these relationships are structured in Chapter 3. These basic types of human relationships do not, however, define the specific acts of working members of an organization in their daily work performance.

When we analyze in this chapter the specific behavior systems surrounding work, we will find that each exhibits the three fundamental types of human relations, but in special and distinctive ways.

TYPES OF BEHAVIOR SYSTEMS

We will distinguish four basic behavior systems characteristic of every job. These are the *technological* behavior system, the *formal* behavior system, the *non-formal* behavior system, and the *informal* behavior system. Each will be examined separately.

Behavior systems define the specific acts by which various aspects of work are carried out. Each system has its unique features relating to special aspects of work. Each system supplements and complements the others. Every member of the work organization, in performing his job, operates in all four systems. However, his behavior in each system is quite different and distinct. Therefore, to understand working behavior, we must understand these four systems within which it is carried out.

The fundamental types of human relations are the *how* of behavior in organizations. We know that human beings will interact with each other in power, authority, and status relations to get work done. The four behavior systems of work are the *what* of behavior in organizations. The technological, formal, nonformal, and informal behavior systems tell us what people actually do when they are at work and working.

TECHNOLOGICAL BEHAVIOR SYSTEMS

The technological behavior system comprises the job or task activities. They are always specific to the job, and include what must be performed to get the job done. These activities are usually performed in standard ways. Each person filling the job has to perform these actions.

The actions are technological in character because they are technical acts related to equipment and its use, or to production processes and operations. Technical devices and technical knowledge are used to perform the acts required by the technological behavior system of a job.

We can grasp the nature of the technological behavior system best by taking a specific example of a job description. From the United States Employment Service we have the following description of a Strip Roller, who rolls out wire strip for subsequent processing into springs. Here is the description of the work performed, as shown on the job analysis schedule.

Finish rolls cold strip steel in a two-high rolling mill to reduce it to specified gage for processing into mechanical springs.

1. Loads Mill: Reads work ticket to ascertain type of steel to be rolled and total reduction specified. Refers to record book for directions on number of passes (consecutive reductions) and thickness to be achieved on each pass. Positions coil of strip on take-off reel (unwinding device), using an electric hoist; secures coil by clamping self-locks of reel and removes binding wires, using pliers. Manually threads end of steel strip through mill, inserting it between, over, or under a series of guide posts, pressure rollers, and felt-covered wipers. Clamps end of strip in lock of take-up reel (re-winding device). Alines threaded strip so that it lies in a straight path, by observing its direction and making set-screw or bolt adjustments to guideposts on bed of machine and take-off mechanism.

2. Sets up mill: Starts machine by clutch and reduces a few feet of strip on a trial pass. Stops mill and takes hand micrometer measurements to determine if specified reduction has been achieved. If tolerance for pass is not met, decides whether to raise or lower rollers to decrease or increase pressure on strip and alters position of rollers accordingly by turning handbar of screw-downs (control pistons) a slight degree, guided solely by sense of touch. Repeats trial runs and roller adjustments until tolerance of first pass is achieved. Similarly sets rollers for each sucessive reducing pass.

3. Operates mill to reduce strip: Observes action of mill and condition of metal to detect defective operation or roller wear. Frequently stops machine and takes micrometer measurements of rolled steel to determine accuracy of reduction. Makes required adjustments to rollers by shifting screw-down handles in order to achieve steel reduction, modifying degree of adjustment to compensate for expansion of rollers due to friction or variation in quality of steel, exercising care when adjusting screw-downs to avoid unbalanced pressure on rollers which would result in stretching one side of strip (edge sweep). As necessary corrects excessive thickness on one side of stock by increasing roller pressure on opposite side. Infrequently varies degree of reduction per pass upon approval of Foreman, Steel Mill. Infrequently rolls special orders on which written specifications are not available, by milling small sample strips until satisfactory standards are obtained. Occasionally operates two mills simultaneously, setting one for a finer degree of reduction than the other and treating the steel successively in the two mills.

4. Maintains equipment in good working con-

dition: oils parts as required. Dismantles rollers that require resurfacing by unbolting their supports in preparation for removal by Maintenance Men. Glues replacement felt pads to wipers and makes other minor adjustments as required. Verbally requests repair work by electrical or mechanical maintenance departments.

Note that the Strip Roller has to do many technical things to get his job done. He also has to do them in a particular order. A good deal of his behavior when he is operating the rolling mill is predetermined for him by the technological behavior system necessary to operate the mill and produce the wire for springs. It is also important to emphasize that all of this routine prescribed work for the Strip Roller takes place without reference to other people except a foreman at one point.

We could get even more specific about the details of the technological behavior system by making motion studies of a Strip Roller. Here we would have literal descriptions of physical movements; of hand movements like grasping, carrying, placing, moving, and turning, and also the motions through which the body goes while at work on the particular operations. These motion studies could be used for training the operator to run the strip mill.

It is quite clear that the technological behavior system is technical in character. It is also clear that it is a system of actions whose performance is necessary to get a job done. Every job, however simple, has a technological behavior system associated with its performance. It is a minimum condition of being able to hold a job that the person be able to perform the technological behavior required by it.

The technological behavior system is the one most divorced from a social setting. The requirements of technical behavior on a job are not determined by interpersonal relations. They are not determined by the human structure of the work organization. Technical behavior is determined by the relationship of the human body as a machine, or the person as a repository of knowledge, to the technological process and production equipment.[1]

Every work assignment has a technological behavior system necessary for its performance. In most production jobs the technical behavior is set forth in great detail. In administrative and executive positions technical behavior systems may be less specific in detail, involving the use of systematic knowledge in decision making. For salaried professions the technical behavior system may be highly specific, although very complex in character.

TECHNOLOGICAL BEHAVIOR AND POWER RELATIONS

Power relations involve the connections between separate functions. The technical behavior system for each job defines, through the job activities, the boundaries between separate functions.

Job activities are the most objective definition of functions. What an individual does in a specific technical sense in getting his job done is the most concrete way of describing his functions. Every individual knows, or should know, what he does on his own job. This tells him his own functions in the work complex of which his job is a part.

When a person has any awareness of the fragmentary character of his own job in the total work process, he then knows that somebody else, or many other people, will have to perform the other operations to complete the total task. A man working on an engine assembly line in an automobile plant, inserting the piston assemblies on one side of a V-8 engine, can observe directly that his task is only one of many necessary to assemble the complete engine. The motor block, as it reaches his position, already has assembled in it many of its components. After the block leaves his position on the line additional components are added to complete the motor. If the worker is inserting pistons on only one side of the motor block, then a corresponding worker must be inserting them on the other side.

In this example it is clear that the piston inserter knows his own function and has at least an awareness that other functions have to be performed in assembling the motor before it is complete. Furthermore, he knows that at least one other person does exactly the same operations as his own.

We can generalize by saying that the technical behavior system for each job makes specific for the worker on the job the functional division of labor, or the power structure, of which he is a part. Each technical work station in the total job complex is interdependent with others. A given job can be performed only if preceding jobs are performed first. In turn, the job is necessary for those which follow.

Job complexes are tied together through the power relations specifying the dependence of individual tasks in the job complex. Each individual knows his own functions by knowing the technical behavior required in performing his job. He also knows how his functions relate to others. Thus the technological behavior system is the fundamental action aspect of power relations.

TECHNOLOGICAL BEHAVIOR AND AUTHORITY RELATIONS

When the boss gives an order he specifies the situation to be covered, the actions necessary in the situation, and the timing of the required action, including its starting and ending points. These are the basic characteristics of an order or command.

A subordinate's technological behavior system makes it possible for the boss to foreshorten his order. Instead of specifying the action required in the situation, the boss may leave out this aspect of his command, or only partially specify it. The boss can ignore that part of his order which directs his subordinate to do specific things, because the subordinate already knows what these things are through his knowledge of his own technological behavior system.[2]

An example will make this point clear. Suppose the boss declares: "We will start producing walkie-talkie radios four weeks from today and will run 100,000 at the rate of 10,000 per week." This is a command specifying the production situation, to produce walkie-talkie radios; setting forth the starting time, four weeks from today; indicating the timing, 10,000 per week; and declaring the end point, 100,000 units, or ten weeks' run. The boss does not have to incorporate in his specific order the detailed operations required by the production department to carry out the production order. The boss knows what each department in the production process will do to produce walkie-talkie radios. The departments also know what their tasks will be in the production. Accordingly, the boss can issue his order in short, concise terms.

The technological behavior systems of work are therefore exceedingly important in making effective the exercise of authority. If each worker in every department, and each specialist, knows his own required technical behaviors, these do not have to be specified when an order is given. The boss' decision is therefore made much simpler because he can exclude any detailed statement regarding the behaviors required in carrying out his order.

We can state the relationship between technical behavior systems and authority relations more generally. The technological behavior systems specify the individual activities and tasks in a division of labor. A command initiating activity for a work complex need not specify the individual tasks and operations involved. Thus, technological behavior systems simplify direction and command of work operations.

TECHNOLOGICAL BEHAVIOR AND STATUS RELATIONS

Technological behavior provides important kinds of status marks. At least six fundamental features of technical behavior become marks of status distinction.[3]

There is, first of all, a status distinction between doing handwork and doing brainwork. Typically, the latter is more highly valued. An individual whose technical behavior is predominantly brainwork is very likely to have higher status than one whose technical behavior is largely physical or handwork. This distinction is found at all levels of the work organization.

A second technical feature of work that creates status distinctions is the difference between skilled work and routine work. An individual whose job is skilled generally ranks higher than one whose work is routine. The distinction between what is skilled and what is routine is usually measured by the amount of repetitiveness in the job activities. The more routine a job, the more repetitive it is likely to be.

A third feature of technical job activities that leads to comparative rating of people is the difference between creative and routine work. Almost invariably creative work is valued more highly than routine work. An individual who has to design a product, or develop a production operation, is usually accorded a higher status than one who continuously performs the same operation.

A fourth distinction in job operations is the one between individual responsibility and job standardization. A man whose work requires some exercise of judgment and the assumption of responsibility for his work behavior is typically ranked higher in status than one whose job is so completely standardized that he has a minimum of responsibility in determining how to fulfill it.

A fifth aspect of status distinctions attaching to technical behavior is the higher status generally accorded to complex jobs as over against simple jobs. Complex jobs requiring the use of distinctly different technical activities, or a series of related, intricate acts, generally stand higher in value than those which are simple in their details.

The difference between a long learning period and a short one may constitute a sixth feature of status in the technical behavior system. The man who has had a four-year apprenticeship in learning to become a journeyman is rated higher in status than a machine operator who can learn to run his machine in a matter of hours, or days. The engineer whose four years of college are a prerequisite to his profession rates higher in status than a foreman, who may be promoted overnight from the rank and file of workers.

These six aspects of technical behavior are sufficient to indicate how the characteristics of job operations become one basis for the assignment of status at work.

It should now be evident that the technological behavior system of each work assignment is a specific and concrete set of acts necessary in getting the job done. It is largely independent of the interpersonal aspects of work and relates the man to his machine or to the production process. At the same time the technological behavior system exhibits the basic human relations of work. It describes the division of labor and makes clear the chains of dependence among workers. It makes order-giving and order-receiving a very much simplified task in the authority relations of the organization. Finally, the specific characteristics of technical behavior determine status ranks, and thereby some of the actual kinds of preference and deference in work organizations.

FORMAL BEHAVIOR SYSTEMS

The formal behavior system relates each individual to the total work organization. The formal behavior system specifies the minimum conditions of acceptable membership in the work organization, just as the technological behavior system specifies the minimum conditions for holding a given job in the organization.

Generally speaking, the formal behavior system is a set of broad rules, regulations, and procedures governing conduct and behavior while at work. Such codes of behavior are very often incorporated in employee handbooks. They may be further amplified in company rules and regulations, posted as shop rules, or distributed in bulletin form to all the members of the organization.

The first general function of the formal behavior system is to specify the broad goals of the organization and the behavior necessary to achieve them. The organization goals include its specific reasons for existence. Thus a sales organization constantly emphasizes its sales activities. A factory places paramount emphasis on production. A service organization like a beauty shop, for example, constantly calls the attention of its employees to the need for satisfying customers by maximizing services to them. An oil exploration company orients all its employees toward the task of finding and exploiting oil resources.

In addition to specifying the general organization goals, the formal behavior system also indicates broad choices of behavior designed to achieve these goals. The maxim, "the customer is always right," is an important cue for behavior of sales people in a selling organization. Most organizations have similar slogans designed to specify the broad behavior necessary for functioning in them.

A second general function of formal behavior systems is to specify the rules of personal conduct. Members of the organization may be enjoined to display honesty, courtesy, willingness, obedience, and other desirable attributes in their personal business conduct. These codes of personal conduct, when abstracted from the organizational context, often have the quality of the simple moral rules of the society.

The third major function of formal behavior systems is to specify the duties and responsibilities of the individual to his employing organization. These set forth, in affirmative fashion, the concrete actions necessary to fulfill the rules of personal conduct, and the general behavior patterns expected. For example, the individual may be enjoined to report all absences from work; he may have the duty of accounting for all monies handled; he may be directed to keep adequate records of his work; or he may be required to accept the authority of his boss. The duties and responsibilities represent the formal requirements placed on the person by his work organization.

The fourth major function of the formal behavior system is to specify concrete values expected of all members. These values relate specifically to behavior. Every individual member of the organization may be expected to be loyal, faithful, willing, and bound by a sense of duty to his employer. In some kinds of organizations these values may take on a less moral character. The individual may be expected to be a "sharp" salesman, a shrewd bargainer, or a cunning production man. The values characterizing formal behavior systems of an organization provide significant cues for membership behavior.

The formal behavior systems of a work organization provide a broad framework of behavior standards for all its members. Each member learns, through the formal behavior system applying to him, the general goals of the organization, and his expected behavior designed to achieve these goals. He also learns the going values of the organization with respect to its goals. In addition, every member becomes aware of the rules governing his personal conduct, and his specific duties and responsibilities to the whole organization.

FORMAL BEHAVIOR AND POWER RELATIONS

The formal behavior system tends to be neutral with respect to the power structure and power relations of the organization. The reason for this is not hard to find. Formal behavior systems tend to apply to large classes of individuals and even to an entire company membership. Accordingly, there are few features of the formal behavior system that differentiate between groups of people according to their functions. If courtesy is expected in personal conduct, then all members of the organization are expected to be courteous. If the organization is declared to be a dynamic and growing one, then all its members' behavior is expected to be oriented toward a dynamic action pattern.

The formal behavior systems of work organizations have little to do with power relations. As we have already seen, the technological behavior system for each job is the major method by which the organization specifies the power structure. When the formal and technological behavior systems are combined, we have the minimum basis upon which new members of the organization can operate. From these two behavior systems they know what their job consists of and what their general orientation toward the organization ought to be. These two things permit the person to take his place immediately in the organization and begin effective work in it.

FORMAL BEHAVIOR AND AUTHORITY RELATIONS

The formal behavior system is the central one for legitimizing authority relations in the organization. The authority structure may be explicitly recognized in the formal behavior system by specifying for each member the need for being loyal, obedient, and willing in his participation. The class of people called bosses, at every level of the organization, are the people to whom loyalty, obedience, and willing subordination are given. So long as the individuals in the organization recognize the need for accepting authority relations, there tends to be little challenge to the exercise of authority.

Most individuals entering a work organization have had experience with authority relations in other organizations, like schools, churches, and even the home. It is therefore not necessary for the formal behavior system to spell out in detail the nature of the authority structure at work. The existence of an authority structure can be taken for granted. It can also be readily assumed that all new members have previously experienced authority relations, and accept them as necessary to direct the affairs of a complex organized group.

The formal behavior system, therefore, does not have to specify the need for authority, or convince new members that they must submit themselves to authority. The formal behavior system simply restates the fact that authority relations exist, and that in working in the organization every individual is expected to respect its legitimate authority holders.[4]

FORMAL BEHAVIOR AND STATUS RELATIONS

High status may attach to the degree to which an individual adheres to the requirements of the formal behavior systems. The relationship between status and compliance is probably not a linear one. The great bulk of people comply in an average way with formal behavior systems. They probably occupy a middle status position. For the smaller group of members who tend to behave with slavish conformity there may be a higher status accorded by superiors. Such people may be labeled "good company men," or "solid citizens," or "dependable characters." The same people viewed from the standpoint of their peers or subordinates may be viewed as "apple polishers." Thus, over-compliance may lead to a differential status assignment by superiors as against peers or subordinates.

At the other end of the scale those who do not comply with the requirements of the formal behavior system fall into two classes. There is first of all a group of rebels. These are the people who make a fetish out of evading social requirements and social responsibilities. The rebel has low status, particularly in the eyes of his superiors. Even peers and subordinates generally do not value rebellion for its own sake. The rebel, therefore, is likely to have low status even in the eyes of his equals and those over whom he exercises authority.

The second class of non-conformists are those who are driven by energy and initiative to be innovators. Such people do not conform to the formal behavior system because, from their view, they can do it better. The innovating non-conformist is likely to have a fairly high status so long as his innovations appear constructive. However, there is limited time period during which the innovation has to prove out. A bright young man eventually has to prove himself. His status declines rapidly if his energies continually are directed at innovations without any substantial record of accomplishment behind him.

The degree of compliance, and direction of compliance, with the formal behavior system constitutes one basis upon which status is assigned. Status ascription is most important at the extremes of over-compliance or non-compliance. For the bulk of people with average compliance with their formal behavior systems there is no differential status.

NON-FORMAL BEHAVIOR SYSTEMS

Non-formal behavior systems orient the individual with respect to his specific working objectives. The non-formal behavior system provides a means for modifying the technical behavior system within the allowable limits of the formal behavior system.

Suppose an individual is assigned a lathe to produce metal parts according to blueprint instructions. His technological behavior in operating the lathe is specified for him. His formal behavior is described by the expectation that he will operate his lathe, will do so at a speed sufficient to produce the metal parts in the required time, will do so with a minimum of wastage and tool breakage, and can expect to receive his allotted pay for getting the work done. Suppose further that this individual worker knows his lathe and its operating intricacies very well. With certain changes in his technological behavior in operating the machine he can produce more metal parts than expected by the company output standards. The worker then proceeds to produce the parts his way, rather than in the prescribed way, His behavior in deviating from the formal and technical requirements of his job can be called non-formal behavior.

Let us analyze the previous example in terms of its components. It will be noted, first, that the worker accepts the goal set for his work. He does produce the metal parts as expected by the company. Note also that the worker operates within the general limits of the formal behavior system. He is doing his work and only his work as the company expects. It will be seen also that he does not accomplish the work exactly as it has been specified for him by the company. Finally, it can be seen that the outcome of his deviant behavior is to produce a result, in number of pieces turned out, that is either equal to or greater than what the company expected.

In general the non-formal behavior system represents the actual way in which a job gets done. This reality may deviate from the planned scheme of things. It deviates, however, only in its operating features and not in terms of the goals toward which the behavior is directed.[5]

The non-formal behavior system permits the individual to do his work as well or better than the company expects, but to do it in unofficial ways. In this sense, we can say that the non-formal behavior system orients the individual with respect to his specific work goals. It also permits the individual to achieve these work goals in ways that may be either unique to himself, or shared only with colleagues.

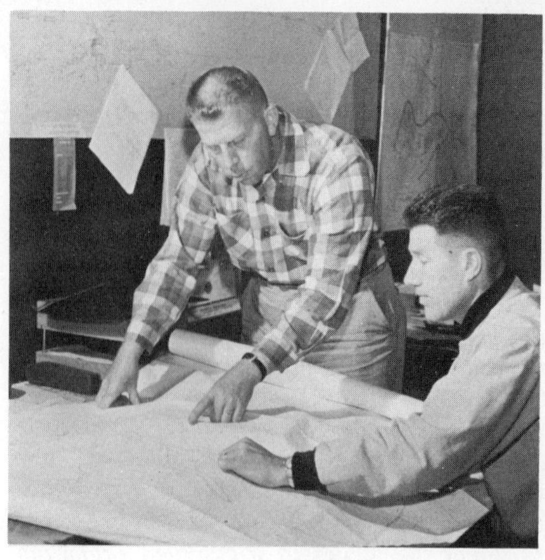

Field engineers, away from direct supervision of the "home office" may devise non-formal ways of getting their assignments done. The very nature of non-formal behavior systems, however, is that they are not readily visible, except to the members of the work organization privileged to use them.

We can see, then, that the non-formal behavior systems of work are the systematic ways in which corners are cut in getting work done. The non-formal behavior systems represent the constant inventiveness of people at work. They discover new and better ways of doing their work or discover different means for achieving the same work objectives.

Non-formal behavior systems always tend to be invisible to strangers observing a work group. For the newcomer to work, one of his most difficult learning tasks is to discover the non-formal behavior system surrounding his particular job. This discovery usually takes the form of being told by colleagues that "if you really want to get the the job done, this is the way you do it."

It is generally true that most positions and jobs have a significant proportion of the technological and formal behavior that is actually a part of the non-formal behavior system. The amount of working behavior in the non-formal system will vary according to the job. The more concrete the technological and formal behavior surrounding a job, the less will there be need for non-formal behavior systems to "really get the work done." With wider latitude in the technological and formal behavior system, a greater percentage of the behavior will be in the non-formal realm.

NON-FORMAL BEHAVIOR AND POWER RELATIONS

Non-formal behavior may modify the distribution of tasks in the work organization. When this happens there are changes in power relations and structures. A simple example from the literature will make the point clear.

In the Bank Wiring Room where the Western Electric sociological study was made, Taylor was a man of high status. His behavior is described in part as follows. When the wiremen were having difficulties with some defective wire, the foreman refused to replace it until it was used up. Two workers left the department and came back shortly with good wire for themselves. Taylor then left the department and returned with a large coil of good wire on a hand truck, enough for the entire work group. Here we have an example of a man who knew how, through "unofficial requisitioning" to secure needed materials even in the face of failure of the man officially responsible for providing proper materials. Taylor's behavior was in the non-formal realm since he, in all probability, did not go through proper channels in the correct manner in his "unofficial requisitioning" of good wire. Taylor had, in fact, taken over one of the functions of the foreman. This act of his succeeded in redistributing the power within the work group between himself and the foreman.[6]

Still another way in which power may be redistributed occurs when non-formal behavior modifies the relationships between tasks. A person may be able to cut corners in getting his job done by omitting or foreshortening related tasks. For example, the requisition procedures of a work organization may require a series of authorizing signatures before the requisition will be accepted by the purchasing department. In the normal course of business the requisition might move through the company mail to each person whose signature is required, and then to the purchasing department where a written order would be placed with an outside vendor. A person requiring an item in a hurry might foreshorten the procedure by hand carrying the requisition to each man whose signature is required. He might even secure alternate signatures in the absence of a person whose authorizing approval is necessary. Having accumulated all the necessary authorizations, our man in a hurry might then take the requisition personally to the purchasing department, and make a plea for expediting his order. He might succeed in convincing the purchasing agent to issue a verbal purchase order to a vendor and save additional delivery time.

This example suggests that the non-formal behavior system is one in which corners can be cut in getting work done by changing the normal relationships between tasks. In effect, the man in a hurry to purchase an item performed other functions than his own (that of the mail boy, for example), and succeeded in getting others to modify their tasks to accommodate him (the purchasing agent's use of a verbal rather than a written order to the vendor).

We may summarize by suggesting that the non-formal behavior system modifies power relations and power structures in two ways: (A) Functions may actually be shifted from one job to another through unofficial behavior, and (B) Related tasks are modified in order that a given task may be accomplished more expeditiously.

NON-FORMAL BEHAVIOR AND AUTHORITY RELATIONS

Non-formal behavior may modify the authority structure in two ways. In the first instance the non-official behavior may have the result of "making the boss look good." In the second instance the non-official behavior may circumvent an authority holder, lessening or destroying his authority.[7]

In the case where the non-formal behavior is designed to make the boss look good, subordinates are concerned with doing their jobs as they know they must be done, rather than doing them as the boss directs. The fact that an authority holder has highly legitimate authority to exercise does not guarantee that he will be right in all his orders, commands, and decisions. For subordinates the dilemma then arises as to whether they will follow orders literally, doing what they know is "wrong" in performing their tasks, or whether they will make personal modifications in the boss' orders so as to do their jobs "right."

There is typically an illusion of infallibility about a boss. This illusion is heightened by the fact that he may appear to be right even when his decisions are wrong. The boss turns out to appear right because his subordinates make his decisions effective by doing what their knowledge and experience tell them must be done, instead of what the boss commands. The non-formal behavior system is the realm in which subordinates can operate to do the right things in getting their jobs done even if the boss has ordered otherwise.

The second case where authority structure is modified by non-formal behavior occurs where an authority holder is a figurehead. In such instances, the form of subordination may be followed, but the actual practice will be to follow the directions of the real authority rather than the figurehead boss. The non-formal behavior systems may be the area where the real structure of authority relations operates. The real structures and relations may differ from the blueprinted, or organization chart, assignment of authority positions.

NON-FORMAL BEHAVIOR AND STATUS RELATIONS

Status ascriptions relating to behavior in the non-formal realm are largely made by peers and co-workers. The very nature of the non-formal behavior systems makes them relatively private areas of behavior. Those persons who have knowledge about, and facility in handling, non-formal behavior patterns are likely to be known primarily to their peers and colleagues. These experts in non-formal behavior will be accorded high status by their co-workers. Such experts in non-formal behavior may have their status further enhanced because they become the instructors for the newcomers to the organization. They become the fountainhead of knowledge about how one "really gets work done around here," and exercises considerable discretion as to whether and when the neophyte will be instructed in the mysteries and art of doing his job. Status ascriptions of high standing are therefore made to those who have considerable knowledge about their non-formal behavior systems, and who can pass on this knowledge to newer generations of workers.

INFORMAL BEHAVIOR SYSTEMS

Informal behavior systems cover the area of direct interpersonal relations of a voluntary character. Informal relations occur, therefore, in addition to the relationships required of people to get their work done. We can look at informal relations as filling up the time during which people at work have some freedom to interact with each other above and beyond the requirements of their work assignments.

Informal interaction with others at work is not necessary in order to get work done. On the other hand, few kinds of working assignments so completely demand the full attention of their occupants that they do not have time for informal interaction with colleagues. Informal relations with other people at work are a natural consequence of being brought together while working, and having free time to interact.

Informal relations are grounded in conventions governing the ways people behave toward each other in situations of free choice. So long as these conventions are shared with other people, we can look upon the behaviors resulting from them as systems. We give to them the name informal behavior systems.

Informal behavior systems serve as means for ordering the free interpersonal relations of people on jobs. They are the connective links between persons based on individual personality characteristics, and permit social relations that recognize the unique qualities of each person.[8]

It is desirable to distinguish at this point between non-formal and informal behavior systems. We can illustrate the difference in the "grapevine" as a channel of communication. We are likely to think of the grapevine as operating at the informal level to transmit gossip and non-official information from one person to another. Further reflection about the grapevine suggests that it is part of non-formal behavior systems, and not informal behavior systems. The grapevine supplements the information channels of the formal organization. The information passed along the grapevine is highly relevant to work. It serves to amplify official communication, or substitute for it. Thus, what appears to be an informal aspect of work turns out to be a non-formal feature of getting work done. It is true that the grapevine requires face-to-face interaction in passing gossip along. The gossip, however, is usually directly related to the work situation and may be highly important in doing an effective job. Put another way, communication along the grapevine is not random. The subjects about which people talk and gossip are relevant to work, and their work organizations.[9]

The two girls are engaged in animated conversation as they assemble a mimeographed report with their male associate. Such informal behavior is above and beyond the interaction required to get work done. When continued over a long period of time, such informal relations become systematic for their participants.

INFORMAL BEHAVIOR AND POWER RELATIONS

Informal behavior takes place outside required job activities. Accordingly, there can be at best only an indirect relationship between informal social relations and power structures. Generally, informal behavior is independent of the functional division of labor and distributions of tasks.

What people do in their informal relations is largely concerned with personal experiences, and events that lie outside the scope of work itself. The sexual exploits of single male workers, real or imagined, may be the subject of endless informal discourse at work; the state of professional athletics; the probable winners in today's horse races; politics; love; distress; personal tragedies or disasters; discontents and hatreds; rest-period poker, cribbage, or crap games; and a host of other commonplace subjects are the content of talk in the informal relations of people at work.

In Chapters 6 and 16, detailed analysis is presented of group life of work organizations, and its impact on work. In those chapters consideration is given to informal groups as aspects of the working environment. In this chapter, we will therefore consider only general aspects of informal behavior systems. What we have said here about the connections between informal behavior and power relations deals with the relations inside a group that are informal in character. We will note later on in Chapters 6 and 16 that an informal group, like a clique, is important in organizing people for the pursuit of power in a work organization.

INFORMAL BEHAVIOR AND AUTHORITY RELATIONS

When boss and subordinate are in each other's presence a minimum of informal relations occur. This is true because each feels constrained to maintain his own position in the authority structure. Neither the boss nor his subordinate feels perfectly free to "be himself" when the two are together.

Informal relations require a person to be able to behave as he "really is," rather than as he thinks he ought to behave in doing his work. When an authority holder fraternizes too freely with his subordinates, it may result in too much knowledge about his personal idiosyncracies and personality characteristics, some of which may diverge from the image of him as an authority holder. Subordinates may have too much opportunity to perceive the all-too-human qualities of the authority holders and, perhaps, have some of their faith in the competence and adequacy of the boss shaken. This is one of the most important reasons why an authority holder typically has a confidant who is not part of his work organization. The confidant is the person to whom real confidences can be expressed and with whom completely relaxed discourse can take place. So long as the confidant is not part of the authority structure in which the person works, these confidences will have no "feedback" to the work organization.

Viewing informal relations with a superior from the subordinate's standpoint we find other kinds of constraints operating. It is quite difficult to "be yourself" in the company of the boss because he may use this information in deciding on promotions, salary increases, or other rewards. It may, of course, be advantageous for the boss to know an individual as completely as possible, in order that the boss' impressions will be most favorable. On the other hand, there is always the chance that the boss will discover personal qualities that he thinks undesirable, and react unfavorably.

It is characteristic of informal relations that those interacting accept each other for what they really are, rather than what they would like to be. So long as either the boss or the subordinate has any concern that his informal behavior will present a picture to the other that might have unfavorable consequences in their official relations, there is an important constraint on his entering into informal relations.

There may be a number of situations in which people with different authority can interact on informal grounds. These are, however, structured situations in which a common focus of attention occupies them. They may, for example, be members of the same bowling team, or play golf together in the company golf tournament. They may picnic together at the firm's annual picnic, be lodge brothers, or members of the same post of a veteran's organization, or the same congregation of a church. It should be noted that the interaction that takes place in such contexts is always centered around the common interest that brings them together in the first place. With their attention centered on this common interest, there may be no conflict betweeen their informal behavior and their authority relations at work. Indeed, it may even be possible for the authority relations to be reversed in the non-work associations. A man might be an officer in his lodge while his boss is only an ordinary member. They interact in the lodge context quite differently from the way they behave toward each other at work. These two realms of behavior are kept separate from each other.

We may conclude that the informal relations do not provide a channel for modifying the authority structures of work organizations. Informal relations are not readily substituted for authority relations.

INFORMAL BEHAVIOR AND STATUS RELATIONS

Through informal relations two or more people get to know each other on a highly personal basis. They come to know each other at work as persons and not merely as job holders or functionaries. This knowledge of personal characteristics becomes highly relevant to the ascription of status based on these personal characteristics.

It is through informal relations that status is assigned to people on the grounds of their personal and more or less private characteristics. Thus, a person may be rated as thoughtful, tense, generous, frivolous, sympathetic, or withdrawn, as a result of informal interaction with him. It is only through informal interaction that these characteristics of the person become evident. Indeed, it is often true that a considerable difference emerges between the official image of a person, and the image we secure through informal relations with him. This may often lead to surprise that the person turns out to be different from the image of him secured from his official behavior in carrying out his work assignment. The tough boss who turns out to have a heart of gold is but one of countless illustrations. In his official relations this boss appears tough and hard-hearted. When his fellow managers get to know him as a personality they may discover that he is relaxed and kindly in his relations with them, in sharp contrast to his tough and aloof behavior when he is acting as boss toward his subordinates.

There may be variations in the ascription of status that are the consequence of informal relations. These variations are the result of different kinds and degrees of informal contact. Informal relations are restricted to face-to-face circumstances. The number of people who can enter into informal interaction is limited. Furthermore, the interaction may be more intensive with some people than with others. A "buddy" is the object of intense and continuous interaction, while a friend may be met less frequently and more casually. This variation in kind and intensity of interaction leads to different amounts of knowledge about each other. Consequently a person may be assigned different status rankings by those who are his informal associates, but who have different degrees of intimacy with him. The old folk saying that "familiarity breeds contempt," and its parallel, "familiarity develops respect," summarizes the graduations in status standings that come from different kinds and amounts of informal relationships.

Status ascriptions resulting from informal relations establish privileges and develop obligations. Privileges are the free choices permitted individuals in their behavior toward others, at the informal level. The higher a person's status, the greater the number of privileges he may be accorded by his informal associates. A respected person may be permitted the privilege of crotchety views about the world, and acid evaluations of his informal colleagues. He is accorded the privilege of expressing himself in such terms without offending his informal associates. A low status person attempting to exercise the same privileges of criticism might be rapidly cut off by his colleagues.

A sense of obligation arising from informal relations is the feeling of commitment and loyalty to associates. Obligations are reciprocal in character. A high status person, like the one just described, may feel a strong obligation to defend his informal associates against the external world, at the same time he is running them down to their face. This is reciprocated by his informal colleagues in their feeling of obligation to accept and even respect his views.[10]

We may conclude that informal behavior has its primary significance for work in affecting the status relations among peers or colleagues. This effect is limited to ascription of status based upon personal characteristics that can only be known through informal relations.

BEHAVIOR SYSTEMS AND THE PERSON

We can now view the person as entering into his work assignment through his actions in four different behavior systems. These behavior systems cover his major relevant working-time activities.

Each behavior system has its special realm covering a distinctive area of necessary working behavior. It should not be concluded, however, that these four areas of behavior are independent in the sense that a person can do his work by only learning one, two, or three of the behavior systems surrounding it. It is necessary for the individual worker to operate in all four of the behavior systems while working.

There is an obvious order in which the behavior systems of a work assignment are learned. Usually the technical behavior system is learned first. It is the principal subject matter of all job training, and obviously of central importance in learning job tasks. The formal behavior system is learned along with the technical, or right after it. Formal behavior is learned through orientation training. The

CHART 4.1

BEHAVIOR SYSTEMS RELATE WORKERS TO THEIR WORK ENVIRONMENT

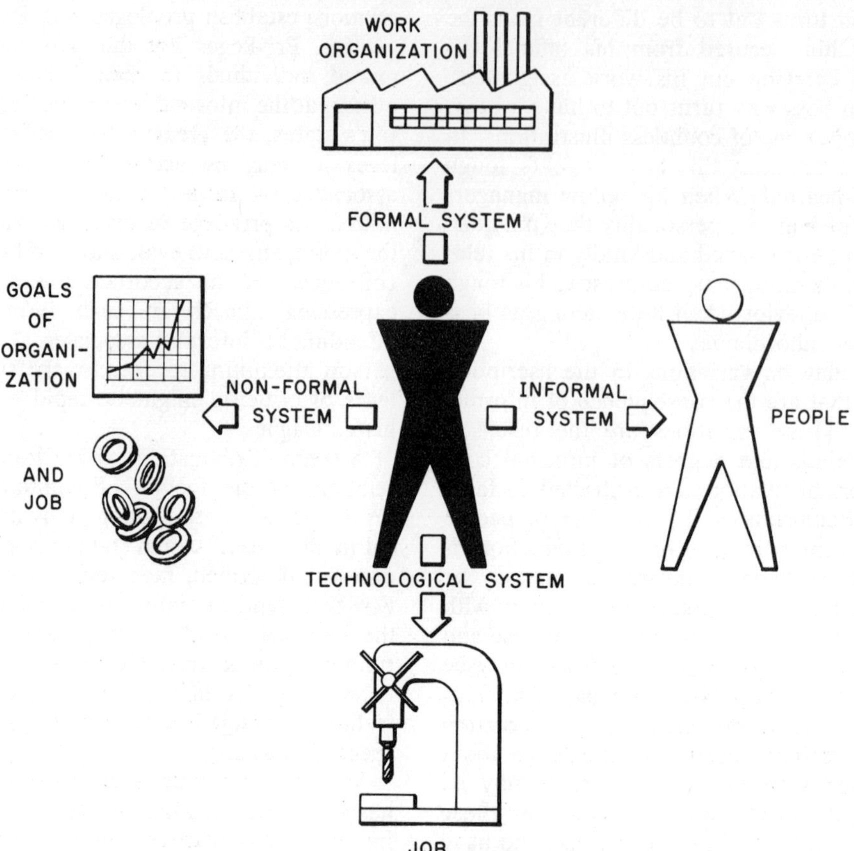

newcomer is given knowledge about the rules, regulations, goals, and purposes of his work organization. After learning these two behavior systems of his work, the new employee is largely on his own in finding out about the non-formal behavior appropriate to getting his work done, and in developing informal relations with his working colleagues. The adjusted worker is one capable of operating in all four behavior systems surrounding his work assignment.

In Chart 4.1 we summarize the ways in which the behavior systems relate the person to his working environment.

Task activities are developed through the technological behavior system. The relations of a person to his job or organization goals and their effective achievement are developed through the non-formal behavior system. This behavior system is important also in developing personal skill in unofficial but effective ways of performing his technical tasks.

The formal behavior system relates the person to the organization in which he operates. He learns here the broad rules of standard behavior as well as the general objectives of his participation as a worker. In the informal behavior system we have the means by which the person relates himself to other persons in his working environment.

This chart summarizes the view of a person at work from the standpoint of the actions and activities that he has to learn in getting his work done.

Chapters 2 and 3 set forth an analytical scheme for understanding the fundamental human relations of working behavior. All interactions between positions can be viewed as power relationships, authority relationships, or status relationships. This is the general view of all working behavior regardless of the systems in which the behavior is found.

When we turn our attention from the general types of human interaction, and ask how the person develops his own behavior at work, we find that there are four behavior systems within which his activities occur. These systems are the technological behavior system, the formal behavior system, the non-formal behavior system, and the informal behavior system. These two views of working behavior give us an analytical scheme by which we can understand the processes of human interaction and cooperation at work.

In Chapter 5 a way is developed for locating each person in relation to all others in the work organization. At the end of that chapter we will show that the fundamental human relations and the behavior systems are the component parts of an analytical scheme for understanding what happens to the person when he moves from his general social environment into the special environment of his work organization.

NOTES FOR CHAPTER 4

[1] It is precisely because of the non-human aspect of the technological behavior system that modern analysts of human relations have largely ignored this work behavior system. Part of this neglect is also associated with a rejection of earlier industrial studies that focused upon the technological behavior systems in trying to understand such phenomena as fatigue and inattention. There has also been a rejection of the mechanistic assumptions involved in exclusive emphasis upon the technological behavior systems of work as being determinate of working behavior. The point at which modern analysts turned away from considering technological behavior systems as even relevant was the publication of the research of the Mayo school: Elton Mayo, *The Human Problems of an Industrial Civilization* (New York: The Macmillan Company, 1933); but especially F. J. Roethlisberger and W. J. Dickson, *Management and the Worker* (Cambridge: Harvard University Press, 1939). *Management and the Worker* was an open admission that working conditions, if varied, did not produce expected changes in working behavior. This led to a very fruitful emphasis on the social aspects of work. Unfortunately, it has also led to an implicit rejection of the technology of work, as being insignificant for working behavior. We are concerned with restoring a meaningful balance in which the technological behavior system takes a coordinate position with the other work behavior systems in the analysis of people at work.

[2] The analysis of authority acts has emphasized many of their aspects but no treatment has placed such stress on the way in which technological behavior systems make commanding more efficient. Cf. Herbert A. Simon, *Administrative Behavior* (New York: The Macmillan Company, 1947), especially Chapters 7 and 8.

[3] The status distinctions of technical behavior are implicit in all job evaluation schemes. We make them explicit here simply to show how status relations result from technical behavior. Carroll L. Shartle, *Occupational Information* (Englewood Cliffs, N.J.: Prentice-Hall, Inc., 1952), is the best single volume dealing with job description and evaluation. See also Joseph Tiffin, "The Joint Committee on Job Evaluation," in Arthur Kornhauser (ed.), *Psychology of Labor Management Relations* (Champaign: Industrial Relations Research Association, 1949), which summarizes some of the more technical points of current controversy in the job evaluation field.

[4] This is a simplified way of stating that loyalty in the work organization is given to the impersonal order, the formal behavior system, rather than the person of authority, or his traditional office. See Robert Dubin, *Human Relations in Administration* (Englewood Cliffs, N.J.: Prentice-Hall, Inc., 1951), pp. 195-198.

[5] It is interesting that very much analytical attention has been focused upon the ways in which actual working behavior thwarts organization goals. Since the pioneering work of S. B. Mathewson, *Restrictions of Output among Unorganized Workers* (New York: Viking Press, 1931), it has been fashionable to call attention to worker behavior that deliberately goes against management expectations. What has been almost completely overlooked is the fact that unofficial ways exist to accomplish the objectives of the organization, and that these too are practiced by the rank and file of a work organization. The most immediate example of the constructive contribution of non-official behavior systems is contained in Melville Dalton, "Unofficial Union-Management Relations," *American Sociological Review*, 15:611-619 (October, 1950), in which it is demonstrated that in unofficial ways the union contract is made to work.

[6] As reported and discussed in G. C. Homans, *The Human Group* (New York: Harcourt, Brace and Company, 1950), p. 78.

[7] This is elaborated in Dubin, "Organization Fictions," *Human Relations in Administration*, pp. 341-345.

NOTES FOR CHAPTER 4 (CONT.)

[8] The classic analyses of informal relations are: Georg Simmel, *The Sociology of George Simmel,* translated and edited by K. H. Wolff (Glencoe: The Free Press, 1950), and C. H. Cooley, *Social Organization* (New York: Charles Scribner's Sons, 1909). The students of human relations in industry have placed major emphasis on informal relations in work organizations. An excellent summary of almost fifteen years' work by W. F. Whyte and his students is contained in his *Money and Motivation,* (New York: Harper & Brothers, 1955). This volume is rich in illustrative material showing informal relations at work, and their consequences for the work organization.

[9] Cf. Herbert A. Simon, *Administrative Behavior,* pp. 160-162, where he discusses the grapevine as an aspect of informal communication.

[10] One of the classic studies of informal relations in the setting of a boy's gang is W. F. Whyte, *Street Corner Society* (Chicago: University of Chicago Press, 1937). Whyte places great stress on the reciprocity of relations. This same emphasis is given a more formal presentation in Homans, *The Human Group.*

Job holders meet with a top office holder. Henry Ford II, President of the Ford Motor Company, chats with some foundrymen outside the company's Dearborn iron foundry.

Chapter 5

JOBS, POSITIONS, OFFICES

In this chapter we will examine the complex relationships between the working person and his organizational setting. We are concerned with what happens to the person when he brings his experiences from the larger society into his place of work. How is his self-conception as a worker formed? What features of his work assignment and his work organization mold him into a productive worker capable of adequate performance?

In the three previous chapters we have examined the basic human relations of work, the structuring of these human relationships into enduring patterns, and the behavior systems through which working activity is expressed. In this chapter we want to discover the focal points of the work organization at which the molding processes take place in making good workers out of new employees. In the process of our analysis we will illustrate the discussion with pictures of top executives, middle management, first line supervision, staff personnel, and production workers.

From this chapter you will gain a view of

how people come to be functionaries of work organizations. You will also have an initial picture of some of the broad classes of personnel making up work organizations.

DIVISION OF LABOR

We need something like a system similar to the horizontal and vertical lines on a mercator map in order to place people in a work organization. The map, with its reference lines at right angles to each other, is indispensable in finding a particular place. Similarly, organizational coordinates are necessary in locating each individual within the work organization. These guide lines are the starting point for locating people at work.

The fundamental locating coordinates of work are *operation* and *activity*. By operation we mean the general steps through which a person goes in doing his daily work. By activity we mean the functional role his work plays in the operating scheme.

OPERATING DEPARTMENTS AND DIVISIONS

When we consider work in terms of the actual operations involved in its performance, we secure a horizontal dimension of the organization. We can view the organization as being subdivided into specialized areas of operation. Typical broad operating areas of commercial and industrial firms are: producing, selling, purchasing materials and supplies, accounting for income and expenses, maintaining plant and equipment, financing, and recruiting and servicing employees.[1]

Usually, these distinctive operations of a firm are organized into separate groups called divisions, branches, departments, sections, or units. In Chart 5.1 we have a typical picture of the separate broad operations of a business, divided into departments whose titles describe the operations involved.

This is the horizontal division of labor. It is the first division of labor to be noted on entering a work organization. Operations are classified by departments whose designation generally reveals the special operations carried on in them. A customer wanting to buy some goods knows he must go to the sales department for service. A salesman trying to sell the company some new machine tools knows that he can do his business with the purchasing department. A job seeker knows he must go to the personnel department to apply for work. A foreman needing repairs on a machine will call the maintenance department.

There is no theoretical limit to the extent to which operations can be specialized in departments. Indeed, it is one of the characteristics of large scale organizations that they exhibit growth by continual specialization of the horizontal division of labor.

Extension in the horizontal division of labor

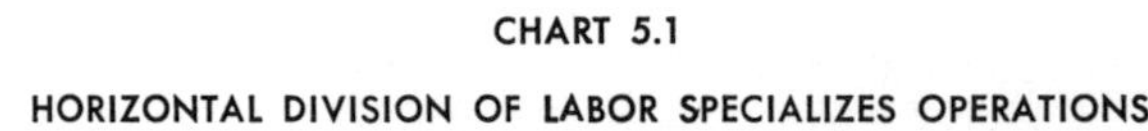

CHART 5.1

HORIZONTAL DIVISION OF LABOR SPECIALIZES OPERATIONS

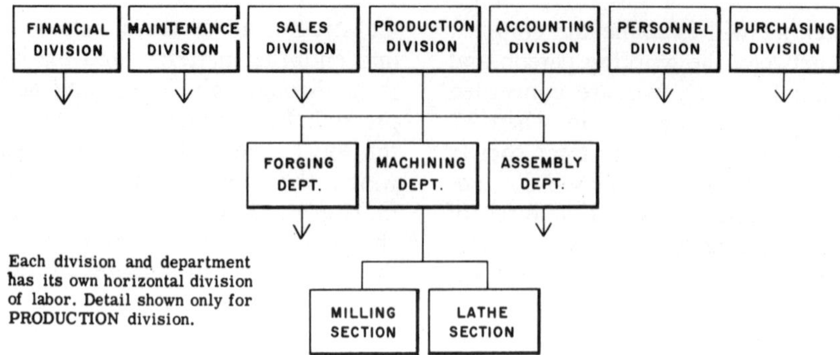

takes place in one of two ways. A given department may have an operation carried on in it that, over a period of time, takes more and more attention of a growing number of people. When the operation is continuous enough, and the group is large enough, a supervisor is appointed and the group is given independent designation as a unit, section, or department.

The second manner of growth in the horizontal division of labor is to start a new operation. This operation may gradually grow in the amount of time devoted to it until it, too, is given independent status as a unit, section, or department. When this growth in the horizontal division of labor is rapid, it may become the vehicle for opportunists in the organization to seek supervisory positions, or to make more important their present positions of supervision. This is popularly called "empire building" when it exceeds the actual needs of the organization, and when it results from a desire for personal aggrandizement.[2]

There is no immediate and obvious basis upon which we can rank operations in an order of importance. We can view the work organization as a collection of necessary operations, all of which are essential to the total functioning of the organization. Who is to say that salesmen are more important than production men (except, of course, salesmen themselves)? Does it make any sense to assert that the purchasing operation is more important than the production operation, because the latter cannot go to work until supplies are on hand with which to work?

Departmentalizing divides the organization into separate working units, but the same goals that dictate division of parts also require the dependence of each upon the others. It is only the total complex of all operations that makes the whole organization.

We can conclude, then, that knowing an individual's place in the scheme of work starts with knowing the department in which he is employed. We have to know his place in the horizontal division of labor. When we do, we already know some important things about him. We know the general operations he performs in doing his work.

DIFFERENTIAL KINDS OF ACTIVITY

It will be recalled that the second general organization coordinate is that of activity. We are here concerned with the functional role that an individual's work plays in the total operation of getting work done.

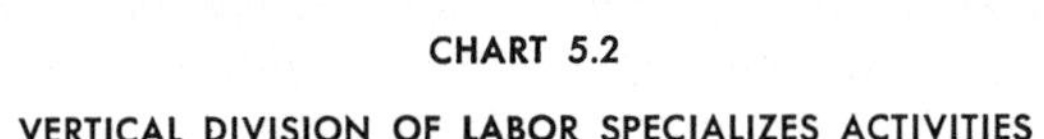

CHART 5.2

VERTICAL DIVISION OF LABOR SPECIALIZES ACTIVITIES

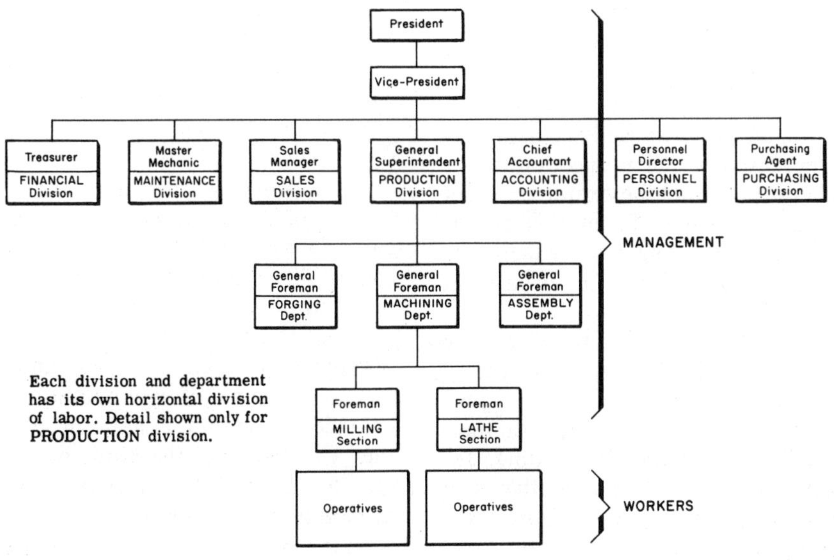

Each division and department has its own horizontal division of labor. Detail shown only for PRODUCTION division.

We can distinguish five general functions in work: (A) actually *doing the work* of the organization; (B) *directing* others who do the actual work; (C) *coordinating* those who direct the work operations; (D) *controlling* the quality and quantity of work performed; and (E) *innovating* for the organization.

The most general distinction in every work organization is between those who do the work and those who direct it. This is the common distinction between workers and management, between rank-and-file and those in authority. Typically this distinction is viewed as a vertical dimension of organization. Thus, in Chart 5.2 we have illustrated the two broad vertical layers of work organizations, workers and management. It will be noted that the distinction between workers and management cuts across each department.

We now have a primitive two-dimensional set of reference coordinates for locating every person in the organization in terms of his position in the horizontal division of labor, and in terms of the broadest vertical division of labor. We can say that a person performs specific operations required in a given department, and that he is actually doing productive work, or directing others at it.

TYPES OF AUTHORITY ACTIVITY

We now consider the differences among directing, coordinating, controlling, and innovating as distinctive forms of authority activities. We are here concerned with the different kinds of activity carried out by management. Not all managers do the same thing. Functional roles do differ among management personnel.[3]

Not all persons directing others at work have the same *amount* of responsibility for decision, nor do they have the same *kinds* of decision making responsibilities. It is therefore necessary to analyze the different types of authority activities in terms of the amount and kinds of decision making responsibility.

AMOUNT OF AUTHORITY

The amount of authority activity a person has is best measured by the proportion of his working time during which he exercises direct control over subordinates. From this standpoint the amount of directing activity increases as the authority is delegated downward in the organization.

The top executive of an organization may have a relatively small amount of directing activity. He does not undertake direct supervision of his immediate subordinates, or their subordinates, for very much of the time. Indeed, we often think of a chief executive who is capable of keeping his desk cleared for action as being the "best" kind of executive. Such a chief executive exercises relatively small amounts of direction over others, and delegates completely to his immediate subordinates the responsibility for their own actions. Nevertheless, as we shall see in the discussion of the kinds of direction exercised, the chief executive in this instance has not given up his responsibility for the over-all direction of the organization. We might call this the "responsibility paradox." It is seen particularly in the case of the chief executive that the amount of direction of others decreases while the kind of direction of others becomes more far-reaching.[4]

We can put the situation the other way around and suggest that for the lowest level of line supervisor the opposite may be true. The first line supervisor may exercise a large amount of direction, but of a limited sort only, over his immediate subordinates.

It is probable that from the top to the bottom of the organization there is a reciprocal relationship between the amount of responsibility for direction of subordinates, and the kind of direction that is given. This analysis suggests, that at the middle reaches of an organization, administrators and executives face a dilemma of maintaining an adequate balance between the amount of supervision they exercise, and the kinds of direction they give to subordinates. For the middle reaches of management, there may well be difficulty in working out an adequate supervisory pattern to encompass the sometimes incompatible demands of continuous directing supervision as over against coordinating, controlling, and innovating activities.[5]

It is certainly possible to differentiate jobs, positions, and offices in the organization in terms of the *amount* of authority exercised. This, however, is an incomplete basis for the analysis of responsibility. The *kind* of direction exercised is also important in understanding the delegation and execution of responsibility.

We have already indicated that there are four kinds of authority, namely, directing, coordinating, controlling, and innovating. We will now examine them individually.

DIRECTING AUTHORITY

The individual with directing authority is given the task of seeing that a fixed and established operation is carried forward in accordance with predetermined expectations. Thus a foreman may be expected to fulfill a production schedule with the assigned materials, machines, and men in an established period of time, with a minimum amount of scrap loss and machine maintenance. We can consider operating authority as involving the actual productive or "doing" part of an organization. It is what one typically sees when he looks at the day-to-day operations of an organization.[6]

A foreman spends most of his time directing the work of his work group. The foreman goes to the scene of actual work and has visual and verbal contact with his workers. Here the foreman (in tin hat) is supervising a crew welding sections of an oil pipeline together.

Directing authority is essentially of a conserving, or conservative, nature. A foreman, for example, attempts to repeat an already established and successful production pattern, continuing to repeat it to the satisfaction of those who set the standards for him. Those with directing authority are concerned essentially with any and all elements that stabilize an operation, making it highly predictable and relatively easy to manipulate in terms of the desired operating goals. It is for this reason that we often find collusion at the foreman level, for example, where the foreman will go along with his subordinates' preferences because by so doing he is able to achieve a stable and highly predictable system of operation.[7] Furthermore, from this stable operating system he is able to develop adequate bases for satisfying higher management expectations.

We can see the possibility that management demands for increased efficiency, for innovation, for reduction in scrap loss, for any change that might affect a stable and going system of operations, may not be cordially received by those who have directing authority. To them any factor introducing change in the operating situation may be unstabilizing.

In resistance to change at the directing authority level we can begin to see the origin of specialization in such things as safety, industrial engineering, cost control, personnel, and the like. It is the experience of management that to depend upon individuals having operating authority to be innovators is to lose the spirit of innovation and the exercise of initiative in the organization. It is too much of a demand to expect that a person with operating responsibility can, at the same time, fulfill an innovating, coordinating, and controlling responsibility as well.

CONTROLLING AUTHORITY

A responsibility for controlling the behavior of others involves establishing and policing recognized standards of behavior. In more highly organized situations we have such operations as production control, safety control, inventory control, and scrap control, all having to do with establishing adequate limits, and then making sure that the operators stay within these limits. Controls are designed to provide instantaneous information as to the adequacy of any given production or operating unit, so as to be able to analyze those situations requiring special attention or correction because they are no longer within acceptable control limits.[8]

Controlling authority is one that basically lends itself well to a high degree of specialization within the organization. Thus, we are likely to get a production control department with sole responsibility for controlling the flow of production on the production floor itself. In other areas we have budget control and a host of other operating controls.

Where the immediate supervisor is required to meet controlling limits established by another agency, he is likely to view this as (A) an intrusion on his area of responsibility, and (B) an invitation to "beat the system." Every organization of any size has its "statistical virtuosos" who can prepare reports on their operating departments in ways to make themselves look good. When this becomes possible on a wide scale, it is clear that the operating responsibility and the controlling responsibility have become so intermingled that the latter loses a great deal of its effectiveness. Those who are responsible for maintaining the systems of control become the victims of statistical tricks that deprive the organization of desirable and necessary knowledge. The systems of control become burdensome statistical operations without producing adequate returns for the investment of time and energy expended.

COORDINATING AUTHORITY

With the work organization composed of many special departments, supervised by people with different amounts and kinds of authority, it is clear that there has to be adequate responsibility for coordination at some points and levels. This coordinating responsibility tends to increase as one goes higher in the organization. The reason for this is obvious. At the higher levels of the organization, specializations come together and require balancing for effective performance of the total organization.[9]

For example, one of the characteristic problems of the business organization is to balance the demands, needs, and desires of the sales department with those of the production departments. Sales personnel are likely to ask for things that make products more salesworthy, over the objections of the production staff which sees these as difficult or costly to incorporate in the product. In an educational institutional there is likely to be a similar kind of conflict between the academic staff and the non-academic staff. For the academic staff all other members of the organization exist to provide the necessary services for teaching and research. For the non-academic staff, the academic people may be considered visionaries and impractical souls who have no sense of neatness, orderliness, and businesslike methods. The administration of an educational institution demands, at the top reaches, someone who can keep in balance academic and non-academic aspects of the organization. Add to this the problems of the athletic association, and it becomes clear that the task is not only necessary but, indeed, a difficult one to fulfill in the academic institution.

In general, coordinating authority requires vastly different kinds of background, experience, and outlook from that of persons maintaining directing responsibility or controlling responsibility. The individuals vested with coordinating responsibility have to have breadth of background and ability to comprehend the ideas, points of view, and special demands of a wide number of different technologies and different outlooks. In some respects, executives with coordinating authority are a different breed of people from those with directing or controlling authority. This explains why it is possible for a relative stranger to come into an organization and do a first-rate job of filling a position of coordinating responsibility. It also helps to explain why a cabinet officer in the Federal government or a cabinet minister in the British government is able to take over, with relative ease, the operations of complex departments and bureaus without having any special training or background in the areas over which they exercise coordinating control. Indeed, as Harold Laski has observed, every organization needs the wisdom of the coordinating executive to balance the narrowness and sectarian point of view of the specialists. The wisdom with which the coordinating responsibility is exercised may have more than any other single thing to do with the effectiveness, efficiency, and ultimate survival of an organization.

INNOVATION AUTHORITY

Innovating is a special kind of responsibility that is typically found in many organizations. There are, of course, some kinds of organizations which operate with little thought toward innovation. There are other organizations having special departments, or special individuals, whose primary function is that of innovating, and changing the organization. In many modern organizations there are planning staffs, for example, or research staffs that are always oriented toward the future with an eye towards improving, changing, modifying, or in some way affecting the future operations or products of the firm.

Responsibility for innovation is the one least likely to be related immediately to the day-to-day activities of the organization. For that reason innovators are likely to be somewhat isolated from the organization. In many industrial firms research activities are set up in a separate unit that is distinct, and often physically separated, from the main activities of the firm. This isolation is designed to insure that individuals will view the process of innovation with relative freshness and originality rather than continue an existing line of development by further refinements and improvements. It is for this reason also that many industrial concerns invest in fundamental scientific research with the hope that eventual application of basic discoveries can be made to their products and operations.[10]

The innovating function is usually carried out by a staff. Sometimes the innovating function may have immediate practical applications as its goal, as is the case of an industrial engineering department. In such a department new operating lines, new production processes, and new plant layouts will be worked out. It is also in such departments that ideas may originate for the purchase and use of new equipment and machines that have come on to the market.

An innovating staff like the industrial engineering department may often encounter great difficulties in working out adequate relations with line or operating departments. There is a basic conflict between directing and innovating authorities. As has already been suggested, those with operating authority want a stable, relatively unchanging, and highly predictable set of operations over which to exercise control. For those with innovating responsibility there is a tendency to look upon the established as old fashioned, needing revision, change, and modernization. Thus the engineers with innovating authority may be constantly introducing change, and therefore threats, to those who have operating authority. The resultant conflicts are well known in the literature and in practical experience.

Sometimes the outcome of such battles impels the innovators to try to move into positions of operating authority so that they can carry out their reforms. Top management, exercising coordinating responsibilities, may have to step in to adjudicate the conflicts, and to make decisions approving one course or another.

COMPLEXITY OF AUTHORITY ACTIVITIES

We can conclude generally that the kinds of authority activities to be found in an organization are substantially different from each other. In any given position there are likely to be elements of all four kinds intermingled. Yet at different levels of the organization and in different operations or functional specializations we can see that certain kinds of authority activities predominate over others.

Where the individual must exercise simultaneously various kinds of authority he may have an exceedingly complex job to perform. He may encounter frustrations and difficulties in trying to satisfy contradicting demands. At the same time, we would anticipate that those who have different kinds of authority would be more likely to be in conflict than in harmony with each other. We might therefore expect that the kind and amount of authority attaching to a person will relate significantly to the way he fits into the work organization.

There is a differential kind of authority that distinguishes the levels of an organization. This difference between levels of the organization occurs both in the amount of authority, and in the kind, that is to be found at each level. The amount of directing authority increases as one goes downward in an organization. However, the amount of responsibility for coordinating and integrating diverse operations of the organization increases as one goes upward in the organization. At the middle and upper reaches of the organization, and usually in a staff capacity, are to be found controlling and innovating authority.

CHART 5.3

AUTHORITY ACTIVITIES VARY WITH LEVEL OF AUTHORITY

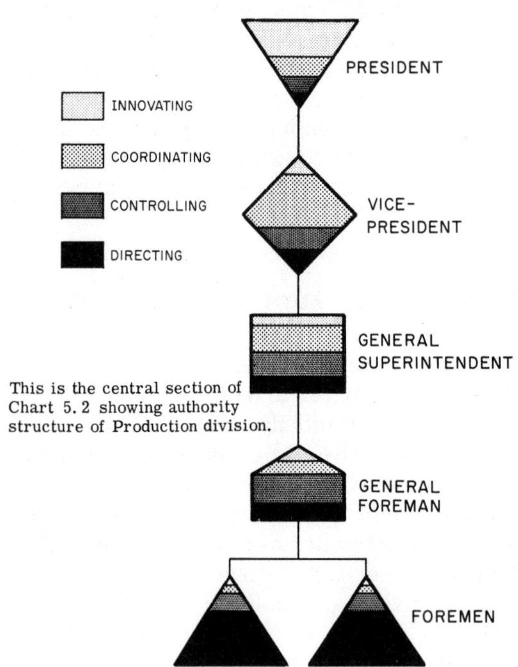

We are now in a position to introduce significant additional variables into our picture of organization coordinates. We will redraw a segment of Chart 5.2. In so doing, we will superimpose on the operating and activity coordinates the differential amounts and kinds of authority.

Each member of management is now seen, in Chart 5.3, as having defined for him his sphere of operations, his level of activity, his kinds of activities, and their amounts. The size of each area in the symbol for each work location is an indication of the amount of that activity carried out in the position. The shape of the symbol helps to give you a visual image of the activities most important for each work location.

Chart 5.3 is an idealized picture. Nevertheless, it now gives us a charting device comparable to a map for visualizing a work organization.

We have now completed the first task of this chapter which is to provide a manageable framework for understanding some of the broad features of the work organization that mold people into effective personnel. Using charts comparable to Chart 5.3 together with the analysis upon which it rests, we have the fundamental organizational coordinates of *operation* and *activity* set forth in a manner to facilitate further analysis of working behavior.

INTERACTION IN AUTHORITY STRUCTURES

At the lowest level where operating authority is typically found, it is clear that the managers are largely concerned with directing the actual behavior of their subordinates. Thus, operating responsibility comes to be closely identified with direct supervision. The significance of person-to-person interaction is most obvious at the operating levels. Direct supervision is vitally concerned with maintaining an adequate system of personal relationships between superior and subordinate.

For top executives of an organization, who exercise largely coordinating, innovating, and controlling authority, and have a minimum of responsibility for direct supervision, the importance of developing and maintaining adequate personal relations is not nearly as great. The very nature of coordinating functions is such that they affect relatively few people who are themselves in positions of supervising responsibility.

Chief executives are in primary contact with the middle and upper reaches of management. It is here, where the background of the individuals is more likely to be homogeneous, that it is possible to work out satisfactory personal relations with relatively little training, effort, or concentration. Even without satisfactory personal relationships, the organization can still operate fairly effectively because the nature of coordinating responsibility does not depend on personal loyalty, or smoothness in interpersonal relationships. We can see this principle operating in a military organization during situations of battle. In a sense, the most dispensable and most easily replaced casualties are among the higher ranks of officers. It is at this level that the replacement can come in, and without working out an adequate network of personal relations, assume command in accordance with the established military pattern. On the other hand, battle casualties among platoon leaders or squad leaders may seriously damage the effectiveness of the outfit unless a man can be promoted from within the ranks to take over, at least temporarily, the immediate supervising and directing functions.[11]

In the industrial situation it is also true that at the levels of immediate direction and supervision it is probably more desirable to bring men up through the ranks, men who have gained the confidence of their peers and who are likely to retain this confidence as supervisors and foremen.[12] It does not follow that the upper ranks of management should be, or need to be, recruited from within the organization. Indeed, it may turn out that the recruitment of top executives on the basis of merit, and not on the basis of their personal relationships with the executive ranks of an organization, may have a good deal to recommend it. That is looking at the recruitment problem entirely from the standpoint of the knowledge, skill, and ability of the particular person selected. However, from the standpoint of the frustrated aspirations of those who may have seen themselves as candidates for top positions, there is an obvious drawback. Disappointed candidates for promotion to top positions may be able to sabotage the regime of their successful competitors.[13]

Those who have substantially different kinds of authority in an organization are likely to have a great deal of difficulty in communicating with each other. The kind of authority an individual has inevitably molds his point of view. Some of the most frustrating disagreements and conflicts in organization are the consequence not of the ill-will of people, but rather of the failure of people to communicate effectively across their different spheres of authority.

JOBS, POSITIONS, OFFICES

For analytical reasons it is desirable to distinguish in work organizations among jobs, positions, and offices. The discussion up to this point has used "job" as a general term covering all three categories. Like all distinctions, there is an arbitrary element about this one. Yet, we will find that work assignments called jobs are different from those called positions, and both differ from organization offices. We will now examine the differences, and discover how this classification of work assignments is useful in understanding the relationships between the person and the work organization.[14]

There are three grounds on which we can note differences among jobs, positions, and offices. (A) The three classes of work assignments are given different kinds of titles in the work organization. (B) There is a significantly different basis upon which personnel is selected to fill each class of work assignment. (C) There is a marked difference among the three classes in the degree to which personal initiative operate in getting work done, and, therefore, the degree to which the organization molds working behavior.

TITLES

In general, *jobs* have very specific titles, descriptive of the operating area and activity carried on in them. Positions, on the other hand, carry titles that may be common to several operating areas, with less specification of the activities carried on in them. Offices usually are named to indicate organization-wide responsibilities whose specific activities are not likely to be stated in the title.

Illustrations of job titles are: automatic screw machine set-up man, floor moulder, punch press operator, typist I, file clerk, maintenance electrician, washroom attendant, receptionist, overhead crane operator, crane hooker, turret lathe operator, die sinker, gear hobber, fur beater, doughnut pumper, and grinding wheel dresser. It will be noted that these illustrative job titles indicate both the operating area, and the specific activities carried on in doing the work. For example, the automatic screw machine set-up man is clearly in a production operation. His specific activities have to do with making and installing cams and cutting tools in an automatic screw machine into which bar stock of steel is fed to be cut, machined, or ground into complex finished shapes. The set-up man does a highly skilled job in preparing the machine for rapid, continuous output of large quantities of the desired metal pieces. This job is clearly different from the screw machine operator whose primary task is to feed the bar stock into the machine periodically, and sometimes to make process inspections of the output, insuring that measurement tolerances are maintained. There may even be another related job called automatic screw machine tool adjuster whose activity involves adjusting the cutting tools if they show wear or get out of alignment.

Positions in the work organization carry titles that may be common to more than one operating area. Furthermore, the position title tends to be less specific than job titles in detailing the activities of the position. Examples of position titles are: foreman, supervisor, department head, administrative assistant, accountant, and engineer. It seems clear that for the titles designating management positions, the names meet the two tests, namely, application to several operations or departments, and less specificity as to the activities involved. Foreman, for example, will be found in a number of departments. The title, foreman, does not specify foreman activity with nearly the detail that is characteristic of a job title. In the instance of accountant and engineer the position titles suggest rather specific activities, but upon closer examination it would be necessary to inquire beyond the title to be certain as to what a particular engineer or accountant does at work.

Organization *offices* carry names indicating organization-wide responsibilities with the title giving relatively little clue as to the specific activities carried on in the office. It is also typical in naming people who occupy organization offices to use the adjective "the." Thus, one talks about *the* president, or *the* treasurer. The very fact that organization offices are spoken of as being occupied by a given individual, or only one person, suggests that members of the work organization view the office as unique. Furthermore, organization offices often have their occupants designated as officers. The officers of a business firm, for example, are the president, vice-presidents, secretary, treasurer, and perhaps others, like the controller.

It is clear that if we were to use only titles to differentiate among jobs, positions, and offices, we would find many work assignments that lie at the borderlines between the categories. It is necessary to consider the two additional criteria of personnel selection and degree of personal initiative, in order to clarify further the differences between the three general classes of work assignments.

RECRUITMENT

Jobs, by virtue of the high degree of specification of activities, are the most readily filled in an organization. It is possible to enter the labor market and advertise for people with specific training in the jobs being filled. The classified section of a newspaper makes clear, in the help wanted columns, that most firms seek job holders by advertising for the specific kinds of workers they want. Failing to find already trained workers in the labor market, a firm may have a well established training program to take unskilled people and train them in the necessary job skills.

Positions in an organization usually require prior experience or equivalent education to fill them. For many of the technical positions the requisite is usually prior education. Thus for accountants, engineers, and similar specialists four years of college training are a minimum necessary to be a candidate for such positions. In other kinds of positions, like that of foreman, the person may go through a period of job training as an assistant foreman, a sub-foreman, a working group leader, or straw boss, prior to his elevation to the foreman position. It is generally true that some technical schooling is necessary to fill most positions, and, in many cases, experience in handling the varied activities of the position may also be necessary.

Organization *offices* tend to be filled by personnel who have exhibited prior successful performance in high level positions or lower level offices. The recruitment to organization offices tends to be highly selective on the grounds of past successful fulfilment of work assignments.

We can now briefly characterize working jobs as being filled from the unskilled and relatively untrained portions of the labor market. This is by far the greatest number of work assignments as well as the largest labor supply. Filling work positions is selective with respect to prior technical training, usually in schools, or prior experience that is roughly equivalent to schooling. Recruitment for organization offices places particularly heavy emphasis on the past history of successful work performance in positions of managerial responsibility. This suggests obvious differences in the personnel to be found in jobs, positions, and offices. Job holders would have the least formal training and require a short learning period in developing the skills necessary to hold their jobs. Those in positions would tend to be college graduates, or people with extensive experience. Those in organization offices have a period of demonstrated executive competence behind them.[15]

INITIATIVE

From what has already been said about the nature of *jobs* it seems clear that this category of work assignments tends to have the largest amount of specific work activities. A person holding a job has most of his technical and formal behavior specified for him by the organization. A job holder operates within more or less rigid limits established for his job. In general, the job holder uses very little initiative in carrying out his job, except as he is able to exercise initiative in the non-formal behavior systems, or in the informal behavior systems.

Those who have *positions,* on the other hand, have a good deal more opportunity to exercise individual initiative. Where technical background is important in filling a position, it is clear that many work activities are governed by technical learning. An engineer, for example, applies his engineering knowledge with relative freedom from constraint by his work organization. Indeed, he is expected to do so in making his working contribution to the organization. A foreman similarly is expected to exercise judgment and discrimination in handling his supervisory problems. He is expected to make decisions relevant to his activities and to be able to discriminate among the choices open to him in his behavior. In general, those occupying positions have a great deal more initiative expected of them than job holders, and greater opportunity for displaying initiative, or personal decision, in filling their work assignments.

People in organization *offices* have the largest amount of initiative in carrying out their work. Typically office holders establish the tone and value standards of the organization they direct. The office holder, wittingly or unwittingly, in almost all his actions provides a model, or gives cues to his subordinates, as to how they are expected to behave. For example, an easy-going president may be succeeded by a tough president in the direction of a firm. The character of subordinate behavior will change markedly between the two regimes. Each type of president may be successful, but on quite different grounds, and with quite different kinds of organizational behavior displayed in getting work done.[16]

We have now pointed out why it is significant to distinguish among jobs, positions, and offices: The actual titles of work assignments differ for the three classes; the types of personnel recruited into the three classes of work assignments tend to be different; finally, the degree to which personal initiative is free to operate in fulfilling work assignments varies markedly among the three classes.

COMPONENTS OF JOBS, POSITIONS OFFICES

We can analyze every job, position, and office in terms of six components. These six components are: (A) tasks, (B) duties, (C) responsibilities, (D) rights, (E) obligations, and (F) privileges. These components of work assignments combine in varying degrees to differentiate among jobs, positions, and offices. We will examine each component separately, indicating briefly how they distinguish jobs from positions, and both from offices.

TASKS

Every work assignment is a task or combination of tasks. The task is the actual action through which the person goes in doing his work. For people in jobs, the task is largely technological in character. For people in positions there is a combination of technological actions and authority actions that constitute the total tasks of the position. Organization officers have their tasks defined almost completely in terms of authority activities with a minimum of technological behavior involved. In general, the tasks of a work assignment are the specific behaviors that a person performs in filling his assigned place in the work organization.

DUTIES

The duties of a work assignment represent the formal organization values surrounding the performance of work. These values specify for each working person the ranges and limits of his behaviors. Typical organization duties are the requirements to be at work on time, actually to do work during assigned work periods, and, in general, to follow the letter of all rules and regulations applying to work.

Duties are essentially formal in character. They do not depend on personal conviction for their fulfillment. A person may do his duty even though he is indifferent or even opposed to the duties required of him. Duties tend to be uniform for large segments of work organizations.

The major difference among jobs, positions, and offices with respect to organization duties lies in the assumption that those in positions and offices will tend to have greater conviction about the rightness and desirability of duties, than job holders. Job holders tend to view duties as a formal requirement. Those in positions and offices are more likely to be intellectually and emotionally committed to the duties required of them.

RESPONSIBILITIES

Responsibility is the sense of correctness a person feels about carrying out the tasks and duties of his work. A responsible person is one who is convinced that it is desirable to carry out his tasks and duties, and who can be depended upon to do so within the limits of his capabilities. Responsibilities have, therefore, both an intellectual and emotional component. The intellectual aspect of responsibility is the ability to comprehend the tasks and duties of a work assignment. The emotional component represents the personal conviction that it is desirable to make every effort to carry out assigned tasks and duties.

In general, there is a minimum management expectation of responsibility among job holders. Accordingly, most work organizations surround jobs with a maximum number of controls to insure responsible behavior, whether or not workers are convinced that responsible behavior is desirable. In positions and offices, on the other hand, there is a greater management expectation that the person will be responsible and, therefore, need not be surrounded by as many, or as stringent controls on work performance. A simple example will make the point clear. Job holders typically are subject to frequent checkups by supervisors. Those in positions and offices usually receive few if any supervisory checkups, on the assumption that they are responsible enough to be at work when required, and to remain there as long as necessary.

RIGHTS

The rights surrounding a work assignment represent the legitimate expectations a person has of his working colleagues and the organization employing him. Rights are conferred and made legitimate by either the work organization or fellow workers. Rights are always legitimate in that they depend on consensus by others for their existence. For example, a person has the right to exercise authority only when this right is conferred upon him by the organization, and when those responding to the authority acts agree to the legitimacy of his performing them. Rights tend to be irrevocable in character. Once conferred they are normally not rescinded.

The rights surrounding jobs, positions, and offices differ. In general, job rights tend to be uniform for all job holders. Rights in positions usually involve some discretion as to when they will be used. Rights of office may usually be exercised with the greatest amount of discretion by the office holder.

OBLIGATIONS

A sense of obligation is a moral compulsion a person feels to behave in particular ways. Obligations represent personal commitment to chosen behavior. Obligations are therefore the internalized values guiding behavior.

Obligations come into play only when the person is faced with a personal choice among alternatives. In situations where alternatives for behavior are specified by the work organization, or an informal social group, the sense of obligation may not operate.

Illustrations of obligations are to be found in a number of realms. Weber's and Tawney's emphasis on the relationships between the Protestant ethic and the spirit of capitalism shows one kind of moral obligation that develops out of the religious values of Western society. The Protestant ethic proclaims a moral obligation for a person to render adequate services for his pay. Another example of obligations is revealed in the instances of engineers, accountants, and attorneys employed in a work organization who, as professionals, have moral obligations to follow the ethics of their profession, as well as to render required services to the employing organization. Where organization requirements conflict with professional ethics the professional is constrained to make a moral decision as to his personal stand. Still another example of a sense of obligation is revealed in the behavior of an executive who displays *noblesse oblige* toward his subordinates. Such an executive sees himself as obeying a moral imperative of his office.

PRIVILEGES

Privileges are the opportunities for behavior accorded in interpersonal relations. They represent what working associates are willing to permit and accept in the behavior of a person. Privileges are conferred by associates but they may also be withdrawn. The realm of privileges is that of personal association. Since privileges are the product of direct interaction of people with each other, the bases upon which privileges are accorded or withheld are personal attributes, and the evaluation of personal characteristics.

A few examples of privileges will make their character clear. A group of co-workers may accord to its most senior member the privilege of having the "last word" in a discussion. A president may extend the privilege of free comment on worldly affairs to the company chauffeur while driving the president to his appointments. A female work associate may be permitted the privilege of joining male colleagues in the coffee break, or this privilege may be withheld from her. A company "clown" or "screwball" may be accorded the privilege of publicly kidding superiors. A superannuated employee may be accorded the privilege of demanding inordinate attention to his personal needs. A "jet job" (man who is promoted more rapidly than his peers; a "fair-haired boy") may be denied the privilege of association with those he has passed on the promotion ladder. Favored individuals may have the privilege of "getting around" rules and regulations accorded them by others who could insist upon observance of the letter of the law.

SUMMARY OF COMPONENTS

For any job, position, or office, there are six categories, in terms of which their characteristics can be set forth. These six features of working assignments represent the sociologically relevant aspects of working roles as they are defined in the organization context. The discussion of tasks, duties, and rights reveals that these features of work assignments are independent of the worker. On the other hand, responsibility, obligation, and privileges are associated with the personal characteristics of the worker.[17]

CITIZENS INTO EMPLOYEES

We are now in a position to summarize the materials of this chapter and the preceding three, to demonstrate the relationships between a person and his work. Chart 5.4 shows this set of relationships.

Central to Chart 5.4 is the working person. He is shown as encompassing both his self image, and his organizational location represented by his job, position, or office. These two are connected by arrows showing the mutual interaction. The heavier arrow going from organization location to self image is intended to indicate the strong influence that the organization has in molding behavior.

On the left hand side of the chart, the person's social experience is shown as influencing his self image. The social experience in turn comprises experiences in primary groups, family, general social institutions, formal organizations or reference groups outside the work organization, and schooling, training, and prior technical experience.

On the right side of the chart, the fundamental human relations of work organizations, power, authority, and status, are shown as the connecting links among all the jobs, positions, and offices of the organization. In turn, these fundamental human relations are also shown as the basis from which are derived the four behavior systems of work, the technological system, the formal system, the non-formal system and the informal system, examined in detail in Chapter 4.

We can see jobs, positions, and offices linked together into structures according to the distributions of power, authority, and status for the particular work organization. There is derived from these fundamental human relations particular systematic ways of behaving that give to each person established action patterns for carrying out his working assignments.

The four behavior systems have differential impact on the components of jobs, positions, and offices. Some of the behavior systems are significant for one or only a few of the components. The arrows connecting the behavior systems with the components of jobs, positions, and offices indicate the major bonds of relationships. These components of organization location are also shown as influenced by aspects of the person's social experience. Finally, the six components of organization location are shown as the determinants of job, position, or office.

In Chart 5.4 we have organized the analytical materials of the three preceding chapters and this one into a model of the relationships between a person and his work. It will be recalled that we started this chapter with the problem of determining what happens to the person when he brings his experience from the larger society into his place of work. We asked how his self-conception as a worker was formed, and sought to locate the features of his work assignment that mold him into a productive worker capable of adequate working performance .

Chart 5.4 presents the general outlines of the connections between a person and the basic features of his work and working environment. This provides a theoretical framework you will find useful in the remainder of this volume, in research on working behavior, and in your personal experience as members of work organizations.

CHART 5.4

WORKING BEHAVIOR IS THE PRODUCT OF COMPLEX INTERACTIONS BETWEEN SOCIETY AND WORK ORGANIZATION

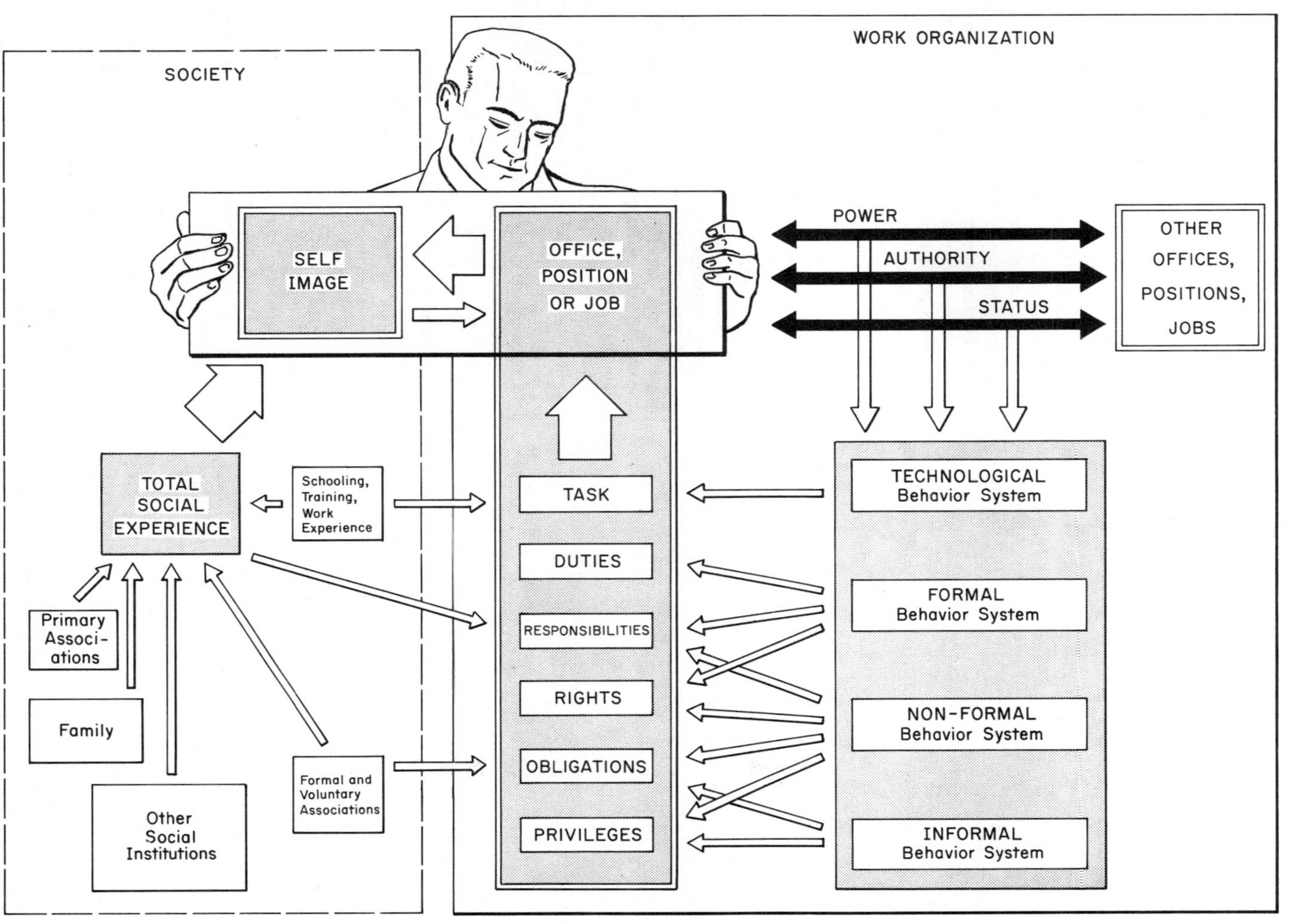

NOTES FOR CHAPTER 5

[1] Specialization of operations is recognized as the fundamental feature of the horizontal division of labor in the leading studies. One of the more thoughtful analyses of complex problems of subdivision by specialization, and the resulting need for coordination, is found in J. D. Mooney and A. C. Reiley, *The Principles of Organization* (New York: Harper & Brothers, 1939).

[2] R. W. Porter, *Design for Industrial Coordination* (New York: McGraw-Hill Book Co., Inc., 1941), has given particular attention to the issues raised in defining the boundaries between operations in Chapter 4, "Jurisdiction Processes of Industrial Coordination."

[3] All analysts of management define the functions performed by management. Fredrick W. Taylor urged that functional specialization be extended throughout the ranks of management, making specialists of all managers, the description of whose functions could be made in terms of the requirements of their specialty. F. W. Taylor, *Shop Management* (New York: Harper & Brothers, 1911). Chester I. Barnard has declared the functions of executives to be: "first, to provide the system of communication; second, to promote the securing of essential efforts; and, third, to formulate and define purpose" *The Functions of the Executive* (Cambridge: Harvard University Press, 1938), p. 217. Robert Tannenbaum has defined managers as "those who use formal authority to organize, direct, or control responsibile subordinates in order that all service contributions be coordinated in the attainment of an enterprise purpose." "The Manager Concept: A Rational Synthesis," *Journal of Business*, 22:225-241 (October, 1949).

[4] Mary P. Follett, "The Meaning of Responsibility in Business Management," in H. C. Metcalf (ed.) *Business Management as a Profession* (Chicago: A. W. Shaw Co., 1927) lays stress on the balance between functional authority and final authority.

[5] Some sense of these dilemmas can be secured from M. C. Niles, *Middle Management: The Job of the Junior Executive* (New York: Harper & Brothers, 1941).

[6] Directing, as we use the term, is equivalent to supervision. There is a vast literature of the "how to do" character dealing with supervision. Some of the better analyses of supervision include: Ernest Dale, *The Development of Foremen in Management*, American Management Association Research Report No. 7, (1945); Melville Dalton, "The Role of Supervision," Chapter 13 in A. Kornhauser, R. Dubin, A. Ross (eds.), *Industrial Conflict* (New York: McGraw-Hill Book Co., 1954); Floyd Mann and J. Dent, "The Supervisor: Member of Two Organization Families," *Harvard Business Review*, 32:103-112 (December, 1954); F. J. Roethlisberger, "The Foreman—Master and Victim of Double Talk," *Harvard Business Review*, 23:283-298 (Spring, 1945); W. F. Whyte and B. B. Gardner, "The Man in the Middle: Position and Problems of the Foreman," *Applied Anthropology*, 4:1-28 (Spring, 1945); and D. E. Wray, "Marginal Men of Industry: The Foremen," *American Journal of Sociology*, 54:298-301 (January, 1949).

[7] An interesting example of collusion between foreman and workers is reported by Donald Roy, "Efficiency and 'The Fix': Informal Intergroup Relations in a Piece-work Machine Shop," *American Journal of Sociology*, 60:255-266 (November, 1954).

[8] Special kinds of industrial controls, such as cost control and production control, have elaborate technologies developed for their accomplishment. The human consequences of organization controls and the exercise of controlling authority are especially examined in: Melville Dalton, "Industrial Controls and Personal Relations," *Social Forces*, 33:244-249 (March, 1955); Edward Gross, "Some Functional Consequences of Primary Controls in Formal Work Organizations," *American Sociological Review*, 18:368-373 (August, 1953); and Alexander Vucinich, "The Structure of Factory Control in the Soviet Union," *American Sociological Review*, 15:179-186 (April, 1950).

[9] Mooney and Reiley, *The Principles of Organization*, place particular emphasis on the authority activity of coordination in management. Their analysis of the complex coordinating problems in the management of large scale industry is outstanding for its insight.

[10] Analyses of business leadership are always torn between recognizing the conserving functions of authority, and its innovating functions. A good treatment that seeks to state the balancing points between conserving and innovating is: Chris Argyris, *Executive Leadership* (New York: Harper & Brothers, 1953). The extent to which innovation can be physically removed from the organization is revealed in the role of industrial consultants, who are hired to develop specific innovations. Universities have even established large consulting activities to serve business firms. Stanford University has the Stanford Research Institute, with world-wide offices, and Illinois Institute of Technology has associated with it the Armour Research Foundation. Both research organizations provide extensive development and innovation services to business firms and government agencies.

[11] This conflicts with Barnard's conclusion that upper levels of management also need habituation in a particular organization to make it work. See "Education for Executives," Chapter 7 in Chester I. Barnard, *Organization and Management* (Cambridge: Harvard University Press, 1948), pp. 201 ff.

[12] An interesting and rather unusual dilemma created by promotion from the ranks is illustrated in the printing industry, where foremen retain their union membership and are confronted with conflicting loyalties. See E. F. Baker, "The Printing Pressroom Foreman—Union Man: A Case Study," *Indus-*

NOTES FOR CHAPTER 5 (CONT.)

trial and Labor Relations Review, 4:367-385 (April, 1951).

[13] See Chapter 16, "Work Groups and Work," where the organizational significance of cliques is analyzed.

[14] An excellent treatment of organization offices is contained in E. C. Hughes, "Institutional Office and the Person," *American Journal of Sociology,* 43:404-414 (November, 1937). Our distinction between jobs and positions is based upon the criteria established in the subsequent discussion of this section of the chapter.

[15] It should be noted that we are emphasizing the differential recruitment criteria for jobs, positions, and offices. Parsons has emphasized that the industrial division of labor has led to the use of universalistic recruitment criteria. That is, criteria of selection cut across the entire population and do not depend on previously established social ties. Talcott Parsons, *Essays in Sociological Theory, Pure and Applied* (Glencoe: The Free Press, 1949), Chapter 9, The Motivation of Economic Activities." Parsons' point serves to distinguish recruitment for industrial organizations from recruitment for other types of social organizations, for example, a voluntary association. Our distinction differentiates the various recruitment criteria used *within* industrial organization for selecting various classes of personnel.

[16] The way in which the individual faces the requirement of exercising initiative is tied up with his personality. In this connection see: E. C. Hughes, "Personality Types and the Division of Labor," *American Journal of Sociology,* 33:754-768 (March, 1928); and W. E. Henry, "The Business Executive: A Study in the Psycho-dynamics of a Social Role," *American Journal of Sociology,* 54:286-291 (January, 1949).

[17] The components of jobs, positions, and offices are analytical categories generally used. Specific references will be given later in the volume where aspects of work assignment components are analyzed in detail.

People working together get together. Social interaction is the normal consequence of personal contact. When personal contacts are repeated the relationship may become a group. These two men, cutters in a glove factory, make up a close-knit two man group.

Chapter 6

GROUP LIFE OF ORGANIZATIONS

Work in modern society typically requires working with others to produce the goods and services expected. It is, therefore, necessary to examine the human consequences of rubbing elbows with other people at work.

In the preceding chapters we have examined the formal aspects of work organizations and the relations of individuals to them. In this chapter we will view work organizations as continuous associations of human beings. We are concerned here with (A) the roots of sociability at work, and (B) the forms group interaction takes.

BASES OF SOCIABILITY AT WORK

Human beings at work are not simply substitutes for machines. They are motivated people with sentiments, ideas, emotions, and feelings. There are goals towards which workers strive that may or may not be compatible with those of their work organization. There are interests that each person carries to his job that may be more important to him than his work. At any given moment, a worker's attention is likely to be divided, focusing partly on the tasks before him, and partly on interests only remotely related to work. Furthermore, in most kinds of employment, there is constant interaction with other human beings. Out of long prior experience people react to each other at work as they would anywhere else in the society—with interest, affection, good humor, indifference, contempt, and anger. However demanding are the requirements of a job, people manage to surround their work with satisfying human relationships that have little or nothing to do with filling the job.

The very nature of human personality has within it the roots of group life in organizations. The social life in organizations results from the human qualities of persons, as they find and hold a place among fellow workers.

We will first examine some of the bases of group life in organizations. An understanding of why we find social groups in any kind of organized activity will give us a better understanding of the forms such social life takes.

HUMAN SOCIABILITY

A human being, once socialized, needs to continue to be with other people. In a more rigorous fashion we can state this proposition as follows: to remain human requires continuous meaningful relations with other human beings.

Reflection on education and socialization through adulthood reveals the significance of this proposition. Maturing involves communication with other persons. At birth, interaction is limited almost exclusively to the family, and particularly the mother.[1] Patterns of learned behavior gradually broaden out to include non-family members. Eventually in adulthood the preponderance of interactions in the daily round of life tends to be with people outside the immediate family.[2] The social personality of the individual is both a product of his interaction with others, and dependent on such interaction for its continuation.[3]

We start with the assumption that there is at least a minimum amount of social interaction of a relatively free and unstructured sort each person requires in his daily life. Once we have learned to communicate with others, we feel strained when opportunities for communication are limited. Learning to interact meaningfully with other people makes us depend on interaction as a normal part of daily living. We have a striking example of what physical isolation means in the analysis that the late Admiral Byrd made of his lengthy period alone in the Antarctic.[4]

The extent to which informal interaction is valued in our society is revealed in our systems of punishment. One of the most extreme forms of penal punishment is solitary confinement. The notable thing, of course, about solitary confinement is that the punishment is social, not physical. It is isolation from fellow human beings that is punishing.[5]

In most work there is a relatively high demand for attention to the job. Each individual is expected to carry out his allotted tasks, and to put its accomplishment first. Indeed, it is one of the consequences of mass production that the worker's attention and pace of work are geared to the production process.[6] Under such circumstances opportunities for informal interaction with fellow workers tend to be limited.

Yet the simple fact of the matter is that almost all workers find one way or another to establish informal relations with other people on the job. In some kinds of jobs it is possible to work and talk at the same time. An observer may be surprised to see a worker doing a relatively intricate task, to which he has long since become habituated, and at the same time carry on animated conversations with those around him. However, such circumstances are not wholly typical in industry and commerce. There is the opposite extreme in which people are in close physical contact, but because of the speed of operations, the noise surrounding the work, or other barriers, they are not in a position to exchange even the simplest pleasantries.

Work itself has first claim on the time and attention of workers. The need for informal associations at work is amplified by the very pressures of work that minimize opportunities for such interaction. Where informal relations do not develop naturally while working, or during slack or rest periods, the needs for sociability will be satisfied in the comradeship of the washroom, during lunch periods, or by extending official interactions to include "passing the day" and "shooting the breeze" kind of talk.

The origin of informal relations at work lies in the demands of the human personality for free interaction with other people. In the very nature of work organizations, like business firms, government bureaus, or even educational institutions, it is difficult deliberately to design informal relations into the organization. Management would appear ridiculous in its own eyes, and certainly to its employees, if it took seriously a claim that "this firm is just one big happy family." A lathe operator would certainly feel sheepish if he took the notion just to pop over to see Bill in the maintenance department, turning off his lathe and forgetting about the production schedule to satisfy an urge to chat with a "family" member. The collective stacks of management, from foreman to president, would blow at such behavior.

Being able freely to choose the people you want to talk to, and the times for being with them, is inimical to work regimes and production schedules. The best management can do is provide opportunities for informal association. These must be legitimized by management, like the coffee break, or the personal relief period. Out of informal relations will develop groups with relatively permanent existence. These groups are the locus of most informal interaction in work organizations.

When a person takes his place at work he does not lose his interest or desire to establish satisfactory and continuous informal relations with fellow workers. This is a need of his personality. This need will be satisfied in the informal relations at work and in the groups that sustain them.

COMMON INTEREST

The one location most continuously occupied during waking hours is the work place. Most individuals at the present time spend approximately eight hours a day working at some paying job. This is the longest continuous segment of their daily life. It should hardly be surprising, then, that at work each individual finds a common set of interests with co-workers. This common set of interests extends well beyond immediate work problems and job subjects.

Any attentive listening to the kind of talk taking place among workers will reveal common interests like sports, sex, public affairs, personalities, and many others.[7] During eight hours each day these common interests are brought to the fore and made topics of conversation. It is important to note that almost all of the informal interaction is verbal. Conversation is the major mode of interaction, and gossip is its major subject. There may, of course, be games and horseplay like that displayed in the Bank Wiring Room among the wiremen and soldermen. These men engaged in "binging," a hard blow to the upper arm, whose recipient was always privileged to repay the attacker.[8]

The group life of work organizations is also a consequence of daily eight-hour interaction among co-workers. In this continuous association there are expressed the common interests, aspirations, hopes, and desires of men at work. A bond of unity is forged around common interests that become the basis for informal groups.

REQUIRED INTERACTION

Minimum activities necessary to fill a job successfully are usually defined in advance for the individual who takes a job. This includes work activities, authority relations, and power relations with individuals whose co-operation is necessary in order to get the job done. There are relatively few jobs in commerce and industry which do not require, at some point in their daily performance, significant interaction with other people. There is "built into" the structure of an organization, in dependent jobs, need for interaction among fellow workers, and between those in authority and those subordinate to them. The organization is built on channeling interactions between people.

There is no guarantee that conversation and contact demanded by organizational requirements and technological needs will be limited solely to business. Indeed, it is a familiar observation that the business of an organization could be conducted in a relatively short time by those who communicate with each other to carry it out. Nevertheless, communication is prolonged, and talk is usually carried over into areas that are only remotely related to business at hand. Out of required interaction come free talk and neighboring that provide an outlet for informal relations.

Interactions necessary to get work done are often continued beyond work needs. Group life at work grows up during these periods of freely chosen association.

INDIVIDUAL JOB DECISIONS

Manuals of operations, and job descriptions of work organizations, contain a tremendous amount of detail. Yet if workers on the job are asked if their written and spoken instructions typically cover every activity confronting them, the answer is usually "no." Almost every job has problematic characteristics about which the job holder can make decisions.

The personal decisions about work activities usually involve other people. A worker may consult his foreman about what to do. The choice may involve a joint decision on the part of several people before the activity can continue. In other instances, a worker may consult with more experienced fellow workers before reaching his own job decision.

The general point is that no organization can completely eliminate the need for consultation with others in order to carry out job activities. This becomes particularly evident in the advice sought and given in making job decisions. The person being helped values the advice of his more experienced co-workers, who usually appreciate the compliment of being asked. There is then built still another bond among fellow workers making possible informal groups and personal allegiance to them.

PERSONNEL TURNOVER

Turnover of personnel, because of quitting, retirement, firing, or transfer, necessarily changes the patterns of existing ties among people working together. No two people behave in precisely the same fashion. When a person succeeds another in a job, new patterns of interaction with co-workers are developed, different from those of the predecessor. The new man and his working associates go through a period of mutual adjustment to each other.[9]

Every time a new person comes onto a job, there is a heightened self-consciousness about him and his place among his peers. The new man becomes aware of the need to secure cues for informal relations from the behavior of the people around him. They, in turn, "size up" the new man preparatory to reaching a collective judgment about him.

Turnover of workers is very frequent in American work organizations. Rapid turnover keeps people self-conscious about judgments regarding each other. Turnover also leads to more or less self-conscious reaffirmation of valued informal bonds.[10] In this sense, then, personal turnover establishes the initiation procedures for bringing new people into informal groups, and leads to an affirmation of the boundaries of the group.

JOB LEISURE AND FREE TIME

Workers either find free time on their jobs, or make it. This free time ranges from complete idleness[11] to relative inattention while an activity is being carried out.[12] Between these extremes lie many and varied situations in which leisure time while working is available to the worker.

Free time on the job is typically filled by voluntary association with co-workers. A man with time on his hands seeks the company of other people.

Job leisure leads to a number of relatively annoying personnel problems, such as talking and gossiping while working, and prolonging of smoking and coffee breaks. Another example is the person whose job leisure permits him to become a rover, going from place to place, and from desk to desk, just to pass the time of the day. These are just a few among many possible examples of the ways in which job leisure is used to seek human company.

There is always a neat problem for management to balance reasonable job leisure against prudent use of the free time. Members of management are often irritated into wanting to restrict the amount of job leisure because of their dislike for the ways in which it is used. Men who shoot craps, or tell dirty stories in the wash room during a break may appear to be wasting a rest period in the eyes of management, perhaps justifying shortening or eliminating the rest period. What is not so obvious is that the break period is used for social relaxation as well as physiological rest. There is as much need to be in the easy company of friends as there is need to rest weary muscles.

Job leisure is used to seek and enjoy the company of friends and associates. The mere availability of free time on the job permits informal associations to develop, out of which come the social groups of work.

ENVIRONMENTAL CHANGES

Any organization operates in an environment larger than itself. This environment has many uncontrollable features, that cannot be influenced by any action taken within the organization. Thus, a downward or upward swing of the business cycle can only be anticipated—it can scarcely be influenced by actions taken within a single firm.

Some degree of flexibility is "built into" a work organization to permit tactical moves for adjusting to changes in the larger environment. This organizational flexibility is based upon an expectation of indeterminacy. Indeterminacy is being acknowledged when a person is called upon to exercise initiative in carrying on a task. Indeterminacy takes an even more positive expression where staff organizations are given the specialized tasks of forecasting or predicting the future of business affairs.

However indeterminacy is handled in the organization, it produces another possibility for interaction among co-workers. People talk to each other, trying to assemble the best knowledge, information, and judgments to face an uncertain future. A good deal of time is spent with other members of the organization and superiors seeking approval or support for decisions that will affect future operations.[13]

The environment of operations is also the work organization itself. This environment changes too. A company may be growing rapidly, adding new plants and personnel. It may be diversifying and adding new products, or changing designs and production processes on existing products. In general, work organizations tend to be dynamic and therefore to change much of the time. Adjustments to internal changes produce the same kinds of personal discourse as adjustments to changes in the external environment. People are thrown together to talk about the impending changes and their direction and consequences.

Any environmental changes affecting a work organization provide additional reasons for person-to-person interaction among its members. Changes become the natural subjects of gossip. Changes demand decisions, and prolonged discourse to make them. Uncertainty about the future heightens social interaction among work organization members and provides still another basis for informal relations and groups.

INNOVATION AND NEW DISCOVERY

A number of different methods exist for finding new ways to perform established tasks of an organization. Individual workers may be permitted leeway in the behavior systems of work so that new discoveries may be made about work. Formal suggestions systems may be established to encourage employees to share new ideas with management. The organization may even establish special research departments to develop innovations. Seeking after better ways of doing things is part of the broad secular trend in our society toward increasing rationality in the design and management of the formal organizations of society.

The introduction of discoveries follows an elaborate course. Ideas may be tried with colleagues first. There may follow elaborate steps of testing, reworking, and continuous consultation with those affected about design and operations.[14] Later the suggestion may be submitted to the officials of the organization for formal management action. If affirmative action is taken, there usually follows a testing period in which further modifications may be suggested and adopted.

Introducing new ideas entails a high degree of interaction and communication among members of an organization. Even when new ideas are rejected, their consideration usually involves prolonged deliberations, not to mention the kind of griping and public disgruntlement displayed by the originator of the new ideas when the adverse decision is announced.[15]

Change is one of the most universal characteristics of working life. It is always a signal for comment and evaluation. Indeed, where we have had experiments with deliberate changes, they have not only been noticed and talked about, but they have even affected working behavior because of a presumption about the effects of the change. In the Western Electric studies, workers increased output when they saw the janitor change the light bulbs where they worked, even though the replacement bulbs were of identical wattage, or even gave less illumination.[16]

Change, which is usually justified as a new idea or innovation, heightens human interaction at work. Sides are taken approving or condemning the changes. People are thrown together, faced with the problem of confronting change, and find much of their discussion taking place at an informal level. Here is still another source of informal groups in work organizations.

ROOTS OF GROUP LIFE—SUMMARY

We can now outline the sources of group life of organizations as follows:

I. Fundamental condition for social life of organizations is *human sociability*.

II. In the organization
  - A. Large amount of continuous time spent together develops *common interests* of co-workers.
  - B. Technological and formal systems *require interaction* and necessitate *individual job decisions* which also entail interaction.
  - C. Established interaction patterns between co-workers are always interrupted and re-established by *turnover of personnel*.
  - D. Social void created by *leisure and free time* on job is typically filled by informal social interaction.

III. Environment of the organization
  - A. Both external and internal environmental changes result in heightened interaction among organization members.
  - B. Markedly heightened interaction occurs during *innovation and new discovery* affecting established behavior systems within organization.

TYPES OF VOLUNTARY GROUP LIFE

The social life of organizations takes many forms. Individuals in isolation may play a significant role in the organization. We can also see fairly large organized groups performing certain functions, and affecting significantly an organization. Between these extremes, there lie a number of different forms of group life. In this section we will examine some of the more commonly found social groups of work organizations. In Chapter 16, we will analyze in detail the many ways in which social groups affect work.

THE PAIR

A common form of interpersonal association within the organization is the pair. Two individuals may often be thrown together in the performance of their job so that they constitute a technologically oriented team of two. While this may provide an initial basis for association, it is not always certain that there will develop the kind of social interaction between two people so related that they will take on real group characteristics.

The pair is usually united by a number of reciprocal ties of affection, shared ideas, loyalty, common ideals, and similar norms. These qualities shared between the members of the pair give them a great deal of sympathy for each other and an ability to understand and accept each other's behavior.[17]

Under some circumstances, the members of the pair may behave toward each other as relative equals. There may be no outward evidence of domination by one or the other member. Observing their actual behavior, it is possible to see them interchanging roles as they interact with each other. Thus, for example, if they are in the habit of eating together there may be an established system of informal exchange of favors, like buying each other's drinks. Typically, this exchange of favors balances out over the long run so that neither of the individuals is permanently indebted to the other.

The pair relationship involves identity of personality, ideas, feelings, and emotions of the members. They appear to an observer as sharing a number of common characteristics. The members of the pair tend to behave and act alike.[18]

Another kind of a paired relationship is one in which the members of the pair have unlike characteristics. For example, a sophisticated person may have a relative fool as a close informal associate. The smarter person may use the fool as the butt of his jokes and ridicule. The fool may accept such a position in the relationship. He may return to his more gifted colleague a kind of admiration and hero worship that reciprocates and solidifies the relationship.[19]

The organizational significance of the pair lies in its exceptional cohesiveness. The pair, by virtue of the strong identification between its members, is very closely knit. What affects one member either positively or negatively is rapidly communicated to the other member, and he tends to respond in like fashion. Thus, if a foreman "bawls out" one member of a pair, the resentment against such criticism is likely to be transmitted rapidly to the other member. The foreman is faced with discontent not in one individual but in two.

These two men, the very nature of whose work requires continuous cooperation, have every opportunity to solidify their relation into a two man group. A division of work assignments on an individual basis is determined by them. They are a telephone construction crew, erecting poles, stringing wire and putting up aerial cable.

The pair, then, is a highly cohesive social unit in which two people are capable of behaving as one. There are many situations in which, for want of knowledge of the way in which a pair functions, an organization supervisor or executive is at a loss to understand why an individual seems discontented for no apparent reason. It may often be found that the discontented person may be a member of a pair whose other half has been subjected to circumstances about which he is unhappy. The unhappiness is transmitted to the pair member, and two people share this feeling.

THE TRIAD

A social group that has significant differences from both the pair and larger units is the triad. The threesome is significant because it involves some of the elements of unity that is found in larger informal groups.

We have said that in the pair there is a high degree of intimate associations and sharing of feelings, ideas, attitudes, and reactions. In the triad this sharing may be a good deal less complete, in particular as it relates to the number of areas covered. The threesome may have a single or at best several areas of common interest. These areas of common interest tend to lie outside the immediate intimate experience of the three members.[20]

have informal sanctions in the event there is a violation of the group expectations. These sanctions are typically of an informal character involving the use of ridicule, sometimes physical punishment, and even occasionally temporary isolation from participation in the group.

The functional significance of the triad lies in the fact that its center of interest may be external to the group; that is, the realm of its operations is likely to be something outside the subjective life of the individuals involved.

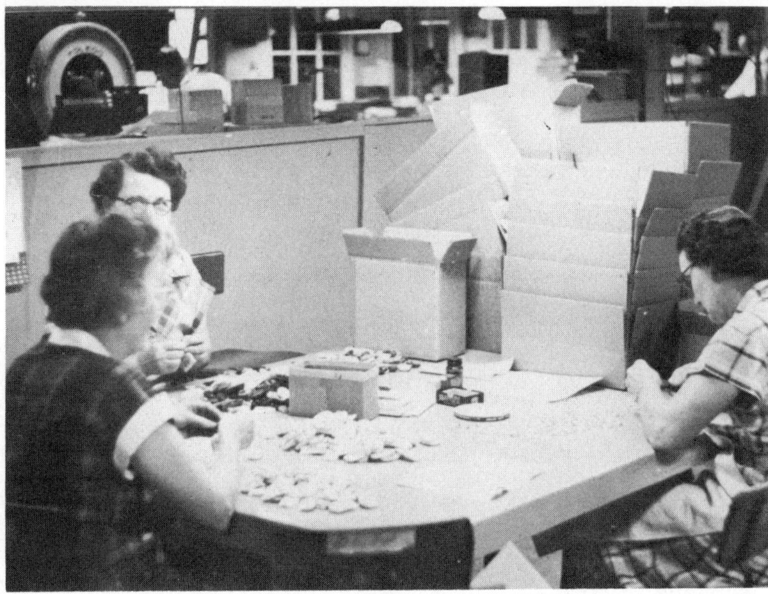

Here are three women doing identical work assembling plastic novelties, whose physical relationship to each other makes it possible for them to become a voluntary triad. They can talk while they work and are in literal face-to-face contact with each other.

The beginnings of division of labor can be noted in the emergence of one individual who is likely to play a leadership role. There may also emerge some minor contest for the leadership position in terms of which the third or non-competing member of the group may play a balancing position. The group is likely to exhibit its unified action as a consequence of the direction of its leader.[21]

Unified action is expressed as the result of a more or less conscious consensus. In the pair relationship the unified action is more nearly the consequence of a feeling of identification and a kind of sensing of the agreement of the other. In the triad, the grounds for agreement are likely to be stated explicitly and agreed on as the basis for unified action.

Furthermore, the threesome is likely to

In an organization, the triad may focus its attention on aspects of the organization. It may operate against the organization because of dislike for what its members view as undesirable aspects of it. It may operate in the direction of the organization because there is satisfaction with the organization's environment. Thus, the triad constitutes a significant grouping of people whose loyalty has to be gained and held, or whose dissatisfaction may be damaging to the organization.

THE PRIMARY ASSOCIATION

The literature is full of references to what has come to be known loosely as the informal group.[22] It is typical to contrast the informal group with the collectivity that we call the formal organization. It is desirable, however, to examine the informal group concept in somewhat greater detail. There is no single kind of group called an informal group. There are two distinctly different kinds of group formations which we will designate, respectively, the primary association and the clique.

The primary association is a group of people who are in a more or less continuous face-to-face association with each other. This association involves regular interaction from which several things result.

The group comes to define a boundary including within itself its members, and excluding those who are beyond the boundary. The boundary may be difficult to observe under some circumstances. In general it is defined by the relatively greater frequency of interaction among those who fall inside its limits.[23]

Highly skilled workers hand assembling klystron electronic tubes. This department is contained in the room pictured. The similar work, high level of shared skill, and physical separation establishes a high probability that primary associations will develop among the members of this department.

The continuous face-to-face interaction suggests that there are limits on the size of the primary association. These limits vary, but they tend to be related to the circumstances under which people work and therefore to the ways they contact each other.

Mayo and Lombard, in studying an aircraft plant during World War II, found 12 out of 69 work groups that were primary associations. The largest of the 12 groups had 7 members.[24] In the much studied Bank Wiring Room at Western Electric, there were two primary associations of 6 and 4 members each, out of 14 men in the room.[25] It is probable that the upper limit of a primary association is about 10 members.

The primary association exhibits a more pronounced division of labor than is found in the threesome. There may be a leader, and in addition there may be individuals who play specialized roles in the life of the group. There may be heroes and fools, the highly skilled and drudges. This division of labor is usually related to group interest and objectives. Where the group is involved primarily in conversation in and about the work place, the skills that may mark different members are cleverness in repartee, and the ability to turn a phrase, or toy with an idea. In such a group, there may be those who are always the butt of the jokes and the sharp remark. There may be one or several individuals who play the role of the straight man very much as would be found in a team of comedians. In other words, the differentiation of roles within the primary association is related to the on-going activities of the members in the group. If the informal group is operating as an athletic team of some sort, then obviously skill in the athletic endeavor would be important in differentiating the roles that the members play.[26]

The primary association tends to have a sense of likemindedness among its members. There is usually explicit agreement as a consequence of discussion among the members. This may be reenforced by certain areas in which there is implicit agreement as well.

The group tends to focus its attention on common activities which are of primary concern to the group members and of relatively little concern to those outside the group. In this sense, the primary association can be viewed as being inner-oriented, or self-oriented, rather than oriented primarily with respect to groups around it.[27]

The primary association may serve to fill organizational voids by satisfying needs for certain kinds of human interaction. The primary association can be viewed as a group context that exists parallel to the formal organization but not necessarily in competition with it. When we put the formal organization together with the informal association or primary association, we are likely to find the two most significant group contexts in which organized co-operation among a group of individuals is both possible and probable.

THE CLIQUE

The clique within an organization is a form of informal group distinguishable from the primary association. The basis on which the distinction can be drawn lies largely in the degree of like-mindedness among the members of the two kinds of groups and their respective centers of attention.

The primary association is oriented towards the group itself and its activities. The clique is typically oriented against other groups, cliques, or factions within its environment. Thus, we can think of a clique within a business firm seeking to gain control of a department or even of the entire firm. We can think of a faction within a political party seeking to dominate its affairs. We can view the possibility of a faction within a church organization ultimately leading to schism and the establishment of a new sect.

A clique is likely to achieve its unity in terms of the combined resentment and antipathy of its members against some other group. The common interest binding the clique together is shared animosity, rather than feelings of like-mindedness and fellowship found in the pair, the triad, and the primary association. Viewed in these terms, the clique is likely to be more extensive in size than the primary association. Furthermore, it is capable of sustained action without necessarily having continuous and face-to-face interaction among its members.[28]

This kind of a group tends to exhibit a high degree of internal division of labor with clearly defined leadership and special roles for dissemination of gossip, spreading innuendo, and the like. Under some circumstances, there may also be roles involving use of physical force against groups in the environment which are the focus of animosity of the clique.

The clique seeks always to increase its membership and thereby to decrease the relative strength of opposing cliques. This is not a characteristic of a primary association, which tends to limit and restrict its membership. The clique does not ask questions about the interests and background of its recruits, and only demands loyalty to the cause for which the clique is crusading. Thus, the membership is likely to be a good deal more diverse in background and much less well knit as a group than is true in the primary association.

The very nature of the clique, and its goals, suggests that it can be highly inimicable to the interests of the organization of which it is a part. There may even be a tendency to destroy the organization rather than permit rival cliques to gain and hold authority. In justification of its activities, the clique is likely to claim that it has the right answer or solution to organization problems and all those opposed to its aims and goals are the real enemies of the organization.

We can differentiate the primary association from the clique by the fact that the primary association has a network of we-feelings that unite its members. The members of a clique, on the other hand, are united by feelings of hostility toward some other group.

The clique is likely to be a great deal more unstable than the primary association, for it is possible to wean away its members by convincing them that their interests lie with a rival clique. Since there is only a minimum loyalty that unites the members of the clique, this loyalty can be readily shifted to some other faction. To guard against this defection from the ranks there is likely to be employed in the clique a maximum of abusive condemnation of all rival cliques, in order to convince present members that their best interests lie in remaining members of the clique.

TYPES OF ORGANIZED GROUP LIFE

There is still another general kind of grouping within work organizations, called "organized groups." In many respects, these are the most common groups found within most formal organizations, for they include all work groups.[29]

Looking first at the work group as a form of organized group, we note that it tends to be oriented primarily towards the technology of work itself. Thus, if the technology includes the production of an item on an assembly line basis the workers are organized in assembly line positions. The organized group takes a wide variety of forms as a work group. It may involve a pair of workers, as operators on a press or a shear. It may encompass a pair of workers, as crane man and hooker. It may include a pair of workers as engineer and fireman in a locomotive. There may be a triad of pilot, co-pilot, and engineer as in an aircraft. The organized group may cover an entire production line of many workers. We can thus see that the size of the organized group is not the feature that distinguishes it from other types.

The organized group takes on its characteristics from the fact that people are thrown into association with each other without any choice. They are performing tasks in a dependent system of jobs that is designed by the managers of the organization.

An organized group therefore has a minimal basis for unity in the interdependence that knits the various related jobs together. It is an interesting feature of an organized group of this sort that it can operate very effectively without any real sense of identification among its members. Indeed, it is possible for it to operate effectively with little or no consensus among its members. The minimum element of consensus necessary for cooperation in technological operations is an agreement simply to continue operating in one's own job. It is possible for two people who are bitter enemies to operate effectively in a chain of dependent jobs. The interaction between such individuals can be limited exclusively to that required to carry out the jobs. There is even evidence to suggest that where we-feelings and a sense of identification are developed the efficiency of a group may, under some circumstances, actually decline.[30]

The organized group may be of a relatively temporary character. For example, there may be a volunteer fire department in a small community, or an industrial plant, whose operation is called into being only in the face of fire. Once the fire is over, the organization ceases to function. Another example of a temporary group is that having to do with a drive to raise funds for the Community Chest.

There are three types of organized groups that are distinguished on the basis of the degree of initiative left to the members of the group in executing their tasks.

TEAM GROUP

One type of organized group is a team, with initiative in the hands of the team members to designate the positions to be filled and the people to fill them. Thus, we can view a telephone truck crew that erects poles, strings wires, and makes repairs as an example of a team. Within such a group, there may be interchange and rotation of jobs as a consequence of the decision of the members of the group. In such a group, the management of the organization in effect says: "Here are the tools; here is the task; and here are *x* number of men to accomplish the job. We now leave it up to you men to determine how best to complete your work."

TASK GROUP

A second type of organized group is one in which the jobs are clearly defined, and each individual is assigned to one and only one job within the group. In such a group, there is little if any exchange of jobs and little if any opportunity to determine, by decision of the group, who shall perform which jobs in the execution of its task.

There may still remain, however, an opportunity for the members of the group to choose their own method of executing their task, and, within limits, an opportunity for the group as a whole to determine the pace at which it will operate. A task group has a great deal of the activity of its members specified in advance for them by the management. There still exists, however, some degree of choice within the group as to certain aspects of its operation; namely, the individual steps in each job, and the group work pace.

An organized team group, with maximum autonomy among the members in determining work pace and task assignments.

TECHNOLOGICAL GROUP

A third type of organized group is perhaps best exemplified in an assembly line. Here each work station is specifically assigned to an individual and his pace is determined no longer by himself, or his fellow workers, but by a mechanically moving line with which he must keep up. Furthermore, because of the speed of the line and the single operation to which each individual is assigned in the line, the actual content of work tasks is usually clearly specified. The worker is trained to do his particular tasks in only one way. Thus, on the assembly line there is nothing that lies within the control of the individual either in the choice of his tools, his methods of work, the pace at which he works, or the location at which he operates.

This technological group is almost the analog of the machine, in which human hands are considered simply as cogs. In this kind of a group, perhaps the only choice remaining to members is social interaction independent of job activities, or complete cessation of work.[31]

The extreme development of the technological group eliminates all opportunity for social intercourse among its members. In such a situation, the individuals not only have prescribed their behavior and activities, but are prevented from any kind of social interaction in the course of filling their jobs. Thus, the pace may be so rapid or the physical barriers of equipment, machinery, or noise so pronounced that it is impossible to communicate in any way with fellow workers.

The writer has observed a production line in a foundry, for example, in which adjacent workers were actually brushing against each other, but working at such a pace, and with such intense concentration and rigidity of expected operations, that there was neither time nor opportunity for communication among the individuals on the line.

In technological work groups, we see the ultimate reduction of the human being to the status of a machine. At this level it is possible and indeed probable that some kind of mechanical equipment will be developed to replace the human being, providing human labor becomes relatively costly enough to warrant the substitution. In technological work group organization, we can find some of the real roots of dissatisfaction with the lot of an industrial worker.[32]

THE ISOLATE

Our analysis of the forms of social life in an organization would be incomplete without some consideration of the isolate. In general, we can view the isolated individual as the product of personality factors which bar him from significant communication with his fellows, or as being isolated by virtue of the kind of work he does.

The individual who is isolated because of his personality may present real problems in the organization. These problems become more acute as the individual is expected to operate effectively not only within the requirements of the formal organization, but to participate as well in the voluntary groups found in connection with his work. There are some kinds of jobs where the social life in the work place is minimized and where the individual, who has personality quirks that isolate him from his fellows, can operate effectively by meeting only the formal requirements of his job. From the standpoint of placement of individuals in the organization, it is thus possible to find certain kinds of tasks in which the personality misfit turns out to be a genuine round peg in a round hole.

The other kind of isolate in the organization is the individual who is isolated by virtue of kind of task that he performs. This isolation is most often grounded in the technological requirement that the individual not be in communication with his fellows while executing his job. But there are social dimensions of such isolation as well. Thus, the inspector who has responsibility for condemning unacceptable work may be effectively isolated from the people whose work he is inspecting. The member of a minority when first thrown into a work group in which he is the only representative of his group may be effectively isolated by virtue of his minority group characteristic.

The isolate may be important in the organization because he performs some kind of technological tasks that require isolation. He may also be important in the organization as a potential focus of dissatisfaction and therefore of grievances with consequent trouble for the managers of the organization. Only in the instance where the personality quirks of the individual lead to his assignment to a technologically isolated task are we likely to find isolation posing no threat to the organization. Where there is either social or technological isolation real problems of dissatisfaction may arise.

These three men weld the top to frame members in assembling an automobile body. Each man has his assigned task and working spot while lifting the top into place and then welding it to the frame with gun welders. This is an organized task group.

A typical technological group composed of workers doing separate tasks in assembling an electronic device. Each device is pushed along the roller assembly line from one work station to the next.

VARIETIES OF WORKING GROUP LIFE

We can now summarize the forms of group life in work organizations. Our first broad distinction is between voluntary social groups, and organized ones. The voluntary social groups are entered through acts of individual choice. Organized social groups are the product of a technology and management decision, limiting the personnel available for membership. Within each one of these broad categories there are special kinds of groups. These are shown below.

- Voluntary Social Groups
  - Pair
  - Triad
  - Primary Association
  - Clique
- Organized Social Groups
  - Team Group
  - Task Group
  - Technological Group

The task of this chapter has been two-fold. We first examined the roots of sociability at work to determine why people seek each other's company during working hours. We then turned to a description of the forms human sociability takes in work organizations. Our analysis shows that there are seven different kinds of recognizable human groupings that may occur when people are brought together to work.

It is a major task for Chapter 16, to analyze the many consequences for work of the fact that people are sociable, and work in groups. The present chapter provides a substantive framework within which much of what follows in this volume, and especially the content of Chapter 16, takes on added meaning.

A man doing paint touch up on an automobile body just before drive off from the end of the final assembly line. He works with a number of people close at hand, but the need for wearing a face mask, and the desire of other workers to avoid the floating spray, tend to isolate this worker from on-the-job social contacts.

NOTES FOR CHAPTER 6

[1] Cf. J. M. Whiting and I. L. Child, *Child Training and Personality* (New Haven: Yale University Press, 1951).

[2] P. A. Sorokin and M. Berger, *Time Budgets of Human Behavior* (Cambridge: Harvard University Press, 1939).

[3] G. H. Mead, *Mind, Self, and Society* (Chicago: University of Chicago Press, 1934), and C. H. Cooley, *Human Nature and the Social Order* (New York: Charles Scribner's Sons, 1902), are basic representations of this view of personality development.

[4] Richard E. Byrd, *Alone* (New York: G. P. Putnam's Sons, 1938); other reports of the effects of solitude in polar regions are: J. M. Scott, *Portrait of an Ice Cap with Human Figures* (London: Chatto and Windus, 1953); A. Courtauld, "Living Alone Under Polar Conditions," *Polar Record,* 1:66-74 (July, 1932); Christiane Ritter, *A Woman in the Polar Night* (New York: E. P. Dutton & Co., 1954). Solitude among sailors is reported in: Captain Joshua Slocum, *Sailing Alone Around the World* (London: Rupert Hart-Davis, 1948; and New York: Dover Publications); Patrick Ellam and Colin Mudie, *Sopranino* (New York: W. W. Norton & Co., 1953); Alain Bombard, *The Voyage of the Heretique* (New York: Simon and Schuster, 1953); Jean Merrien, *Lone Voyagers* (N. Y.: G. P. Putnam's Sons, 1954); and Louis Bernicot, *The Voyage of the Anihita* (London: Rupert Hart-Davis, 1953). Scientific and experimental consequences of isolation on the human personality are contained in: M. H. Small, "On

NOTES FOR CHAPTER 6 (CONT.)

Some Psychical Relations of Society and Solitude," *Pedigogical Seminary,* 7: 13-69 (April, 1900); W. Heron, W. H. Bexton, and D. O. Hebb, "Cognitive Effects of a Decreased Variation in the Sensory Environment," *American Psychologist,* 8:366 (August, 1953); W. H. Bexton, W. Heron, and T. H. Scott, "Effects of Decreased Variation in the Sensory Environment," *Canadian Journal of Psychology,* 8:70-76 (June, 1954); D. O. Hebb, E. S. Heath, and E. A. Stuart, "Experimental Deafness," *Canadian Journal of Psychology,* 8:152-156 (Sept., 1954); and J. C. Lilly, "Effects of Physical Restraint and of Reduction of Ordinary Levels of Physical Stimuli on Intact, Healthy Persons," paper presented at a meeting of the Group for the Advancement of Psychiatry, November 13, 1955.

[5] An excellent account of the prison situation is contained in Christopher Burney, *Solitary Confinement* (New York: Coward-McCann, 1952). There are a number of fictional accounts, notable among which is included in Arthur Koestler, *Darkness at Noon* (New York: The Macmillan Company, 1946; and New York: New American Library); the story of a purged commissar, thrown into prison during a Soviet purge.

[6] See Georges Friedmann, *Industrial Society,* edited with an introduction by H. L. Sheppard (Glencoe: The Free Press, 1955), for a wide-ranging marshaling of evidence on machine pacing of production and its human consequences.

[7] There are very few studies of actual conversations among workers. A study of several factories in Northern Italy revealed that politics, sports, and women were the three topics of conversation that represented the widest common interest and served to provide the basis for acceptance or rejection of new workers by primary associates. See Franca Magistretti, "Sociological Factors in the Structuring of Industrial Workers' Teams," *American Journal of Sociology,* 60:536-540 (May, 1955).

[8] Described in F. J. Roethlisberger and W. J. Dickson, *Management and the Worker* (Cambridge: Harvard University Press, 1939), pp. 421-423.

[9] The familiar process of "hazing" is a characteristic feeling out approach to a new person before his induction into a work group.

[10] This is well illustrated in the way in which a New England factory group rejected management's choice of a Yankee to fill a job traditionally held by a person of Irish descent—the valued informal bond here being ethnic origin. Orvis Collins, "Ethnic Behavior in Industry: Sponsorship and Rejection in a New England Factory," *American Journal of Sociology,* 51:293-298 (January, 1946).

[11] The dial watchers in oil refining operations are good examples of people who have long stretches of idleness while working.

[12] See Elton Mayo, "Revery and Industrial Fatigue," *Journal of Personnel Research,* 3:273-281 (December, 1924), and also his "Day Dreaming and Output in a Spinning Mill," *Journal of the National Institute of Industrial Psychology,* 2:203-209 (January, 1925). Mayo started his pioneering work in the study of industrial work with an interest in the psychic life of workers. These two early papers were the result.

[13] A rare study of the actual behavior of working people when a company decision is being formulated is: Neil Chamberlain, *Management in Motion, The Corporate Decision-making Process as Applied to the Transfer of Employees* (New Haven: Labor and Management Center, Yale University, 1950). Chamberlain shows the almost endless hours spent by all levels of the organization in conversation and consultation while a major company policy was being worked out.

[14] A considerable movement has grown up in industry based upon a "group dynamics" approach to cooperation through collaboration. One of the pioneering experimental studies in which consultation with workers whose work load was raised was used in order to overcome their resistance to the change is reported in: Lester Coch, and J. R. P. French, "Overcoming Resistance to Change," *Human Relations,* 1:512-532 (August, 1948).

[15] Very adverse consequences to union leaders who cooperated with management resulted when management finally refused to continue the formal cooperation. Worker satisfaction with cooperation was turned into disgruntlement and vicious attack upon the union leaders most active in the cooperation venture. See W. R. Dymond, "Union-Management Cooperation at the Toronto Factory of Lever Brothers Limited," *Canadian Journal of Economics and Political Science,* 13:26-27 (February, 1947).

[16] Roethlisberger and Dickson, *Management and the Worker,* pp. 15-18.

[17] One of the most important analyses of the pair as a sociological group is by the great German sociologist, Georg Simmel. See *The Sociology of Georg Simmel,* edited and translated by K. H. Wolff (Glencoe: The Free Press, 1950), pp. 122-135.

[18] *Ibid.,* especially the section beginning on p. 126, titled "Intimacy."

[19] *Ibid.,* particularly p. 137.

[20] *Ibid.,* Chapter 4, "The Triad," pp. 145-169.

[21] *Ibid.,* pp. 145-153.

[22] An entirely new direction was given to the Western Electric researches when its principal staff was unable to explain the observed behavior and turned to the sociological literature for guiding ideas from men like Durkheim, and the functional anthropologists like Malinowski. W. L. Warner, then conducting the "Yankee City" studies, was one of the people who opened up the new area of ideas by suggesting to the researchers at Western Electric that they turn in the new direction. Roethlisberger and Dickson, *Management and the Worker,* consistently

NOTES FOR CHAPTER 6 (CONT.)

use the term "clique" to label what we call primary association. Subsequent researchers have been inclined to use the term "informal group" as a generic term for all types of human groupings not specifically designated by an organization chart. Cf., W. F. Whyte (ed.), *Industry and Society* (New York: McGraw-Hill Book Co., 1946).

23 This has become the actual criterion used in sociometry for measuring the boundaries of a group. It is instructive to examine almost any issue of *Sociometry* through 1955 when it was edited by the inventor of sociometric methods, J. L. Moreno. There are literally hundreds of studies of groups whose characteristics are analyzed in terms of the choices or rejections members make of each other.

24 Elton Mayo and G. F. F. Lombard, *Teamwork and Labor Turnover in the Aircraft Industry of Southern California* (Cambridge: Research Studies No. 32; Boston: Harvard Business School, Division of Research, 1944), p. 22. They called the primary association a "natural" group.

25 The interaction charts on the basis of which the primary associations were determined are redrawn and analyzed with great clarity in G. C. Homans, *The Human Group* (New York: Harcourt Brace and Co., 1950), pp. 48-80. The two primary associations are actually charted on p. 71, where they are labelled "cliques" following the practice of the original authors, Roethlisberger and Dickson.

26 *The Sociology of Georg Simmel,* Chapter 5, pp. 170-189.

27 It must be remembered that we are distinguishing the primary association from the clique. The latter is other-group oriented where the primary association is very much less so. Cf. C. H. Cooley, *Social Organization* (Charles Scribner's Sons, 1909) where the in-group, out-group distinction is elaborated.

28 A recent study of union political behavior in the printing industry has analyzed the on-the-job social relations of printers in relation to their political behavior inside the union. This part of the study is relevant to the analysis of cliques. See S. M. Lipset, M. A. Trow, and James S. Coleman, *Union Democracy: The Internal Politics of the International Typographical Union* (Glencoe: The Free Press, 1956), especially pp. 163-171.

29 We have adopted Mayo and Lombard's term from *Teamwork and Labor Turnover,* p. 23.

30 It has been shown, for example, that too much social cohesion of a voluntary group kind may be detrimental to the effectiveness of a technical team, in this case basketball teams. See F. E. Fiedler, "Assumed Similarity Measures as Predictors of Team Effectiveness," *Journal of Abnormal and Social Psychology,* 49:381-387 (July, 1954).

31 A poignant description of the tension that builds up when workers on a production line "pull the switch" and stop work is contained in Henry Kraus, *The Many and the Few* (Los Angeles: The Plantin Press, 1947), pp. 47-55. Kraus describes the first strike on the job in Fisher Body Plant No. 1, Flint, Michigan, in the days just preceding the sit-down strike which led to the recognition of the United Automobile Workers union.

32 The most consistent and well documented case against the degradation of workers in technological teams is: Georges Friedman, *Industrial Society.* It is very easy and often tempting to overdraw the consequences for human personality of modern production methods. It should be clear from our analysis that there is no simple black and white set of conclusions about the human consequences of work regimes. For example, it is possible that the depersonalizing effects of being a member of a technological team can be more than overcome by a vigorous voluntary group life in the work place. Most of those who take violent sides in the machine *vs.* man arguments do not see the possible combinations of the voluntary and organized work groups which can function jointly to provide satisfying human relationships. This very point is given detailed analysis in Chapter 16.

The continued existence of a business, or any work organization, is an important institutional pressure playing on executive decisions. The mere possession of assets, like buildings, equipment, and skilled employees, generate strong pressures to perpetuate them.

Chapter 7

INSTITUTIONAL BASES OF DECISIONS

There are many sources of regularity in human behavior. Some of the principal influences tending to make human behavior uniform, and therefore predictable, lie in the customs, mores, laws and moral principles, and in the habits and mutual expectations that grow up when human beings associate with each other.

Human behavior also becames regularized through institutional practices. In particular, important regularities appear in work organizations that are the consequences of their institutional behavior systems. In this chapter we want to investigate those institutional practices of work organizations having particular importance for executive decision making by executives and administrators of work organizations.

INSTITUTIONAL PRACTICES

By institutional practices we mean simply the content of the general behavior systems of the work organization. You will recall that in Chapter 4 we analyzed the behavior systems surrounding work. In Chapter 5 we discovered how these behavior systems constitute important facets of jobs, positions, and offices.

The behavior systems of work organizations establish the actions that occur regularly. We would expect the executive's and administrator's decision making behavior to take systematic forms. Executives approach and solve their problems requiring decision through acts learned from participating in the behavior systems surrounding their work. The behavior systems partially determine the *ways of making* executive decisions.

We might also expect that the problems on which decisions are necessary are problems of the four work behavior systems. Hence, these systems determine the *subject matter* of much executive decision making.

We are looking for factors that determine the subject matter and the ways of making management decisions. We want to understand what an executive has to take into account, and how he takes it into account, when making a decision.[1]

An individual joins an organization with a wide range of choices for behaving, based on prior experience and personality characteristics. However, the actual behavior exhibited while a member of the organization results from limitations that membership in the organization places on him. The organization clearly molds the individual in the sense that he may behave quite differently as a consequence of membership in it.[2]

The man who is a husband and father in his family makes decisions and behaves in family contacts quite differently from the way he behaves as an executive of the XYZ Corporation. These differences in behavior cannot be accounted for by personality changes as he moves from the family to the business setting. The differences in his behavior are largely the consequence of differential demands made on him by the business organization and by his family.

In this chapter we want to examine the evidence that demonstrates the existence of institutional bases for organization decision making. We will also examine some of the areas in which decision making has come to be institutionalized. We will look, too, at the consequences of institutionalizing decision making from the standpoint of human relationships and human behavior.

PERPETUATING THE ORGANIZATION

Institutionalized decision making results from activities for perpetuating organizations.[3] With few exceptions, business organizations are designed to have a considerable life history. In the course of maintaining the continuity of the organization there grow up certain connections between past history, present conditions, and future prospects.

Certain kinds of decisions become appropriate for executives and members of the organization because they are like the decisions that they, or their predecessors, made in the past. Expectations of future behavior are similarly colored by what people are now doing, or have recently done. A work organization has a style that tends to remain relatively unchanged through time. People may move in and out of the organization as officers and employees. While operating as members of the organization, they tend to orient their behavior to going patterns and expectations.

Even in the instance where the organization may change direction and make some sharper break with its past, there may be some logical connections with its past condition. For example, a business executive may decide to diversify the products of his firm, proceeding either to establish new divisions, or to buy other companies. The institutional imperatives playing on such a decision may be viewed as (A) the prior high degree of specialization in product, and (B) the belief that fluctuations in the business cycle can be minimized in their impact if diversified products, affected differently by swings in the business cycle, are produced by the company. As in this example, the direction of change can probably be predicted for a firm, knowing the conditions of its previous stability and knowing something of the environment within which it operates.[4]

RATIONAL CHARACTER OF BUSINESS ORGANIZATIONS

It is one of the features of modern business and industrial organizations that they are grounded in rationality. They are planned organizations that have carefully thought out relationships among their parts, and carefully delineated objectives for the parts as they contribute to the whole organization. A business organization is systematic, having been constructed on the basis of certain systematic ideas, and designed to operate in accordance with these ideas. It is the conscious development of systems of jobs, positions, and offices, systems of communication, systems of production, systems of control, systems of authority, systems of rewards and incentives, and power systems, that represent the rational aspects of organizations.[5]

Those officials habitually making decisions affecting operations will tend to bring their decisions into some relationship with the organization's systems. Thus, knowing the systems, or the rational models, on the basis of which behavior is expected to be ordered, it becomes possible to predict the specific behaviors of members. This is also true of decisions those in authority make. Consequently, the rational bases of business organization are another source of institutional rather than individual roots of decision making.

AUTHORITY AND INSTITUTIONALIZATION

The authority structure of a work organization is supported by institutional practices. These practices are designed to reinforce the authority structure and to insure its relative stability. In particular, every member of the work organization is expected to accept the proper exercise of authority in getting work done.[6]

There are two major aspects of institutionalized authority. The first relates to the legitimacy of the authority structure and those who exercise it. Here the organizational problem is a simple one. Exercising authority is decision making about aspects of work. Decision making, to be effective, requires willing acceptance of it. When workers feel that a legitimate person makes decisions, accepting his decisions is facilitated.

Surrounding each position of decision making, therefore, will be features of the task or position that signalize legitimacy. The job title may denote legitimate order giving. A foreman, by definition, legitimately gives orders. So does the executive vice president. The organization chart describes the chain of command. The daily round of work life confirms who habitually gives orders, and in what realms. These are but a few examples of the position or task features confirming decision making responsibilities.

The second major aspect of institutionalized authority relates to the kinds of executive decisions that are made to support authority. This has two facets. The first involves making decisions supporting exising authority structures. It is important to recognize that "going through channels" is vital in the downward flow of authority. The executive can undercut a subordinate's authority by ignoring him in the chain of command. This provides an important institutionalized base for executive decisions. The executive is constrained to make his decisions with an eye to their execution in the chain of command. He takes the authority structures of his work organization into account in making decisions affecting them.

The second facet of executive decisions supporting authority structures is the consistent pressure on executives to "stand behind" decisions of subordinates. An executive's first impulse is to declare publicly that his subordinate's decision is proper, whether it is in fact good, bad, or indifferent. It is not solely out of human weakness, or kindness, that the executive does this. He is also compelled to support his subordinate since, frequently, failure to do so would call into question the legitimacy of the authority structures.

We can now suggest that executives, in making decisions, are operating within limits placed upon them by the authority structures. Executives have to be certain that their management of the work organization insures symbolic conferring of legitimacy on all subordinate authority holders. Secondly, executives have to support authority structures by going through channels, not ignoring authority holders who are in the chain of command. Finally, executives are constrained, at least publicly, to favor their subordinate's exercise of authority even when it is questionable. By so doing the integrity of the authority structure is sustained.[7]

Executives are not completely free to make decisions without reference to the authority structures of their organization. Indeed, the authority structures provide important institutional limits on executive's decisions.

STATUS AND INSTITUTIONALIZATION

The status structures of work organizations also place limits on decision making. Here the executive's decisions largely affect personnel matters.

One of the most vexing problems for the executive is to insure that status is adequately conferred and maintained for the members of his organization. Executives operate in a kind of fish bowl where their every action is viewed by subordinates as having potential status conferring significance.

Examples are numerous; a few will illustrate the point. An executive has to be careful with whom he publicly passes the time of the day. Talking with one subordinate more frequently than others at the same status level will lead to the inference that he is favored; i.e., has higher status. In designing office layouts, the executive has to be sensitive to the proper location of people in terms of their relative status. Failure to consider this in decisions regarding layout will have the effect of changing the status structure in the eyes of subordinates. Care has to be taken in distributing all external marks of organization status, to be sure they correspond with the official and informal ascriptions of status.

An important constraint on an executive's decision is the status conferring character of his own actions and decisions. Where status structures are consciously taken into account in making decisions, the executive has to know their nature. Such knowledge will help to guard against decisions, otherwise good, that wittingly or unwittingly do violence to the current distribution of status symbols.

Another important constraint on executive action and decision is the need to be sure that violation of the status structures are not an unplanned-for consequence. Every decision, however remotely it seems to affect status, requires review to determine its possible influences on status. As people carry out decisions, they scrutinize their manner of determination as well as their content for status implications. If undesirable status changes are even implicit in decisions, their successful execution may well be in doubt. Organization members may rebel against decisions because their fulfilment endangers established status, quite aside from whether or not the decision is desirable on any other grounds.[8]

POWER AND INSTITUTIONALIZATION

The power structures of work organizations provide still other limitations on executive decision. In general these limitations have to do with assignment of responsibility throughout the organization.[9]

Power structures are stable because they define the existing distribution of work activities. Where activities are transferred, shifted, or discontinued, for whatever reasons, strong resistance usually develops from those losing the activities. Most executives know this. Their decisions regarding the distribution of power often reflect knowledge about such resistances. Assignment and reassignment of work activities usually start from the assumption that things ought to be done where they have always been done. Change in location of activities is usually suspect.[10]

Many activities have their established locations within the scheme of work. Decisions regarding their location are not difficult to make. However, many new activities, or those changed by new technologies, may lie between established divisions of work. A number of departments or divisions may be fighting to get the new activities. Some kind of executive decision is required to settle the issues. These decisions are often most difficult to make. The contending parties can marshal pertinent arguments favoring assignment to them. When the decision is made, the losing contender may have to be placated. These power struggles are constantly occurring, and their solution occupies a major share of executive attention.[11]

We can illustrate such power struggles with classic examples drawn from business operations. An area of constant struggle is between staff and line units. The line units involved in direct production operations resist any staff efforts to take over, or change, production operations. Many kinds of staff units like engineering, production control, and cost accounting constantly find their work penetrating into production operations. The struggle for control over activities and the power conferred by this control is a constant one between line and staff. Another example of power conflict is that between central office and branch operations. The issue here centers on the virtues of local *vs.* central direction of activities.[12]

From the executive's standpoint the power structures of the work organization are additional limiting considerations in his decisions. Any change in the current arrangement of work assignments will disturb existing power structures, and will inevitably change them in some respect. In short, decisions affecting power structures may have serious operating consequences. There is little wonder, then, that executives tend to favor decisions about power structures and power relations that produce as little change as possible.[13]

EXPERTS AND INSTITUTIONALIZATION

When specialists operate in relation to each other, order is possible only if the specialists remain in their area of competence, and the rules governing their interrelationships remain relatively unchanged. Thus, in the interests of maintaining order in relations among specialties, there are important limitations on the kinds of decisions that can be made by specialists, and the directions they take. Each specialist must make his decision without disturbing the going relations with other specialties.

Furthermore, the coordinating executive limits the range of his decisions holding special activities together. He will tend to act as though each specialty is stable and unchanging. He will also tend to make his decisions about their coordination as though they interrelated in fixing and established ways.

The expert can operate successfully in his limited and specialized sphere if two general conditions are met: (A) that the scope of the expert's operations is clearly differentiated from the specialized areas of others; and (B) that the relations between spheres of specialization are systematized and standardized. Granting these two conditions, it is possible for the expert to maintain professional independence.[14]

For example, the legal counsel or legal officer of an organization may often be remote from the ways of thinking of his colleagues in the organization. The financial officer may make decisions that are based on highly specialized knowledge of the money market, and and the relations of the company to it. The public relations officer may similarly operate in an area of highly specialized knowledge that is shared with few if any other members of the firm.[15]

The expert may operate within his sphere of competence in accordance with standards and values that are independent of his work organization. In a very real sense, the legal officer is more responsive to the requirements of being a lawyer, and of filling the institutional expectations of a lawyer, than he is responsive to fulfilling the institutional expectations of the business firm for which he is legal counsel. Put another way, the professional institution within which the individual operates may have more to do with the kinds of decisions he makes than the organization in which he is employed.

On the face of it this may appear to give rise to potential conflict between professional standards and organization expectations. Usually, the organization recognizes the professional characteristics of the realm within which the expert operates. The expert is usually given the right of "last word" in the areas of his professional competence. Thus, the lawyer has the final say on legal aspects of the company's business; the public relations man approves executive speeches and public relations activities; and the engineer has the responsibility of certifying adequacy of engineering designs. Consequently the expert is integrated into the business organization in terms of his expertness, not in spite of it.[16]

Where the realm of the specialist is inappropriately integrated into the organization untoward consequences may result. For example, in some electrical and aircraft manufacturers and other firms that employ large numbers of engineers, management has made serious errors in understanding the professional expectations of engineers. One result has been organization of engineers into independent trade unions to bargain collectively with employers who have failed to accord to the engineers the semi-independence they feel their profession requires. It has recently been estimated by *Fortune* magazine that there are forty thousand such engineers presently organized in independent company-wide unions; this, in spite of the fact that the professional engineering societies frown upon collective bargaining. The reason for this "non-professional" behavior lies in the failure of management properly to guarantee professional job independence to the employed engineers.

From what has been said it seems apparent that some of the institutional foundations of work organization decision making may be found in institutions other than the operating organization.[17] This is true in the case of experts who are professionals. The basis of professionals' decisions may lie in the principles and institutionalized expectations of the profession itself, rather than in the organization where the profession is exercised. Coordinating executives take this into account as a limitation on their decisions affecting experts.

OPERATIONS RESEARCH AND LINEAR PROGRAMMING

There have been two very recent developments in the application of scientific methods to business organization. These are interrelated applications called operations research and linear programming.[18] The essential feature of these two developments is the application of probability theory to the analysis of business problems.

It is instructive to look at the history of this development. It comes largely out of World War II where physical scientists were asked to work on problems of military logistics and tactics. The scientists came up with effective answers to (A) the relative efficiency of ocean convoys as over against single sailings in transporting goods across submarine infested waters; (B) the most effective bombing patterns for maximum damage on the target with a minimum investment of bombs and planes; (C) the most effective evasive action of a submarine under attack while submerged; and (D) the kind of firing pattern for an artillery battery that would be most destructive.[19]

The solution to these problems was based upon an objective knowledge of the operating situation, and a maximum knowledge of probability theory and its applications. Indeed, in one of the first texts on operations research, the point is strongly made that the operations researcher is better off by virtue of a specialist staff position in the organization in which he is applying this method.[20] The implication is drawn that those who have been operating in the organization by traditional methods are blocked from seeing new problem solutions. It is lack of commitment to a given solution that permits operations research experts to be effective in solving problems.

The development of linear programming is essentially the direct application of operations research to business operations. Effective applications of operations research and linear programming have already been made in practical situations by a number of progressive corporations. For our purposes it is desirable to ignore the techniques of operations research and to look at it as a form of decision making, illustrating how the decision making process works in business organizations.

Operations research provides a method for making business decisions. This method of decision making (A) provides an invariant operation for reaching the decision, and (B) insures in advance the decision made will be the best possible one within the limitations specified for the problem.

The mechanical nature of this method of decision making, and the certainty of outcome, represent important developments in business decision making. These developments are essentially twofold. The actual operation of decision making may become more and more of a technique, effectively carried out by technicians rather than executives. Relative certainty of outcome will permit longer range planning and fuller understanding of future developments, with a consequent improvement of business forecasting.

Operations research and linear programming represent, therefore, one of the highest developments of the institutional bases of organization decision making. We can see in this development the convergence of the rational character of business organizations, the focus on perpetuating activities in organizations, the intensive use of experts—all combined to produce conditions where decision making loses most of its artistic character and develops precision never before achieved.

There are three aspects of operations research that deserve particular attention. First, the "rules of the game" are defined in general models. These models are the theory about the behavior being studied. Thus, the theory of probability is a general theory, important in building models of business problems. When probability theory is used in the solution of a business problem it represents an application of the theory, just as the theory may be applied in the studies of public attitudes, voting behavior, or celestial movements.

A second feature of operations research is that the applied situation becomes one of "putting the data into a theoretical model and cranking out the answer." Once the theoretical model is fully understood, formulas can be established for routine application of the theory to standard situations. The theory and its operations guarantee, in advance, certainty of an answer, and its validity. Under these circumstances, decision making becomes a technology and is no longer a matter of "judgment" or of "art."

The third feature of operations research as applied to business decision making is that the construction of the theoretical models and the selection of variables to put into the model become the important intellectual steps. It is here that the businessman *as* a businessman functions to make decisions by which operations research or linear programming are effectively applied to business problems. If the wrong variables are chosen to build into theoretical models, or if the relationship among the variables is inappropriate, then the model may grind out an answer, but the answer will not be to the questions asked.[21]

Decision making operations are becoming more and more technical. The areas of executive judgment may shift from that of reaching a conclusion, to that of being able to define a problem and specify the proper variables and their interrelationships for its analysis.

With further development of operations research and linear programming still another kind of expertness will be introduced into the business realm. This expert's area of competence is mathematics and probability theory. The subject matter of mathematics is highly abstract and often "impractical." In the development of operations research we probably have the best single example of how abstract thinking becomes ultimately the basis for the most practical kinds of solutions to practical business problems.

EXAMPLES OF INSTITUTIONALIZED DECISIONS

In principle, every area of business operation is subject to some degree of institutionalized decision making. We can say this another way by suggesting that there are no areas of business decision where there is not a model by which to go.

There are some areas of business in which decision models are less complete and less precise than in other areas. It is in such operations that decision making is still considered an art. Differences between artistic aspects of decision making and systematic aspects are ones of degree rather than kind. Pressures in business organizations are in the direction of systematizing models for decision making and, therefore, the certainty with which decisions will be appropriate and effective for the organization.

We can say, in general, that every area of business decisions displays some degree of institutionalization.[22] It may be instructive to examine briefly how institutionalized decision making is exhibited in various parts of work organization operations.

TECHNOLOGY

American business operations are based on a philosophic assumption that technology is always subject to improvement. This faith in technological progress is the foundation for institutional pressure to value technological change.

Such emphasis on innovation is historically unique. The history of technological advance makes clear that innovation tended to be resisted rather than welcomed. Only since the Industrial Revolution has the reverse been generally true.[23]

The impact of faith in change on executive decision has been marked. The term "progressive management" derives its meaning almost exclusively from belief in technological advance. Executives are under pressure to give active expression to this idea by favoring improved technology in their decisions. This is truly an institutional imperative affecting executive decisions even though the influential factor is an idea. Ideas, too, can be institutionalized, as this instance illustrates.

PRODUCTION

In the production realm a conservative institutional influence operates. High speed production is dependent on long runs for its efficiency. Orders for products have to be in sufficient quantity that items can be produced for relatively long periods of time with no change in machine set-up, materials, or operations. Once a production line is operating effectively, there is a strong disinclination to change it.

Emphasis on stability in operations is a characteristic feature of production units. Production people tend to oppose changes in materials, machines, or operating arrangement that will halt production and require reorganizations of the production unit.

Reasons for this conservative orientation are not hard to find. Pressure is on production units to get the most out with the least effort and expense. Any interruptions in work flow will be costly, and will lower volume of output. Production men are under constant pressure to keep output at a high and stable volume. Consequently, they oppose any disturbances that will affect stability of output.

It is interesting to note that faith in technological innovation, and desire for high volume of output are in conflict in the short run. On a day-to-day basis, the production man is opposed to technological innovation that will temporarily upset his stable producing unit. In the long run he may share faith in technological advancement, and accept improvements where they can be planned into his producing unit so that he is not held responsible for lowered output while the innovation is being "run in." This, incidently, partly accounts for the pilot line or pilot plant technique for introducing major technological innovations. The pilot operation is completely separated from the producing operations. All "bugs" are worked out of the process before it is "put on the line." This removes responsibility from the production man for having to maintain high volume of output with untried methods.

The major institutionalized factor in production affecting decisions is the demand for continuous high level output. This leads to favoring those operating conditions that will minimize change once a satisfactory operating level is reached.

ACCOUNTING

Accounting as an aspect of executive control of work organizations has an interesting influence in institutionalizing rationality in operations. The basic operation of accounting is the precise assignment of a cost or income factor to an accounting category for summarizing it. Thus, an item of expenditure may either be a direct or overhead cost. It has to find its place in some category that accounts for it.

Business operations are not quite as clean-cut and neat as acounting practice would have them. Yet the acounting sheets must be filled with figures, placed in the proper column. There is a spurious kind of precision demanded in making up accounting reports. Things seem more precise than they really are.

This is not to be taken as a criticism of accounting. The point is simply that the appearance of rationality and knowledge that a column of figures gives is not exactly matched by the reality it represents.

On the other hand, the need for precision in accounting reports has had a genuine influence in making more accurate assignments of costs and income. With better knowledge about the distribution of costs and income has come more adequate and rational executive decision making.

The functions of an accountant force him into precision analysis. His very precision has a feedback on the organization, making its operations more precisely known, leading to greater rationality in management by increasing the volume and quality of knowledge about operations.[24]

SALES

One of the principal institutional factors affecting sales is the fact that this is the major area in which the work organization is outwardly oriented. It is through product sales that the work organization is tied to its consuming public. The behavior of sales personnel and sales decisions are almost exclusively oriented toward the customer, who is not part of the work organization.

Customer orientation of sales tends to present a special face of the organization to the outside world. There is a vast difference in appearance between the booming, noisy, dusty, drab, hot, cluttered production shops where refrigerator bodies are stamped out on huge forming presses, and the plush sales floor of a retail shop where the gleaming refrigerator is sold. Furthermore, the kinds of behavior in the production shop are much more subject to control. In relations with customers, the control of the situation is shifted in the customers' direction. As a result, sales personnel are likely to be much more "other directed" in their orientation and behavior.[25] In the instance of sales activities we see the impact on institutional decisions of groups and persons external to, but functionally necessary for work organizations.

These very brief summary statements are intended simply to illustrate the character of some institutional imperatives playing on work organization behavior and executive decision making. The examples are not exhaustive. They should give you a notion of some of the subtle connections between the environment in which executives operate and their behavior as decision makers.

DECISIONS AND STABILITY

The most pervasive imperative playing on decision making is the need to solve problems. Work organizations are rational in structure, goals, and operations. They operate with scarce resources and have limited time periods for "paying off." Any problems that represent significant blocks to continuous operations and goal achievement threaten the very existence of the organization. Such problems must be solved, however imperfectly, so that work can move ahead toward planned goals.

An unsolved operating problem is a visible threat to the organization. It means that a planned-for outcome may not be achieved. Control systems are often designed to give literal and visible signals that a problem has arisen. The common symbol of "red ink" to represent a financial loss, or deficit, is a literal signal of a problem. Visual production control schemes similarly employ colored or shaped warning signals indicating present or prospective operating problems.

The simple fact of the matter is that a business organization is a finely balanced operating system. Any evidence that a part of the system is malfunctioning poses an immediate threat to the stability of the whole organization.

Executives attempt to design their organizations so that there is a maximum of stability, achieved partly through self-stabilizing actions. Any control of work activities not only tells those subject to it what is expected in the way of behavior, but also signals when they fail to comply. This signaling of failure in doing what is expected is an important form of self-stabilization; it immediately calls into action the "trouble shooters" who are prepared to make decisions solving the problem.

Executives are constantly faced with the need for being organization "trouble shooters." A significant per cent of all executive decisions made are concerned with restoring stability in circumstances where planned-for results do not materialize.

A major goal of all work organizations is stability of operations. This does not imply stagnation. Stability may mean a stationary level of output. It may mean a regular cycle of output varying with the seasons. It may mean a systematic increment of output through time, or it may even mean an orderly decline in output.

The central point about business stability is this: some systematic plan for operations is developed with the full anticipation that it will be achieved. It is a major responsibility of executives to direct their decisions at insuring a reasonable organizational effort to achieve the planned for operations. This means that there is a strong institutional imperative to solve immediately all operating problems constituting roadblocks to the realization of plans and schedules.

DECISIONS AND CHANGE

The picture that we have up to this point portrays the organization in relative equilibrium. It is nevertheless true that business organizations particularly are subject to contingencies making change an essential feature of their operations. We, therefore, have to examine the relationship between institutionalized decision making and change in business organizations.

A new technology may give rise to a whole new set of operations, the development of new products, new marketing procedures, and new personnel problems requiring immediate solution. Indeed, it might be argued that the real "art" of the executive lies in confronting and handling changes impinging on his organization. The executive can leave to the technician development of standardized procedures for decision making in stable situations. The technician is probably incapable of handling situations in which significant change occurs affecting areas of stable behavior.

It is here that the executive has to take into account the nature of the changes and their impact on the internal and external environment of his organization. He may have to redesign his decision models to incorporate the changes in operations of his firm.[26]

There may be some areas of business operations in which change is accepted as a normal and standard feature. This is particularly true of sales promotion, and technological development. However, there are other areas in which the impact of change may be viewed as undesirable, and the whole goal is to stabilize operations and systems in human behavior. This appears to be true in the personnel area[27] and in the area of business financing.[28] Thus, areas of business operations are affected differently by change.

Sociologists have developed a term "cultural lag" to deal with the degree of permeability that change has in various aspects of human behavior. The "cultural lag" concept suggests that systematic ways of behaving tend to persist, and to exclude alternatives that upset the system. Consequently, while knowledge may exist of desirable changes that could be incorporated in the business firm, the dependent behaviors requiring modification in order to incorporate the proposed change would be so extensive that the change may be rejected.[29]

For example, the undepreciated value of a piece of equipment may necessitate its continued use because it still has a book value, even though a successor piece of machinery is demonstrably more efficient in turning out the identical product. Here the system of accounting, and the allocation of costs in the firm, become all important, and the production objective may have secondary value in keeping an obsolete piece of equipment in production.

LIMITS OF CHANGE

There is probably no example of a perfectly static work organization. Change occurs, however slow its progress. On the other hand, there are business firms that appear to change very rapidly. There is probably always an effective balance between stability and change, between institutionalized bases for decisions and opportunistic decisions to meet changing conditions. It is not possible to specify the exact balance between stability and change. It is probably true that the former outweighs the latter in organizations that have the capacity to survive over long periods of time.

We can gain some perspective on the limits surrounding change by examining technological advance. It has already been noted that industrial management has a strong belief in the virtues of technical improvement. This is one area of business operations where change is valued over stability. Yet, as we will see below, opportunities for technical advance are not unlimited.

It is a sociological truism that a change in culture proceeds from existing cultural complexes. Consequently, we would expect that the development of a particular technical advance grows out of existing technical knowledge. For example, effective utilization of atomic fission was dependent on theoretical developments in physics and chemistry as well as engineering developments in modern industry. Their fusion was the great accomplishment of the Manhattan Project, which produced the first atomic bomb. Only the war emergency could have impelled the government to make the vast investments necessary to produce fissionable material. The amount of capital investment necessary far exceeded the financial resources of any of the typical institutions that develop technology, like private companies, or industrial cartels. World War II was a necessary cultural element in the development of controlled atomic fission.

There is a certain logic and order in the development of technology out of the preexisting culture. This often provides a basis for predicting the future course of technology. We can see, for example, that the electronics industry, which has produced electronic devices and "thinking machines," will have great impact in the next quarter or half century on the machine equipment of modern industry. The automatic plant is already a reality, and will come into general use in the next half century.[30]

This is a safe prediction, for the technical elements necessary for its fulfillment are already evident. Two general considerations will slow up the rapidity with which electronics and electronic controls will be used in modern production. First, the present tremendous capital investment in machines and processes must be written off before substituting the more modern equipment. Second, the ideas, values, and sentiments that surround present methods of production will have to undergo modification in the direction of accepting and working out the social consequences of the new systems of production. Both of these considerations are conservative influences that will slow up the introduction of the newer technology.

Institutional practices are habitual ways of behaving that have become routine through constant usage. Once established, the institutional practices tend to persist because there is both a physical investment in cultural artifacts, and a psychological investment in habitual performance that places relatively high value on current institutional arrangements.

Is it not possible to argue that a free enterprise system implies relatively great freedom for industrial managers to introduce such changes in their operations that they deem prudent? Or, are the executives of industry subject to considerations that limit choices about future development?

There are important limitations on the unchecked exercise of authority even for those who are in the controlling positions in our large scale organizations. First of all, the legal system provides important checks on decisions in a number of directions. Private decisions are limited by certain social objectives that must be met and which are embodied in the laws and regulations of the society.

Second, the complex dependence which is characteristic of industrial society places certain limits on the direction in which individual companies, or individual industries, may move. For example, the vast development of aluminum production required that new uses be found for aluminum sheet and barstock before the increased production could become economical. During World War II, with the aluminum industry expanded considerably, the output for its products went into aircraft manufacture. However, after the war with a cutback in aircraft production, alternative uses had to be found. During this period aluminum output temporarily fell off. In a sense, therefore, the evolving technology can move only as rapidly as there is a reasonable accomodation to the changes produced in the other segments of industry and the whole economy.

A third factor that affects the range of private decisions in managing organizations that control our technology is the method of industrial financing. Investments in capital goods are typically written off, or amortized, over a period of years. There is an expectation that a piece of equipment not fully amortized will be continued in operation until it is paid for out of future production. This provides a brake on too rapid introduction of new changes in technology.

Consumer resistance to changes in products may constitute still another brake on full freedom in the exercise of organizational decisions with respect to technology. Mass consumers may be unwilling or unaccustomed to accept new products that could be produced. Until consumer acceptance is built up the products will not be successful on the market.

Labor organizations will, through their union contracts, provide additional limits within which organizational decisions have to be made. This may cover the rapidity with which technological changes are introduced, and the rapidity with which job changes will be permitted. The union contract will also cover important decisions affecting labor costs, and thereby cost pressures affecting changes in technology.

We can see that there is not complete freedom of choice among decisions governing the introduction of new technologies. Therefore there is not complete freedom to exercise total influence over the development of our industrial society. In this sense, we can say that even though control of the developing technologies may be centered in executives of work organizations, it does not follow that they have unlimited social power.

FREEDOM AND DECISIONS

It is an important element in Marxist philosophy that control of the means of production is the key to social power in modern industrial society. A more modern view suggests that ownership or control of industry is not the crucial factor in social power deriving from industrial technology. More important is the ability to determine the direction in which the new technology will evolve. It should now be clear that this is not solely the consequence of private decisions of business executives. Technology changes as a consequence of composite decisions of directors of business firms, legislators, competitors, consumers, and labor union officials, made in the light of present institutional practices defining the nature of work, the division of labor among industries, investment policies, and the conditions of organization stability.

The social power of those who control industry is great.[31] The managers of industry make highly important decisions that affect the lives of many people who are employees and customers.

In the context of the whole society, executive decisions are neither unlimited in range, nor capricious in their content. It is the central point of this chapter that most of the influences playing on executive decision center on maintaining stability in complex industrial organizations. It is difficult either to be willful or imaginative in making executive decisions. Indeed, one of the central problems of industrial leadership is the development of broad imagination in guiding industrial firms through a changing environment, as we shall see in Chapter 21, "Management as Leadership."

NOTES FOR CHAPTER 7

[1] Three general references dealing with the institutional aspects of executive decision making are: A. A. Berle, Jr., *The 20th Century Capitalist Revolution* (New York: Harcourt, Brace and Co., 1954); Kenneth Boulding, *The Organizational Revolution* (New York: Harper & Brothers, 1953); and an excellent summary of the state of research on aspects of business decision making, H. R. Bowen, *The Business Enterprise as a Subject for Research* (New York: Social Sciences Research Council, 1955).

[2] The classic example of the molding effects of organization is the transformation of civilian conscripts into military men in a very short space of time. Basic training seldom extends beyond three months, at the end of which time major reorientations have been achieved in the conscripts. See S. A. Stouffer *et al., The American Soldier: Adjustment During Army Life* (Princeton: Princeton University Press, 1949).

[3] Cf. E. Wight Bakke, *Bonds of Organization* (New York: Harper & Brothers, 1950), where the ties between the individual and his organization are viewed in a larger framework of activities designed to perpetuate its life.

[4] A very sophisticated treatment of strategy always takes into account the things an opponent has to do because of limitations of his environment or the demands of his past history. See, for example, John von Neumann and Oskar Morganstern, *Theory of Games and Economic Behavior* (Princeton: Princeton University Press, 1947).

[5] See the treatment of rationality in organization behavior in H. A. Simon, *Administrative Behavior* (New York: The Macmillan Company, 1947), especially Chapter 4, "Rationality in Administrative Behavior." Simon has attempted a more general model of rational behavior in "A Behavioral Model of Rational Choice," *Quarterly Journal of Economics,* 69:99-118 (February, 1955). Max Weber placed particular stress on the rational aspects of business organizations in *The Theory of Social and Economic Organization* (New York: Oxford University Press, 1947), pp. 329-341; and *From Max Weber: Essays in Sociology* (New York: Oxford University Press, 1946), pp. 196-244. A summary of the rational characteristics of business organizations will be found in Robert Dubin, *Human Relations in Administration* (New York: Prentice-Hall, 1951), pp. 156-163.

[6] A unique analysis of the ideological bases for legitimizing authority at work, and the institutional frameworks within which the ideas of legitimacy develop, is Reinhard Bendix, *Work and Authority in Industry* (New York: John Wiley & Sons, 1956), especially Chapter 1.

[7] Chester I. Barnard has an exceedingly interesting discussion of authority relations and their legitimation in *Organization and Management* (Cambridge: Harvard University Press, 1948), Chapter 2, "Dilemmas of Leadership in the Democratic Process."

[8] Barnard has concluded that "The resistance to loss of status is in general stronger than desire to achieve higher status . . . . " *Ibid.,* p. 238.

[9] A sweeping picture of the changes that have occurred in the responsibilities of management itself is contained in "The Transformation of American Capitalism," *Fortune,* 43:79-83 (February, 1951).

[10] An interesting plea for the location of greater responsibility in the hands of operating management as over against an owning or controlling group is contained in J. D. Mooney and A. C. Reiley, *Onward Industry* (New York: Harper & Bros., 1931). A very sophisticated argument for the actual transfer of power to the managers of industry, and the predicted consequences, is developed in James Burnham, *The Managerial Revolution* (New York: John Day, 1941). Thorstein Veblen, *The Engineers and the Price System* (New York: B. W. Huebsch, 1921), urged the transfer of power to the experts from the controlling oligarchy.

[11] Cf. W. H. Newman and J. P. Logan, *Management of Expanding Enterprises* (New York: Columbia University Press, 1955).

[12] Peter F. Drucker, *The Concept of the Corporation* (New York: John Day, 1946), is careful to avoid undue controversy about the centralization *vs.* decentralization in General Motors, but his analysis seems to make clear that this is a persistent problem of the distribution of power in that firm.

[13] Henry Ford, in building the Ford Motor Company, took great pride in the constant change he introduced in manufacturing processes and the resulting organization structure of the company. See Henry Ford, *Moving Forward* (New York: Doubleday, Doran, 1930). In the later years of Mr. Ford's active management there was a shift in emphasis toward maintaining rigid organization.

[14] The clearest exposition of the interrelations of

NOTES FOR CHAPTER 7 (CONT.)

specialists is contained in Harold Laski, "The Limitations of the Expert," *Harper's Magazine,* 162:102-106 (December, 1930).

[15] The specialized outlook and the limited perspective of specialists are emphasized in R. K. Merton, "The Machine, The Worker, and the Engineer," *Science,* 105:79-81 (January, 1947).

[16] An interesting device for insuring that the expert is accepted as a specialist in the work organization is to keep the non-specialist in a state of ignorance about the specialty. The role of ignorance is developed by W. E. Moore and M. M. Tumin in "Some Social Functions of Ignorance," *American Sociological Review,* 14:788-789 (December, 1949).

[17] Leonard Reissman, "A Study of Role Conceptions in Bureaucracy," *Social Forces,* 27:305-310 (March, 1949), has stressed that the functional bureaucrat and specialist bureaucrat have strong ties to the professional organizations to which they belong.

[18] There is a scientific journal in the field, called *The Journal of Operations Research,* any one of the issues of which will provide ample illustrations of the kinds of problems that are being handled by this application of science to organization behavior.

[19] See P. M. Morse and G. E. Kimball, *Methods of Operations Research* (New York: John Wiley & Sons, 1951).

[20] *Ibid.,* Chapter 1.

[21] *Ibid.,* pp. 5-6.

[22] A careful reading of H. Maurer, *Great Enterprise: Growth and Behavior of the Big Corporation* (New York: The Macmillan Company, 1955), reveals the many areas in which institutionalization has been achieved in the decisions of large corporations.

[23] The following general references are particularly important in giving historical perspective to the value placed upon technical innovation. Stuart Chase, *Men and Machines* (New York: The Macmillan Company, 1937); S. Giedion, *Mechanization Takes Command* (London: Oxford University Press, 1948); Harry Jerome, *Mechanization in Industry* (New York: National Bureau of Economic Research, 1934); L. L. Lorwin and J. M. Blair, "Technology in Our Economy," United States Congress, Temporary National Economic Committee, *Investigation of Concentration of Economic Power,* Monograph No. 22 (Washington: Government Printing Office, 1941); W. J. Marx, *Mechanization and Culture* (St. Louis: B. Herder Book Co., 1941); Lewis Mumford, *Technics and Civilization* '(New York: Harcourt, Brace and Co., 1934); and S. McK. Rosen and Laura Rosen, *Technology and Society: The Influence of Machines in the United States* (New York: The Macmillan Company, 1941).

[24] An excellent summary of some of the institutional factors in economic and accounting decisions is contained in Joel Dean, *Managerial Economics* (Englewood Cliffs, N. J.: Prentice-Hall, 1951); see also in this connection Trygve Haavelmo, "The Notion of Involutary Economic Decisions," *Econometrica,* 18: 1-8 (January, 1950); and E. M. Hoover, "Some Institutional Factors in Business Investment Decisions," *American Economic Review,* 44:201-213 (Supplement) (May, 1954).

[25] Cf. D. J. Riesman, *The Lonely Crowd* (New Haven: Yale University Press, 1950; and New York: Anchor Books), and his delineation of the "other-directed" personality type. Eric Fromm has suggested the "marketing orientation" as a distinctive relationship to the social world in *Escape From Freedom* (New York: Farrar and Rinehart, 1941), pp. 270 ff., and *Man For Himself* (New York: Rinehart and Co., 1947), pp. 67 ff.

[26] For example, the businessman has increasingly been concerned with his public image as a moral leader of the society. The pressures to consider the moral leadership of the business man are generated through past attacks on immoral business behavior and subsequent discoveries by businessmen that the public view of them is less negative than was thought. This, in a sense, gives the businessman a standing to live up to. Attitude surveys like B. R. Fisher and S. B. Withey, "Highlights from Big Business as the People See it: A Study of a Socio-Economic Institution" (Ann Arbor: Survey Research Center, University of Michigan, 1951), present the images of business leaders to which they react. Shady business practices are always publicly rejected although sometimes widespread in actual operations as a recent study has shown: M. B. Clinard, *The Black Market* (New York: Rinehart & Co., 1952). A number of recent attempts have been made to develop a positive ethic for business, notable among these being: H. R. Bowen, *Social Responsibilities of the Businessman* (New York: Harper & Brothers, 1953); and M. W. Childs and Douglass Cater, *Ethics in a Business Society* (New York: Harper & Brothers, 1954; Mentor Books), based, in part, on the previous volume. This is simply an example of how the business environment changes, requiring changes in the outlook and decisions of executives.

[27] Cf. Robert Dubin, "Decision-Making by Management in Industrial Relations," *American Journal of Sociology,* 54:292-301 (January, 1949).

[28] Long-term financing of business operations requires some stability on the basis of which both borrowers and investors can predict the economic environment of the future.

[29] The concept of cultural lag was developed by W. F. Ogburn, in *Social Change* (New York: Viking Press, 1922).

[30] Scientific American Editors, *Automatic Control* (New York: Simon and Schuster, 1955, paper), especially "An Automatic Chemical Plant," pp. 41-52.

[31] See C. W. Mills, *The Power Elite* (New York: Oxford University Press, 1956).

Part III

WORKING POPULATION

The millions of men and women who daily work in the factories and offices of the country constitute its labor force. These men and women (can you find them?) are employees of the Ford Motor Company.

Chapter **8**

LABOR FORCE

In any society, the labor force is that group of people who work for a living. We are concerned, in this chapter, with determining how the labor force of our society compares with that of other societies, and why there are the differences that we find. The United States is a fabulously wealthy country and this fact leaves its mark on our labor force. We will also make a detailed examination of the U.S. labor force to determine its distribution among the broad categories of remunerative work, according to the skill of the people working and, finally, in terms of the places where they carry on their work.

The human profile of an industrial society is revealed in the distribution of its working members. Our task for this chapter is to sketch out the main features of Americans at work.[1]

TOTAL AMERICAN LABOR FORCE

The labor force has received different definitions, depending on the ways in which its size has been estimated. The U.S. Census Bureau's *Monthly Report on the Labor Force* publishes the results of a sample survey of people who are asked to report themselves as employed, unemployed, or not in the labor force. Those now employed for pay, or unemployed but seeking work, are counted as part of the labor force.[2]

CHART 8.1

THE AMERICAN LABOR FORCE IS A STABLE PROPORTION OF THE TOTAL POPULATION

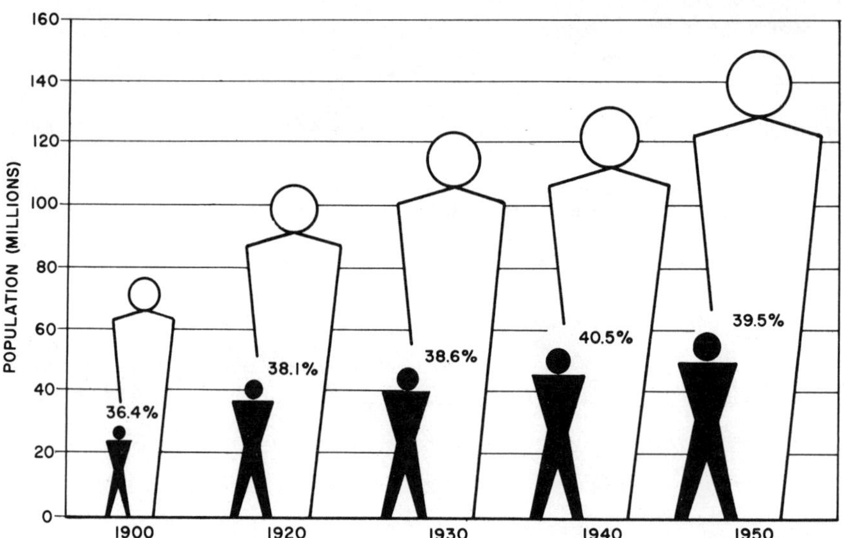

Jaffe and Stewart have pointed out that the working force, on the other hand, is composed of those who are economically active, whether or not they are paid for their work.[3] In primitive societies the working force is hardly distinguishable from the total population, most members of the society having to work to provide means for subsistence. In our society more people are part of the working force than are part of the labor force. Included in the working force of the United States are housewives and other unpaid workers who perform socially desired services without drawing pay for the work done.

The concept of the working force, then, is the most general one dealing with those who are economically active in the society. The more limited concept of the labor force covers those who are now working for pay, or who seek such work. This is admittedly an arbitrary distinction made useful by the fact that knowledge of the labor force is important for making socially meaningful decisions about economic policy.

The simplest way to grasp the picture of the American labor force is to view it in its absolute numbers, and as a percentage of the total population. Chart 8.1 presents the facts graphically. The large light figures represent the total population for each census year from 1900 to 1950. It will be noted that the population has exactly doubled in the fifty-year period. The dark figures represent the labor force. The labor force has a little better than doubled over the same period. This suggests that the labor force percentage of the total population has been relatively stable. These percentage figures are shown on the chart, and have increased from 36.4 in 1900 to 39.5 in 1950.

An immediate conclusion is obvious. The American labor force has grown in numbers; in the long run, almost entirely as a consequence of general population increase. There has been only a slight increase in the proportion of all citizens who are part of the labor force.

RECENT HISTORY OF THE AMERICAN LABOR FORCE

We can now look at the American labor force in a historical perspective. We want to examine some of the basic trends among the people who do the work of our society.

Table 8.1 shows the fifty-year record of the proportion of the population 14 years and older in the labor force. This table differs from Chart 8.1 in an important respect. The table excludes the very young who do no productive work of any magnitude. We are measuring here the size of the working population in relation to the number of citizens potentially available for work. In Chart 8.1 we measured the labor force against the whole population. Accordingly, the percentages in the table are higher than those shown on the chart.

TABLE 8.1
THE LABOR FORCE IS A STABLE PROPORTION OF THE PEOPLE AVAILABLE FOR WORK

	Per Cent Age 14 and Over in the Labor Force		
Year	Total	Male	Female
1900	55.0	87.7	20.4
1910	54.3	84.4	22.7
1920	54.5	84.1	24.3
1930	55.2	82.6	27.9
1940	63.0	89.2	37.3
1950	57.5	83.7	32.1

SOURCE: Reprinted with permission from A. J. Jaffe and C. D. Stewart, *Manpower Resources and Utilization,* 1951, John Wiley & Sons, Inc., p. 164.

It can be noted, first, that the proportion of the population available for work and in the labor force has been remarkably stable over the entire fifty-year period. The figure has stabilized between 55 and 60 per cent, except for the World War II period whose impact was already felt in the figures for 1940.

The second notable observation about Table 8.1 is that the proportion of males in the labor force has been equally stable. More than eight out of ten males 14 years of age and older are in the labor force.

The third major fact about Table 8.1 is that over the years an increasing proportion of females have entered the labor force. As the American economy expanded its demands for labor, a higher proportion of our female population has been drawn into industrial and commercial work.

Another aspect of the historical development of the American labor force is revealed in Table 8.2 showing the proportion of children between the ages of 10 and 15 who were gainfully employed. In the sixty-year period from 1890, child labor has virtually disappeared as a significant element in the American labor force.[4] This is a consequence of conscious social policy directed at keeping children from having to work. It has been accomplished through compulsory school attendance laws, and legislation restricting employment of children below certain ages.

TABLE 8.2
CHILD LABOR HAS LARGELY BEEN ELIMINATED

	*Per Cent Age 10 to 15 Gainfully Occupied**		
Year	Total	Male	Female
1890	18.1	25.9	10.0
1900	18.2	26.1	10.2
1910	15.0	21.7	8.1
1920	11.3	16.8	5.8
1930	4.7	6.4	2.9
1940	1.8	2.7	0.8
1950	5.3	7.8	2.8

SOURCE: Reprinted with permission from A. J. Jaffe and C. D. Stewart, *Manpower Resources and Utilization,* 1951, John Wiley & Sons, Inc., p. 168.
* See footnote 2.

Over shorter periods of time the number of persons in the labor force can vary markedly. This is particularly true in periods of national stress. During World War II, for example, the labor force of the United States showed a temporary increase of more than 10 million. This is graphically pictured in Chart 8.2 where the civilian labor force and the armed forces are shown separately. It is clear from Chart 8.2 that many people who were not regularly in the labor force went to work to carry out war production.

In Table 8.3 we have displayed the wide fluctuations that occurred in the Armed Forces of the United States in the two World Wars. There was, for example, a sixty-fold increase in the Army and Navy combined from 1935 to the World War II peak. The civilian labor force during World War II remained relatively stable. The total labor force, including the Armed Forces, increased substantially.

We may conclude, therefore, that for every person withdrawn from the normal labor force to serve in a fighting capacity, another worker entered the labor market to take his place producing war goods. The American people showed a remarkable capacity to shift into the labor force under the demands of a national emergency. The readjustment was possible, of course, only by putting to work people not normally in the labor market.

It is a sociological generalization that rapid social change occurs in periods of social stress. This is well illustrated in the capacity of the American population to move into war production and recruit upwards of 12 million for its Armed Forces. During the short-run period of the War, new ideas about who shall work were accepted by our citizens, and the total labor force expanded accordingly. After the emergency was passed, the more normal ideas about working were restored. By 1950, as Chart 8.1 shows, the long term relationship between the total population and the labor force has been re-established with 39.5 per cent of the population being reported in the labor force.

CHART 8.2

DURING WAR THE TOTAL LABOR FORCE SHOWS A LARGE TEMPORARY INCREASE

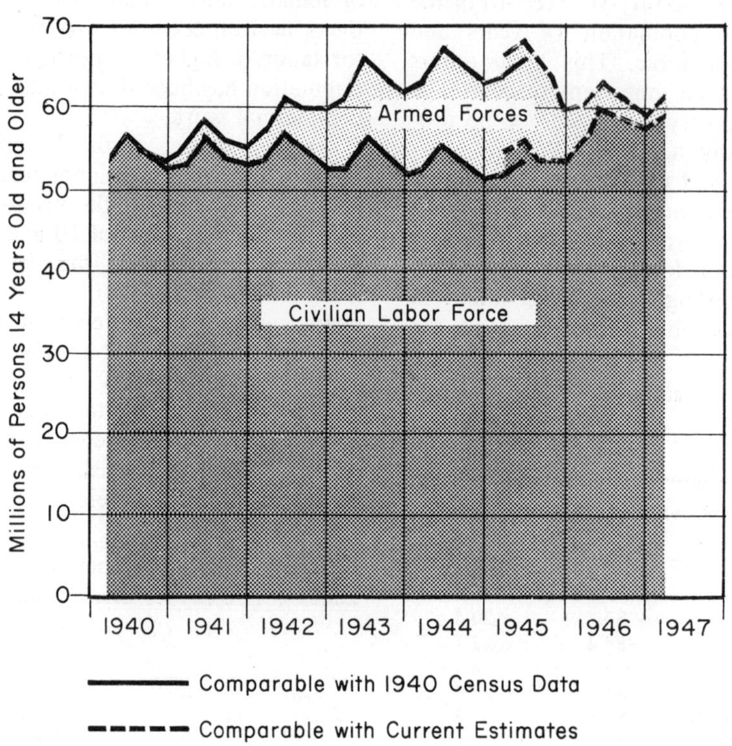

TABLE 8.3

THE ARMED FORCES RAPIDLY WITHDRAW SUBSTANTIAL NUMBERS FROM THE LABOR FORCE DURING NATIONAL EMERGENCIES

	U. S. Military Strength (in thousands)			
Time Period	Total	Army	Air Force *	Navy
Average Strength 1915	173	106	–	67
World War I Peak	4,265	3,665	–	600
Average Strength 1935	244	132	–	112
World War II Peak	12,178	8,291	–	3,887
June, 1950 (Pre-Korea)	1,458	591	411	456
June, 1951 (1 Year after Korea)	3,186	1,550	737	899
June, 1953	3,515	1,485	975	1,055

* Included with Army through World War II.

SOURCE: Reprinted with permission from William Haber, *et al* (eds.), *Manpower in the United States: Problems and Policies,* 1954, Harper & Brothers, p. 171.

CHART 8.3

MALES ARE THE PRINCIPAL BREADWINNERS IN AMERICAN SOCIETY

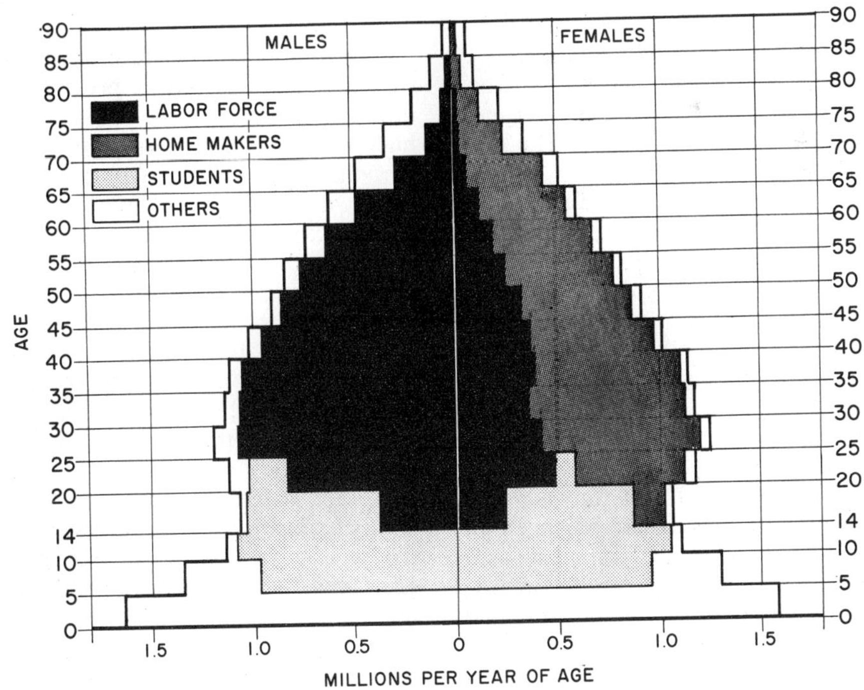

ACTIVITY OF THE TOTAL POPULATION

It is instructive to consider how the whole population relates to the labor force. We can secure a picture of the broad categories of activities of the population from Chart 8.3 which is in the form of a population pyramid. This population pyramid shows the numbers of persons in each five-year age interval. To the left of the center line of the pyramid are shown the males; to the right, the females. Vertical divisions on this population pyramid show the labor force, the homemakers, those in school, and all others.

Chart 8.3 makes very clear that the American labor force is asymmetrical with respect to sex. There are many more males in each age level in the labor force than there are females. Obviously, our society makes the male the principal bread winner. The characteristic balancing activity for females 20 years and older is that of homemaker, as revealed in the population pyramid. Observing that a high proportion of males ages 20 through 65 were already in the labor force, it is clear that expansion in the number of people working means bringing more females into the labor market. Females constitute, in our society, a reserve labor force.[5] They enter remunerative work during times of emergency, like a war, or during periods of increased labor demand, such as was experienced in post World War II days.[6]

The reserve labor force represented by women is further illustrated in Table 8.4, where the labor force participation rates for married women living with their husbands is shown. The husband may normally be presumed to be the primary provider so that when his wife goes to work it is usually as a secondary breadwinner. During this period of more than a decade the proportion of married women at work, or seeking work, almost doubled.[7] It will be noted that for each age group, except 14-19 years, there has been an increase in the percentage of married women in the labor force. In our high level economy, the growing demand for labor has already had its effect in putting homemakers to work for wages. We will leave to students of the family the task of determining the impact of an increased proportion of working wives on American family behavior.

TABLE 8.4
PROPORTION OF WOMEN AS SUPPLEMENTARY BREADWINNERS HAS INCREASED SHARPLY

Age of Women	*Labor Force Participation Rates of Married Women Living with Their Husbands*		
	1940	1950	1955
Total	14.7	23.8	27.7
14 to 19 years	10.7	24.0	19.8
20 to 24 years	18.6	28.5	29.4
25 to 34 years	19.0	23.8	26.0
35 to 44 years	16.3	28.5	33.7
45 to 64 years	10.3	21.8	29.8
65 years and over	4.1	6.4	7.5

SOURCE: U. S. Bureau of the Census, *Current Population Reports,* Series P-50, Nos. 22 and 39; and *Statistical Abstract of the United States,* 1956.

A second notable feature of the population pyramid is the picture it presents of the future labor force of the United States. The high level of present birth rate has made the pyramid bulge in the age groups under 10 years. These same children, starting in the 1960 decade, will begin to reach normal working ages. Since these children are already born, and since the death rates for the first thirty years are relatively low, we can predict that the labor force will show a marked increase after 1960, due to the present age distribution and the present high birth rate. Based solely on the number of workers available, America's capacity to produce will increase.[8] If we also consider increased productivity due to technology, it seems clear that the productive capacity of our economy can grow very considerably during the last four decades of the twentieth century.

SEASONAL LABOR FORCE VARIATIONS

Another way of grasping the fluid nature of the labor force over the short run is shown in Chart 8.4 where the labor force is pictured during a single year. Here the total population 14 years of age and older is distributed according to its status in the labor market. The shaded portion of the chart shows the number of men and women who would be in and out of the labor force at some time during the year. Seasonable employment for those not normally in the labor force is what draws them to work temporarily, and, of course, would account for their leaving the labor force at the end of the work season.

The total number of men and women in the labor force at any time during a year is relatively stable. The particular people who are working or seeking work may vary at any given time.

We now have a picture of the general features of the American labor force in terms of its numbers and its sex composition. The long-term trend is for an increase in the size of the working population, but with no marked increase in the proportion of all people who work. Women constitute the major reserve labor force for the country, although in the last four decades of this century, the present birth rate will guarantee an increased number of people available for work. During periods of crisis, people not normally in the labor market go to work if production demands are high. There is some indication for our society that women are exchanging their homemaker roles for that of supplementary breadwinner, which, if the trend continues, will mean that the total labor force will increase even more rapidly than what is already guaranteed by the present high birth rate.

CHART 8.4

PEOPLE MOVE IN AND OUT OF THE LABOR FORCE EACH YEAR

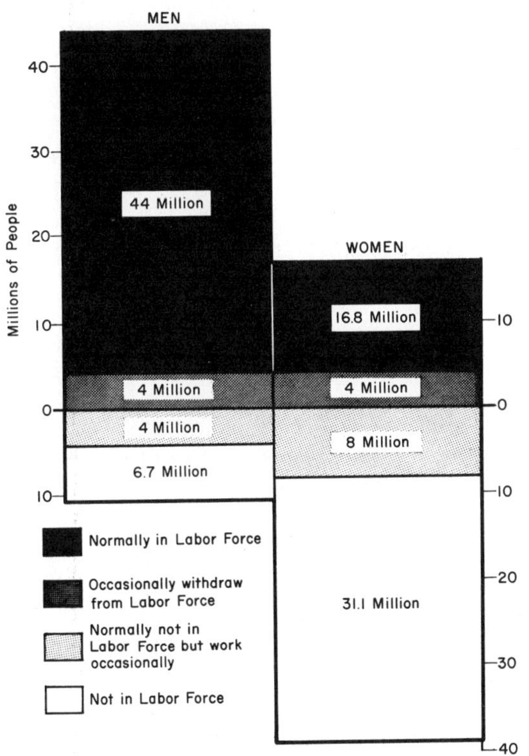

Reprinted with permission from W. S. Woytinsky and Associates, *Employment and Wages in the United States*, The Twentieth Century Fund, 1953, p. 315.

INTERNATIONAL LABOR FORCE COMPARISONS

There are wide differences in the participation of people in the labor force among various countries of the world. Basically, these variations are the consequences of differences among the economies represented.

In Table 8.5 the gainful worker rates for men in three age groups are shown in selected countries. Three basic facts are revealed.

We first note that in the normally productive ages of 20 to 64 all countries show more than 90 per cent of the males as gainful workers. Thus, we can see that the labor force of each country, irrespective of its economy, draws upon the basic core of males in the age group of 20 to 64.

The next general observation about Table 8.5 has to do with the proportion of males 65 years and older who are still gainful workers. Here the range is more than two and one-half times, from the low of 29.7 per cent in Germany to 86.3 per cent in Egypt. An examination of the array of countries shows that there is a marked tendency for agrarian and "poor" societies to retain a higher percentage of their older males in the labor force. On the other hand wealthy countries, and those more highly

TABLE 8.5
CORE OF THE LABOR FORCE IS AGE 20 TO 64 WITH FEWER OLDER PEOPLE WORKING IN INDUSTRIALIZED COUNTRIES

	*Gainful Worker Rates for Men **		
Country and Date	65 Years and Over	20-64 Years	15-19 Years
Egypt (1937)	86.3	97.0	91.1
Hungary (1930)	83.3	98.3	87.6
Peru (1940)	82.6	93.5	61.2
Panama (1940)	82.0	96.8	77.1
Rumania (1930)	77.8	98.0	†
Brazil (1940)	74.3	95.3	†
Italy (1936)	72.6	96.3	88.0
Ireland (1936)	67.3	95.4	71.1
Bulgaria (1934)	67.1	96.7	79.6
Greece (1946)	64.0	95.3	65.3
Japan (1930)	63.0	95.3	78.5
Switzerland (1930)	62.5	96.1	78.4
France (1931)	59.4	94.5	82.3
Australia (1933)	57.0	97.0	80.8
Philippines (1939)	53.3	94.5	69.2
Norway (1930)	53.1	95.5	76.6
Czechoslovakia (1930)	53.0	94.4	82.2
Sweden (1930)	49.8	95.6	82.3
United Kingdom (1931)	47.9	96.7	88.3
Canada (1941)	47.2	96.0	59.3
Belgium (1930)	45.3	95.3	80.4
Netherlands (1930)	42.6	95.0	78.2
United States (1940)	*41.7*	*98.7*	*36.5*
New Zealand (1936)	40.0	96.3	87.9
Denmark (1940)	35.1	95.9	85.1
Germany (1939)	29.7	92.7	86.1

SOURCE: Censuses of individual countries and various issues of the *Yearbook*, International Labour Office. The years were selected to make the comparisons for similar time periods.
* See footnote 2.
† Not available.

industrialized, permit leisure for older citizens, no longer requiring their services for productive labor. The correlation is not high, but the general trend is evident.

The third observation regarding Table 8.5 is that the relationship between type of economy and the employment of younger males is not strong. The country using the highest proportion of its young males in the labor force, Egypt, exceeds by approximately two and one-half times the figure for the lowest country, the United States. This accords with our general expectation that industrialized countries can afford to give leisure to their younger citizens. However, some highly industrialized countries, like Germany and the United Kingdom, also employ a very high percentage of their young males for productive work, while agrarian countries, like Peru and Greece, use a relatively low proportion of this segment of the population for production. Some of the lack of relationship can be attributed to the vagaries of statistics, which are uneven in their quality, and based on varying definitions from country to country.

It is clear, however, that the United States presents an exceptionally favorable comparative picture relative to the rest of the world. In general, more industrialized societies afford leisure for a higher proportion of their older citizens than do agrarian societies, but the United States also confers freedom from productive labor on its younger males, even when they have reached the age of physical capacity for labor. American society is unique in its ability to provide its citizens with freedom from paid work in their younger and older years.[9]

LABOR FORCE AND ITS SOCIAL CONTEXT

From the facts so far considered, a generalization emerges. The labor force, through its productive efforts, supports the total population. At the same time, some parts of the population can be relieved from work and yet there is evidence to suggest that the people as a whole are economically better off. This apparent paradox, of economies that are better off while a significant proportion of their citizens enjoys freedom from work, needs further elaboration. We will shortly see that the paradox is resolved when we observe that it is not human energy alone that produces the goods and services for consumption.

In examining the social context of the labor force comparatively, Jaffe and Stewart have correlated various aspects of social life with an index of the labor force structure.[10] Their data are presented in Chart 8.5, where the relationships of the number of males over 65 in the working force to selected social and economic facts are shown. It will be recalled that leisure is one of the rewards of a high-level economy, so that countries with a relatively low proportion of older men still working are those that are economically better off.

People have more and better food in more advanced economies. There is greater food consumption per capita, a higher caloric intake and a higher proportion of animal proteins in the diet. This is true in spite of the fact that the nations requiring more of the old to work are more agrarian and have a lower percentage of their working forces in mining, manufacturing, construction, and service pursuits.

In the less advanced countries there is a higher birth rate, a higher death rate, and a higher rate of natural increase. At the same time there are fewer physicians to attend to the health needs of the people. The more advanced countries have more school teachers and lower rates of illiteracy than the poorer countries. In terms of personal convenience, the advanced countries have more automobiles and telephones per citizen than the backward states.

Measured on these various yardsticks, it seems quite clear that a country's advance in economic development results in accumulated leisure for its citizens, better and more abundant food, higher levels of health, more education for more people, and better provision of goods for personal consumption and convenience.

CHART 8.5

LEISURE AND THE BETTER LIFE GO TOGETHER

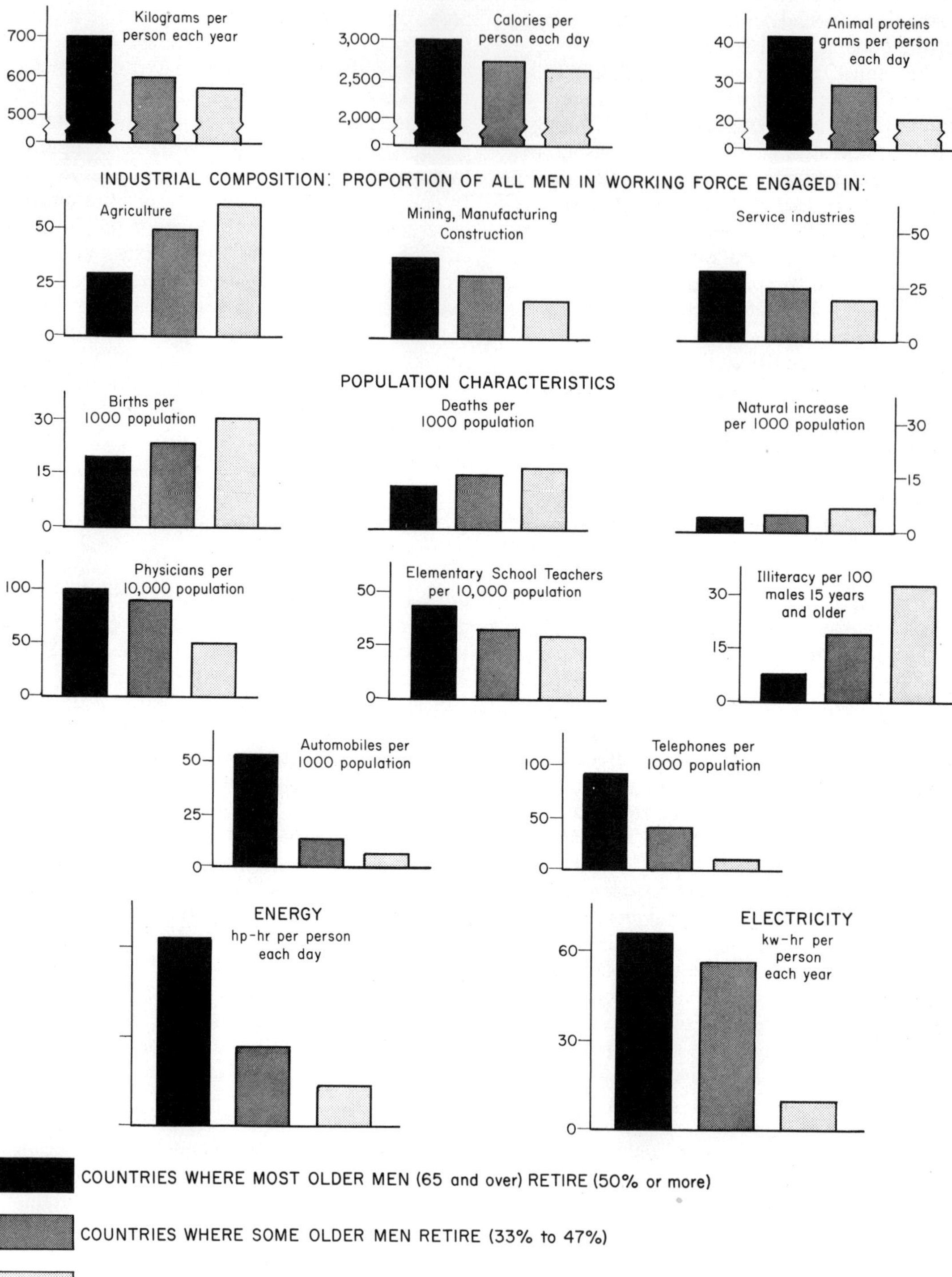

Reprinted with permission from A. J. Jaffe and C. D. Stewart, *Manpower Resources and Utilization*, John Wiley & Sons, Inc., 1951, pp. 408–409.

How can we explain the paradox that leisure and the better life go hand in hand? The answer lies in the use of sources of energy that supplement human effort in production. In the high-level economies there is a much greater consumption of all kinds of energy units per person than in low-level economies. This is confirmed in the consumption of electricity as a major source of energy for work operations. It seems clear that the difference between economies of low and high output relates to the amount of energy used per person in the society. Where much energy in the form of burnable fuels—like coal, oil, and electricity—is available and utilized, the economy is likely to be advanced.

Put another way, we can conclude that where only human energy is available for production the economy will be generally at a low level, and its citizens will have to work long and hard to produce necessary goods and services. Where supplements to human energy are available, a high production economy can develop, with more of the better things in life available to its citizens.

WHAT THE AMERICAN LABOR FORCE DOES

We can now turn to a consideration of the areas of productive labor engaging the American labor force. We will first of all examine the kinds of output that come from the economy. Then we will analyze the more detailed distribution of the labor force according to the major industry groups in which it is employed.

The United States has undergone a marked shift from an economy producing largely physical goods, to one in which services now account for the employment of the majority of the labor force. This is vividly shown in Chart 8.6 where the entire labor force is distributed into the two main categories. In 1870 about three out of every four workers were producing physical goods. That means they were working in agriculture, forestry, fishing, mining and manufacturing—producing the foodstuffs, raw materials, and manufactured products of the economy. By contrast, in 1950, over half of all American workers were providing services for the economy in retail and wholesale trade, business and personal serv-

CHART 8.6

MORE AMERICAN WORKERS NOW PROVIDE SERVICES THAN PRODUCE GOODS

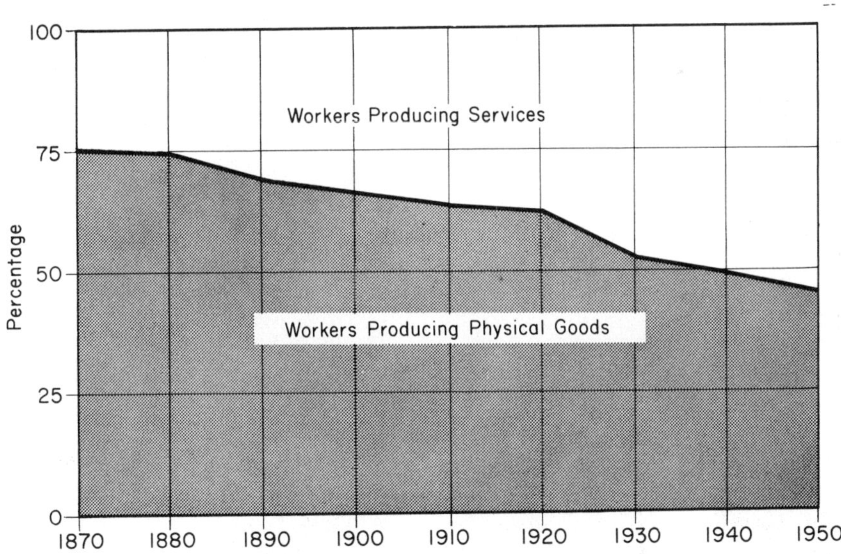

CHART 8.7

PROPORTION OF ALL EMPLOYED WORKERS IN TRADE, PROFESSIONAL SERVICE, AND MANUFACTURING HAS INCREASED CONSIDERABLY IN FORTY YEARS

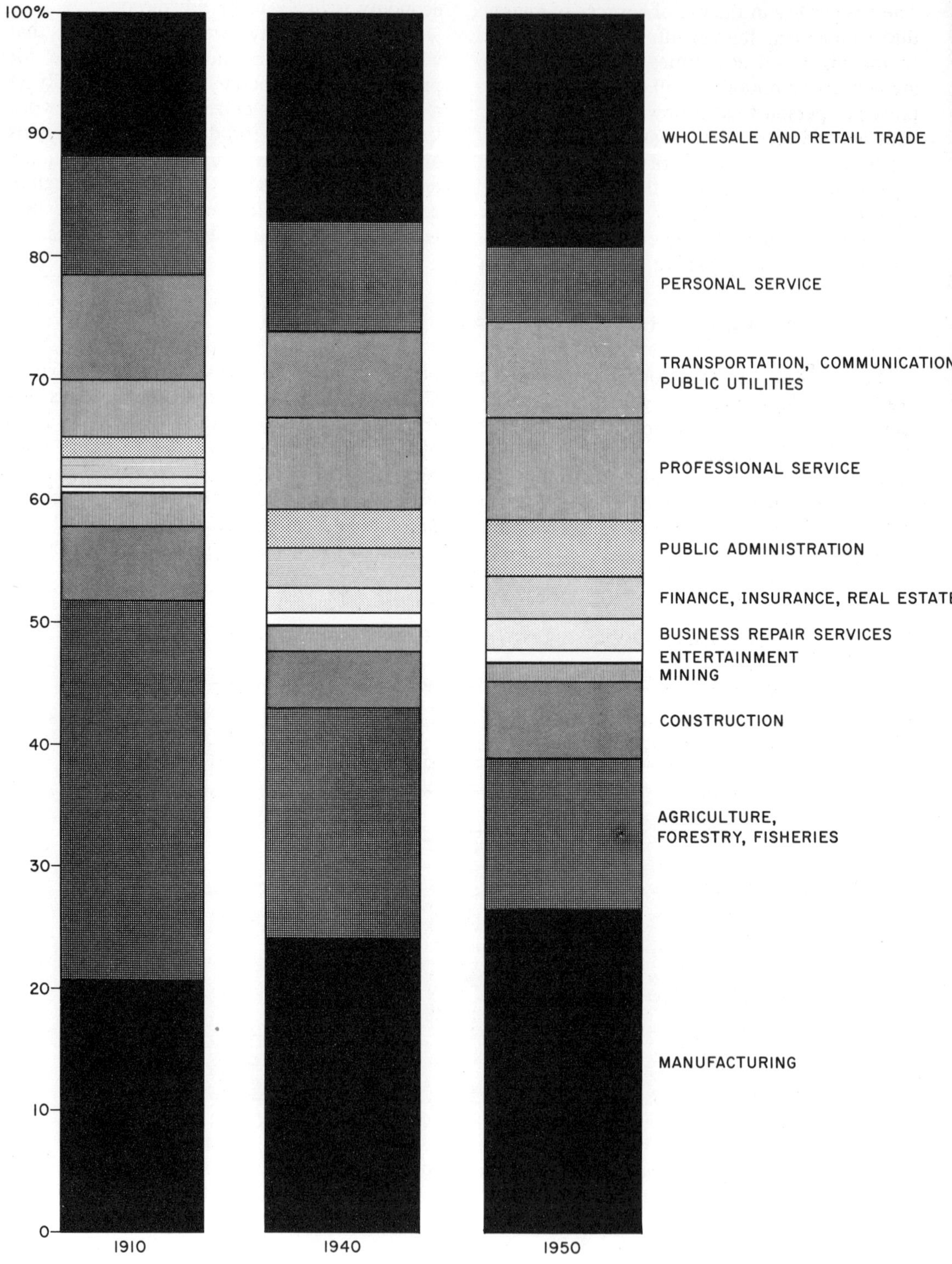

ices, transportation and other public utilities, professional activities, and government.

We can put the contrast between the beginning and end of the eighty-year period this way. At about the end of the Civil War it took three workers out of every four to produce the physical goods necessary for the American economy. Shortly after World War II a little less than two workers out of every four were necessary to turn out the physical goods for a vastly expanded population at a high standard of living.

The American economy has been transformed so that a majority of all employed people are no longer engaged in primary production. It can be truly said that we are a nation of white collar and service workers. This general fact deserves particular emphasis. It means that the social environment of work for the majority of American employees is not the field, mine or factory. It means that more than half of all working people work exclusively at providing services, or that they are members of the office and sales staffs of organizations turning out physical goods. It is notable that most of our studies of people at work analyze those engaged in primary production. We need many more studies of persons at work in service occupations and in stores and offices, since they now constitute the majority of all working people.

Just exactly how is the labor force distributed among the major industries of the country? In Chart 8.7 are displayed the twelve major industrial groups of the economy showing the proportion of all employed workers in each major industry for the past forty years.

Among the industries involving primary production, two things are notable. We know that there has been an over-all decline in the proportion of workers engaged in primary production. This decline has been particularly strong among those in food production, since these workers constituted only 12 per cent of the labor force in 1950, where they had accounted for 31 per cent of all employed people in 1910. We have indeed become a nation in which farming, forestry, and fishing are distinctly minority occupations. At the same time, in spite of the total relative decline among primary producers, there has been a proportional increase in the size of the labor force devoted to manufacturing. Thus, manufacturing is becoming more important and has displaced food and fiber harvesting as the major primary production activity of the American labor force.

Turning to an examination of the eight major categories of service industries, we note that all save two have increased very considerably during the four decades since 1910. Public utilities (including transportation), and personal services have declined relative to all other industries in the proportion of workers employed in them. Trade now bulks largest in the service field, with almost exactly one out of every five American workers involved in selling and distributing goods.

Some of the smaller service industries have shown the largest relative gains. Government service, the field of finance, and businesses involving repair services have shown the most vigorous growth relative to other categories over the forty-year span.

We may conclude generally that manufacturing is becoming more important as a source of livelihood for American workers in spite of the general decline in primary production. Indeed, over one out of every four employed persons is engaged in manufacturing, making it the single most important source of jobs in the economy. Our second summary conclusion is that service industries as a whole now employ the majority of workers resulting in much greater prominence of white collar workers. Most vigorous in growth within the service group have been the industries farthest removed from primary production—those providing financial, government, and repair services. Finally, the production of goods together with their distribution now account for almost half of all employed people.

It is fair to characterize the American economy as a "make and trade" one. We are no longer a people who "grow and dig" the materials for sustaining life, as our major economic activities. This significant transformation has come about in the twentieth century. The present trends promise to continue, if not to accelerate in the future.

WORKING SKILLS OF THE AMERICAN LABOR FORCE

People of various levels of skill are distributed throughout all the branches of industry. If we look at the skill level of the labor force, therefore, we secure another picture of Americans at work. From a skill standpoint we see the labor force composed of people with different kinds of work training and different kinds of functions to perform at work.

Chart 8.8 shows an array of skill levels commonly used to summarize the jobs, positions, and offices filled by people in work organizations. It will be noted that we have excluded people employed in agriculture as farm owners, managers, foremen, or laborers. This is a book about commerce and industry and we want to focus attention on that segment of the labor force.

Any broad classification of people is a compromise between precise distinctions and comprehension. This is especially true when we try to compress the wide range of working skills into only eight classes. Furthermore, the classification scheme is mixed. For example, we use a kind of functional classification in distinguishing among factory workers, sales workers, and service workers. At the same time, we use a skill criterion to separate craftsmen and foremen from factory workers. This lack of clarity as to the grounds for classifying is one of the prices we pay for ease in grasping the picture. Recognizing these limitations we can follow some of the main trends in the working skills of the American labor force.[11]

In a time perspective there are several notable features of Chart 8.8. The first is that only one skill group showed a marked decrease in the proportion of non-agricultural employees in it. This is the laborer group. The proportion of workers who were laborers declined sharply, shifting from about one in six in 1910 to less than one in fifteen by 1950. Indeed, the class of laborers was the only one to show an actual numerical decline in the forty-year period.

The clerical class is the one that showed the most marked increase. This class' proportion of all non-agricultural workers almost doubled from 1910 to 1950. It is also of special interest to note that almost two-thirds of the people who were clerks in 1950 were women, whereas only one-third of them were women in 1910. (The chart shows the percentage of workers in each class who were women.) It is clear from this fact, and from the change in the proportion of women in the other classes of workers, that women have entered the labor force primarily as clerks.

Another significant characteristic of the American labor force revealed in Chart 8.8 is that professional and technical workers have increased by fifty per cent in the period covered. This is the second most important increase for the entire array of non-agricultural workers. Our economy is obviously demanding a higher proportion of people with professional and technical skills to satisfy the demands of our complex technology and to care for the health needs of our population. Indeed, this marked increase in the need for highly trained people has already had its impact on our educational system. There is growing concern in our society that the common schools, colleges, and universities are not training enough people with professional and technical skills to satisfy existing demands. Citizens and organized groups are agitating for more emphasis on professional and technical education.

The remaining occupational classes—including managers, officials and proprietors, craftsmen and foremen, sales workers, operatives or factory workers, and service workers—have accounted for a relatively stable percentage of the work force during the period of rapid industrialization from 1910 to 1950. This is a rather remarkable finding. It suggests that the skills demanded by the economy have changed more slowly than has the industrial habitat of the labor force, as we have seen from the previous section of this chapter.

We can summarize the distribution of skills among the American labor force in the following ways. Highly trained people (professional, technical, managers, officials, and proprietors) now constitute one in every five persons in the non-agricultural labor force. The least trained people (service workers and laborers) are actually a smaller proportion than those highly trained, accounting for only

CHART 8.8

PROPORTION OF ALL WORKERS IN EACH OCCUPATIONAL CLASS HAS SHIFTED IN FORTY YEARS

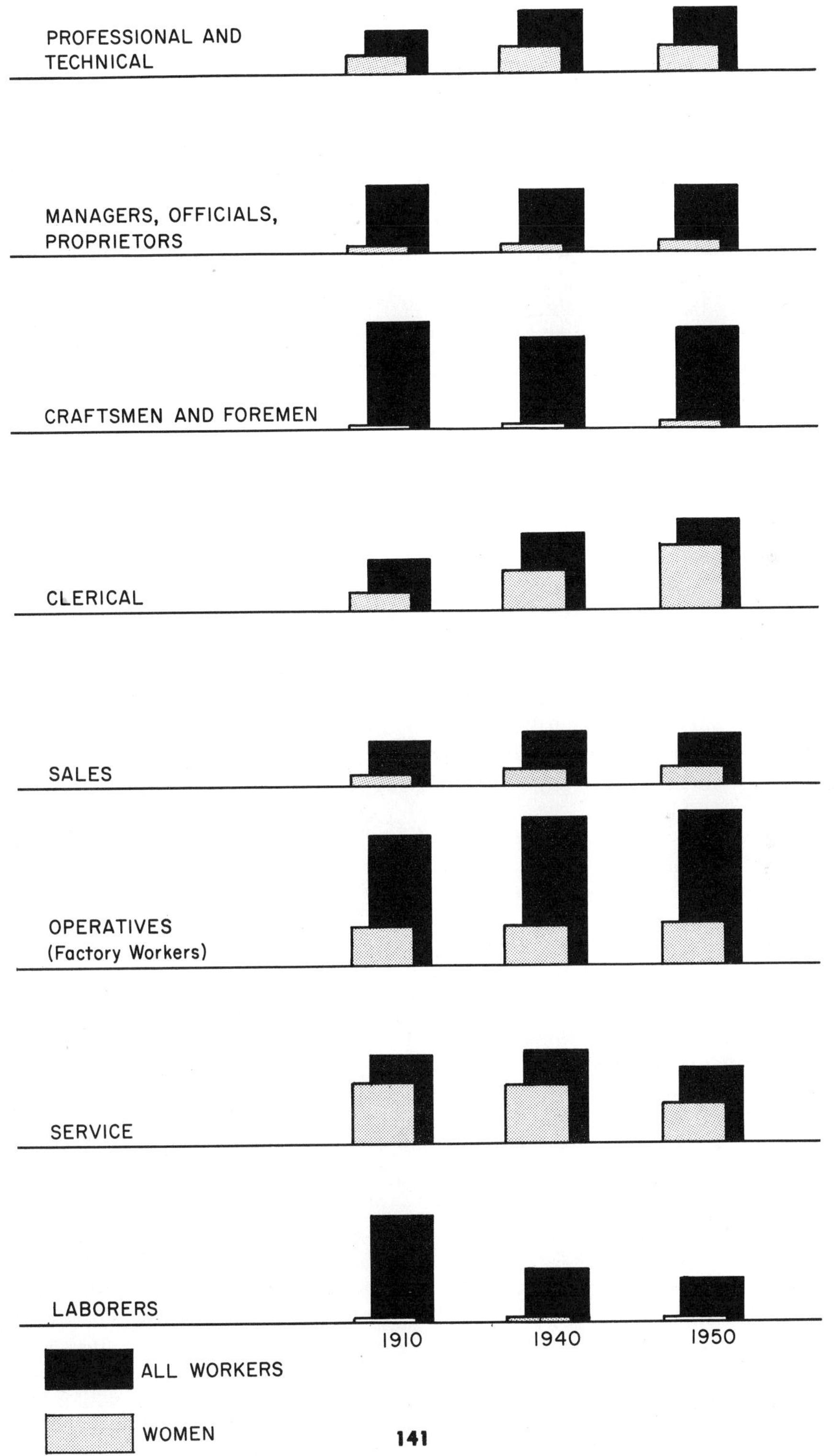

18.4 per cent of the labor force. Between these two extremes are to be found the skilled manual workers, the office and store workers, and the semi-skilled factory workers, with each class accounting for between 15 and 25 per cent of the remaining labor force.

Table 8.6 clearly reveals that the present non-agricultural labor force of the United States can be viewed as composed of five general skill classes whose sizes are roughly comparable. This relatively crude measure suggests that the American labor force does not show present marked dominance by a single class of any given skill level.

TABLE 8.6
NO SINGLE SKILL CLASS DOMINATES THE AMERICAN LABOR FORCE

Skill Class (non-agricultural)	1950 *Per Cent* *
Highly Skilled	20
Highly Skilled Manual	16
Skilled and Semi-skilled Office and Sales	22
Semi-skilled Factory	24
Unskilled	18
Total	100

* Rounded to whole numbers.

GEOGRAPHY OF THE AMERICAN LABOR FORCE

We know that the total population of the United States is not evenly distributed over the country. We also know that industrial plants draw workers to their location. For service industries, work opportunities exist where the people are who need the services.

We would then expect that the geography of the non-agricultural labor force corresponds to the location of past and present expanding industrial areas. In general, this is exactly the picture of the geographic distribution of the non-agricultural labor force.

In Table 8.7 are shown the fifteen leading states in size of manufacturing employment. These same states, except for substituting Connecticut for Florida, led in manufacturing employment in 1939, just prior to our entry into World War II. In the decade and a half up to 1955 the centers of industrial America have remained approximately the same.

One immediate qualification needs to be added to the last statement. The present centers of industrial concentration are continuing to grow, but the less industrialized parts of the country are growing even more rapidly, in non-agricultural employment. The consequence is that these less industrialized areas are also the most rapidly expanding with respect to all non-agricultural employment. Manufacturing has sparked the general growth of the labor force in all its other major industry divisions.

We can gain some picture of the dynamic growth of the labor force from Table 8.8 where the total non-agricultural employment is shown for 1955, together with the percentage increase since 1939. The figures for each region and state should be compared with the United States average. When such comparisons are made, a pattern emerges. The older industrial regions of the New England, Middle Atlantic, East North Central states have increased less than or about the same as the United States average, while the remaining

TABLE 8.7
THE FIFTEEN LEADING STATES IN NON-AGRICULTURAL EMPLOYMENT

State and Geographic Area	*1955 Employment*
New York (Middle Atlantic)	5,907,000
California (Pacific)	4,018,000
Pennsylvania (Middle Atlantic)	3,663,000
Illinois (East North Central)	3,375,000
Ohio (East North Central)	3,065,000
Michigan (East North Central)	2,438,000
Texas (West South Central)	2,292,000
New Jersey (Middle Atlantic)	1,852,000
Massachusetts (New England)	1,788,000
Indiana (East North Central)	1,387,000
Missouri (West North Central)	1,280,000
Wisconsin (East North Central)	1,106,000
North Carolina (South Atlantic)	1,037,000
Florida (South Atlantic)	933,000
Georgia (South Atlantic)	928,000

SOURCE: *Statistical Abstract of the United States, 1956.*

TABLE 8.8
WHERE DOES YOUR STATE AND REGION FIT IN THE PATTERN OF LABOR FORCE GROWTH?

Region and State	1955 Non-Agricultural Employment (000)	% Increase over 1939	*Region and State*	1955 Non-Agricultural Employment (000)	% Increase over 1939
New England	3,499.6	35.5	*South Atlantic Cont.*		
Maine	272.4	28.7	West Virginia	470.9	27.9
New Hampshire	179.0	23.4	N. Carolina	1,036.9	69.3
Vermont	101.8	36.1	S. Carolina	518.4	71.5
Massachusetts	1,787.7	32.4	Georgia	927.8	81.1
Rhode Island	294.7	22.1	Florida	932.7	142.1
Connecticut	864.0	54.5			
			East South Central	2,484.0	72.7
Middle Atlantic	11,422.0	41.1	Kentucky	601.0	59.5
New York	5,906.8	41.4	Tennessee	846.2	82.6
New Jersey	1,852.2	48.9	Alabama	684.1	72.1
Pennsylvania	3,663.0	37.1	Mississippi	352.7	75.6
East North Central	11,369.8	65.6	*West South Central*	3,868.7	95.0
Ohio	3,064.7	74.3	Arkansas	314.5	60.4
Indiana	1,386.6	70.4	Louisiana	705.1	79.2
Illinois	3,375.0	48.1	Oklahoma	556.7	72.2
Michigan	2,437.8	80.8	Texas	2,292.4	114.1
Wisconsin	1,105.7	65.9			
			Mountain	1,509.6	90.4
West North Central	3,914.3	59.4	Montana	160.1	47.7
Minnesota	865.1	60.6	Idaho	134.2	60.0
Iowa	634.1	48.4	Wyoming	84.2	56.2
Missouri	1,279.5	55.8	Colorado	427.6	87.0
North Dakota	112.9	55.7	New Mexico	179.9	128.6
South Dakota	122.5	43.4	Arizona	217.8	131.2
Nebraska	354.2	63.1	Utah	221.5	100.8
Kansas	546.0	86.1	Nevada	84.3	142.9
South Atlantic	6,257.0	73.6	*Pacific*	5,236.8	110.0
Delaware	141.2	89.0	Washington	749.9	76.8
Maryland	817.8	67.8	Oregon	468.5	82.1
District of Columbia	493.7	50.4	California	4,018.4	121.8
Virginia	917.6	72.1	*United States*	49,561.8	63.5

SOURCE: *Statistical Abstract of the United States, 1955.*

regions of the country have increased more than the average. The West South Central, Mountain, and Pacific states have had the most spectacular growth of all in non-agricultural employment.

The rate of growth favors the newer industrial areas. However, some sense of proportion is gained when we recognize that all of the Middle Atlantic states and all of the East North Central states make up eight of the fifteen leading states in size of manufacturing employment. Indeed, these two regions together employ about 40 per cent of all non-agricultural workers. Industry has certainly not abandoned its older habitats and is not likely to in the near future.

What we are experiencing in the United States is a rapid expansion of non-agricultural employment with new centers of industry supplementing and only very gradually dis-

TABLE 8.9

THE SOUTH AND WEST SHOW LARGEST PROPORTIONATE INCREASES IN NON-AGRICULTURAL EMPLOYMENT IN THE MAJOR INDUSTRIAL DIVISIONS

(showing 1955 employment in thousands and per cent increase since 1939)

			Moderate Increase, 1939 to 1955				*Large Increase, 1939 to 1955*				
Industrial Division		*U. S.*	New England	Middle Atlantic	East North Central	West North Central	South Atlantic	East South Central	West South Central	Mountain	Pacific
Construction	No.	2,737.1	168.1	522.9	568.9	239.2	397.5	132.3	256.4	112.1	339.7
	%	132.5	105.3	94.0	163.7	131.3	120.6	95.4	130.6	170.8	220.8
Government	No.	6,928.1	422.7	1,316.1	1,208.4	599.7	1,123.8	422.9	631.2	312.5	890.8
	%	73.7	43.4	52.1	60.8	38.0	98.5	78.7	98.3	96.3	147.0
Manufacturing	No.	16,469.6	1,455.9	4,164.1	4,816.8	961.9	1,861.9	793.7	768.1	205.7	1,441.5
	%	63.2	24.6	42.7	73.1	84.7	54.6	77.0	108.4	117.9	146.9
Trade	No.	10,807.1	680.3	2,323.5	2,310.2	1,016.4	1,369.7	549.3	997.4	370.4	1,189.9
	%	63.7	34.3	41.6	59.3	52.9	94.4	99.1	99.4	92.4	79.0
Service	No.	5,579.7	396.0	1,390.8	1,106.9	462.1	667.0	255.7	445.9	199.6	655.7
	%	67.1	55.1	56.5	63.0	53.4	77.0	80.1	76.8	97.2	90.0
Transportation, Public Utilities	No.	4,073.9	212.5	949.7	847.6	400.7	480.7	185.3	386.4	167.3	443.7
	%	39.9	23.3	21.6	42.3	42.9	47.4	33.8	60.3	54.2	65.4
Finance	No.	2,194.9	162.3	643.2	429.1	180.4	247.1	81.1	159.8	56.4	235.5
	%	60.8	61.2	23.4	49.9	69.4	129.6	136.4	137.4	182.0	95.0
Mining	No.	772.7	2.2	111.9	82.1	54.0	109.2	64.0	223.5	85.7	39.9
	%	−8.1	−8.3	−46.7	−22.0	23.2	−21.0	−32.6	79.2	13.4	−12.5

SOURCE: *Statistical Abstract of the United States, 1956.*

placing the old. States like Florida, Tennessee, Texas, and California are undergoing considerable industrialization with very substantial increases in non-agricultural employment. Other states like Colorado, New Mexico, Arizona, Utah, and Nevada in the Mountain Region have shown exceedingly high per cent increases, but these are based on very small actual numbers. The total non-agricultural employment in all of the five states just mentioned does not equal that of Indiana, for example, and is only about one-fifth of New York's labor force.

We can secure a broad picture of the ways in which other employment follows industrialization from Table 8.9 where the per cent increase in employment is shown for the major industries in each region. Based on these percentages, it seems clear that the Old South, the Southwest, and the Mountain and Pacific regions of the country are the areas of most rapid economic growth. The old adage, "Go West, young man," must now be revised. The rapidly expanding opportunities for work are west and south.

MOBILE AMERICANS

A general picture of the American labor force emerges. Its most striking characteristic is its fluidity. We have noted the remarkable transformation of the economy from one engaged in primary production to one with a majority of employed people in service industies. This has made opportunities for women to work and they have moved into the labor force, particularly into clerical occupations.

The skills of the working force have also changed, but somewhat less rapidly than the distribution of the industries in which they are practiced. It seems evident that there is no single class of people at a particular skill level who dominate the non-agricultural labor force. Older centers of industry continue to grow. Supplementing them are the new centers of industry in the South and West, where very rapid increases are being achieved.

Types of industry are changing, types of industrial skills are changing, and even the locale of work itself is shifting. The American labor force is truly a mobile one.

NOTES FOR CHAPTER 8

[1] The field of demography, and its sub-field, the labor force, is widely studied and has a vast literature. Following are some of the best general references covering this area: J. D. Durand, *The Labor Force in the United States, 1890-1960* (New York: Social Science Research Council, 1948); William Haber, F. H. Harbison, L. R. Klein, and G. L. Palmer (eds.), *Manpower in the United States: Problems and Policies* (New York: Harper & Brothers., 1954); A. J. Jaffe and C. D. Stewart, *Manpower Resources and Utilization: Principles of Working Force Analysis* (New York: John Wiley & Sons, 1951); United States National Resources Committee., *The Problems of a Changing Population* Washington: Government Printing Office, 1938); and P. M. Hauser, "The Labor Force as a Field of Interest for the Sociologist," *American Sociological Review,* 16:530-538 (August, 1951).

[2] Because of the way in which statistics are collected, it is necessary later in this chapter to use figures for "gainful workers" instead of statistics on the "labor force." The gainful worker concept is generally used throughout the world. It emphasizes work for pay and aims to provide a measurement of the number of persons classified by occupational experience. See in this connection: P. M. Hauser, "The Labor Force and Gainful Workers—Concept, Measurement, and Comparability," *American Journal of Sociology,* 54:338-355 (January, 1949); W. E. Moore, "The Exportability of the 'Labor Force' Concept," *American Sociological Review,* 18:68-72 (February, 1953); and Social Science Research Council, *Labor Force Definition and Measurement,* Bulletin No. 56 (New York: The Council, 1947).

[3] Jaffe and Stewart, *op. cit.,* pp. 14-15.

[4] For an excellent account of the working child problem see: Grace Abbott, *The Child and the State,* Vol. I (Chicago: University of Chicago Press, 1938).

[5] An excellent discussion of earlier materials on working women is S. P. Breckinridge, "The Activities of Women Outside the Home," in *Recent Social Trends in the United States* (New York: McGraw-Hill Book Company, 1934).

NOTES FOR CHAPTER 8 (CONT.)

[6] It is necessary to reconcile the fact that the labor force is a stable proportion of the total population for male workers and for the entire labor force at the same time that the proportion of females in the labor force has increased (See Table 8.4 as well as the discussion of this paragraph). The explanation is simple. The proportion of men who are in the labor force has remained stationary, but the number of men of working age has not grown in proportion with total population growth. Consequently, for the total labor force to remain a stable proportion of the total population, females have to fill in where the number of males of working age is deficient. This has been a "demographic pull" on females to enter the labor market to satisfy the manpower demands of commerce and industry.

[7] Cf. J. D. Durand, "Married Women in the Labor Force," *American Journal of Sociology,* 52: 217-223 (November, 1946).

[8] In making this statement about the future labor force we are really using a "manpower" concept. Manpower is used to define the potential available supply of labor. Social practices may, of course, modify the age of entry into the labor force, the age of retirement, and the constancy of membership in it. Consequently, a statement about manpower usually predicts the upper limits of physical possibility, not the actual outcome that might occur. See Jaffe and Stewart, *Manpower Resources and Utilization,* pp. 16-17.

[9] There are other, less desirable, consequences of this leisure too. Juvenile delinquency, poor education, and general economic loss of the goods and services not produced by the economically idle are but some of the more obvious undesirable results.

[10] Jaffe and Stewart, *Manpower Resources and Utilization,* pp. 408-409.

[11] Cf. A. M. Edwards, *A Social-Economic Grouping of the Gainful Workers of the United States* (Washington: Government Printing Office, 1938).

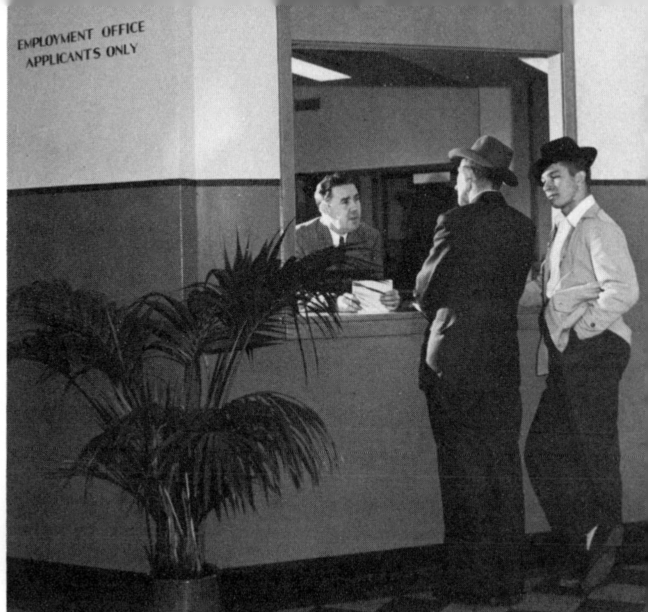

At the company employment window the worker conveys, explicitly and indirectly, his background. The earnestness of this older job applicant is in sharp contrast with the cockiness of the youth next in line. Does the young man feel that he has more than the older one to offer the company?

Chapter 9

BACKGROUNDS OF WORKERS

If the United States is a social melting pot, this is equally true of the country's labor force. A central characteristic of the labor force is its heterogeneity. The American labor force is composed of people with widely different ethnic and racial backgrounds, who have been reared in a variety of different social environments. Older workers differ as to amount and quality of education from the newer recruits to industrial work.

American industrial firms cannot depend on the society fully to prepare workers to assume traditional work assignments guided by customs of social behavior. A remarkable transformation is wrought by work organizations when people of diverse backgrounds are brought together to work in industry. Employing organizations have to develop techniques for standardizing working behavior of employees with varied backgrounds.

Standardization of mass produced products requires uniformity in working behavior to achieve it. American industry makes an "organization man" out of the worker because the mass production of goods and services in large companies necessitates standardization of work behavior. We can better understand the problems of molding a company work force when we appreciate the diversity of background in those recruited to it.

In this chapter we will examine five aspects of the social backgrounds of American workers. Age, education, ethnic origin, rural-urban background, and racial composition will be analyzed. These factors, together with what we have already examined in Chapter 8 (males and females in the work force, skill levels, and the productive distribution of the labor force), give us a broad picture of the diversity of Americans at work.

AGE OF WORKERS

The American labor force is an aging one. By this we simply mean that the average age is increasing, with higher percentages of workers found in older age brackets.

Aging of the labor force is a consequence, of course, of the aging of the total population. As more people are kept alive through better medical knowledge and improved sanitation, a higher proportion than formerly survive to older ages. Accordingly, we would expect that the United States, with highly developed medical professions, widely diffused medical facilities and services, and advanced sanitary facilities protecting water supplies and sewage disposal, would exhibit this aging characteristic in its population and labor force.

A sense of the rate at which the labor force is aging is gained from Table 9.1 showing the percentage distribution of the working population from 1900 to 1950. In the first fifty years of the twentieth century, the working population has shifted markedly to older ages.

TABLE 9.1
THE AMERICAN LABOR FORCE IS AGING

	*Per Cent in Each Age Group**		
Year	16 through 44	45 through 64	65 and over
1950†	65.0	30.0	5.0
1940	68.8	27.2	4.1
1930	69.5	25.7	4.6
1920	71.5	24.1	4.1
1910	74.5	21.3	3.9
1900	74.0	21.2	4.4

* The figures do not add to 100% for each year since those whose ages were reported in the Census as "unknown" are not shown.

† Based on the Labor Force for 1950 and 1940, and Gainful Workers for earlier years.

SOURCE: U. S. Bureau of the Census, *Historical Statistics of the United States, 1789-1945,* and an estimate of those aged 14 and 15, based on *Current Population Reports,* P-57, No. 94, p. 9, applied to the 1950 Census count.

About one out of every five workers in 1900 was between the ages of 45 and 64 years. Fifty years later almost one out of three workers was in the same age group. As the proportion of the labor force in this age group has increased, the proportion in the younger age class has declined.

The American labor force is an early middle aged one. We can secure a more detailed picture of the labor force from Chart 9.1, which reproduces the labor force portion of Chart 8.3. This chart shows the distribution of the labor force by five-year intervals.[1] It will be noted that the total length of the bar for each age interval is about the same for the ages from 26 to 40. This suggests that the workers presently in this age range will survive in large numbers to become older workers with the passage of time. It will also be noted by looking back at Chart 8.3 that there is a deficiency in the total population in the ages 11 to 20 years. This is a consequence of the very low birth rates during the Great Depression. Accordingly, as that group enters the labor force, we can expect a decrease in younger people available for work.

The general consequence of the even distribution of present labor force members 21 to 40 years of age and of the deficiency in the total population between 11 and 20 years, is to make the future labor force have an even higher proportion of members in the older age groups than now. This condition will prevail until about 1965 when the youngsters born in the post-World War II baby boom first begin to enter the labor force. After 1970 we can anticipate a slowing down in the aging of the labor force as the new population boom begins to show its influence on the working population.

CONSEQUENCES OF AN AGING LABOR FORCE

There are four major consequences of the aging American working population. First and foremost is the effect on industrial incentives to work. Incentives will be analyzed in Chapter 13. An important distinction is drawn there between incentives to be mobile, to change jobs and move ahead, and incentives to stay put in present jobs. As the labor force ages, pressures on management to provide stability incentives in preference to mobility incentives will increase. In general, older workers are more concerned with security and stability than they are with advancement and its attendant unstabilizing problems. In Chapter 15 we examine individual job and occupational mobility in detail. It is concluded there that most movement upward on the occupational ladder occurs generally between the ages of 25 and 45. With an aging population, and an increasing proportion of the labor force in the ages above 45, the expectations of advancement diminish rapidly. Attention becomes focused on stability and security. Thus, we can expect that the shifting of the labor force to older age groups will have important consequences for the kinds of incentives offered to work.

CHART 9.1

THE AMERICAN LABOR FORCE AT MID-CENTURY

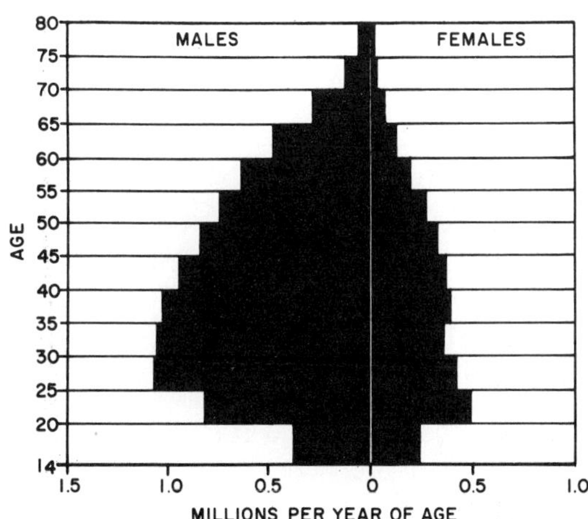

A second consequence of the aging labor force is that labor unions, covering a major portion of the labor force, will respond to the security needs of its older members by fostering collective bargaining demands and supporting legislative programs tending to make employment opportunities more secure and stable. It is significant, for example, that the emphasis on guaranteed annual wages and support of government intervention to maintain general economic stability have occurred in the recent period when labor union membership reflects the aging labor force.

A third consequence of the middle age character of the American labor force is that it may give rise to problems of occupational advancement for younger workers. Better jobs and positions are typically held by older workers. Their seniority usually entitles them to first choice of such jobs and positions. Consequently, the aging of the labor force may make fewer total opportunities for advancement available to young workers. For the younger worker it is, perhaps, fortunate that the Second Industrial Revolution is upon us. In Chapter 11 we analyze this new industrial revolution, the product of automation. We show in that chapter that entirely new kinds of skills and higher levels of education and experience will be necessary to fill the jobs and positions in automated employment. By and large, it is more economical to educate and train new workers than it is to retrain and amplify the education of older workers in order to fill the new work assignments created by automation. It may very well be, therefore, that the younger worker in industry and commerce today will have very rapid advancement opportunities in entirely new occupations, the product of automation. We may conclude, then, that the Second Industrial Revolution will save younger workers from the need to develop patience in aspiring to higher jobs and positions.[2]

A fourth consequence of an aging labor force is that it may have an influence on the "tightness" of supervision in industry. With a higher percentage of the labor force in older ages will come a longer average exposure to industrial work and experience with it. This means that the labor force, in general, will be a more experienced one in skills and habituation to industrial discipline. Consequently, we might expect that the need for maintaining tight industrial discipline will be less in the supervision of older workers when they constitute an even higher proportion of all workers.

EDUCATION OF WORKERS

The amount of total education of younger workers in the labor force is markedly greater than that of older workers. This is shown in the population of pyramid, Chart 9.2, which was constructed by taking the years of school completed, by age, for the entire population and applying it to the males and females in the labor force for each age group. It is reasonable to assume that education in the labor force will be comparable to education in the total population.

The proportion of young male workers who have had at least some college education, or who are college graduates, is generally higher than for workers over 35 years of age. Half of the male workers between ages 20 and 29 have had twelve or more years of schooling, while 36 per cent of those aged 30 to 34 have had a similar amount of schooling. There is a marked decline after 35 years in the proportion in each age group having at least 12 years of schooling; 35 per cent of those aged 35 to 39 have had that much schooling but only 19 per cent of those aged 60 to 64 have had at least twelve years in school. The same pattern holds for female workers except that higher proportions of younger women have had twelve or more years of schooling.

CHART 9.2

YOUNGER WORKERS HAVE MORE EDUCATION THAN OLDER WORKERS

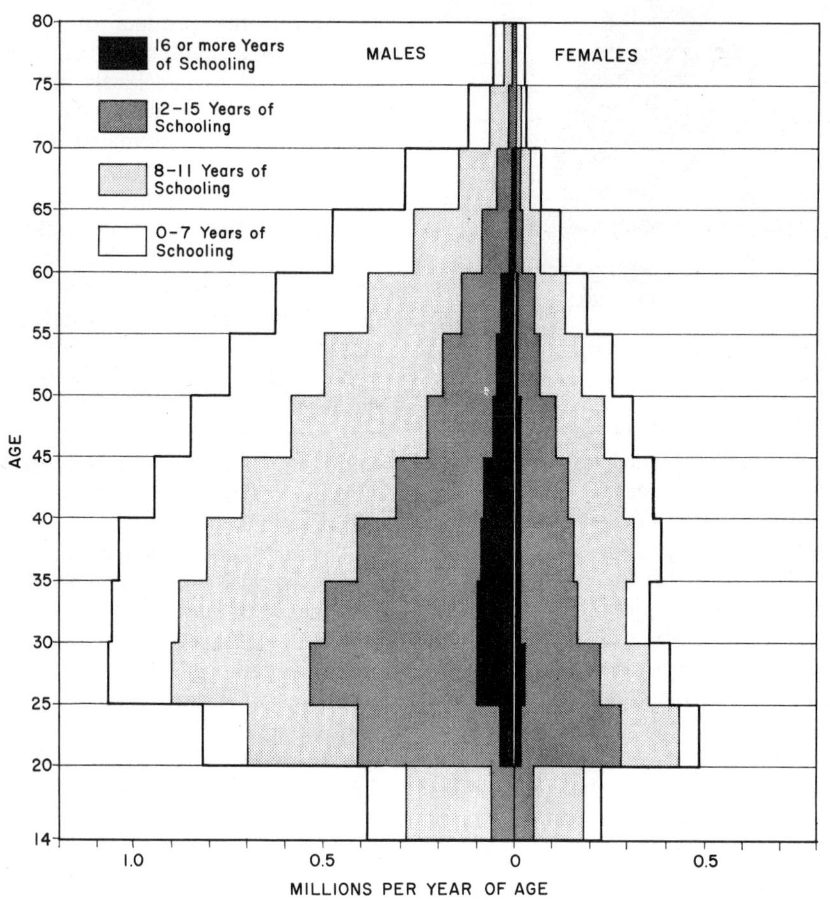

It seems clear that the labor force is characterized by diversity with respect to the amount of schooling of its members. Younger people have the advantage of a greater amount of schooling than older members of the labor force. It will be recalled from Chapter 8 that the United States has a very low proportion of its entire population ages 15 to 19 who are gainful workers. This is shown in Table 8.5. This same general fact is revealed in the population pyramid in Chapter 8 showing the distribution of the total population by activities. It is concluded in Chapter 8 that the wealth of the American economy permitted late entry of younger people into the labor force. The major alternative activity is to continue schooling. Thus, a significant consequence of the wealth of the economy is to improve the total amount of education in the labor force.

There is another aspect of employment that may also have led to increasing the average amount of schooling for more recent entrants into the labor force. Much industrial and commercial work requires a minimum of literacy for its performance. This literacy includes facility with language and arithmetic. It may also include competence in technical subjects as well, which in turn is grounded in reading, verbal, and numerical literacy (reading blue prints, for example). We have already seen, in Chapter 8, that there has been a rapid increase in clerical and sales occupations. There has also been a sharp decline in the proportion and absolute numbers of laborers. These facts would suggest that the demands of commerce and industry have been for greater and greater numbers of people possessing a minimum amount of literacy to perform jobs. For example, in the clerical and sales group, spelling, language usage, and mechanical skills with a typewriter are important to being a typist, stenographer, or file clerk. In sales, ability to do simple sums and competence with spoken English are requisites for doing such work. Thus, the changing nature of the economy has demanded a higher level of education to fill an increasing number of jobs and positions for which this education is necessary.

We may conclude, then, that the wealth of the economy has permitted leisure for more younger people, and that the leisure has been used for additional schooling, better to prepare them for work in industry and commerce. Leisure in the society and the demands of work organizations have both been important influences on the increasing amount of education found among younger workers.

A great deal of controversy exists today regarding the quality of American common school education. In particular, grave concern is often expressed over the apparent shifts away from "hard" subjects like mathematics, physics, and chemistry. These subjects and allied ones are necessary in preparation for working in complex industrial processes, and with automation.[3] Professor Hand has demonstrated that the conclusions regarding the move away from hard subjects are erroneous.[4] For example, he points out that in contrast to 1900, high schools in 1950 had five times as many students enrolled in mathematics and science courses.[5] Furthermore, he points out that the proportion of children of high school age actually in school has increased sharply from 8 per cent in public high school in 1900 to 64 per cent in 1950.[6] Hand also goes on to point out that about 7½ times as many high school students in 1950 as in 1900 are in a position to take mathematics, chemistry, and physics because they are offered in schools they are attending.[7] In general, Hand concludes that the present student body in American high schools has exposure to "hard" subjects, and a much higher proportion are taking these subjects than in 1900. The real block to further expansion in teaching such courses is the supply of teachers, not educational policy giving preference to other kinds of subjects. Hand also cites "now and then" studies to show that students today do as well or better than their predecessors on appropriate tests.[8]

It seems apparent that the American labor force exhibits wide diversity with respect to educational background, as measured by amount of schooling and its quality. In general, younger workers have better education, and more of it.

CONSEQUENCES OF EDUCATIONAL DIFFERENCES

There are problems that age-associated differences in education raise for company promotion policies as well as jobs of first entry into the labor force. Younger workers may be preferred over older workers when promotion opportunities are available to jobs and positions requiring higher levels of education. Furthermore, younger workers may actually enter jobs and positions at a level considerably higher than their fathers and, indeed, higher than the workers presently employed.

This may have important consequences for the status valuations placed on jobs, and on people who occupy them. To the extent that older people look upon those younger than themselves as "upstarts" and "smart alecks" they will tend to be resentful of younger workers who can rise more rapidly than they, and who can start in better jobs and positions. Thus, it would appear that the differences in amount and quality of education, favoring younger workers, may be an important disturbing factor in the status structures of industry, where age is considered the important criterion of status.

We can expect an increasing tendency for more younger people to be supervising older workers, and for more younger people to be in responsible technical positions than their older working associates. This is the "educational revolution" that is having important consequences in the organization of industry and commerce.

ETHNIC BACKGROUND OF WORKERS

The United States has historically been the land of opportunity for millions of immigrants, principally from Europe.[9] The flow of immigrants accelerated after the Civil War and continued to be an important factor in the growth of America until 1930. In Table 9.2 the number of immigrants by decades is shown.

TABLE 9.2
BULK OF IMMIGRANTS CAME TO THE UNITED STATES BETWEEN 1840 AND 1930

Period	*Total Number of Persons*
1821–30	143,000
1831–40	599.000
1841–50	1,713,000
1851–60	2,598,000
1861–70	2,315,000
1871–80	2,812,000
1881–90	5,245,000
1891–1900	3,688,000
1901–10	8,795,000
1911–20	5,736,000
1921–30	4,107,000
1931–40	528,000
1941–50	1,035,000

SOURCE: U. S. Bureau of the Census, *Historical Statistics of the United States, 1789-1945;* and *Statistical Abstract of the United States: 1953.*

It is estimated that about 70 per cent of the immigrants remained as permanent citizens.[10] This immigrant flow to the United States was important in making immediate additions to the labor force when new labor was required for growing American industry. Indeed, for a period in the last quarter of the nineteenth century and extending into the early years of this century, labor recruiters were sent to Europe to encourage able bodied men to come to America to work in the mines, mills, and transportation systems of the growing country.[11]

The immigrant has left his mark on many aspects of American culture. He typically brought with him the culture of his birthplace, often combining it in strange and wonderful ways with that of his adopted country. The immigrant and his children are present in our labor force in large numbers. Their ethnic backgrounds still play a role in diversifying the social characteristics of the American labor force.

One quarter of the entire white population of the United States in 1950 was foreign born, or had at least one foreign born parent. We call this group the foreign stock of the country. Approximately one in thirteen of the total white population in 1950 was foreign born, while almost one in five was a child of foreign or mixed parents. These proportions are relatively high in spite of the fact that the flow of immigrants to this country was drastically limited by the Quota Acts of 1921 and 1924. Table 9.3 shows the data on the total for-

Ethnic diversity is revealed on the faces of these men lined up at the pay window to receive their wages.

TABLE 9.3
FOREIGN STOCK STILL BULKS LARGE IN THE AMERICAN POPULATION
(population figures rounded to the nearest thousand)

			Per Cent of White Population		
Year	Total White Population	Total Foreign White Stock	Foreign Stock	Foreign Born	Children of Foreign or Mixed Parents
1950	134,942,000	33,751,000	25.0	7.5	17.5
1930	110,287,000	39,886,000	36.2	12.7	23.5
1910	81,732,000	32,243,000	39.5	16.4	23.1
1890	55,101,000	20,626,000	37.4	16.5	20.9
1870	33,589,000	10,818,000	32.2	16.3	15.9

SOURCE: Reprinted with permission from E. P. Hutchinson, *Immigrants and Their Children, 1850–1950,* John Wiley & Sons, Inc., 1956, p. 3.

eign stock of the United States from 1870 to 1950.

In general, we might expect that about one in every four white workers was born outside the United States or had one or both of his parents who was. As a matter of fact, however, the percentage of foreign white stock in the labor force is even higher. This is due to the fact that the foreign-born white people and their children are, on the average, much older than native white persons of native parents. Accordingly, a higher proportion of foreign stock is eligible for work because of age, and is therefore likely to be working. The median ages of the native white population and the foreign stock are shown in Table 9.4.

TABLE 9.4
THE FOREIGN STOCK IS OLDER THAN THE NATIVE STOCK

Population Group	*Median Age of the White Population*						
	1950	1940	1930	1920	1910	1900	1890
Children of Native Parents	26.1	26.1	23.4	22.7	22.0	21.2	21.0
Children of Foreign or Mixed Parents	36.8	29.4	24.7	21.6	20.0	18.2	16.2
Foreign Born	56.1	51.0	43.9	40.0	37.2	38.5	37.1

SOURCE: Reprinted with permission from E. P. Hutchinson, *Immigrants and Their Children, 1850–1950,* John Wiley & Sons, Inc., 1956, p. 15.

Due to the generally higher age of the foreign stock, they are represented in greater proportion in the labor force than in the population as a whole. The data on labor force participation rates for white workers are shown in Table 9.5 which is similar to Table 9.3 except that the base is the working population and not the total population.

TABLE 9.5
ALMOST A THIRD OF WHITE AMERICAN WORKERS ARE STILL OF FOREIGN STOCK

Year	Total White Workers	*Total White Workers of Foreign Stock*	*Per Cent of White Workers*		
			Foreign Stock	Foreign Born	Children of Foreign or Mixed Parents
1950	52,479,000	16,588,000	31.6	9.2	22.4
1910	32,699,000	14,791,000	45.2	23.8	21.4

SOURCE: Adapted with permission from E. P. Hutchinson, *Immigrants and Their Children, 1850–1950,* John Wiley & Sons, Inc., 1956, p. 200. Based on gainful workers 10 years of age and over in 1910 and experienced civilian labor 14 years of age and over in 1950.

It is clear that almost half of all workers in 1910 were of foreign stock. The foreign stock was, in turn, about equally divided between foreign-born workers and the children of foreign or mixed parents. By 1950 almost a third of all white workers were still of foreign stock. By that date, however, two-thirds of the foreign stock were native-born children of foreign or mixed parents, and only one out of three of the foreign stock had been born abroad.

Foreign-born people tend to have at least some of the elements of their native culture incorporated in their present way of life. This is certainly true of language, with the native language often spoken along with English. It is also true of social customs and practices. Even their children are likely to carry some of the culture of their parents' native land. These children are reared in bi-cultural homes and experience their parents' native culture as well as the American culture in which they live.

We might, therefore, expect that industrial workers of mid-century America still had sizeable elements of European cultural features in their rearing and background. This is certainly true for the 10 per cent of foreign-born workers, and at least partially true for the one worker in five who was reared in a bi-cultural home.

It seems clear that ethnic factors still play an important role in the American labor force. This factor has declined in importance over the years, and with continual restriction on immigration will decline further. Nevertheless, people at work still exhibit ethnic diversity that is a product of the historic flow of millions of European workers to the United States.

OCCUPATIONAL SPECIALIZATION OF ETHNIC GROUPS

It is an old adage about Boston that "the blue bloods own it, but the Irish run it." This saying suggests that ethnic origin may be an important factor in making employment opportunities for relatively low-status job seekers. In general, immigrants have been low-status compared to people born in this country. Accordingly, we would expect that immigrants to the United States entered the labor force in low-level occupations.

This is exactly what happened to the bulk of immigrants. The flow of workers up the industrial occupational ladder was constantly augmented by additions of the newest immigrants at the bottom rungs. People last off the boats from Europe were given their first chances in the land of opportunity at the bottom of the heap. They accepted these chances and eagerly anticipated the time when they could look down on still newer arrivals.[12]

Immigrant labor was concentrated in unskilled and low-paid jobs, tended to be underrepresented in the professions, and avoided agriculture.[13] It has also been observed that even when they brought with them some industrial skill, they tended not to follow their established occupations after going to work in the United States.[14]

The consequence of layers of ethnic groups regularly entering the occupational structure at the bottom is that these layers remained relatively intact as the immigrant workers rose in occupational status. For example, in coal mining, the original wave of immigrant workers came from England, to be succeeded first by the Irish and later by "Slavs"—a commonly used term to designate eastern and southern Europeans.[15] As the "Slavs" came into mining, the English and then the Irish moved up into skilled jobs and supervisory positions. In the iron and steel industry, by 1870, the English who were early immigrants had a very high concentration as rolling mill operatives, a relatively high-skill group of occupations. The English were still concentrated in other iron and steel occupations, but these were jobs increasingly being filled by the Irish, who were more recent immigrants than the English.[16]

The layering of ethnic groups in industry is still evident today.[17] Collins has pointed out that ethnic background is important in distinguishing between middle management and foremen, with the ethnic group (in this case, Irish) being "acceptable" only as high as the foreman level.[18] It is probably generally true today that "ethnic layering" of the labor force is much more evident within the ranks of management than among workers. In the analysis of a sample survey of the foreign-born in 1950, Hutchinson has found that there has been a distinct upward movement of the foreign-born workers between 1910 and 1950 away from manual and unskilled work and toward more skilled employment.[19]

One important consequence of the layering of ethnic groups in industry is that ethnic background becomes an important status-conferring characteristic of the person. When ethnic origin is less visible, it is less likely to confer low rank. It is significant in this connection that the second generation foreign stock (children of foreign or mixed parents) had, by 1950, much less marked occupational specialization than their foreign-born parents. Indeed, the second generation had an occupational distribution close to that of the entire white labor force.[20] As the obvious characteristics of ethnic origin (language difficulties, education, "clannishness," and "foreign air") become less marked, attribution of low status to those possessing these characteristics also diminished. Consequently, the American-born children of immigrants dispersed more widely through the occupational structure than their parents.

The politics of labor unions has reflected "ethnic layering" of the labor force. In the needle trades, for example, many of the top union leaders are of Russian-Jewish ethnic background. As their ethnic group was supplanted by later immigrants in the industry, principally southern Europeans and especially Italians, union leaders of that ethnic group rose in the needle trade unions. Today there are important union posts held by people of Italian origins. Similar representation of ethnic groups through elected union officials is to be found among New England textile workers where French Canadians are an important ethnic component; among shoe workers where southern Europeans are important in the industry, and in the automobile and steel industries where southern and eastern Europeans constitute large segments of the work forces.[21]

In general, the long range trend has been away from ethnic specialization in particular occupations, or industries. Nevertheless, certain stereotypes of ethnic association with particular occupations and industries were once real characterizations. For example, the Census of 1870 revealed that working people born in Germany had especially heavy concentrations among barbers and hair dressers, professional musicians, restaurant and bar keepers, milkmen, peddlers, operators of cigar, clothing, and liquor stores, and as bakers, butchers, basket-, cabinet-, candy-, clothes-, barrel-, cigar-, liquor-, and piano-makers, engravers, gun- and lock-smiths, upholsterers, and woodworkers.[22] We can certainly see in this list of trades and occupations some of our still persisting stereotypes of the German as the jolly host and saloon keeper, the noisy brass band musician, the heavy handed butcher, the baker of rich delicacies, and the skilled artisan. However, the Germans did not hand down many of their early specializations to their children (or perhaps it could as well be said that their children did not prefer to follow in daddy's footsteps). In an abbreviated, and perhaps not wholly comparable analysis made of workers of foreign stock in 1900, first and second generation Germans appear to be heavily concentrated as saloon keepers and bartenders, merchants and dealers, cigar makers, as industrial workers in iron and steel, and in the machinist trade.[23] Thus, ethnic occupational inheritance seems to have diminished markedly over a relatively short period of time as measured by the number of occupations in which there is continuing heavy concentration of ethnic Germans.

We may conclude generally that ethnic identification is still important in diversifying the American labor force. Successive waves of immigrants, coming from different countries—each entered the labor force at the bottom and moved up, making room for the more recent arrivals. This led to a layering of ethnic groups in industry, with the early arrivals moving toward the top and the later immigrants taking their places below in the occupation structure. In recent times there has been very little occupational specialization of ethnic groups. The ethnic factor still plays a role as a status-conferring aspect of the individual, principally in the ranks of management. The ethnic factor is also important in industry insofar as people reared in ethnic-oriented homes have to learn common ways of working cooperatively on the job.

REARING AND MOBILITY OF AMERICAN WORKERS

A large segment of American workers do not go to work in the community in which they were reared. This suggests that the influences playing on the upbringing of American workers are not the same as those affecting their adult lives as workers.

In the ten years preceding 1950 there was an increase of almost 20 per cent in the urban population of the United States. By 1950 two-thirds of the population were urban residents. Much of this change represented moves made to urban areas by farm-reared people, and involved important shifts to non-farm employment as well.[24]

With the closing of American shores to foreign immigrants, industrial America has turned to the rural sections of the population to recruit work forces. Continuing flow of new workers into industry has come increasingly from the farm-reared portions of our population. The sons and daughters of farmers are the native immigrants to American industry who have replaced their foreign-born predecessors. It has been pointed out by Freedman, for example, that one out of every three adults now living in non-farm areas was reared on a farm.[25] Freedman also reports that for the metropolitan area of Detroit almost one out of three adults was farm-reared.[26]

Some evidence of the extent of moving around in the labor force is given by Bogue's analysis. In March, 1950, almost 12 million out of a total of 62 million labor force members lived in houses different from their residences a year earlier.[27] Thus, almost one in five workers had changed his residence in the course of a single year. About one in 20 of the workers in 1950 also moved out of his county of residence into another county during this sample year.[28]

Where is the future labor supply of the United States to be found? From what geographic areas will the future labor force come? In Chapter 8 the geographic distribution of the labor force was analyzed and the areas of rapid growth were noted. From that analysis it appeared clear that the Southeast, the Southwest, and the Far West are areas of rapidly growing labor forces, attributed to industrial expansion in those areas of the country. In general, to the extent that the distribution of jobs and birthplaces of workers do not coincide, then people have to move to jobs; jobs have to move where potential workers are to be found; or both may move to find each other. In examining the geographic distribution of the labor force in Chapter 8 we noted the movement of industry, creating jobs, into the southern and western areas of the country.

We now want to examine the probability that people will move to find existing jobs. It will be recalled that in Chapter 8 we emphasized the fact that the older industrial areas of the country still employed a major share of

TABLE 9.6
THE SOUTH HAS MORE PEOPLE THAN IT HAS JOBS TO OFFER THEM

Geographic Division	*Percentage Distribution of—* Jobs Available: Employed in 1950	People Getting Ready to Work: 10–14 Years Old in 1950	People Starting Work in 1965: Births in 1950	*Difference Between Ready to Work and Jobs Available* (— is a shortage, + a surplus of people)	*Difference Between Start Work in 1965 and Jobs Available* (— is a shortage, + a surplus of people)
United States	100.0	100.0	100.0		
South					
South Atlantic	13.6	16.0	15.4	+2.4	+1.8
East South Central	6.8	9.6	8.7	+2.8	+1.9
West South Central	9.8	10.9	10.9	+2.0	+2.0
East					
New England	6.4	5.4	5.4	—1.0	—1.0
Middle Atlantic	21.0	17.3	17.2	—3.7	—3.8
Middle West					
East North Central	21·1	19.2	19.8	—1.9	—1.3
West North Central	9.5	9.4	9.3	—0.1	—0.2
Far West					
Mountain	3.1	3.8	4.0	0.7	0.9
Pacific	9.5	8.3	9.4	—1.2	—0.1

SOURCE: Donald J. Bogue, "Residential Mobility and Migration of Workers." Reprinted with permission from William Haber, *et al* (eds.), *Manpower in the United States: Problems and Policies,* 1954, Harper & Brothers, p. 147.

the labor force. The north central and eastern manufacturing belts were also growing in size of labor force, although less rapidly than the newer indsutrial areas.

If we contrast the 1950 labor force with the number about to enter it (in the ages of 10 to 14 years), and those whose survivors will begin to enter it between 1965 and 1970 (childern born in 1950), we have a measure of the areas of surplus people and the areas of surplus jobs. This is done in Table 9.6 which is a rough measure of the regional distribution of jobs and of people now born who are available to take them. It will be noted immediately that the southern group of states are the only states with a significant surplus of future workers over jobs. The older industrial areas of the East and the Middle West have a significant shortage of future workers compared with present job opportunities.

It is very clear that the breeding ground of the future labor force is the South. People with southern background and the particular cultural features associated with being reared there are the migrants who will move north, northeast, and west to take jobs in commerce and industry. There may be significant problems in assimilating the southern migrants, white and Negro, into the working culture of the North and West. It is conceivable that industry receiving southern workers will have problems of assimilation not entirely unlike the problems raised by incorporating foreign-born immigrants.

The problem of assimilating rural-reared people into urban work and ways of life is mediated somewhat by the fact that cityward migration tends to take place in two stages. Migrants often move from the farm to smaller cities, then move on, in a second stage, to larger urban centers.[29] Furthermore, the distance traveled tends to be relatively short with each move.[30] Accordingly, some of the southern migrants being recruited for industry tend to take first jobs in the South, later moving to the East, Middle West, and Far West. Habituation to industrial work discipline is thus acquired in the cultural setting in which the southern workers have been reared. Therefore, their adjustment to industrial work and to a different community cultural setting may not have to be made at the same time.

The stream of migrants going into industry is not a cross section of those with whom they were reared. Migration is generally more frequent among better educated people, those with higher income, and those who have some professional training. Workers of comparable ages but of lower socioeconomic standing move less frequently. The least mobile segments of the population are those who have low incomes, who have experienced long periods of unemployment, and laborers or low-skilled workers.[31] There is no marked preference of males or females, but younger people of both sexes migrate more frequently than older people.[32] The movement of people to jobs therefore tends to be selective, favoring younger people who are better educated, better trained, and having higher incomes. Industrial and commercial jobs attract people to them especially among those with high skill and training who can be utilized at their highest performance levels.[33]

An excellent picture of the cross currents of labor force mobility is revealed in Table 9.7 These data are based on Palmer's extensive study.[34] The table shows the migrants into six industrial cities of the United States. Migrants were defined as those who had less than 12 years of residence in the metropolitan area of the city. Chicago and Philadelphia, two large northern cities, recruited 35 and 36 per cent, respectively, of all their new workers from the South. More than one out of every three migrants into these two major metropolitan centers came from the South. It is notable that most of the southerners going to Philadelphia came from the southern seaboard, while their brothers going to Chicago came from the central tier of southern states. These findings are paralleled by other studies of migrants to the Detroit metropolitan area. The Detroit Area Survey in 1953 found in a sample of 1157 homes of Detroiters that 22 per cent of adults over twenty years of age had previously lived in the South.[35] Hawley, in an earlier study of people moving into the Detroit-Willow Run area between 1940 and 1944 (the peak war employment years), found that 37.2 per cent had lived in the South in 1940. He also found that Detroit recruited the bulk of its southern workers from the central tier of southern states.[36]

TABLE 9.7
WORKERS MOVE TO THE CITIES TO FIND JOBS

(persons with less than 12 years of residence in the metropolitan area of the city were classified as migrants)

Region of Previous Residence	Workers Who Move Showing Region of Residence Before Moving to Cities—1951 (numbers in thousands)											
	Chicago		*Philadelphia*		*Los Angeles*		*San Francisco*		*St. Paul*		*New Haven*	
	No.	Per Cent	No.	Per Cent	No.	Per Cent	No.	Per Cent	No.	Per Cent	No.	Per Cent
Total	426	100	201	100	721	100	226	100	152	100	20	100
Home State	37	9	45	22	109	15	61	27	22	42	4	20
South	152	35	71	36	133	18	36	16	2	4	3	15
South Atlantic	27	6	62	32	18	2	8	4	1	2	3	15
East South Central	99	23	7	3	19	3	6	3	*	*	*	*
West South Central	26	6	2	1	96	13	22	9	1	2	*	*
East	41	10	55	28	118	16	23	10	2	4	9	45
Midwest	106	25	10	5	230	33	38	17	20	38	1	5
West	38	9	5	2	95	13	39	17	4	8	1	5
Outside U. S.	46	11	14	7	34	5	27	12	1	2	2	10
Previous residence unknown	6	1	1	*	2	*	2	1	1	2	*	*

* Less than 0.5.

SOURCE: Adapted with permission from Gladys Palmer, *Labor Mobility in Six Cities,* 1954, Social Science Research Council, p. 167.

If we look at Los Angeles and San Francisco on the west coast, only 18 and 16 per cent of their labor migrants came from the South. In absolute numbers, southerners moving to Los Angeles were somewhat fewer than went to Chicago, but almost twice as many as migrated to Philadelphia. One-third of the Los Angelinos came from the Middle West, while San Francisco recruited almost a third of its new workers from the home state of California. Looking at the smaller cities of St. Paul and New Haven, we discover that they both recruit almost completely from their home state or their home region. St. Paul recruited 80 per cent of its migrants from Minnesota and the Middle West. New Haven recruited 65 per cent of its new workers from Connecticut or the East, although it did draw 15 per cent from the South Atlantic seaboard. This migration pattern to the smaller industrial cities suggests the two-stage migration cycle previously noted. Many of the migrants going to St. Paul and New Haven to work are in the first stage of movement. They are probably moving from farms, villages, and small urban communities to their earliest industrial work.

Chicago, Detroit, and Philadelphia are certainly recipients of a major flow of new workers from America's breeding ground, the South. This pattern is duplicated for the other major industrial centers of the East and Middle West. The flow of workers to the West coming from the South is augmented by a large movement out of the Middle West and a significant number who come from the East.

In general, we can now conclude that about one-third of the people living in cities were reared on farms. Their early social experiences tended to differ from their adult ways of life. For them, personally, some kinds of adjustments had to be made to urban living patterns.[37] It is also probably true that industry accommodated its working methods and work customs to the rural qualities of its recruits.[38] As international immigration diminished, the flow of workers into industry was sustained by rural-born citizens of the United States. The real excess of available people in relation to jobs is now in the South. The South is, and will continue to be the breeding ground of a major share of the industrial labor force. The imprint of being reared in rural areas, in the South, or both will add to the diversity of the social characteristics of the American labor force.[39]

It is interesting to speculate about the consequences of the two great streams of industrial recruits for American labor unionism. European immigrants often brought with them their own ideas about the role and functions of unions. They gave to the labor movement a political and sometimes even a radical outlook. Business unionism in mass industries, characterizing the modern labor movement, has the bulk of its membership among native-born migrants to our industrial centers. These rural-reared people have grown up in the larger traditions of the American society. Many—whose families belonged to organizations like the Grange, the Farm Bureau Federation, and farmers' unions—have also experienced organizational power. It may very well be that the characteristic business unionism of American labor—vigorously making a place in, rather than materially modifying, present economic arrangements–is at least a product of the background and rearing of a major portion of its membership.

RACIAL BACKGROUND OF WORKERS

About 10 per cent of the American labor force is composed of non-whites. These non-whites are principally Negroes, with other non-whites composing a relatively small portion of the labor force.

The central feature of the employment of non-whites is the discrimination exercised against them. Negroes have relatively greater difficulty than whites in securing managerial positions, and work in clerical occupations and sales. Furthermore, they are vastly over-represented, compared to whites, among laborers and service workers.[40]

Chart 9.3 shows the Negro labor force in relation to the entire labor force. It will be noted that the age distribution of Negroes is approximately the same as that for whites. There is a slightly higher proportion of very young Negroes working than is true for whites. There is also some slight tendency for Negro women to represent a higher proportion of all working people than Negro men. In general, however, the population pyramid suggests that the Negro labor force is substantially like the white labor force in terms of age and sex.

Discrimination against Negroes in employment has tended to exclude them from higher-level jobs, and to force them into less-skilled and lower-paid occupations. Even when the amount of education is held constant so that there is a fair presumption that a Negro and white job applicant are not markedly different in school training, discrimination in employment definitely favors the white worker. In Table 9.8, the distributions of Negroes and white workers in broad occupational groups are shown for comparable amounts of education. In order to determine whether job dis-

CHART 9.3

1950 NON-WHITE LABOR FORCE IS NOT MARKEDLY DIFFERENT IN AGE FROM WHITE LABOR FORCE

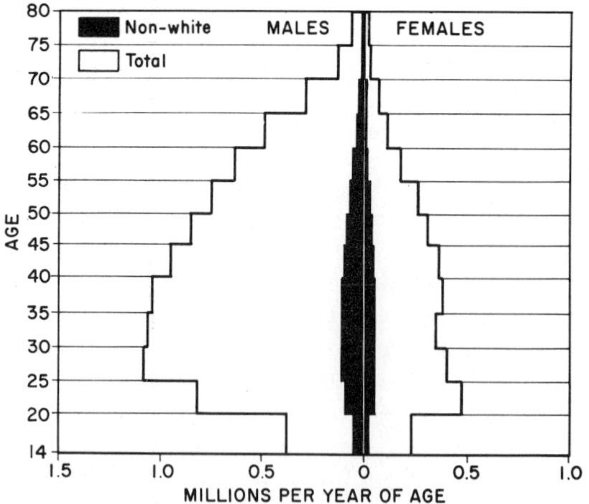

crimination is a regional or a general characteristic, working persons of the North and West are grouped together and contrasted with those of the South.

It is notable that outside the South, Negro high school graduates have a much smaller percentage of their group among managerial occupations and in clerical and sales occupations than white workers with the same amount of education. Furthermore, the Negro high school graduate more than half the time finds a job in laboring or service occupations, while only one out of ten of his white peers who graduated from high school is in this group. The same pattern of differences is also to be seen in the comparison of Negro with white college graduates. Of particular significance is the fact that more than one out of five of the Negro college graduates go to work in laboring or service jobs, in contrast with only one in a hundred white college graduates. These figures are for working people in the North and West where we can presume that job discrimination against Negroes would be less than in the South. The same pattern of discrimination against Negroes is to be found within the South, when education is held constant. The whole country is apparently about equally disinclined to afford equal employment opportunities to Negroes.

The Negro has been the traditional object of employment discrimination in the United States European immigrants, as we have already noted, have tended to enter the labor market in low-level jobs but eventually they and their sons and daughters worked their ways up the occupational ladder. Negroes also entered industry and commerce at the bottom of the occupational heap. However, they have not succeeded in securing the same kinds of opportunities to rise occupationally as characterize the white population.

A familiar Pittsburgh street scene: steelworkers leaving the mill for lunch. Negroes have been recruited in large numbers for work in heavy industry.

Discrimination against Negroes has been widespread. Labor unions as well as employers have erected barriers against the Negro.[41] There is some evidence to suggest that workers tend to discriminate less against the Negro than members of management.[42] During World War II significant advances were made in Negro employment, largely under the pressures of labor shortages created by the war.[43] The Federal government required then, as it does now, non-discrimination in employment on government contracts. In addition, some states

TABLE 9.8
NEGROES DO NOT FARE AS WELL AS WHITES IN EMPLOYMENT WHEN EDUCATIONAL DIFFERENCES ARE ELIMINATED

Occupational Group	*High School Graduates*		*College Graduates*	
	White	Negro	White	Negro
	NORTH AND WEST			
Professional	6.0	4.1	54.6	48.5
Managerial	15.7	2.7	16.1	6.1
Clerical & Sales	32.5	11.4	22.6	15.2
Craftsmen & Foremen	16.5	10.3	2.9	3.3
Operatives	18.8	19.3	2.4	4.6
Laborers & Service	10.3	52.2	1.4	22.3
Total	100.0	100.0	100.0	100.0
	SOUTH			
Professional	5.4	4.1	53.0	65.0
Managerial	20.6	3.1	18.8	4.6
Clerical & Sales	35.4	9.8	22.2	11.9
Craftsmen & Foremen	15.8	7.6	2.9	2.0
Operatives	15.8	17.6	1.9	3.0
Laborers & Service	7.0	57.8	1.2	13.5
Total	100.0	100.0	100.0	100.0

SOURCE: U. S. Bureau of the Census, *U. S. Census of Population, 1950, Special Reports,* Part 5, Chapter B,"Education"(Washington: Government Printing Office, 1951). Computed from Table 11, using "non-white" as equivalent to Negro.

and cities have passed fair employment practices acts. The legal ban against job discrimination serves to buttress the hands of an employer or labor union pressing to use Negro workers at their highest skills. Attitudes of discrimination, however, are not readily changed by laws. It takes vigorous action to achieve reasonable integration of white and non-white workers. A number of industrial and commercial companies have pursued forthright policies of hiring workers regardless of race. Notable success has been achieved in local public transportation, government service, in some areas of manufacturing, and in retail trade.

Where substantial numbers of Negroes enter the labor market, they encounter caste barriers that are effective blocks to occupational advancement.[44] Segregation is a common outcome, with Negroes given special jobs—usually low-skilled and low-paid—or segregated on separate shifts or in separate departments. Insofar as caste barriers continue to be effective, management practices in handling personnel become complicated by the implicit or explicit special treatment accorded Negroes. These caste barriers also create special problems in the social interaction of workers on the job.[45]

DIVERSITY OF THE LABOR FORCE

The American labor force is heterogeneous in its social origins. Vast streams of European workers moved to the United States throughout the nineteenth century and the first three decades of the twentieth. Today the foreign-born and their children—the foreign stock—account for almost a third of the entire labor force. About another third of the urban labor force is made up of people who were born and reared in rural communities and have since moved to cities to find jobs. Another ten per cent of the labor force is composed of Negroes. Thus, three major factors—foreign origin, rural origin, and race—account for roughly three-quarters of the people working in industry and commerce.

The age distribution of the working population, and the amount and quality of its education, increase distinctions among labor force members. The "middle age" dominance in the labor force tends to favor those past 35 years as against younger workers. The younger workers, however, have distinctly more and better education, which gives them advantages not enjoyed by their older associates.

The American labor force does not have firmly rooted traditions and a common heritage governing work. Its diversity in social origins and personal characteristics mitigates against the development of widely held customs governing who does what kind of work, in what manner, at what ages, and under what circumstances.

American society is, therefore, less controlling than more traditional societies in providing a common work heritage to its children as they grow up—a heritage they can take with them into commerce and industry to govern working behavior and social relations in the work place. It is perhaps for this reason as much as any other that American work organizations are so tightly and self-consciously organized as compared with European counterparts. Industrial discipline and rationalization of operations are distinctly more highly developed in American industry.[46] Every aspect of working tends to be controlled and organized because little of working behavior can be left to common tradition or social heritage for its control.

Even in the ranks of management, the "organization man" of Mr. Whyte's business world, is a man of varied background, certainly not born to management.[47] The need for rapid socialization of large numbers of members of the managerial bureaucracy has placed pressures on management to emphasize conformity to a common image in molding people with diverse social backgrounds into a "management mold."[48]

It is also significant that American labor unions have developed their own philosophy and goals, distinct from the European labor movement. Labor unions have had mixed streams of traditions playing on them, fed by the heterogeneous social backgrounds of their members. Under the circumstances we would expect innovation and experimentation with a high probability that American unions would develop unique features of their own. This they have done.

In these two chapters on the labor force we have secured perspective on how the human material that makes up work organizations comes to the work place with divers experiences and expectations. Workers must be molded into some semblance of uniform behavior so that delicately balanced productive processes and complex economic interdependencies can be made to work. Implicitly, American industrial management has recognized this problem of standardization, and has developed management techniques to achieve it. The next eight chapters on "Getting Work Done" examine the detailed ways in which uniform work behavior is developed and sustained.

NOTES FOR CHAPTER 9

1 A comparable population pyramid showing the labor force in the entire population for 1940 constructed on the same basis as this one is contained in J. D. Durand, *The Labor Force in the United States, 1890–1960* (New York: Social Science Research Council, 1948), p. 39.

2 In the next section of this chapter dealing with education of workers we point out that younger workers have more and better education than older ones, and that this is an advantage for them.

3 The "scare" quality of this public controversy has sometimes obscured the facts upon which the arguments ought to rest. Those who think the "educationists" are ruining American education with emphasis on "life adjustment" in preference to intellectual competence buttress their case with statistics to prove deterioration. See A. E. Bestor, Jr., *Educational Wastelands* (Urbana: University of Illinois Press, 1953), which sparked a good deal of the protest against professional educators' dominance of the

NOTES FOR CHAPTER 9 (CONT.)

American common school system. The article by H. C. Hand, next cited, is an attack on a charge made by Bestor (reported in *U. S. News and World Report,* November 30, 1956) that we are less educated than 50 years ago.

[4] H. C. Hand, "Black Horses Eat More than White Horses," *AAUP Bulletin,* 43:266-279 (June, 1957).

[5] *Ibid.,* p. 273.

[6] *Ibid.,* p. 272.

[7] *Ibid.,* p. 275.

[8] *Ibid.,* pp. 277-278.

[9] Three prime sources of statistical and interpretative materials on immigrants in the labor force of the United States are: Niles Carpenter, *Immigrants and Their Children, 1920,* Census Monograph VII (Washington: Government Printing Office, 1927); T. J. Woofter, Jr., *Races and Ethnic Groups in American Life* (New York: McGraw-Hill Book Co., 1933); and E. P. Hutchinson, *Immigrants and Their Children, 1850–1950* (New York: John Wiley and Sons, 1956), this being the most recent and complete treatment of the immigrant components of the labor force.

[10] See W. F. Willcox, *Studies in American Demography* (Ithaca: Cornell University Press, 1940), p. 390.

[11] That European immigrants were immediate additions to the labor force is confirmed by the fact that the bulk of them were men. Over the century since 1820, there have been approximately 150 males for every 100 females among immigrants. Hutchinson, *op. cit.,* p. 18.

[12] The classic American study of the continuities with Old World life, and the breaks with it encountered by immigrants to the United States, is W. I. Thomas and Florian Znaniecki, *The Polish Peasant in Europe and America,* 2 volume edition (New York: A. A. Knopf, Inc., 1927). The persistence of ethnic life-ways in America is amply demonstrated in W. L. Warner and Leo Srole, *The Social Systems of American Ethnic Groups* (New Haven: Yale University Press, 1945), which documents the social standing and special features of ethnic life for a New England industrial city, Newburyport, Mass. An historical treatment of the immigrant showing his impact on American culture is Oscar Handlin, *The Uprooted* (Boston: Little, Brown and Co., 1952).

[13] Hutchinson, *Immigrants and Their Children, 1850–1950,* pp. 64-66.

[14] Louis Bloch, "Occupations of Immigrants before and after Coming to the United States," *Journal of the American Statistical Association,* 17:762-763 (June, 1921).

[15] See Hutchinson, *op. cit.,* pp. 64 and 84; also Handlin, *op. cit.,* pp. 71-72.

[16] Hutchinson, *op. cit.,* p. 84.

[17] Cf. E. D. Beynon, "Occupational Succession of Hungarians in Detroit," *American Journal of Sociology,* 39: 600-610 (March, 1934); and Samuel Koenig, "Ethnic Groups in Connecticut Industry," *Social Forces,* 20:96-105 (October, 1941).

[18] Orvis Collins, "Ethnic Behavior in Industry: Sponsorship and Rejection in a New England Factory," *American Journal of Sociology,* 51:293-298 (January, 1946).

[19] Hutchinson, *op. cit.,* p. 275.

[20] *Ibid.,* pp. 275-276.

[21] The best and almost the only analytical treatment of the impact of ethnic factors on the labor movement is Jack Barbash, "Ethnic Factors in the Development of the American Labor Movement," in G. W. Brooks *et al.* (eds.), *Interpreting the Labor Movement* (Madison: Industrial Relations Research Association, 1952), pp. 70-82.

[22] Hutchinson, *op. cit.,* pp. 82-84.

[23] *Ibid.,* pp. 172-173.

[24] See Gertrude Bancroft, "Trends in the Labor Force," Chapter 10 in William Haber *et al.* (eds.), *Manpower in the United States: Problems and Policies* (New York: Harper & Bros., 1954), p. 134.

[25] Ronald Freedman *et al., Principles of Sociology,* revised edition (New York: Henry Holt & Co., 1956), p. 462.

[26] *Ibid.,* p. 463.

[27] Donald Bogue, "Residential Mobility and Migration of Workers," Chapter 11 in Haber *et al., op. cit.,* p. 145.

[28] *Ibid.*

[29] A. H. Hawley, *The Population of Michigan* (Ann Arbor: University of Michigan Press, 1949), p. 82, found that 81.8 per cent of those moving into the Detroit-Willow Run area between 1940 and 1944 did not have a farm residence in 1940. Even among those coming from the South, 3 out of 4 had not lived on a farm in 1940. These data are important in establishing the evidence for the two-stage character of city-ward migration.

[30] Bogue, *op. cit.*

[31] *Ibid.,* p. 151.

[32] Cf. U. S. Bureau of the Census, *Population: Internal Migration, 1935–1940; Age of Migrants* (Washington: Government Printing Office, 1946).

[33] In a sense, then, education tends to make people mobile, especially if the opportunities to use their education are not available where they receive it.

[34] See Gladys Palmer, *Labor Mobility in Six Cities* (New York: Social Science Research Council, 1954).

[35] See University of Michigan, Detroit Area Study, *A Social Profile of Detroit* (Ann Arbor: University of Michigan, 1954), p. 18.

[36] Hawley, *op. cit.,* p. 82.

[37] Cf. E. D. Beynon, "The Southern White Laborer Migrates to Michigan," *American Sociological Review,* 3:333-343 (June, 1938).

[38] When foreign immigrants constituted the bulk of new recruits to industry, it was pointed out that job simplification and mechanization were intro-

NOTES FOR CHAPTER 9 (CONT.)

duced to compensate for the relatively low-skill level at which the immigrant entered industry. See *U. S. Immigration Commission Report,* Vol. i (1911), p. 494.

[39] See in this connection: R. B. Vance, *All These People: The Nation's Human Resources in the South* (Chapel Hill: University of North Carolina Press, 1945).

[40] The classic study of the American Negro is: Gunnar Myrdal, *An American Dilemma,* 2 volumes (New York: Harper & Brothers, 1944). An early examination of the minority races in American industry is Herman Feldman, *Racial Factors in American Industry* (New York: Harper & Brothers, 1931). A specialized volume dealing with the major aspects of Negro employment is R. C. Weaver, *Negro Labor, A National Problem* (New York: Harcourt, Brace & Co., 1945).

[41] An early study of the Negro and the labor movement is: S. D. Spero and A. L. Harris, *The Black Worker: The Negro and the Labor Movement* (New York: Columbia University Press, 1931). A more recent account of Negroes in industrial unions is H. R. Cayton and G. S. Mitchell, *Black Workers and the New Unions* (Chapel Hill: University of North Carolina Press, 1939).

[42] See in this connection B. A Reed, "Accommodation Between Negro and White Employees in a West Coast Aircraft Industry, 1942–1944," *Social Forces,* 26:78-84 (October, 1947).

[43] A good short treatment of this is in R. C. Weaver, "The Employment of Negroes in United States War Industries," *International Labour Review,* 50:141-159 (August, 1944).

[44] Caste lines may appear particularly visible in the South but they are readily apparent in the North also. For the analysis of the impact of caste on Negro employment in the South see: C. S. Johnson, "The Conflict of Caste and Class in an American Industry," *American Journal of Sociology,* 42:55-65 (July, 1936), for an analysis of the tobacco industry; H. A. Bullock, "Racial Attitudes and the Employment of Negroes," *American Journal of Sociology,* 56:448-457 (March, 1951), dealing with employment in Texas; and Donald Dewey, "Negro Employment in Southern Industry," *Journal of Political Economy,* 60:279-293 (August, 1952).

[45] Three relevant studies are: Wilson Logan and Harlan Gilmore, "White Employees and Negro Workers," *American Sociological Review,* 8:698-705 (December, 1943); R. D. Minard, "Race Relations in the Pocahontas Coal Fields," *Journal of Social Issues,* 8:29-41 (1952); and L. M. Killian, "The Effects of Southern White Workers on Race Relations in Northern Plants," *American Sociological Review,* 17:327-331 (June, 1952).

[46] In the post-World War II period, productivity teams were brought to the United States from European countries to study industrial rationalization as a basis for improving productivity in their home countries.

[47] W. H. Whyte, Jr., *The Organization Man* (New York: Simon and Schuster, 1956; and Anchor Books).

[48] W. H. Whyte, Jr., *Is Anybody Listening?* (New York: Simon and Schuster, 1952), contains a series of sketches of how large industrial companies extend the selection and molding processes for their young executives into their personal lives.

Part IV

GETTING WORK DONE

Chapter **10**

TECHNOLOGY AND PRODUCTION

The technology of modern industry and commerce is the most important single determinate of who does what kind of work, when, and in what manner.

There is widespread respect for the genius of Americans in developing modern industrial technology. Indeed, our technology of production is so generally acclaimed that we tend to accept it, almost without analysis for its meaning and consequences, as a permanent feature of the American industrial environment.[1] This reaction to technology is also probably found in industrialized Europe where modern methods of production have a respectably long history.

In this chapter we will examine the human consequences of modern technology. Our first focus of attention will be on the relations between technology and human work skills. We will then turn to the methods by which modern technology is incorporated into actual production processes, establishing the industrial division of labor. Lastly, we will examine the human consequences for people at work of the requirements imposed by technology and production processes.

MACHINES AND MEN

Machines utilize energy for performing work. Industrial machines perform work by using energy sources other than men or animals. Work output is a direct result of the amount of energy spent in doing the work. The greater the amount of energy used, in general, the greater will be the amount of work performed.

ENERGY, MACHINES, AND PRODUCTIVITY

The first Industrial Revolution, usually dated from Watts' first patent on the steam engine in 1769, involved the utilization of energy from coal and wood and, later, from natural gas, electricity, and petroleum. This industrial revolution was characterized by the replacement of men and animals as sources of motive power.

CHART 10.1

SINCE 1910 THE DOMINANT SOURCE OF INDUSTRIAL POWER COMES FROM MACHINES

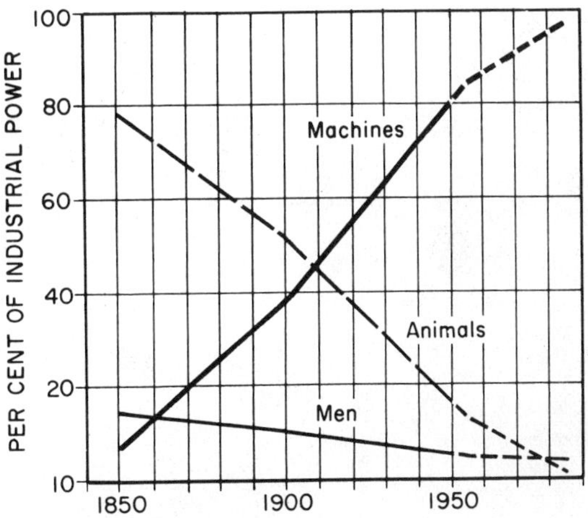

From K. T. Compton, "Engineers," *Scientific American*, September, 1951, p. 66.

Technology supersedes local culture in determining how industrial work gets done. Oil well drilling on three continents: at Norman Wells, Northwest Territory, Canada; El Centro, Columbia; and Abquiq, Al Hasa, Saudi Arabia. Racial background and culture of the workers are obviously different. The kind of work they do in drilling for oil is dictated by the universal technology of this industry, and not by local custom and practice.

Some measure of the magnitude of the changing power base can be secured from Chart 10.1 where the percentage of industrial power is shown for men, animals, and machines. In the hundred years since 1850 machine power has increased from about 7 per cent of the total of industrial power to 80 per cent. Men and animals as sources of power have become negligible factors in industrial output. Estimating the curves to 1985 throws the balance even further in favor of machines.

TABLE 10.1
INDUSTRIAL COUNTRIES USE MORE ENERGY THAN AGRARIAN COUNTRIES
(energy derived from coal, electricity, wood, petroleum and natural gas)

Country	*Estimated Million Calories per Capita (1946)*	*Index (U.S. = 100)*
United States	*12,507*	*100*
Great Britain	5,304	42
Sweden	3,960	32
Belgium and Luxembourg	3,503	28
Iceland	2,734	22
Czechoslovakia	2,480	20
Finland	2,430	19
Switzerland	2,313	18
France	2,211	18
Netherlands	2,045	16
Poland	1,353	11
Ireland	944	8
Spain	814	7
Rumania	726	6
Hungary	476	4
Greece	464	4
Bulgaria	437	3
Albania	292	2
Turkey	257	2

SOURCE: *Etudes et Conjoncture Economie Mondiale,* Institut National de la Statistique et des Etudes Economiques, Nos. 17, 18, 19 (Oct., Nov., Dec., 1947).

Our modern industrial world is one almost totally dependent on non-human and non-animal sources of motive power. The importance of power is graphically displayed in Table 10.1 where energy consumption per capita is shown for selected countries in the world. A glance at this table shows clearly the contrast between industrial and agrarian countries in terms of their power consumption. The United States uses more than twice as much energy per citizen as any other country listed. (Data was not available for the USSR.)

Motive power, however, is not usable until it is converted into working energy. Industrial machines perform this conversion process. They take energy and literally put it to work in producing the goods of the economy. It is through machines, and the industrial complexes of which they are a part, that the vastly increased output of goods in our industrial economy is achieved.

For the United States, there is approximately a 3 per cent increase in output per man-hour each year for manufacturing industries. This rate of increase has been fairly steady since 1909. In mining and railroad transportation the annual rate of productivity increase has been about the same. In the electric light and power industry productivity has increased about 8 per cent annually since the early 1930's. In these industries, output per man-hour has approximately doubled between 1919 and 1939, with rates of increase being at least as great or greater since then. The future holds prospects of even further increases in man-hour output. This increased productivity is graphically displayed in Chart 10.2, showing the American industries for which trend data on man-hour output are available.

It should be noted immediately that American workers did not work any harder in 1939 than they did in 1919, although output per man doubled during this period. The greater output was the result of machines doing the increased work.

When we fully realize the central position that technology and production machines play in industrial output, in getting the work of the society done, we can grasp the overriding importance of technology in modern work.

There can be no significant analysis of modern work without recognizing the pervasive influence that technology has on all its aspects.[2] Work organizations are characterized by technological behavior systems governing human work. We have also seen that the power structures of work organiza-

CHART 10.2

PRODUCTIVITY IS INCREASING

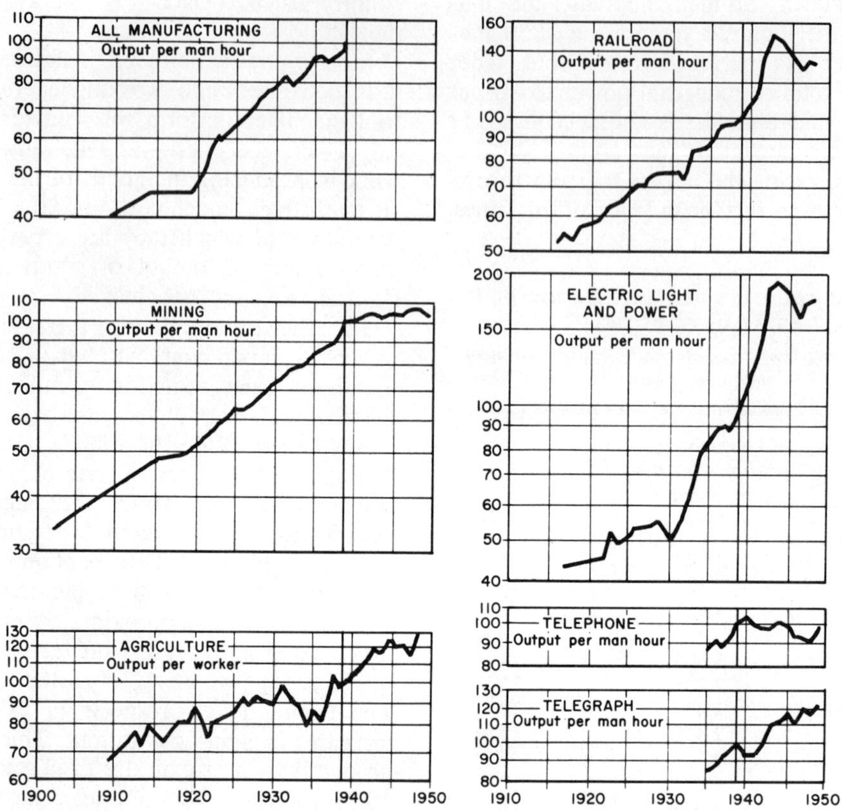

Reprinted with permission from A. J. Jaffe and C. D. Stewart, *Manpower Resources and Utilization*, John Wiley & Sons, Inc., 1951, p. 236.

tions are grounded in the performance of work functions that, in turn, are the product of the technology of work. Even the authority and status structures of work organizations have some of their principal features determined by technology.

MACHINES AND MEN—AN EXAMPLE

We can see the impact of technology most vividly by examining the evolution of a task that has retained the same general title for centuries. Weaving is a common occupation found throughout the world. Here are descriptions of three stages of weaving.

Weaving is the crosswise interlacing of at least two sets of parallel fibers or threads of any kind. The interlacing may be done entirely by hand if reeds, grasses, leaves or other relatively stiff, short fibers are to be woven into grass mats, for example. This is achieved by laying the warp in parallel rows on the ground or on lap boards, and guiding the weft fibers alternately over and under the warp strands, thus locking the two groups together.

The method is not, however, practical for weaving long lengths of cloth. Most hand loom weaving is done on a frame to which the warp threads are attached and held at a suitable tension to keep them in an even, parallel position. A Navajo weaver, for example, uses the simplest frame for holding

The time-honored way of primitive peoples in weaving cloth. Tewanaemtewa, Hopi Indian of Shungopavy village, 75 miles north of Holbrook, Arizona, is working at a blanket loom.

the warp threads as he weaves a blanket. In this way the weft may more easily and quickly be guided into place either with the fingers alone or with the aid of a shuttle. The shuttle, which may be merely a twig or thin stick, holds the supply of weft thread. Each passage of the weft across the alternate warp threads is called a shot or pick.[3]

A second stage in the improved technology of weaving is represented in an early American loom where a mechanical treadle worked by foot power is used to separate the warp threads. The weaver seated on a long wooden bench in front of the loom, pushes back with her left thumb the swinging reed, presses down the treadle, thereby drawing apart the warp threads, and through the opening thus formed casts from right to left the wooden shuttle that holds the weft thread. The shuttle through, she withdraws her thumb, and the reed swings forward, driving home the weft, the process being reversed for the passage of the shuttle from left to right.

The modern power loom differs from the hand loom of colonial days only in the multiplicity of parts necessary to take the place of the human hands and feet. The movements of the harnesses, the let-off and take-up motions of warp and cloth, the self-acting temple which regulates the width of the cloth, the fly shuttles and drop boxes move smoothly without attention. A detector acts when the bobbin in a shuttle is empty, and causes the magazine to pass a new bobbin to the waiting shuttle. If a shuttle leaves its race and plunges into the warp, technically called a "smash," an electric stop halts the loom before harm is done. The breaking of warp yarns is also detected by an electrical device. The drawing in or entering is still done by hand.[4]

The evolution of the power loom has simply added complex parts and mechanisms to take the place of hands and feet. The old operations of the loom are present but they are all done mechanically. The weaver merely has to watch the machine. In the power loom pictured one man can tend from twenty-eight to thirty-four looms. The shuttle makes up to 162 trips a minute through the warp.

This example of the evolution of weaving should make clear the consequences of technology in getting work done. The first step from complete hand work was to use additional human energy in operating the warp separating treadle mechanism by foot power. This increased the speed of work, but required more human energy to gain the added output. When power was applied to weaving, and the machine designed to utilize non-human motive power in almost all its operations, shuttle speeds were increased at least six times. But note also, a single operator could now attend many machines, since his principal task did not involve physical work, but was simply to *watch* the machines for stoppages and breakdowns. The substitution of non-human motive power and its utilization by machines have increased output many

A battery of modern Automatic Bobbin Changing Dobby Looms making gingham cloth. There are twenty-two looms visible in this picture, with the attending weaver at the far end examining one of them.

times, at the same time reducing the amount of direct expenditure of human energy and need for human skill. This is indeed the miracle of modern work technology.

SKILL IS MACHINE ORIENTED

It is perhaps safe to suggest that the difference between the craftsman of a handicraft era and the craftsman of a machine era lies in one simple fact. The handicraft artisan was specialized in terms of the product he made. He was a shoemaker, a tailor, a candlestick maker. The basic hand tools with which he worked had relatively little specialization for the accomplishment of his task. Thus, drills, hammers, chisels, knives, and the like, were to be found in almost all handicraft operations.

The modern factory artisan's skill is specialized with respect to the kinds of machines he is capable of using and working.[5] Thus, a roller in a rolling mill gets this title and develops his skill by being able to pass hot billets of metal repeatedly through giant rolls until the heated metal takes on the desired shape. The roller is an exceptionally skilled person in a steel or brass mill. Yet his skill has no relationship to the skill of, let us say, a machinist in the same plant who is capable of operating equipment like lathes, milling machines, drill presses, and screw machines with high precision, having the ability to translate a blueprint into reality by virtue of his skill with the machines. What the machinist knows, and the kinds of skills he uses, are not the same as what the roller knows and does. The significant difference between their skills and abilities lies in the technical equipment each uses.

We can conclude, then, that the introduction of machine technology has tended to specialize skill according to machine operations rather than in terms of product. In this respect the handicraft artisan and the modern skilled craftsman are markedly different.

NON-TRANSFERABILITY OF SKILLS

Another feature of machine technology is that skills tend to be less and less transferable from one kind of operation to another.[6] This may be true even to the extent of specialization on a particular kind of task that is accomplished on one make of machine. For example, it is common to train bookkeeping machine operators on a particular brand of bookkeeping machine. It is often difficult for one trained on, let us say, a Burroughs bookkeeping machine quickly to transfer her skill to the operation of a National bookkeeping machine. Neither of these bookkeeping operators, in turn, would be very useful without intensive re-training in doing the bookkeeping operations on a punch card system.

Skill specialization according to task or machine reduces transferability of the skill to another operation or machine.[7] This has several consequences. First, it requires more and more emphasis on job training for specific tasks. A second consequence is that the tasks themselves come to be highly standardized in order to facilitate training, among other things. Third, workers are likely to place relatively little value on skill because of its ready obsolescence. Fourth, emphasis on machine and process skill specialization has increased considerably the general problems of managing men. More men doing many more different tasks place greater burdens on management to coordinate the operating diversity coherently.

TECHNOLOGY AND LABOR SUPPLY

It is one of the characteristics of machine technology of the past hundred and fifty years that it required an increasing number of industrial and commercial employees. As the technology developed, the need was quickened for a supply of people capable of manning the technical, industrial positions created.

Machine technology requires large numbers of people in its development, and in distribution of the goods it produces. Throughout the Western world the major source of labor has been agrarian areas. This source of labor gave a particular direction to the design of the technology. Work positions and jobs were designed to utilize relatively unskilled labor.[8]

Under these circumstances of labor supply, the technology moved inevitably in the direction of simplifying work. Tasks were made as simple as possible. The number of different tasks that an individual might be expected to perform was also limited. Coupled with the large demand for goods and the consequent development of mass production, it became possible for the individual to specialize on relatively simple tasks. The relatively unskilled labor supply available for manning industry led to the conscious design of machines and production processes to emphasize the low skill levels widely utilized in industry today.

MASS PRODUCTION AND STANDARDIZATION

Mass production of items for consumer purchase, coupled with standardization of the product in order that each successive consumer could expect to receive substantially the same product, led to stabilization of production technology. Stabilization took the form of insuring that each employee produced precisely what was expected of him with minimum individual variation permitted.

There has been a vast growth of inspection and control techniques designed to insure minimum variation in product. Little or noth-

Mass production requires standardization. Uniformity is built into the production process, and not left to the skill or discretion of the individual worker. Here two men are tending flat glass grinding machines that surface continuous sheets of glass.

ing was left to the whim or initiative of the worker. The greatest emphasis was placed on standardization of his product. Control and inspection methods have played an important role in permitting mass production, and in broadening the markets for industrial goods.

Standardization has tended to operate against the assumption of initiative on the part of the individual worker, or the exercise of any taste, discretion, or judgment about the product he turns out. The area of the discretion left to the worker came more and more to be focused on the *amount* of work, not the *quality,* turned out in a given time.[9] Quality was guarded by managerial controls incorporated in standardized production processes, and the inspection of products to conform with engineering and design standards.

SPECIALIZATION OF WORK

We are now going to examine the division of labor as it worked out in actual operations. We are concerned here with how the technological division of labor is achieved.

In general, the division of labor occurs as a consequence of three distinctive developments: (A) specialization of tasks; (B) subdivision of tasks; and (C) creation of new tasks. We will first analyze specialization of work.

The most pervasive division of labor is that among specialized functions. This is obvious if you contemplate your daily round of life. From the moment of arising in the morning until retiring at night, great areas of dependence on the industry of other people are evident. You could not be warm, fed, clothed, transported to and from work, have the raw materials to work on, have markets for distributing your product, without a host of other people doing highly specialized work in performing these tasks, making possible your daily life. The coal miner, farmer, bus driver, steel worker, railroad man, wholesaler, retailer, butcher, baker, and light-bulb maker—all are a necessary part of your life for the services that they perform and the goods they produce.

One of the primary distinctions between a primitive society and a modern one is that individuals in modern societies tend to specialize their productive activities.[10] The citizen of a primitive society will grow his own food and process it for eating; will make his own clothes and build his own shelter; will manufacture his own tools; and fashion his own musical instruments. In our society each one of these tasks tends to be specialized in the hands of an individual or group, performing the tasks exclusively.

SPECIALIZATION AND SOCIAL STRUCTURE

The broad specialization of labor that occurs society-wide influences the occupational and other social structures of a society. Most of the analyses of class structure of modern societies start with an analysis of what people do. The product of a citizen's work or how he does it, is important in determining where he stands in the society.[11]

What an individual does often determines his relative social position. Some occupations come to be valued more highly than others. Some occupations are paid, or rewarded, more highly than others. Some occupations are considered to be distasteful, dishonorable, or both. Out of such evaluations of what people do arise evaluations of what people are, and what they merit in the way of social standing and esteem.

Every division of labor based on specialization necessitates a complementary bond of dependence. Every specialization implies that the special activity is an integral part of a larger whole.

Specialization of work has the major consequence of building important ties of dependence among the citizens of a complex society. We are likely to observe the nature of these ties most clearly in situations of stress, or in situations in which the normal flow of goods and services is disrupted. Thus, in a disaster, or in a labor strike where the flow of goods and services is temporarily halted, each citizen becomes acutely aware of the degree, and pervasiveness, of his dependence on a host of other citizens of the society.

The development of industrial complexes, specialized in their product, or products, is another direct consequence of specialization of functions within the society. We find that the common designation of an industry is based on the product it turns out: for example, the steel industry, automobile industry, electrical goods industry, machine tool industry, canning industry, clothing industry, and so on through a whole list of industrial complexes.

SPECIALIZATION AND SOCIAL COHESION

For the person the social specialization of work has three general consequences. (A) Each individual finds his place in a class structure to be a consequence of the specialized tasks he performs in the broad division of labor. (B) Each person has a feeling, however dimly perceived, of the dependence that encircles the society of which he is a part. He finds that his own specialized work can be performed only if a host of other people perform theirs. Everyone especially perceives his dependence on others in situations of stress, or disaster, which temporarily stop the expected flow of goods and services. (C) Each person comes to identify his productive role with an industry, or an industrial or commercial complex.

This three-fold relationship of the person with the specialized division of labor in society serves to give him a point of anchorage in the productive activities of the society, a social or class position within the general structure of the society, and a sense of symbiotic dependence, or social bond with the other citizens of the society.[12]

SPECIALIZATION IN PRODUCTION OPERATIONS

Looking at actual production processes, rather than the broad, society-wide division of labor, another kind of specialization of work is found. For example, observe the dentist in action. Most of the professional activity will be carried on by the dentist himself. However, he will have a female assistant who does simple tasks like cleaning teeth; and a receptionist who also contributes to the performance of the dental service, although indirectly. This group of two, three, or four people constitutes the team that provides dental services. This team is in constant operation whenever the services are being performed, and is held together by the basic unity of the operation as each contributes to it.

In the factory, a similar kind of specialization of functions occurs.[13] Specialization within a given technology, or within a given industry, is grounded in high demand for the output. If the demand is sufficiently steady for a product or service, it is then possible to employ specialists continuously to perform individual tasks in a cooperative effort. When, for example, the demand for automobiles is great enough, toolmakers can devote themselves exclusively to their operation; diemakers have enough work to spend full time making and repairing dies; and a host of specialized machine operators can produce parts that are put together by other operators called assemblers, into the finished automobile. If, however, only one or several automobiles were produced by each company at a time, there is a high probability that only those would be employed who were all-around workers, capable of doing any of the operations, and usually performing them in the manufacture of a single vehicle. The industrial and commercial division of labor, as it works out in the specialization of tasks, is the product of a continuous demand for products.

From the standpoint of the individuals involved in technological specialization of functions, there are a number of consequences. First, there is a growth of groups of specialists with specific vocational or occupational outlooks. The designation of areas of work, like tool and die maker, machinist, or set-up man, provides labels for permanent and lifetime careers. Technological specialization leads to the development of technical careers, professional and semiprofessional pursuits.

A second consequence of technological specialization is that the degree of expertness in the specialty may be enhanced. To be able to concentrate fully on being a diemaker may lead to a higher degree of skill than might otherwise be achieved. If a worker had to make and repair dies, make and repair tools, and also be a general machinist, there is every reason to believe that his degree of skill would not be as great in the diemaking part of his performance. Intense concentration on a specialty may improve skill. To the individual there may be a great deal of satisfaction in highly expert performance.

A third consequence of technical specialization is paradoxical in character. It seems obvious that each specialist would recognize his dependence on other specialists in their joint contribution to the ultimate product. Yet it tends to be true that each specialist views his particular operations with undue narrowness. This has often been referred to as the "trained incapacity" of the specialist to perceive or understand the operations and theory that underly other specialties tying in with his own. The specialist displays a narrowness and provincialism of outlook. This creates important problems in coordinating the division of labor among specialists incapable of understanding each other.

A fourth consequence of extreme specialization of tasks is to limit the ability of the general citizen of the society to designate social standing or class position in terms of occupational titles. When a broad occupation like journeyman machinist is transformed into specialties like set-up man, toolmaker, diemaker, machinist A, machinist B, and machinist C, it becomes increasingly difficult for citizens to place individuals carrying one of these specialized occupational titles.[14] Uncertainty may result in using occupation to place an individual within the class structure of the society.

The basis for classifying people according to their occupation may lead to a whole series of indeterminacies if specialized occupations are not clearly understood by the larger community. When this development occurs, there is a strong likelihood that recognition of class position by fellow citizens comes increasingly to be the result of industrial rather than occupational attachment. Or class position may be assigned according to very broad occupational categories like "white collar" and "blue collar."[15]

SPECIALIZATION AND ORGANIZATION STRUCTURE

Management usually encourages technical specialization, in the prevalent belief that specialized performance of a single task is more efficient than serial performance by the same people of related tasks. Much of what goes under the name of "rational administration" consists of working out adequate and reasonable work specialties, and training or hiring people to fill them. There is constant pressure in organizations further to specialize tasks and the individuals who perform them.

A simple example of a specialized job: telephone installation man who wires and connects telephones to the service line. His is a specialized task, completed in all its phases by himself. The wide range of tools and equipment he uses, including the truck in which he travels, is shown.

This leads to a curious paradox. Often specialists are incapable of operating in the higher reaches of management where a general outlook rather than a special outlook is usually required. One of the consequences has been the multiplication of top management positions at and near the vice-president level. Even vice-presidential positions are usually highly specialized in character. Thus, the vice-presidents in charge of finance, production, sales, legal aspects of the firm, public relations, industrial relations, and even in charge of "happiness," represent the ultimate realization of specialization in the highest reaches of management.

Specialization of work within the technologies of a given enterprise represents one of the fundamental ways by which rationality is introduced into the organization. The consequences of specialization are not entirely constructive. We will deal in detail with this problem when we consider, in later chapters, the issues of coordinating specialists and building cooperative activities out of their diverse and very intensely specialized work.

SPECIALIZATION AND TASK UNITY

In general, specialized tasks tend to retain a wholeness and integrated character that make them complete in themselves. The tasks that a specialist performs tend to have a beginning and end that are recognizable, and that define the limits of his operations. Furthermore, his activities may be highly complex and entail a great deal of knowledge and training to accomplish them successfully. Finally, there is an exclusiveness that attaches to the performance of specialized work making it improbable in the absence of a given individual that anybody but a comparable specialist will undertake to perform his tasks. This is partly out of recognition of the difficulty of a specialized task, and partly out of recognition of the exclusive jurisdiction that the specialist has over such tasks.

SUBDIVISION OF WORK

Subdivision of work is based on quite different grounds than specialization. Where specialization leads to more intensive development of skill and ability, subdivision leads to a limitation of skills and ability.

The general drive to subdivide work is based on the character of labor supply, and the relative lack of trained personnel in mass labor markets. Employing large numbers of people, and training them rapidly for tasks that might change in short periods of time, necessitate having simple tasks for which the training time is rather short, a matter often of hours and usually not more than a day or two. Subdivided tasks are relatively simple, and therefore can be learned rapidly.[16]

The basic objective of work subdivision is to break a job down into its simple component parts and distribute these task parts to individuals who perform them exclusively. Work subdivision necessarily involves two related steps: (A) methods for integrating subdivided tasks, and (B) methods for controlling output. These three organization features provide a basis for understanding the subdivision of work.

METHOD OF WORK SUBDIVISION

Subdivision of work is based on the general assumption that all tasks can be divided into objective, component parts. These parts of tasks are identified as physical or bodily movements.[17] The totality of movements are then analyzed for possibilities of improvement by changing the kind of movements, or their grouping.

When task activities are grouped together in some organized fashion, it is usually discovered that the new groupings of activities can each be performed by different persons in sequential operations. The other alternative is to have each of the new groupings of activities performed by the same person, but in a new and preferred sequence. When the total task is broken up into groups of activities performed by different persons in sequential operations, we have work subdivision. This is the fundamental feature of all continuous production lines.

Motion study methods of modern job analysis play an important part in determining work subdivision.[18] Each operating task is analyzed for the physical movements and motions necessary for its performance. In those tasks in which some degree of mental effort is required, the nature of this mental effort is taken into account, including the kinds of discriminations or judgments the operator may have to make in performing his task. Subdivision leads to breaking down larger tasks into smaller units of activity, each to be handled by a separate individual.

Work subdivision satisfies the requirements for minimum schooling time in training a relatively unskilled, or ill-trained work force. At the same time, it permits reduction of operating costs, since it is assumed that subdivision increases the total output of the individual.[19] The amount of time lost in changing from one activity to another is minimized if the worker does not need to change. Thus, the subdivision of work minimizes lost motion or lost time.

The subdivision method rests, first of all, on the notion that tasks can be rationally described, and each of their parts carefully delineated. Work subdivision also depends on the assumption that more complex operations can be transformed into mechanical or machine activities, thereby relieving the operator from the need for concern with them. Indeed, examination of subdivided tasks in industry reveals the degree to which it is really a product of technology and machines that largely replace the uniquely human attributes of choice and decision. The engineer who subdivides tasks in the process of rationalizing the production scheme is dependent, by and large, on the cash investment he can make in machinery and tools to replace human skill, choice, and decision.

The engineer looks upon the human being as being capable of controlled movements and intellectual judgments. An important motivation in designing subdivided tasks is to make the most continuous use of these human faculties. A task that might require simultaneous use of both hands and both feet may not represent a rational task only because it is a difficult physical feat to accomplish.[20] For the engineer, the integrity of the individual as a human being is judged largely on the basis of potential conflict in demands on the simultaneous exercise of human faculties. So long as the engineer cannot anticipate such conflict, he is satisfied that the tasks which he has built into the subidivision of work are perfectly compatible with the human being as a physiological mechanism. It is this physiological compatibility that is the touchstone for the engineer in designing operating tasks, using the subdivision method.

METHOD OF WORK INTEGRATION

Work integration is a necessary and obvious corollary of work subdivision. Subdividing tasks is breaking down a larger task complex that has been previously performed as a whole task by single individuals. In the process of subdivision, it becomes necessary to re-establish the unity that had formerly been achieved by having one person do a variety of different things in serial order. This is the problem of work integration.[21]

It would not be economical, for example, to bore a hole in a piece of metal, and then store the pieces until such time as they move to another operation where threads are cut in the hole. The need for multiple handling and storage of the items suggests the desirability of having the bored pieces of metal move promptly to a threading operation, and having the two activities occur immediately in serial order.

We see, then, that in subdividing tasks the engineer is faced with the simultaneous need of putting the subdivided work steps back together in some kind of integrated whole. This leads directly to linear production methods in which subdivided activities are placed in order along a production line, and are performed one right after another in a continuous and everflowing sequence.[22]

Integration of subdivided work requires that the amount of time each task takes should be roughly comparable to the time spent on all other tasks. There are variations in this general principle of timing, but the principle is simple in its basic dimensions. If a manufactured item is to flow continuously along a production line, then each stop should be neither longer nor shorter than any other stop. Once the line is filled with moving items in various stages of manufacture, each individual will be performing a task which takes just as much time as all other tasks on the line. It is obvious, of course, that some variations can be introduced in this scheme. But all variations take into account the multiples of operating time required at any given work station.

THE ENGINEER AND WORK SUBDIVISION

The kind of emphasis on technology that derives from both subdivision and integration of work tends to dehydrate the engineer's view of the work situation, focusing him only on its technological aspects.[23] From this standpoint, human operators become simply cheap machines whose virtue lies only in the fact that they are less expensive to employ than mechanical substitutes.

The engineer is concerned largely with the physiological limitations on task performance of human operators. Only so long as these are genuine limitations is the engineer at all interested in the human operator as a living organism.

The engineer displays his "trained incapacity" as a production specialist when he designs production lines.[24] The rationality with which he views and solves his technological problems is unquestioned. The human being is indeed only a living organism and can be treated as such from the standpoint of the design of a technical process, particularly where work subdivision is used. However, this necessarily ignores the human qualities of the organism. We will examine below some of the potential and actual consequences of ignoring these human qualities when subdividing work.

METHOD OF WORK CONTROL

Control of work is necessary when tasks are subdivided. Control of work means this: operations are so ordered with respect to each other and the time schedule that the flow of manufactured items through the production process is adequately controlled for timing, quantity, and quality.

Subdivision of work requires in general a more rapid flow of manufactured items through the manufacturing process. Timing becomes an increasingly important aspect of production. A second and equally important consequence of high speed production is the need for controlling quality. If items can be produced on a cycle of, let us say, one per second, then a machine operating for several minutes could produce 120 defective items if the machine got out of adjustment. This can lead to very substantial wastage of material, or high costs in reworking defects.

Work control operates to insure organization of the work, maintenance of the rate at which work flows through the production process, and uniform quality at each step in the process.

Each of these aspects of work control has highly complex technological facets. However, in general we can see that the control of speed and coordination of steps in the line operation are problems of design of the production setup. The lay-out of work stations, and the work flow between work stations are essentially problems of plant layout and production process design. They are primarily engineering problems.

Control of quality has a number of aspects in addition to the control of speed and work flow. The control of quality introduces an additional set of operations into the production process. It may be necessary to use go, no-go gauges so that a sampling of products in process can be tested by the operator. It may be necessary to institute 100 per cent inspection or, at some points, the inspection process may be built directly into the work flow and become entirely mechanical. For example, when cartridge cases are filled with a charge of powder, each case is put on an arm which is a long spoke of a wheel. The wheel revolves between two fixed stops. If the cartridge case is too light, indicating a shortage of powder, the spoke will rise above its fellows and the cartridge case will be knocked off by the top stop. If the cartridge case is too heavy, the spoke will be pressed down below its fellows, and the cartridge case will be knocked off by the lower stop. This is a good example of mechanical process inspection that is built into a continuous operation.

The quality control aspects of work subdivision illustrate how new operations are developed in the person of inspectors or whole inspection departments. It often happens that the subdivision of tasks can seldom be a simple division of a complex task into a series of simplified tasks. There is typically involved, because of the need for establishing work control, the addition of at least new control functions in the subdivided task complex. It may turn out that more people are required when tasks are subdivided. In addition, new kinds of people with new kinds of skills may also be needed in the subdivision of work.

TYPES OF WORK SUBDIVISION

In general, there are two different types of work subdivision: (A) where the original job complex performed by a single person, or small group, is subdivided into component parts, and the parts distributed to separate individuals, and (B) where an original job complex is subdivided technically so that the new tasks are not the same as the components formerly performed in the integrated operation.

In simple work subdivision, the job is taken for granted, and the series of tasks that were performed by a single individual are divided into parts and distributed among several persons. A good example of this is found in welding. Where there is a sufficient volume of work to be performed, it is common to have a tack welder, whose task it is to make temporary and periodic welds on pieces to be joined so that they are held in position for the finish welder to lay his welding bead. There may be one tack welder for a number of finish welders. It is perfectly feasible for the finish welder to do his own tack welding since it requires less skill. However, it may turn out to be desirable in the interests of increased work pace to subdivide the work into that of tack welder and finish welder. It is evident here that there has been no change in the total operation. It is simply a question of who will do it, and whether or not the degree of subdivision is justified by the more rapid flow of work.

There are many instances in which the original job complex can be subdivided and distributed to separate individuals. This typically happens where the same kinds of instruments or tools are used in all the related operations in a job complex. Thus, both welders use exactly the same welding equipment. In the case of a sewing operation, the same kinds of sewing machines may be used, and the work is simply passed from one operator to another as successive tasks are performed on a garment.

Subdivision of work, without changing the tasks involved in the original job complex, is a relatively simple process. It has to meet the single criterion of whether more per unit of labor cost is produced than was true when it was an integrated operation.

Where the original job complex is subdivided and the component parts are *not* the same as they were originally additional problems arise. For one thing, the determination of whether to go ahead with subdivision in-

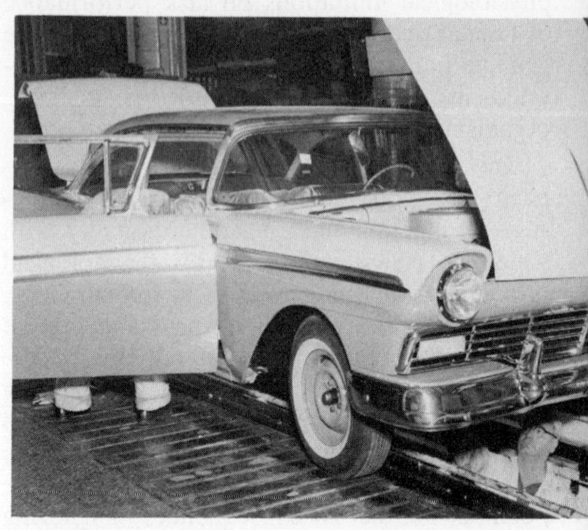

Simple work subdivision is shown in the automobile final assembly line very close to the drive-off point. The man in the pit is tightening a bumper bolt; the man leaning into the car is checking the front seat; and the barely visible man on the far side is having a final look under the hood. One man could do all of these tasks, but at a slower sustained speed.

cludes weighing the costs of the additional tools or equipment necessary to perform the new job complex by different methods.[25] In general the subdivision of work that leads to new tasks is a much more complex process, requiring a great deal more concern with costs, and technology, than is true in simple subdivision of work.

A good example of technical work subdivision is illustrated in the difference between custom molding and production molding. In custom molding, the skilled craftsman, known as a molder, takes a metal form and partially fills it with fine sand, tamping the sand down to firm it. He then takes the pattern of the piece to be molded and sets it in the sand, filling the form or flask to its brim. After further tamping, and levelling, a separation fluid is brushed on the surface of the sand. Then the upper flask is put in place, and more sand tamped in. Riser and gate holes are formed, and the two halves of the flask are then separated. The pattern is removed and any cores needed to produce inside cavities are set in place. The surface of the molded shape, now exposed with the pattern removed, is treated with a special liquid. The top flask is then replaced and the mold is ready to be poured full of metal. All of these tasks are done by the same man, the molder.

In production molding, each step is done by a different individual. Starting with an automatic molding machine that mechanically tamps the sand, the flask moves down a roller line to have cores set, surfaces sprayed, the two halves of the flask joined, and the metal poured at the end of the line. The mold may even continue through a cooling room and be shaken out only minutes after the hot metal was poured in.

Only where long runs and large quantities of relatively small cast items are needed does it become economical to substitute a production molding set-up for a custom operation. In making automobile parts, for example, production molding is highly economical. It will be noted, of course, that the subdivision of work on the production line changes completely the skills necessary. No single man on the line has the total skill of a custom molder. Furthermore, there is actual change in the technical features of the work, most notable being the substitution of the molding machine for hand tamping.

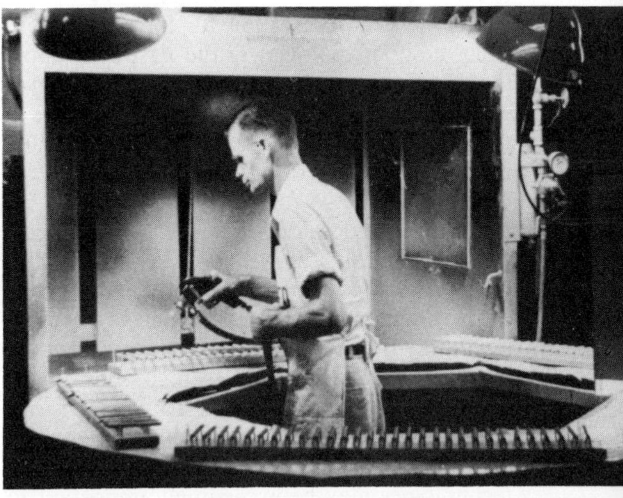

Technical work subdivision usually involves special production processes and investment in new equipment. In this operation, special spray painting equipment and spray booth are used because the items being painted are produced in sufficient quantity to warrant this subdivided task.

NEW WORK TASKS

Division of labor may result from establishing fundamentally new technologies. A machine may replace another to produce similar items, but the kind of skill required to operate the new machine may shift significantly. For example, when the Linotype replaced hand type setting, the printers who set type by hand had to learn an entirely new technology in order to qualify as Linotype operators. The Linotype really required new skills that had not previously existed. At the same time, the use of Linotypes did not wholly supplant handsetting, for in many cases the larger "display" type is still set by hand.

It is one of the fundamental characteristics of the new Industrial Revolution through which we are presently going that it gives rise to the invention of many new skills that had not previously existed. We are destined to see the rapid obsolescence of many skills and their replacement by newly created ones.[26]

TYPES OF NEW WORK TASKS

There are two types of new work tasks: (A) where the development of a technology creates an entirely new set of tasks not previously performed, and (B) where the development of technology substitutes new operations in fulfilling the same production functions.

Much of modern technology involves the creation of entirely new tasks not previously performed. Generally there are limitations on the extent to which old methods and old forms of production can be improved and perfected. The basic advances in industrial technology come as a consequence of new inventions and processes completely supplanting the old. Invention of new production processes is essentially a consequence of advances in knowledge, and the application of basic scientific discoveries to industrial production.[27]

The general motivation for introducing entirely new technologies is the desire to apply the rapidly growing body of scientific knowledge. The context of these motivations is a general notion of progress. It is not specifically related to a given operation, product, or factory. The impetus for basic technological innovation is seldom derived directly from operating problems. It has its roots in the attitudes of the society to experiment, to be imaginative in the creation of new technologies. Developments on the frontier of science are used to create new products, and to revolutionize the manufacture of old products. This point is important to note. It is clear that the obsolescence of a skill as a consequence of entirely new technologies may be exceedingly important to the individual whose skill is abandoned, and he may react personally to the situation. The reason for his being thrown upon the industrial scrapheap is not the consequence of the malice of management, or the desire to hurt him personally.[28]

Making a final test and inspection of a Klystron electronic tube. The product is new and much of its testing equipment had to be specially designed. This operator learned a special set of skills in order to fill this job.

The development of new technologies can be seen, for example, in the metals field where the newer metals like aluminum and magnesium, requiring quite different technologies in their production, have been developed to a high degree and are seriously competing with the older and more common metals like iron and copper and their alloys. At the time of this writing a new solid fuel has just been announced. It will replace petroleum products for jet and missile propulsion. The fuel is made from borax, and although manufacturing details are secret, it is safe to assume that the production technology is unique.

The second general form that creation of work tasks takes is the replacement of old tasks by entirely new ones that fulfill the same functions.[29] In simpler cases like clerical work, for example, the hand posting of ledgers may be supplanted by machine posting, and this in turn may be succeeded by a punchcard system, which is designed on an entirely different principle. The hand-poster, the machine-poster, and the punchcard operator really do quite different activities, and for all intents and purposes are performing quite different tasks. Yet, their functions are identical—to keep a set of ledgers, important in the conduct of the business. Often the changes in tasks created by technical developments are very great, and the old operators may not be really competent to undertake the new tasks.

The major human consequences of new tasks are to make obsolete and obsolescent certain skills, creating new jobs at the same time. In individual instances, the worker whose job is no longer necessary may face very severe readjustments in order to find another job. At the same time, those seeking work may find a real opportunity to develop a career in the new tasks that have been developed out of new technologies.

HUMAN CONSEQUENCES OF DIVISION OF LABOR

We have noted that in the engineering view of the subdivision of work, the human being is viewed essentially as a physiological organism. The limits to which subdivision of labor can be carried are a consequence of this narrow consideration of the human being.

When we take into account the social aspects of the human organism, we discover that there may be additional important limitations on division of labor.[30]

REPETITION AND MONOTONY

Repetition of task typically accompanies the breakdown of more complex tasks into simpler parts. What the subdivision achieves is limitation in number and complexity of task activities with a consequent increase in their repetition.

There has been a long record of research on the impact of work repetition on human beings.[31] The evidence is by no means conclusive. Repetitiveness of the tasks, together with the monotony that it is likely to engender, has at least the following consequences for workers.

First, the task itself comes to be viewed as a mechanical activity having relatively little emotional or symbolic value. The worker finds little basis for attaching his sentiments to his work. As a consequence, the work itself has very little meaningful content to him. It seems improbable that a worker can become highly excited and interested over a long period of time in the continual tightening of bolt number 63 on a moving sub-assembly that passes before him at the rate of 30 a minute. Thus, one of the first consequences of work subdivision is to provide a basis for alienating the worker from his work. He finds no grounds on which to feel attached to his work out of a sense of pride in workmanship, or out of the challenge that is likely to arise in connection with performing varied and sometimes difficult tasks.[32]

A second consequence of the monotony of work is the opportunity which repetition provides for reverie and "letting the mind run away." The very minimal involvement required of the worker's attention permits him to perform his activities with his interests focused elsewhere.[33] The extent to which the attention of workers can be completely divorced from their work can be noted in the conversations that occur on assembly lines. On grounds of a basic lack of emotional attachment to his work, and the opportunities it provides for non-working behavior on the job, the worker is likely to be alienated from his work as a source of satisfaction.

The continuous strip mill produced a major technological revolution in the steel industry. It increased output many times, at the same time displacing thousands of workers. Part of the continuous strip mill involves passing the strip steel through an acid bath as a "pickling" process to remove oxidized scale before the steel goes to the cold rolling mill to be reduced to its final thickness. This operator controls the rate at which the ribbon of steel is fed into the acid bath.

FRAGMENTS VS. UNITY IN WORK

A second human consequence of the subdivision of work is the worker's relative feeling of incompleteness about his job. It has been noted by Walker and Guest and others, in their studies of industrial workers, that there is an almost nostalgic concern with having the opportunity to do a complete thing, or produce a complete item at some time.[34] The worker clearly recognizes that he is, in fact, a cog in a machine. Out of lack of a sense of wholeness about his work, the worker comes to recognize that his particular job has relatively little subjective meaning in a final product that may be very remote and difficult to perceive.

In psychological terms it can be said that there is lack of closure on the part of the worker, so that he fails to see his role in an integrated operation. As a consequence there may result indifference to the work, indifference to the quality of the work, and a focus

On the chassis assembly in an automobile plant, this worker does five operations. Here he is connecting the exhaust pipe to the manifold with a power driven wrench that hangs convenient to the work spot where he needs it. Walker and Guest report that similar workers in an automobile assembly plant openly express a wish for the opportunity to put together an entire automobile, not just fragments of it.

on means as ends in themselves. When the end product is either difficult to see, or so complex that the individual input into the product is hidden or disguised, attention is likely to shift to the instrumental aspects of the work rather than its goal aspects. A worker may become preoccupied with keeping his work place clean because this is necessary in fulfilling his particular task. But the more he thinks about his work the more it seems to become only a matter of keeping his work place clean, rather than really turning out the products for which he is responsible. The instrumental aspects of work become ends.

In general, it can be suggested that the subdivision of labor tends to make the final product so remote from the particular task as to further alienate the worker from his work. It has been shown, for example, in the case of a number of companies that have queried their workers as to the products turned out, that there is a high rate of ignorance even as to the basic products the firm produces.

Subdivision of work tends to leave the worker indifferent to the small contribution he makes to a larger whole. Without any further attempt on the part of management to make clear the relationship to the final product, the worker is likely to find himself highly indifferent to it.

FATIGUE AND WORK PACE

A third and equally important human consequence of the subdivision of tasks results from the methods of work control. The degree to which individual behavior results from technological requirements is emphasized when there is need for control of speed, quantity, and quality of output in subdivided work. In regular line production it may reach the point where the individual is not even free to leave the line for matters of personal necessity unless and until he has been replaced by a relief operator.

The sense of being tied to an impersonally operating and mechanically determined work tempo and pace tends further to emphasize the machine-like aspects of work. Those studies that have been made of the effect of measured pace on workers seem to indicate that the objection is not basically to an over-extended physical demand on the body, but rather to the lack of variation and personal control of work pace. This is particularly true in the objections that workers often express to the fact that they cannot themselves vary the pace at which they operate.[35]

OUTPUT STANDARDS AND EXCEPTIONAL PERFORMANCE

Steadiness of pace has still another effect which is an unplanned-for consequence of work control. In the interests of keeping a steady rate of output, and minimizing variations in quality, the control standards have to have both a maximum and a minimum level. Consequently, in subdivided tasks, there is likely to be little opportunity for exceptional perfomance by an individual above and beyond the maximum requirements for his task.

Consequently, management is faced with the need for setting upper limits on output and upper limits on performance as well as lower limits. This of course does not accord with the typical management exhortations for maximum output by individuals. It can be seen here that the requirements of the technology supersede the requirements of morality in the situation. Management faces the interesting dilemma of how to keep up the moral pressure to produce at a high rate in a situation where the top limits of production are determined necessarily by technical interests.

In those situations where the technology sets upper limits on output, individuals may still manage in rather limited cases to show exceptionally high output above and beyond the maximum limits. However, under these circumstances the worker typically takes his reward in the form of increased leisure. For example, the worker may be able to build up a "bank" ahead of the production line, and slack off for a period of time until his bank has been used up.

It is interesting to note that typically management does not want to know about these things. Workers, of course, usually hide such exceptional performance from management. The reason management is relatively uninterested in the opportunities for such outstanding performance is that should it become the standard, then the whole line has to be redesigned in order that the flow of work may be speeded up to satisfy the rate of output of the maximum operation.[36] In the end there may be involved a great deal of technological change and a great deal of restudy, and sometimes retooling, in order to bring the total unit up to the level of the fastest subdivided task within it. This constitutes one of the significant, difficult problems for mechanical engineers in designing production processes.

For example, on a highly efficient foundry production line, the author has heard engineers asserting that they had hundreds of additional technological changes they wanted to introduce. Their main problem was not to find these individual changes that would improve the rate of output or lower the unit cost. Their problem was to figure out how to incorporate each change, and the correlating changes that it necessitated. For in accordance with the need for work integration, the production unit is always affected when any of its parts is changed.

There are important pressures on those who manage production lines to minimize the changes at any point once the subdivided tasks have been integrated into an operating unit. The delicate balance of an operating unit may be severely distorted and disturbed if untoward production on either the high or low side is obtained at any point in the work complex.

WORKERS AND TECHNOLOGY

Highly complex integrated production units are delicately balanced systems. To make a production unit too complex may build rigidities into it that make it less susceptible to further change and further improvement. Therefore, one of the limits on additional subdivision of tasks may well be the cost of making further change once the production unit is established. When flexibility in operations becomes limited, it may be important to consider whether or not the subdivision of functions has been carried too far.

In general, it should be pointed out that the subdivision of work has as one of its major consequences the reduction of importance of work itself as a center of interest for workers. The job simply does not provide significant meaning and value to the individual. The worker finds it difficult to attach himself to work as a central feature of his life.[37]

Specialization of work has largely positive human consequences. It does not threaten the integrity of the human personality, but rather tends to support it. Subdivision of work, on the other hand, reduces man to the lowest social common denominator. It alienates man from industrial work. New technologies may either further specialization of work or further its subdivision. In the next chapter we will give special attention to the influences of automation on man's relations to his work.

NOTES FOR CHAPTER 10

1 Some general perspective on industrial technology can be gained from the following sources: S. Giedion, *Mechanization Takes Command* (London: Oxford Univeristy Press, 1948); Harry Jerome, *Mechanization in Industry* (New York: National Bureau of Economic Research, 1934); Emil Lederer, "Technology," in *Encyclopaedia of the Social Sciences,* 14:553-560; L. L. Lorwin and J. M. Blair, "Technology in Our Economy," United States Congress, Temporary National Economic Committee, "*Investigation of Concentration of Economic Power,* Monograph No. 22 (Washington: Government Printing Office, 1941); and A. P. Usher, *A History of Mechanical Invention* (New York: The Macmillan Company, 1929).

2 As Chapter 7 points out, a central theme in the rational management of business enterprises is the application of modern technology to operations. In the European literature the application of technology is given the name "rationalization" which is most descriptive of scientific management. See for example C. S. Myers, *Business Rationalization* (London: Pitman, 1932).

3 Adopted from H. J. Brown, "Weaving, Hand Loomed," *Encyclopedia Americana,* 29:136 (1953 edition).

4 Adopted from M. S. Woolman and E. B. McGowan, *Textiles* (New York: The Macmillan Company, 1943), p. 53.

5 This point was given particular emphasis by Hyacinthe Dubreuil, *Standards* (Paris: B. Grasset, 1929).

6 Cf. U. S. Department of Labor, Bureau of Labor Statistics, "Productivity of Labor and Industry, Technological Changes and Labor Displacements," *Bulletin 616* (Washington: Government Printing Office, 1936).

7 A good general reference dealing with this point is: Mary Fledderus and Mary Van Kleek, *Technology and Livelihood: An Inquiry Into the Changing Technological Basis for Production as Affecting Employment and Living Standards* (New York: Russell Sage Foundation, 1944).

8 This is one of the major conclusions in the pioneering study of the effects of industrialization on under-developed areas, W. E. Moore, *Industrialization and Labor: Social Aspects of Economic Development* (Ithaca: Cornell University Press, 1951); see also his "Labor Attitudes toward Industrialization in Underdeveloped Countries," *American Economic Review,* 45:156-165 (May, 1955).

9 That this is not a phenomenon in capitalist production alone is revealed in a comparative study of mechanization in the Soviet Union and the Western world: Georges Friedmann, *Problems du Machinisme en URSS et dans les Pays Capitalistes* (Paris: Editions Sociales Internationales, 1934).

10 Cf. Lewis Mumford, *Technics and Civilization* (New York: Harcourt, Brace and Co., 1934).

11 A widely used socioeconomic classification of occupations designed to measure class position is Alba M. Edwards, *A Social-Economic Grouping of the Gainful Workers of the United States* (Washington: Government Printing Office, 1938); the Warner six-fold division of class structure, which emphasizes occupation and source of income, was first presented in W. L. Warner and P. S. Lunt, *The Social Life of a Modern Community,* first volume of the "Yankee City" series (New Haven: Yale University Press, 1941).

12 The symbiotic interdependence with respect to industrial activity is emphasized in S. H. Slichter, *Modern Economic Society* (New York: Henry Holt and Co., 1931), especially Chapter 6, "Specialization." The sense of class solidarity that is the consequence of industrial specialization is revealed in an analysis of worker cohesion, E. J. Hobsbawm, "The Machine Breakers," *Past and Present,* 1 (February, 1952). The most complete analysis of social solidarity resulting from industrial specialization of workers is: Clark Kerr and Abraham Siegel, "The Interindustry Propensity to Strike—An International Comparison," Chapter 14 in A. Kornhauser, R. Dubin, and A. Ross (eds.) *Industrial Conflict* (New York: McGraw-Hill, 1954).

13 An early and excellent study of specialization in four firms is M. Fairchild, "The Significance of Skill," *Personnel Journal,* 9:128-175 (August, 1930).

14 Otto Lipmann, "Der Anteil des Menschen am Produktionseffekt," in 4me. Conference Internationale du Psychotechnique, *Report* (Paris: 1929), pp. 224 ff, makes the point that small job differences are important to the worker but scarcely recognizable to the outsider.

15 W. L. Warner and J. O. Low, *The Social System of the Modern Factory: The Strike, a Social Analysis* (New Haven: Yale University Press, 1947), especially Chapter 5, "The Break in the Skill

NOTES FOR CHAPTER 10 (CONT.)

Hierarchy," and Chapter 9, "The Workers Lose Status in the Community."

[16] Daniel Bell, "Adjusting Men to Machines," *Commentary,* 3:78-88 (January, 1947), criticizes human relations research in industry as reflecting management's conception of workers as means for getting out production. Whatever the moral consequences of this position, the fact of the matter is that people are an integral part of the production process and are viewed as means, as we have indicated in analyzing their training for simplified tasks. A very early view of the alleged degredation of skilled labor in industry is contained in Andrew Ure, *Philosophy of Manufactures* (London: 1835).

[17] A classic study that laid principal foundations for time and motion study is F. B. Gilbreth, *Bricklaying System* (New York: M. C. Clark, 1909).

[18] Gilbreth systematized his ideas about motion study in *Motion Study* (New York: Van Nostrand, 1911), and with his wife, Lillian, later published *Applied Motion Study* (New York: Sturgis and Walton, 1917). Fredrick W. Taylor did some earlier work than the Gilbreth's, and is often acclaimed as the father of scientific management and work subdivision. See his *The Principles of Scientific Management* (New York: Harper & Brothers, 1911). From these beginnings there has been a very rapid development of motion and time study as a standard set of techniques for designing jobs and determining their work pace. There have been at least 60 major titles published in this field which can readily be found in the library card catalog.

[19] See C. R. Walker, "The Problem of the Repetitive Job," *Harvard Business Review,* 28:54-58 (May, 1950) who reports on a study of jobs at International Business Machines Corporation and concludes that more output and lower costs do not indefinitely result from continuous subdivision of jobs.

[20] Cf. H. C. Weston and S. Adams, "Observations on the Design of Cotton Machinery in Relation to the Operator," *Journal of the National Institute of Industrial Psychology,* 5:97-107 (April, 1930), in which the authors criticize the machine design because it requires either artificial or dangerous movements of the operator. They propose that machines be tested with human operators before designs are accepted, to make sure that bodily movements required are physiologically compatible. This general period in the development of industrial engineering was probably the high point of the mechanistic and physiological approach to human operators.

[21] Also called work flow. See F. L. W. Richardson, Jr., and C. R. Walker, "Work Flow and Human Relations," *Harvard Business Review,* 27:107-122 (January, 1949).

[22] The prototype of the modern assembly line was established at the Highland Park Plant of the Ford Motor Company in 1914.

[23] The typical narrowness of emphasis is revealed in D. W. Harding, "A Note on the Subdivision of Assembly Work," *Journal of the National Institute of Industrial Psychology,* 5:261-264 (January, 1931). A well reasoned defense of the engineer and his outlook contrasted with an "artistic" view of work is contained in H. S. Person, "Man and the Machine: The Engineer's Point of View," *Annals,* The American Academy of Political and Social Science, 149: 88-93 (May, 1930).

[24] The mechanistic position has always had its attackers even from within engineering itself. See: C. S. Myers, "The Efficiency Engineer and the Industrial Psychologist," *Journal of the National Institute of Industrial Psychology,* 1:168-172 (January, 1923); and G. H. Miles and P. Angles, "Psychology and Machine Design," *Journal of the National Institute of Industrial Psychology,* 3:159-161 (July, 1926); both articles stress the psychological aspects of work performance. A modern statement of the same position is contained in F. C. Bartlett, "Men, Machines, and Productivity," *Occupational Psychology* 22:190-196 (October, 1948); with the final culmination of this emphasis on individual psychology being reached in laboratory experiments for studying work movements and positions as in: A. Chapanis, W. R. Gardner, and O. T. Morgan, *Applied Experimental Psychology: Human Factors in Engineering Design* (New York: The Macmillan Company, 1951). Engineering of work activities has even been taken over by labor unions with the union using its own staff engineers to advise management on work design; see Solomon Barkin, "The Technical Engineering Service of an American Trade Union," *International Labour Review,* 61:609-636 (June, 1950).

[25] Cf. A. L. Gitlow, "An Economic Evaluation of the Gains and Costs of Technological Change," in Solomon Barkin, *et al.* (eds.), *Industrial Productivity* (Champaign: Industrial Relations Research Association, 1951), pp. 172-193.

[26] See for example Martin Segal, "Introduction of Technological Changes in Industrial Plants," *Explorations in Entrepreneurial History,* 6:41-61 (October, 1953); and Solomon Barkin, "Job Redesign: A Technique for an Era of Full Employment," in William Haber, *et al.* (eds.), *Manpower in the United States: Problems and Policies* (New York: Harper and Brothers, 1954), pp. 39-50.

[27] The following references are particularly pertinent: Yale Brozen, "Research, Technology, and Productivity," in Solomon Barkin, *et al.* (eds.), *op. cit.*, pp. 25-49; Pierre Chevenard, "On the Function of Science in Works," *The Engineer* 162:279-281 (September, 1936); R. W. Maclaurin, The Process of Technological Innovation: The Launching of a New Scientific Industry," *American Economic Review* 40:90-112 (March, 1950). A general treatise on cultural change dealing with the entire culture is: Homer Barnett, *Innovation: The Basis of Cul-*

NOTES FOR CHAPTER 10 (CONT.)

tural Change (New York: McGraw-Hill Book Co., 1953). A preview of the extent of future change resulting from scientific advance and technological change is given in "People, Products, and Progress: 1975," *Nation's Business* 43:9:56 ff. (September, 1955).

[28] See Robert K. Merton, "The Machine, the Worker, and the Engineer," *Science,* 105:79-84 (January, 1947) where the suggestion is made that at least some technological advance is planned by management as a threat to workers to make them more tractable. Over the broad sweep of changing technology this is at best only a transitory reason for introducing technical change, or threatening to do so.

[29] For specific examples see: J. H. Mitchell, "The Mechanization of the Miner," *Human Factor,* 4:139-150 (April, 1933); J. W. Riegel, *Management, Labor and Technological Change* (Ann Arbor: University of Michigan Press, 1942); and E. L. Trist and K. W. Bansforth, "Some Social and Psychological Consequences of the Longwall Method of Coal-Getting," *Human Relations,* 4:3-38 (December, 1951).

[30] Three general references dealing with these limitations are: International Labour Office, *The Social Aspects of Rationalization,* Studies and Reports, Series B., No. 18, (Geneva: The Office, 1931); E. D. Smith and R. C. Nyman, *Technology and Labor* (New Haven: Yale University Press, 1939); and Thorstein Veblen, *The Instinct of Workmanship and the State of the Industrial Arts* (New York: The Macmillan Company, 1914). Two recent case studies that show some of the limiting factors affecting the application of technical changes in production are : S. B. Levine, "Union-Management Relations and Technical Change: A Case Study," *Current Economic Comment,* 13:24-41 (November, 1951); and H. O. Ronken and P. R. Lawrence, *Administering Changes: A Case Study of Human Relations in a Factory* (Boston: Harvard University Graduate School of Business Administration, 1952).

[31] The English psychologists were particularly interested in the study of repetition and boredom. See, for example, the early works like C. S. Myers, *Mind and Work* (London: Putnam, 1920); and representative studies like the following that were published among the *Industrial Fatigue Research Board Reports:* S. Wyatt and L. A. Fraser, "The Comparative Effects of Variety and Uniformity in Work," No. 52 (London: His Majesty's Stationery Office, 1928); and H. M. Vernon, S. Wyatt, and A. D. Ogden, "The Extent and Effects of Variety in Repetitive Work," No. 26 (London: His Majesty's Stationery Office, 1926).

[32] See: Georges Friedmann, "Outline for a Psycho-Sociology of Assembly Line Work," *Human Organization,* 12:15-20 (Winter, 1954); and the fictionalized account of workers' reaction to automobile assembly line work, Wessel Smitter, *F.O.B. Detroit* (New York: Harper & Brothers, 1938).

[33] Cf. S. Wyatt, "Boredom in Industry," *Personnel Journal,* 8:161-171 (October, 1929).

[34] The fragmentation of work with its resultant loss of meaning was recognized early. See, for example, E. Sachsenberg, "Psychologie der Arbeit am Laufanden Band," *Maschinebau* 4 (1925). It took only experience with subdivided tasks and not trained observational skill to see this consequence of such work as William Green, then president of the A.F. of L. revealed in: "The Effect of the New Standardization Programs of American Industry," *Annals,* The American Academy of Political and Social Science, 137:43-46 (May, 1928). See also C. R. Walker and R. H. Guest, *The Man on the Assembly Line* (Cambridge: Harvard University Press, 1953).

[35] A work summarizing lengthy research on fatigue and work pace is G. C. Homans (ed.), *Fatigue of Workers* (New York: Reinhold Publishing Co., 1941). A shorter summary of the conclusions of English industrial psychologists is contained in G. H. Miles, "Fatigue from the Industrial Point of View," *Human Factor,* 11:8-15 (January, 1937). The relationships between fatigue and rest periods are given particular emphasis in: S. H. Bartley and Eloise Chute, *Fatigue and Impairment in Men* (New York: McGraw-Hill Book Co., 1947); and G. H. Shepard, "Effect of Rest Periods on Production," *Personnel Journal,* 7:186-202 (October, 1928), in which it is reported that optimal rest periods are about 16 percent of total work periods. The rest period argument, although largely depending on the need for rest for recovery from physiological fatigue, must also take into account the break in work pace that a rest introduces. If Shepard's findings are general, then approximately one-sixth of the working time should be devoted to rest as a break from routine.

[36] This is suggested in C. R. Walker, "Adjustment, Individual and Social, to Technological Change," in Solomon Barkin, *et al.* (eds.), *Industrial Productivity,* pp. 194-211.

[37] This is perhaps the major conclusion of Georges Friedmann, *Industrial Society: The Emergence of the Human Problems of Automation,* edited with an introduction by Harold L. Sheppard (Glencoe: The Free Press, 1955). Friedmann's book is a major attempt at a cross cultural analysis of the human problems of modern industry. Sometimes the polemic positions of the author obscure his conclusions or substitute for them, but this volume is important to anyone interested in more detail on the human consequences of industrial technology.

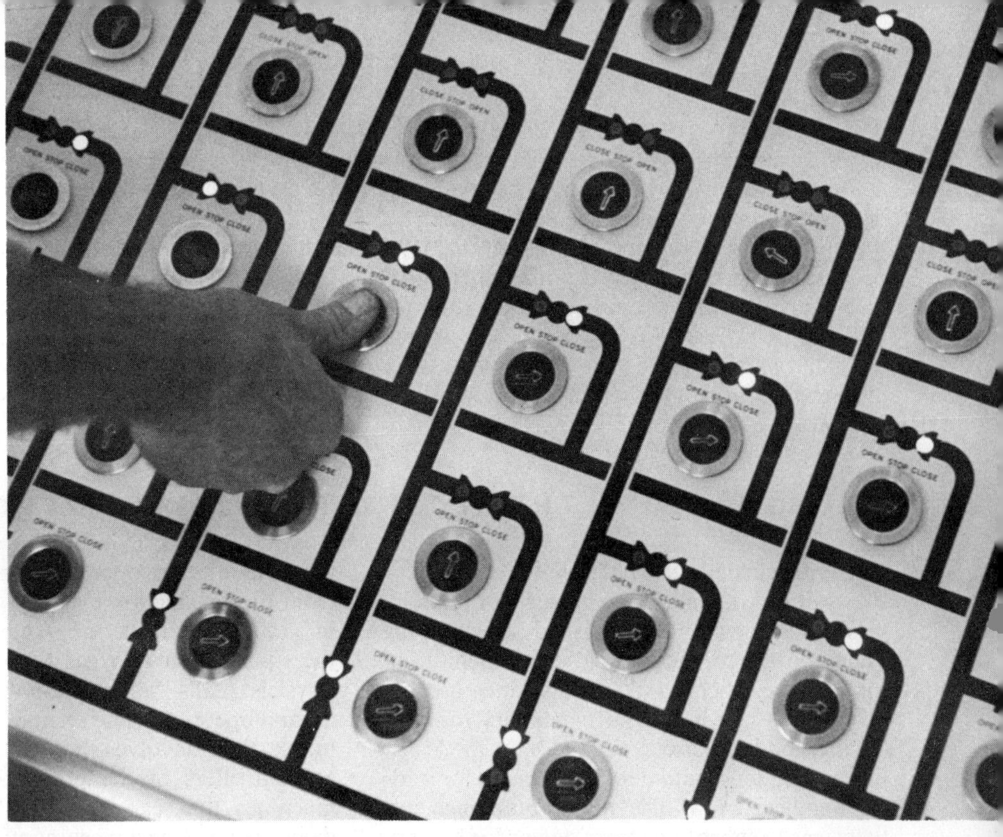

We are likely to think of automation as push button production. Actually, in true automation even the human hand is removed from the push button, and electronic controls take command. This picture shows the control board on a petroleum pipeline.

Chapter **11**

AUTOMATION AND HUMAN RELATIONS

Automation is a new form of industrial technology. The central human issue in automation is this: will automation of production processes result in specialization or subdivision of work assignments?

When automation results in greater *specialization* of work, people can tolerate working in automated factories and offices, with very much of the same social environment that now exists in work organizations. Should automation lead to more *subdivision* of work, then most assuredly we need to invent new kinds of social structures for organizations to make it possible for human beings to work in them.

The answers to this basic alternative are still being sought. We have some evidence, and a lot of opinion to guide us. The evidence, however, is not conclusive. This chapter, therefore, is partially speculative in character because no one has yet demonstrated unequivocally the consequences of automation for working behavior. It is nevertheless essential to analyze automation, for its revolution in industrial technology is already upon us.

There are two basic objectives of the chapter. We first want to make clear what is meant by automation. We then want to see what automation does to work assignments. In satisfying this second objective, we will examine the impact of automation on actual work operations; on the skills and training needed in the labor force; and on the nature of management functions.

AUTOMATION: THE SECOND INDUSTRIAL REVOLUTION

The original Industrial Revolution saw the substitution of machine power for human power. This was accomplished by applying steam power to mechanical equipment used for turning fibers and metals into useable products. Much industrial machinery for producing goods followed very closely in design the production equipment used in the preceding handicraft era. The major difference initially was to substitute steam power for human, water, wind, and animal power.

The subsequent evolution of production equipment took the general form of building machines that included the human operator as an essential part of the cycle of operations. The first stage in early production equipment was one in which output was speeded up with steam power, still using basic handicraft technology. Things could be done faster with outside sources of power. Therefore, the human operator could turn out more goods per unit of working time.

The second stage in the evolution of production equipment came when machines were designed to operate with very small tolerances allowed in the variation of dimensions of finished products. This was achieved by designing precision into the equipment, rather than leaving it in the hands of the operator. With the development of greater speed and greater precision, the principal features that distinguish the first Industrial Revolution from the preceding handicraft era were firmly established. Further developments in industrial technology emphasized greater speed, higher precision, or both.

The second Industrial Revolution, which has been named "automation" by John Diebold, is based on the fundamental assumption that the human operator can be eliminated from the production cycle as an essential link in getting work done.[1] Automation permits the substitution of what Louis Ridenour, the physicist, calls "information machines" for the human operator.[2] The second Industrial Revolution, then, involves the displacement of men as controllers of the production process, by machines that can exercise this control. Indeed, in some instances control can be exercised more adequately by machines than by human operators, especially where extremely high speed controls are necessary.

In the broadest terms, therefore, we can view automation as finally freeing production equipment from dependence on human operators. The first Industrial Revolution changed the form of working behavior for the human machine operator, but throughout the whole development of our subsequent technology we have consciously designed the human operator into the production processes as an essential controlling machine, indeed, the only generally available. The second Industrial Revolution, through automation, eliminates the direct control of output by human operators. The first Industrial Revolution sharpened man's intellectual faculties as these were applied to industrial output. The second Industrial Revolution eliminates the need for man's intelligence in direct operations, substituting machines that are equal to or better than man's intelligence in controlling production operations.[3]

OLD TECHNOLOGICAL ELEMENTS IN AUTOMATION

There are two old technological elements present in automation. The first is the use of power-driven equipment. The second is the use of mechanical or automatic transfer systems for moving work from one operating station to the succeeding one. Both of these technological elements are obvious in any present production line; they represent the refinements of the older production technology, which Diebold has called "Detroit automation."[4]

The use of power driven machinery is evident in any factory. Motive power is used to drive the machines that process fibers, metals, liquids, and gases. The most common type of motive power is the electric motor. Indeed, even the current conceptions of the use of atomic power involve converting the power potentials of fissionable materials into electric energy for use in industrial output. All automated operations need sources of power to energize equipment doing the work. In this respect, automated equipment will not differ materially from production equipment now used in industrial operations.

The second old technological element in automation is the use of mechanical means to move work in process from one operation to the next. The classic example of such transfer equipment is the continuous production line. An assembly line, for example, may start with the basic structural member of the assembly placed on the line. As this piece moves toward the end of the line, items are assembled onto it at succeding work stations. The assembly of an automobile engine is an excellent illustration. The motor blocks start at the beginning of the line all machined, bored, and tapped to receive the operating parts like pistons and carburetors, as the assembly moves toward completion. The block moves either on a power-driven line that transfers it from one work station to the next, or else it is shoved on a roller bed by each worker to the next. Sometimes the parts are even assembled while the block is in motion.

An automated transfer mechanism on an automobile engine block line. The mechanism at the center turns the block 90° and then flips it over so that its top faces down, as the blocks move from lower left to upper right. The mechanism, furthermore, sends more blocks to the far line, which is longer than the near line, so that the two lines will each have a constant flow of work on them. In principle such transfer systems are old, but refinements like this example are of recent origin.

Some of the highly developed transfer equipment is a good deal more complicated than a moving production line. This equipment may use mechanical, hydraulic, or other devices to position, turn, flip over, and otherwise manipulate the work in process. As the piece being worked reaches a given place in the transfer system, it is shifted into a new position, readying it for the next operation. Such transfer equipment is used, for example, in the machining of automobile engine blocks. This involves manipulating a heavy casting into a number of different positions as the succeeding machining operations are performed. The transfers from one operating stage to the next are handled automatically by the transfer equipment.

These two elements of modern automation —power-driven equipment and mechanical transfer—are basic elements in our present non-automated technology. Their fullest development is "Detroit automation," which has symbolized to the world some of the most advanced applications of machine design in the first industrial Revolution. Powered production machines and transfer equipment will remain basic elements in the automated technology of the second Industrial Revolution.

NEW TECHNOLOGICAL ELEMENTS IN AUTOMATION

Two technological elements have been introduced that are new to modern production.

A good example of automatic programing. When this machine is operating it is programed to drill 20 holes in a crankshaft from four different directions. Automation moves the crankshafts into place before each battery of drills, starts and stops the drilling action, and then sends the crankshafts to their next machining operation. This machine is stopped while the worker changes worn drill bits.

These, combined with the two existing technological elements, provide the basis for automation. The first new element is the programing of the operations of equipment in advance, rather than depending upon the operators' programing of the equipment while it is running. The second, and more fundamental, new element is the development of "feedback" mechanisms for automatic self-control and self-regulation of equipment.

Programing of operations means telling a machine what to do in an orderly series of steps. The usual programing, involving a human operator, consists of training him to follow a sequence of predetermined activities. Once trained, the operator knows what to do at each point in the sequence, and is the controller of the sequential operations. In more complicated programing, still using human operators, a mechanic may start with a set of blueprints showing what is to be produced. He operates his equipment in ways he has already learned, often at very high skill levels, to produce the blueprinted product. A craftsman may take a blueprint of a metal object and turn a piece of metal on a lathe; mill some of its surfaces on a milling machine; use a drill press to drill holes in it; tap some of the holes with threads; and hone other of the holes or some of the surfaces. In the end, the piece of finished metal duplicates what is called for in the blueprint. The mechanic has programed each step in turning out the finished item.

In the illustrations just examined, the operator acts as the programing agent. He decides what is to be done, and operates machines in doing it. He is the one who starts the machine, stops it, makes checks of accuracy in process, adjusts the settings on the machine, and sharpens or changes the cutting tools. In an office, a typist will take either dictation or written materials and reproduce them with her typewriter. The typist programs the typewriter to produce what is required.

When the programing phase of production is automated, the equipment is given its instructions in a mechanical or electronic prearranged form. This may be a punched tape, like the one used with the MIT experimental milling machine.[5] The tape is fed into a decoding machine that translates the punches on the tape into electrical impulses that are sent to the machine's controls. These controls are operated in accordance with the instructions that the decoded tape gives to the machine. A teletype machine, such as is used in communicating messages over long distances, does essentially the same thing. An operator, manipulating the typewriter keyboard at the point of origin of the message, activates electrical impulses that are decoded at a receiving machine, which then automatically types on paper the message being sent.

Automatic programing enters into the operations of machines at two essential points. The regular operations of the machine may be predetermined and programed for it. Once done, the programed series of operations is then transmitted as instructions to the machine. The machine carries out exactly those instructions given to it.

In some operations, particularly high speed operations, programing may also be used to keep the machine, or the production process, within the range of acceptable error set for it. That is, operating changes may also be programed. For example, in all metal cutting equipment there is inevitable wear on the cutting tools. It is then necessary to adjust, or even replace, the cutting tools when they no longer cut the metal to required tolerances. Machines may be programed in advance to make in-process tool adjustments or replacements as required.

There are important technical problems involved in automatic programing of machines or production processes, but it will suffice here to mention that a central problem is that of oscillation. By oscillation is meant an under or over response by the equipment to the directing signal given to it. A good example is in the use of radar fire control equipment on anti-aircraft guns. The radar tracks planes and is continually searching the sky. The movements of the massive gun follow its radar tracking equipment, but there is usually a slight lag. By the time the gun has moved from angle A to angle C to follow the radar, the radar may be back at angle B, issuing signals to return to that position before the gun has fully complied with the original signal. Such conflicting signals, under certain conditions, may amplify the erroneous, random motions of the gun instead of correcting them, even to the point of rendering the whole system ineffective. Many of the problems of oscillation in automatic programing of operations have been solved, while others still await analysis.[6]

Programing with mechanical and electronic directions to operating equipment replaces the human operator as the controller of the equipment. The programing of a piece of equipment may be done either by a human operator, or by directions given to the equipment from non-human controls. Automation is increasingly replacing the human operator as the director of operating equipment and production processes.

The second fundamentally new technological aspect of automation is the development of "feedback" systems. A feedback system is a mechanical or electronic way of securing information from an on-going operation. This information is then used as a basis for controlling or programing that operation.

Feedback systems are of two sorts: closed and open systems. An open feedback system is one in which information, not solely a product of operating conditions, is fed into the programing of operations. For example, a thermostat set outside a house will control the heating system in response to atmospheric conditions out-of-doors. The information brought into the control system is not a product, in this instance, of the operation of the heating system itself.

A closed feedback system is one in which only that information having to do with the on-going operation is fed back into the programing mechanisms to control the operation. Thus, when the thermostat is put in the room, a fall in room temperature turns the heating system on, raising the room temperature to a programed point, at which time the heating system is turned off. The heat in the room is a product of the room temperature and the output of the heating system. These two are kept in balance by the settings on the thermostat. The thermostat is a combined mechanical and electronic closed feedback system. Some closed feedback systems are entirely electronic and others are entirely mechanical.

The feedback element in automation requires three essential mechanisms. The first is a system of receptors to receive information about operating conditions that are to be controlled. The second mechanism is a center where the received information is translated, in accordance with the desired operations, into directions for the operating scheme. The third essential mechanism for a feedback system is a set of effectors for sending out messages to control production operations. Using a biological analogy we can describe a feedback system in production operations as consisting of receptor "nerves" for securing information about the production scheme, a "brain" for transforming this information into a set of directions for future operations, and finally, effector "muscles" for giving directions for the next stages of operations.

In principle, control can be removed, through succeeding stages, from the points of actual operations. That is, each "brain" can be connected through receptors and effectors to a "higher level brain." Finally, the total control of all operations can be vested in a "super brain." This is the automatic factory![7]

The enormous significance of automation should now be apparent. Automation, through automatic programing and feedback of information, can do all the essential operations that formerly used man's unique contribution to production. The human operator was able to remember instructions and to think through the meaning of operating information for succeeding steps in work. Automatic programing takes the place of man's memory. Feedback systems take the place of thinking through the meaning of information about the operating system for future operations.

Man has finally lost his unique monopoly of memory and thinking as applied to work! Gadgets can do it as well in many instances. Indeed, in especially fast or complex operations the gadgets can do it even better than man.[8]

It really staggers the imagination to contemplate the significance of automation for work and our civilization. Edward Bellamy, at the turn of the century, wrote a prophetic novel that foretold man's ultimate leisure from work as machines increasingly were able to look after themselves.[9] But even he did not dare contemplate the science-fiction-like drama of machines capable of reproducing themselves. Von Neumann, one of the most distinguished modern mathematicians, did exactly that, and demonstrated that, in principle, self-reproduction is possible![10]

The second Industrial Revolution is upon us. You who read this book will live through some of its major developments. Out of our new automated technology will come profound social changes with such rapidity that each succeeding year will show measurable differences from the past. It is a challenge, knowing some of the potentialities of the second Industrial Revolution, to predict its far-reaching consequences.[11] In this book we must reluctantly restrict ourselves to the consequence of automation for work and the worker.

AUTOMATION AND WORK OPERATIONS

What will automated technology do to men at work? That is the fundamental question of this chapter.

On the face of it it seems entirely clear that many jobs using human operators can be redesigned to eliminate them. Control equipment can be substituted for human operators. This displacement of human operators will occur differentially, however. That is, there is little point in introducing automatic controls on a pick and shovel. On the other hand, there may, indeed, be great savings achieved in introducing automatic controls on a coal cutting machine in a mine. It must be remembered that automatic controls are always coupled with machine driven equipment.

This suggests immediately that traditional hand work for which power machinery has not been developed or found economical, will remain relatively untouched by automation. The man with a pick and shovel can feel fairly secure that his job will not be taken by an automated robot until he is first replaced by power digging equipment.[12]

On the other hand, where we now have power driven machines, we can expect immediate and general adoption of automatic controls. It is in the factory and office that automation will move forward most rapidly.[13]

REPLACEMENT OF HUMAN OPERATORS

Human operators will be replaced in work operations that are already mechanized. The one major restriction on this is the cost of replacing or modifying present equipment. Where capital costs justify the replacement of human operators, it will come rapidly. In the present phase of our economy, with unprecedented capital expansion in production facilities, the situation definitely favors rapid automation of production.

What happens, then, to production operations from the standpoint of workers? It is clear that entirely new kinds of jobs will come into being, requiring large numbers of people. Most observers of present-day automation seem agreed that the first impact of automation will be to eliminate highly repetitive and extensively subdivided jobs. That is, the growth of Detroit automation, which led to further and further subdivision of work operations, prepared the groundwork for true automation.

Detroit automation carries the subdivision of tasks using human operators to its logical limits, and also results in making control operations simpler and more specific to given tasks. The very processes of subdividing operations and simplifying the necessary controls required at each operating step set the stage for true automation. Building automatic control equipment to take over the simplified controls exercised by the human operator becomes relatively simple.

We can then expect that in the first stages of true automation, our production lines will resemble those of the older mechanized technology. The major difference will be the substitution for human operators of automatic controls that will function as direct analogues of human operators. Much of our present specialized production equipment which has been designed for single purpose operations will continue to be used, operating with automatic rather than human controls.

Before the second stage in automation is reached, there will be a transitional stage of full automatic controls but with specially designed single purpose machine tools. Here is a description of this transition stage as applied to the machining of automobile engine blocks. "We have a 300 foot factory line, consisting of five transfermatic machines, hooked together, which perform 495 machining operations and 106 inspection operations. More than 100 engine blocks are in process at one time."[14]

A second stage in automation will see a fundamental redesign of production equipment itself. This redesign will take advantage of the opportunities to generalize production operations in machines and equipment. Human operators as controllers have to be trained in their work tasks. This makes for a "stickiness" in changing tasks because of the time and money involved in retraining operators. Automatic controls, on the other hand, simply require a new set of programed instructions, e.g., a tape, to do a new job. There is no training time or cost. It is highly probable, therefore, that we will begin moving away from single purpose machine tools toward a species of machine tools that is universal in character.

In this second stage of true automation we should see a gradual evolution from present machine design toward more general purpose equipment whose operations can be programed at will through the controlling information machines.

We can then conclude that the first impact of automation on the labor force will be to displace machine operators in presently mechanized tasks. These mechanized tasks are generally highly subdivided and repetitive.

What will then happen to the character of the work force in automated plants? It seems clear that there will be a rapid growth in demand for workers with professional and semiprofessional training. Special emphasis will be put on engineering and science backgrounds.[15]

Workers with engineering and science training will be used in two general capacities. The first is programing operations and setting up programed controls. The second is in the maintenance of both the operating and control equipment.

The special skills necessary in programing and maintaining the control equipment involve learning coding and decoding systems and understanding mechanical and electronic circuits. In simpler kinds of control equipment, such as that used in controlling automatic calculators and tabulators, the operator learns how to link jack connections on a control board, which then programs the machine's operations. In more complex programing, the information fed to the machine may be punched out on tape; unequivocal instructions are insured through the application of number theory in the coding procedure. Thus a binary number system may be used to translate involved operating instructions into code form as a basis for programing production.

The kinds of skills required in programing operations, maintaining control equipment, and servicing control circuits are of a high order. It should also be noted that these skills are characteristically specialized rather than subdivided. A person who programs automatic equipment has specialized knowledge of electronic circuits and information theory. He may apply this knowledge over the whole control system.

The second major area of work activity that will be increasingly emphasized is the maintenance of operating equipment and control machines.[16] Automation will permit more continuous operations at higher speeds, often extending over twenty-four hours instead of the more normal eight-hour shift; these in turn will require new refinements in machine maintenance. Speed will become a keynote in putting equipment back into operation.[17] This will require highly skilled maintenance mechanics. Such mechanics will be specialists rather than operators in subdivided tasks.

In the longer run prospect, twenty-five years from now and more, we can expect that some of the programing and even some of the maintenance may become automated. In principle this certainly seems feasible. When this occurs we can expect that both programing and maintenance will require even higher levels of specialization in work behavior. Those doing programing will become really top level professional and scientific specialists whose primary functions will be the design and control of automation itself. Similarly, the maintenance personnel will become increasingly specialized in knowledge of operating and control equipment, concerning themselves with the design of automatic maintenance systems.

Another major consequence of true automation for work operations is a general shift toward employment in distribution and sales of goods. The vastly increased output of goods that can be anticipated from automation will exaggerate the problems of distribution. We have already noted in Chapter 8 that the American economy is a "make and sell" one. Even greater emphasis will be put on distribution and sales in the future. Thus, part of the displacement of workers from factories may be into sales and distribution occupations.

WORK BEHAVIOR

A very considerable change in work behavior can be anticipated as a consequence of the inevitable increase in the amount of "leisure on the job." It is one of the paradoxes of automated operations that the human work force associated with it will be more productive, yet require less attention to on-going operations.[18] Furthermore, the specialists who are associated with automated operations will behave in ways characteristic of professional and semi-professional personnel.

The on-the-job leisure and professional outlook of workers in automated operations will inevitably have consequences for the social organization of work. In servicing on-going operations, a good deal of time will be spent in watching and waiting. Furthermore, this time will typically be spent in the company of other specialists who are also watching and waiting. As a consequence of being thrown together and having the leisure for interaction, there will be a growth of voluntary social groups at work. The nature of these voluntary social groups is examined in Chapter 16. It is sufficient to suggest at this point that the "tightness" of industrial discipline that has grown up to control behavior of machine operators will tend to be relaxed in favor of accommodating automation specialists in their self-image as professionals capable of policing their own personal behavior. These specialists will have greater freedom to associate freely with each other, doing their work as necessary, rather than having to give the appearance of being continually busy.

A second major shift in work operations will entail the redefinition of traditional working

Watching and waiting in automated production processes is well illustrated in this picture of men who work at the control board in an oil refinery.

days. With a greater use of twenty-four hour operations, the work forces will tend to be distributed more equally around the clock. Our present labor force is primarily employed during the standard work day, starting in the morning and ending in the late afternoon. Second and third shift operations, carrying the work cycle around the clock, are now considered abnormal, except in continuous process industries. These additional shifts are even discouraged by workers and their unions through exacting premium pay for work on second and third shifts. This practice will probably be modified in the future as it becomes more normal to work on the traditionally less desirable shifts.

We will not discuss the implications of the change in the work day for the society as a whole. It seems obvious, however, that many of our social arrangements, ranging from family life to recreation, will have to be modified to provide opportunities for community life for a growing proportion of workers whose work period will be late evening or early morning hours. It is not unlikely, for example, to see our future homes designed with a completely darkened and soundproofed bedroom for the breadwinner to use after a night shift, undisturbed by his family following a more usual daily round of life.

INDIRECT CONSEQUENCE OF AUTOMATION

A very important indirect consequence of automation will be felt in non-automated areas of industrial production. Non-automated production will move increasingly in the direction of Detroit automation. Non-automated operations will have to compete with more efficient automated ones. This competition will result in increasing mechanization, still using human operators, in less advanced industrial sectors.

As we have already seen, Detroit automation leads to greater and greater subdivision of work activities. Consequently, we can predict that at the same time that automation is leading to specialization of the work force, mechanization of non-automated operations will further subdivide its tasks.

In viewing what will happen to the entire labor force, to discover the impact of automation on working behavior, we will observe two contradictory trends. Automation will promote specialists. Mechanization of non-automated production will lead to subdivision of tasks. Over the entire labor force, both of these trends will be evident. It can be concluded, then, that automation will directly lead to greater specialization of work tasks, and indirectly lead to more widespread subdivision of working activities.

AUTOMATION AND THE LABOR FORCE

Automation of industrial production will have at least five major consequences for the labor force. (A) The creation of new specializations will change the skill composition of the total labor force. (B) The needs for much higher skills will have an inevitable impact on formal schooling preparatory to entering industry. (C) Retraining of displaced workers will constitute a major problem for the total economy. (D) A probable shift in the assignment of work by sex may be anticipated. (E) There is a high probability that the areas of more recent economic growth will be favored by automation. Let us examine these five consequences for the labor force in order.

NEW SPECIALISTS

It was noted in Chapter 8 that for the entire non-agricultural American labor force, about one in five working persons was classified as highly skilled. This, of course, includes all professionals, even those in the so-called free professions. It was also observed in Chapter 8 that semi-skilled factory operators accounted for twenty-four per cent of the non-agricultural labor force. Furthermore, semi-skilled and skilled office and sales workers accounted for twenty-two per cent of the labor force.

We can anticipate that automation, by creating a large corps of specialists in automated production, will lead to a significant increase in the proportion of the labor force classified as highly skilled. It is likely that the highly skilled group of manual workers will also show some proportionate increase as maintenance of automated operations becomes more important.[19]

An operator at the signal board of the automated controls governing feeding and unloading of cylinder blocks in a Barnes drill. Vari-colored signal lights tell the operator all he needs to know about on-going operations. The installation and maintenance of such complex equipment requires highly skilled and trained workmen.

The pressures generated by automation to mechanize further the non-automated sectors of industry will result in some additions to the semi-skilled office and factory ranks. That is, as some workers are being up-graded into skilled jobs, others will move from hand work and unskilled labor into semi-skilled mechanized work.

Part of the recruitment of the highly skilled specialists needed for automation will come from the annual additions to the labor force. This recruitment will be largely among college graduates and those receiving technical training. Some of the recruits will also come from the ranks of those retrained to fill the more highly skilled automation specialties.

We can then summarize the broad changes in the labor force by suggesting that needs for highly skilled automation specialists will lead to an increase in the proportion of all non-agricultural workers in the highly skilled professional and technical categories. We can also expect that the need for maintenance people will lead to a relative increase among the highly skilled manual workers.[20] At the same time, semi-skilled factory workers, and unskilled workers generally, will decline in relative importance. The greatest relative decline will be seen among unskilled workers.

It has already been suggested in this chapter that demand for office and sales work will probably increase as a consequence of the need to distribute and sell the increased output of automation. At the same time office automation is leading to very rapid replacement of people by machines. This is particularly true of accounting and record keeping. Thus, even though there is generated a need for sales and distribution personnel, at least a part of the labor requirement will be met by installing automated office machines.[21] Even in selling, mechanical sales devices appear to have a bright future. Many kinds of vending machines—beverages and cigarettes for example—have already made their appearance, and the end is not in sight.

SCHOOLING OF SPECIALISTS

The kinds of knowledge necessary for specialization in automation are highly technical.[22] Consequently, the task of educating people to become specialists will fall largely on the schools. This is particularly true for later high school and college levels of schooling. The current concern with the alleged decline in teaching mathematics and science in high school and college is but one evidence of the fact that demands are already exceeding supplies of students trained in these subjects. Schools have tended to lag behind in anticipating the labor market demands for their students.[23]

It is fortunate to have some leverage on school curricula from an unrelated source. We can claim the Soviet threat as a justification for new emphasis on mathematics and science. Alarmists have repeatedly pointed to the growing emphasis on science and engineering training in the USSR. By comparison we are at a disadvantage. The Russians are presently turning out more engineers and scientists each year than we are. We are thus using our competitive position in relation to the Soviets as leverage on school curricula. The simple fact of the matter seems to be that we need all possible justification, direct and remote, to swing our schooling into some adequate relationship with the needs generated by automation.[24]

Existing shortages of trained people are being met by emergency schooling programs. Some companies are even sending people back to school at company expense in order to gain the necessary science and engineering knowledge. In the long run, these emergency programs will be replaced as curricula are changed to reflect the new labor force needs.

RETRAINING OF DISPLACED WORKERS

A major social problem already exists, and will be intensified, in the need for retraining people displaced by automation. The problem is not now as acute as it will become. At the present time our high level economy is capable of absorbing most of the displaced workers into similar or related occupations.[25] As automation is adopted more widely, the retraining of displaced workers will become more imperative.[26]

It is reasonable to suggest that the movement of people from displaced occupations will increasingly take the form of shifting to quite different kinds of work. Some of the displaced machine operators will move up to more highly skilled automation specialties after a period of intensive training.[27] Others, and perhaps the majority, will move out of their own companies and even their customary industry. They will move to other sectors of the economy where their relatively low skill level will still be useful. Continued mechanization of non-automated industry will become a source of job opportunities for people displaced by automation.

This accelerated movement of workers in the labor market will have profound effects on company security programs. Pensions and other benefits that accrue to workers for continued service in a company may be lost through displacement from automated jobs. This will create demands in the work force, and through the unions representing it, for company emphasis on retraining displaced workers for further employment in the company.[28] Only through continuity of employment with the company will security aspects of the employment contract be protected. We will see, later, in Chapter 13 that financial and other security guarantees provided by a company are important incentives for work. Their incentive value may be diminished, however, with mass displacement from jobs and consequent loss of employment with the company. It would appear that many companies, placing heavy emphasis on employment security, will find this an important limitation on the rate with which they can introduce automation and still retain the incentive value of security guarantees.[29]

It is notable that labor unions are also increasingly concerned with the retraining problem. Obvious pressures arise from union memberships to protect people from displacement. This may result in demands for restriction in the rate of automation, or coordinated training to fit displaced workers into newly created jobs.[30]

The retraining problem entails large financial burdens. It also means great human costs to those who are displaced from their regular jobs. Unions have emphasized the human strains involved in giving up a job and retraining for another. Management has been concerned with the financial costs of retraining large parts of the labor force. Actually the retraining issue rests with the country as a whole. To what extent are the citizens of the country to be displaced from their jobs and left as free agents to find the best possible substitute employment? To what extent will, and should, society assume some responsibility for retraining people to continue their productive careers? Who is to bear the tremendous financial burden of job finding and job retraining programs, and perhaps even the cost of moving families to new geographic areas where suitable jobs are available? Unions in the traditional language of collective bargaining demands are insisting that business bear a significant proportion of the social and financial responsibility for job changing and retraining.

The most likely outcome is that attempts will be made to transfer the financial costs of retraining to our society as a whole. This can be accomplished by using the school systems of the country to undertake the retraining programs.

MALES VS. FEMALES

An interesting consequence of automation is that it may change employment opportunities for females. We saw in Chapter 8 that females have entered the labor force in increasing proportions. Their work opportunities have been found particularly in clerical and sales occupations. We also discovered that a large proportion of all females working were employed as semi-skilled factory operatives. With increasing automation in the office, and the high skills required for automation specialists, it is highly probable that the monopoly of office jobs now held by women will be broken. More and more male specialists will come into the offices to program and maintain automated equipment.[31] The same general shifts can be expected to occur in semi-skilled factory jobs now held by women.

Science and engineering are traditionally male specializations. As opportunities for applied science and engineering open up in the office and factory, a major problem will be posed for women to find jobs in their present areas of dominance.

These limitations on future employment opportunities may be very threatening to women. There may not be sufficient alternative employment opportunities for them. This problem may be worked out, in part, by shifting our traditional preference for men in science and engineering. Women could then more easily gain entrance into schools in these disciplines preparatory to becoming automation specialists.

It is within the realm of probability that women will refuse to work as their traditional job opportunities disappear. Up to now each succeeding decade has seen a higher proportion of women going to work. Women may simply retreat to the home as their real alternative to working for wages. The consequences of this for family and home life are not for us to consider here, although they may be very far-reaching. For example, should such a shift into the home take place, the birth rate may rise more rapidly than at present, and family size may increase. The consequences of this for population growth, for the home building industry, and for industries servicing children's needs are obviously great.

Office automation showing a view of various types of data processing machines using punched cards The absence of females is notable among this office staff.

GEOGRAPHY OF INDUSTRY

Automation, in its initial phases, is not particularly disruptive of existing production arrangements, but as it becomes necessary to consider new plant layout and new machines, it is often more profitable to start anew, building new factories to house the automated production lines. Automated plants will increasingly be entirely new from the ground up.

When automation demands the abandonment of old plant sites, or complete replacement of old factories, the issues of plant location can be re-examined by a company.[32] Areas of rapid industrial growth become potential plant sites for new automated factories. We can anticipate, therefore, that the areas of rapid industrialization may also be the areas leading in automation of production.[33] In the newer industrialized areas—the South, Southwest, and West—we already have evidence that the industrial complex is favoring automation. This may sharpen the contrasts in productive efficiency between the newer areas of rapid industrialization and the older.

The mobility of industry is increased by automation and the development of instantaneous communication networks tying together far-flung plants. Centralized executive direction can readily be maintained over vast geographic distances. The Sylvania Electric Company has already accomplished this by scattering its plants in relatively small production units, maintaining centralized direction through an extensive private communication system.[34]

One of the initial effects of automation will be further geographical dispersion of industry. The consequences of this on population shifts are obvious. People will follow job opportunities. Not so obvious, but perhaps equally important may be the defense significance of industrial dispersion. The Federal government defense proposals for minimizing bomb damage to industrial output by moving industry out of places of heavy concentration have not been successful. However, automation may be the spur to industrial dispersion that will have as an unanticipated consequence greater protection of our industrial output from possible war damage.

AUTOMATION AND MANAGEMENT FUNCTIONS

Four major consequences of automation for management can be predicted. (A) Top management decision making will become more complicated and more rational. (B) Recruitment and background of managers will change markedly. (C) Supervisory functions of management at the middle and lower levels will become more standardized. (D) Managers' interests will broaden beyond the present emphasis on production and distribution.

MANAGEMENT DECISIONS

The amount, quality, and timing of information affecting business operations will all improve as a consequence of automatic data processing, so that decisions guiding business affairs will be more complex and more rational.[35]

Automatic data processing is a new, and highly significant development of automation. Information about on-going operations is reduced to electrical impulses for purposes of feedback and programing of these operations, as we have already seen. This same information can become immediately available as permanent recorded data about what is going on. This information can be treated independently of the on-going operations. It is fed into automatic data processing machines to provide immediate information to business decision makers.

Such information previously had to be accumulated in written reports, summarized and then put on the executive's desk. With hand operations, the time lapse between data gathering and final report to the executive was often days, weeks, or months. With automatic data processing machines, information can be made available in hours or even minutes.[36] Furthermore, the amount and complexity of the information made available are no longer limited by human observation of on-going activities, and the opportunities to record their consequences. Observing and recording can now be done automatically. Automatic control equipment provides the receptors and recorders for the data processing machines.

The significance of automatic data processing can be illustrated in inventory control. Automatic recording can give continuous information on inventory levels for every item. Automatic data processing machines can be programed to record and give automatic instructions to reorder when individual items of inventory have reached a minimum level.[37] The Army now uses automatic data processing machines to control world-wide inventories of spare parts and components in supply depots. Mail order houses use similar data processing to control inventories.

In the telephone industry, the latest central switchboard equipment has built in feedback and recording circuits that automatically punch out on a card the nature and location of any difficulties in operating circuits. Here an engineer is reading such a card. This is a form of data processing which makes a continuous record of operations and their difficulties.

It is now possible with data processing machines to have nearly instantaneous information made available to executives about their businesses. This means more rapid and more complex decisions. The increase of available information permits more variables to be considered in decisions, rather than "holding them constant" because nothing is known about them.[38]

Another significant feature of automatic data processing equipment is that it in turn may be programed to manipulate a given set of information so as to provide the best possible answer to a given question.[39] The answer is the result of complex means of interrelating the whole body of information in ways beyond the timely grasp of the human brain. For example, in forecasting future sales, a typical starting point is the recent past history of sales. Recent sales information, together with relevant information about the economy, consumer's habits, competitor's potential moves, and the company's output possibilities can all be fed as information into automatic data processing machines programed to digest all this information and compute one or more answers about future sales.[40]

The human mind tends to take complex information and deal with only one pair of variables at a time. Automatic data processing machines do not have this limitation. For example, automatic data processing machines are used in air defense. The air defense information machine takes information from radar observations to compute the presence, speed, direction, and probable course of enemy planes. It also has fed into it the strength and disposition of defense forces. The machine is able to turn out a set of tactical instructions giving the best military response to the enemy attack. These are complex decisions, made rapidly. They are presumed to be better decisions than could be made by a human being digesting the same kind of information. Automatic data processing machines have built into them memory devices. Such memory devices are essential, for they permit the machines to store up information as well as to process it. Such stored information can be programed for recall when needed. Hence automatic data processing machines can receive and process data rapidly, relating it as desired to stored-up information.

The President of the International Business Machines Corporation has estimated that by 1966 at least ten thousand such machines will be in use by business and government. Something of the order of 170,000 people will be needed to program, maintain, and process information received from all these machines.[41]

It seems clear that automation of information gathering and analysis will make business decisions more complex and more rational. Less and less dependence will be placed on executives' memories, or their "feel" for a situation. Great stress will be placed on maximum acquisition of information, and its complex analysis, as a basis for operating decisions. Senator Ralph E. Flanders, Republican of Vermont, illustrated this in his testimony before the Joint Congressional Sub-committee studying automation. In a company about which he had knowledge an early type of data processing machine was installed, primarily as a labor saving step. It was discovered that so much more important information became available to management that the company executives asked more and more questions about their business. The result was that more people were employed to use the automatic data processing equipment than had been true with hand accounting methods. Furthermore, management felt it was doing a much better job of running the company because its decisions were improved.[42]

Top management will increasingly ask more penetrating questions about its business. There are relatively few questions about business operations that cannot, in principle, be answered. It will no longer suffice for an executive to say, "If we really knew, then we could decide."[43] Executives can now ask "what" or "why" and be reasonably certain that automatic data processing can produce answers better than the most "educated guess" of any of their colleagues.[44]

The period of the intuitive executive and the overpowering tycoon seems to be closing.[45] Future executives will be men with sensitive intelligence, schooled to comprehend information theory and the relation of information to decision making.

EXECUTIVE RECRUITMENT

Undoubtedly there will be a marked shift, over the long run, in kinds of men and training suitable for executive positions.[46] We can expect to see growing numbers of executives drawn from the ranks of automation technologists and specialists. Such executives will be men thoroughly familiar with automation, but most important, these future executives will be capable of comprehending the broad sweep of the Industrial Revolution.

Ultimately, programing of data processing machines and of production equipment depends on asking an imaginative set of questions. Executives of our automated technology are going to be under continuous pressure to exhibit real ingenuity in asking questions about the affairs over which they exercise direction. There will be constant incentives to be curious about things in ways productive of usable answers.

An interesting paradox will result from the new background training needed by automation executives. On the one hand, their knowledge must inevitably be specialized with respect to science and technology. On the other hand, knowledge of science and technology may not generate constructive imagination to see the full potentiality of the new technology. Consequently, the training of future executives may, of necessity, require a strong emphasis on broad liberal arts schooling to develop, to a maximum, facility with constructive imagination. Human consequences of automation must necessarily enter into the calculations of its growth and development. To ask significant questions about these human consequences, the future executive will need schooling in depth in the social and behavioral sciences. Social values and value judgments will also enter into future business decisions controlling and using automation. Future executives will want adequate preparation in philosophy, history, and other liberal disciplines in order to understand the past history of social values as a basis for future value judgments.

In Chapter 21 we examine managerial leadership. A number of the problems of leadership are there analyzed in detail. It is enough to suggest at this point that the leadership functions of the future executive will be more complex and taxing than at present.

STANDARDIZING SUPERVISORY FUNCTIONS

The concepts of programing machine operations will be carried over into the control of management organizations. This will be particularly true in the control and direction of supervisory functions.

In Chapter 20 we will examine management as bureaucracy. One of the central themes of that chapter is the continual rationalization and standardization of command functions. Command functions can be viewed as an analogue to programing of automatic operations. Programing is giving command to the equipment being controlled. In an analogous way, supervisory functions can be programed so that they become highly standardized for the functionary.

It is probable that the parallel between automatic programing of equipment and standardization of command functions will be quickly recognized by the upper echelons of management. The inevitable result will be standardization of supervisory functions along the lines of automatic programing.

As in the control of machines, command functions are essentially concerned with insuring that expected behavior will be carried out. To insure expected behavior from human beings entails rules, regulations, and other methods of predetermining choices of action in given situations. In our present mechanized technology supervisors perform other functions in addition to command. As these other functions—like scheduling of output, or control of scrap loss are incorporated into the automatic controls, supervisors will be left primarily with command over human work forces as their major function.

Many of those directed will be specialists largely controlling their own work behavior. Supervisors will then have fewer functions to perform regarding their many subordinates capable of directing their own activities. The remaining command activities of supervisors will be subjected to standard procedures for which supervisors become the administrators.

We are suggesting that the leadership functions in business organizations will be further centralized at top executive levels. In the middle reaches and supervisory levels of management, command activities will be emphasized and these will be standardized.

INCREASED SCOPE OF MANAGEMENT

Automation does not merely change production technology. Automation has very wide implications for the whole web of society. Industrial managers who are initially responsible for introducing the technological changes will have impressed upon them the correlated consequences for the society as a whole.

A laissez-faire outlook simply will not suffice for the future. Indeed, the feedback of the consequences of industrial automation on the welfare of the business community will be immediate and direct. Industrial executives will have to take this feedback into account in their business decisions. This will move them rapidly into areas of social welfare that have been the traditional province of other institutions.

FURTHER CONSEQUENCES OF AUTOMATION

A number of additional consequences of automation are readily evident. We cannot here deal with them in detail. However, we can at least indicate some of the central issues involved.

MASS CONSUMPTION

The potential for vastly increased output that automation promises requires a balancing increase in consumption.[47] This problem is epitomized in the reported conversation between Walter Reuther, President of the United Automobile Workers Union, and a Ford executive. On a visit to the highly automatic Cleveland plant of the Ford Motor Company, one of the Ford executives, pointing to a series of automatic loading machines, teasingly said to Mr. Reuther, "You will have a hard time collecting overtime for those guys." Reuther replied, "And you will have a hard time selling them Fords."

Our economic system may be modified in order to provide mass consumption for increased output. Labor unions are now pressing for such devices as guaranteed annual wages and automatic increases in hourly rates, so that workers may share the increased output of automated equipment. These programs are already incorporated in important collective bargaining agreements. They may become more widespread in the future.

Management's general answer to union demands for guarantee of income to provide mass purchasing power has been this. The lowered unit costs of products of automation will continue to provide the mass markets for such goods. Furthermore, the continual growth of the total economy will absorb all displaced workers and the estimated 700,000 new workers annually added to the labor force. From management's standpoint, lower unit prices and continual growth in the gross national product will sustain mass markets for the output of our automated technology.

Unions, operating on a "here and now" outlook, see immediate prospects of technological unemployment, lower total purchasing power as a result, and the severe personal problems of those displaced from present employment. It is probable that union demands for protection represent realistic ways for handling the transition to automation. At the same time, management predictions of lower unit costs and a continually expanding economy may be a realistic forecast of the long run solution to the problem of mass consumption. It may turn out that the views of these contending groups are complementary rather than opposed. Union programs cover the short run; management predictions take a broader outlook.

WAGES

The general upgrading of the labor force that automation promises will raise average wage levels. This will, of course, contribute to the solution of the mass purchasing problem.

Our present systems of wage determination, as discussed in Chapter 13, take skill and training as fundamental. If these systems are retained, there is no question that the upgrading of the labor force into higher skill jobs will raise the general wage level.

WEALTH DISTRIBUTION

There are opposing economic needs that accompany automation. Vastly increased capital investment is required to purchase expensive automated equipment, but the maintenance of purchasing power requires sufficient spendable income in the hands of consumers.

It is estimated that the investment for machinery and equipment in automated production is roughly ten times as great per worker as in our present technology. Thus, in the United States in 1952 the average machinery investment for a production worker in an automated plant was as much as $100,000. For automation to be accomplished, it is necessary that the amount of investment capital be materially expanded.[48]

Paralleling the need for large amounts of capital is the need for large amounts of consumption income if our level of living is to be sustained, let alone improved. Some examples of the increased output potentials of automated equipment will highlight this point. New automatic machines enable four men to turn out eight times as many phonograph records as 250 men had previously produced. An automobile engine part that was once produced at the rate of 38 an hour by five men and two machines is now produced by one man with one machine at the rate of 750 an hour.[49]

The contrast between capital needs and consumer needs neatly poses the issue of wealth distribution in the economy. Will there be a shift in favor of capital funds to finance the new machine? Will there be a shift toward consumer income to provide sustaining purchasing power for output? Will the total level of spendable income be increased sufficiently to satisfy the needs of both of these expenditure categories without changing the relative distribution to each? These are serious questions of economic policy whose analysis is beyond the scope of this book.[50] We assume that social policy forbids a decrease in the level of living in favor of building up our new technology.

COLLECTIVE BARGAINING

In a companion volume, *Working Union-Management Relations,* we present a thorough consideration of collective bargaining. At this point we can only suggest that the revolutionary change in production technology caused by automation will have important effects on collective bargaining.

Automated production will lead to new types of workers. This will affect present jurisdictions of labor unions. It will create problems of membership recruitment. It will mean labor unions will recruit more and more well trained people, many of whom will have a self-image of a professional or semi-professional.

The issues of collective bargaining and their methods of resolution will also be modified. The use of automatic data processing by management will provide management bargainers with many more facts at the bargaining table. It is not unlikely that unions will make use of similar automated data processing equipment to buttress their own factual position at the bargaining table. We may then anticipate a growing need for highly sophisticated bargainers on both sides. Furthermore, the conduct of bargaining will place greater reliance on the preparation and presentation of the facts than on their interpretation.[51]

The power of unions and their memberships to face management will probably be increased as a consequence of automation. That is to say, the specialists in automated production and the workers who keep automated equipment going will have more important functions to perform in production. They will also have more exclusive control over these functions by virtue of specialized and technical training. Consequently, we might anticipate that the unions of the long run future will have enhanced bargaining power because of the increments of power held by their memberships in production operations. Granting that our present free collective bargaining will continue, it seems likely that, over the long run, labor unions will be able to make better deals for their members than now.

It can also be anticipated that the issues of hours of work, and number of days of work will become more prominent.[52] As automation is extended, unions will increasingly emphasize payoff for work in the coin of leisure time.

We can also expect that with standardization of supervisory command functions will come greater centralization of bargaining on both sides. The basic issues in collective bargaining will be handled directly by top company and union executives. Top executives will come into the discussion of issues earlier, and fewer issues will be handled by lower level officials.

LEISURE

It is safe to predict that those who work in the future will have more leisure than workers of today.[53] It also seems likely that the young and the old can be assured of freedom from productive labor. The young will be kept in schools until later ages to equip them with the necessary technical training and knowledge to become effective workers with automation. Older workers may be retired at relatively early ages to enjoy freedom from productive labor in their later maturity.[54]

If more leisure seems to be the prospect for the future, we can look for new industries to cater to leisure-time needs of the population.[55] For the young, greater emphasis will be put on schooling and vast investments made in our school systems. For workers and those who are retired, organized recreation and cultural activities will probably grow very rapidly to fill the increased leisure time available. It is not too far-fetched to suggest, for example, that we will preserve handicraft skills in our society by an accelerated growth in "do it yourself" activities.[56] Such activities will result in only minor economic output, but will have significance as a source of personal satisfaction in craftsmanship and creativity.

AUTOMATION IS FOR THE FUTURE

We opened this chapter by suggesting that automation is already upon us, but only in its beginning phases. There is still a considerable period of time, perhaps as much as a generation, before automation will become the characteristic technology of modern production. Therefore, many of the predictions contained in this chapter are necessarily speculative in character. Nevertheless, it is believed these predictions are well grounded on available facts. They may be modified in detail, but their general outlines appear highly probable.

We are still living with a mechanized technology. We still have to understand and analyze what now exists, as well as ponder the future.

The present state of our industrial technology is a period of rapid transition. We are moving from the climax of the first Industrial Revolution into the infancy of the second. The next six chapters of this section of the book are oriented primarily toward the climactic phase of our first Industrial Revolution. That is, we are analyzing the current reality of getting work done in the major sectors of our economy. Keep in mind, however, that our present stage of technological evolution is but prelude for a vastly different future.

NOTES FOR CHAPTER 11

1 See Norbert Wiener, *Cybernetics* (New York: John Wiley & Sons, 1948). This is a pioneering work dealing with control systems.

2 "Information Machines," in Scientific American Editors, *Automatic Control* (New York: Simon and Schuster, 1955) pp. 111-121. This book will be referred to hereafter as *Automatic Control.*

3 The most complete picture yet assembled on the nature and future of automation is contained in *Automation and Technological Change,* hearings before the Subcommittee of the Joint Committee on the Economic Report, Congress of the United States, 84th Congress, 1st Session, October 14-28, 1955 (Washington: Government Printing Office, 1955). We will refer to this hereafter as *Automation and Technological Change.* The subcommittee subsequently published "Automation and Technological Change," *Report* of the Subcommittee on Economic Stabilization to the Joint Committee on the Economic Report, Congress of the United States, 84th Congress, 1st Session, November, 1955. This will be cited as *Report.*

4 John Diebold, "Automation: Its Impact on Human Relations," address before the NAM Congress of American Industry, December 3, 1954.

5 William Pease, "An Automatic Machine Tool," *Automatic Control,* pp. 53-62.

6 Arnold Tustin, "Feedback," *Automatic Control,* pp. 15 ff.

7 Ridenour, "Information Machines," especially pp. 118-120. See also E. W. Leaver and J. J. Brown, "Machines Without Men," *Fortune* 34:165 ff (November, 1946).

8 Eugene Ayres, "An Automatic Chemical Plant," in *Automatic Control,* pp. 41-52, and also Ridenour, *op. cit.,* especially pp. 120-121.

9 Edward Bellamy, *Looking Backward* (New York: Houghton Mifflin Co., 1898 and Modern Library College Editions).

10 J. C. Kemeny, "Man Viewed as a Machine," in *Automatic Control,* especially pp. 142-146.

11 Cf. G. P. Shultz and G. B. Baldwin, *Automation—A new Dimension to Old Problems* (Washington: Public Affairs Press, 1955.)

12 See Norbert Wiener, *The Human Use of Human Beings* (New York: Houghton Mifflin, 1950), especially pp. 159-160.

13 "Most experts agree that electronic displacement of human beings will go farthest and fastest in the office. . . ." Howard Coughlin, President, Office Employees International Union, in *Automation and Technological Change,* p. 213; see also p. 228.

14 Quoted from Ralph E. Cross in a speech before the American Society of Tool Engineers in 1953.

15 "The most significant feature of any shift in employment that may result from automation is that much of the shift will be from menial labor to higher skilled, better paid, safer, and more interesting jobs," D. J. Davis, Vice President—Manufacturing, Ford Motor Company, *Automation and Technological Change,* p. 58. The volume contains many repetitions of these conclusions.

16 "The preponderance of automatic equipment and other complex machinery makes maintenance skills . . . particularly important," Otto Pragan, Director of Research, International Chemical Workers Union, *ibid.,* p. 155.

17 "We have . . . discovered some of the basic difficulties which may be expected in the operation of an automatic shell plant. For example, day-to-day operations are severely handicapped by the inadequate . . . maintenance designed into the special-purpose machinery . . . With an automated production process material moves more continuously than in a conventional plant . . . the temporary inability of the weakest link in the chain to perform effectively is much more serious in an automated process than in a conventional one." J. I. Snyder, Jr., Chairman of the Board and President, United States Industries, Inc., *ibid.,* p. 570.

18 Testimony of John Diebold, *ibid.,* pp. 28-29.

19 Testimony of James P. Mitchell, Secretary of Labor, *ibid.,* p. 264. James J. Nance, President, Studebaker-Packard Corporation, testified (p. 417) that the Packard engine plant at Utica, Michigan ". . . provides . . . an increase in skill levels and in the number of maintenance employees." See also testimony of Otto Pragan, p. 154.

20 See *Report,* p. 7.

NOTES FOR CHAPTER 11 (CONT.)

[21] See testimony of Dr. A. V. Astin, Director, National Bureau of Standards, *Automation and Technological Change,* p. 576.

[22] See testimony of Dr. Vannevar Bush, President, Carnegie Institution of Washington, *ibid.,* especially p. 616.

[23] "The most disturbing thing that has come to the Sub-committee's attention during the hearings was the near unanimous conclusion of the witnesses that the Nation is faced with a threatened shortage of scientists, technicians, and skilled labor." *Report,* p. 7.

[24] See testimony of Walter P. Reuther, then President, Congress of Industrial Organizations, *Automation and Technological Change,* especially p. 106.

[25] Management representatives tend to favor the position stated here. See for example the testimony of: D. G. Mitchell, Chairman and President, Sylvania Electric Products, Inc., *ibid.,* p. 182; Robert C. Tait, President, Stromberg-Carlson Company, and Senior Vice President, General Dynamics Corporation, p. 202, who even argues that without automation production will not be able to keep up with the growth of population; Cledo Brunetti, Director, Engineering Research and Development, General Mills, Inc., p. 384; Marshall G. Munce, Vice President, York Corporation, p. 404; Ralph J. Cordiner, President, General Electric Company, pp. 427-428; Professor T. J. Walsh, Case Institute of Technology, p. 487; Ralph E. Cross, Executive Vice President, The Cross Company, p. 499; and C. W. Phalen, President, Michigan Bell Telephone Company, p. 530. Labor representatives see the dangers of immediate unemployment and worker dislocation. See the testimony of: J. B. Carey, Secretary-Treasurer, C.I.O., p. 227; J. A. Beirne, President, Communication Workers of America, p. 346; and W. P. Kennedy, President, Brotherhood of Railroad Trainmen, p. 462; Mr. Edwin G. Nourse, former Chairman, Council of Economic Advisers, stated: "Nor can the problem be left entirely to the curative or preventative powers of population growth, which is one of the chief reliances of the economic faith healers." p. 623.

[26] Walter Reuther emphasized particularly the retraining problem in his statement *Ibid.,* p. 103.

[27] Clarence C. Donovan of The Ford Motor Company, made this statement about the labor force in the automated engine plant: "The average length of service of our operators on the cylinder-block line and in the new Berwin engine plant is 25 years. Those people have been trained in the old processes and then retrained in the new processes, and we found that we were able to accomplish it with very little difficulty." *Ibid.,* p. 63.

[28] The case study on the introduction of an electronic computer in a large insurance company showed that retraining and job shifting within the company was a major factor in limiting the undesirable effects of automation. *Ibid.,* p. 262.

[29] Marshall G. Munce in his testimony stressed particularly that normal attrition will take care of much of the problem of labor turnover caused by automation. *Ibid.,* pp. 401-402.

[30] J. A. Beirne lists the demands that labor makes upon management to develop programs for handling labor displacement. *Ibid.,* p. 346.

[31] When an automatic computer was installed in one operation of General Electric, 30 women had been employed for manual calculation. After installation, 20 were still employed for manual calculation, and 40 more for programing. Eight of the 40 had professional standing. In addition, *50 males were added to the staff* to analyze and program problems and operate the night shift. *Ibid.,* p. 444.

[32] See statement by Walter P. Reuther, *ibid.,* p. 103.

[33] J. J. Nance suggested that, with the wider use of automation, smaller companies would increase their ability to compete. In new areas of industrialization the companies tend to be smaller in size. *Ibid.,* p. 417.

[34] See the testimony of President Mitchell, *ibid.,* pp. 184-185.

[35] John Diebold emphasizes the impact of automatic data processing on the rethinking of management problems and decisions. *Ibid.,* p. 19.

[36] See further statement by Diebold, *ibid.,* p. 22.

[37] *Ibid.,* p. 125.

[38] Testimony of Dr. Nourse, *ibid.,* pp. 625-626.

[39] "The computer can answer the 'What would happen if?' questions that cannot now be answered. Computers can analyze and report end results of projected operations set up by management according to various hypotheses and alternatives." *Ibid.,* p. 24.

[40] President Cordiner of General Electric describes sales forecasting in his company, *ibid.,* p. 446.

[41] Newspaper article quoting Thomas J. Watson, Jr., January, 1957.

[42] *Automation and Technological Change,* p. 241. This is confirmed in Cordiner's testimony, pp. 444-445.

[43] *Ibid.,* p. 576.

[44] Professor W. S. Buckingham, Georgia Institute of Technology, makes this point in his statement. *Ibid.,* p. 33.

[45] See Buckingham's testimony, *ibid.,* p. 31.

[46] Diebold emphasizes this point. *Ibid.,* p. 28.

[47] The purchasing power problem is discussed, *ibid.,* p. 42.

[48] One of the spokesmen for the machine tool industry emphasizes the cost aspect of automated equipment as well as the write-off problem for older tools. *Ibid.,* p. 497.

[49] Cited in W. A. Faunce and H. A. Sheppard,

NOTES FOR CHAPTER 11 (CONT.)

"Automation: Some Implications for Industrial Relations," *Transactions,* Third World Congress of Sociology, 2:166.

[50] Norbert Wiener, *The Human Use of Human Beings,* p. 162, predicts that automation "... will produce an unemployment situation, in comparison with which the present recession and even the depression of the thirties will seem like a pleasant joke." A much more optimistic view that does not foresee the mass unemployment predicted by Wiener is that of Wassily Leontief, "The Economic Impact," in *Automatic Control,* pp. 72-80.

[51] Dr. Nourse cites specific examples to support these conclusions. *Automation and Technological Change,* pp. 626-627.

[52] These and further issues are listed, *ibid.,* pp. 156-158.

[53] *Ibid.,* pp. 110-111.

[54] *Ibid.,* p. 106.

[55] Professor Buckingham lists some examples, *ibid.,* p. 43.

[56] This point is made by David Riesman, *Individualism Reconsidered* (Glencoe: The Free Press, 1954), Chapter 14, "New Standards for Old: Conspicuous Consumption to Conspicuous Production," pp. 219 ff.

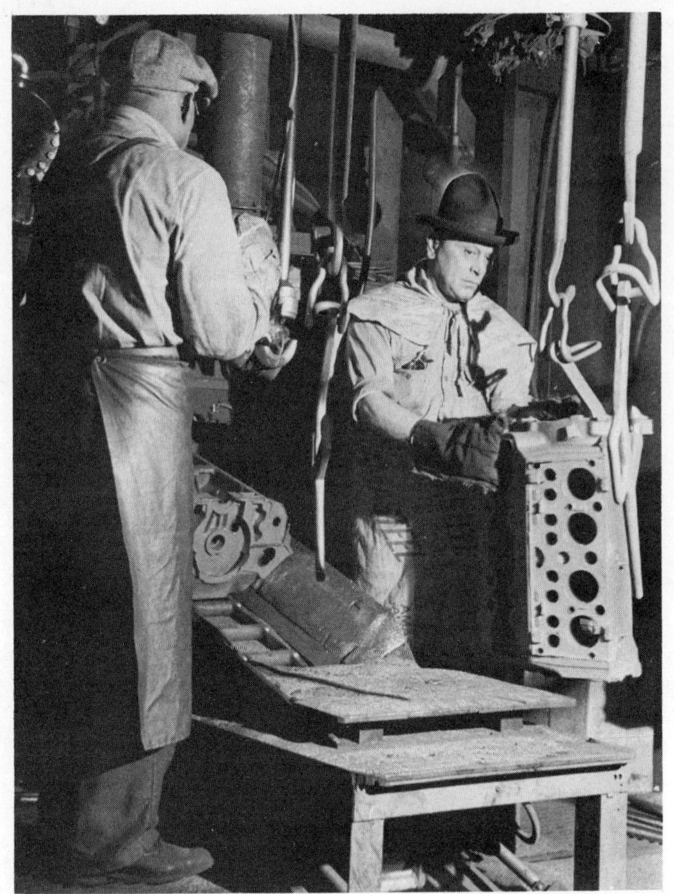

Cylinder blocks coming off the roller conveyor are picked up and hooked by these foundrymen onto the chain conveyor that takes the blocks to a sand blasting operation for cleaning. These men are motivated to work by the expectations built into the society that able-bodied men will work for a living. They will continue to work at hard and unchallenging jobs because this social motivation keeps them at work. Does the reflective mood of the man facing you suggest the level of his morale?

Chapter **12**

MOTIVATION AND MORALE

How are people motivated to work and keep working? What happens to their work as their morale changes? We want to discover how motivation and morale relate to work organizations, and the extent to which they are built-in features of them.

MOTIVATION

Motivation may be seen as the forces maintaining human activity. Morale is the amount of zeal and zest people have for their activities. The next chapter deals with incentives, which are intimately related to motivation and morale. We will therefore suggest at this point a definition of incentives, reserving for the following chapter their detailed analysis. Incentives are the inducements placed along the course of on-going activities, keeping the activities directed toward one goal rather than another. Motivation, morale, and incentives are distinctive aspects of a person's connections with his work organization.

MOTIVATION DEFINED

Motivation may be defined as the complex of forces starting and keeping a person at work in an organization. To put it generally, motivation starts and maintains an activity along a prescribed line. Motivation is something that moves the person to action, and continues him in the course of action already initiated. Furthermore—and this is important—motivation is part of an activity at work.

Clearly there are forces inside the person starting and maintaining activity. Whether we call them drives, instincts, wishes, or tension states, they can be described as mechanisms of the organism. Psychologists and physiologists analyze these mechanisms.[1]

It is also clear that behavior is highly organized. Impulses to act have to find appropriate channels of expression. The social setting of behavior defines these channels of expression. Analysis of the channels of systematic behavior—or behavior systems as we have called them—as part of the motivational field surrounding behavior is the task of the sociologist. This is the viewpoint of our study of work.[2]

BIOLOGICAL MOTIVATION IS DIFFUSE

A wide variety of schemes have been proposed by different kinds of behavioral scientists for describing and analyzing motivation. We can take our choice. There is the relatively simple formulation of W. I. Thomas, who saw people motivated towards new experience, response, recognition, and security.[3] There was the very complex formulation, now discarded, of psychologists of the instinctivist school who assume an instinct as the basis for each separate and distinct kind of human activity.

In recent years behavioral scientists are more or less agreed that there is not a general cause and effect connection between specific psychological motivation mechanisms and specific behaviors. The reasons for this are simple. It has been found repeatedly that the same activities can apparently be the consequence of quite different motivating forces. It has also been found that the same motivating force can give rise to widely different activities. As a consequence it is difficult, if not impossible, to see a one-to-one relationship between something called a motivating force inside the person, and a resulting activity. The current view suggests that internal motivating forces start the human being in action, and keep his activity going, but that we have to look outside the person for the determinants of particular action patterns.[4]

Do biological drives like sex, hunger, or the reduction of bodily tension make these men work hard in cooperation with each other? Biological motivations are diffuse, but the social motivations for working, and working together, are specific to the society, the industry, the company, the job.

The situation clarifies from an analytical standpoint if we turn our attention to the social practices that organize human activities. It is here, in the analysis of social structure, that we find the pathways along which human activity is directed. The society comes to define each activity as to the point of its origin, the nature of its initiating behavior, the manner in which it is continued, and the point of its termination. The society defines, for example, what earning a living means; what being a father means; and the activities that are related to being an entertainer.

It is, in a sense, immaterial from the standpoint of society what drives underlie the activity of men who are fathers, for example. Some might become fathers as a consequence of an incidental sex act; others because they like children; and still others because of the authority the position would give them in directing the lives of their offspring. In the social system these internal motivations, however diverse, are of relatively little import in defining what a father is and how he shall behave.

Similarly, it makes relatively little difference to a business firm whether its junior executives are motivated toward advancement by vanity, by keeping up with the Joneses, by lust for authority, by a miserly desire to accumulate wealth, or by a dedication to the interests of the business firm. Any and all of these personal motivations in any combination might be found in a typical cross section of junior executives. To the business firm the main thing is that all of this cross section of its future principal officers are strongly motivated towards achieving the terminal positions of leadership in the firm.[5] Granting these diverse drives toward promotion and success, the business firm can use various forms of incentives to encourage the junior executives to keep striving toward their success goals.

It should be clear, then, that if we view motivation from the standpoint of driving forces within the person, it must be considered a general, rather than a specific attribute of the individual. The sum total of human drives can be seen as the forces that keep the human being in a state of sustained activity. These forces are, in most instances, difficult to detect in or infer from a given line of activity.

From the standpoint of the society, or any given organization within the society, the minimum test that is made of each individual is his capacity for activity. Only those individuals incapable of purposeful activity are rejected. Thus, society and its formal organizations tend to set aside those individuals who are so dissociated from reality that their activity bears no relationship to their immediate environment.[6] Also rejected are those individuals who are so overpowered by their environment that they are in a state of literal paralysis for meaningful activity.

Granting the capacity for meaningful activity on the part of most human beings, their behavior can be directed in specific and concrete ways. The systems for achieving direction of activity are the systems of motivation with which we are primarily concerned here. We will see below that motivation is sustained by social structure. We will examine specific ways in which this is done.

MOTIVATION AND SOCIAL STRUCTURE

Social structure channels and sustains motivation. We can examine this proposition from two standpoints: (A) from the standpoint of the basic socialization of the person as a citizen of society; and (B) from the standpoint of learning to behave in specific organizations in which the individual carries out much of his daily activity.

The social structure sustains motivation in a specific way. When a person internalizes a value, norm, goal, or behavior pattern, these become guides for future activity.[7] Internalization means acceptance into the personal behavior systems, and ways of thinking. It means, literally, putting inside the social personality, modes of activities and thoughtways so they become, in the future, the bases for behavior and thought. These activities and thoughtways, in turn, have their origins, for any given person, in social experience.[8]

We can now recognize the circular course of social motivation. Social experience provides the substance internalized by the person. Once internalized, the behavior systems and thoughtways become the motivational bases for future behavior.[9] After they are learned the social behavior patterns become the person's chosen channels for initiating, sustaining, and completing activities.

Of particular consequence as a motivation is the "payoff" resulting from chosen behaviors. Society defines the "payoff" for acceptable individual behavior in the rewards they bring. These rewards are general rather than specific. For example, a youngster is constantly reminded to be a good child. The adults fostering childhood "goodness" reward the right responses with affection, approval, and acceptance. This kind of reward can be summarized as payment in "status coin." Adults, and particularly parents, pay good children in the currency of higher ascribed status than bad children.

From this same example we can also learn the difference between motivation and incentive. Offering a child a piece of candy if he eats his spinach is an incentive to complete a specific activity. According the same child high status for being a good youngster in all his activities builds a motivational system. When the notions of goodness are internalized by the child, he has standards for choosing channels of behavior in all areas of social interaction.[10]

Social motivational systems define their rewards for acceptable individual behavior in terms of basic human relationships.[11] The "payoff" is in "power pay," or "authority pay," or "status pay." Correct behavior may be rewarded by the opportunity to perform more important functions, or to assume exclusive control of some functions; the reward is power. Such behavior may lead to the assumption of a decision-making position in relation to others; the reward is authority. Finally, socially appropriate behavior may be accorded higher ranking, being rewarded in "status pay." It is in this sense of broad types of rewards that the "payoff" of motivational systems is general rather than specific.

We are constantly learning to value and exhibit the behaviors that are defined by our society as important and desirable. From early childhood we learn correct and proper behavior and their appropriate rewards as well as the punishments that go with incorrect and improper activity. By the time we reach adulthood we have already learned a great deal about the specific channels of behavior that are acceptable in our society. In subtle areas we learn that there are kinds of rewards that are not so obvious and yet extremely important. The esteem of one's peers, the ceremonial recognition from one's parents or superiors, or the applause of an audience are all kinds of

Once committed to working, the motivations that sustain productive activity come out of an experience in a work organization. Many American women go to work even though they are not compelled to by pressures in the larger society. Such work usually does not represent a permanent career. Yet these women do good work because they internalize the motivation patterns of their organization, whether it be in office or factory.

rewards to which we are early conditioned to respond as systems of motivation. The family, school, church, play group, and athletic team are all institutional settings in which the growing child learns channels of proper activity and systems of reward and punishment. In this sense, then, the individual has already learned the basic motivational patterns of his society before he is thrown as an adult into active participation in work organizations.

In the work organization the adult learns the motivation system that is specific to that institutional setting. There is real continuity between childhood experiences in the society and adult experiences in the work organization. The work organization builds its motivation systems on societal foundations. What happens at work, however, is that these social motivation patterns are made more specific. They are also made appropriate to the work performed.

Motivational rewards in the form of "power pay" become, at work, the conferring of increased responsibility for job functions. For example, a man may be rewarded by being given sole responsibility for turning a valve at a critical moment in a liquid distilling process, a responsibility that he alone has, and that is highly essential in producing the proper distillates. The reward of "authority pay" may be promotion to the ranks of management, directing others in doing their work. High "status pay" may come as a result of exceptional skill in doing a task.

The motivation systems are not the same for all kinds of work organizations. The motivational patterns for a clergyman in a church organization will differ markedly from those of an accountant in a business firm. Furthermore, the motivational patterns of the United States Steel Corporation will differ, in some respects, from those in the General Motors Corporation. Particular systems of motivation have some characteristics that are unique for each work organization.

There is a very real learning process through which every individual goes in becoming a member of any organization. One of the most important things learned is the nature of the specific motivation systems of the organization.

Once a person becomes acclimated to his work organization, his church, his fraternal clubs, his recreational associations, and the like, he finds that his particular motivation is largely automatic in each organizational setting. That is to say, once accepted by, and accepting membership in, an organization, the person acknowledges his internalization of the motivational patterns established by that organization. It is in this sense that the systems of motivation are sustained by the organization, or the social structure.

CONTINUITY AND STABILITY OF MOTIVATION

Motivation in the organization is continuous. The persons composing the organization, once they become a part of it, automatically fall into a pattern of motivation initiating and sustaining their organization activities.

The continuous and built-in character of motivation has already been examined in detail in Chapters 2-5. There we analyzed the behavior systems of work as they influenced the components of jobs, positions, and offices. At the end of Chapter 5 the relationships are summarized. In the context of motivation, three features of the work assignment—tasks, duties, and rights—are seen as impersonal environmental forces molding behavior in each work assignment.[12] They channel technical activities and the activities concerned with general behavior in the work organization. The rights associated with a job are some of the specific rewards for adequate work performance.

In Chapter 5 we also analyzed responsibility, obligation, and privilege as components of each job, position, and office. These three components represent, respectively, the personal internalization of the work values, the emotional commitment to these values through the sense of obligation about work, and the rewards coming out of interpersonal relations, in the form of privileges.[13] Each member of the work organization discovers that some rewards of his work come in the form of rights and privileges. These rewards, in turn, require that he carry out the tasks and duties of his work and that he do so with at least minimum responsibility and sense of obligation.

We may conclude, then, that in the very components defining work assignments are to be found the channels of behavior appropriate to work, and the rewards that re-enforce compliance with these selected channels of behavior. The molding character of the work environment results in built-in, continuous, systematic motivation.

There is a permanence to the systems of motivation in organizations that tends to be little affected by personnel turnover and many other kinds of changes. There are several sources for this stability. The first and most obvious lies in the general purpose and philosophy governing the existence of the organization. In a business organization where the financial balance sheet is one of the primary indicators of economic health, it is scarcely surprising that emphasis is put on channeling motivational patterns in financial terms. However, in an educational institution the academic staff can scarcely be said to be motivated by strictly financial gain. In many instances professors could do far better financially in other pursuits. We can understand professors' motivational patterns if we know that the purpose of a college or university is not to earn money, but to produce educated persons. The way in which the goals of the organization affect the motivational systems is even more evident in a religious organization. Here the creed of self-sacrifice and devotion to an idealistic goal becomes the center around which the motivational system is built. One tends to hold suspect the preacher who drives a Cadillac, but considers saintly the one whose clothes are threadbare.[14]

A second source of the stability of a motivational system lies in the fact that it affects a primary bond of organization.[15] The motivational system deals directly and immediately with the attachment of the person to the organization. Changes in the motivational system may entail vital and often disastrous changes in the bond between member and organization. Consequently, when members become acclimated to a particular motivational system in the organization in which they operate, they are often very reluctant to accept any significant changes that would tend to redefine their individual relation to the organization. We can see here the roots of the kind of resistance that workers are likely to display towards changes in the financial systems of rewards that are introduced as forms of incentives. The very changes in the pay system are likely to be viewed as a fundamental change in the worker-manager relationship, and to be opposed as a consequence.

We can then conclude that a system of motivation is an essential ingredient in any organization.[16] Furthermore, it is a permanent feature of an organization and tends to reflect the nature of the organization, its goals, objectives, and underlying philosophy.[17] The motivational system is usually well-understood by all the participants in the organization. It is, furthermore, stable and permanent, known to the managers of the organization as well as its members. Indeed, a motivational system could hardly be effective unless it is understood, and its operations evident to all those affected by it.[18]

MORALE

There have been times in reading this book when you were easily distracted by people around you, when you tired beyond your physical fatigue, and when you felt you were missing points. It is an author's hope that at times you read with interest, profit, and comprehension. These differences were in you. Your morale fluctuated, and with it your reading performance. In this section of the chapter we will analyze the character of morale and its influences on performance.

MORALE DEFINED

Morale is the zeal with which an activity is carried out. The higher the morale, the greater is the zeal displayed by the people engaged in an activity.[19] The level of morale may determine the speed and competence with which a task is carried out.

In instances where much is at stake in an operation, morale may be crucial in affecting the responsibility with which the operation is executed.

Morale can be viewed as an additive to motivation. We are suggesting that the level at which activity once motivated is carried out can vary widely, the determinant of the level being morale.

Most people have experienced low morale in group situations. Even though morale was low, it was possible for the group to carry out tasks and complete business. Motivation kept the group on the track, but the level of its output was low because of low morale. Every organization activity requires motivation for it to be initiated and carried forward and even in the situation where morale is extremely low, the group activity can go forward and be completed.[20]

MORALE AND INTERPERSONAL RELATIONS

Morale is the product of a specific group situation. It is the consequence of the immediate operating reality in which the person participates. Morale is determined by a person's relations to his associates in a group, and the circumstances surrounding the group's activities.[21]

The morale of an individual may fluctuate widely even in a single day. He may feel in good spirits and full of zest with his family in the morning. He may then go to work and feel dispirited, exhibiting little interest in his work. A return of zeal may come that evening when he engages in his weekly bowling session with friends. A downward swing of morale may end his evening as he returns home beyond the accepted hour and meets an irate wife unwilling to accept the usual excuses. The thing to be noted about this example is that we can think of the morale of the individual as being specific to the context in which he is currently operating. He has different levels of morale at home, at work, in his recreation, and back home again. Not only who he is with, but also the circumstances in which he is interacting with them, can determine the level of his morale. It is in this sense that we can think of morale as being immediate, direct, and the consequence of the specific group situation.

In the life history of a group there may be wide fluctuations in morale. Its members may have periods of high zeal and complete devotion to group goals. At other times, there may be much bickering and fighting and lack of unity. These variations in morale level, if analyzed carefully, would correspond to changes in relations among group members, or changes in the group environment.[22]

Morale is developed and sustained by interpersonal relations. Direct face-to-face contact with other people affects morale. When contact is indirect but maintained by a symbolic bond, the situation may have the same consequence for morale as direct face-to-face contact. The worker may still be preoccupied at work about his relationship with his wife, even though they are separated by the distance between home and work place. A soldier may have his morale boosted or shattered by letters from home that maintain a symbolic group bond, months after the last previous face-to-face contact.

The zeal for a task results from the responsive relationship with others performing the task.[23] There is involved here first of all the entire network of social interrelations among people. Much of this relationship takes place at a conscious and verbal level. We see it, for example, in the banter, the "horse play," and the running flow of conversation among co-workers. At another level there is implicit interaction that is born of continuous association. There may be an unspoken agreement, an unspoken unity, and an unspoken bond of sympathy that tie the members of the group together. When such a bond unites a group, there is little need for reenforcing its cohesion by talking about the things making for unity in the group.

The morale of a group is particularly a consequence of the network of interpersonal relations among its members. Where unity and solidarity exist we might expect the morale to be high. Conversely, where there is discord and disunion we might expect the morale to be low.

MORALE AND LEADERSHIP

Some kinds of groups have leaders who are in direct, face-to-face contact with their followers. In such groups the interpersonal relations between leader and followers will have consequences for group morale. Indeed, it is often true that the morale of a group results from the leadership exercised in it. This is a major function of leadership in an organization (to be considered in detail in Chapter 21). By virtue of a personal relation between the leader and his followers, the leader is in a key position to make or break the morale of the follower group.[24]

While it is true that the leader may be crucial to the level of morale in the group, it may also be true that groups can function with high morale in the absence of a leader. Such groups may be able to operate temporarily or in crisis situations almost as effectively without a leader as with one. This occurs when groups are composed of people who have been in long-time association with each other, or who have a high degree of familiarity with the circumstances under which the group operates, and who share a high degree of confidence in each other. The removal of a leader from such a group may, indeed, change the composition of the group by reducing its numbers by one, and the network of interactions correspondingly, but it is no assurance that the group's effectiveness will be destroyed. We can see examples of this in military units, in prisons, and in industrial situations in which a recalcitrant group may be punished by having its leader removed. The removal of a leader can often backfire because of the sustained quality of morale in the group, and its capacity to direct its zest toward a new objective of thwarting authority for having removed the group leader.

Leaders in face-to-face work groups can gradually build and sustain the level of morale of the group.[25] Indeed, it can be suggested that one major function of leadership is building and maintaining the level of group morale.[26]

MORALE FLUCTUATES

Morale tends to vary through time. There are points at which the morale of a group may be high, and other points at which the morale may be very low. The modern organization, composed of many groups, may also exhibit unevenness in the level of morale at any given time in a cross section of all its groups.

The fluctuating character of morale makes it one of the most difficult areas of management concern. Morale is not only basically difficult to manipulate, but it is also difficult to predict very far into the future.[27] The predictions usually made about levels of morale in a work organization are based on highly simplified models of what affects morale. A management, for example, that has persisted in the practices of paternalism, may assume that the morale of its employees is high because they have been given something by management. This may be a convenient fiction in terms of which management can predict levels of morale to its own satisfaction. But like all fictions, the accuracy of the prediction may be very low.

We can find the roots of the varying character of morale in several factors. There is, first of all, the delicate nature of interpersonal relations to be taken into account. People interact with each other in subtle and often indirect ways. A single word, a particular inflection, or a simple gesture may be sufficient cues to affect the behavior of a worker. The effect of the cue and its interpretation by its recipient may continue for many hours, or even days, after the moment at which the cue was received.

On the other hand, a high volume of interaction in a peculiarly stylistic fashion may be observed in a group. The interaction may be continuous over long periods of time, but have very little emotional impact on its participants. A great deal of the running conversation among workers focusing on sex, sporting events, and personal reminiscences can take on a stylistic character that has little immediate effect on the morale of the group. It simply represents a way of passing time that cannot be spent anywhere but at the work place. It was notable, for example, that among early hand cigar makers the monotony of the task was broken by hiring one of their fellows to be a reader. Each cigar maker contributed a portion of his earnings to the reader, who made no cigars, but entertained his fellow workers. The interrelationship between the reader and his listeners was well-defined and continuous. Yet there was probably relatively little emotional effect from the inflection, the rapidity, the expression with which the reader said his lines, or the way in which his reading was interpreted by his listeners.

A second cause of variable morale lies in the fact that each individual brings his outside life into the group relationship. What has happened to each person in the time that he has been away from the group may affect how he will reenter the group the next time. If a worker has left home after a serious quarrel with his wife, he may disturb the established network of personal relationships with his fellow workers when he reaches the job. This may have the effect of changing the level of morale not only of himself but of the entire group. Thus, the level of morale of a group is peculiarly subject to the differential participation of each of its members.

A third factor affecting morale of a group is its sensitivity to its environment. Most intimate face-to-face groups are dependent on other groups, and on continuous ties with management for their operating effectiveness. Furthermore, the environment in which the group operates may change from day to day, or even from hour to hour. Consequently, work groups are constantly alert to changes in their environment, and react to such changes.[28]

Changes in the group environment may either heighten or reduce morale. In crisis situations like a disaster, for example, the group may rise to the situation with superb morale, performing above and beyond the call of duty. On the other hand, the discharge or transfer of a fellow worker from an intimate work group may leave the remaining members unhappy and in low morale.

Morale does vary. Small changes, and sometimes intangible factors, that influence morale within a group make it difficult to manipulate morale from the outside. Managers of work organizations often seek gadgets and gimmicks that are supposed to raise morale. The intrinsic difficulty with all contrived devices for changing morale is the fact that interpersonal relations are not easily manipulated from the outside. Only those who are party to the relationship can directly affect its character. We emphasize, again, that morale is developed and sustained by interpersonal relations.

MORALE AND OUTPUT

There are two problems encountered in determining how morale affects output. The first problem is to determine whether heightened morale is related to increased output, and how strongly. The second problem is to determine the direction in which the morale is displayed. If, for example, a work group is antagonistic to management, its activities may be directed with great zeal at opposing management, resulting in low output even in the face of high morale.

We can say with some certainty that output tends to increase with heightened morale. The Western Electric studies demonstrated this at several points.[29] In the early experiments it was shown that the work group reacted with heightened morale, as measured by increased interaction, and more output, when management appeared to be changing the level of illumination in the work room. This was one of the first demonstrations of how a change in environment, in this instance by management, changed group morale. In other aspects of the Western Electric studies, changes in personnel of the work group increased morale, or decreased it, with corresponding changes in output.

Other studies in which morale was measured directly also show a positive relationship with output. The research of the Survey Research Center at the University of Michigan has demonstrated that an increase in work group morale is usually accompanied by an increase in output.[30]

Our real problem is to determine how much of an influence a change in morale does have on output. The answer to this question suggests important limits on the amount of increased output that will result from higher morale. For example, in a study by Morse, Reimer, and Tannenbaum two groups of clerical workers in a large insurance company office were subjected to two different kinds of supervisory patterns.[31] The first group had democratic supervision with a great deal of downward delegation of authority. The second group had a tightening of management authority with an increase in external pressures for output and regimentation of the work situation. The results of this experiment are exceedingly significant for our problem. The members of the work group with democratic management atmosphere liked their work more, liked their supervisors more, and displayed a significantly greater amount of internal cohesion. The work group with autocratic management was characterized by greater hostility among its members with more reports of friction, tension, disagreeableness, and "fighting jumpiness" in its interpersonal relations. We would certainly conclude that the morale of the autocratically led work group was lower than that of the democratically led one. Here is the astonishing result of the study. Over a year after the experiment began both groups had increased their output significantly above the starting level. Furthermore, the autocratically led group with its measurably lower morale had increased its output more than the higher morale, democratically led group!

What is the relationship between morale and output? It is probably a positive one.[32] When morale is increased, output will also increase. But it is equally clear that many other variables also determine the amount of output. We have seen, for example, in Chapter 10 that technology is the most important single determinant of output. What then, can we say about the magnitude of the influence of morale on output? Such studies as we have indicate a positive correlation in the range of .30 and .40 between morale and output.[33] This suggests that something of the order of ten to twenty per cent of the variance in output can be accounted for by the variable called morale, since the square of the correlation coefficient is the coefficient of determination. Thus, if we knew all the variables that affect output, we might expect the morale variable to account for one-tenth to one-fifth of the variation in output. This is a significant relationship. It indicates that morale is worth considering as a determinant of output. But it also cautions us to remember that other variables are important, and that taken together they account for more of the total variation in output than does morale.

Let us now turn to examine the direction in which a work group displays its morale. A work group may operate toward the goals set for it by management. As its morale increases, its output (which is what management wants) will also increase. But suppose the group is antagonistic to management goals. A heightening of group morale under these circumstances may lead to deliberate lowering of output and sabotage of management expectations. This is exactly what happens in industrial work when workers engage in restriction of output as Mathewson, Dalton, Collins, and Roy have pointed out.[34] It is the high level of the group's morale that sustains its opposition to management, and makes possible a deliberate slowdown in output. In a military unit the same phenomenon might result in covert sabotage of orders. In a religious organization schism might be the consequence of high morale in a dissident group.

The relationship between morale and output appears to be positive and significant, but of a relatively low magnitude. All other factors affecting output apparently account for 80 to 90 percent of variation in it. On this relatively simple task of shaping leather gloves over steam heated forms, output is stable and satisfactory to management even though physical surroundings and opportunities for high morale are not the best.

We then come to a more complicated answer for our question about the connection between morale and output. Where the work group accepts management goals, a heightened morale will be accompanied by increased output. Where the work group rejects management goals, a heightened morale will be accompanied by decreased output. The magnitude of the change in output in either direction is probably about ten to twenty per cent.

MORALE, MOTIVATION, AND WORK

It is at this point that we can see another connection between motivation and morale. The systems of motivation are designed to insure a correspondence between the goals of the work organization and the goals of its individual members and work groups. Motivation systems attempt to insure that employees and work groups will always tend to operate in the direction that the organization management expects. Morale affects the level of membership participation. The motivational systems cannot police the level of morale, but they can, if effectively designed, police the direction of work activities.[35]

In modern work organizations considerable attention is given to motivation and incentive systems. In the process an implicit assumption is often made that morale is elusive and beyond management influence or manipulation. Part of the reason for this assumption lies in the fact that morale can fluctuate. In keeping delicately integrated production operations in balance so that only the proper amount of output is forthcoming from each step, management must seek to minimize the influence of uncontrolled factors that might cause output to vary. A work group with high morale might overproduce one day, but with lower morale lag behind output goals the next. This output variation is disruptive of continuous production. Consequently management emphasizes the channeling of behavior through motivation systems to insure steady output, and controls deviant behavior. This emphasis on steady output may conflict with the morale states of work groups.

At times when work groups feel like "putting out," their extra output is not welcomed; at other times when group morale is low, great pressures generate to keep production up. This leads to the dilemma of being unable to relate morale states to output needs. One major result of the dilemma is that workers and work groups become alienated from the production process and the organization in which it is carried out.

Many top leaders of modern American industry are concerned about the fact that morale is low or unrelated to the demands of production in the organizations they direct. At the same time these organizations produce record volumes of goods at high level profits. The reason for this paradox should now be clear. Motivation—getting people to the work place and channeling their productive effort in desirable ways—is sustained by social structure. Morale—the level of zeal for the work—is sustained by interpersonal relations.

The social structure supporting motivation, and the interpersonal relations sustaining morale, are not always compatible with each other. This is one of the important issues we examine in later chapters. The issue is given very special attention in Chapters 20 and 21, where we deal with management of work organizations.

NOTES FOR CHAPTER 12

1 See, for example: M. R. Jones (ed.), *Nebraska Symposium on Motivation* (Lincoln: University of Nebraska Press, 1954); Wayne Dennis *et al., Current Trends in Psychological Theory* (Pittsburgh: University of Pittsburgh Press, 1951), especially David Krech, "Cognition and Motivation in Psychological Theory," pp. 111-139; D. O. Hebb, *The Organization of Behavior* (New York: John Wiley and Sons, 1949); and B. F. Skinner, *The Behavior of Organisms* (New York: Appleton-Century-Crofts, 1938).

2 See: John Dewey, *Human Nature and Conduct* (New York: Modern Library, 1930); and Kurt Lewin's *Resolving Social Conflicts* (New York: Harper & Brothers, 1948), and *Field Theory in Social Science* (New York: Harper & Brothers, 1951).

3 First set forth in W. I. Thomas, *The Unadjusted Girl* (Boston: Little, Brown and Company, 1923).

4 See, for example: A. H. Maslow, *Motivation and Personality* (New York: Harper & Brothers, 1954), especially Chapter 5, "A Theory of Human Motivation," pp. 80-106; Talcott Parsons *et al., Towards a General Theory of Action* (Cambridge: Harvard University Press, 1951); John Gillin (ed.), *For a Science of Social Man* (New York: The Macmillan Company, 1954); and one of the classics of the field, George Herbert Mead, *Mind, Self, and Society* (Chicago: University of Chicago Press, 1936).

NOTES FOR CHAPTER 12 (CONT.)

[5] As a general reference on this point see: Clyde Kluckholn *et al., Personality in Nature, Society and Culture* (New York: Alfred A. Knopf, Inc., 1953), which has a number of papers dealing with various facets of the problem of relating motivation to action. W. E. Henry, "The Business Executive: The Psycho-Dynamics of a Social Role," *American Journal of Sociology,* 54:286-291 (January, 1949), shows the diverse motivations of successful business executives as revealed in their responses to Thematic Apperception Tests.

[6] In our society they are usually labeled psychotics and institutionalized.

[7] See Mead, *op. cit.,* and also James Olds, *The Growth and Structure of Motives* (Glencoe: The Free Press, 1956), especially Chapters 2 and 3.

[8] This is the general point made by Talcott Parsons, "Motivation of Economic Activities," *Canadian Journal of Economics and Political Science,* 6:187-200 (May, 1940).

[9] Compare, Olds, *op. cit.*

[10] See for example J. M. Whiting and I. L. Child, *Child Training and Personality* (New Haven: Yale University Press, 1951).

[11] See Chapter 2, "Human Relations of Work."

[12] Page 88 above.

[13] Pp. 88-89 above.

[14] It sometimes happens, however, that the management's philosophy does not, in fact, determine the organization's motivation system. For example, paternalism in industry was supposed to generate a grateful response by workers to management's *noblesse oblige.* It seldom did. For a general discussion of paternalism, see Herbert Blumer, "Paternalism in Industry," *Social Process in Hawaii,* 15: 26-31 (1951). For a specific case example, see Robert Dubin and D. E. Wray, in *Labor-Management Relations in Illini City,* Vol. 1 (Champaign: Institute of Labor and Industrial Relations, 1953), "The Metal Products Company."

[15] E. Wight Bakke, *Bonds of Organization* (New York: Harper & Brothers, 1950), makes this general point.

[16] See Rensis Likert, "Motivational Dimensions of Administration," in *America's Manpower Crisis* (Chicago: Public Administration Service, 1952). See also Daniel Katz and Robert Kahn, "Human Organization and Worker Motivation" in Solomon Barkin *et al.* (eds.), *Industrial Productivity* (Champaign: Industrial Relations Research Association, 1951).

[17] This is the central point made by Rensis Likert, *et al.,* "Motivation: The Core of Management," *Personnel Series,* A 155 (New York: American Management Association, 1953), pp. 3-21

[18] A general treatment of motivation together with an analysis of studies dealing with it is Morris Viteles, *Motivation and Morale in Industry* (New York: W. W. Norton & Company, 1953).

[19] The literature is devious in the ways in which morale has been defined. It has been made equivalent to motivation and incentives, to generalized feeling states, and to the zeal with which goal-directed activity is carried out; our preference is for the last. See the following, which fit this general position: Daniel Katz, "Morale and Motivation in Industry" (Ann Arbor: Institute for Social Research, 1949), mimeographed; and Nancy Morse, Floyd Mann, and Robert Kahn, "The Meaning of Morale" (Ann Arbor: Institute for Social Research, 1952) mimeographed; Ronald Lippitt, "Morale of Youth Groups," in Goodwin Watson (ed.), *Civilian Morale* (Boston: Houghton Mifflin Company, 1942), where morale is equated to satisfaction with group life, interpersonal relations, and group structures; and H. S. Sullivan, "Psychiatric Aspects of Morale," *American Journal of Sociology,* 47:277-301 (November, 1941), where the opposite of demoralization produces the conditions of personal morale. For Sullivan, chronic demoralization ranges from discouragement to despair. Demoralization is viewed by Sullivan as resulting from interpersonal and biological factors.

[20] This is illustrated in an excellent study by W. J. Goode and Irving Fowler, "Incentive Factors in a Low Morale Plant," *American Sociological Review,* 14:619-624 (October, 1949), where they show how motivation is built into the organization and serves to keep work going even in the face of low worker morale.

[21] The development of "human relations in industry" research stems essentially from this insight that the level of work activity is more dependent upon social interaction than upon the physical environment (lighting, heating, and so forth). See, for example Elton Mayo, *The Human Problem of an Industrial Civilization* (New York: The Macmillan Company, 1933). J. A. Hobson, *Incentives in the New Industrial Order* (New York: Thomas Seltzer, 1923), emphasized the importance workers attach to control of their immediate social environment while working; see especially Chapter 5, "Incentives to the Efficiency of Labour."

[22] See C. M. Arensberg and Douglas McGregor, "Determination of Morale in an Industrial Company," *Applied Anthropology* 1:12-34 (January-March, 1942); and R. E. Bernberg, "Socio-psychological Factors in Industrial Morale: I. The Prediction of Specific Indicators," *Journal of Social Psychology,* 36:73-82 (August, 1952).

[23] This is especially evident in the study of personnel in a large department store: Nicholas Babchuk and W. J. Goode, "Work Incentives in a Self-determined Group," *American Sociological Review,* 16:679-687 (October, 1951).

[24] See, for example, Fritz J. Roethlisberger, *Management and Morale* (Cambridge: Harvard University Press, 1941). Roethlisberger points out (p. 38) that the foreman sometimes finds it "impossible to uphold strictly the logic of efficiency without some-

NOTES FOR CHAPTER 12 (CONT.)

times demoralizing the group." The strict demands of efficiency sometimes cut the personal bonds between the leader and his subordinates.

[25] See Daniel Katz *et al., Productivity, Supervision, and Morale Among Railroad Workers* (Ann Arbor: Institute for Social Research, 1951), a study of section gangs where direct supervision is particularly important as the only visible evidence of management when the men are working on the road bed; and R. L. Kahn and Daniel Katz, "Leadership Practices in Relation to Productivity and Morale," in D. Cartwright and A. Zander (eds.), *Group Dynamics* (Evanston: Row Peterson, 1953).

[26] As suggested, for example, by C. I. Barnard, *The Functions of the Executive* (Cambridge: Harvard University Press, 1938), especially in Chapter 17, "The Nature of Executive Responsibility." See also J. C. Worthy, "Factors Influencing Employee Morale," *Harvard Business Review,* 28:61-73 (January, 1950). Rensis Likert, *Morale and Agency Management* (New York: Life Insurance Sales Bureau, 1941), places particular emphasis on characteristics of the supervisor's relationship with his employees that produce high morale: recognition of accomplishment, and insight into personal motives and personality factors of subordinates.

[27] One of the major manipulative techniques employed by management to affect morale is the use of group participation in decisions. Such experiments are almost invariably limited to single problems—like introducing a particular technological change, J. R. P. French and Lester Coch, "Overcoming Resistance to Change," *Human Relations,* 1: 512-532 (August, 1948)—and dropped when the problem is "solved," or to trivial problems where participation is of only minor consequence to the total work environment—see some of the examples in N. F. R. Maier, *Psychology in Industry* (New York: Houghton Mifflin Co., 1946), and pp. 95 ff., where the advantages of participation are summarized.

[28] See: C. R. Walker, "Work Methods, Working Conditions, and Morale," Chapter 26 in A. Kornhauser, R. Dubin, and A. Ross (eds.), *Industrial Conflict* (New York: McGraw-Hill Book Co., 1954), pp. 345-358, where the technical environment is explored for its influence on morale; and A. J. Marrow, "Human Factors in Production," *Personnel,* 25:341-349 (March, 1949), where organizational environmental factors like turnover and transfer are discussed as influences on morale.

[29] F. J. Roethlisberger and W. J. Dickson, *Management and the Worker* (Cambridge: Harvard University Press, 1939), *passim.*

[30] *Productivity, Supervision, and Employee Morale,* Human Relations Series 1, Report 1, Survey Research Center, University of Michigan, 1948; Daniel Katz, "An Overview of the Human Relations Program," and R. L. Kahn, "An Analysis of Supervisory Practices and Components of Morale," in Harold Guetzkow (ed.), *Groups, Leadership, and Men* (Pittsburgh: Carnegie Institute of Technology Press, 1951); Daniel Katz and R. L. Kahn, "Some Recent Findings in Human Relations Research in Industry," in G. E. Swanson *et al.* (eds.), *Readings in Social Psychology,* revised edition (New York: Henry Holt & Co., 1952).

[31] N. C. Morse, E. Reimer, and A. Tannenbaum, "The Experimental Change of a Major Organizational Variable," as reported by Daniel Katz, "Satisfactions and Deprivations in Industrial Life," in Kornhauser, Dubin, and Ross, *op. cit.*

[32] An important critical look at the present confused state of the research in this area is contained in Harold Wilensky, "Human Relations in the Workplace: An Appraisal of Some Recent Research," Chapter 3 in C. M. Arensberg *et al.* (eds.), *Research in Industrial Human Relations* (New York: Harper & Brothers, 1957).

[33] A general conclusion reported by N. C. Morse and Floyd Mann at a conference sponsored by the Organization Research Project of Princeton University and the Social Science Research Council in 1952. See also: N. C. Morse, *Satisfactions in the White Collar Job* (Ann Arbor: Survey Research Center, 1953); and Robert Kahn and N. C. Morse, "The Relation of Productivity to Morale," *Journal of Social Issues,* 7:8-17 (1951).

[34] S. B. Mathewson, *Restriction of Output Among Unorganized Workers* (New York: Viking Press, 1931); Donald Roy, "Quota Restriction and Goldbricking in a Machine Shop," *American Journal of Sociology,* 57:427-442 (March, 1952); and Orvis Collins, Melville Dalton, and Donald Roy, "Restriction of Output and Social Cleavage in Industry," *Applied Anthropology,* 5:1-14 (Summer, 1946).

[35] For example, the general rules of business organizations define the requirements for attendance at work, and the penalties for absences. There will, however, be variations in absence rates by departments, depending upon such factors as the morale of the workers in each department. This was the finding of Elton Mayo and G. F. F. Lombard in *Teamwork and Turnover in the Aircraft Industry of Southern California* (Boston: Harvard Business School, 1944). See also J. B. Fox and J. F. Scott, *Absenteeism: Management's Problem* (Boston: Harvard Business School, 1943).

A $250.92 award went to this man for his production suggestion that spring clips replace tape in holding rubber and chrome moldings in place during installation of automobile windshields. What was the incentive for the suggestion: pride in workmanship, devotion to the company, or the probable cash award for a usable suggestion?

Chapter 13

INCENTIVES

At the beginning of the last chapter we defined incentives as the inducements placed along the course of ongoing activities keeping the activities directed towards one goal rather than another. Incentives are what the working person gets from his employing organization for being a productive member. These incentives are pay for working. The pay comes in some form that is tangible. It is recognized as pay for work by both its recipient and those who make the payoff. Incentives must, therefore, be part of the working environment. Various kinds of incentives are built into the work organization, paying off in systematic ways as work is performed.

People work because they expect something out of it. They are likely to work for the Widget Company instead of the Gadget Company or the Trinket Company because they think Widget has a better payoff. Whatever incentives are important to the person may become the basis for his preference for his employer rather than another. Incentives are therefore important in keeping members in a work organization, as well as keeping them productive while working.

TYPES OF INCENTIVES

We can look at incentives from two different but related standpoints.[1] If interested in designing incentive systems we concentrate on the form they take. If we are concerned with how people react to the incentives offered for working, then attention is focused on their subjective reaction to them. We will first examine the general forms of work incentive systems. Then we will consider subjective reactions to incentives. Having established our groundwork, we will turn to a detailed consideration of work incentive systems, showing how they are developed, and how they operate.

FORMS OF INCENTIVE SYSTEMS

A common distinction is that made between financial and non-financial incentives. Any incentive that pays off either directly or indirectly in money is a financial incentive. Wages and salaries are the major financial incentives. However, bonuses, profit sharing, retirement pay, vacation pay, health insurance, and free, company-sponsored medical service are obvious extensions of financial incentives that either pay out directly in money, or provide services that might otherwise require personal expenditures.

Non-financial incentives are forms of payment for working where the inducement is not a monetary one. Non-financial incentives may take the form of earning higher status, being given greater responsibility and participation in work decisions, receiving public praise from superiors, or receiving token rewards like service pins. Non-financial incentives are based on the clear recognition that people respond to a wide variety of inducements that are not expressed in monetary terms.

Many incentives have both a financial and non-financial aspect. A promotion, for example, can be viewed as a non-financial incentive in which the reward is greater authority and status. Promotions typically, however, also carry increased pay, so that they reward doubly. People seek promotions because they pay off in both financial and non-financial ways. Other examples of incentives that combine financial and non-financial inducements are: recognition for merit (pay increases within the job rate range *plus* public recognition); seniority standing (retention on the job during layoffs, or preference for advancement *plus* rights and privileges); and designation as a permanent employee (often signalized by an increase in pay *plus* protection from firing except for cause).

The distinction between financial and non-financial incentives rests on the difference in the form of the payoff. It is important to recognize the different forms of inducements in order to design incentive systems of work organizations. We will analyze in detail below these two basic forms of incentives for work.

SUBJECTIVE RESPONSES TO INCENTIVES

Incentives can also be viewed from the standpoint of their impact on the working person. Here we are concerned with the subjective response to inducements in whatever form they might be presented. From this subjective standpoint we can distinguish three types of incentives: (A) those based on present satisfactions; (B) those based on present dissatisfactions; and (C) those based on providing functional equivalents.

Incentives based on a person's present satisfactions are those features of his work that he likes, and wants to see continued. These kinds of incentives cut across the whole spectrum of job features towards which a liking may develop. Once a person likes aspects of his work, he develops an interest in seeing them preserved. Furthermore, these interesting features of work give the person reasons for wanting to continue work, or for wanting to continue employment in his present place of work. Examples of incentives based on present satisfactions are pride of craftsmanship, sense of creativity, feeling of meaningfulness of the task, enjoyment of the company of co-workers; finding a "home" at work, habituation to pleasant routines; attachment to physical objects like a particular machine tool (truck drivers often have violent preferences for "their" truck and may even give it a name, usually feminine); a comfortable relationship with superiors, and the pleasure of being powerful (e.g., the only file clerk who can really find things in the files).

Incentives based on a person's present dissatisfactions are focused on those features of his work that he likes, but wants more of. Here again, almost all aspects of work can arouse dissatisfactions whose dissipation depends on getting more of what you now have. Indeed, the most common view of incentives is based on the dissatisfaction principle. We tend to think that a man works hard because he wants more pay, more authority, more power, or more status. Businessmen not uncommonly assert, for instance, that when their employees get hungry then they will work harder. We can surely recognize that incentives based on present dissatisfactions are important in making people want more of what they now have. We must also be prepared to acknowledge that people work because of the incentive value of preserving present satisfactions. As we will see immediately below, they also work to secure from the work organization things that are equivalent to what they might otherwise have to provide for themselves.

The third subjective response to incentives is based on the ability of the work organization to provide its members with functional equivalents of services or rewards that also can be secured on a private basis. The most general functional equivalent is the replacement of personal actions by organization programs for enhancing security. These company security programs take a number of forms. Included under the security heading are health and welfare services, hospital and life insurance, disability and retirement pay, job tenure, and security of employment through annual employment, or annual wage schemes.[2] All of these aspects of personal living can be taken care of on an individual basis. It is significant that the work organization takes over the maintenance of features of personal security. This has important incentive value for members of the organization who typically lose benefits of security plans if they leave their employment.

The second kind of functional equivalent incentive is provision of substitutes for private activities. These substitutes may or may not be used by organization members. For those who use them, participation in the activity may have important incentive value. Examples of substitute activities include: company sponsored recreation and cultural programs; company lunchroom and coffee service facilities; company medical, counseling or psychiatric services; and credit unions or other financial aid services.

We can now summarize types of work incentives. They take the form of either financial or non-financial systems of payoff. From the personal subjective standpoint, incentives either play on present satisfactions, present dissatisfactions, or substitute company services and rewards for those usually secured on a private basis. Generally, these three subjective aspects are intermingled for any single form of incentive. We can best organize our view of incentives by visualizing an example of the relations between their forms and the subjective response to them. This is done in Table 13.1 where illustrations are presented. The chart shows only single illustrations. It should not be interpreted as representing an exhaustive list of possible examples.

In this chapter we are concerned with understanding how incentives are made systematic. We want to know how incentive systems are developed and why they take particular forms. Consequently, we will continue our analysis by focusing on the *forms* of incentive systems, dealing with financial and non-financial incentives, in that order.

TABLE 13.1

THERE ARE CHARACTERISTIC SUBJECTIVE RESPONSES TO EACH FORM OF INCENTIVE

(some illustrations)

Subjective Response to Incentives	*Form of Incentive* Financial	Non-Financial	Financial and Non-Financial
Present Satisfaction	"My wages are tops."	"My boss treats me like a human being."	"My seniority standing protects me."
Present Dissatisfactions	"Hope that raise comes through."	"Watch my smoke when I learn the ropes around here."	"I'm 'bucking' for a promotion."
Functional Equivalent: (1) Security	"I'd rather let 'them' worry about paying me than work for myself."	"My wife may not understand me but my boss sure does."	"When you work for this company for a long time you know they'll take care of you."
(2) Substitutes	"It's cheaper to eat in the company lunchroom than outside."	"Our department bowling team will win tonight."	"I had a rough time until the counsellor in Personnel set me straight."

FINANCIAL INCENTIVES

"It is literally true that most workers in the United States do not make a living. They make money and buy a living."[3] This conclusion by Noland and Bakke views the financial rewards of work as providing the worker with income to live in his community. It is a way of viewing money as a medium of exchange in which work is traded for income, and the income is then spent for personal consumption.

For our purposes we want to emphasize another aspect of income from work. The dollar is also a medium of evaluation.[4] The financial payoff for working becomes an important way of stating the value of a man's work. If one man earns more than another, his productive efforts may be presumed to be more valuable. This concern with money as a measure of a man's value to a productive enterprise is the keystone of all financial incentive schemes.[5]

The views that money provides a yardstick for measuring work performance, and that money is also a medium of exchange, supplement each other. The first statement tells us that money is a common measure of work performance. The second tells us that money income is useful only when it is spent for personal consumption.

Ideally, all financial incentive schemes are planned to pay for work in accordance with the importance of the worker's contribution. Again ideally, it should be possible to take the jobs, positions, and offices of a work organization and range them on a dollar scale, so that the importance of the work assignment corresponds to the amount of pay received.

Two problems arise in achieving the objective of making performance and pay correspond. (A) The first problem is to determine the relative standing of the company scale of pay in the community pay ranges. This is the problem of being sure that on similar jobs the people in one company get something like the same financial rewards as those in other companies. (B) The second problem is to establish, objectively if possible, a scale for measuring the importance of work assignments so that financial returns to everyone within the company can be assigned on a uniform basis.

COMMUNITY PAY LEVELS

What a man expects to be paid for his work is affected by what he knows other people are getting for the same work. In classical economic theory it was assumed that, if every worker were entirely free to change his job, a small wage increase offered by another employer would be an incentive to make the job change. In the operation of actual labor markets we discover that employers have pay scales that tend to be uniform among them. Workers in the labor market also tend to know the "going" pay for their kind of work. Consequently, there is not nearly the amount of job shifting between employers as classical economic theory would predict. We have to examine this aspect of labor market stability and ask: How does the individual worker come by the knowledge of what others like himself are getting? and Why do employers tend to match each other's pay scales?

There has been a very rapid growth in communication about pay rates.[6] The U.S. Bureau of Labor Statistics and some of its state counterparts publish regular statistics dealing with occupation and industry wages. Trades associations provide their members with survey statistics on their industry's wages. Unions do the same thing for their locals and members. Public and private employment services disseminate pay information when they refer job seekers. Help-wanted advertisements in newspapers generally feature the pay for open jobs. Federal and state minimum wage legislation establishes wage floors that become generally known throughout the community and are policed by the punitive provisions of the law. In general, we can conclude that job seekers have many avenues of information about what other people get paid for the kind of work they are seeking, and that employers share the same kinds of information. In terms of wage rate information, the sharing of knowledge in the labor market about wage levels is an important force making for community-wide uniformity in wage levels.

What keeps these women at their sewing machines day after day and year after year? They certainly do not work for the laughs that occasionally brighten a face. The incentives to come to work are largely financial, as are the incentives to stay put in the same old job.

If we now view the labor market as a competitive market in which many employers seek to hire the available labor we find still another factor making for wage rate uniformity.[7] From the standpoint of management decisions regarding wage rates, we are not here concerned with the detailed economic problems of labor costs as costs of production. We assume that an employer is going to hire labor to produce the number and kinds of items he estimates necessary for the market he sees before him. Faced with the need for hiring labor, from what standpoint can an employer view the general wage level he will offer?

It is a common experience to talk to employers and have them point out that their general wage and salary levels are as good or better than the average for the community in which their company is located. Implicit in this viewpoint is the concept that community pay levels determine the going rates for the company. Sometimes the employer statement is phrased in terms of the industry rather than the community. In either instance, however, the general pay levels for the company are related to the levels of the community or industry.[8]

This is basically a labor market concept of wage determination. Each employer is willing to make the necessary adjustment to keep in line with community or industry pay rates. General wage levels tend to be set in terms of the broad social forces operating in the community as a whole. In this sense, general pay levels may not be set, as economic theory suggests, by the employer's calculation of worker pay as a cost of production. The employer's alternative for not following the general levels of pay in the community or industry is to take his chances of not having sufficient labor to produce his goods during periods of high level employment. Under such circumstances, the employer is much more likely to meet the going price of labor and to cover any increased costs by adjusting upward the selling prices of his finished products.[9]

It is notable that the labor market concept of wage determination is actively fostered by labor unions. Unions consciously follow the policy of "equal pay for equal work." In terms of general wage levels this takes the form of arguing with individual employers that their wage rates are below community levels and should be raised. As unions have extended bargaining on a community-wide or industry-wide basis, they have been able to achieve uniformity in pay levels among employers.[10] Unions contend that there is discrimination against any workers employed at wages below community levels, and seek to rectify the discrimination by bargaining for pay raises. Thus, unions use the labor market view of wage determination as a logical basis for raising substandard wage levels. We will see below that unions use additional arguments to move the entire wage structure upward.

We may conclude, in general, that there are strong pressures institutionalized in the labor market that lead employers to make their pay rates comparable to community rates. These institutionalized aspects of the labor market are: (A) broad knowledge of pay levels shared by employers and employees alike; (B) the employer's competitive need for labor, making it necessary to meet the pay offers of other employers; and (C) strong union pressures to force low-paying employers up to community pay levels.

Fundamentally, the labor market concept of wage level determination rests on the view that pay is a measure of services rendered. From this standpoint, equal services should be equally compensated. This view is supported by employers because it provides a practical way of ordering relative pay rates. It is supported by workers and their unions because it tends to eliminate below-average pay levels from the labor market. Finally, government action, through minimum wage legislation, sets legal floors under the labor market wage structure and acts as a force pushing low-level wages up toward the average.

We have so far examined the institutional pressures that tend to keep pay levels grouped around the average. We have seen that this "averaging" of pay derives from working income viewed as the payoff that evaluates equal productive contribution as requiring comparable financial reward. We now turn to a second important question about community pay levels. How does the whole structure of pay move upward or downward? What sociological factors are important in contributing to such movements?

GENERAL MOVEMENT OF PAY LEVELS

There are four broad arguments used in moving pay levels as a whole upward or downward. The first is that employees are also consumers and need to be paid enough to buy back the goods and services they produce. The second is that wages should be tied to the cost of living so that working income will be able to buy approximately the same amount of goods and services when their price goes up or down. The third argument for general wage movements is to tie them automatically to productivity increases that are the consequences of technological innovation. Finally, labor unions sometimes argue that wage payments should be used to redistribute the national income in favor of workers.

The consumer income argument for moving wages upward or downward rests on the view that workers are also consumers. As consumers they have to have enough spendable income to buy back their share of the goods they produce. When Henry Ford in 1914 introduced a minimum $5.00 a day pay at the Ford Motor Company, he was using the consumer income argument to justify his move. Mr. Ford actually raised his wages above the industry and community level of the period. From an incentive standpoint he was saying that workers will work hard if they feel their income from work will buy them an adequate standard of living. Henry Ford was also saying that the prosperity of the economy depends on the ability to consume its output. Union policy generally accepts the consumer income view of wages.

The cost of living argument for general wage movements is an extension of the consumer income viewpoint. If consumer prices vary, and particularly if they move upward, then workers' income will not buy the same amount of goods as previously. To overcome this difficulty, wage levels are tied to price levels, and move with them. For example, wages may move automatically with changes in the consumer price index published by the Bureau of Labor Statistics. It is estimated that over two million workers in the United States are now covered by union contract agreements where their wages move automatically with shifts in consumer prices.

The incentive value of the cost of living view for changing general pay levels is clear. Workers are more likely to feel secure in their present employment if they are not caught in the squeeze of fixed wages and rising consumer prices. Since the cost of living argument provides an automatic way of raising wages with each change in the consumer price index, unions have accepted this position, and many have incorporated the idea in union contracts. The American economy has not had a great deal of experience with automatic downward adjustments of wages when consumer prices are falling. In such circumstances it is highly probable that unions will temporarily abandon the cost of living position. They will urge that wages should serve to redistribute the national income, and should not be cut when prices are falling.

A recent innovation in the determination of general wage levels is the viewpoint that technological productivity should be shared with workers. The General Motors-UAW union agreement of 1950 gave general currency to this position. The argument is essentially this. American productivity per man hour has been increasing at the rate of about 3 per cent each year for as far back as there are reliable statistics to measure it. This advance has come through better technology. If a man with the same physical and mental effort can turn out more goods because the machines he works with are better, then who shall benefit from his increased output? General Motors answered by saying it would grant its workers an automatic wage increase of 3 cents per year. This represents the workers' share of the increased output resulting from improved technology.

The technological improvement argument says that workers shall share the returns from the increased output of industry even though management was responsible for making the technical advances. As a minimum this has incentive value in keeping workers from opposing new machines and technical advances by guaranteeing they will get more pay from the anticipated increase in output. Needless to add, labor unions have accepted this contention, and can be given some responsibility for initiating it.

In addition to encouraging the three previous views of why general wage levels should move, unions have advanced a fourth, not shared by management. Unions have sometimes viewed their economic role as leading to the redistribution of the total income of the society in favor of workers. In terms of the redistribution of income view, labor argues that it is necessary to impose bargaining power in order to insure that labor gets an increasing share of the national wealth. This is another way of saying that if the rich get too rich, the poor are going to get too poor. The result will be economic stagnation because of the inability of the bulk of the population, which happens to be workers and their families, to buy the productive output of the society.

During the period of the 30's the notion of "under-consumption" gained wide currency. It led to the contention that wages should be raised during the depression years in order to redistribute purchasing power to the working population. It is of no importance whether this concept of the redistribution of income reflects reality or not. Studies indicate that workers' share of the national income has not been increased through union activity.[11] The point to emphasize here is that leaders of labor and union members are likely to act as though they believed that union economic action served to redistribute the wealth of the society in favor of workers.

Up to this point in analyzing financial incentives we have dealt with two issues. The first was to examine the institutional forces leading employers to "average" their pay levels with those of the community. Underlying this result is the belief that pay for work should be related to the productive contribution made. We have just analyzed the general movement of pay levels upward and downward on the dollar scale. Here we concluded that general wage movements are rationalized in terms of the four notions of wages as consumer income, the need for adjusting wages to the cost of living, sharing technical innovation through automatic pay increases, and the redistribution of national wealth.

It should be noted that we have not included the traditional economic viewpoint. Economists tend to view wages as one of several major costs of production. They see the employer setting his wage rates in terms of his analysis of the cost of hiring labor to produce a given number of items at a given price. The employer modifies his cost view of pay levels only to the extent necessary to take into account the balance between current demand and supply of labor in the market.

Our emphasis on the sociological aspects of pay as incentives is entirely deliberate. Looking at pay as a financial incentive we have to answer the question: How does the worker view the financial payoff he gets from working? The worker knows little about his own pay as a cost of production to his employer, and cares even less. For the man getting the payoff, the crucial questions are: (A) "Do I get at least as much as others making a comparable working contribution?" and (B) "On what grounds can all of us who are working get more?" We have shown why he gets about as much as comparable people because of employers' tendency to average their pay scales with those of the community. We have also shown the bases on which all those working get more pay, or less, through time. We have in effect given answers to the man for whom pay is one incentive to work.

COMPANY PAY SCALES

Let us now turn our attention to what happens inside a work organization. What incentive values do pay scales provide for employees, or what purposes do the pay scales serve as incentives? How are pay and salary systems established and administered? What are some of the unanticipated consequences for working behavior of company pay scales and the methods by which they are designed? These questions will be answered in order.

INCENTIVES FOR MOBILITY AND STABILITY

Differences in pay received by different persons have two incentive objectives. These objectives are: (A) to make employees want to move from lower to higher jobs, increasing their payoff as they move; and (B) to make employees want to stay in their present work, increasing their payoff for staying. Pay differentials are used to make people want to be upwardly mobile. They are also used to make people satisfied with their present job. These two objectives are achieved simultaneously by a method called job evaluation.

The mobility incentive is built into the job evaluation scheme by paying higher level jobs more than lower level jobs. The company president gets more pay than the general manager, and both get more than machine operators. In achieving the mobility incentive the company pay scale is graduated from low to high to correspond to the evaluation of jobs in terms of their productive contribution. It is assumed that many people will want to get ahead. Part of their reward for striving for advancement is the increased pay with each job promotion.

schemes contain these two financial incentives. Individual job evaluation plans will vary in the amount of incentive pay attached to mobility as over against stability.

JOB EVALUATION

Job evaluation is a method by which a series of jobs can be put in some rational order according to their productive contribution.[12] Once the jobs are ranked from low to high, the community pay scale is projected onto the job classes to determine the pay they will carry. Chart 13.1 shows the essential structure of any job evaluation plan.

The first operating problem is to establish some way for ranking work assignments ac-

CHART 13.1

PAY SYSTEMS HAVE STABILITY AND MOBILITY INCENTIVES

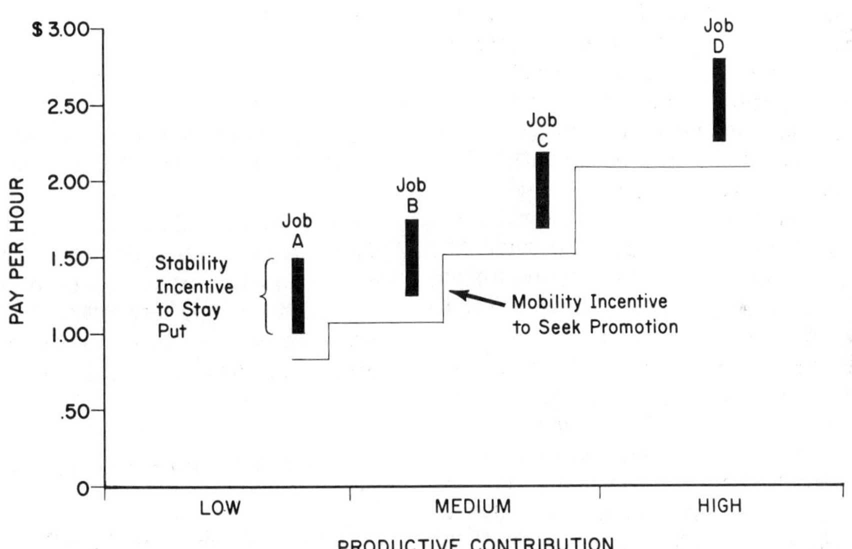

Not everybody, however, will make the promotion grade. In addition, not everybody will want to strive for promotion. Yet it will be desirable to provide an incentive for staying put on present work assignments. The incentive for keeping people stable in their present work is built into the job evaluation scheme by providing a pay range for increases within the same work category.

The two incentives are pictured in Chart 13.1 where the mobility and stability incentives can be visualized. All job evaluation

cording to their productive contribution. The least complicated way to do this is informally. Informal job evaluation simply says that within the ranks of management, positions and offices should be paid in accordance with the amount of authority attaching to them. All management members should get more pay than job holders, and the latter should be paid according to the difficulty and/or importance of the tasks performed. On these simple grounds it is possible to develop a usable job evaluation plan.

More formal methods exist for ranking work assignments. For example, a schedule of job factors may be set up including such items as job fatigue, physical effort, manual dexterity, intellectual effort, prior training required, and supervision needed. A long list of job components may be used. For each job, all the job components are evaluated on a point scale, and a number score is determined for each job factor. The individual scores may be summed, or weighted and then summed. The total score then becomes the evaluation of the work assignment. All jobs having the same score, or scores within a prescribed range, are paid alike. The jobs are then placed in rank order according to their job evaluation scores, and the step-like array of jobs, as shown in Chart 13.1, results.

Regardless of the particular system of job evaluation used, and we have illustrated the features of only a point scoring scheme, the end result is to obtain a standard score for each work assignment that ranks it against all others. Jobs, positions, and offices are ranked by the job evaluation method so that the financial payoff corresponds to the evaluated rank.

It would be possible to have a single wage or salary for each job or step in the evaluation plan. This, however, would not provide any incentive for staying put on a work assignment. Consequently, a range of pay is established, applying to the jobs in a given step. For shop jobs, the range may be relatively narrow, perhaps ten per cent of the starting wage for the job. For example, if the job pays a minimum of $2.00 per hour, the top rate for the job may be $2.20 per hour. This ten per cent range may be sufficient incentive for at least some workers to want to get to the top of the job pay range. In general, however, the incentive for job stability has to be based on a range greater than ten per cent. The stability incentive, if it is effective, has to come closer to twenty or twenty-five per cent of the lowest rate for the job. In the ranks of management, the stability incentive may be as much as fifty per cent. Thus, a position having a starting salary of $10,000 may have a ceiling of $15,000, permitting substantial increases for the incumbent, as a financial incentive to stay put in his present position.[13]

All job evaluation plans provide an objective way for ranking work assignments in relation to each other. The pay differences assigned to the succeeding ranks are the financial incentives for upward mobility, or promotions. Within a given rank, and for every job, position, or office, there is a range of pay provided. This differential pay for the same work assignment constitutes the incentive for stability, for staying put but receiving merit increases for effective performance. These are the two fundamental features of all job evaluation plans. These features build into the financial incentive schemes of the work organization the basic incentives for mobility and stability.

Both mobility and stability are necessary for the organization. Mobility provides a ready reserve of promotable people available to fill higher work assignments as they open up (people do die, leave, and retire from the organization, and new work assignments are established). Stability is necessary to maintain a trained and permanent work force capable of carrying on the organization tasks year after year. The bulk of employees reach promotion ceilings relatively early and have many years of future work at the same task. These are the "Thank God for" people who are a blessing because they do stay put. For them, merit increases on their present work assignment constitute financial incentives for continued effective performance. They, of course, also benefit from any upward movement in general pay levels.

ADMINISTERING COMPANY PAY SCALES

There are four major problems in administering company scales. These are: (A) maintaining flexibility of work assignments once they are established in the job evaluation scheme; (B) handling worker claims of inequities in the dollar value placed on their work as compared with other work; (C) striking a balance between stability and mobility incentives; and (D) making stability incentives effective. We are using "problem" here in the sense that unanticipated consequences result from job evaluation. Management has to face these consequences in administering company pay scales.

FLEXIBILITY OF WORK ASSIGNMENTS

In order to evaluate work assignments it is necessary to have a good job description. The job description must set forth all the tasks performed so that each task in the work assignment may be evaluated. Complete job descriptions make explicit every activity contained in the tasks performed. You will recall that in Chapter 2 we gave a job description for a Strip Roller, setting forth the detailed activities of his work.

Every worker comes to know, through his job description, what is included in his work, and what is excluded. Making the job description objective, by describing its details, also makes it specific, with its content and boundaries clearly defined. Under such circumstances, the worker most likely reacts by contending that only those activities contained in his job description are the things for which management can hold him. Consequently, the worker may refuse to do any work that is not specifically set forth in his job description. In short, to achieve objectivity in job descriptions for purposes of job evaluation, work assignments become rigid, and workers hold management to them by refusing to do work not contained in their jobs.

Two examples will make this point clear. In a plant employing 10,000 workers, as a result of a newly instituted job evaluation plan, machine operators were refusing to perform jobs they considered to be part of a higher job classification. The machine operators were ordered by management to make minor adjustments of the cutting tools on their machines while they were operating. The workers refused, claiming that tool adjustment was part of machine setup work. Under the job evaluation plan machine setup work was a separate job paid at a higher rate. Prior to the establishment of the job evaluation plan there was no question that tool adjustment was part of the operator's task. The job evaluation plan had served to emphasize the difference between machine operator and machine setup man (who prepared the speeds and feeds on the machine and adjusted the cutting tools prior to operation). When this distinction became focused in two separate job classifications, the machine operators argued that they would do only their assigned tasks, or would do the additional work only if paid the higher setup man rate while doing it.

The second example also occurred in a large plant employing 12,000 production workers. On production welding, finish welders were refusing to do tack welding and fitting work. Before making the finish welds requiring high uniformity and accuracy, large parts were put in a fixture holding the pieces in place. Then temporary "tack" welds were made at regular intervals to hold the pieces together rigidly for the finish weld. Fitting and tack welding were lower skilled and lower rated jobs, but the finish welders were ordered by management to do them in the interests of maintaining continuity of production. Management guaranteed the finish welding rate even while tack welding and fitting were being done. The finish welders refused, claiming tack welding and fitting did not come within their job description. The finish welders had been segregated by their job descriptions as a high class work group. They refused to perform lower level work even though it involved no financial sacrifice, and had they done it, would have increased over-all output. Job descriptions made work assignments rigid and actually impaired output efficiency in this case.

We may conclude that an inevitable consequence of establishing accurate job descriptions for job evaluation purposes is that work assignments become more rigid. This inflexibility may, in turn, have adverse consequences for productive efficiency.

The most typical method for handling the issue of worker unwillingness to take on new tasks is to provide a systematic standard for determining when a new job description must be made. Usually, any change in equipment, materials, or product is declared in advance, as the signal for a new job description and a new evaluation of the work assignment. These standards are even written into union contracts so that management and workers know when to expect a new job study, and the circumstances justifying it. Obviously, the need for making many new studies of changing jobs places a considerable burden on the company job evaluation staff. Such a staff, once established, finds a heavy work load and tends to grow rapidly. Thus, in order to preserve some flexibility in work assignments, management must undertake to operate a new staff department, adding to the indirect costs of production.

JOB INEQUITIES

A second problem in administering company pay scales involves the accuracy with which comparative pay rates are established. If a group of workers feel that they are not being paid enough, compared with the pay for other jobs, considerable dissatisfaction may result. The dissatisfaction usually takes the form of claiming an inequity in pay. Workers will contend that they work just as hard, but get paid less; or that their work is just as skilled but is paid for at a lower rate.

The central feature of all claims of job inequity is that the job evaluation plan itself has made an error. Through some mishap a particular job has not received as high an evaluation as it should. It is notable that the claim of discrimination is always made from the vantage point of the lower rated job. The benchmarks for measuring inequities are always higher rated jobs, against which it is contended that a lower rated job has suffered by comparison. The correction of inequities, therefore, takes the form of raising the lower rated job to a higher pay level, if the raise can be justified.

BALANCING STABILITY AND MOBILITY INCENTIVES

Every financial incentive scheme attempts to provide stability and mobility incentives at the same time. It is necessary to organize the relationships among jobs so that it becomes attractive financially to move from a lower to a higher job. It is also necessary to provide some range of pay for each job so that over a period of years the worker can feel he is making some financial progress without changing his job.

A compromise is always required in achieving these two objectives. In order to achieve the incentive value of taking job promotions, the differences in pay between present and higher work assignments have to be relatively great. In order to maximize the incentive value of staying on the present job, the pay range for the job has to be increased. As the second is accomplished, there is a greater likelihood of overlap in pay between jobs, thereby diminishing the attractiveness of moving to the next higher job. Therefore the pay scales of a company reflect a compromise between these two non-compatible objectives. This dilemma is visualized in Chart 13.2 where the two objectives are separately pictured.

The compromise between mobility and stability incentives is usually achieved in the light of the requirements of the particular company or industry. If the organization is a fast grow-

CHART 13.2

CONFLICT BETWEEN STABILITY AND MOBILITY INCENTIVES

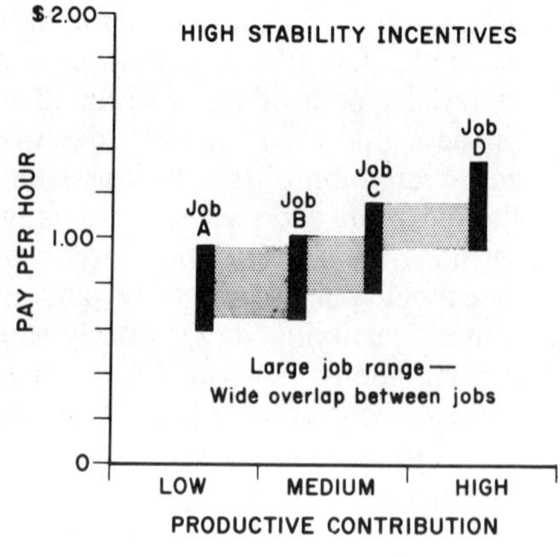

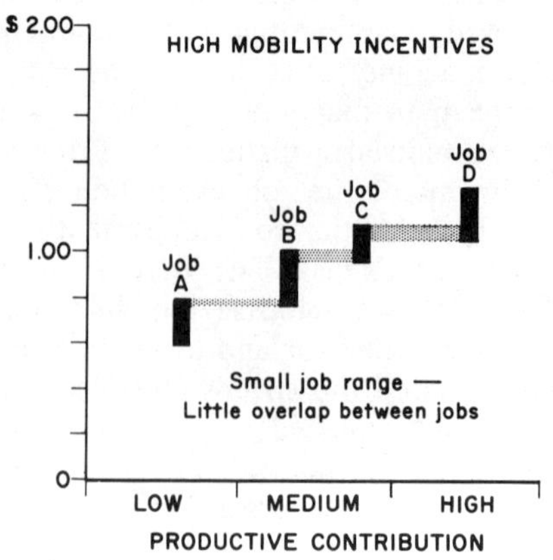

ing company, there are likely to be relatively narrow job and salary pay ranges accompanied by sharp differences between jobs in order to encourage people to move upward to fill the rapidly opening higher positions. If, on the other hand, the company is a stable one, not requiring rapid expansion of personnel, there are likely to be relatively wide pay ranges for each job in order to hire people for those jobs and keep them there for long periods of time until needed for promotions. At the same time, such companies will have narrower differences between jobs and a great deal more overlap between the pay scales of adjacent work assignments.

MAKING STABILITY INCENTIVES EFFECTIVE

To keep a man on the same work assignment for a long period of time and still provide him with adequate financial incentives is not easy. There is a crucial administrative problem in making stability incentives effective. This problem is: how does the employee progress up the rate range for his work?

The stability incentives must be effective in the occupation of printer. The younger man still learning his trade can see his long time career moving just a few steps to the place of his older colleague. To all intents the younger man reached about as far as he will go, with many years of work still ahead of him.

A person can move from the bottom to the top of the wage range for his work assignment in one of two ways. His pay increases may be automatic, or they may be based on some measure of performance.

Where it is difficult to measure work performance, as would be true in most managerial positions, and some office and shop jobs, an automatic progression policy is likely to be used. Such a policy defines a beginner's rate for the work. After a fixed period of time (say six months to a year) the employee is given a permanent rating and a pay increase. Future increases may be given at periodic intervals, in stated amounts. After a period of several years or more, the person has progressed to the top pay rate for his work assignment. This progress has been up a step-like pay scale for the job. Movement to the next higher step results from a given period of service with at least an average level of performance. It should be clear that automatic progression from bottom to top of the job pay range is simple to administer. Everyone makes the move upward, unless he is below average, in which instance he is likely to be fired or transferred. Thus over a relatively short period of time more and more employees tend to reach the top of the pay scale for their work.

Even though it is easy to administer, the automatic progression system tends to destroy the incentive for stability. When the majority of fellow-workers are at the top pay for your work along with you, there is no effective future pay target, and no satisfaction at being higher paid than the others. Indeed, an automatic within-job pay increase system is likely to generate real pressures for general wage increases as an increasing proportion of people reach the top of their job pay scales. The general wage increase then becomes the only way employees can stay on their present work assignment and still get more money.

Where stability incentives are based on meritorious performance an added burden is placed on management to measure or evaluate merit. The problem is essentially this: How will management know the people who perform above average so that they can be given a pay increase as a reward? What management is trying to do is reward exceptionally meritorious performance.[14] Ordinarily, for poor performance, management does not give a pay or salary cut; it simply withholds a pay increase to signalize its displeasure with the person's performance.

It is clear that merit increases in pay within the job classification require some way to measure merit. Let us look at the fundamentals of merit rating as a process that are the same for all systems used. All systems of merit rating are methods for gathering opinions about an employee from one or several other members of the work organization. Merit ratings are always opinion data.[15]

All merit rating systems suffer from the usual limitations of opinion data. The first general limitation of opinion data is the "halo effect": that a general opinion will influence specific opinions about single items. If I think an employee is generally good, I will rate him "excellent" or "good" on all the individual items (ability, dependability, loyalty, skill, cooperativeness, and so forth) for which a rating is asked. If I think the man is below average, I will rate the individual items as "poor" or "below average." This halo effect is an important limitation of the opinion data used for merit ratings.

A second general limitation of opinion data is the personal orientation of the rater toward others. Some people tend to rate very favorably, while others tend to be tough in their ratings. Each person expresses his particular biases in the opinions he holds of the people around him. In order to have some degree of uniformity when the opinion data of several raters are used, the bias of the individual raters has to be discounted.

A third limitation of opinion data is that the more general the item being evaluated, the less discriminating is the opinion about it likely to be. In an effort to standardize merit ratings, a company will often have all incumbents of jobs, positions, and offices rated on the same items. For example, they may all be rated on "cooperativeness." This may be an important item to measure for an executive, or a sales person serving the public. It may be a wholly irrelevant item in measuring the performance of the night watchman. In some instances, as in the case of the inspector, he might have to be rated "low" on cooperation to be considered good, since that indicates he is not likely to be in collusion with the workers whose output he is inspecting.

Granting the three basic limitations of opinion data, and correcting for them, it is possible to design a merit rating system that does point out the above-average personnel eligible for pay increases. Under a good merit rating plan, employees in a given job classification are likely to be distributed more evenly than under an automatic increase plan, along the pay range for the classification. This avoids bunching at the top limit of the pay scale, characteristic of automatic pay increases.

However, every time an individual does not get a merit increase due to a low rating by his boss, the subordinate's enthusiasm for the boss is likely to decrease. Merit rating schemes are notorious for placing strains on authority relations in the work organization. The stress is particularly great on the authority holder. He is placed under great pressure to justify low ratings to subordinates who receive them. It is not always easy to face an irate employee, who, having little to lose by complaining, comes storming into the boss' office demanding an explanation of his low merit rating.

We may conclude, generally, that it is not easy to make the financial incentives for stability operate effectively. We have looked at some of the technical problems involved in making stability incentives work. Insofar as an employee is satisfied to stay in his present work assignment for a long time, we are justified in concluding that the financial rewards for job stability are less important than other kinds of rewards. The non-financial incentives will be examined later in this chapter.

UNANTICIPATED CONSEQUENCES OF PAY SYSTEMS

There are two interesting and important consequences of pay systems that are not always expected when the systems are established. The first is the way in which financial rewards are used to encourage and enforce conforming behavior by subordinates. The second consequence is the impact on the destiny of the authority holder of the fact that he is part of the financial reward system.

The responsibility of the authority holder for determining whether a person gets a pay increase or promotion becomes one key incentive for the subordinate to orient himself acceptably toward his boss. The boss can recommend merit increases, or he can block them with a low rating. The boss can recommend promotion, or he can advise against it. The supervisor is in a key position to influence the working destiny of his subordinates. Where a merit rating plan is used, the periodic ratings are made a part of the employee's permanent personnel record. This can mark a man, and he has a hard time living down a bad reputation established by past merit ratings. The way in which pay systems are administered provides the work organization with significant control over the behavior of its members.

An undesirable consequence of the connection between pay systems and authority structures is the possibility of favoritism being displayed by supervisors. A supervisor may use pay increases and promotions in a discriminatory fashion. Without a grievance procedure and the protection of a union, the supervisor's authority may be abused, destroying whatever incentive the pay system may have for high level performance, and substituting "apple polishing" as the single criterion for advancement.

The fact that the authority holder is important in administering the financial reward system has two important consequences for his own destiny. In the first place, his evaluation of his subordinates becomes a test of his own effectiveness as a supervisor. In the second place, he is given the responsibility for sponsoring his own successor.

If a supervisor rates his crew members low, his own boss is likely to question the advisability of keeping the low rated people, and may even wonder why the supervisor took them on in the first place. A supervisor's low ratings of his subordinates may raise questions about his capacity to pick and develop people. On the other hand, should the supervisor have many highly rated people in his unit, he may suffer serious personnel turnover. Under the circumstances the supervisor may develop the reputation for knowing how to pick good people, but at the same time, experience difficulty in running his own unit because the company will constantly steal personnel away from him to promote to jobs in other departments.

The destiny of the supervisor is also involved in the selection of his own replacement. It is a common belief in industry that every supervisor should always be training his successor. Every management position should be two deep, and preferably three or four deep. Management presses each authority holder to select and develop a replacement. By manipulating promotions and merit increases, the supervisor is in a position to sponsor his own successor.

There are some subtle issues involved in choosing a replacement. An obvious designation of an heir apparent may be punishing to the man selected. His peers may consider him a "fair haired boy" and make his life miserable. The judgment of the supervisor may also be called into question by management. Is the supervisor really capable of selecting the best possible replacement? Finally, the supervisor may feel threatened by having his own replacement breathing down his neck, ready to take over. In short, every supervisor develops a sensitivity about the mixed blessings attaching to his involvement as an authority holder in the financial incentive systems of his work organization.

We can now summarize financial incentive systems, as they stimulate mobility and stability, in the following terms. The intention of financial payoff is to reward better than average performance with more pay. But we have now seen that the payoff is partly for conforming behavior as well as above average output. Men given periodic pay increases and promotions may be sociologically the most deserving of reward. This is so because both their output records, and their conforming behavior, are being measured and rewarded. It may even be true that the highest producers do not get the top rewards because they rebel against conforming to authority!

INDIVIDUAL AND GROUP PAYMENT METHODS

Payment to the individual for his work performed is based on the assumption that it is easiest to be induced to work hard when you can see a direct relationship between your own output and its reward. In measured day work (pay is by the hour with a fixed minimum number of units of output) the individual is supposed to see the connection between his own work behavior and his payoff for it. Where graduated pay is used (more pay for more output, often called an "incentive" system) the connection between efforts and output is supposed to be even clearer to the individual.[16] The management motive for paying the individual for his own output is that it will make each worker develop a deeper sense of responsibility for his work assignment.

Payment to a group of workers for their joint output is largely justified on the grounds that the group becomes self-policing. If everyone's pay depends on the joint effort, laggards will be urged on, or punished, by their eager fellow workers. Consequently, the burden of supervision is reduced. At the same time, the group payment method mobilizes the work group in the interests of the work organization. Paying the group, then, can also utilize morale as an important ingredient of production.

The literature on group *vs.* individual methods of payoff tends to extol the virtues of one method over the other.[17] The fact of the matter is that both methods work, and work well. The reason for this is clear. The goals or objectives of each of the methods are different. If management is seeking to develop individual worker responsibility, then the individual method is preferable. If management is trying to reduce administrative overhead, and wants to mobilize the work group for organization purposes, then the group method should be used.[18]

The only limitation on either method is that the unit of payment be appropriate to the output situation.[19] Where an individual's output is clearly evident in the flow of work, then the payment to him is appropriate. Where it is difficult to follow the individual contribution of a worker, or where his contribution is intimately dependent on the work of others, then a group payment system is called for. The group should be a natural production unit, with the group output clearly measurable.

OTHER FINANCIAL PAYOFFS

There is a wide variety of financial incentives other than wages or salaries. Profit sharing, bonuses, free medical and other services, suggestion systems that pay in dollars, and at the executive ranks, the generous expense accounts, company limousines, and "working" vacations, are all examples of added financial incentives for working.[20]

Periodically, interest turns to the additional financial incentives in a search for new ways to stimulate employee effort. Perhaps the central reason for such interest lies in the fact, already examined, that companies are less and less different from each other in their straight financial payoffs. The averaging of wages and salaries with those of the community or industry means that the distinctive company has to have added financial incentives.

The literature is full of special pleading for particular ways of making the additional financial payoffs. It is probably true that all added incentives work, more or less successfully. That is, they work in the sense that employees will gladly accept any methods for "sweetening the take-home."[21]

One of the pitfalls involved in using added financial incentives is the effort sometimes made to substitute uncertain special incentives for certain wages or salaries. In the most extreme case, where a salesman works on a straight commission for each sale made, with a bonus for exceeding a quota, the incentive value of the added earnings may be overwhelmed by the insecurity of no earnings in a bad week or month. In short, special financial incentives can only be effective when added to the basic financial incentives. The added incentives cannot take the place of a regular payoff for work performed.

MONEY MAKES THE WORLD GO ROUND

It has become part of the folklore of industrial management to assert that wages and salaries are not the most important incentive for work. Studies are cited to show that workers rank earnings below the top when asked what they like most about their work. Does this really prove that other incentives really take precedence over income from work? The answer is a clear negative.

If wages and salaries are comparable to the going community or industry rates, then they are likely to be taken for granted, as Haire and

Gottsdanker and others have pointed out.[22] If employees feel that their basic financial payoff is at an acceptable level, then and only then will they rate other incentives as more important to them. This is illustrated in the case of the Detroit Edison Company where job security was excellent, but where wage levels fell below the going rates in the automobile plants. When the 8,075 workers were asked, "What do you like least about working for Detroit Edison?" one out of every five reported earnings. In this study, 19 per cent would not or could not give an answer to this question, so that almost one quarter of all those responding gave earnings as the most disliked aspect of working for the company.[23] Twenty-two per cent of these same workers rated chances for promotion as the most disliked aspect of their work. Eight other reasons for not liking work in the company drew only one to seven per cent of the responses. It seems clear from this evidence that when the basic financial payoff is not considered adequate, employees have no difficulty in recognizing this, and being unhappy about it.

In our society money does make the world go around. As Katz has pointed out, a worker wants economic advancement and economic security for himself and his family.[24] Taking a job is a means to this end. In our society, as Veblen long ago suggested, we have measured most forms of human activity in money terms. Money is the universal medium of exchange that can buy anything from man's brainpower to, it is alleged, woman's virtue. Income remains the all-important means for satisfying human wants and needs. Income from wages and salaries is the major incentive to work.[25]

NON-FINANCIAL INCENTIVES

We have already suggested that non-financial incentives are forms of payment for working where the inducement is not a monetary one. The affirmative definition of non-financial incentives is: the psychic rewards, or the rewards of enhanced position, that can be secured in the work organization.

There are two general forms of psychic rewards with which we will deal. The first is satisfaction with the work assignment, sometimes called job satisfaction. The second is "privilege pay," which is the free access to interaction with those in a superior organization rank.

There are three major forms of position rewards that can be won at work. The first is "power pay," which is an increase in the essentiality or exclusiveness of a work assignment. The second is "authority pay," an advancement into a position of greater authority. The last is "status pay," an increase in value attaching to a person on some comparative standard of judgment.

JOB SATISFACTION

One of the rewards for some people at work is the satisfaction they get from their tasks. The work assignment itself is a source of job satisfaction. The big question is this:

Service pins awarded for 10, 20, 30 years service in a company may have little monetary value. However, they are widely accepted as a symbol of the contribution made by individuals in terms of service. Perhaps these awards symbolize for those who draw satisfaction from them, as this man obviously does, an inner feeling of job achievement that is given ceremonial support by the company.

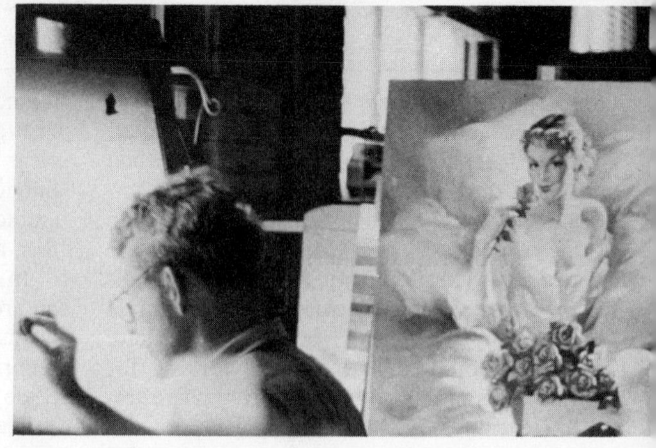

An industrial artist retouching photograph plates preparatory to making multicolor printing plates. His work will result in faithful reproduction of the picture standing beside him. This kind of skilled work can bring out positive feelings of job satisfaction.

what is there about work assignments that provides personal satisfaction? Studies do not give us conclusive answers to this question. However, the partial answers are suggestive.

In general, there is strong evidence that job satisfaction increases with the skill required to do work. Harrell summarizes a number of studies reaching this general conclusion.[26] A series of studies by Hoppock shows that more than 90 per cent of a group of 500 teachers like their work, while among a cross section of over 300 people in a Pennsylvania town an index of job satisfaction increased as one moved up the skill ladder.[27] In a study of working youth, Bell found that 98 per cent of those working in canning factories and textile mills as unskilled laborers hated their jobs.[28] In a study of an automobile assembly line, Walker and Guest found that most of the workers did not get satisfaction out of their work and wished that they did.[29]

In a cross section of thousands of industrial workers who were asked about their satisfaction with work, Hull and Kolstad concluded that people in highly skilled trades responded with greater satisfaction about their work than did unskilled labor.[30] Studies by Thorndike,[31] Uhrbrock,[32] and Super,[33] confirm the increase in amount of job satisfaction that comes with higher skill and more complex work.

In an attempt to separate out the intrinsic job satisfaction factors from the general liking for all aspects of one's work, Morse studied 580 clerical employees of an Eastern insurance company.[34] In responses to interview questions only 7 per cent of high level technical employees revealed low satisfaction with the specific work they were doing, while 41 per cent of those doing repetitive clerical work had low job satisfaction scores. The relationship was not changed by holding constant length of service and salary.

If we ask what there is about a work assignment that makes it satisfying, some partial answers are suggested by several studies. In the Morse study those who had higher job satisfaction scores tended to describe their jobs as being more varied, and giving them some chance for decisions about their work. This conclusion is also reached by Walker and Guest in their study of the automobile assembly line. Another study by the Michigan Survey Research Center of 5,700 production workers in heavy industry revealed that 51 per cent would like to have more to say about the way their work is done, although 40 per cent were not interested in having more decision making responsibility about their jobs. In this same study 65 per cent of the people felt that their work could be done better if they had more chance to make suggestions about such things as design, layout, and set-up of their own work.[35]

We may conclude, then, that people doing more difficult and more skilled tasks get more rewards from their work in the form of job satisfaction. In particular, they seem to enjoy the variety of their work and the sense of personal responsibility they have for doing it.[36]

These general conclusions suggest that at the lower reaches of most work organizations the non-financial reward of job satisfaction probably does not operate generally as a significant incentive. It is also true that most industrial workers start their working life at the lowest skill levels. This poses an interesting administrative problem. As some of these workers gradually move up into higher skill work assignments, they probably have to change from an indifferent or even hostile attitude toward job satisfaction, to an outlook in which they value the satisfaction rewards they get from doing their tasks. This is another way of suggesting that different incentives operate at successive stages in working life histories. Industrial managers might well ponder this conclusion, and not expect job satisfaction comparable to their own from unskilled and semi-skilled subordinates.

PRIVILEGE PAY

Privilege pay, like job satisfaction, is essentially a psychic reward. Both result in a feeling or attitude of wellbeing and pleasure. We mean by privilege pay the freedom with which authority holders permit subordinates to interact with them. People in authority can accord to their subordinates opportunities for interaction, or these opportunities can be withheld. It is a genuine privilege to a subordinate to be able to talk with his boss as another human being.

Privilege pay is highly valued. Subordinates like to feel, in particular, (A) that they are free to talk to the boss about working problems, (B) that their boss values their professional and technical opinion, and really wants them to be free to express their opinions about operating problems troubling the boss (e.g., to be the opposite of "yes men"), and (C) that there is an area of discourse with the boss where they can be man-to-man with each other. When the boss is able to create an atmosphere in which these goals of subordinates are achieved, then the subordinates have been paid off in privilege pay. They have earned the privilege of setting aside the boss-subordinate relationship, under some conditions, and at some times.[37]

There has been a very vigorous movement in personnel circles to encourage bosses to make more liberal use of privilege pay as a work incentive. This general movement goes under the name of "group dynamics." The formal rationalization for using a group dynamics approach as a boss is that it succeeds in unlocking hitherto unused human resources of the organization. By involving people in making decisions about their own work, more effective brain power is mobilized on behalf of the work organization. Many studies, of which the report by Kahn and Katz[38] is representative, establish this conclusion.

The fact that people enjoy and value participation in determining their own working destiny appears undisputed. The "group dynamics" approach, initiated through the research of Kurt Levin,[39] has been extremely valuable in providing an alternative to what Worthy[40] has called the "machine theory of organization," or what Mayo[41] had earlier called the "rabble hypothesis" of industrial administration. In the more mechanical view of industrial administration it is assumed that the work organization operates most effectively only by using its formal structures and official channels and means of interaction.

In the group dynamics view, it is recognized that human beings respond to a wide range of incentives, of which privilege pay is an important one. It has not generally been recognized by the proponents of the group dynamics approach that what the subordinate gets out of the group dynamics situation is privilege pay. Most of the studies of employee reaction do not go beyond pointing out the greater satisfaction reported by subordinates.[42] It should be recognized, however, that the principal reason for such satisfaction is the opportunity to interact with the boss as a relative equal, under particular circumstances. It is the boss who is conferring this privilege on his subordinates. He is giving them privilege pay. Indeed, the management literature makes this crystal clear. The great difficulty in making a group dynamics approach work is getting the boss to accept and use it.[43] Only when the boss is willing to accord this privilege pay to his subordinates will the method work.

Privilege pay is an important non-financial incentive for work. In particular, it works because it modifies the authority structure of work organizations. It changes the boss from an "oracle" to a troubled administrator, seeking the best help he can get from his working associates and subordinates. Privilege pay substitutes for an unquestioning response to authority by subordinates, an attitude of cooperation. In order for privilege pay to be an effective incentive, the boss must be willing to admit that he "doesn't know," and be willing to pay off his subordinates with the privilege of expressing their best ideas to him, in helping him be a more effective boss.

POWER PAY

We have already indicated that power pay, authority pay, and status pay are rewards of enhanced position that can be secured at work. Each form of pay serves to improve the position of the person receiving it.

Power pay is the reward conferred on a person by making his tasks more important in the organization. It is one of the precepts of management that subordinates should be encouraged in many ways to feel that their work is important to the organization. This is the way in which power pay as a non-financial incentive is usually discussed. When we stop to ask what is meant by importance, we discover it can be described in two ways. The work is important because its performance is essential; or the work is important because no one else does it or can do it.

The most direct forms of power pay are to make the work more important, or to give the worker more exclusive jurisdiction over it. This usually involves actual changes in tasks and the assignment of work responsibility. For example, a man operating a machine tool may be told that the accuracy of his work determines the functioning of a finished product. He may not only be told the tolerance dimensions within which he is expected to hold the items he produces, but may, in addition, be given instruction in using micrometers and gages to measure his output. He may also be given the responsibility for checking his own work, and making adjustments in the machine to correct for inaccuracies. The worker now knows that his output is considered highly essential and is given the means for insuring that he will fulfill his critical responsibility. He has been paid off in power pay.

To take another example of power pay, a branch plant accountant may be given the sole responsibility for forwarding accurate accounting reports to the home office of the firm. Here the person is impressed with his critical importance as the only link between the records of the branch plant and the home office. The power pay comes in the form of exclusive jurisdiction over a work assignment.

The subjective response to power pay is clear. A person feels his own importance when he is aware of the position of power he holds. Whiting Williams long ago reported this sense of power among the lowly workers with whom he worked as an observer.[44]

This man controls the oil well drilling operation. His is a job of considerable responsibility, being both essential to the drilling operation, and performed exclusively by him. Does his obvious interest and alertness suggest that he responds favorably to his "power pay"?

Power pay can be an exceedingly strong incentive. It applies at all levels of the organization. The satisfaction resulting from it does not depend on the absolute amount of power a person actually holds. The satisfaction with this kind of non-financial payoff results from a clear recognition that work is somehow important, and that superiors recognize its importance. In short, there is a real reward in knowing that one's work has an important function in the organization.

AUTHORITY PAY

Authority pay is the promotion to a position of greater authority. It is the most generally used of the non-financial incentives. For all those employees who aspire to get ahead at work by moving into the ranks of management, authority pay is a potent incentive.

In relatively simple organizations the authority pay is reasonably clear-cut. For such organizations there tends to be a close correspondence between promotions in management and increased authority.

In more complex organizations promotions and authority may not have a simple relation to each other. If we examine the kind of authority involved, the reason wil become clear. As persons are promoted to higher levels of management, they tend to move from directing authority to coordinating and controlling authority as we have already seen in Chapter 5. They may also move from a staff to a line position, or move in the opposite direction. Under the circumstances of a change in kinds of authority, or kinds of management position, it is not always clear that a promotion is necessarily accompanied by more authority pay. Indeed, one of the ways to get rid of people without firing them is to "kick them upstairs." This involves a nominal promotion accompanied by actual lessening of authority —some of the authority pay is taken away from the person.

Authority pay is a not very subtle form of payoff for working. People tend to measure authority pay in very practical terms. "How many people do you supervise?" or "How many departments are under your jurisdiction?" are obvious questions designed to determine the level of authority pay. For those employees who are particularly attracted by authority pay, "empire building" may become a method for forcing more authority pay from management.

Of all the non-financial incentives for working, authority pay comes the closest to being a substitute for a financial payoff.[45] It is not uncommon in industry to encounter supervisors who make less money than some of their subordinates. What probably accounts most for the supervisor's tolerance of the situation is his greater authority pay, although he is fully aware of his income disadvantage and actively seeks to overcome it.

STATUS PAY

Status pay is the increased value that management places upon you. This sense of value may be grounded in any scale of measurement that permits comparative judgments. Members of management may consider one employee the neatest, another the most loyal, and another the most skilled. If there is some public acknowledgment of these evaluations, each employee is being rewarded with status pay by management.

We recall, however, that status conferred by management is not to be confused with status accorded by the primary group at work. When management and worker goals differ, the former may backfire on the recipient, who has accepted some token of company approval; the latter seems thus to be more durable. Status pay accorded a person by peers is potentially a large element in the payoff of a given job, conceivably enough to keep a man from starting elsewhere.

The difference between status pay and power pay is real, although in an operating situation they may be confused at first glance. Status pay is the reward for some valued attribute of the person. Power pay is the reward for some valued attribute of the work assignment. For example, all secretaries in a firm may be expected to produce neat letters. Some will, in fact, do neater work than others and will be accorded higher status for it. The president's secretary may or may not turn out the neatest letters of them all (she is probably near the top in neatness anyway), but she has a powerful job in the organization if only because she controls access to her boss.

Status pay is the "cheapest" form of payoff for the organization. It involves only some kind of public recognition by a member of management of a person's particular merits. The individual so singled out receives some acknowledgment that he is valued, usually in a way that other employees will be aware of the high regard of management.[46]

The incentive value of status pay depends on the good judgment of those according it. The attributes of a person that are valued should have some relevance to the work situation. To prefer an employee for the way he parts his hair, or because he is tall, is to accord status, but for reasons irrelevant to the work situation. This kind of preferential selection does not turn out to be status pay at work because it does not use a criterion of selection that could apply to all employees for their work performance.

Because status pay is so cheap to give, it is likely to be given lavishly, and thereby lose its incentive value. If everyone gets praised for something, then the value of the praise is diminished, and it becomes a debased form of payment. The very value of being accorded high status lies in the fact that this is a position shared with few others. Differentials in status must be recognized and preserved if status pay is to have incentive value.

Status pay is a nonfinancial incentive found in all kinds of work organizations, and providing incentives for all kinds of personnel. We have elaborated elsewhere (especially in Chapters 2 and 3) the various forms taken by status pay.

INCENTIVE SYSTEMS

The financial and non-financial elements of incentives for work tend to form systems. Each work organization puts various forms of incentives into effect in different combinations; some kinds supplement others, while other combinations may be incompatible with each other.[47]

Each work organization develops its special incentive systems. A government bureau, for example, with more limited opportunities to exploit financial incentives by paying high salaries, will give greater emphasis to non-financial rewards in working out its system of work incentives. Power, authority, and status pay tend to take on a great prominence for the government bureaucrat, and job satisfaction coupled with privilege pay ("the Secretary of State called me in for consultation today") become highly valued as his psychic income.

To take another example, an oil company recruiting for work in a foreign oil field may give great prominence to the direct financial incentives of high pay, low-cost quarters, and favorable income tax treatment in order to attract and hold men for such work. Here the opportunities for non-financial incentives to operate may be small, so that the emphasis is put largely on the financial ones.

Note also that some kinds of incentives go together while others do not. If part of the payoff is in the form of power pay by giving exclusive jurisdiction over an operation, then it does not make sense to determine the wages or salary on a group output basis. The very exclusiveness with which the tasks are performed calls for individual salary payment. To take another example, there are sometimes wide overlaps in the salaries of assistant, associate, and full professors in a university of college. The professorial ranks are largely status differences. Some teachers value status pay almost as much as their salary check, so that it is not completely impossible for them to accept a lower ranking colleague who draws more pay. On the other hand, it would be difficult, if not impossible, to recruit chemistry and physics professors into a business research activity without making the financial payoff comparable to the status title of the positions being filled. The differences in the character of the two organizations determine the differences in the incentive systems they employ.[48]

We have given detailed consideration to incentives for work. Incentives are complex in their form and content. We have also discovered that they are built into systems that differ among work organizations. Finally, we have seen that the incentives for work are built into work organizations. They are the product of rational planning, and are carried out through careful administration and management.

NOTES FOR CHAPTER 13

[1] Some general references include: C. C. Balderston, *Group Incentives* (Philadelphia: University of Pennsylvania Press, 1930); Z. C. Dickinson, *Compensating Industrial Effort* (New York: Ronald Press, 1937); and G. H. Miles, *The Problem of Incentives in Industry* (London: Pitman & Sons, 1932).

[2] For excellent discussions of the security implications of annual wages see: Bureau of National Affairs, *The Guaranteed Annual Wage* (Washington: The Bureau, 1955); and A. D. H. Kaplan, *The Guarantee of Annual Wages* (Washington: The Brookings Institution, 1947).

[3] E. W. Noland and E. W. Bakke, *Workers Wanted* (New York: Harper & Brothers, 1949), p. 149.

[4] See, for example, Melville Dalton, "Economic Incentives and Human Relations," in Solomon Barkin *et al.* (eds.), *Industrial Productivity* (Champaign: Industrial Relations Research Association, 1951), pp. 130-145.

[5] Some general references dealing with wage and salary payment plans are: C. C. Balderston, *Wage Setting Based on Job Analysis and Job Evaluation* (New York: Industrial Relations Counselors, 1940); D. W. Belcher, *Wage and Salary Administration* (Englewood Cliffs, N. J.: Prentice-Hall, Inc., 1955); M. J. Dooher and Vivienne Marquis (eds.), *The AMA Handbook of Wage and Salary Administration* (New York: American Management Association, 1950); J. T. Dunlop, *Wage Determination under Trade Unions* (New York: The Macmillan Company, 1944); R. W. Gilmour, *Industrial Wage and Salary Control* (New York: John Wiley & Sons, 1956); and J. O. Hopwood, *Salaries, Wages, and Labor Relations* (New York: Ronald Press, 1945).

[6] Cf. Ernest Dale, *Sources of Economic Information for Collective Bargaining* (New York: American Management Association, 1950).

[7] See, in this connection, Thomas Kennedy, *The Significance of Wage Uniformity* (Philadelphia: University of Pennsylvania Press, 1949).

[8] Two recent studies bear on this point: L. G. Reynolds and C. H. Taft, *The Evolution of Wage Structure* (New Haven: Yale University Press, 1955); and F. C. Pierson, *Community Wage Patterns* (Berkeley: University of California Press, 1953).

[9] The arguments and counter-arguments on the "wage-price" spiral come down to contending that advances in wages force prices up, or vice versa. See, for example, Chamber of Commerce of the United States of America, Committee on Economic Policy, *Wage-Price Spirals and Economic Stability* (Washington: 1949) which points to wages as the initiator of price moves. The conclusion that unions do not start the spiral is reached by Daniel Bell, "Do Unions Raise Wages: The Illusion of the Wage-Price Spiral, *Fortune,* 43:65 ff. (January, 1951).

[10] The coal miners bargain separately for hard and soft coal workers, and establish regional wage rates. In steel and automobiles, the unions have achieved an operating industry-wide wage scale, although bargaining is done with individual companies as though they were reaching independent contracts with each. The Teamsters have established area wage contracts that govern truck hauling over large geographic areas. There are many local agreements in service industries and in printing and building trades covering wage rates for an area.

[11] See, for example, Paul H. Douglas, *Real Wages in the United States, 1890–1926* (Boston: Houghton Mifflin Co., 1930); he found that for the period up to 1914 unionists did benefit more than non-unionists, but from then to 1926 this was not true. A. M. Ross, *Trade Union Wage Policy* (Berkeley: University of California Press, 1948), shows some influence of unionism on the redistribution of wealth; and H. M. Levinson, *Unionism, Wage Trends, and Income Distribution* (Ann Arbor: University of Michigan Press, 1951) concludes that unionism was not a factor in redistributing income from 1919 to 1947, except within the working population from non-union to union workers in the period 1929 to 1947. At best, the evidence is by no means conclusive that unions really redistribute the national income in favor of their members. See also: K. E. Boulding, *The Organizational Revolution* (New York: Harper and Brothers, 1953), Appendix, pp. 275 ff.

[12] See E. J. Benge, *Manual of Job Evaluation* (New York: Harper and Brothers, 1941).

[13] Good examples are R. B. Fetter, *Compensation and Incentives for Industrial Executives* (Bloomington: University of Indiana Press, 1952); and G. T. Washington and V. H. Rothschild, *Compensating the Corporate Executive,* revised edition (New York: Ronald Press, 1951).

[14] See: Fred Massarik, I. B. Weschler, and Robert Tannenbaum, "Evaluating Efficiency Rating Systems Through Experiment," *Personnel Administration,* 14:42-47 (January, 1951).

[15] See the excellent discussion of merit rating in J. F. Mee (ed.), *Personnel Handbook* (New York: Ronald Press, 1951).

[16] For general references on graduated pay systems see "Incentive Wage Systems: A Selected Annotated Bibliography," (Princeton: Industrial Relations Section, Princeton University, 1955). Some specific references are: American Management Association, *Incentive Plans for Direct and Indirect Workers* (New York: 1950); K. J. Louden, *Wage Incentives* (New York: John Wiley and Sons, 1944); C. W. Lytle, *Wage Incentive Methods* (New York: Ronald Press, 1942). A specialized incentive plan is described in J. F. Lincoln, *Incentive Management: A New Approach to Human Relationships in Industry and Business* (Cleveland: Lincoln Electric Company, 1951); and a critical examination of graduated

NOTES FOR CHAPTER 13 (CONT.)

pay from the standpoint of union policy is contained in Van Dusen Kennedy, *Union Policy and Incentive Wage Methods* (New York: Columbia University Press, 1945).

17 See, for example, National Industrial Conference Board, *Some Problems in Wage Incentive Administration,* Studies in Personnel Policy No. 19 (New York: The Board, 1940).

18 The particular form of wage payment can also have a reverse effect on work groups as suggested in: L. R. Sayles, "The Impact of Incentives on Intergroup Work Relations—A Management and Union Problem," *Personnel,* 28:483-490 (May, 1952).

19 An interesting illustration is found in R. C. Stone, "Mobility Factors as They Affect Workers' Attitudes and Conduct toward Incentive Systems," *American Sociological Review,* 17:58-64 (February, 1952).

20 Two attempts at supplementing straight compensation have been profit sharing and stock ownership. See: L. W. Cooper, "Profit Sharing," *Encyclopaedia of the Social Sciences* (New York: The Macmillan Company, 1933); B. M. Stewart and W. J. Couper, *Profit Sharing and Stock Ownership for Wage Earners and Executives* (New York: Industrial Relations Counselors, 1945); and R. A. Gordon, "Ownership and Compensation as Incentives to Corporate Executives," *Quarterly Journal of Economics,* 54:455-473 (May, 1940).

21 The March, 1957, issue of *Industrial Bulletin,* published by the New York State Labor Department, reports that a teamsters' local in New York has an agreement that permits bakery employees to take home two dozen free bagels (rolls) at the end of each working day; another teamsters' local has a contract with a brewery allowing workers unlimited free beer during specified parts of the day; and a painters' union has an agreement with Staten Island contractors providing for birthdays off with pay and a present of $5.00. These are trivial, yet real, examples of ways in which the take-home is sweetened, even though the brewery workers have to take it home under their belts.

22 Mason Haire and J. S. Gottsdanker, "Factors Influencing Industrial Morale," *Personnel,* 27:445-454 (May 1951). Where wages are not satisfactory, then they definitely are not taken for granted. See, for example, the study of industrial workers of Calcutta, India where wages ranked first in the most desired feature of the job, interpreted by the author as the result of low level of wages: H. C. Ganguli, "An Enquiry into Incentives for Workers in an Engineering Factory," *Indian Journal of Social Work,* 15:30-40 (June, 1954).

23 See *Findings of the Employee Questionnaire* (Ann Arbor: Survey Research Center, 1949).

24 Daniel Katz, "Satisfactions and Deprivations in Industrial Life," Chapter 6, in A. Kornhauser, R. Dubin, and A. Ross (eds.), *Industrial Conflict* (New York: McGraw-Hill Book Co., 1954), pp. 96-97.

25 Contrast this with incentives to work in non-industrial societies: F. L. K. Hsu, "Incentives to Work in Primitive Communities," *American Sociological Review,* 8:638-642 (December, 1943).

26 T. W. Harrell, *Industrial Psychology* (New York: Rinehart & Co., 1949).

27 R. Hoppock, *Job Satisfaction* (New York: Harper & Brothers, 1935).

28 H. M. Bell, *Youth Tells Their Story* (Washington: American Youth Commission, 1937).

29 C. R. Walker and R. H. Guest, *The Man on the Assembly Line* (Cambridge: Harvard University Press, 1952).

30 R. L. Hull and A. Kolstad, "Morale on the Job," in Goodwin Watson (ed.), *Civilian Morale* (New York: Reynal and Hitchcock, 1942), p. 257.

31 E. L. Thorndike, "Workers' Satisfactions: Likes and Dislikes of Young People for Their Jobs," *Occupations,* 13:704-706 (May, 1955).

32 R. Uhrbrock, "Attitudes of 4,430 Employees," *Journal of Social Psychology,* 5:365-377 (August, 1934).

33 D. Super, "Occupational Level and Job Satisfaction," *Journal of Applied Psychology,* 23:547-564 (October, 1939).

34 N. C. Morse, *Employee Satisfaction, Supervision and Morale in an Office Situation,* Part II (Ann Arbor: Survey Research Center, 1953).

35 Survey Research Center, *Attitudes and Opinions of Hourly Employees* (Ann Arbor: The Center, 1950).

36 A study of a naval research laboratory suggests that management practices in which professionals are "restrictively" led does not decrease output by management standards when compared with permissively led groups in the same setting. This simply underscores the fact that job satisfaction may even supersede management practices as a psychic reward, for some classes of professionals, at least. See I. R. Weschler, M. Kahane, and R. Tannenbaum, "Job Satisfaction, Productivity and Morale: A Case Study," *Occupational Psychology,* 26:1-14 (January, 1952).

37 For general insight into the nature of "privilege pay" see: Henry DeMan, *Joy in Work* (New York: Henry Holt & Co., 1929); Russell Davenport, "Enterprise for Everyman," *Fortune,* 41: 55-59 (January, 1950); and T. H. Hargrave, "Working Conditions and Morale," *Human Factor,* 6:382-84 (October, 1932).

38 R. L. Kahn and Daniel Katz, "Leadership Practices in Relation to Productivity and Morale," Chapter 41 in Dorwin Cartwright and Alvin Zander (eds.), *Group Dynamics* (Evanston: Row, Peterson and Co., 1953), pp. 612-628.

39 See especially his *Field Theory in Social Science* (New York: Harper & Brothers, 1951).

NOTES FOR CHAPTER 13 (CONT.)

[40] J. C. Worthy, "Factors Influencing Employee Morale," *Harvard Business Review,* 28:61-73 (January, 1950).

[41] Elton Mayo, *Social Problems of an Industrial Civilization* (Boston: Harvard University, Graduate School of Business Administration, 1945), Chapter 2.

[42] See, for example, R. B. Wolf, "Non-Financial Incentives," *Advanced Management,* 5:168-170 (October-December, 1940).

[43] Cf. Stuart Chase, *Roads to Agreement* (New York: Harper & Brothers, 1951); and Elizabeth and Francis Jennings, "Making Human Relations Work," *Harvard Business Review,* 29:29-55 (January, 1951).

[44] Whiting Williams, *Mainsprings of Men* (New York: Scribners and Sons, 1925), especially Chapter 4, "What the Worker Wants in His Job."

[45] Cf. C. A. Drake, "When Wages Incentives Fail," *Advanced Management,* 7:42-44 (January-March, 1942).

[46] See a simple, yet effective treatment of this in Walter Brown, "Our Way of Putting Creative Interest into Humdrum Jobs," *Factory,* 33:39-137 (July, 1924).

[47] The best single statement of this, together with ample illustrative material, is in W. F. Whyte, *Money and Motivation* (New York: Harper and Brothers, 1955), in which Whyte summarizes his own research and that of his students over a fifteen year period. His principal conclusion is that incentives for work do form systems, whose efficiency is the consequence of minimizing the conflicts and disparities among their parts. See an early statement in W. F. Whyte, "Economic Incentives and Human Relations," *Harvard Business Review,* 30:73-80 (March-April, 1952).

[48] A study of the failure of an incentive plan owing to its exclusive dependence on financial payoff is W. F. Whyte, "Incentives for Productivity: The Bundy Tubing Company Case," *Applied Anthropology,* 7:1-16 (Spring, 1948).

An oil field "roughneck." The world of work takes on an entirely different perspective when viewed through the eyes of the worker, rather than the organization employing him. Personal life history then comes to the fore. The purposes of work, its technologies, factories, and offices may be of wholly secondary importance.

Chapter 14

THE INDIVIDUAL WORKER

In this chapter we will consider the individual as a unit of an operating organization. We will first examine the individual's career and the typical patterns it seems to follow. In the course of this we will see some of the consequences personal life history has for occupations. In the second and third sections of this chapter we will consider the relationship between personal satisfaction and the daily routine of working.

LIFE HISTORY AND OCCUPATIONAL CAREER

We can tell a great deal about the life history of an individual if we know something about his occupational career. The work career of an individual tends to follow established patterns of development, but there is a great deal of variation in the pattern among different occupations. It is therefore desirable to focus attention on the way in which careers unfold, and to examine the impact this has on the individual as he lives out his own life history.[1] In this chapter we will consider some general features of a career from the standpoint of those who follow them. In the next chapter we will draw a more precise distinction between a career and just working for a living.

OCCUPATIONAL CHOICES

There are many occupations in industry and commerce to which a transition is made immediately from the high school or grade school level. In such occupations there is little, if any, direct relationship between common school education and the kinds of skills and abilities required to fill them. In occupations of this sort, schooling is only indirectly preparatory to assuming a job, and effectively performing on it.

In contrast there are other kinds of occupations for which schooling is an absolute prerequisite. For such occupations long and intensive formal education is pursued prior to entering a career. Thus, an industrial chemist may take a minimum of four years of college and typically additional post-graduate work as well, before becoming a member of the technical staff of a business firm. An accountant usually has a minimum of four years of college training. Most engineers are college graduates, as are an increasing proportion of salesmen, production executives, and such specialists as purchasing agents, advertising executives, and personnel men. Within a business firm there are wide differences in the preparation for career, differences that can be characterized largely in terms of the amount of education required to enter into them.[2]

It is notable in our society that occupational choices are commonly made relatively early in the life history of the individual. Also typically in our society these occupational choices are for general fields, rather than specific work assignments.[3]

Many occupational choices are the consequence of limitations on individual opportunity. If an individual knows he will not have the opportunity to attend college, his choice of occupations, or the range of probable jobs for which he will point himself, is limited by the fact of the termination of his formal education. In such an instance we have a negative selecting factor operating through the exclusion of a large number of individuals from occupational opportunities that are dependent on formal education.

It should be emphasized, however, that not everyone who fails to get the necessary formal education regrets the corresponding lack of opportunity to enter occupations for which such training is a prerequisite.[4] It is typical for college students to asume that all people would like to go to college, and have chances to become white collar or professional workers. It is necessary to remember, however, that this may be a preferred set of occupations only to those actively preparing themselves for them.[5]

During World War II, when there was a shortage of trained people, many promotions were made from the ranks to foreman and other positions of supervision. Surprisingly enough, there was a great deal of difficulty in recruiting people for these positions. Furthermore, there was not an inconsiderable number of temporary foremen who returned to the ranks willingly and with a great deal of relief to be rid of their responsibilities and newfound authority. The point illustrated is that the upwardly mobile individual who is seeking a higher level of occupation that seems preferred to him, is not necessarily emulated by all those who work in what he would consider less desirable occupations.[6]

The amount and kind of schooling, then, play an important role in distinguishing among the initial stages of different work careers. There are those who have suggested that formal schooling beyond the high school level provides an opportunity to enter industrial organizations and commercial firms at the middle levels of opportunity rather than at the lowest levels. It is possible to bypass some of the initial and more difficult stages in getting ahead in a work organization.[7]

OCCUPATIONAL COMMITMENT

There are vast differences among occupations about the point at which commitment is made to a particular career in the life history of the individual. There are also occupational differences in the degree to which this commitment is more or less irrevocable.[8] In the case of a doctor, commitment begins early in undergraduate training. Once the commitment is made, it is difficult for the doctor to change his occupational course. The reason for the total commitment to the occupation lies in the fact that training of a medical practitioner is specialized and has relatively little carry-over to other occupations.[9] This kind of almost irrevocable occupational commitment is most pronounced in the so-called free professions. It tends to be largely true in other professional and semi-professional fields as well. The accountant tends to be committed relatively early in his college training to his profession. Once immersed in special training he is likely to continue in this field with little opportunity to move in other directions.

We should not conclude, however, that early commitment to career and relative permanency of the choice, once it is made, are characteristic only of professional occupations. A young man of eighteen who enters an apprenticeship to become a tool and die maker, for example, will devote himself to two or more years of intensive training in his trade. He will enter the trade committed to one line of work for the rest of his career. Tool and die making is highly skilled work. Fortunately, however, for many of the skilled trades, the stages through which the individual goes in developing his high skill are stages that are comparable to lower levels of machine work. Consequently, with the need for finding substitute employment, particularly in periods of slack work, the highly skilled craftsman is often able to move downward into less skilled work since, in the process of becoming a craftsman, he had learned the lesser skills. Whatever this may do to the man's self-esteem and feeling of pride in his skill, he is still able to meet the technical requirements of a lesser position, and will take it if nothing else presents itself.

At even lower levels of skills and competence there may be sociological barriers, keeping a man committed to his occupation after he has pursued it for a period of time. Thus, a janitor, once he has established his skill in this occupation and has been labeled a janitor by his associates and his employer, is likely to find it very difficult to move to other kinds of work. The tasks of janitorship are viewed as having relatively little relationship with any families of jobs. Consequently, it is not often viewed as an initial stage in an evolving career. It is a terminal job. There are other kinds of lonely occupations of this sort that are terminal jobs, often involving relatively isolated work, or difficult or undesirable tasks.

Occupational commitment by the individual tends to be one of the overriding considerations in his entire life history. It is comparable to marriage, which is another great decision having long time consequences for the individual's life.[10]

It is remarkable that major decisions, like choice of a general area of occupation, or a specific occupation, or profession, are often made in considerable ignorance. There may be very real lack of knowledge about the requirements of an occupation, or about the kind of life, working conditions, and expectations that surround it.

Accompanying the ignorance of career conditions is the fact that choices are usually made at a critical juncture of life. Many children move from household chores to some kind of part-time paid work, like delivering papers, or Saturday work in a retail store. The adolescent is still centered in his home and family. However, when a person enters his first full-time job, he does so with the expectation of earning a living, and also a belief that this confirms his passage into adult status. Thus, the individual simultaneously adjusts to two major changes in his life—the change from adolescent to adult status and the change from economic dependence to economic independence.

Since these two changes occur simultaneously, it is perhaps to be expected that there will often be difficulties of adjustment for the very young worker as he enters industry. At the same time, the individual is likely to learn at work many adult patterns of behavior, and to acquire behavior patterns and an outlook he will follow throughout the rest of his adult life. In this sense, the work place becomes one of society's socializing agencies even though it is not intended as such, nor is it generally viewed in that light.

LABOR MARKET AND CHANCE

The individual frequently enters the labor market in ignorance of available jobs and potential opportunities. At different phases of the business cycle the opportunities may change drastically. Variations in regional work opportunities, and even in work opportunities among different sections of a city, may set the limits within which the individual can make occupational choices.

In general, there are market factors that govern appearance and disappearance of available kinds of work. As a result, the individual may have a sense that chance plays an important part in the determination of his occupation. This is revealed in surveys that ask individuals why they chose particular careers or occupations. The reasons given are often superficial, or represent a definite inability to assign any reasons for the occupational choice. This is another way of saying that the choice appears to the individual to be largely a consequence of chance factors over which he exercises little or no control.[11]

OCCUPATIONAL CAREER STAGES

Miller and Form have pointed out that the occupational career pattern of the typical industrial worker has five phases. There are preparatory, initial, and trial phases, a stable period, and the period of approaching retirement.[12]

In the view of these writers, the preparatory stage is typically the stage in which generalized orientation toward work is learned in doing family chores and odd jobs, often without pay. In the initial work period the first real paid job is secured. At this stage there is the possibility of severe adjusments having to be made by the individual as he learns how to work, and also learns how to become an adult at the same time.

Following the initial period there is a trial period in which the individual begins to see opportunities for careers and begins to test out his capacities and the labor market by moving from one job to another, searching out a final career. The stable phase of the unfolding career represents the point at which a commitment has finally been made to an occupation. This continues through most of the individual's lifetime and is finally succeeded by approaching retirement from industrial employment. In the last phase there may be part-time work, or leisure, depending on personal interests, financial need, and the availability of work opportunities.

These phases of the occupational career pattern are modified in the instance of those individuals who pursue their education to higher levels. There is a tendency, with a college education, for the person to go immediately into the trial phase of his career, or even directly into its stable period. College education–particularly where it is of a specialized, semi-professional, or professional character—tends to skip the individual over the first phases of the typical career pattern. In a sense, occupational commitment has already been made in the educational process and does not come, therefore, as a consequence of work experience and experimentation with different kinds of work opportunities.

STABLE WORK PERIOD

The stable work period is characterized by final and more or less irrevocable commitment to a career. It is during this period that the individual is labeled as attached to a particular occupation. He also has developed attachments to and investments in a particular employing organization. He may build up seniority rights in his job, or retirement expectations, both valuable to him in his career. Furthermore, he is likely to have been confirmed in his career choice by virtue of rising to the higher wage levels for his occupation, being paid at or near the top of the rate range for his job. Consequently, the individual's commitment to a career is re-enforced by institutional arrangements that make it relatively more attractive to continue the career.[13]

At this point the individual recognizes in his career a new dimension. He is committed to a specific occupation. He is also usually committed to employment in a particular firm. In the stable work period the career is finally rounded out to include both occupational choice and organizational commitment. It is these two aspects of the total career, the occupation and the employing organization, that constitute the two broad features of work history.

EMPLOYER VS. JOB

Through the stable work period there is likely to be a transformation in the interests and loyalties of the individual. This transformation consists of a shift from interest in a specific job, to interest in the specific employer. The institutional arrangements that tie the individual to his employer tend to facilitate this shift.

In his later years, for example, the employee is likely to be more interested in the kind of security that his employer can provide than in the satisfactions he gets, if any, out of the job he performs. He loses interest in the job partly because he has done it so long. He increases his interest in the employing organization because it is here that his security and income and, therefore, his general social welfare, are affected. This is one of the important factors often accounting for the high loyalty that older workers have for their employers. Enhanced loyalty is a result of a shifting perspective in which the career is viewed as primarily associated with the employing organization, rather than with a specific job or occupation.

Life histories are lived out in many social contexts, only one of which is the work organization. The total life of industrial workers must have some bearing on their view of work and working.[14] At the same time, what they work at, and how they do it, will have an impact on living in the community. Life histories tend to have some consistency and pattern to them.[15] Work may be of central importance to some people, but only instrumental in the lives of others. This difference should affect the ways in which the two types of people adjust to work, and their attitudes toward it.[16]

IMPORTANCE OF WORK

There is a curious assumption that often underlies discussions of personal adjustment to work. The assumption is that all people like to work; that all people are strongly attached to their particular work or the organization employing them. The obvious consequence of this point of view is that all workers ought to be filled with zeal for their work, displaying high morale in their employment. Furthermore, if the zeal is lacking or if the morale is low, it is assumed that something is amiss and corrective action needed. This point of view assumes that all workers are a kind of homogeneous mass of work-oriented and work-interested people.[17]

This white-haired gentleman, a janitor sometimes called a "maintenance engineer" for status enhancing purposes, has long been in a stable work period. This is his job for the rest of his working life. He is very likely to turn his loyalties toward his employing organization as a source of security rather than focus them on his work as a source of job satisfaction.

An alternative view suggests that work, like many other routine portions of life, can have varied meaning to different people. At one extreme are the people whose work and employment are the very center of life. These job-oriented people live and breathe their work and find their major satisfactions and sorrows in connection with their employment. To such people everything that happens at work, or is connected with it, takes on major significance.[18]

At the other extreme there are people whose

primary orientation towards living is outside of work. These non-job oriented people may operate in a work environment to which they can be relatively indifferent regardless of its ups and downs, and regardless of its specific content. To such people the real center of life is to be found in other areas than work, perhaps the family, the church, a hobby, or recreation. In terms of many kinds of industrial occupations, it is probable that as many as three-quarters of the workers are in the non-job oriented category, as a recent study has shown.[19]

If the industrial scene generally reflects the results of this particular study, it is evident that there are at least two major kinds of workers. There are those who are job-oriented, and those who have a community orientation. Both of these groups of people have a significant core around which they build their lives. To the first group it is the job. To the second group it is something outside the job of vital and immediate importance to them.[20]

There is a third type of person in a marginal category who does not have any center of strong interest, either on the job, or in non-job areas. This relatively indifferent type of person is partially alienated from all the usual centers of life interest. Such people, in general are capable of operating in routine areas of life with little difficulty. However, the extent of their emotional involvement is relatively slight. They are capable of moving from one life area into another, maintaining only superficial attachment. Indifference constitutes another kind of orientation that is found in industrial and commercial employment.

WORK-ORIENTED PERSON

The work-oriented person is an individual centering his life on his job. To him the most important single institutional unit within which he operates is the work place. He is, perhaps, best characterized as finding his major satisfactions and rewards, as well as his deepest disappointments and frustrations, in connection with his work. Being job-oriented has important implications for the way in which the individual behaves on the job, and for the systems of management that secure the most effective results from him.

The job-oriented individual is much more sensitive to the incentives of his work organization; he is likely to place high values on work incentives, if they are reasonably appropriate.[21] Furthermore, he is likely to be highly sensitive to the rules and regulations that govern the work situation. The very sense of dedication and attachment he feels for his work is likely to heighten his attention to all aspects of his job.

The work-oriented individual has built into his own viewpoint the going demands and expectations, rewards, rights, duties, and obligations, that center on the organization and its work that he is doing. He may become the "perfect" employee, embodying the ideal image of a willing and devoted worker.

This man is only a boiler room attendant in the steam and power plant of a large factory. His demeanor suggests a work-oriented outlook.

The individual whose work is the center of his life is also likely to be very sensitive to the inadequacies that usually attend any job environment. By making work the center of his life, he becomes committed to adjusting to the job environment, and also to changing those aspects of the job environment that demand too much of an adjustment. In a situation conducive to dissatisfactions, the work-oriented person is likely to feel great indignation precisely because the job is so central in his life. He is the kind of individual who may be most upset if he fails to make an adequate adjustment to work, or if he considers demands of work to be improper, unjust, or impossible. The most loyal employees, and the most bitter critics of the organization, are to be found among work-oriented people.

Greater knowledge about work is one consequence of interest in it. Workers interested in their tasks are likely to become highly skilled.[22] This suggests that supervision of work-oriented people must take into account highly developed competence and general sense of devotion to the organization. The supervision can be relatively loose in the technological area, since a job-centered worker can be assumed to have a self-interest in establishing technical competence. At the same time it is necessary that he achieve real satisfactions from work. These satisfactions can be fortified, more or less constantly, by supervisory encouragement and recognition, and other responses to a capable job well done.

Thus the work-oriented person demands less technical supervision, on the whole, but more personal interaction with supervisors. His supervisors have to confirm actually and symbolically his wisdom in choosing this work as the central interest of his life.

COMMUNITY-ORIENTED PERSON

The community-oriented person has his life centered on institutions outside the job. From the standpoint of job performance it is more or less immaterial what is the individual's real life interest. He may be a stamp collector, detective story enthusiast, devoted family man, gardener, horse-race fan, or bridge player. These are obviously not comparable kinds of interests, but they nevertheless are all characteristically pursued outside the place of employment.[23]

The principal fact about the community-oriented individual is that his life is focused just as intensively and just as devotedly as the work-oriented person. The difference between the two lies in the fact that one makes work the center of his life while the other chooses some non-job activity.

Community-oriented workers are likely to exhibit a distinctive kind of adjustment to work. The necessity to work is accepted as conforming to social expectations. The central meaning of work is that it provides the wherewithal to pursue real life interests. Work may represent pretty largely a source of income, necessary to pursue the things that are really important. To the community-oriented individual, then, the job is viewed as a means to an end rather than as an end in itself.[24]

As an instrument, work can be viewed with a kind of dispassionate detachment. If there is not forthcoming from work enough payoff, for example, if the income is inadequate to pursue real interests, then community-oriented individuals may become extremely dissatisfied.[25]

In the most extreme case the individual may have such an overriding non-job interest that he will exploit his job and his employer. Such circumstances may lead to embezzlement of company funds, for example, for purposes of gambling, though this is a relatively rare phenomenon. Ordinarily the community-oriented individual does not seek to exploit either his job or his employer to satisfy his non-job interests. He is generally willing to accept the legitimate payoff from work as the instrument for achieving his non-job satisfactions.

The community-oriented person tends to be indifferent to a total evaluation of his job, and the kinds of satisfactions it gives him. To him the major gratification the job provides is money for satisfying his non-job interests. So long as these interests are satisfied, the job is viewed as adequate. It is to such individuals that management often refers in saying that they are "not interested in anything but their pay checks." That is certainly an effective characterization of an individual who sees his work as a source of income for pursuing his satisfaction and pleasure at some other point in the society.[26]

The community-oriented person is likely to operate at a technological level of competence somewhat below that of the work-oriented person. He can perform effectively, and certainly can meet minimum job standards. However, community-oriented workers are not moved to perfect operating techniques, nor to develop skills beyond the level of job retention. At the same time, the non-job oriented person is less upset by any technological inadequacies that may exist on his job. He will be a pragmatist, not a perfectionist, with respect to maintenance of his equipment, for example.

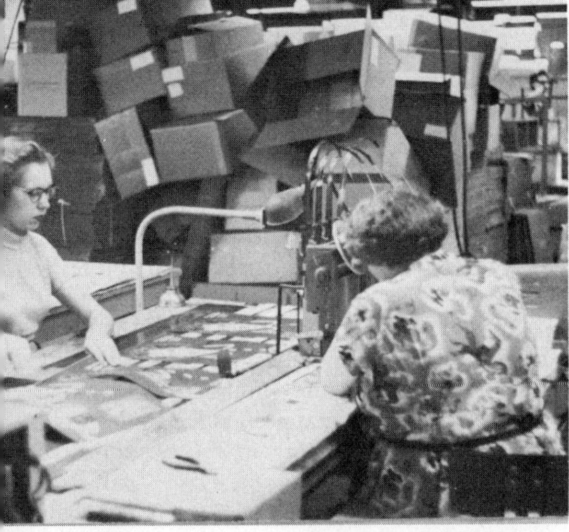

What do these women think about as they do this repetitive job of feeding and operating a machine that binds together the separate sheets of a calendar? Are they essentially community-oriented workers who can accept and be largely indifferent to job conditions like the carelessly stacked boxes in the background?

The community-oriented person is not emotionally involved in his work to any extent. His relative indifference permits him to accept frustrating conditions with a feeling that they make relatively little difference to him. He is likely to view inadequacies in terms of their interference with his creature comfort, not as stumbling blocks to doing a good job. The community-oriented individual is essentially materialistic toward his job. So long as his material expectations of the job are satisfied, he can tolerate many inadequacies in the job situation. Such an individual can work in a dirty shop. He can work with inadequate tools. He can accept crude and unsympathetic supervision with relative equanimity.

The community-oriented person demands little personal approval and commendation. For him the amount of personal contact between supervisor and worker is slight in comparison with interaction for the work-oriented person. Indeed, the humanly warm supervisor may find himself very much frustrated by the indifferent response of community-oriented people upon whom he lavishes praise and encouragement. This helps account for the fact that many supervisors and foremen with relatively little human relations skill can nevertheless be successful; a large majority of their subordinates, community-oriented people, do not require the finesse of subtle human relations.

INDIFFERENT PERSON

The indifferent person is an individual who has not found a central area of life that commands his interest and emotional involvement. Such an individual has shallow and temporary interests and tends to change them frequently. In the more serious development of indifference, there may be actual withdrawal from most routine social contacts and situations. The end result of withdrawal is the inability to behave adequately in any social situation.

The indifferent person is the least animated of the three types of industrial workers. He has a kind of dogged, slow system of reaction, or a degree of inattention that exemplifies his indifference. Perhaps the most important single index of the indifferent person is his relatively shallow emotional response to anything.

There are many routine jobs for which the indifferent individual is acceptable or even desirable. The very fact of his indifference prevents him, for example, from reacting with boredom or frustration to a highly repetitive job. There may also be menial tasks that are of a very low status to which the indifferent individual can adjust with minimum dissatisfaction. In general, it can be suggested that there may be important niches in the organization in which indifferently-oriented people can be used very effectively.

The supervision of people with indifferent orientation entails unique problems. Supervision can be generally oriented towards a custodial approach. That is, the supervision may involve continuous visual control over the workers who are in the indifferent category. Such workers are more likely to be adequate in jobs entailing limited responsibility, with a fair degree of repetitiveness, and a short learning period. The supervision of job performance is largely a question of maintaining standards of quality and quantity. This may be relatively difficult under the circumstances of a withdrawal from significant social relations by the indifferently-oriented person. However, it is probably best maintained by an impersonal method of supervision in which the standards expected in work performance are clearly set forth, and the individual then held to them.

For the indifferently-oriented individual, failure to meet work standards is not a consequence of the competition of another set of interests. It is simply a consequence of relative inattention to any interest. Accordingly, being forced to focus attention on work is likely to produce less of a negative emotional response on the part of the indifferent person than might be true in the instance of the community-oriented person. Because of this, supervising indifferent workers will entail less of a strain on the supervisor than any other type of person.

TYPES OF WORKERS AND WORK BEHAVIOR

We have delineated three general types of industrial employees largely in terms of their reaction to the work environment. No mention has been made of personality types directly, nor have we considered individual differences and personal variability in behavior. We have classified types of workers from a sociological viewpoint.

It should be obvious that there can be different personality types within each class of worker. This should not be surprising. The evidence in the fields of psychology indicates that there is very little, if any, relationship between central life interests, or special niches in the society, and personality types.

SUPERVISION STYLES

People react to their social environment in different ways. The differences result from whether a particular segment of experience is central to their life, is viewed as simply necessary, or lies at the very margin of their interest. Whether work and the employing organization are a central area of life, or of secondary importance, makes a difference for reactions to work. These differences exhibit themselves in the way employees behave, and in the systems of supervision necessary for the different types of employees.

In examining the problems of supervision, it should be noted that a supervisor's work group is not typically composed of only one type of worker. Consequently, the supervisor is faced with the responsibility of differentiating his systems of supervision to fit variations in types of workers. The supervisor is called on to behave toward the work-oriented individual in a special way. He has to deal with the community-oriented individual in a somewhat different fashion, and the indifferently-oriented employee has to be treated in still another way.

It is a common failing in the literature of supervision to assume that there is only one best way to deal with subordinates.[27] The view presented here suggests that there is no single method of supervision that is best. There are people, poles apart in their supervisory behavior, who are nevertheless successful in their particular departments, or in their particular area of supervision. This fact has seldom been given the attention that it deserves. The analysis in this section suggests that varied supervision styles may be equally successful when used with different types of workers.

We can speculate about the relationship of types of workers to various kinds of work situations. For example, where a "revolutionary" regime takes over an organization, employees who are work-oriented are likely to prove effective allies of the new power holders. Second most loyal group would be the indifferently-oriented employees. Community-oriented people might be much involved in the non-job features of the struggle for organizational power and oppose vigorously a new regime for which there are community reasons to dislike.[28] Warner and Low pointed out that the new management of the shoe factories in Yankee City, coming from another city, was strongly opposed as "foreign" although it was no more antagonistic to workers and their unions then the displaced local owners. The shoe workers were strongly community-oriented and therefore tended to react to management from that standpoint.[29] This also, incidentally, is the basis on which "cooption" of leaders of special employee groups, like ethnic or racial groups, focuses community-oriented employee interests on organizational goals, and thereby build employee loyalty, or at least neutrality.[30]

It has been noted in military organizations that company, platoon, and squad units composed largely of non-job oriented people can nevertheless function effectively at their military tasks. Indeed, the history of most large scale armies shows that they have been composed of conscripts who are typically unwilling, and in their view temporary, soldiers. They are either non-job oriented or indifferent. Yet they have managed to fight the battles and win the wars through world history.

The very nature of military administration and command is predicated on the implicit assumption that the rank and file of soldiers will be either indifferent or non-job oriented. Accordingly we find of all forms of administration the military is most mechanical, most highly structured, and most impersonal and indifferent to personal variability. This is not the consequence of the limitations of the military mind, although it is in part at least due to the limitations and necessities of the military task. It makes good sense for a military organization to supervise enlisted personnel on the assumption that they are not job-oriented. Indeed, if our analysis of the relation between forms of supervision and worker types is accurate, we would expect these aspects of supervision to dominate in the military situation.

CHANGING LIFE INTERESTS

Up to this point we have examined types of workers in static terms. There has been an implicit assumption that the individual remains oriented in a particular way throughout most of his life. This assumption may be false.

In entering on his permanent work career, the individual may still be community-oriented. However, as he develops his career and finds gratification in work, he may shift his interests more and more to a work-centered outlook. This kind of development is something that should be taken into account, for it means that the organization plays a significant role in shifting the orientation of the individual.

It should also be noted that the individual may shift his orientation away from work after an initial burst of enthusiasm. There may be a counter movement of growing loss of interest in work with increasing service on the job, and a corresponding shift of interest to non-work centers.

Consequences of shifting life interests for company personnel programs are clear. Personnel services and activities emphasize both job and off-job interests. Job-centered personnel activities, like suggestion systems, on-the-job services, and non-financial incentives secure affirmative responses from work-oriented employees. Such personnel activities appeal to people with fixed job-oriented outlook, and to other employees who may shift to such an outlook. Community-centered personnel activities, like recreation and hobby programs, and "good works" in the community, appeal to workers with non-job perspectives as evidence of company good will and support of their interests. The total personnel program is well rounded to capture employee sympathy in the areas of their life interests, wherever they may center.

ORGANIZATION CRISES

It is constructive to consider possible differences among types of workers in situations of crisis. Many organizations undergo important crisis in their history, and their success or failure may depend on reactions of their employees. Furthermore, there are types of operation that entail constant crises in individual parts of plants and firms. Here, too, the differential reaction to the crisis may be crucial to the organization.

It is likely that the work-oriented individual would react most adequately in the interests of the organization when facing a crisis. Because the job in the employing firm is all-important to him, such an individual is predisposed to do everything possible to protect his source of employment, and his particular job. Where the crisis is general, or where the crisis is clearly to be solved in the interests of the firm, job-oriented individuals can typically be expected to take every action necessary to bring the crisis to a sucessful conclusion. Such a group responds readily to appeals when the firm faces difficulty, and can be expected to react pretty much as management desires.

The same conclusion cannot be reached, however, with respect to community- or indifferently-oriented employees. The kind of uncertainty that is implicit in a situation of crisis is a threat principally to the instrumental value that the organization has for them. In a period of relatively easy job shifting the community-oriented or indifferent individual is very likely to view the fate of his particular employer with relative indifference. Such workers would be much more difficult to interest in solving the crisis, or saving the firm from possible harm. This group reacts by leaving it to management to handle the crisis situation. We would expect relatively little coperation to be spontaneously offered, and a great deal of difficulty in eliciting cooperation, where it is sought by management.[31]

Some of the puzzlement about the reaction of employees that management displays in crisis situations is the consequence of managerial expectations that people will react in a job-oriented fashion. Where employees are not job-oriented, they will be difficult to mobilize. Consequently, management may feel a deep sense of disappointment with the relative indifference of a fair proportion of employees.

SEPARATION FROM EMPLOYMENT

For the work-oriented individual, separation from employment either prior to retirement or at retirement may constitute a major point of readjustment. In a sense, the center of the individual's life is suddenly closed to him, and he must find alternate interests and activities on which to center his life. This is especially true in retirement from active employment. It is notable that many individuals who were strongly job-oriented have extreme difficulties in entering retirement gracefully.

In the case of the job-oriented individual who is fired or separated from employment for reasons beyond his control, the loss of the job in that particular employing firm may constitute a severe blow. This is usually implicitly recognized by executives and administrators. It accounts for the often repeated experience in which an individual, who is strongly job-oriented but who has outlived his usefulness, is retained in the organization in spite of clear recognition that he can no longer be fully justified as a productive employee. Managers come to recognize the supreme dependence that the individual has on his job, and cannot bring themselves to exercise cold-headed judgment in firing the person because of his declining usefulness.[32]

Devotion to the job may become an important consideration in management's personnel decisions. The more devoted the individual, the greater is the probability that he will "be taken care of" in partial repayment for his dedication. While this may introduce inefficiencies in the organization, it may have hidden functions in serving to develop a job orientation, and make the job a central life interest to those whose interest might otherwise lie elsewhere. When they come to recognize that the work-oriented individual is, in fact, rewarded for his job interest, they may seek to emulate him. Thus, the apparent economic loss in maintaining devoted employees beyond the period of their usefulness to the firm may be compensated for, at least in part, by providing incentive for others to develop job orientation.

Separation from employment is viewed with relative unconcern by community and indifferently-oriented people, where alternate employment is readily available. In periods of high level employment such people may move readily from one employer to another, so long as the economic disadvantage is not too great. Where great loss of seniority or pension rights may occur, resistance to job shifting may develop. This resistance, however, stems from economic or other instrumental considerations, not from attachment to the company. For community and indifferently-oriented people the institutional bonds of organization and not the moral ones provide the basis for attachment to a work organization.

PEOPLES, CAREERS, AND WORK

Working is only part of a whole life. For those who work, the careers offered in their employment have importance to some, and only instrumental significance to others. This makes a difference in the kind of employees that they are in their employing organizations.

In Chapter 12 we examined motivation; our analysis of incentives in Chapter 13 placed emphasis on organization and social structure as the molding forces guiding work behavior. People typically have many choices, from among which they select the guide posts for their behavior. In this chapter we have given special attention to the general orientations that workers can take toward their work, and the organization in which they pursue it. It has particularly been noted that the organization does not always have "the last word" in molding work behavior.

What the person brings with him to work, and the interests he develops in the community, can shape his resistance to the total influence on his behavior of organization requirements. This does not mean that anarchy prevails in the work-place, or that sabotage is characteristic of worker behavior. It does mean, however, that workers do not "kill themselves" to fulfill or over-fulfill management expectations. They remain people with wide and discriminating interests which sometimes center on work and, apparently, more often do not.

The real miracle of modern industrial and commercial work organizations is that they can be so efficient in spite of, rather than because of, the commitment their employees have to them.

We have already examined many facets of the ways in which the miracle is achieved. More will be considered in the following chapters.

NOTES FOR CHAPTER 14

[1] A great deal more analysis of careers is contained in Chapter 15, with its perspective of occupational mobility.

[2] For example, Warner and Abegglen show that 76 per cent of business leaders—men who have already achieved executive positions—have had some college education, contrasted with only 13 per cent among all U. S. males 30 years and older; W. L. Warner and J. C. Abbeglen, *Occupational Mobility in American Business and Industry* (Minneapolis: University of Minnesota Press, 1955), p. 96.

[3] Cf. Eli Ginsberg, *et al., Occupational Choice: An Approach to a General Theory* (New York: Columbia University Press, 1951).

[4] Cf. Richard Centers, "Motivational Aspects of Occupational Stratification," *Journal of Social Psychology,* 28:187-217 (November, 1948).

[5] See, for example, Paul Meadows, "The Motivations of Industrial Man," *American Journal of Economics and Sociology,* 6:363-370 (April, 1947).

[6] Cf. R. R. Dynes, A. C. Clarke, and S. Dinitz, "Levels of Occupational Aspiration," *American Sociological Review,* 21:212-214 (April, 1956).

[7] The most recent evidence is contained in Warner and Abegglen, *op. cit.,* pp. 131-132, and, by the same authors, *Big Business Leaders in America* (New York: Harper and Brothers, 1955), pp. 215-216. See also William Miller, "The Business Elite in Business Bureaucracies," Chapter 11 in William Miller (ed.), *Men in Business* (Cambridge: Harvard University Press, 1952), pp. 286-305.

[8] For some indirect evidence on this see: D. Super, "Occupational Level and Job Satisfaction," *Journal of Applied Psychology,* 23:547-564 (October, 1939).

[9] Some alternate careers are in hospital administration, medical research, medical politics in professional associations, popular education (especially through medical advice columns in newspapers), and public health administration. A clearly lower status substitute career is "detail man" (salesman) for a pharmaceutical firm.

[10] See: David MacKaye, "The Fixation of Vocational Interest," *American Journal of Sociology,* 33: 353-370 (November, 1927).

[11] See the next chapter for an extended discussion of chance in job changing, and evidence on the extent to which random factors operate.

[12] See: W. H. Form and D. C. Miller, "Occupational Career Pattern as a Sociological Instrument," *American Journal of Sociology,* 54:317-329 (January, 1949); and by the same authors, *Industrial Sociology* (New York: Harper & Brothers, 1951).

[13] Cf. B. C. Rosen, "The Achievement Syndrome," *American Sociological Review,* 21:203-211 (April, 1956).

[14] This is suggested, for example, in M. G. Dickson, "The Factory Worker's Philosophy," *Sociological Review,* 28:295-312 (July, 1936).

[15] A general theoretical position that gives centrality to W. I. Thomas' notion of the "definition of the situation" as the consistent feature of personal-

NOTES FOR CHAPTER 14 (CONT.)

ity is stated in E. H. Volkart, *Social Behavior and Personality* (New York: Social Science Research Council, 1951).

[16] The earlier emphasis of industrial psychology, in which personality traits were correlated with work behavior, tended to obscure the relations between general orientation and work behavior. See, for example M. S. Viteles, *Industrial Psychology* (New York: W. W. Norton and Co., 1932). However, Hugo Munsterberg, over fifty years ago, noted that the feeling of monotony was less associated with the conditions of work than with the dispositions of the workers. This suggested the kind of position presented here. See his *Psychology and Industrial Efficiency* (Boston: Houghton Mifflin Co., 1913).

[17] A war-time study of shipyard workers clearly suggests that workers compartmentalize their lives into job and non-job areas which may or may not interact with each other. See D. Katz and H. Hyman, "Morale in War Industry," in T. Newcomb and E. Hartley (eds.), *Readings in Social Psychology* (New York: Henry Holt and Co., 1947), pp. 437-447. See also D. Katz, "Satisfactions and Deprivations in Industrial Life," Chapter 6 in A. Kornhauser, R. Dubin, and A. Ross (eds.), *Industrial Conflict* (New York: McGraw-Hill Book Company, 1954). See also A. R. Heron, *Why Men Work* (Stanford: Stanford University Press, 1948).

[18] The classic work on vocational interests and their correlates is E. K. Strong, Jr., *Vocational Interests of Men and Women* (Stanford: Stanford University Press, 1943). The study of vocational interests as pursued by Strong and his students represents a transitional position in which the total interests of successful people in specific occupations are established as profiles, against which the expressed interests of job applicants or young people can be matched as a basis for vocational guidance or employee selection. This work is really the basic starting point for the transition from an individual industrial psychology to a social psychology of industry. An excellent critical treatment of the continuation of the individual psychology approach is: M. E. Steiner, "The Search for Occupational Personalities," *Personnel,* 29:335-343 (January, 1953). A good example of the personality trait approach is A. F. Dodge, "What are the Personality Traits of Successful Clerical Workers," *Journal of Applied Psychology,* 24:576-586 (October, 1940).

[19] Robert Dubin, "Industrial Workers' Worlds: A Study of the Central Life Interests of Industrial Workers," *Social Problems,* 3:131-142 (January, 1956).

[20] This is suggested in Melville Dalton, "Worker Response and Social Background," *Journal of Political Economy,* 54:323-332 (August, 1947), where machinists are analyzed in terms of their social characteristics and their differential response to wage incentives.

[21] A good example will be found in Melville Dalton, "The Industrial 'Rate-Buster': A Characterization," *Applied Anthropology,* 7:5-18 (Winter, 1948).

[22] The engineer as a work-oriented employee is studied in H. B. Moore and S. J. Levy, "Artful Contrivers: A Study of Engineers," *Personnel,* 28:148-153 (September, 1951).

[23] A persistent theme in American life is the ability to become economically independent, usually by establishing a small business. A. M. Bingham, *Insurgent America* (New York: Harper & Brothers, 1935), examines this myth as it relates to work. Ely Chinoy, *Automobile Workers and the American Dream* (New York: Doubleday and Co., 1955), and in an earlier paper, "The Tradition of Opportunity and the Aspirations of Automobile Workers," *American Journal of Sociology,* 57:453-459 (March, 1952) points out the persistence of this dream of independent small business opportunity. On this same general point see also R. H. Guest, "Work Careers and Aspirations of Automobile Workers," *American Sociological Review,* 19:155-163 (April, 1954). It is particularly significant to note that these aspirations are not work centered but income centered, and envision the income as originating elsewhere than in employing organization. Furthermore, and this is particularly emphasized by Chinoy, the workers' aspirations for advancement come to be realistically focused on their children, and their chances for social mobility through education. Thus, the family becomes the central life interest, with hopes resting on better opportunities for the children. These workers seem clearly to exhibit community orientation.

[24] This is certainly a fair conclusion to be drawn from Joseph Shister and L. G. Reynolds, *Job Horizons: A Study of Job Satisfaction and Labor Mobility* (New York: Harper & Brothers, 1949), especially their general summary conclusions as to why people move, which includes as one of the three most important features of the job its wages in an absolute or standard-of-living sense (pp. 33-34). They are undoubtedly reporting here the response of community-oriented workers.

The particular virtue of financial incentives lies in their ability to induce effective work output in both work-oriented and community-oriented people. Work-oriented individuals respond because they are interested; community-oriented workers, because pay is instrumental to their community life.

[25] Some notion of variation in total financial payoff for different occupations and professions is contained in H. F. Clark, *Life Earnings in Selected Occupations in the United States* (New York: Harper & Brothers, 1937); and L. I. Dublin and A. J. Lotka, *The Money Value of a Man* (New York: The Ronald Press Co., 1946).

[26] In this connection see, for example: A. W. Rose, "How Negro Workers Feel about Their Jobs,"

NOTES FOR CHAPTER 14 (CONT.)

Personnel Journal, 29:292-296 (January, 1951); and Allison Davis, "The Motivation of the Underprivileged Worker," Chapter 5 in W. F. Whyte (ed.), *Industry and Society* (New York: McGraw-Hill Book Co., 1946).

[27] A rather subtle variation on the "one best method of supervision" is the approach which sees employees as malleable, if "properly handled." Thus it is considered possible to change workers' reactions and behaviors by changing the "psychological field" in which the work is carried out, and particularly the boss-worker relationship. See, for example: Dorwin Cartwright, "Achieving Change in People: Some Applications of Group Dynamics Theory," *Human Relations,* 4:381-392 (November, 1951). I have serious doubt that community-oriented workers will be transformed into work-oriented people by any amount of manipulation of the psychological field of the work place.

[28] It is not uncommon for strong union members to have marked preference for one management faction over another in a particular company. The union member attitude is based upon a belief that the preferred management group is more sympathetic to the union organization.

[29] W. L. Warner and J. O. Low, *The Social System of the Modern Factory—The Strike: a Social Analysis* (New Haven: Yale University Press, 1947). The authors emphasize the importance of community status for the workers.

[30] See Philip Selznick, "Foundations of the Theory of Organization," *American Sociological Review,* 13:34-35 (February, 1948). "Cooption" is a term invented by Selznick to designate the process of bringing leaders of opposing groups into the fold of the group holding authority.

[31] A different interpretation based upon a psychological approach is given in R. N. McMurry, "The Problem of Resistance to Change in Industry," *Journal of Applied Psychology,* 31:589-593 (December, 1947). Here the assumption is made that removal of general fears and insecurity will change resistance into cooperation. No room is left for the possibility of an indifferent response.

[32] This attitude is sometimes facetiously said to result in creating an "industrial WPA."

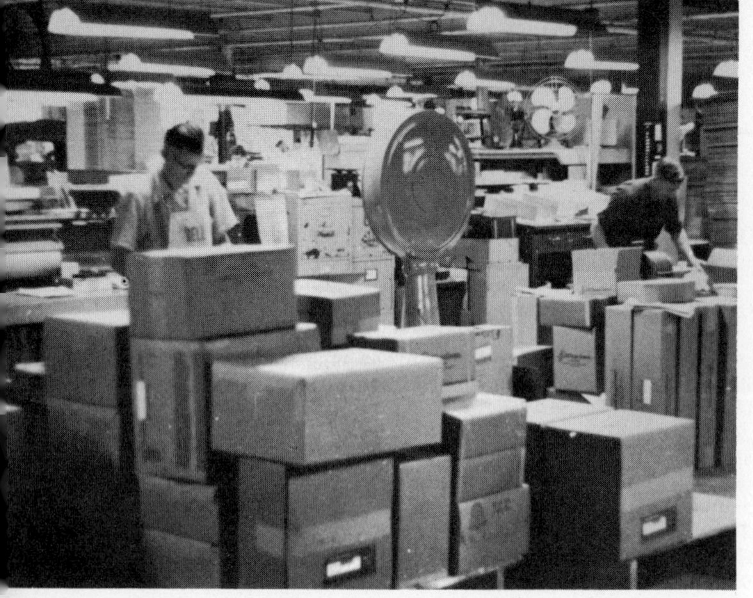

The packing and shipping department is usually near the bottom of the heap where many workers start their climb to better jobs. Some never make it, but many do. A very few move way up—in the office boy to president tradition—but most of those who better their jobs make moderate advances. Some even slip downward from the beginning to the end of their working lives, but more move up than down.

Chapter **15**

INDIVIDUAL MOBILITY

It is the rare person who does not change his job, or at least his place of employment, during the course of his working life. Indeed, changing jobs and employers is often evidence of success.

In this chapter we will examine the general magnitude of job mobility, together with the directions in which people move from one occupation to another. We will then consider work as a career. Here we will extend the analysis of careers begun in the last chapter, focusing on the ways careers are fitted into work organizations. In the last sections we will examine the general kinds of work organization mobility that are represented by promotions, and separations.

WORK AND MOBILITY

How many different jobs does a person hold in his working lifetime? This appears to be a simple question. Yet, it divides into two important and separate issues.

We can be concerned simply with job changes. Here we are interested in how many employers a person has worked for, or how many different job titles he has carried either with the same, or different employers. This does not tell us anything about the status of the jobs held. We might then ask, Has he changed his occupation as well as his job? We will examine both of these questions for the American labor force.

LENGTH OF WORKING LIFE

Before answering what a person has done during his working life, it is necessary to know how long he will work, on the average. What is the length of working life?

If a person begins working at 18 and retires at 65 years of age, he will have worked 47 years. School attendance is typically required to the age of 18, which is also the usual age for graduation from high school. Sixty-five is a standard retirement age in this country. This rough calculation of 47 years of working life is confirmed by refined estimates based on statistical analyses of large population data.

Wool calculated that a young man aged 14 in 1940 could expect, on the average, to be in the working force for 46.6 years.[1] Jaffe and Carleton, by analyzing a fixed group of people, concluded that the average length of working life was about 46 years for the entire working force in the census years 1950 and 1940.[2] For the year 1930 it was about 47 years, the difference being the consequence of deferring entry into the labor force almost a year in the more recent period.

There is wide variation among major occupational groups in the length of working life. The Jaffe-Carleton study concluded that there is a −.82 correlation between the status of occupations and the average length of working life in them.[3] The better or higher status occupations, as measured by earnings and education, demand shorter working lives of their participants, than do lower rated jobs. Table 15.1 shows the average number of years in the working force, together with the age of entry and retirement, for ten major occupational categories.

This table makes clear the meaning of the correlation between type of occupation and the length of time it is pursued. In general, for higher status occupations, a longer time is spent in preparing to get into them, and retirement comes relatively early. For lower status occupations, typical workers start early in life, and stay in them longer. Obviously, for the higher status jobs, the deferred entry into the occupations is either the result of lengthy schooling (the professions particularly), or apprenticeships. The lower than average retirement ages for these higher status occupations are undoubtedly a result of higher incomes earned while working, and the consequent ability to retire from choice.[4]

TABLE 15.1

PEOPLE IN LOWER SKILLED OCCUPATIONS WORK MORE YEARS OF THEIR LIVES THAN SKILLED PEOPLE
(data for United States, 1950)

Major Occupational Group	*Mean Number Years in Working Force*	*Average Age of Entry*	*Average Age of Retirement*
Professional and Technical	40	above average	below average
Managers, Officials, Owners	41	above average	below average
Craftsmen and Foremen	44	above average	average
Operatives	45	below average	below average
Sales Workers	47	below average	average
Clerical Workers	47	below average	average
Laborers (except Farm and Mine)	51	below average	above average
Service Workers	52	below average	above average

SOURCE: Reprinted with permission from A. J. Jaffe and R. O. Carleton, *Occupational Mobility in the United States, 1930–1960,* King's Crown Press, 1954, p. 50.

JOB SHIFTING

In the 46 years of average working life, how many different jobs does a person hold? Here we are concerned with jobs, whether they are the same job with different employers, or different occupations. In the next section we will deal specifically with shifts among occupations.

Stable data on a substantial number of working life histories simply do not exist. We therefore have to estimate the number of jobs held during the average 46 years of working life by the average employed person. From the largest single study of labor mobility, that reported by Gladys Palmer, we discover that in the six cities studied, there was an average of 2.6 jobs held for the ten-year period from 1940 to 1950.[5] This covers all occupations. If we project this figure over a 46-year working life, we arrive at almost 12 jobs held by the average worker during his working lifetime.

A much more limited body of data derived from the study of 935 working heads of families in Oakland, California shows that there was a mean of 4.8 jobs for an average of 25.3 years in the labor force. This study by Lipset and Bendix leads to the conclusion that about 9 jobs will be held through the whole working lifetime of 46 years.[6]

Twelve jobs in a working lifetime may be an overestimation. We know that older workers change jobs less frequently, for example. If we take a lower and more conservative figure of 9 jobs in 46 years of working, it appears that American workers change their jobs on the average of once every five years. People do move from their jobs to others. They do this with relative frequency.[7]

The implications of this job-shifting characteristic of the American labor force are clear. Many people do not stay long enough on particular jobs to develop strong attachments to their company. Their attachment to occupations as a way of life may be lessened by the frequent moves from one job to another. Their aspirations about future jobs may be higher. Experience with frequent job changes may lead to the belief that, because jobs can be changed relatively frequently, the next one will be a better one. Indeed, as we will see in the next section there is a considerable upward mobility in the occupational structure.

Job changing is not evenly distributed throughout the work force. Some people change jobs more frequently than others. Therefore, any figures showing average job changes tend to obscure the fact that a good share of the job changing is done by the frequent job shifters. We have a measure of the impact of frequent job changers in Table 15.2 where their proportion in major occupational categories is shown.

TABLE 15.2

JOB CHANGES OCCUR MORE FREQUENTLY IN LESS SKILLED OCCUPATIONS

(data for six American cities*)

Occupation of Longest Job Held in 1950	*Workers in Thousand*	*Mean No. of Jobs Held (1940–1949)*	*Workers with 3 or More Jobs as Per Cent of Total Group*	*Workers with 5 or More Jobs as Per Cent of Total Group*
All occupations	3,396	2.6	42	13
Managerial workers	453	2.4	36	9
Professional workers	311	2.4	34	10
Sales workers	215	2.5	41	12
Clerical workers	514	2.6	42	13
Service workers	397	2.7	41	13
Operatives	803	2.8	46	15
Craftsmen	539	2.8	46	15
Laborers	164	3.1	56	22

* Excluding persons with no work experience 1940–1949, persons not reporting number of employers, and persons not reporting occupation. The six cities are: Chicago, Philadelphia, Los Angeles, San Francisco, St. Paul, and New Haven.

SOURCE: Reprinted with permission from Gladys Palmer, *Labor Mobility in Six Cities,* Social Science Research Council, 1954, p. 72.

From the first line of this table it is clear that during the ten-year period, more than four out of every ten workers shifted their jobs three or more times, which is above the mean of 2.6 jobs held by the average worker. A little more than every tenth worker had five or more jobs during the same period, or twice as many jobs as the average worker.

When we examine Table 15.2 for occupational differences we note that at lower occupational levels a larger percentage of workers change their jobs more frequently than in higher occupations. Two important inferences follow from this fact. The first is that people in lower occupational groups are changing jobs in order to get ahead. The second inference is that higher occupations tend to be careers, with consequent less job shifting as the career unfolds. We will examine both of these conclusions later in this chapter.

What happens to people when they change jobs? Unfortunately the data are not available for all kinds of job changes. However, Palmer's study does show what happened to people when their job changes involved moving from one employer to another. These data are contained in Table 15.3 showing job shifts for men during the ten years studied. The job shifts for women show approximately the same pattern.

Table 15.3 reveals several outstanding facts. Most notable is that 55 per cent of men, if they changed employer, also changed their occupation and the industry in which they worked (the comparable figure for women is 46 per cent). This figure is stable for each of the six cities studied. It is of the same magnitude even when we consider layoffs that are a result of slackened work. The magnitude does not change when separations from the job for other reasons including personal choice are shown separately.

Looking at Table 15.3 from another standpoint we can say that when a man changes his employer, only about one in five will return to work in the same industry and at the same occupation. The figure is slightly higher, one in four, when the change in employer is the result of layoffs due to business conditions.

It seems very clear, then, that when men move from one employer to another, somewhere between 76 and 84 per cent of them will change their occupation, or the industry in which they work, or both. The higher percentage will make such changes if their separation from their previous employer was for reasons other than being laid off; the lower percentage if they were laid off because of their employer's business conditions.

Moving from one job to another is indeed a significant change for the worker. In the vast majority of instances it means changing industry, or occupation, or both. More than half the time it will involve changing both.

Americans are a mobile people. Their mobility is no better illustrated than in the amount of shifting they do from one job to another. Such shifting of jobs usually also entails changes in the industrial environment in which work is performed, and the occupations pursued.

OCCUPATIONAL MOBILITY

Where the kind of job pursued is valued as a measure of social standing, we might expect patterns of shifting from one occupation to another to reflect the valued preferences of a society. If everyone wants to get up to the top of the heap, then the patterns of shifting from one occupation to another will show an upward movement in social standing.

This basic feature of American social values is summed up as "getting ahead in the world." When we get ahead, we mean that our present occupation is a better one than the last, and that the next one will be better still.

Occupational mobility is, therefore, meaningful to people according to the kinds of shifts among occupations that represent getting ahead, standing still, or falling behind.[8] We are, of course, concerned with what happens in the working life history of the people now working. There is a literature dealing with generational shifts in occupations. Typically father and son occupations are compared to find out what happened between these two generations. Interesting as that literature is, our attention in this chapter is on what happens in the individual's working life history, not how he compares with his father's place in the world of work.[9]

Lipset and Bendix suggest that the funda-

TABLE 15.3

WHEN MEN CHANGE FROM ONE EMPLOYER TO ANOTHER, MORE THAN HALF WILL ALSO CHANGE THEIR OCCUPATION AND INDUSTRY

(data for six American cities, 1940-1949,* numbers in thousands)

Reason for separation and type of shift	*Chicago*		*Philadelphia*		*Los Angeles*		*San Francisco*		*St. Paul*		*New Haven*		*6 cities*	
	No.	*Per cent*	*No.*	*Per cent*	*No.*	*Per cent*	*No.*	*Per cent*	*No.*	*Per cent*	*No.*	*Per cent*	*No.*	*Per cent*
TOTAL SHIFTS	1,527	100	689	100	1,163	100	424	100	122	100	62	100	3,987	100
Employer only	272	18	102	14	221	19	87	21	16	13	8	13	706	18
Employer and occupation	65	4	35	5	71	6	27	6	7	6	3	6	208	5
Employer and industry	275	18	122	18	173	15	63	15	20	17	10	16	663	17
Employer, occupation, and industry	819	54	400	59	640	55	233	55	71	58	37	60	2,200	55
Other	96	6	30	4	58	5	14	3	8	6	4	5	210	5

LAYOFFS	362	100	194	100	290	100	103	100	36	100	15	100	1,000	100
Employer only	100	27	37	19	65	22	27	26	6	16	3	17	238	24
Employer and occupation	13	4	5	3	20	7	7	7	1	3	1	5	47	5
Employer and industry	75	21	38	20	41	14	18	17	8	22	3	18	183	18
Employer, occupation, and industry	162	45	110	56	150	52	48	48	19	54	7	57	496	50
Other	12	3	4	2	14	5	3	2	2	5	1	3	36	3
SEPARATIONS FOR OTHER REASONS	1,165	100	495	100	873	100	321	100	86	100	47	100	2,987	100
Employer only	172	15	65	13	156	18	60	19	10	12	5	11	468	16
Employer and occupation	52	4	30	6	51	6	20	6	6	7	2	6	161	5
Employer and industry	200	17	84	17	132	15	45	14	12	14	7	15	480	16
Employer, occupation, and industry	657	57	290	59	490	56	185	57	52	60	30	61	1,704	57
Other	84	7	26	5	44	5	11	4	6	7	3	7	174	6

* Includes job shifts reported by all workers reporting more than one employer in 1940–49. Layoffs are those separations that occur because of business conditions affecting the employer initially, such as failure, plant removal, or contract cancellation. Discharges for cause are not included in layoffs. Separation for other reasons includes all other causes of separation, except layoffs.

SOURCE: Reprinted with permission from Gladys Palmer, *Labor Mobility in Six Cities,* Social Science Research Council, 1954, p. 74.

mental cleavage in American society is between those who work with their hands and those who do not.[10] Their study of the Oakland labor market leads to two conclusions on occupational mobility. Those who work with their hands have spent 80 per cent of their working lives in manual occupations, on the average. Those who do not work with their hand have spent 75 per cent of their working lives in non-manual occupations. It appears from their data on 935 working heads of households that white collar and blue collar occupations are two different worlds of work. Once committed to either of these separate worlds, the worker is likely to remain in that world for his working lifetime.

Much more extensive data are available in the Jaffe-Carleton study which makes use of facts from the Palmer study of six cities.[11] The first conclusions to which Jaffe-Carleton come are these. Improvement of occupational position takes place particularly during the first two or three decades of working life. Indeed, most upward mobility occurs generally between the ages of 25 and 45. Men tend to reach their highest position on the occupational ladder by about age 50.[12]

Jaffe and Carleton also reach the same conclusion as Lipset and Bendix, that white collar and manual work tend to be separate realms. Of these who begin working in white collar occupations, 50 per cent will remain in that occupational group. Of these who begin in a manual occupation, about two-thirds will remain in the same general class of work for their working lives.[13]

Turning next to the crucial question of who goes where, and in what numbers, from one occupational level to another, Jaffe-Carleton have developed the best single measure of broad occupational shifting in the United States. Their results are shown in Table 15.4.

This table was constructed as follows. The authors assumed that a thousand boys at each age level from 15 to 24 have entered each of the seven occupational groups. Using the data from the Six City Study on actual interchange among the occupational groups, by age, they trace the movements of these boys from occupational group to occupational group until the survivors of the original thousand in each class have reached the age group 55 to 64 years. In making these computations they assumed that the occupational changes observed during the 1940's in the Six City Study would apply for the entire working lives of their cohorts of a thousand. To the original 10,000 they added the people going to work for the first time, at a rate based on new entries in the labor market in 1940. Thus, the table represents losses through death and leaving working, and gains through new workers for each year. The table sums the results for a forty-year period.

Table 15.4 then shows the occupations in which 10,000 men begin and end their working lives. Jaffe and Carleton used the only body of data available for such calculations, a body of data so costly to gather that it is not likely to be duplicated for many years.[14] This table is much like an insurance life table. Based on the facts about a population, it represents a theoretical picture of characteristics of that population.

Table 15.4 can be read in two ways. Reading down each column we find out what happened to the people who started out in the occupational group. For example, 425 remained craftsmen out of 1254 who started in that group. The other two-thirds who started in the group moved out, approximately one-third moving up and the same proportion moving down. Each column shows the mobility out of the occupational group. This is the data for the left hand side of the figures in Chart 15.1.

Reading across each row of Table 15.4 we learn from what groups will come the people who move into an occupational class. Thus, almost a third of the 2651 men who end up as craftsmen and foremen come from the ranks of operatives. Each row shows the mobility into the occupational group. This is the data for the right hand side of the figures in Chart 15.1.

The seven occupational groups shown in Table 15.4 are listed in the rough order of their social-economic standing. Some questions arise about the relative standing of adjacent groups. In general, however, the listing is from high to low.

For all occupational groups taken together, the chances are better than one in two (55.51%) that a person will end his work-

TABLE 15.4

MEN'S WORKING LIFE HISTORIES ARE FEATURED BY THEIR OCCUPATIONAL MOVES UPWARD
(theoretical working life table for the United States, non-agricultural occupations)

		Occupational Group at Beginning of Working Life						
Occupational Group at end of working life	Total	Professional and technical	Managers, officials and proprietors	Clerical and sales workers	Craftsmen and foremen	Operatives	Service workers	Laborers (except farm and mine)
Total	10,000	548	371	1,854	1,254	3,092	675	2,206
Professional and technical	759	197	29	180	78	167	40	68
Managers, officials, and proprietors	1,785	90	104	402	224	526	119	320
Clerical and sales workers	1,322	80	72	334	133	374	91	238
Craftsmen and foremen	2,651	78	76	413	425	869	150	640
Operatives	1,983	55	53	308	236	680	126	525
Service workers	994	37	25	145	109	315	111	252
Laborers (except farm and mine)	506	11	12	72	49	161	38	163

See text for basis on which this table is constructed.

SOURCE: Reprinted with permission from A. J. Jaffe and R. O. Carleton, *Occupational Mobility in the United States, 1930–1960,* King's Crown Press, 1954, p. 52.

ing life in a higher occupation than the one in which he started. The odds are one in five (20.14%) that no change will be made to either a higher or lower occupation during the working life history. Finally, one out of every four persons will move downward during his period of industrial and commercial employment. Thus, three out of every four members of the labor force will be as well or better off when they leave the labor market as they were when they entered. These are the summary conclusions from Table 15.4. The American labor force not only moves frequently from job to job, and industry to industry, but the majority also "get ahead" in the process.

In Chart 15.1 we have summarized the circulation into and out of each of the major occupational groups as portrayed in Table 15.4. A careful examination of this chart shows the differential mobility of the various strata of occupations. Comparisons among the seven figures reveal that those who start high tend to remain in the upper levels those who start in the middle are most stable although some move up and down; while those who start at or near the bottom do get ahead.

MOBILITY AND CHANCE

We have two generalizations that appear contradictory. The first suggests that job changing leads to changes in industry or occupation in about three out of every four instances where a worker changes employer. We also have discovered that a considerable body of changes among occupations appears to be directed toward improving one's working status. The first generalization suggests random causes operating. The second generalization suggests that occupational changes are not random in character; that these shifts are made in the process of getting ahead.

We need to consider the role that chance

CHART 15.1

OCCUPATIONAL MOBILITY HAS ITS UPS AND DOWNS

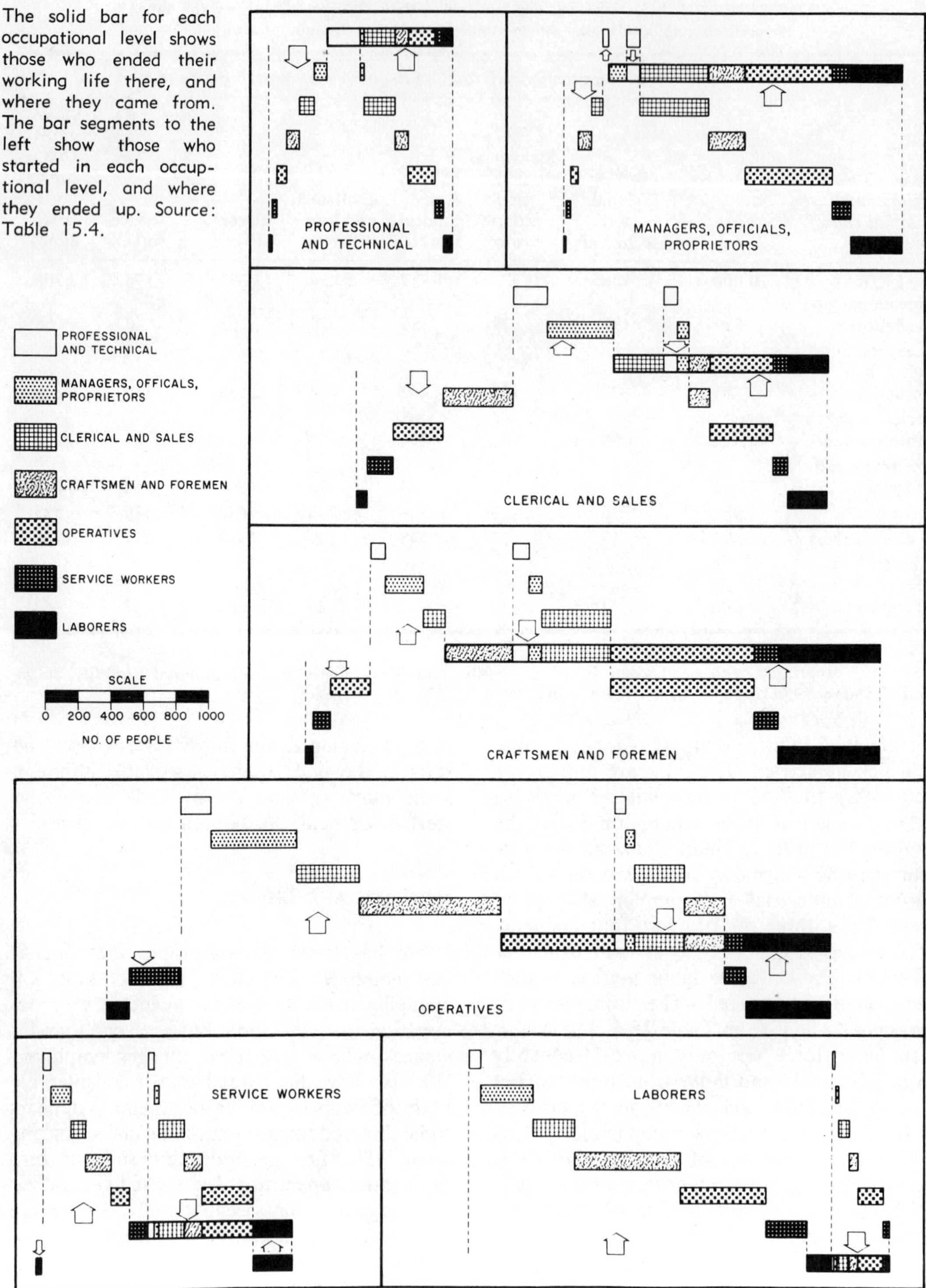
The solid bar for each occupational level shows those who ended their working life there, and where they came from. The bar segments to the left show those who started in each occupational level, and where they ended up. Source: Table 15.4.
PROFESSIONAL AND TECHNICAL
MANAGERS, OFFICIALS, PROPRIETORS
CLERICAL AND SALES
CRAFTSMEN AND FOREMEN
OPERATIVES
SERVICE WORKERS
LABORERS
PROFESSIONAL AND TECHNICAL
MANAGERS, OFFICALS, PROPRIETORS
CLERICAL AND SALES
CRAFTSMEN AND FOREMEN
OPERATIVES
SERVICE WORKERS
LABORERS
SCALE
0 200 400 600 800 1000
NO. OF PEOPLE

plays in job and occupational shifting. To what extent do people plan to get ahead in their work? To what extent do factors not directly related to kind of work affect decisions to change work? Finally, to what extent do people drift more or less accidentally into the jobs they hold?

Data are available on these points. Turning again to the Six City Study, we find that Palmer concludes, "accidental circumstances were largely responsible for the occupations held in 1950 by 23 per cent of all men and 37 per cent of all women 25 years of age and over in the six cities combined. Most of these workers were in manual occupations, and almost half were operatives or kindred workers. They included a nucleus of persons who 'never stay long in a place' and substantial numbers of women with irregular attachments in the labor market."[15]

Thus, one out of every four of the men in major cities of the United States and better than one out of every three women workers were in occupations which, in their own way of looking at them, were not occupations of their choice.[16] Even though there is a large accumulation of workers at the semi-skilled level, the sheer magnitude of this group should make clear how significant the factor of chance is in the occupations followed by a substantial number of our citizens. If chance is the determinant of what people do at work, then we have added reason for understanding why attachments to occupations and places of work may be relatively weak in a substantial proportion of the American working force.

Still another body of data reported by Palmer has a bearing on the operation of chance in occupational choice and job shifting.[17] In Table 15.5, special data for voluntary job shifting among skilled men in the six cities, and for both men and women in St. Paul, Minnesota, are shown. For our present purposes it is necessary to focus on the proportions of those who voluntarily changed their jobs because of personal or family reasons. Among the males about one in every four job shifts was ascribed to personal or family situations. Among women workers who voluntarily changed their jobs almost one in every two was for personal or family reasons.

Now what does this have to do with chance? The connection is this. Ordinarily, personal or family considerations are only remotely, if at all, related to jobs. That is, what is happening at home in emergencies, illness or death, in changing the family residence, or in changing family responsibilities such as new children or old folks to take care of, is not immediately related to the kind of work people perform. These factors are extraneous to work. Yet they enter significantly into decisions to change jobs. It is a matter of chance that a member of the family will become seriously ill, yet this chance event may produce a job shift.

It should be noted that the general magnitudes are similar for both sets of data. One out of every four men in the Six City Study was following an occupation not of his special choosing, but the consequence of accidental factors. Approximately one out of every four skilled men and another sample of St. Paul workers said that they shifted their jobs voluntarily for reasons not directly related to their job, for personal or family reasons. Similarly for women, better than a third in the Six City Study said that chance determined their present jobs, and about a half in the St. Paul sample said that non-job personal or family situations determined their voluntary shifts in jobs.

We may conclude then that chance plays a significant role in occupational and job shifting. As many as a quarter of the American working force may be indifferent to the driving desire to get ahead. They may be willing to "play the labor market" for its opportunities to earn a wage or salary. They may be largely indifferent to the specific jobs they get, leaving the determination of their work to the impersonal, and therefore in their view, chance character of the employment market. They may also be willing to let non-job considerations sway their job changes, viewing these factors as chance factors with respect to their work.[18]

Turning now to a further consideration of Table 15.5, we can focus on the proportion of voluntary job changes that are made for reasons of job improvement. Job improvement was defined as a change improving some aspect of the job including economic position,

These men all work with wire. Their jobs are manifestly different, however. The lineman on the pole, the toll testboardman and the central office repairman may have known little or nothing about these "private" careers in the telephone industry before joining the company. Did chance play a large part in their being in their present occupations? Some opportunities exist to shift from one of these occupations to the other even though they represent a division of labor in the installation and maintenance of telephone lines.

TABLE 15.5

WHEN PEOPLE CHANGE JOBS VOLUNTARILY, OVER A HALF THINK THEY ARE GETTING AHEAD WHILE ABOUT A QUARTER MOVE FOR NON-JOB REASONS *

(numbers in thousands)

Reason for Separation	*6 Cities* Skilled Men 1940-50		*St. Paul* Men 1940-44		Men 1945-50		Men 1940-50		Women 1940-44		Women 1945-50		Women 1940-50	
	No. of shifts	Per cent	No. of shifts	Per cent	No. of shifts	Per cent	No. of shifts	Per cent	No. of shifts	Per cent	No. of shifts	Per cent	No. of shifts	Per cent
All reasons	725	100	31	100	41	100	72	100	14	100	26	100	40	100
Job improvement	402	55	21	67	30	72	51	71	7	53	12	45	19	48
Relationships on the job	69	10	1	3	2	6	3	4	†	1	1	3	1	2
Personal or family situation	214	29	6	20	9	22	15	21	6	41	13	51	19	48
Defense work	40	6	3	10	†	†	3	4	1	5	†	1	1	2

* Derived from counts of all shifts (including 1950 as well as 1940-49) reported in detail by mobile workers in St. Paul and shifts up to and including the seventh (per man) made by skilled men classed as mobile. Excluded are shifts made because of layoffs traceable to business conditions, military service, and miscellaneous reasons, which include (in the study of skilled workers) a considerable proportion of shifts with no reason given, and (in the St· Paul study) a high proportion of shifts with "unemployment" given as the reason. The categories of reasons are defined as follows:

Job improvement includes reasons involving wages or other means of improving the worker's economic position, working conditions, hours, etc.

Relationships on the job includes dislike of management or supervision.

Personal or family situation includes the worker's health or age, family responsibilities such as the care of children or older persons, emergencies such as death or illness in the family, change of family residence, and reasons such as job wanderlust or desire for change of scene.

Defense work includes shifts so specified, except that changing to a defense job in order to maintain deferred status under the draft laws has been class as a personal reason in the study of skilled workers.

† Less than 0.5.

SOURCE: Reprinted with permission from Gladys Palmer, *Labor Mobility in Six Cities,* Social Science Research Council, 1954, p. 73.

working conditions, hours of work, and job status.

We note that something over half of the voluntary job shifts for skilled men in the Six Cities and about seven out of every ten job shifts for St. Paul males were for reasons of job improvement. For women in St. Paul, about half the job shifts were to improve the job. This tells us that between fifty and seventy per cent of the working force will make voluntary job changes to improve themselves in some respect. It will be remembered that the Jaffe-Carleton study showed that more than half of all working people really do get ahead. Thus, there seems to be a good deal of correspondence between the expectation of getting ahead and its reality.

The available data tend to be mutually supportive and provide definite answers to the questions with which we started this section. Somewhere between a half and three-quarters of those who voluntarily change their jobs think they are improving themselves. These are the people who are striving to get ahead. Something of the order of a quarter of those who voluntarily change their jobs let extraneous non-job factors determine their moving. These are the people who may not be very strongly concerned with getting ahead. Cutting through the data in another way we discover that about a quarter of those working feel that they had no control over their job desiny. Whether they liked it or not, whether they were "strivers" or "resters," they felt that chance ruled their job destinies.

CAREERS AND MOBILITY

Each person is involved in working at a series of jobs in his work lifetime. The jobs that a person holds are a consequence of chance, of choice, and of the condition of the employment market in which he seeks employment. Under some circumstances we can consider his work experience as a career.

OCCUPATIONAL CAREER

An occupational career is the sucession of *related* jobs filled by an individual. The jobs are held in an ordered series, and there is some kind of real relationship among them. Some individuals start in a line of activity which carries on for the rest of their lives. They move progressively into successive stages of their line of work.

There is a great deal of difference between work and a career. Work is the acceptance of employment with the primary objective of securing the income that it provides. Each job is viewed as an isolated interval in the process of earning an income. The entrance on a career carries with it a whole series of future expectations extending through the effective lifetime of the individual. Working usually takes place within a short time perspective. Entering a career usually has a lengthy time perspective for the individual.

The expectations surrounding a career concern the compensation to be received from working in a particular line of activity, the rights, privileges, status, and non-financial rewards that are associated with the work career. The portion of a career yet to be fulfilled represents anticipatory stages of working life development. In a sense, the career provides the broad framework for a long-time planning of the future.[19]

STABILITY OF CAREERS

Some careers are relatively stable, and have a common definition in the society. This is particularly true for the professions which have long-standing traditional definitions. Professions have clear-cut channels of entry. The resulting rewards and expectations that are associated with professions are generally known. On the other hand, there are activities known only to their participants and largely unknown to the public as a whole. Careers in the factory, and many office jobs, may be reasonably clear to those who follow them, but largely unknown to an outsider. Furthermore, the dependence an individual has on a particular technology, or a particular machine, or a particular operation, may, with a change in that technology, machine, or operation, result in the sudden termination of a career.

We can distinguish between two kinds of careers. There is a public career in which work is viewed by the public as following a well defined career pattern having a beginning and an end, and developmental stages throughout its entire length. There is another type, called a private career, whose features are known only to those following it.

Private careers are specialized to a given industry, or a company, or even a unique technology. These private careers are known primarily to those who follow them, or to the relatively few outsiders in occupational contact. Private careers have the special characteristic that they seldom serve to define the general social standing of those following them in the eyes of the public. For example, if I told you that my uncle was a roller in a steel mill (a definite private career)you might conjure up a whole series of mental images about what he does, how important he is, and where he stands in the status structure of the society. Most of you would be at a loss to place this man, perhaps visualizing him as a laborer coiling steel strip, or rolling scrap metal from one place to another, or even forming steel balls by rolling molten metal. The steel mill roller is a man of very high status, well paid and exceptionally skilled, in charge of a giant rolling mill that forms and shapes ingots.

One of the general trends in American society, with its continual elaboration of the division of labor, is the conversion of publicly recognized careers into private ones. At the same time, many new private careers are established having no specific relationship to traditional careers.

The vast increase in the number of private careers makes career planning difficult. You do not know of the available careers until you actually go to work and discover the private careers of your particular company and industry. You may say that you are planning a career in business, for example, but that merely establishes your preference to work for a private company. It is not until you actually go to work that you will discover the private career lines available to you.[20]

The tremendous increase in the number of private careers has another consequence. Relatively few people know of the private careers. Those following private careers, therefore, tend to develop two directions in their attachment to their careers. For the general public they are likely to establish their identity with either their company, or their industry. When asked what they do, their ready response is: "I work for General Motors," or "I work in the auto industry." At the same time, within the occupation, they are likely to identify with others following the same career, as Reissman has pointed out.[21] Those following the same career form associations or unions, and identify with fellows like themselves through the association.

It is notable that some careers may change their form over relatively short periods of time. For example, the engineer employed by a large industrial firm is pursuing a different career, in many respects, from that of his predecessor who was an independent practitioner executing engineering assignments for a client. On problems of engineering design and design theory, these two engineers operate in identical fashion. However, the contexts of the careers are quite different, the one being part of a business firm, the other being an independent professional practitioner. Thus it would be unthinkable, for example, for the independent professional practitioners to organize into a union for purposes of collective bargaining with their clients. However, the engineer as a member of the corporation has, in fact, done this. It is now estimated that there are forty thousand engineers who bargain collectively with their employers.

The career of machinist has undergone significant transformation so that the lineal descendants of the machinists of fifty years ago are men who are highly skilled specialists. In spite of their apprenticeship, the new machinists may not have the all-around skill and ability of their predecessors. Indeed, they may have their titles changed from that of machinist to setup man, production machinist, machine maintenance man, and so forth. Nevertheless, in spite of these changes the new jobs are as clearly careers as were the jobs out of which they grew.

In work where tasks are likely to undergo change over relatively short periods of time, where machines are likely to change, and where the requirements for the individual's performance are likely to be significantly modified, it is difficult to have a sense of career. Thus it is fairly common to designate a whole series of factory jobs as semi-skilled labor, or machine work. Similarly, in the office it is common practice to designate a whole series of related, yet changeable jobs, as clerical work. Ordinarily we would not say the individual who is a clerical worker, or a machine operator, is pursuing a career. Such workers may not know today the kind of work they will be expected to perform tomorrow, nor will they know the rewards and perquisites that will be associated with doing their future but unknown work.

WORK VS. CAREER

It should be clear that not all who work are following careers.[22] Indeed, there is an increasing tendency in the development of factory and office work to destroy traditional career patterns without substituting alternative careers. This is part of what is meant by job dilution, and breaking down skills. It may be also one of the significant roots of disinterest in work, or in the company in which work is performed.

Are these women just working, or pursuing a career? If the girl is "in line" for the job of the woman, and the two jobs actually represent connected stages in the development of a work history, then this represents a career.

The careerless character of much industrial and clerical work may necessitate the development of functional equivalents of careers in order to make such work attractive. This is particularly true if the objectives of making work attractive are to support interest and to have a strong sense of identification with the employing organization. If neither of these objectives is important, then there need be little management concern with the lack of career characteristics in industrial or clerical work.

A career is not a place of employment, it is an occupation. An individual called an assembler can properly carry out his duties even though facing annual changes in the product assembled, in the material worked on, and in the tasks performed. The assembler may be a different worker in the task he does from month to month, or year to year. The only career characteristic his work retains is continuing employment by the same firm at approximately the same wages. However, continuity of employment in the same firm is not the same as the pursuit of a career. One's career is not the XYZ Company; it is a clearly defined occupation, having distinctive features of its own.

All job careers are pursued at some kind of work, but not all work can be considered careers.[23] Furthermore, many careers are undergoing constant modification. Those who enter a career in the early stages of their life may end up doing quite different things when they finally retire from work.

CAREER AS A SYSTEM OF ORGANIZED INCENTIVES

A career is a system of organized incentives. By this we simply mean that the stages of a career, the unfolding and future aspects of a career, stand as guides and goals for the person following it.[24] The career, when it is recognized as such, is important in setting forth lifetime goals in the work world. The individual knows where he begins work, and the kind of work that is expected of him. He knows into what kinds of work he is likely to graduate, and the rewards it will bring. He knows just as importantly where he ends up, what his terminal position will be.[25]

From the relative certainty that the knowledge of a career provides, the individual is afforded an opportunity to develop bench marks for laying out the pattern of his non-work life. A person can anticipate his relative earnings, and his status in the community. From this he can determine a style of life appropriate to his anticipated income and status.[26] Whether the individual views his work as a source of direct satisfaction, or simply as a source of income for living in the community, entering into a career provides himself a way of ordering his future life and giving it direction.

A career provides a degree of predictability about an individual's future. The more nearly work is a career, the more definitely can the individual predict where he will be in the distant future.[27] Predictability about the future is one of the important elements that give stability to a sociey. It is also one of the important elements that give stability to an individual's life history. It does so by defining the full extent of work expectations, and also by defining the limits beyond which these expectations cannot go.[28]

The great emphasis on unlimited promotion that is given lip service by many American industrial managers may be destructive of stability and security among the personnel. One of the effects of the myth of unlimited mobility is to blur the lines between careers. It also gives the impression that every career, however lowly, has an unlimited ceiling. This is manifest nonsense in many instances, and highly improbable in most instances. It is unstabilizing for the personnel of an organization to operate with the appearance of indeterminancy about the terminal point of their chosen careers. Rather than provide incentive the myth of unlimited mobility may create uncertainty. People whose careers are clearly incapable of terminating in top positions may fail to perceive this obvious fact, because of the myth of unlimited promotional opportunities.[29]

Established career patterns develop patience and tolerance in those pursuing the career. Every career tends to have a beginning, developmental stages, and a terminal point. Part of entering a career is the clear recognition of its evolutionary stages. The total career pattern defines, for each individual pursuing it, where he ought to be in relation to the time in his life that he entered the career. However impatient the individual may be, he tends to find greatest ease in pursuing his career by following in the traditional evolutionary stages. Hall has pointed out in the medical career, for example, that the practice of a specialty has in the past been one of the rewards of age and length of previous medical practice.[30] This, of course, is an implicit and not an explicit feature of the medical career. Nevertheless, the young doctor, impatient to pursue a specialty, in the recent past, at least, found himself faced with rather subtle, and sometimes not so subtle pressures, to conform to the career expectations of the medical profession. The military officer who graduates from a Federal military academy similarly has to pass through the appropriate ranks at about the appropriate speed as his career unfolds. He may evoke considerable jealously and often subtle opposition from his fellows if his career appears to be progressing too rapidly.

In the factory and the office there may be certain rights granted to the older members in careers which may be coveted secretly by younger individuals, but which can seldom be openly sought. The opportunity to choose the newest machine to operate may be afforded to the senior man in a job career. The least physically demanding tasks may become the prerogative of senior members who are in the declining years. There may even be retained obsolescent tasks for the people who are at the end of a career in order that they may finish out their career with honor and distinction. These all grow up as expected rights and rewards of those who follow a career. They are seldom violated, either by the younger members or by the organization in which the career is pursued.

A career may be viewed as a channel along which one's work life unfolds. The channel has clearly defined boundaries to it, and moves in a prescribed direction. Furthermore, there are established stages along this channel, achieved at approximately the same time by all those pursuing the career. Finally, the career usually has an established terminal point, and a definite set of rights and expectations that are associated with each of its stages. Typically, these rights and expectations increase in value as the later stages of the career are reached.

CAREERS IN WORK ORGANIZATIONS

Careers in work organizations function to the advantage of the organization in a number of different ways. In this section we want to examine some of the relations between careers and organizations.

CAREERS AND SPECIALIZATION

We have noted before that specialization of tasks is a fundamental characteristic of organizations.[31] These specializations are usually pursued in separate departments of the organization, and are usually performed as tasks having distinctive job titles. Means have to be developed in the organization to keep individuals within the confines of their special jobs. The career is one important device that satisfies this requirement of the work organization.

When a task takes on characteristics of a career it becomes distinctive and is differentiated from all other tasks. The individual performing the job sees himself as associated with other kinds of work through a broad division of labor, but differentiated from every other kind of task as a consequence of specialization. Such incentives as operate, operate only in the special area with respect to the special job. There may be other kinds of jobs with different incentives. In a sense, therefore, the career serves to define the goals towards which the individual works. These goals are typically unique and special to his chosen career. Indeed, it might be argued that the organization, for the individual who is pursuing a career in it, becomes ultimately the provider of opportunity to fulfill the career. The individual's attachment to the organization is through his career.

CAREERS AND TRAINED INCAPACITY

The specialized tasks that are a career in an organization must exclude many other tasks performed elsewhere in the organization. The particular tasks in a career become clearly defined, and the limits of its activities are established. Any individual who is in a stage of a career tends automatically to be absolved from the need for doing work clearly outside the career boundaries.

A career provides for the individual the justification for not being fully competent, or not being capable of doing tasks that fall outside of the career pattern. This is a way of suggesting that the specialist's trained incapacity[32] is sustained by his concept of his career and its limits as a set of working tasks.[33] The specialist who can see his work as a career is fully justified in being indifferent to operations and tasks performed around him.

CAREERS AND LIMITED AMBITION

Individual career lines in the organization establish the range of limited ambitions that people may pursue. It becomes respectable to have modest expectations about one's terminal position if that terminal position is the last stage of a career. It is perfectly respectable for an individual not to aspire to the top positions of a company, or organization, if he can see that his own work has its special goal and special terminal position. By way of example, the enlisted man achieves real respectability if he retires in the rank of Master Sergeant or Chief Petty Officer. He is not condemned by either service men or civilians for lack of ambition. He has reached a terminal point in a career and this is respectable, however lowly this terminal point may be in the general scale of social status. Similarly it is perfectly respectable for a company-grade officer to retire in the rank of Captain, or a field-grade officer to retire in the rank of Colonel.

Every organization needs those people who fill the lowly jobs faithfully and continuously throughout their working life. The extent to which the lowly jobs of an organization can be developed into careers determines the ability of individuals to derive genuine satisfaction out of filling them. When janitor's work becomes a career rather than a job, the janitor can retire after fifty-two years of service with a great feeling of satisfaction that he has performed well a necessary function in the organization.

The elaboration of careers in organizations establishes the bases on which the "thank God for" people build a significant working life history in lowly jobs.[34] Such people are the individuals filling the largest number of jobs in every work organization, commonly referred to as production jobs, and whose incumbents are designated as the rank-and-file.

It has often been suggested that dirty or low grade work, or work that is generally valued poorly in the status systems of a society, may often require special rewards in order to induce people to hold such jobs. Alternatively it is suggested that the personal failures of society are likely to be found performing such tasks.[35]

Both of these positions ignore the reality of making careers out of any and all jobs, regardless of where they fall within the status systems of the community. So long as work is perceived as a career, it can be pursued with dignity and devotion by those who find their satisfaction in it. The chimney sweep of British tradition not only wore his top hat, but was often rewarded by a cup of tea by those whose dirty flues he swept. He was clearly a man with a career. There was an almost professional aura surrounding his self-image of what he did and where he fitted into a scheme of things.

A number of personnel procedures in industry have been inimical to the development of careers. One of the most common practices is the broad designation of relatively homogeneous tasks under titles like "common labor," "machine operator," "clerical pool." Put in its most ridiculous form we might ask, "Who would ever pursue a career as a common laborer?" or "Who could make a career of being a clerical pooler?"

In the very usage that is implied here, the individual loses his identity by being lumped together into a labor pool having a common designation with no distinctive characteristics. There is no career in being a common laborer, but there may very well be a career in being a ditch digger. The tasks performed may be identical, but the identity of the individuals is clearly defined in the latter case, and obviously lost in the former case.

The status position of any given task does not determine its potentiality for being a career. The personal importance of a career is not related to the terminal social status that the career affords. Careers are, in this sense, independent of status. However, as we will note in our discussion of upward mobility or promotions, for the individual within given career lines there are clearly defined increments of status that are associated with stages of the career.

PROMOTIONS AS A FORM OF INDIVIDUAL MOBILITY

Promotions represent a change in status within the organization. Different kinds of promotions represent different forms of mobility for the individual; four of these relate to career patterns.

PROMOTIONS WITHIN A CAREER

Once entered on a career, the individual develops appropriate expectations regarding his own advancement. He knows that after so much service, or a certain quality of task performance, he can expect to move forward to the next career stage. These expectations are general for the career. The career expectations are shared by all those pursuing the career and are a matter of common experience and common expectation in the group.

This suggests that promotional opportunities are not the sole proprietorship of management. Advancement becomes the expectation of career employees as incorporated by management into appropriate systems of incentives. Thus there may be periodic increases in salary or wages associated with length of service or improvement in task performance. There may be changes in title, or other added marks of status awarded by management. Withholding of promotion or other rewards for progress is ordinarily viewed as an undue disturbance of career patterns. The promotion becomes a fixed expectation, to be fulfilled by management except where cause can be shown for failure to promote.

On the other hand, promotion out of line of normal career development, more rapidly than the general career expectations associated with a job, may be resented as interference with the career pattern. In some companies it is common to talk about "jet-jobs," which is a designation of individuals moving more rapidly than their career warrants. There is typically a resentment against both the individuals who move too rapidly, and the management that violates the established career expectations in promoting "fair-haired boys."

Promotions within a career pattern are neither freely withheld nor freely granted by management. Promotions tend to conform to the expectations of those who pursue the career. The career provides a basic solidarity among those pursuing it. This is typically expressed through insistence that progression within career lines be honored more or less rigidly by management.

PROMOTION BETWEEN CAREERS

One of the most interesting and yet most difficult transitions to make in an organization is to move from one career line into another. This entails a number of obvious adjustments.

In the first place, the individual who moves from the top of one career pattern into the bottom of a higher career pattern may be shifting his vantage point from one of achieved success to one of uncertain prospects. The top of a career pattern is an assured position. The bottom of another career line, even though it may culminate at a higher level, may represent a position of great insecurity to the individual.[36] He has a whole new ladder to climb with his foot resting only on its bottom-most rung. It is not uncommon in many organizations for individuals to hestitate to accept a promotion that represents moving from one career into another. This hesitancy is the consequence of the relative insecurity that is associated with a new start.

A second kind of adjustment must be made when the new career represents a changed style of life, and level of living. The individual has to adjust to a whole new pattern of life. When given the opportunity to move into an entirely new and higher career line there may be serious readjustment in life patterns outside the job in order to bring general behavior into accord with different expectations of the new career line. This may require important adjustment which the individual has to choose either to make, or attempt to ignore.

An individual is, when at the apex of one career, absolved from the general social pressures of moving ahead. He has gained his objective and is no longer motivated towards upward mobility as he was during the lower stages of his established career. However, when forced into a new and higher career pattern he has to reactivate all his drive toward upward mobility, and reassemble his resources to climb toward the pinnacle dictated by his new career. The habit of upward mobility may have been lost by this time; or interest in moving upward may have diminished. Consequently, the individual who moves from a lower to a higher career line may face the additional disadvantage of having lost some of his earlier drive when climbing the new promotional ladder.[37]

PROMOTIONS AND PARALLELING CAREERS

It is obvious that not all careers terminate at the same level. There can be paralleling careers overlapping for a major portion of their length, but with one extending to a higher terminal rank. Sometimes promotions are offered to individuals to move from one career into a paralleling one that has a higher ceiling. Such promotions provide relatively few problems of adjustment for the individual, providing the careers are truly parallel in character. In parallel careers, the tasks are largely similar, or require relatively easy adaptation from the old tasks to the new.

Sometimes moves between parallel career

The young engineer may often start with a company doing field work, like the men surveying. At the much higher reaches of the engineering profession is the research engineer like the member of an industrial research group shown consulting with a research chemist. If the young engineer aspires to the research position, and makes it, his promotion will be between paralleling careers.

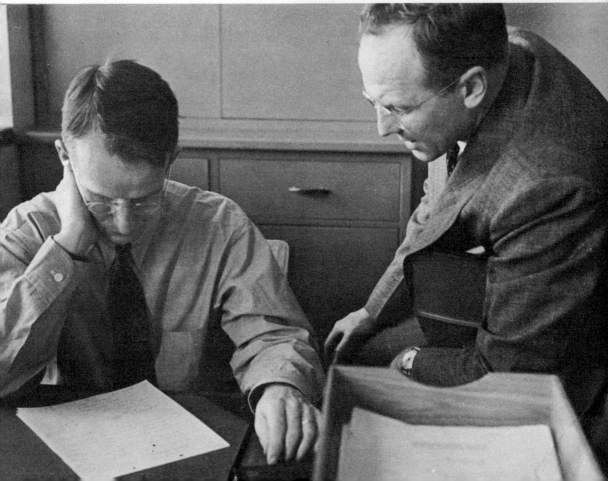

patterns simply involve transfer from a branch department into the central office, for example. Here the paralleling careers have almost identical features but the height at which the career can culminate in the central office may be greater than in the branch office. In other instances, like the move from a staff to a line position, an individual may continue to perform his accustomed duties, but do so in a career pattern that affords him greater opportunity for moving upward in the organization. Very many of the promotions available in work organizations consist of moving from one career into a paralleling one.

PROMOTION FROM WORK INTO A CAREER

The simplest kind of promotion, and the most common in work organizations, is promotion from work into a career.[38] This takes place when the individual is removed from a general classification, or designation, and put into an occupational career. Very often there is a clearly designated period of probation, or temporary employment, during which the individual is tested for his capacity to fulfill the career.

There may be formal training programs, including executive training programs, in which new members of the organization are placed. They undergo a trial period during which they get the "feel" of the organization in performing minor and largely non-essential tasks. Having, however, passed the trial period successfully, they are formally introduced into careers, at the lowest rungs, from which they can move upward as the career affords the opportunity.[39]

TRANSFERS AS A FORM OF INDIVIDUAL MOBILITY

We can see transfers as involving a number of distinct moves of individuals within the organization. We can examine these transfers as they relate to moves between different kinds of career patterns.

TRANSFERS INTO PARALLEL CAREERS

It has been suggested above that transfers moving from one career pattern into a paralleling one can be viewed as a promotion. At the same time, it is evident that where the move is made at the same level, with no change in status, rewards, or pay, we can call the move a transfer rather than a promotion. The transfer serves to move the individual horizontally in the organization into the new career pattern.

The net effect of transfer is to increase the probability that the individual will end higher in the organization by virtue of the higher ceiling that the new career pattern affords. On the other hand, the transfer may not even provide this. It may simply provide an opportunity to do a different kind of work, or do it in a different place. There may be no effective change in the unfolding career that the individual will pursue. Thus, transfers between parallel careers (as distinct from promotions between parallel careers) are a way of accommodating the individual and his particular skills to the requirements of the organization.

TRANSFERS FROM OBSOLETE CAREERS

One of the perennial problems of organizations is the obsolescence of careers. Technological changes are the major influences destroying or changing careers. In general, companies pursue a policy of "taking care of" people whose skills are no longer required. This may involve the transfer of individuals whose careers are still in mid-stream, or those who have reached the apex of their career, into new lines of work.

Transfers from obsolete careers may entail a number of difficulties, for those already established in the new career lines as well as those who are transferred. There may be antagonism against the invaders because they have not themselves undergone the early stages of the career pattern into which they are transferred. The newcomers may be uncertain of their capacity to fill the new jobs by virtue of their lack of experience in the career.

In general, the overriding desire to "look after" the displaced people may take precedence over all other considerations. A kind of humanitarian consensus will prevail that makes the transfer acceptable to all concerned. However, such transfers may not always meet the test of efficiency of performance, and only humanitarian grounds render them acceptable to management.

SEPARATIONS AS A FORM OF INDIVIDUAL MOBILITY

The unfolding work career is often intimately associated with the organization in which it is pursued. This is particularly true where the job is distinctive and the tasks are unique to that particular organization. Consequently, when a job is lost, or the individual is separated from his employment, he is not simply losing his job or his income. He may see his whole career cut off in mid-stream. He may see his career expectations destroyed in not having an opportunity to pursue it elsewhere, since it was unique to his former organization.

There may be very subtle dimensions to career uniqueness. A president's confidential secretary who is discharged on the retirement or dismissal of her boss, may be uniquely suited to fill only the job of secretary to that particular president. Although her secretarial skills may be general, little of her special knowledge is transferrable to some other president in some other company. Consequently, on being fired, the secretary may find herself severely down-graded in her career. The termination of employment for one who is engaged in a career may have degrading consequences to the extent that the career is unique to an employer or company.

When separation from work is temporary, as when there is a cut in production, most careers are not interrupted. Accordingly the individual may accept temporary unemployment with relatively little antagonism. He is likely to view it essentially as a loss of income and not as a loss of career. There is the full expectation that this temporary layoff will at most delay the unfolding of the career, and certainly will not interrupt it.[40]

In Table 15.3 we have evidence regarding the causes of separation from employment. These data deal with an actual change in employer. When a worker leaves one employer for another, approximately a third of the time this is because of business conditions affecting the employer, such as failure, plant shutdown, plant removal, or slackening of business. Caught up among this third of the workers who change employers are undoubtdedly a large number who suffer some career dislocation through no fault of their own. They are thrown out on the job market because of a drop in their employer's business.

The two-thirds of the workers who change employers for reasons other than layoffs, as revealed in Table 15.3, include those who quit to get ahead, those fired for incompetence or other causes, and those who quit for reasons not related to work. This group, then, includes people who are judged not to be competent in their chosen careers or jobs, those who think they can move ahead faster with another employer, and those who are more or less indifferent to their work. The "strivers," the "resters," and the "skidders" are all part of this group.[41]

The Six City Study tells us that one-third of the time people change employers because of economic conditions having nothing to do with their work performance or work preferences. The other two-thirds of the job changes are made because of reasons having to do with actual work performance and occupational expectations, or because non-job factors dictate the change. The major inference we can draw from these data is that two times out of every three, voluntary action by either the employer or the employee will lead to a shift in employment from one firm to another. This highlights the magnitude of the personnel problem involved for the average business firm resulting from separations and consequent turnover of employees.

AMBITIONS, CAREERS, AND WORK ORGANIZATIONS

The majority of Americans want to get ahead in their work. This leads to a vast amount of job shifting. Somewhere between a half and three-quarters of the voluntary job changes are made in expectation of advancement.

The occupational ladder, however, can be climbed in both directions. Some people actually go downward during their working lifetime. We have examined the extent of this back-sliding and discovered it to be of considerable magnitude, happening to one worker out of four.

One way of giving some assurance that jobs will improve with each succeeding change is to follow an occupation that is a career. Once engaged in a career, progression is made through its stages to a definite terminal point which, when reached, provides an honorable and satisfying end for a lifetime of work. Careers have incentive values in establishing the milestones for job progression. When careers are built into work organizations they serve to give stability to the work force, and enhance identification of employees with their work and the firm employing them.

NOTES FOR CHAPTER 15

[1] Harold Wool, *Tables of Working Life, Length of Working Life of Men,* Bulletin 1001, U.S. Department of Labor (Washington: Government Printing Office, 1950).

[2] A. J. Jaffe and R. O. Carleton, *Occupational Mobility in the United States, 1930-1960* (New York: King's Crown Press, 1954), p. 49.

[3] *Ibid.*, p. 50.

[4] The same general results regarding total working life are reported in Ewan Clague, "The Working Life Span of American Workers," *Journal of Gerontology,* 4:285-289 (October, 1949); and S. L. Wolfbein, "The Length of Working Life," *Population Studies,* 3:286-294 (December, 1949).

[5] Gladys Palmer, *Labor Mobility in Six Cities* (New York: Social Science Research Council, 1954).

[6] S. M. Lipset and Reinhard Bendix, "Social Mobility and Occupational Career Patterns," *American Journal of Sociology,* 57:366-374 (January, 1952).

[7] For an interesting analysis of mobility as an established pattern of life see: Theodore Caplow, "Transiency as a Cultural Pattern, *American Sociological Review,* 5:731-739 (October, 1940).

[8] An excellent treatment of social mobility in its principal aspects is contained in P. A. Sorokin, *Social Mobility* (New York: Harper & Bros., 1927). A general source on occupational mobility is Omar Pancoast, Jr., *Occupational Mobility* (New York: Columbia University Press, 1941. The best summary to date of some of the research problems involved in mobility is H. S. Parnes, *Research on Labor Mobility: An Appraisal of Research Findings in the United States* (New York: Social Science Research Council, 1954).

[9] An original study of the stability and shifts in occupations between fathers and sons is: P. E. Davidson and H. D. Anderson, *Occupational Mobility in an American Community* (Stanford: Stanford University Press, 1937). A specific study of intergeneration inheritance of coal mining occupations is found in William Wance and Richard Butler, "The Effect of Industrial Changes on Occupational 'Inheritance' in Four Pennsylvania Communities," *Social Forces,* 27:156-162 (December, 1948); while the transmission of business leadership positions from father to son is treated in W. L. Warner and J. C. Abegglen, *Occupational Mobility in American Business and Industry* (Minneapolis: University of Minnesota Press, 1955), especially Chapter 6, "A Man's Family and His Career," Still another recent study of shifts in occupations between fathers and sons is Reinhard Bendix, S. M. Lipset, and F. T. Malm, "Social Origins and Occupational Career Patterns," *Industrial and Labor Relations Review,* 7:246-261 (January, 1954).

[10] S. M. Lipset and Reinhard Bendix, "Social Mobility and Occupational Career Patterns," *American Journal of Sociology,* 57:366-374 (January, 1952).

[11] A. J. Jaffe, and R. O. Carleton, *op. cit.,* p. 51.

[12] There is some differential in the age at which occupational stability and the highest occupational level are reached according to the occupation followed. For higher level occupations that tend to be career, entry is made earlier than in lower level occupations. See for example F. L. Babcock, *The United States College Graduate* (New York: Time, Inc., 1941), who concluded that stability in the highest occupations is usually achieved by college trained adults between thirty and forty years of age. See also the conclusions in: Stuart Adams, "Regional Differences in Vertical Mobility in a High Status Occupation," *American Sociological Review,* 15:228-235 (April, 1950); and A. J. Reiss, Jr., Occupational Mobility of Professional Workers," *American Sociological Review,* 20:693-700 (December, 1955).

[13] A. J. Jaffe and R. O. Carleton, *op. cit.,* p. 57.

[14] Contrast it, for example, with the limited sample represented in such a study as: Richard Centers, "Occupational Mobility of Urban Occupational

NOTES FOR CHAPTER 15 (CONT.)

Strata," *American Sociological Review,* 13:197-203 (April, 1948).

[15] Quoted with permission from Gladys Palmer, *Labor Mobility in Six Cities,* pp. 135–136.

[16] Some indirect evidence showing comparable results for English data is contained in Margot Jefferys, *Mobility in the Labor Market* (New York: Grove Press, 1954).

[17] Gladys Palmer, *op. cit.,* p. 73.

[18] This, of course, raises a whole series of questions about the ways in which employees are selected by employing firms. From the firm's standpoint it is desirable to minimize turnover of labor, and especially that portion of the turnover attributable to employee's indifference to work. It would, therefore, be desirable to have some means for culling out of the group of job applicants those who are likely to let non-job considerations affect their future employment with the company. Much less attention is given to this feature of employee selection than is given to the skill and personality traits of job applicants. See, for example, R. M. Dorcus and M. H. Jones, *Handbook of Employee Selection* (New York: McGraw-Hill Book Company, 1950); and R. K. Burns and H. W. Johnson, "Personnel Selection and Employment,' in J. F. Mee (ed.), *Personnel Handbook* (New York: The Ronald Press, 1951), pp. 417-462.

[19] This is particularly well revealed in the study of students in the college phase of their occupational careers. See H. S. Becker and J. W. Carper, "The Development of Identification with an Occupation," *American Journal of Sociology,* 61:289-298 (January, 1956).

[20] This is one of the thorny problems of incentives among new employees. Since job applicants tend to be ignorant of a company's private careers, they have to be "sold" on the general features and benefits of working for the company. After employment they may learn of the real career opportunities and develop attachments to the private career. This problem is implicit in most discussions of employee selection. See for example M. S. Viteles, "Selection and Placement of Employees," in Arthur Kornhauser (ed), *Psychology of Labor-Management Relation* (Champaign: Industrial Relations Research Association, 1949), pp. 9-22.

[21] Leonard Reissman, "A Study of Role Conceptions in Bureaucracy," *Social Forces,* 27:305-311 (March, 1949).

[22] Professor Foote has made a provocative analysis of automobile labor in Detroit and concludes that important forces are operating to make careers out of line production jobs. We agree with 'his general conclusion, as elaborated later in this chapter, that all kinds of jobs can become careers. We would not agree that this has already happened in the automobile industry. See N. N. Foote, "The Professionalization of Labor in Detroit," *American Journal of Sociology,* 58:371-380 (January, 1953).

[23] Cf. H. M. Case, "Two Kinds of Crystallized Occupational Choice Behavior: A Problem in Delineation and Relationship," *American Sociological Review,* 19:85-87 (February, 1954), and the addendum in 19:350 (June, 1954). Students of labor markets have noted that work goals and satisfactions often seem to fluctuate widely in response to shifts in local labor market conditions. We would suggest that this is much more true for those whose jobs are viewed as work and not as careers. See, for example, L. G. Reynolds, *The Structure of Labor Markets* (New York: Harper & Brothers, 1951).

[24] When commitment is made to a career early in life, as is sometimes done by parents who dedicate themselves to bring up their children "to be a doctor (lawyer) (engineer)" then it becomes interesting to find out how far back in the person's life history his knowledge of personal dedication to a career affected his outlook. Some indirect evidence on this is found in P. J. Allen, "Childhood Backgrounds of Success in a Profession," *American Sociological Review,* 20:186-190 (April, 1955).

[25] Cf. S. M. Lipset, Reinhard Bendix, and F. T. Malm, "Job Plans and Entry into the Labor Market," *Social Forces,* 33:224-232 (March, 1955).

[26] It has been shown, for example, that such non-work aspects of behavior as political party, religion, and lodge membership are important as part of the style of living of those who "get ahead" in their careers. See Melville Dalton, "Informal Factors in Career Achievement," *American Journal of Sociology,* 56:407-415 (March, 1951).

[27] An attempt to answer the question: "To what extent do first jobs serve as predictors of career patterns?" will be found in S. M. Lipset and F. T. Malm, "First Jobs and Career Patterns," *American Journal of Economics and Sociology,* 14:247-261 (April, 1955).

[28] A particularly interesting examination of the impact of career patterns on mobility in business firms, with special emphasis on the limitations set by career channels, is found in N. H. Martin and A. L. Strauss, "Patterns of Mobility within Industrial Organizations," *The Journal of Business,* 29:101-110 (April, 1956).

[29] The belief in unlimited opportunity is so widespread that children with common school education are likely to discover a work world quite different from their images of it. For example, a post-depression study concluded: "... for about 85 per cent of the youth who will enter the labor market upon leaving school, their rendezvous are not with scientific laboratories, courtrooms, and pulpits, but with such unglamorous things as picks and shovels, filing cabinets, sales slips, and production lines." H. W. Bell, *Matching Youth and Jobs* (Washington: American Council on Education, 1940), p. 68. Another study made at about the same time indicated that a third of the high school graduates in Rochester, New York felt that their schooling provided only gen-

NOTES FOR CHAPTER 15 (CONT.)

eral preparation for work, and a sixth said that it was no help at all. See: H. C. Seymour and C. E. Tremer, *We Left School a Year Ago* (Rochester: Rochester, New York Public Schools, 1941).

30 Oswald Hall, "The Stages of a Medical Career," *American Journal of Sociology,* 53:327-336 (March, 1948).

31 See Chapter 5 for the general statement, and Chapter 10 for the analysis of specialization in terms of its technological roots. In this same connection see Helen Wood, "Trends in the Specialization of Occupational Requirements," in William Haber, *et al* (eds.), *Manpower in the United States: Problems and Policies* (New York: Harper & Brothers, 1954), pp. 103-116.

32 "Trained incapacity" is a phrase originated by Thorstein Veblen. For two very insightful discussions of it see: H. J. Laski, "The Limitations of the Expert," *Harper's Magazine,* 162:102-106 (December, 1930); and R. K. Merton, "Bureaucratic Structure and Personality," *Social Forces,* 18:560-568 (May, 1940).

33 There is always the dilemma in personnel selection between hiring a job applicant to fit his first job, and hiring him to fit higher level jobs into which he might later move. This is one basis on which Professor Haire suggests caution in uncritical use of tests in employee selection: Mason Haire, "Use of Tests in Employee Selection," *Harvard Business Review,* 28:42-51 (January, 1950). The more traditional position of fitting the job applicant to a particular job opening is set forth in Donald Super, *Appraising Vocational Fitness* (New York: Harper & Brothers, 1949). Where selection is for the initial stags of a career, the fit of man to current job secures emphasis. Where growth potential is sought, then personality traits that permit an individual to break out of the confines of career restrictions should perhaps be emphasized in making the selection.

34 E. C. Hughes used the phrase " 'thank God for' people" in describing "the unambitious people who can be counted on to stay where they are, and who keep things running while others are busy climbing the mobility ladder from one job to another." E. C. Hughes, "Queries Concerning Industry and Society Growing Out of a Study of Ethnic Relations in Industry," *American Sociological Review,* 14:218 (April, 1949).

35 Cf. C. A. Meyers and G. P. Schultz, *Dynamics of a Labor Market* (Englewood Cliffs, N. J.: Prentice-Hall, Inc., 1951).

36 The insecurity involved in career shifts even when they result from promotions out of one career into another is discussed in Walter Weisskopf, "Industrial Institutions and Personality Structure," *Journal of Social Issues,* 7:1-6 (1951).

37 Cf. Chris Argyris, "Top Management Dilemma: Company Needs vs. Individual Development," *Personnel,* 32:123-134 (September, 1955).

38 "The American Factory Worker," *Fortune,* 35:5ff (May, 1947), contains a discussion of worker reaction to promotion opportunities that sheds light on the promotion from work to a career.

39 A study designed specifically to test the ease with which opportunities for promotion were afforded workers as over against college-trained people does not indicate a marked advantage for the latter, unless the modernity of the production methods was taken into account. Among the four production units studied, those with more modern production methods showed a lower mobility rate for workers than for college-trained people. R. C. Stone, "Factory Organization and Vertical Mobility," *American Sociological Review,* 18:28-35 (February, 1953).

40 A series of papers dealing with labor turnover in an English factory relate job shifting to the various aspects of the social system of the factory. Their conclusions tend to support the general notion that ease with which people leave jobs or accept separation from them is related to the extent to which the jobs are viewed as careers. See: A. K. Rice, J. M. M. Hill, and E. L. Trist, "The Representation of Labour Turnover as a Social Process; Studies in the Social Development of an Industrial Community (The Glacier Project)—II," *Human Relations,* 3:349-372 (1950); J. M. M. Hill, "A Consideration of Labour Turnover as the Result of a Quasi-Stationary Process; With a Case Illustration (The Glacier Project)—IV," *Human Relations,* 4:255-264 (1951); A. K. Rice, "An Examination of the Boundaries of Part Institutions; An Illustrative Study of Departmental Labour Turnover in Industry (The Glacier Project)—VI," *Human Relations,* 4:393-400 (1951); A. K. Rice, "The Relative Independence of Sub-institutions as Illustrated by Departmental Labour Turnover (The Glacier Project)—VII," *Human Relations,* 5:83-93 (1952); and A. K. Rice and E. L. Trist, "Institutional and Sub-institutional Determinants of Change in Labour Turnover," *Human Relations,* 5:347-371 (1952).

41 A British study confirms that the turnover rate of an industrial plant is a consequence of the proportion of those who feel committed to a career to those who are still experimenting in the labor market. J. M. M. Hill, "A Note on Labour Turnover in an Iron and Steel Works," *Human Relations,* 6:79-87 (1953).

These two men constitute an organized team having specific tasks to perform in making the complicated cable wire connections. Their constant and literal face-to-face association while working makes it highly probable that they will also constitute a voluntary social group. This dual basis of association between the men can have important consequences for the amount and quality of work they do.

Chapter **16**

WORK GROUPS AND WORK

Many if not most of the tasks of work organizations are accomplished in working groups. We have already seen, in Chapter 6, that *organized* work groups are the team, the task group, and the technological group. Each organized work group has a different relationship to the technology of its operations, and there is further variation in the types of social interaction taking place in each kind of organized work group.

We also examined in Chapter 6 the *voluntary* social groups in work organizations. We discovered these voluntary social groups to be the pair, the triad, the primary association, and the clique. Voluntary social groups are distinguished from the organized social groups in work organizations. Voluntary groups gain and hold their membership through the operation of some free choice on the part of their participants. Members of organized groups are thrown together through the interdependence of their working tasks. Little or no choice is left to the members of organized groups as to who shall join them, or remain members.

It is our purpose in this chapter to consider the concrete relationships between work groups and getting work done. Specifically, we are concerned with (A) the functions of group life at work, and (B) the relationships among the different kinds of social groups in work organizations.

FUNCTIONS OF GROUP LIFE

It should be clear by now that all save those who work in isolation are members of some kind of organized work group. It should also be clear that all workers, except those whose personality traits isolate them, typically find some kind of voluntary group life in which to participate at their place of work. Organized working groups are a part of the functional division of labor. Voluntary social groups at work are a part of the sociological character of human interaction. Most working members of an organization have a place in an organized work group, and the opportunity to enter into one or several voluntary social groups.

We now turn to a consideration of the function of the organized and voluntary groups in work organizations. What significance does the "groupness" of work have for getting work done, and for the people who do the work? This is the fundamental question for which we seek answers in examining the functions of group life.[1]

We will place particular emphasis on the following functions of the social groups of work: (A) as the operating units within which the broad plans of the work organization are interpreted as specific operating procedures for getting work done; (B) as the environment that stimulates and supports personal invention and innovation; (C) as the carriers of standards of conduct; (D) as the realm in which personality integrity is confirmed and maintained; and finally (E) as the social units within which morale is built and sustained.

CASUAL ASSOCIATIONS

It is necessary to distinguish casual associations from the permanent group life of work organizations. Casual associations are superficial interactions between people. Casual associations occur when people interacting know each other in the simple sense that they can place each other; they are the kind we mean when we talk about a "nodding acquaintance."

Casual associations are always superficial in their content. They are also usually discontinuous, or if continuous, formal in character. The general characteristic of casual interaction is summed up by the fact that the words and gestures exchanged serve to acknowledge the presence of the other. To say "Hello," or to comment on the weather or other neutral topic, lets the other person know that you are aware of his presence, and that you are neither hostile nor indifferent towards him.

Casual associations are the realm in which people recognize each other as specific human beings, and signal this recognition by "passing the time of the day" with each other. In the most general sense, casual relations relieve the deadly serious business of people interacting with each other as occupants of jobs, positions, and offices. Casual associations permit them to behave like "just folks" towards each other too.[2]

Casual associations can serve a ceremonial democratic function in the authority structure. Through casual relations an authority holder can set aside his position of authority without damaging it. For example, it may be the habit of the company president to pass the time of the day with the elevator operator as he goes up to his office. The words passed between them and the limited content of their conversation become a ritual both parties recognize and continue. The elevator operator is pleased to be acknowledged each time as a human being by his superior. Indeed, most fraternizing by authority holders is precisely this kind of casual relationship in which subordinates are made to feel that they exist as human beings, and not merely as cogs in the productive scheme.

Casual associations also serve to facilitate rapid identification of people so that official business can be carried on more efficiently. It is desirable that those who have to interact in carrying out their tasks have some degree of knowledge about each other. The minimum amount of knowledge is that of names and responsibilities so that the proper person can be asked to provide help, to supply information, issue tools and stock, or whatnot. Casual relations help people carry out their work assignments because through casual associations additional knowledge is gained about who does what, where, when, and how.[3]

We can summarize casual associations by suggesting that they make it possible to identify a person with his work assignment. They are the minimum form of interaction that transforms the occupant of a work assignment into a human being known to us. Casual associations are universal when people meet. They serve to permit democratic behavior by authority holders outside the authority structure, and facilitate official interaction by identifying those whose business brings them into contact.

It would be a mistake, however, to assume that casual relations are of the same importance for behavior as work groups.[4] The very meager and stylized content of casual interaction makes it of only transitory importance to working behavior. Casual relations are something like the systems of polite behavior that one displays toward strangers. They facilitate interaction but are only the beginning phase of the more intensive and permanent relationships that are always imbedded in a group structure, though it be as small as a pair, or as large as a clique.

GETTING WORK DONE

One of the primary functions of the social group in a work organization is to carry out work efficiently. This is accomplished through informal cooperation, group operating decisions, and shared knowledge, important in defining what is to be done.[5]

For most operating situations it is impossible fully to specify the totality of expected behavior. This rests, in part, on the inefficiency of trying to detail all the actual behavior patterns involved. Were this attempted for each work assignment, it would be necessary to reduce the information to micro-motion facts, on the one hand, and voluminous verbal and written instructions, on the other. Under some circumstances this is attempted in order to standardize an operating procedure. The logical conclusion of such efforts is to eliminate the human factor in production.

We can, therefore, conclude that most work assignments do not reach the point of making man into a machine. Most tasks require some operator judgement and even decision, however minor, for their execution. In the vast majority of instances, judgment and decision are shared among several people whose work is interdependent. At this point the social group becomes important as the operating unit within which judgment and decision are exercised to get the work done. The social group takes the general operating decisions of the work organization and supplements them with specific judgments and decisions at the point where the actual tasks are performed.[6]

If we look at the social dimension of work, it will be noted that there are other aspects of behavior that are not directly related to the technology. There may be significant status factors asociated with the members of a work group such that some have privileges in the group not accorded to others. These privileges may be the consequence of length of service, skill, ethnic background, or any other factor which tends to differentiate among people. It would be impossible for the work organization to specify the subtle inter-personal patterns of behavior in terms of these social factors. Thus, for the organization to say that an apprentice toolmaker shall be treated as an individual of markedly lower status than a journeyman toolmaker would entail a description of behavior patterns almost inexhaustible in their detail. Yet, it is certain that there are marked differences in the way in which these two classes of people behave toward each other, and toward others in their immediate environment. It is a function of the social group to define these patterns of behavior, to lay down the lines along which they proceed, and to police the behavior in the interest of group unity.

The social group, by defining the interpersonal relations on the job, particularly the intra-group authority and status relations, makes it possible for people to interact in a more knowledgable and understanding fashion while working. The social group succeeds in defining each person's relations with his fellow workers. In this way the social group makes work more efficient by removing some indeterminancies in social relations.[7]

We can then summarize two broad functions of a social group by suggesting that (A) the group provides the organizational unit for carrying out and administering many broad policies of the organization at the operating level, and (B) the social group serves to define many of the subtle nuances of interpersonal relations that, in the very nature of things, cannot be defined in job descriptions and job analyses.

ORGANIZED GROUPS AND GETTING WORK DONE

Of special importance in getting work done at the operating level are organized work groups. This is particularly true for the team and the task groups. Both of these groups are specialized with respect to a general operation. Some autonomy exists in each type of group for determining work methods, and in the team group, even work assignments.

When an automobile body is dropped onto the final assembly line to meet the chassis for the first time, the men involved are organized into a work group to put these two major units together. The organized work group is work centered.

An organized work group doing office work. This is one accounting operation in the billing department of a metropolitan telephone company. Collection slips from telephone pay stations are sorted in the rack at the back of the department and then given to the girls at the left who do the figuring on them. The work then moves to the right hand line of girls where entries are made in the company books and each customer is credited with his percentage of pay station receipts. The department supervisor, shown standing, has a desk which faces the department giving her constant surveillance of its operations.

Voluntary groups in the work place fill the social voids of work routines. During breaks, for example, people are free to choose their associates, and the things about which they will talk. Free-flowing interaction occurs in such situations.

The autonomy of team and task groups is exercised principally with respect to the work they do.[8] It will be recalled from Chapter 6 that team and task groups take on their group character initially in relation to an operating assignment. The members of such groups are organized in relation to each other around an operation and the technology with which it is executed. For the group members, there is some freedom in working out their activities to get the group work done. If the members of a team or task group feel responsible for their work, they will make positive efforts to execute their operating assignment with imagination and skill.[9] The group members will move affirmatively to make effective the general goals set by management for their operations.[10]

The technological group is one whose membership is an incidental product of a rigid technology. The production line is the prime example of a technological group, as we saw in Chapter 6. The overriding importance of the technology allows the group members little autonomy in determining or varying the operating activities. The group factor is, therefore, of small importance in making a positive contribution toward getting work done for the technological group. In the same way, the technological group is not capable of obstructing the flow of work short of shutting down the work process itself. This is illustrated in the sensitive account by Kraus of the beginning of the sitdown strike at the Flint plant of General Motors.[11]

All three types of organized work groups operate to define subtle aspects of interpersonal relations. This is most pronounced for the team group and successively less so for the task and technological groups. In the working team, authority and status relations are elaborated much beyond the demands of the work organization, but usually in a direction to amplify them.[12] Least elaborate interpersonal relations are derived from the technological group. Here interpersonal relations are much more likely to be established and maintained in a paralleling voluntary social group. This shift from organized to voluntary group will be examined in detail in a later section of this chapter.

VOLUNTARY GROUPS AND GETTING WORK DONE

Voluntary work groups as discussed earlier in Chapter 6, do not focus their attention primarily on the work organization, except in the instance of the clique. Indeed, we took pains to establish that the pair, the triad, and the primary association have particular significance because the content of interaction within them is subject to wide variation, and diffuse rather than focused interests.[13]

It is precisely because voluntary work groups (again excepting the clique) do not focus on the business at hand that they have great sociological importance. We will elaborate their importance later in this chapter. For our present purposes we may conclude that the pair, the triad, and the primary association can have at best only a very indirect impact on getting work done.[14] Such groups function in other areas but not in relation to specific working behavior.[15]

The clique is a group in the work organization whose major reason for existence is to manipulate the power, authority, and status structures. Cliques are organized to develop a following for the purpose of changing some present aspect of the organization. The clique leaders may be seeking to enhance their authority; they may be striving for control of functions that will increase their power; or they may anticipate increased status as leaders of an organized following. All of these goals of clique leaders are pertinent to operations of the work organization. The activities of the clique that they direct will have immediate consequences for work performance.

In its least constructive form the clique is simply against something. In its more constructive actions, a clique will actively seek to substitute its own alternatives to present ways of doing things. Thus, cliques have very much to do with getting work done. They may be major obstacles to effective performance if they are united in a stand against present procedures. They make important contributions to greater efficiency if the alternatives they seek are better than present procedures. Unfortunately, the "fighting" character of most cliques makes the test of their proposals less likely, since established authority usually reacts by fighting back.

The established authorities can destroy clique effectiveness, as Selznick has pointed out, by "coopting" its leaders into the existing authority structure.[16] When the clique leader is taken into the authority group he becomes clothed with important commitments to the policies of the leadership he joins. His clique followers are disorganized because they no longer have a leader who is fighting against the established authorities; the program of opposition to which they give allegiance is generally inseparable from the leader.

CHANGE AND INNOVATION

The social groups of work are exceedingly important to the individual worker as the units within which he is able to produce innovations and changes that affect work. Social groups of fellow workers are the breeding grounds of originality.

Picture the individual immersed in a factory of several thousand, or even a department of fifty or one hundred people. Can he react with anything save a sense of detachment and bewilderment in the face of the colossus that is his work organization? How can he be an innovator of the new ideas, changes, or improvements he may seek for a variety of reasons?

The answer lies in the support and encouragement he receives from fellow workers. In the social groups of work are the personal relations that support originality and give encouragement, and even rewards, to the innovator.[17]

The indeterminacy of many operating procedures as to details of execution provides for the working group the opportunity to interpret, analyze, and finally determine operating procedures. Under these circumstances, the group at the work level has the opportunity not only to carry out the goals expressed in an organization policy, but to determine within itself the method for its execution. In the process of deciding how a thing should be done, it is highly possible that it may be done in ways not anticipated by the policy makers, or even in ways that ultimately change the purpose and intent of policy itself.[18]

In many senses, the actual behavior of an individual is exposed to the view of working associates most of the time. It is difficult if not impossible to hide from fellow workers what one does on the job.[19] It is not so difficult, and is generally more desirable, to hide the actual work behavior or methods of doing work from supervisors and higher levels of management. Perhaps it is the public character of work behavior in the fellow worker group that makes it one important social unit of change in the organization. Failure to secure the acquiescence and acceptance of fellow workers may endanger any innovation the individual makes. On the other hand, the acceptance of an innovation by fellow workers tends to guarantee its continuation, and its protection from management notice if that seems desirable.

The so-called "perfect bureaucrat" is one who considers his working operations as an end in themselves. As Merton has suggested, the bureaucrat converts means into ends, which often do not serve the intended purposes of the organization.[20] The bureaucratic perversion of organization policy is an example of undesirable innovation. It should be emphasized that the bureaucrat's behavior is carried out in an operating group of fellow workers who accept the innovating perversions of policy, encouraging and maintaining them.

Another obvious instance of the innovation being at the level of the social group, and not at a higher point in the organization, is the case where the working group discovers more efficient ways of carrying out its operations. It is not uncommon for the more efficient methods to be hidden from management. When this happens, individuals choose leisure on the job as the reward for their innovation in methods or procedures. It may be possible to accomplish the output standard set by management in six, or five, or even four hours of a standard eight hour day. The work, under some circumstances, will be accomplished in this short time, and the remaining hours used by the employees to "goof off," or to enjoy the leisure to which they feel entitled.[21]

The general point we are making is that at the operating level, in the context of shared relationships with fellow workers, innovations are achieved which may be important in changing the operating characteristics of an organization.

Under some circumstances, the individual may have official opportunities to be an initiator and innovator. This is true, for example, where he occupies a position of authority from which he can introduce change.[22] Again, a person can be an innovator if he has the qualities of leadership such that he attracts to himself a sufficient following for his new ideas. Thus, the informal leader even of lowly organizational rank may develop a following sufficient to give him power to secure attention to his demands and ideas within the hierarchy of organizational authority. It is to be noted in this second case (essentially the case of Max Weber's charismatic leader) that the success of the individual as an organizational innovator is dependent on the size and importance of his group following or clique. The second case is not literally an instance in which the individual acts alone to produce innovations in the organization.

It should be clear that we are not suggesting that the only changes affecting the organization originate in the fellow worker groups. We are suggesting, however, that one of the bases of the individual attachment to such groups is that here he secures the acceptance of his innovations and their perpetuation in the organization. Managerial actions through special staffs and through top level decision are doubtless the most important factors in organizational change. We are emphasizing that an individual, "lost" in a large organization, has the best opportunity to make changes by aligning himself with his fellow worker group and securing its approval.

ORGANIZED GROUPS AND CHANGE

We have focused attention here on changes that affect formal, non-formal, and technical behavior in work organizations. It follows that organized social groups are the ones primarily involved as the fellow worker context within which the individual makes his innovations, since such groups are deliberately established to carry on work operations.

The importance of organized work groups for individual innovation has been repeatedly confirmed in studies of work organizations. Richardson and Walker discovered that organized work groups had to be won over to support changes necessitated by company expansion. These groups were immaginative in finding ways to oppose change.[23] Whyte has shown how countermen invent ways of establishing buffers between themselves and waitresses.[24] Roethlisberger and Dickson discovered in the Bank Wiring Room experiment that work teams will develop means for exchanging jobs—a practice prohibited by management—even when under surveillance by official observers.[25] The same researchers found that production was restricted in the work teams. Mathewson,[26] Roy,[27] Anderson,[28] and others have repeatedly observed production slowdown among organized work groups.

Other studies have shown that "work secrets" are guarded in organized work groups and passed on to newcomers only when they are incorporated in the group. The wide difference between formal and non-formal procedures has been set forth by Turner in his study of the Navy disbursing officer where, again, the emphasis is on the organized work group as the unit in which the innovation is developed and supported.[29] Turner has also pointed out that an unofficial (and perhaps illegal) system for exchanging favors also develops in the relations between organized work groups (in his illustration, alcohol secured by medical corpsmen being exchanged for first purchasing rights on scarce items in the ship's store).

It can also be shown that the vast growth of committee management in American industry is a direct recognition that innovation has its natural habitat in the organized fellow worker group. An industrial committee is an organized work group, a team, composed predominantly of peers. It has a specific assignment, usually to handle an existing problem. Chamberlain ably demonstrated in his study of a telephone company that the committee is successful in its task of innovation because it involves the people who know something about the problems at hand, and its members are mutually supportive in arriving at solutions.[30] Committees are organized to seek changes. Their success lies in their ability to mobilize fellow workers to express their originality in a team effort.

The individual as innovator finds the most natural habitat for his originality in the organized work group. The team with the greatest autonomy provides the largest opportunity for individual innovation. The task group, operating within a more restricting environment, provides somewhat fewer chances for innovation. Furthermore, the changes developed may be in the direction of innovations for private purposes, like increasing leisure on the job. The reason for "anti-organization" innovation lies in the greater restrictions imposed by technology, and the fact that responsibility for the technology typically lies outside the task group. Under those circumstances, individual workers feel no pressure for transmitting inventions and discoveries outside the fellow worker group.

The technological work group is least likely to produce constructive innovations shared with management. In such groups the emphasis is increased to limit developments to anti-organization discoveries. The reasons are the same as for the task group.

It is of considerable importance to note that two opposed management viewpoints focus on change. The first emphasizes the need for mobilizing workers to accept changes introduced by management. This approach is illustrated in a study like that by French and Coch where techniques for explaining the need for change were employed successfully to get production workers in a textile plant to accept new work routines, including greater work loads.[31] The main concern is with ample downward communication from management to enhance employee understanding of the need for the proposed changes.

The contrasting viewpoint is concerned with encouraging employees to make constructive suggestions about their work. Here the emphasis in the past has been on using suggestion systems. Their weakness lies precisely in the fact that they expect the individual, divorced from his work group, and therefore without its support and encouragement, to be an innovator. More recent attempts at mobilizing employee originality have depended on using group dynamic methods. The work group is the unit in which discussions take place and decisions are made about innovations. These newer efforts specifically recognize the supportive value of the organized work group for the individual innovator. This kind of approach to developing creativity takes into account its group foundations, and is therefore much more likely to succeed.

VOLUNTARY GROUPS AND CHANGE

What has already been said about the relationships between voluntary social groups and getting work done applies to their impact on organizational change. The pair, triad, and primary association are largely neutral as to changes in work. The clique is focused entirely on producing changes, of one sort or another.

The clique is an unofficial group mobilized to achieve change. Its program is always set forth as a proposal for change, when given an affirmative cast. When the clique does not have constructive alternatives for present ways of doing things, its program is a bundle of criticism.

It is important to note here that a successful clique, upon achieving its goals, tends to break up. The clique leadership's only remaining obligation to followers is to pay them off in the promised favors. Rewards are usually forthcoming in the form of actual or implied favored treatment for those who were loyal followers. However, successful clique leaders may never reward their followers, either because they cannot, or because they recognize that favoritism will jeopardize their newly won gains. The price that the clique leader pays for disappointed followers is that he will seldom again be able to lead a clique as long as his reputation persists for not paying off after victory.

The breakup of a successful clique is important for organization stability. It removes an organized opposition group from the work organization. New cliques may develop but they need new circumstances around which to focus their opposition.

STANDARDS OF CONDUCT

Face-to-face groups of peers at work are important as the unit within which standards of conduct are established and maintained. Cooley,[32] and Simmel before him,[33] placed great emphasis on the society of close associates as the place where standards of conduct are learned. The social groups of work are the societies of close asociates, which function to establish for the individual many standards of working-time conduct.

The society of close associates is the group in which social standards are made real and operative. Broad social standards of conduct require some kind of reality context to be meaningful for each of us as individuals. Abstract notions like honesty, faithfulness, cooperation, and self-sacrifice have no meaning except as they are put to use. The operating situations in which these ideas of moral conduct are constantly applied are those involving small social groups. It is largely in the peer group situation that there is an immediate response by fellow human beings to an individual's behavior. This response is direct and personal. There is no need for self policing of moral standards. The policing is by one's peers, who react immediately to the conduct either to confirm and approve, or to condemn and censure.[34]

The social groups of work are important in establishing standards of conduct for several reasons. In the first place the large turnover of personnel in industry makes many people strangers to their next job. The general rules of the work organization provide some guides for conduct. The guidance of the work place peer group rounds out the standards of conduct for working behavior. In the second place, many aspects of conduct are special to the group and can only be learned through membership in it. We have already examined in this chapter, and elsewhere, the private aspects of conduct found in the social groups of work. Only on entry into such groups can the person come to share the conduct standards of his peers.[35]

Conduct standards can be differentiated from behavior systems. Behavior systems, or activities that compose behavior systems, are the actual actions involved in going from one step to the next in a task. Conduct standards, on the other hand, are the preferences, or values, attached to one activity rather than another. Behavior systems are composed of the ordered set of activities which, when followed, lead to the performance of a task. Conduct standards are the preferential judgments that one set of activities is better than another.

The distinction between behavior systems and conduct standards is crucial. Throughout this volume we have emphasized the importance of behavior systems for organizing productive operations. We have also indicated the factors involved in establishing preferences for some kinds of working conduct, notably in Chapter 7 where we dealt with the institutional foundations of decision making; in Chapters 10 and 11 where technology was singled out as the most important determinant of work activities; in Chapter 12 where the work organization was seen as organizing and structuring motivations for work; and in Chapter 19 dealing with work rules and their enforcement. In the present chapter we are seeking to establish the actual social units within which some of the standards of working conduct develop. We find these units to be the organized and voluntary social groups in work organizations.

ORGANIZED GROUPS AND CONDUCT STANDARDS

Conduct standards developed by, and learned in, organized work groups are oriented specifically with respect to work. Some of these standards have to do with working activities.[36] The rest of the standards have to do with ideas about the work performed.

Conduct standards for working activities deal with how work will be done. For example, on a lathe the speed with which the metal is revolved against the cutting tool, the rate at which the cutting tool moves across the metal, and the depth of the cut, are the important variables to be adjusted in operating this machine tool. Some operators have distinct preferences for taking deeper cuts at slower speeds and feeds, while others prefer shallower cuts at more rapid speeds and feeds. These are the basic alternatives for the operator. His choice will be highly rationalized into a set of concrete reasons for his own preference. This is an important part of the craftsman lore of a lathe operator. It will be transmitted to succeeding generations of lathe operators within the working group, and may even persist as a working preference in the face of orders from company production engineers to do otherwise.

Another example of a conduct standard for working activities is the preference an accounting clerk may have for checking sums of figures by adding sub-totals instead of checking adding machine tapes against original entries. The clerk may have a whole series of reasons for his choice of work activities, and argue violently in favor of it.

In general, therefore, part of the worker's autonomy on the job is his ability to make some of these kinds of choices about how he will get his work done. He becomes involved in and committed to his tasks because he does make these choices, believing them to be better than other choices. In short, he develops a sense of obligation toward his work assignments—he internalizes values guiding his behavior–as we pointed out in Chapter 5.

Even more fascinating are the conduct standards dealing with ideas about the work being performed. Here we are in the realm of judgments and preferences concerning the value of work assignments, their relationships to other values, and the motives of management.[37]

A good example of conduct standards about work is the perennial problem of smoking on the job. Non-smoking is basically justified as a safety measure where fire or explosion hazards exist. Smoking is a very common habit, withdrawal from which may, even for short periods of time, produce discomfort. Personal preferences are then in conflict with organization choices. The motives of management in forbidding smoking are sharply called into question, and real or fanciful reasons are assigned for management's prohibition. The conflict of values may be resolved by reluctant or antagonistic obedience to the prohibition, or it may be resolved by flaunting the rule openly or secretly. The conflict in values may be even more pronounced where female secretaries are forbidden to smoke at their desks while their bosses smoke constantly in the same environs. Here the safety argument loses all merit, and the female employees are likely to consider the rule simply another evidence of their second-class citizenship. Not only will management motives be challenged within the work group, but rest periods will lengthen and be more frequent to accommodate a smoke or two.

An even more serious example of conduct standards in conflict is the problem of maximum production. In principle, many managers will argue that they want maximum output from each employee. In most instances they could get more than they are now getting if employees felt free to "let themselves go." The work group almost universally reacts to pressure for more individual output by impugning the motives of management and asserting that the only outcome of greater effort will be permanently higher output expectations, and even a lowering of pay per unit of output. Many studies have reported this characteristic reaction of work groups to pressure for more output.[38] We can only conclude that the work group is able to convince its members of the perfidy of management, and to police their actual output so that management cannot hold up examples of "rate busters." Dalton has shown the kinds of work group pressure that are brought to bear on "rate busters."[39] He has particularly demonstrated that such people are alienated from their fellow workers by reasons of social background and present relationships. In short, "rate busters" violate work group standards for individual output because such people resist the pressures of fellow workers to accept group standards of output.

Organized work groups are the socially meaningful units within which are developed conduct standards about work activities, and ideas about work. It is also within the team, the task group, and the technological group that fellow worker pressures are brought to bear to enforce the group standards of conduct, even when they may conflict with management rules or expectations.[40]

VOLUNTARY GROUPS AND CONDUCT STANDARDS

The voluntary work groups have their own special areas of conduct standards. These are largely concerned with interpersonal relations among members. Secondarily, especially in the clique, they concern interactions with outsiders.

Within voluntary social groups at work, conduct standards govern how people will behave toward each other in situations of easy going relations. The group establishes its own atmosphere for conduct. Each member is accepted by the group so long as he conforms to these conduct expectations. Such expectations may establish the quality of interpersonal relations. In a pair or triad, for example, it is typical to have an exchange of very personal confidences. The expectations are that other members of the group will respond with sympathy and understanding to one's confidences, taking them seriously. Failure to be sympathetic will destroy the pair or triad.

In a primary association there may be expectations of a different sort. Here the conduct standards may be less concerned with the exchange of confidences, and more nearly centered on determining the realm of acceptable discourse and play activity. Thus, in the primary association free and vulgar discussion of sex may be accepted, even among happily married men.[41] In the area of play, the primary association may develop special games peculiar to it. The famous bank wiring experiment of the Western Electric researches demonstrated the development of "binging" as a play activity.[42] For real or fanciful reasons one worker would hit a colleague sharply on the arm, "binging" him as the practice was called. The "bing" could then be returned at a later time. This was clearly a play activity, although some have attempted to interpret it as a punishment for violating group standards.[43] The fact that the "bing" was always reciprocated is strong evidence that this activity was primarily a game.

In the clique, the intra-group standards of conduct are largely concerned with public display of loyalty to the group and its goals. Clique members are expected to announce their adherence to the group regularly, and to show by their activities that they can be depended on to support the clique. Intimately tied to this public protestation of loyalty in the clique are the derogatory views taken by its members towards outsiders. The clique leaders are "good" and their goals are admirable; opposing cliques or management are bad and their objectives are "shameful." The clique, unlike the other voluntary groups, always defines itself in relation to outside groups. It establishes conduct standards so that "outgroups" can always be labeled as enemies. This is part of the technique by which clique membership is recruited and maintained.

PERSONALITY INTEGRITY

Fulfilling a work assignment may not ocupy the full attention, energies, and complete social life of many individuals in the modern industrial world. Yet, most persons are required to remain at their work place for the prescribed eight hours, and to put in their time in the interests of the organization. Putting in time may be quite different from being productive, but it should be evident that the requirement of high and continuous attention for an eight-hour period each day may be more than the human animal, as a social being, can tolerate. There may be good reason to believe that social interaction of a relatively non-purposive character may be necessary to maintain a sense of personality integrity.[44]

A minimum amount of sociability is required by every person. Each individual at work has to find some opportunity for carrying out social relations with fellow men. The obvious unit within which such social relations can be established and maintained is the fellow worker group. We can thus see the social group of fellow workers as a unit within which are filled the voids of social life at work. It is in such groups that the social character of man's personality is continually emphasized and re-enforced. It is here that each individual finds himself at the end of a work day still a man, a personality, and not reduced to the status of an adjunct to a machine.

The evidence for this idea of the social group as filling the social voids of the work place is to be found in the nature of the conversation and interaction among people at work. Much of the discourse among workers is usually of a non-work character.[45] For those new to a particular operation, there is probably a tendency to talk shop as a basis for breaking into the circle of interaction. As familiarity is developed with fellow workers, there is an increasing tendency for conversation and interaction to move into more and more remote areas of interest.

The general point, then, is that the group of fellow workers provides the opportunity for rounding out interaction with fellow human beings in the course of the work day. This serves as the individual's tie with humanity. It should not be overlooked as an important basis for his attachment to the social groups in his work life. The social groups at work help each person preserve the integrity of his personality.

ORGANIZED GROUPS AND PERSONALITY

For the most part, the organized work groups are important in defining and evaluating the technical aspects of a person's working behavior. In organized groups the individual is constantly being judged by his fellow workers as to his working competence.

The confirmation of one's own technical skills and abilities may be exceedingly important to his self evaluation. If fellow workers regard him as able, then he has every right to hold the same view of himself. It is in this connection that the compliment of a fellow worker may be more important than the praise of a boss. Fellow workers "really" know what you can and cannot do. If they are willing to acknowledge competence, then the individual need no longer have any doubts about his technical performance.[46]

Self confidence that is born of acknowledged ability is developed through appraisals of fellow workers in organized work groups. These social groups can give to the person a sense of worth; or, by withholding approval, deep doubts about his working skills.

VOLUNTARY GROUPS AND PERSONALITY

In the clique as a voluntary social group, personality integrity is supported in ways similar to those observed in organized work groups. The particular personal competences that are applauded in cliques are skills in fighting other groups, and management. In a limited sense, these skills are technical in character. The ability to start and sustain rumors and vilification, and otherwise thwart the aims of an opposing group are special skills. Clique members develop a sense of personal worth from the approval of their fellows for displaying such skills.

In the pair, the triad, and the primary association, the impact on personality integrity is far-reaching. From such voluntary groups the person secures the major rewards of being accepted, for all his idiosyncracies, as a valued personality. It is instructive to examine the importance of this for personality integrity.

The pair, triad, and the primary association are voluntary groups of people who habitually meet together, during work, during rest and lunch periods, and often after working hours. Such voluntary groups do not have concrete goals and stated purposes. The focus of group attention varies. The members know each other through long association, and interact as familiar associates. Everyone knows the other members intimately, including their backgrounds. A good deal of information is shared about family background and previous social experiences. Furthermore, the members know each other as distinctive personalities. The unique and individual features of the personality of each member are known to all others.

Based on this kind of knowledge, each member of the group is able to act towards all others in a knowing and highly anticipatory manner. It is possible to predict the reactions of the other members, based on detailed and intimate knowledge of them. There grows up in the group a whole series of special meanings and common understandings, known to all members of the group, and evoking uniform responses whenever they appear. The members stand in a familiar relationship to each other, and are able to react sympathetically to each other's needs and problems.

There is wide freedom of contact among the members of the pair, the triad, and the primary association. Each feels relatively free to talk to, and interact with, all other members of the group. Furthermore, there is freedom in reacting to the behavior of associates. A fairly high degree of criticism, of kidding, and sometimes even of disapproval can be characteristic of the relations among group members.

Members of these voluntary groups at work have to have some opportunities to contact each other for the relationships to grow up in the first place. However, the members need not be drawn from the same department, or even from close-by work stations. It is generally characteristic of such groups that they are composed exclusively of men or women, but not both sexes. The reason for this may lie in the fact that voluntary groups in the larger society also tend to be composed of a single sex. It is probable that the familiar character of the relationships in the group precludes the possibility of its being a mixed sex association.

There is usually no set time for the voluntary group to meet, although some such groups have habitual times and places for getting together at a particular lunch table, in the wash room, or in places where loitering is possible. While the time and place for the group to assemble may become routine, it is seldom, if ever, planned and consciously worked out.

This is a primary association at work that has been together for long enough to develop real feelings of mutual attachment. They are celebrating, with an impromptu shop party and presentation of gifts, the departure of one of their members. Such human associations are important in supporting the integrity of personality.

We can picture the voluntary association of fellow workers as resulting in a familiar group in which the same persons habitually interact with each other. In the group there is a wide range of subjects of discourse and a shared familiarity about the reaction and personality traits of all members. Such a group is the one in which simple, direct, and unpremeditated social interaction takes place. It is here that a person can speak his mind openly and freely. His audience is sympathetic, willing to listen, and accepting of the individual in all his uniqueness, recognizing his faults as well as his virtues. The voluntary social group fits the person into an easy-going system of social relationships that has permanence, and yet is flexible enough to encompass the wide range of personal moods and idiosyncracies.

There are two characteristic features of the social bond uniting members of voluntary social groups at work. The members are united by a bond of sympathy; they are also united by a bond of empathy.

A sympathetic response to another person is one in which the action of the other person is judged in terms of his own definition of the situation. Whenever we consider our behavior we first define the situation in which we are behaving. Then our behavior can make sense to ourselves. It is not always certain, however, that others observing our behavior, or hearing us tell about it, will accept our definition of the situation in which the behavior occurred. Only when other people are sympathetic toward us will they accept our definition of the situations in which we act. For example, a worker may assert, "I have been given the dirty end of the stick by my foreman," and then go on to elaborate the circumstances of this mistreatment, and his own actions in the situation. If his fellow workers respond sympathetically, they accept, without question, the declaration or assumption that the foreman was being vindictive, and that their colleague was mistreated.

An empathic response is one in which it is possible figuratively to take the place of another person.[47] When you respond empathically, you can put yourself in the shoes of another person, experiencing vicariously his emotional and subjective states of mind. In the case of our aggrieved worker just mentioned, his friends, reacting empathically to his trouble, feel all the indignation and persecution that he does. They react in sharing his subjective feelings about his asserted mistreatment by putting themselves in his place.

In the voluntary social groups of work, individuals are tied together by a willingness to accept each other, as each defines himself and the situations in which he acts; this is the sympathetic bond. Group unity is enhanced by the ability to develop strong emotional attachments to each other through taking the place of the other; this is the empathic bond.

The voluntary groups of the work organization provide the environment for routine easy-going relationships with other human beings. In such relationships the personality comes to be valued by associates. This valuing of personality is important in maintaining personality integrity.

We may then conclude that the social groups found in places of work are essential for personality integrity. The organized groups provide the setting in which technical skills and competences can be observed and applauded by associates. The voluntary groups are the ones in which personality characteristics are judged and valued. From both kinds of group affiliations the person develops images of himself through the collective judgments of respected associates that sustain a sense of personality unity and social worth.

WORKER MORALE

In Chapter 12 we discussed at length the group basis of morale. It was concluded there that morale is sustained by interpersonal relations. We can now see that one important area of interpersonal relations is the work group. It is in organized and voluntary work groups that organization requirements are made effective in getting work done, that the innovator finds support for his originality, standards of conduct established, and an environment provided to sustain individual personality integrity. Working groups establish for the individual the conditions for his relations with other people. The groups in which working people are members are the groups that make and break morale.

ORGANIZED GROUPS AND MORALE

Organized work groups are the units within which zeal for work itself is mobilized. We have already seen that the organized work groups are task oriented. The team, the task group, and the technological group are the ones that most directly relate to work and are, accordingly, the ones in which morale about work operations is sustained.[48]

We can see the general impact of organized groups on morale in two illustrations. Both examples involve establishing centers around which group identification can develop as a basis for morale. The first example deals with the military practice of using cadres in activating new units. The cadres are experienced men of all ranks who form the skeleton of a new outfit. They bring to the new outfit the necessary technical skills. More important, the cadres carry into the new organization abbreviated work groups into which can be fitted additional soldiers until the unit is up to full strength. The importance of the cadres lies precisely in the fact that they are work groups towards which newly added soldiers can develop an identification. The cadre system permits a more rapid mobilization of a military unit because it starts the new organization with "built-in" work groups that carry existing systems for getting work done, and the necessary conduct standards governing interpersonal relations. Military experience confirms the efficiency of the cadre system, especially when it is contrasted with a system of individual recruitment into organizations that exist only on paper.

The second illustration deals with the fluid personnel situation in California aircraft plants during World War II. Mayo and Lombard have reported significantly higher morale in departments where there existed organized work groups in contrast with other departmens where such groups were not adequately organized.[49] Their conclusion is that the zeal for work was very much higher among workers where recognizable group affiliations had developed. This conclusion has been borne out by other studies, notably Whyte's analysis of restaurant workers,[50] Archibald's study of shipyard work groups,[51] Argyris' analysis of bank employees,[52] Ellsworth's study of a New England factory,[53] Jacques' report on an English factory,[54] and Lombard's study of salespeople.[55]

Organized work groups have their origin in the technological need for people to work intimately with each other, and to depend on each other to get tasks accomplished. This technical dependence creates a genuine social group within which develops shared goals and shared enthusiasm for work.

VOLUNTARY GROUPS AND MORALE

Voluntary work groups affect morale in the non-technical areas of human association at work. We have already seen that an important facet of working behavior is the development of relations with other people on an easy-going basis. This is done primarily within voluntary work groups.

The significant contribution of voluntary group life is to give the individual a feeling of zeal about himself as a person and his place as a personality in association with others. The voluntary group is the locale within which the person feels good about himself because others feel that he is important, or necessary, or at least desirable as an associate. In short, the voluntary group maintains a person's morale about himself by according him the respect of fellow workers.

SOCIAL GROUPS AND WORK

Up to this point we have been discussing the social groups of work as though they were independent of each other. Furthermore, we have made an implicit assumption that the person operates in only one social group at a time. Obviously, neither of these conditions is completely true. We now have to face the issue of how the different kinds of social groups fit together. We also want to know why certain kinds of organized groups are not accompanied by complementary voluntary groups, while others are.

We can start our analysis of the relationships between types of social groups at work by recalling that these groups have two areas of primary importance. The groups are either related to getting work done, or they function to provide the environment for human sociability. Organized groups are work oriented—they are organized to perform productive operations. Voluntary groups develop in response to the need for easy-going human associations.[56]

part of Chart 16.1, centering attention on the relationships among organized and voluntary groups.

In the most general case, we expect that working people will limit their group affiliations to as few as possible, providing those chosen satisfy both the needs for working cooperation and the needs for sociability. If the work group satisfies only the production requirement, then we predict that additional groups will be formed to take care of the needs for sociability. This gives us a dynamic way of expressing the most general connections between organized and voluntary groups at work.[57]

CHART 16.1

ORGANIZED AND VOLUNTARY WORK GROUPS COMPLEMENT EACH OTHER

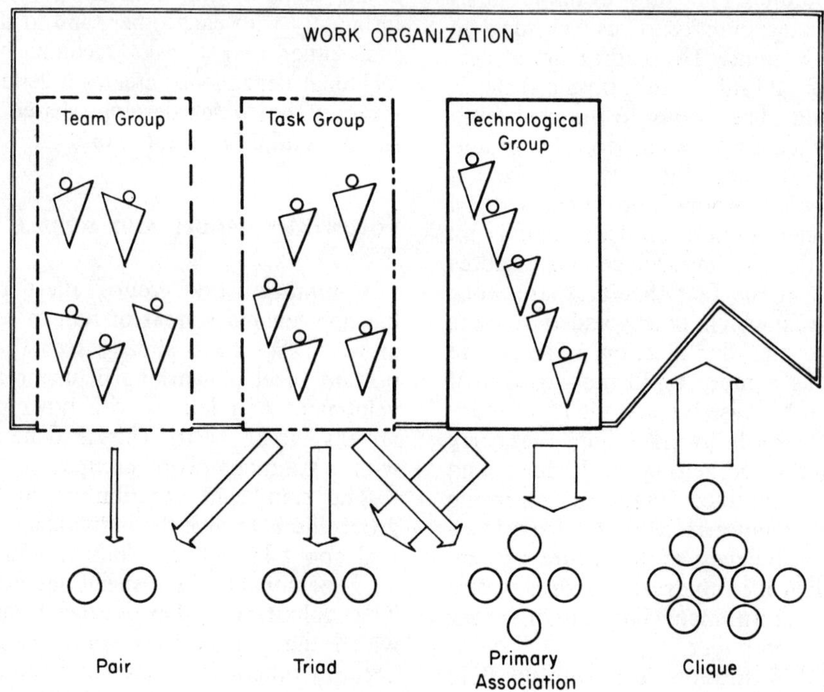

In chart 16.1 the distinction between organized and voluntary social groups is set forth. The team, task, and technological groups are shown as imbedded in the work of the organization. The voluntary groups of the pair, triad, and primary association are shown as functioning to satisfy the needs for human sociability. The clique is pictured as a separate voluntary group that has an impact on the work organization. Indeed, it is pictured as "bending" or changing the "shape" of the organization. We will analyze this feature of the clique after we have discussed the major

We now have to ask which of the organized groups are most likely to provide opportunities for sociability; and which organized groups minimize such opportunities. The answer will tell us the circumstances under which voluntary groups will develop in the work organization.

There are two basic features of Chart 16.1 whose analysis gives us the key to understanding the connections between organized and voluntary groups. It will be noted, first, that each of the organized groups is outlined differently to suggest differences in the degree to which working behavior is specified by the work organization rather than determined by the workers. It will be observed next that the width of the arrows going towards voluntary groups varies, to indicate, as the arrow gets larger, that there is a greater likelihood of voluntary groups being formed.

The team group is pictured as having a relatively open boundary with respect to its behavior. That is, the team has maximum autonomy in determining group activities, as has been pointed out in Chapter 6 and in the earlier sections of this chapter. Consequently there is greater opportunity for its members to develop interactions with each other that take care of the needs of sociability as well as the needs for getting work done. The result is that the team, as an organized group, has a high probability of developing charcteristics of a voluntary group among an identical membership. The organized team group itself will then display all of the characteristics of a voluntary group. For analytical purposes the team turns out to be both an organized and a voluntary group at the same time. Hence, only a narrow arrow connects the team with the voluntary social groups of work, indicating that team groups will not ordinarily have complementary voluntary groups associated with them.

The task group is pictured as having a boundary determining behavior of its members somewhat more restricted than the team. These restrictions are imposed by the technology of work and the degree to which work activities are specified by the work organization. The limitation on behavior that forces attention on work activities generates a strong tendency for members of a task group to form voluntary groups to provide easy-going social relations. Consequently, a broader arrow connects task groups with voluntary groups. This indicates that there is much greater likelihood that paralleling voluntary groups will accompany working task groups.

CHART 16.2

FRIENDSHIPS SHOWED PAIRS, A TRIAD, AND A PRIMARY ASSOCIATION IN BANK WIRING ROOM

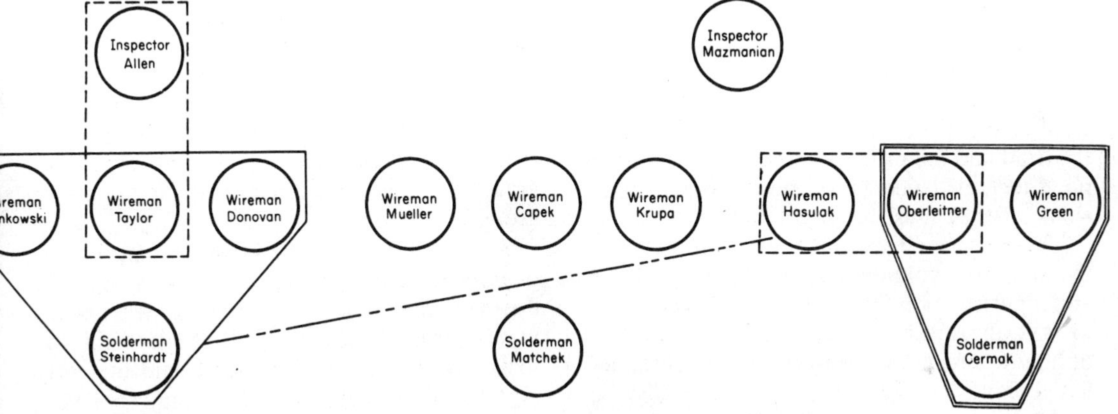

The most adequately studied example of the development of voluntary social groups associated with task groups is to be found in the Western Electric researches.[58] In the Bank Wiring Room, in particular, it was demonstrated that pairs, triads, and primary associations did develop alongside the task groups. These are illustrated in Chart 16.2 where the voluntary groups are shown as closed figures encircling their members, who are shown in their actual work stations. Some sociometric studies of people at work have demonstrated this same characteristic finding.[59]

The technological group, whose classic example is the continuous production line, is pictured in Chart 16.1 as having the most closed or restrictive boundary surrounding the behavior of its members. Here the limits on behavior are set almost exclusively by technological requirements. Opportunities for voluntary social interaction are severely limited. The consequence is that the broadest arrow is shown connecting technological groups with voluntary social groups. That is, in technological groups, extremely strong pressures will develop for the formation of voluntary groups. We can be almost certain that most members of a technological work group will have one or more voluntary social groups within which they spend a part of their working time.

Another feature of Chart 16.2 is the suggestion that the organized work groups tend to be associated with different kinds of voluntary groups. It will be noted that the pair is suggested as the more characteristic voluntary social group to be developed among members of an organized team. From a task group it is probable that a pair, triad, or primary association may develop as the characteristic voluntary group paralleling it. Out of a technological group it is probable that the principal forms of voluntary social groups will be the triad and the primary association. We have no direct evidence to support these conclusions so they must be suggestions.

There is an interesting relationship between the size of a voluntary social group at work and upward mobility. For people who want to "get ahead" there is an important problem of how to break the social ties with colleagues left behind. These ties must generally be broken, because promotion does mean new status and authority. This creates barriers to continued association with former friends who now rank lower.

We would, therefore, expect that upwardly mobile people in work organization would tend to participate in smaller voluntary social groups than would be true for less mobile people. There are two reasons for this. In the first place, it may be easier to break intimate social relations if they are with fewer people. In the second place, a smaller group is more protective in concealing the ambitions of its members. Peers are likely to be contemptuous of overly ambitious associates who proclaim their intentions far in advance of possible accomplishment. In a smaller social group, the chances of revealing, publicly, ambitions to get ahead may be lessened by limiting the number of people who have this knowledge. Furthermore, as we have seen in Chapter 6, the members of a pair and triad are likely to consider their association as relatively confidential in nature, and therefore to view confidences as privileged information. We may then conclude that upwardly mobile people are likely to be members of small social groups at work, although they may belong to large primary associations in the community.

We now have a picture of a man at work living his working hours in two general kinds of social groups. With the exception of a few people who work absolutely alone, the vast majority of industrial and commercial employees are members of organized work groups. If a person is a member of a working team he may find his full social life at work caught up in his total associations with team members. If the working individual operates in a task group or a technological group, and the bulk of them are members of such organized work groups, then the social life at work most likely takes place in both an organized group and one or more paralleling voluntary groups.

Returning now to the clique, which is also pictured in Chart 16.1, it will be noted that this voluntary social group is shown as divorced from both the work realm and the sociability realm. In Chapter 6 and the early portions of this chapter we have indicated why. The clique is a voluntary group whose purpose is to affect some operating aspect of the work organization.

The clique arises as a voluntary grouping of work organization members. This group has limited goals of seeking authority for its leaders, or seeking some change in organization practices that will benefit members. Its successful operation changes the organization, by changing some of its authority holders or operating practices. Although the clique is a voluntary group, it is different in its composition, the bond uniting members, and its functions, from the other voluntary social groups at work. The organizational consequence of a clique is that it threatens the stability of the organization by its combative and divisive tactics. Hence we have pictured the clique as "changing the shape" of the work organization.

A technological group in which management policy can make the greatest difference between group cooperation or antagonism. In this plant management had simple and relatively free rules about talking and "relaxing while working." Other kinds of management might attempt to hold a tight rein on discipline above and beyond the natural discipline determined by the flow of work with a high probability that antagonism among workers would develop.

SOCIAL GROUPS AND COOPERATION

It is one of the continuing management problems of any work organization to mobilize the social groups of work for cooperation with organization plans and goals. Such cooperation is not automatically "built into" the work organization.[60]

Organized work groups exist to carry out productive operations. Consequently they start out with the opportunity for cooperation at the minimum level of being motivated to fulfill the tasks set by management. Their very reasons for existence can only be to perform the allotted tasks.

We have already seen, however, that morale in organized work groups is a product of interaction among their members. This suggests that an important management objective for organized groups is to provide the environmental conditions for developing high morale directed toward achieving working goals. Management actions threatening group unity may lower morale or turn worker zeal against the organization. Actions like frequent personnel changes or transfers, rapid and unexplained changes in working assignments, and restrictive rules for personal behavior may have unfortunate morale consequences by lowering the over-all coperation with management objectives. An over-emphasis on technical needs of production may work against the development of high morale in organized work groups.

Voluntary social groups at work do not ordinarily focus attention on the organization except, of course, for the clique. In the case of pairs, triads, and primary associations, management should make sure that its policies are not directed at, or unwittingly result in, limiting opportunities for development of easy-going social relations. For example, management may impose barriers to voluntary group development by forbidding talking, mild horseplay, or other communication during work and rest periods. This can antagonize workers. As their voluntary groups develop, and they will in spite of management efforts to stamp them out, attention will focus on management inadequacies. There will be a consequent loss in the opportunity for cooperation with, or at least neutrality toward, management.

It is probably most effective to consider the cooperation of voluntary groups as a relatively unattainable goal, primarily because such groups do not have a natural focus of attention on organization activities. At best, management is well advised to recognize the inevitability of their appearance, and to seek to minimize their potential antagonism. This can be done by examining personnel and production policies to determine if they impede the natural development or operation of voluntary social groups. If the policies will have such effects, then they should be re-examined on the grounds that such consequences are undesirable.

The clique is by nature an antagonistic group. There is no way, short of destruction of a clique, to substitute cooperation for antagonism. We will examine the antagonistic character of the clique in a following section of this chapter.

SOCIAL GROUPS AND NEUTRALITY

It is not within the scope of usual management thinking to accept as realistic the possibility that employees can be neutral towards the organization paying their wages and salaries. Management hopes for active cooperation, and combats antagonism. A middle position of neutrality is viewed as untenable —employees should be cooperative, and must not be antagonistic.[61]

Let us examine the constructive features of employee neutrality. The voluntary groups of a work organization concern themselves with human sociability. Sociability is not limited as to subject matter, ranging across the entire spectrum of human experience. If opportunities for sociability are necessary, and therefore naturally develop in voluntary work groups, is there anything to be gained by management's efforts to limit sociable discourse and interaction? Particularly, is anything to be gained by trying to limit the content of sociability at work to working interests? The answer seems to be clearly in the negative.

Citizens of a modern urban-industrial society have ample opportunity for non-work interests. Organized sports, movies, TV, politics, public and personal scandals, sex, and individual experiences are lively objects of interest that typically enter into normal social relations. Recreation and play activities of the group itself are other objects of genuine interest. These are the things that occupy the attention of people in voluntary social relations. All of these objects of attention are neutral with respect to the work organization.

It may be undesirable for management, therefore, to take every opportunity to point out connections between the work organization and the usual subjects of employee discourse.

It may be even worse yet to try to limit the discourse to work-related subjects. Management can afford to accept employee neutrality, and may profit by its very existence. Just to take one example, the disastrous attempts by management to influence voting behavior of employees, especially during the New Deal days, produced strong reactions against management. Management tried to influence elections by urging loyalty to its position. The elections were lost, but more important, so was employee loyalty. It would have strained employee loyalty much less for management to have accepted employee neutrality toward it, regardless of the outcome of elections.

SOCIAL GROUPS AND ANTAGONISM

Antagonism of work groups toward their employing organizations has received the most attention in the literature. In particular, sabotage of output has been studied as a typical consequence of effective group action. It is perhaps for this reason that many managers fear the social groups in their organizations and seek to stamp them out.

An important question arises with respect to antagonism. Is it possible to sustain opposition to your environment for long periods of time? Does opposition arise only when the environment is viewed as undesirable?

Maintaining a long-term position of opposition is difficult under most circumstances. People find it hard to maintain the emotional indignation that is necessary for long periods of time. Antagonism for its own sake is not easy to sustain.

This suggests that when antagonism is encountered in a social group at work, some real and subjectively important cause exists for it. Something is wrong in the environment of the group, and its members are reacting strongly against it. For example, when workers restrict their output, studies show that there is an underlying and shared basis of dissatisfaction leading to this kind of anti-organization behavior.[62] Workers allege that management might lower the pay per unit if output is increased, that the work will be given to fewer workers to do, or that management is not willing to share with employees the income from increased output. These are real bones of contention, but only when they lead to genuinely felt dissatisfaction is antagonism displayed toward the organization and its goals. The removal of the sources of dissatisfaction can turn the antagonism into neutrality, or even cooperation.

The clique is a special case of a voluntary group that exists only to buck the organization. Cliques and their leaders are relatively easy to recognize. They are a special kind of management problem. The counter-moves against a clique may include forming a clique among present management to fight the usurpers. This leads to a head-on struggle.

Another move is to coopt clique leaders into management and thus destroy the group, as we have already pointed out. Finally, justifiable goals or programs of cliques may result in management changes to satisfy them. The struggling clique may actually win the battle with present management and take over the whole organization, or parts of it. Cliques are the only kinds of social groups in the work organization that have avowedly antagonistic objectives. They are not always present in an organization. When they do arise an inevitable struggle will result.

MEN, GROUPS, AND WORK

In this chapter we have analyzed the complicated relationships between men at work, their groups, and consequences for output and working behavior. It is clear that we cannot understand working behavior unless we see it as taking place in work groups.

Of special significance is the distinction drawn between voluntary groups and organized groups in the workplace. On the basis of this distinction we can see that the group life of workers has different functions depending on whether it is a required association in an organized group, or a freely chosen association in a voluntary group.

We have also seen that the two kinds of social groups in the workplace are interconnected. If the organized group does not provide a sufficient amount or satisfying quality of easy primary relations, then voluntary groups will be formed to provide oportunities for sociability.

Groups in which men work are important for their behavior. This is true at all levels of work organizations.

NOTES FOR CHAPTER 16

[1] Two summary volumes are pertinent in the analysis of small group behavior. Both volumes emphasized the analysis of small groups, as such, not the kinds of social groups that form, or are formed, as constituent parts of formal organizations. Dorwin Cartwright and Alvin Zander, *Group Dynamics: Research and Theory* (Evanston: Row, Peterson and Company, 1953)—of particular relevance here is Part III, "Group Pressures and Group Standards"; and Paul Hare, E. F. Borgatta, and R. F. Bales, *Small Groups: Studies in Social Interaction* (New York: Alfred A. Knopf, Inc., 1955), especially the annotated bibliography.

[2] A very interesting study of the consequences of industrial practices for maximizing casual associations is: R. R. Myers, "Inter-Personal Relations in the Building Industry," *Applied Anthropology,* 5:1-7 (Spring, 1946).

[3] The recognition feature of casual associations is illustrated in a Navy setting in C. H. Page, "Bureaucracy's Other Face," *Social Forces,* 25:88-94 (October, 1946).

[4] There is a constant confusion in the literature on "human relations in industry" between casual associations—being friendly and a good fellow with associates—and social group relations. It was Elton Mayo's particular contribution to the analysis of social behavior in industry that he saw the difference between casual relations and social groups, and directed research at the analysis of the latter. See "The Fruitful Errors of Elton Mayo," *Fortune,* 34:180 ff. (November, 1946).

[5] Cf.: J. B. Knox, "Productivity and Human Relations," *Proceedings,* 16th Congress of the International Institute of Sociology, 1954, Vol. IV, pp. 131-138; and R. K. Lamb, "Productivity and Social Structure," in Solomon Barkin, *et al.* (eds.), *Industrial Productivity* (Champaign: Industrial Relations Research Association, 1951), pp. 50-75.

[6] Those students who have focused upon human relations in industry and who have developed training and other programs to maximize individual contributions to work are particularly concerned with developing individual initiative in the social group situation. See for example N. R. F. Maier, *Principles of Human Relations: Application to Managment* (New York: John Wiley and Sons, 1952).

[7] One of the largest bodies of only partially analyzed data on social group behavior in industry is contained in T. N. Whitehead, *The Industrial Worker: A Statistical Study of Human Relations in a Group of Manual Workers,* 2 Volumes (Cambridge: Harvard University Press, 1938). This is the statistical data of the Hawthorne researches in the Western Electric Company. The measured interactions between workers reveal the social groups among them. The bases on which connections are established and maintained between given individuals strongly suggest that interaction in social groups at work serves to organize social relations.

[8] Probably the best single test of the fact that organized social groups develop effectiveness in task performance in spite of the arbitrary manner in which their membership is constituted is reported in F. E. Fiedler, "Assumed Similarity Measures as Predictors of Team Effectiveness," *Journal of Abnormal and Social Psychology,* 49:381-388 (July, 1954). Dr. Fiedler concluded that basketball teams and land survey teams were more effective if there were *not* strong ties of personal attachment among their members. In our framework, this amounts to saying that the coincidence of an organized and smaller voluntary social group among the same members may tend to cancel out group effectiveness.

[9] See in this connection P. H. M. King, "Task Perception and Interpersonal Relations in Industrial Training," *Human Relations,* 1:121-130 (1947); and 1:373-412 (1948). The analysis of social relations among combat infantrymen also reveals the ways in which the team and task fighting groups operate to become effective fighting units. See E. A. Shils, "Primary Groups in the American Army," in R. K. Merton and P. F. Lazarsfeld (eds.), *Continuities in Social Research: Studies in the Scope and Method of the "American Soldier"* (Glencoe: The Free Press, 1950), pp. 19-22 especially.

[10] This is the general point made in Ronald Lippitt and L. Bradford, "Building a Democratic Work Group," *Personnel,* 22:1-12 (January, 1945). See also R. Marriott, "Socio-Psychological Factors in Productivity," *Occupational Psychology,* 25:15-24 (January, 1951).

[11] Henry Kraus, *The Many and the Few* (Los Angeles: The Plantin Press, 1947), pp. 47-55.

[12] A particularly fine study of the self-elaboration of the social group authority and status systems is contained in G. C. Homans, "The Cash Posters: A Study of a Group of Working Girls," *American Sociological Review,* 19:724-733 (December, 1954).

[13] The best single study of verbal interaction in voluntary work groups is an analysis of Italian workers. It was found that politics, sports, and women were the subjects of conversation that served most sharply to select or reject members for voluntary groups in the workplace. It will be noted, of course, that none of these subjects are related to work, and that they provide opportunities for infinite variations on the central themes. In short, the focus of attention is varied and diffuse. See Franca Magistretti, "Sociological Factors in the Structuring of Workers' Teams," *American Journal of Sociology,* 60:536-540 (May, 1955).

[14] A particularly critical study in this connection is A. B. Horsfall and C. M. Arensberg, "Teamwork and Productivity in a Shoe Factory," *Human Organization,* 8:13-25 (Winter, 1949). The authors give a quantitative demonstration that there is a limit beyond which an increase in informal social relations *does not* produce a corresponding increase in productivity. Our own interpretation is clear. Volun-

NOTES FOR CHAPTER 16 (CONT.)

tary social relations are not work-directed, and therefore a significant increase in their amount would not be accompanied by greater output. The importance of distinguishing between organized and voluntary social groups at work is highlighted in such studies as that of Horsfall and Arensberg.

15 An interesting confirmation of this for the academic profession is contained in A. B. Hollingshead, "Ingroup Membership and Academic Selection," *American Sociological Review,* 3:826-833 (December, 1938). Hollingshead shows that voluntary social groups may affect selection of new colleagues—but not how they will work as teachers after selection.

16 Philip Selznick, "Foundations of the Theory of Organization," *American Sociological Review,* 13: 34-35 (February, 1948).

17 Cf. A. T. M. Wilson, "Some Aspects of Social Process," *Journal of Social Issues,* Supplement Series, No. 5 (November, 1951).

18 In this connection see B. M. Selekman, "Resistance to Shop Changes," *Harvard Business Review,* 24:119-132 (Autumn, 1945).

19 This is particularly well illustrated in Donald Roy, "Quota Restriction and Goldbricking in a Machine Shop," *American Journal of Sociology,* 57:427-442 (March, 1952).

20 R. K. Merton, "Bureaucratic Structure and Personality," *Social Forces,* 18:560-568 (May, 1940).

21 The best study of this is Donald Roy, "Efficiency and 'The Fix': Informal Intergroup Relations in a Piece-Work Machine Shop," *American Journal of Sociology,* 60:255-266 (November, 1954).

22 There has been growing recognition that being in a position of authority does not insure automatic acceptance of innovation. Various techniques have been developed for "selling" changes to subordinates. An early plea for consultation with subordinates is contained in H. H. Carey, "Consultative Supervision and Management," *Personnel,* 18:286-295 (March, 1942). A sophisticated treatment of this issue from the standpoint of "group dynamics" is Alex Bavelas, "Some Problems of Organizational Change," *Journal of Social Issues,* 4:48-52 (Summer, 1948).

23 F. L. W. Richardson and C. R. Walker, *Human Relations in an Expanding Company* (New Haven: Yale Labor and Management Center, 1948).

24 W. F. Whyte, *Human Relations in the Restaurant Industry* (New York: McGraw-Hill Book Company, 1948).

25 F. J. Roethlisberger and W. J. Dickson, *Management and the Worker* (Cambridge: Harvard University Press, 1939).

26 S. B. Mathewson, *Restriction of Output among Unorganized Workers* (New York: Viking Press, 1931).

27 Donald Roy, "Quota Restriction and Goldbricking in a Machine Shop." *op. cit.*

28 C. A. Anderson, "Sociological Elements in Economic Restrictionism," *American Sociological Review,* 9:345-358 (August, 1944).

29 R. H. Turner, "The Navy Disbursing Officer as a Bureaucrat," *American Sociological Review,* 21: 342-348 (June, 1947).

30 Neil Chamberlain, *Management in Motion: The Corporate Decision-Making Process as Applied to the Transfer of Employees* (New Haven: Yale Labor and Management Center, 1950).

31 Lester Coch and J. R. P. French, "Overcoming Resistance to Change," *Human Relations,* 1:512-532 (August, 1948).

32 C. H. Cooley, *Social Organization* (New York: Charles Scribner's Sons, 1909).

33 Georg Simmel, *The Sociology of Georg Simmel,* translated and edited by K. H. Wolff (Glencoe: The Free Press, 1950).

34 This principle was used by social psychologists to re-educate supervisory personnel and workers regarding some preconceived notions and attitudes not based on factual information. They used a group involvement method to reinforce the conduct standards being inculcated. See A. J. Marrow and J. R. P. French, "Changing a Stereotype in Industry," *Journal of Social Issues,* 1:33-57 (1945); and A. J. Marrow, "Prejudice and Scientific Method in Labor Relations," *Industrial and Labor Relations Review,* 5:593-598 (July, 1952). The classic experiment testing the effectiveness of the close social group in reinforcing conduct standards was the comparative use of lectures and group discussion to change food preparation habits of housewives in the interests of better food supply utilization. Lewin found that the group definitely did reinforce conduct. See Kurt Lewin, "Group Decision and Social Change," in Theodore Newcomb and Eugene Hartley (eds.), *Readings in Social Psychology* (New York: Henry Holt and Co., 1947), pp. 330-344.

35 This point is made in Elizabeth and Francis Jennings, "Making Human Relations Work," *Harvard Business Review,* 29:29-55 (January, 1951), where it is noted that a conflict of values in the work situation may impair productivity.

36 Experimental support for this conclusion is contained in Leonard Berkowitz, "Group Standards, Cohesiveness, and Productivity," *Human Relations,* 7: 509-519 (1954).

37 This is illustrated for people at work in Milton Oman and R. F. Tomasson, "Disparities in Visualizing Social Norms," *Social Forces,* 30:328-333 (March, 1952).

38 S. B. Mathewson, *Restrictions of Output among Unorganized Workers;* Donald Roy, "Quota Restriction and Goldbricking in a Machine Shop," and C. A. Anderson, "Sociological Elements in Economic Restrictionism."

39 Melville Dalton, "The Industrial 'Rate-Buster'; A Characterization," *Applied Anthropology,* 7:5-18 (Winter, 1948).

40 The most adequately described instance of this is the study of miners and factory workers in a gypsum company. Gouldner, although calling it a

NOTES FOR CHAPTER 16 (CONT.)

study of industrial bureaucracy, really provides the greatest insight into the ways in which work groups develop and police conduct standards. Indeed, it was the circumstance of a change in top plant management that highlighted conflicts in conduct standards and gave the researchers a magnificent opportunity to examine the contests between official company policy regarding work, and the conduct standards developed and enforced in the work group. See A. W. Gouldner, *Patterns of Industrial Bureaucracy* (Glencoe: The Free Press, 1954).

[41] Indeed, the extent to which voluntary work group standards can control conduct is vividly revealed in J. O. Reinmann, "Extra-Marital Relations with Fellow Employees in War Industry as a Factor in Disruption of Family Life," *American Sociological Review,* 14:618-624 (December, 1949).

[42] Roethlisberger and Dickson, *Management and the Worker. op. cit.*

[43] G. C. Homans, *The Human Group* (New York: Harcourt, Brace and Co., 1950), pp. 60-61. It is quite correct, as Homans points out, that "binging" sometimes functioned as a penalty to enforce production standards, but it is also clear that "binging" was begun strictly for play. It was not solely a penalty. It appears to be an instance where play activity was adopted as functional for other purposes. Our major point is that the conduct standards of the voluntary group are diffuse and not work-centered. Such a play activity as "binging" seems to illustrate this well.

[44] Elton Mayo's insight on this point was crucial for his further research interests. His early work convinced him that reverie took the place of social interaction where the latter was not readily available. See Elton Mayo, "Reverie and Industrial Fatigue," *Journal of Personnel Research,* 3:273-281 (December, 1924).

[45] See note 13, page 310 above, and the section to which it refers.

[46] One of the few studies that has penetrated into the work situation deeply enough to discover this phenomenon is Donald Roy, "Work Satisfaction and Social Reward in Quota Achievement: An Analysis of Piecework Incentive," *American Sociological Review,* 18:507-514 (October, 1953). Roy points out that the work group holds down output to agreed standards. But he also points out with illustrations how fellow-worker contempt is directed at workers who fail to achieve work group output standards.

[47] Cf. R. F. Dymond, "A Scale for the Measurement of Empathic Ability," *Journal of Consulting Psychology,* 13:127-133 (April, 1949).

[48] This was suggested speculatively by R. E. Park, "Industrial Fatigue and Group Morale," *American Journal of Sociology,* 40:349-356 (November, 1934). It receives experimental verification in such studies as S. Seashore, "Group Cohesiveness as a Factor in Industrial Morale and Productivity," Ph.D. Thesis, University of Michigan, 1954.

[49] Elton Mayo and G. F. F. Lombard, *Teamwork and Labor Turnover in the Aircraft Industry of Southern California* (Boston: Harvard Business School, Division of Research, 1944).

[50] W. F. Whyte, *Human Relations in the Restaurant Industry.*

[51] Katherine Archibald, *Wartime Shipyard: A Study of Social Disunity* (Berkeley: University of California Press, 1947).

[52] Chris Argyris, *Organization of a Bank: A Study of the Nature of Organization and the Fusion Process* (New Haven: Yale Labor and Management Center, 1954).

[53] J. S. Ellsworth, Jr., *Factory Folkways: A Study of Institutional Structure and Change* (New Haven: Yale University Press, 1952).

[54] Elliott Jacques, *The Changing Culture of a Factory* (New York: The Dryden Press, 1952).

[55] G. F. F. Lombard, *Behavior in a Selling Group: A Case Study of Interpersonal Relations in a Department Store* (Boston: Harvard Business School, Division of Research, 1955).

[56] These two conclusions are supported by the analysis of Professor Gross. He found in the study of an Air Force unit that the organized work group was held together by symbiosis, interdependence, a social bond recognized as necessary to get cooperative work done. He also found that voluntary associations were based upon consensus, feelings of well-being where satisfaction in easy-going human relations was achieved. See Edward Gross, "Primary Functions of the Small Group," *American Journal of Sociology,* 60:24-29 (July, 1954). See also his "Symbiosis and Consensus in Small Groups," *American Sociological Review,* 21:174-179 (April, 1956).

[57] Some evidence on the recognition by workers of the two areas of work group affiliation is given in: Paul and Faith Pigors, *Human Aspects of Multiple Shift Operations* (Cambridge: Massachusetts Institute of Technology, Department of Economics and Social Science, 1944).

[58] Roethlisberger and Dickson, *Management and the Worker.*

[59] Out of the rather extensive sociometric literature, three examples are chosen. Reference should be made to the index of *Sociometry,* the journal in which many such studies have been published, for a more extensive bibliography. J. H. Jacobs, "The Application of Sociometry to Industry," *Sociometry,* 8: 181-198 (May, 1945); Fred Massarick, *et al.,* "Sociometric Choice and Organizational Effectiveness: A Multi-Relational Approach," *Sociometry,* 16:211-238 (August, 1953); and R. H. Van Zelst, "Sociometrically Selected Work Teams," *Personnel Psychology,* 5:175-185 (Autumn, 1952).

[60] The problem of cooperation was given a telling analysis by Elton Mayo, *The Social Problems of an Industrial Civilization* (Boston: Harvard Business School, Division of Research, 1945), where he expounded the general thesis that spontaneous cooperation in industry is one of its central problems. E. W.

NOTES FOR CHAPTER 16 (CONT.)

Bakke, "Teamwork in Industry," Reprint No. 10 of the Yale Labor and Management Center (New Haven: 1948), clearly recognized the difference between organized and voluntary social groups of work and suggested that different mechanisms operated to secure the cooperation of each. Stuart Chase, *Roads to Agreement* (New York: Harper & Brothers, 1951), catalogs the various devices used in industry and elsewhere for developing cooperation. An early attempt to develop techniques for industrial cooperation is described in J. Leitch, *Man to Man: The Story of Industrial Democracy* (New York: B. C. Forbes Company, 1919). The degree to which this sense of problem has diffused from the United States to the industrial centers of Europe, creating an interest in "human relations in industry," is suggested in R. Clemens and A. Massart (eds.), "Human Relations in Industry," *Florence Discussions* (Paris: European Productivity Agency Project, June, 1955).

[61] This dilemma is highlighted in the discussion of Mason Haire, "Group Dynamics in the Industrial Situation," Chapter 28 in A. Kornhauser, R. Dubin, and A. Ross (eds.), *Industrial Conflict* (New York: McGraw-Hill Book Co., 1954), pp. 373-385.

[62] See the references in note 38, page 311. A particularly significant study by Leonard Sayles suggests that degree of militancy against management and its sustained character are related to skill and type of work. Erratic displays of antagonism come from low paid, low skilled people working at the same jobs in work teams. He interprets their erratic militancy as a consequence of technology. It would be our conclusion that the work group serves to drain off some of the antagonism as it functions as a voluntary social group. Consequently, antagonism is erratic rather than sustained. Sayles also finds that more militant people are at least semi-skilled, and characteristically work on separate machines. Our interpretation would be that such people recognize their relatively greater power (individual control of output and machine), and perceive small discriminations against them as having much larger import, not having nearly the continuous opportunity while working to "blow off steam" about them in a social group. Leonard Sayles, *Technology and Work Group Behavior* (Ann Arbor: Bureau of Industrial Relations, University of Michigan, 1956).

A grievance is the occasion for union demands that the company do something about an employee complaint. A great deal of day-to-day collective bargaining is devoted to regular grievance meetings between company and union representatives, like this one in an automobile plant.

Chapter 17

DISCONTENTS AND GRIEVANCES

In this chapter we are concerned with what happens when the individual worker fails to establish an adequate adjustment to his working environment. He may become discontented with his work, and if he remains in the organization, his behavior may constitute a very real problem for his supervisors. If he quits work, then the need for finding a replacement entails other kinds of administrative problems. Either way, individual discontents are something to be taken seriously.

The first general problem has to do with adjusting a working person *in* his working environment. Analysis of this problem views individual behavior as the result of personality factors and environmental working conditions interacting on each other. The general mechanism used to adjust the person *in* his working environment is the grievance procedure.

A second mode of handling working discontents tackles the problem of adjusting the working person *to* his working environment. This approach considers the working environment as relatively stable and unchanging. Attention is focused on better adjustment of the worker so that he may fit more adequately into that environment. The major devices used in adjusting the worker to his working environment are personal counseling and employee services. We will deal first with the grievance process. In the last section we will turn to a consideration of personal discontents that may be handled through counseling and employee services.

AREA COVERED BY GRIEVANCE PROCEDURE

The grievance procedure handles employee problems arising from *administration* of established personnel policy. This point is crucial in defining the area in which the grievance procedure operates. A grievance is an expression of discontent with the ways in which rules governing the work force are administered.

A grievance procedure is a formal system of steps through which a complaining worker can take his discontent to successively higher levels of management. Most grievance procedures require that the discontented worker write down his grievance and present it to his foreman. In all unionized plants this usually means the union grievance man writes up the grievance and takes it up with the foreman. Failing to get satisfaction from the foreman, he has automatic right of appeal to a next higher level of management. This appeal process may go on as far as the company president—or to an impartial arbitrator if one is provided as the last step in the grievance procedure. In short, the grievance procedure formalizes and makes automatic the right of appeal over the head of a supervisor whose decision is disputed by a subordinate.

A grievance procedure revolutionizes the exercise of authority in business enterprises. In particular, it limits the "last word" that the authority holder can have in making his decisions about subordinates, and making them stick. A grievance procedure gives a subordinate a right, and not merely an opportunity, to question his supervisor's judgement and decision. Even beyond that, each employee has the right to question supervisory decisions, from any source, affecting personnel rules or collective bargaining provisions. The grievance procedure of modern industry has been the most important single factor in eliminating arbitrary supervision by subjecting supervisory action and decision to the right of subordinate appeal.

DISCONTENTS WITH WORK

Any attempt to specify the area covered by grievance procedures by listing subjects about which grievances can arise is not particularly revealing. This point has been explicitly recognized by Selekman in his contention that the legalistic approach to the handling of grievances defeats the very purpose for which grievance machinery is established. By the so-called legalistic approach he means determining the legitimacy of a grievance according to a prior definition of a grievance embodied in work rules. In contrast, Selekman proposes a "clinical" approach.[1] Selekman's clinical approach accepts all discontents as legitimate grievances. Any ways used to distinguish among grievances help to determine their particular mode of settlement.[2]

The late National War Labor Board was frequently asked to decide whether certain problems should be treated as grievances. Affirmative answers were given, for example, with respect to discharge,[3] promotion,[4] piece rates,[5] job classifications,[6] medical examinations required by the company,[7] and work assignments.[8]

Any subject can and does come up in the grievance procedure. For example, physical conditions surrounding a job very often find their way into the grievance process. It is important to note that when such subject arises it is always characterized by the complainant's direct or implied charge of maladministration of established personnel policy.

An illustration will make this point clear. Employees complained about the fact that their buildings were uncomfortably cold. It was found that at the time the heating system had been changed from steam to hot water these buildings were storerooms. Since they did not require additional heat, the radiation surface had not been increased. When this location was used for production, the fact that the heat was not up to standard was overlooked until the employees' comments stimulated investigation and the condition was corrected.[9]

The workers' complaint about improper heating derives from their comparative judgement of the heat in their working space and that in other operating departments. Knowing or expecting that it was company policy to provide a uniform level of heat, these employees felt a sense of discrimination against them. They were admittedly less well off than other workers in the plant. The company in administration of its policy on this point had taken no measures to correct the situation. It made no difference that the solution was a mechanical one, and simple at that. Nobody in management had recognized the situation and taken steps required by management policy to effect a remedy.

A grievance may be defined to include any difference or dispute between workers and management arising out of terms and conditions of employment usually outlined in a collective bargaining agreement. This conception of the grievance process emphasizes its relationship to administration of work rules. A typical example of such a contract clause is one ordered by the National War Labor Board in the case of the *Aluminum Company of America:* "A grievance shall include any difference of opinion or dispute by the representatives of the Company and any employee or union representatives, regarding the interpretation or operation of any provision of this agreement."[10]

The War Labor Board in the *Montgomery Ward* case went further by declaring certain subjects outside the realm of the grievance procedure.

> Grievances, within the meaning of the grievance procedure, shall consist only of disputes about working conditions, about the interpretation and application of particular clauses of this agreement, and about alleged violations of the agreement, including alleged abuses of discretion by supervisors in the treatment of employees.
>
> . . . Changes in general business practice, the opening and closing of new units, the choice of personnel (subject to the seniority provision), the choice of merchandise to be sold, or other business questions of a like nature not having to do directly and primarily with the day-to-day life of the employees and their relations with their supervisors, shall not be subject to grievances and shall not be arbitrable. If any question arises as to whether a particular dispute is or is not a grievance within the meaning of these provisions, the question may be taken up through the grievance procedure and determined if necessary by arbitration.[11]

Complaints of employees can also be classified in terms of their real or imaginary content. Here attention is focused on the problem of verifying facts concerning a worker's discontent. This has been well summarized by Roethlisberger and Dickson in their analysis of interview materials secured at the Hawthorne Works of the Western Electric Company. They found one class of complaints about objects that could be seen and touched; another about sensory experiences not dealing with objects that could be seen or touched; and a third category of discontents having nothing to do with sensory experiences. This last group falls into the "imaginary" class.[12]

Other writers have followed this cue to the conclusion that discontent can be very upsetting to a person regardless of whether its source is in real facts or imagined circumstances.[13] Such analysis is illuminating for it makes clear that there is an objective ordering of facts around which discontent arises.

There is one point invariably overlooked in emphasizing the need for getting at the "real" cause of grievances. Grievances arise in a plant situation. This means that they are related to the framework of established personnel policy and rules, as extended or modified through collective bargaining.

The body of rules governing operations of the enterprise are the social reality giving meaning to a worker's complaint or grievance. To be real to the plant situation a grievance must be phrased in the plant context. Let us take a simple example. It would be unthinkable to the employee and meaningless to the company to file a grievance stating: "My wife thinks we ought to have more money and nags me about it. Therefore, I am entitled to a raise." This may very well be the "true" reason for the employee's discontent and desire for a wage raise. Just exactly what can the company do about it? Obviously the problem is outside the scope of company action. If this same man phrases his grievance as: "I am doing work of a higher job classification and am entitled to more pay," or "My work has been satisfactory and I am entitled to a merit increase," then there is a basis for company action on his complaint. He may or may not get the raise, depending on whether his claim can be justified under the company wage payment system. Even if the first statement of his grievance contained the "true" cause of his dissatisfaction, then, it would not enable him to effect a change.

This serves again to emphasize the constraints of the "reign of rules" governing the conduct of working people.

There is another class of grievances only ostensibly expressing worker discontent. One example is the instance where there are competing factions within the union, with some of the grievance comitteemen in the faction opposed to the top officers of the local union. It is posible that such comitteemen might encourage and file grievances of doubtful merit, intending to point the finger of blame at the faction in power for failing to win the grievance case. At the same time, should the case be won, the grievance commiteemen would be prepared to take credit. Such grievances would certainly be phrased to conform to the reality of the work situation. On their face value they would bear no distinguishing mark to indicate their real purpose. To the company, without special knowledge of internal union affairs, such grievances may be handled in the normal course of events.

The simple illustration above suggests that the basis for grievance decisions is sometimes broader than the substantive issues raised by the grievance. Nevertheless, it is true that in such a case and in similar kinds, the real, but unexpressed, cause of the grievance is related to some aspect of the plant situation, or the collective bargaining relationship. In this sense the "reality" of the grievance is meaningful to work-centered factors, and not to factors essentially separate from the work situation as were those in the first example.

A TECHNIQUE OF SOCIAL CONTROL

The basic objective of personnel administration is to provide means for organizing a work force to achieve fixed standards of production. It is necessary that the work force operate according to established standards, which requires at the least that every employee have an assigned job and be trained to perform that job. Standards of performance both as to quality and quantity can be established satisfactorily and controlled by fixing production schedules and inspection of product for quality. The fields of time and motion study and quality control through inspection devote themselves exclusively to these two areas.[14]

POLICING BEHAVIOR

With established standards, however, there remains the problem of administering standards of performance and work rules. This administrative problem provides a key to understanding the grievance procedure's function as a social control device. The grievance procedure serves the role of providing an opportunity for testing the administrative application of rules governing the work force.[15]

Supervisors may make incorrect interpretations of personnel rules. Foremen may ignore established rules and substitute their own. Situations may arise to which the existing body of rules and regulations have no direct application. If a subordinate is subjected to what he considers an injustice, he has available to him a procedure whereby a formal protest can be made with the prospect of righting the alleged wrong. In grievance procedure a substantial substitute exists for protest action that might be injurious to the organization.

The administrative problem to which grievances are relevant has two broad aspects: (A) administration of objective standards of the employment contract or the collective bargain, and (B) administration of the work force considered as a social group.

The first problem includes a wide variety of subjects. Wage rates and the wage payment system are always explicitly set forth in the collective agreement. Similarly, the hours and conditions of work are established in the union contract, or company personnel policy. Generally, objective standards of the employment contract cover those aspects of the work relationship that can be determined in advance. Furthermore, management, union, and employees have or should have full and equal knowledge of them.

The validity of an employee's complaint

that he suffers through administration of objective employment standards can always be judged against the standards themselves. For example, a worker claims he has not received all the seniority due him on the seniority list. His claim can be checked against the seniority clause of the union agreement. To take another instance, an employee working under graduated wage payment system claims that he did not receive correct pay. His pay can be recalculated and the justice of his claim determined objectively within the rules of the particular wage payment plan.

A union grievance committeeman (in striped coveralls) discussing a problem with a worker. This is the first and very informal stage of "grieving." Many grievances stop at this stage as the committeeman is able to offer explanations and advice, or simply talk the disgruntled worker out of his gripe. If a solid grievance is uncovered, then the committeeman is able to mobilize the full resources of the union behind it to secure favorable consideration from the company.

In the administration of the work force considered as a social group, there are two general types of problems evident. On the one hand, we must consider what can be called the "rules of supervision." Such questions as assignment of work, assignment of personnel to jobs, training of employees, and maintenance of the flow of materials to work stations all fall in this category. Furthermore, they all involve a supervisor's organization of his work force, tools, and materials to establish an ordered production unit capable of producing at the rate and to the quality standards set for his unit. In this context employees are viewed as units in the productive process, to be organized in conjunction with machinery and materials.

Certain difficulties occur from the employees' standpoint which may give rise to grievances. An employee on piece work may complain of excessive "down time" because of improper flow of materials to his work station. The worker's complaint centers around loss of earnings, but implicit in his grievance is criticism of his supervisor's organization of the work unit which causes loss of earnings.

The second major aspect of administration of the work force considered as a social group involves the personnel function of the supervisor and his role as a leader of his employees. A supervisor must evaluate each individual under his supervision. He cannot consider them simply as interchangeable units within his work group. There is involved here the whole complex of personal relationships of employee to employee and of subordinate to superior. The worker's grievance in this connection becomes a charge of discrimination by his superiors.

To the workers involved, a grievance procedure means that a problem of improper treatment can be expressed officially and thus handled. It means particularly that they can seek redress beyond their immediate supervisor. This establishes an element of social control over the workers. Ability to give formal expression to management of a dissatisfaction substitutes for other ways that may be harmful to the firm. Absenteeism, labor turnover, and limitation of output are some undesirable forms of expressed discontent.[16]

The grievance procedure acts as a safety valve that channels dissatisfaction in a potentially constructive direction. Of necessity there must be an expectation that a grievance will be judged on its merits and that satisfaction will be achieved if the grievance is well founded.

We have so far considered the function of the grievance procedure as a control mechanism for management. The union also has a vital interest in the grievance procedure, as indicated by the fact that almost every union contract contains some kind of provision for orderly handling of grievances. Lapp estimated in 1945 that more than 50,000 labor contracts had some such provisions, and there must be many more by now.[17]

From the union's standpoint it is important to become an active party in settling grievances. Union participation establishes a relative equality of power on the side of the employee dealing with management in the same sense that this equality of power is evidenced in negotiation of the collective agreement itself. At the same time, decisions in grievance cases become embodied in the work rules of the plant supplementing formal rules set forth in the union agreement. "Such decisions are added to the basic contract, grievance procedure, and local decisions. All these written records become a part of the gradually evolving body of laws governing the Union-Employer relationships."[18] In order that the union maintain some control over development of the body of work rules it is essential from its viewpoint that there be union participation on an official basis.

Where the union does not have a "union shop" or "closed shop" agreement with the employer, the union's participation in the grievance process provides a daily means for impressing nonmembers as well as members with services that the union is able to perform for them. In instructions to grievance committeemen, the Steelworkers' Organizing Committee urged: "Do give everybody a civil and courteous answer. Every fellow employee, union member or not, deserves a decent reply. If he is treated as a friend and fellow worker and sympathetically listened to, he will feel a lot more friendly towards the Union, than he will if given a short unkind answer."[19]

Both management and union have a mutual, but not identical, interest in using their participation in the grievance process for control purposes. At the same time the union has an intra-organizational problem of maintaining loyalty, and thereby control of the membership, which is also served by participation in the grievance process.

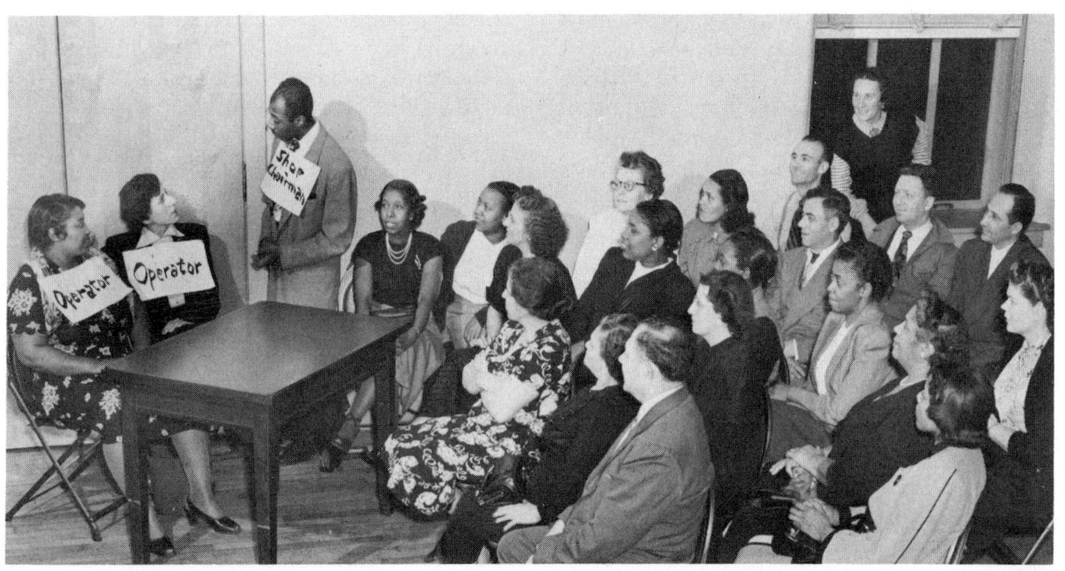

The union interest in the grievance procedure may give rise to carefully planned training programs to make local union officials more effective in handling shop grievances. Role playing is being used in this training session to teach grievance handling.

A SOCIAL INVENTION

Some kind of permanent system needs to be established to make the expression of discontent possible at any time it is felt. We call these permanent systems for handling discontent, grievance procedures.

Grievance procedures are a social invention.

Like many other features of modern work organizations, they are of relatively recent origin. Lapp indicates that a few great industries put grievance machinery into operation as early as 1900.[20] In 1892 the Chicago Publishers' Association and the Typographical Union concluded an agreement providing that all disputes arising out of the interpretation of the contract should be settled by conciliation and arbitration. This agreement was followed on a national scale in 1901, when a nationwide plan was established between the International Typographical Union and the American Newspaper Publishers Association for settling grievances. As a result of the great Anthracite Coal strike in 1902 and the subsequent report of the President's Anthracite Coal Commission, a formal grievance procedure was established by the Commission for the hard coal industry. The flint glass industry, through industry-wide collective bargaining, established a grievance procedure that was first introduced in 1903. After the 1910 strike in the Chicago clothing industry, settlement at the Hart, Schaffner and Marx Company included an elaborate grievance procedure culminating in arbitration of unsettled differences by a permanent Board of Arbitrations.

The subsequent development of formal grievance procedure for handling employee discontent has generally paralleled the growth of collective bargaining and the incorporation of terms of the bargain in a labor contract. During the 1920's when "welfare capitalism" was the vogue and employee representation plans the answer to trade unionism, most of the work of employee representatives was devoted to presentation of grievances.[21]

Handling employee discontents through a grievance procedure is an important social invention for institutionalizing power relations. The grievance procedure does not change the nature of the disputes, nor does it eliminate them. It does, however, provide a fixed and permanent way of handling disputes revolving around worker discontents.

Behavior is institutionalized when it becomes established, recurrent, and generally accepted. It is very clear that in the relationships between management and men, and the relationships between management and union, the grievance procedure is an institutionalized system of behavior for handling employee and union discontents.

ELEMENTS OF THE GRIEVANCE PROCESS

Let us examine in detail the elements of the grievance adjustment process in industry which give it a unique character as a membership adjustment process.

UNION PROTECTIVE DEVICE

The grievance adjustment process is primarily a device for handling employee discontents that center in only a portion of the work force.[22] The grievance procedure provides an effective substitute for direct action by all the work force to get consideration and solution of a problem involving less than all workers.

The union is not called on to marshal all its forces and all its power in handling each individual grievance. In this sense the grievance procedure is a union protective device. It does not have to "shoot the works" in every small case. Consider what would happen to the union if it had to threaten a strike or other drastic action, involving the entire work force, every time a worker had a dispute over a wage rate, or an argument over company discipline meted out to him. It seems evident that the membership as a whole would soon revolt against the uncertainty involved in constant mass action over issues with which few of the workers were personally identified.

MANAGEMENT AS JUDGE

The grievance process involves management in the role of judge.[23] A grievance characteristically involves a management decision for its solution. It is to management that union or individual worker turns with a demand that the cause of the grievance be eliminated.

Negotiation of the collective bargaining agreement involves two parties, of varying power with respect to each other, making demands and counter-proposals. Administration of the bargain places only one party, management, in the role of the arbiter of disputes that fall within the scope of the grievance procedure.

It is important to keep this distinction in mind. It is the difference between bargaining collectively over an agreement and making the agreement an operating code. It is the difference between resolving issues on the basis of relative power, and settling problems through a quasi judicial mechanism in which only one party to the rule-making acts as judge. In this light it becomes clear that strikes over apparently trivial grievances are generally protests against a cumulation of management's grievance decisions which the union feels have been unjust. The last decision only quickens to flame an already smoldering fire. Unwilling to continue adherence to a judicial process that it feels has unjust judges the union has the alternative of return to direct economic action, the strike or slowdown.

This emphasis on the judicial role of management in the grievance process also makes clear the whimsical nature of the sometimes repeated notion that the grievance procedure ought to be a two way street—management should have the right to bring up grievances just like the union.[24] It should be obvious that a so-called management grievance is expressed in direct action by supervision in administering the work force. If shop rule is violated, the worker gets a disciplinary layoff. How ridiculous it would be if management instead brought the culprit up formally on a grievance charge and then ordered itself to mete out appropriate discipline!

We have repeatedly emphasized that large scale enterprise necessitates substitution of explicit rules and standards for personal decisions in administrating large bodies of men. A large corporation, having a master contract covering thousands of workers in many different plants, finds it necessary to live by the letter of the collective bargaining agreement in order to avoid an otherwise administratively impossible situation of varying local interpretations of contract provisions. It is compelled, in other words, to maintain consistency in application of its union agreement in a variety of different situations, and thus is forced to a legalistic outlook as a matter of sound management policy. This obviously places important limitations on the freedom of lower management officials to choose their own basis for decision at the early grievance levels. Thus, freedom to choose any kind of decision is not a consequence of management being the sole judge of grievances.

Still another kind of limitation on arbitrary management grievance decisions occurs where a permanent arbitrator is the final stage in grievance settlement.[25] The office of permanent arbitrator is an important modification of the otherwise one-sided judicial process for handling grievances. By definition, the arbitrator is completely dissociated from either party and does not participate in the initial rule-making involved in collective bargaining. For this reason the development of a grievance procedure which has at its apex a permanent impartial arbitrator tends immediately to change the location of decision-making on grievances by shifting it away from the company to a third party. Under such circumstances management is constantly led to make its decisions with an eye to what subsequently might be done in given cases by the permanent arbitrator.

The arbitrator's area of decision is often limited by union contract provisions. He is forbidden the right to add to or subtract from the union agreement. In some cases he may not have jurisdiction over the entire contract, certain clauses being outside his authority.

There are two consequences of the introduction of a permanent arbitrator into the grievance machinery. The union contract tends to reflect with greater accuracy than it otherwise might, the relative bargaining strength of union and management. The contract provisions become extremely detailed and specific with an eye to providing an explicit set of rules as a basis for the arbitrator's future decisions.[26]

A second consequence of the addition of a permanent arbitrator is to fortify the trend (resulting from management's requirement of administrative consistency) towards legalism in grievance handling. Each case is potentially subject to review by the arbitrator, consequently it is more likely to be prepared by both sides with great care and legal nicety. Legalism in administering a union contract is not, therefore, a sufficient criterion for determining whether a particular union-management relationship can be called conflictful.

MANAGEMENT POLICY QUESTIONED

A grievance procedure is an explicit acknowledgement by management that its right of absolute rule over personnel is subject to open questioning by the employees affected. It represents a concession limiting absolute power with respect to administration of personnel in the enterprise. This is well recognized by both management and labor.

In a National Labor Management Conference, called by the President in 1945, the labor members concluded:

> The Committee, for purposes of clarification, has earnestly endeavored to outline the areas wherein the primary functions and responsibilities of management could be clearly and concisely defined; the area in which management has the function and responsibility to make prompt initial decisions in order to insure the effective operation of the enterprise but where the consequences of the decisions are properly subject to review and adjustment under established grievance adjustment procedures; and finally the area encompassing matters that are clearly subjects for collective bargaining before final decisions can be made.[27]

The management members of the same committee disagreed with their labor colleagues by seeking to limit grievances strictly to personnel matters, in the following words:

> In order to clarify this problem, the Committee has discussed many of the important functions of management involved in operating a business. The management members have classified some of them for the purpose of avoiding misunderstandings and minimizing industrial disputes. We have placed them in two classifications: the first comprises those matters which are clearly the functions and responsibility of management and are not subject to collective bargaining.
>
> The second comprises matters in respect to which it is the function and responsibility of management to make prompt initial decisions in order to insure the effective operation of the enterprise, but where the consequences of such actions or decisions are properly subject to review when they involve issues of alleged discrimination; affect wages, hours, working conditions; or agreed-upon management-labor practices. Such matters should be handled promptly under grievance procedures mutually agreed to as being appropriate for each specific item.[28]

This Committee was unable to reach agreement on the specification of management's absolute rights. It is clear from both reports, however, that there was agreement on the limitation of management's sole power to act in certain areas—restricted to personnel in the management report, although not so limited in the labor report. Review of management's action was acknowledged to come through the operation of the grievance procedure.

ADMINISTRATION CREATES PROBLEMS

A grievance procedure expresses the realization that problems may arise in the future for which no solution can be specified in advance. Because a business enterprise is dependent on a group of operating personnel it is recognized that each individual participant may, at some future date, become dissatisfied with his participation in the enterprise and seek redress short of transfer or resignation. It is impossible to so detail personnel rules in company policies and collective bargaining agreements that they cover all variations of any employee problem. The grievance procedure makes decisions possible in situations not covered by existing rules.

Some grievances will arise as a result of the administration of the union agreement. The union contract makes explicit the duties and responsibilities of each party with respect to the other. There may still arise dissatisfaction, however, with respect to individual wages, or the allocation of hours of work, or the differential treatment of employees regarding working conditions. Such problems arise out of the *administrative application* of the general provisions of the union agreement, and constitute grievances.

UNION AND INDIVIDUALS

A fifth feature of grievance procedures is the dual character of the complainants involved in the grievance process. Individuals have access to the grievance machinery, often represented in the prosecution of a grievance by the union. The union itself has access to the grievance procedure on problems of importance to its whole membership. Thus, the grievance machinery encompasses within its operation two general categories of "grievers."

CHANNEL OF COMMUNICATION

Another aspect of the grievance adjustment process is recognition by management that a channel of communication must be provided for workers to express dissatisfactions arising out of their work situation. This results in establishing specific steps through which a grievance is processed, the grievance procedure proper. The grievance procedure, once established, operates continuously. It is always accessible to the union or workers at the time a grievance arises. The formal procedure thus provides a continuous channel of communication to management about things that make workers unhappy.

STRUCTURE INDIVIDUALIZED

The seventh characteristic of the grievance process is that its structure is designated to fit individual conditions of specific industrial establishments. The later stages through which a grievance must pass if satisfaction is not given by those who first handle it parallels levels of authority in the business organization.

There is no single ideal grievance procedure. A procedure which meets the needs of a steel mill may be totally inadequate for a longshore establishment, an oil field, or a small machine shop. Grievance procedures must be carefully tailored to the nature of an industry, the size of the plant, the number of employees involved, the degree of understanding between the parties, and numerous other factors.

Grievance procedures in existing agreements have varying numbers of steps. Small establishments generally have only two or three steps; large establishments sometimes have as many as six or seven.[29]

The actual structure of the grievance procedure fits the characteristic of the individual enterprise.

MANAGEMENT CONTROL DEVICE

Another operating aspect of the grievance procedure is its role as a control device for management in evaluating the effectiveness of its supervisors. A number of writers have suggested the importance of evaluating supervision in terms of the number and type of grievances that arise from each supervisor's work group. Selekman has summarized this point generally and suggests its application to both the evaluation of supervision, and evaluation of personnel policy.[30]

SCOPE OF APPLICATION

Finally, the grievance process is characterized by an attempt to define the scope of its application within the entire field of personnel administration. Many union contracts specify that grievances are limited to disputes over interpretation of clauses of the union agreement. Other contracts narrow the limits to certain stated clauses. In recent analytical writing there has been a tendency to emphasize the need for removing limits on the definition of a grievance in the interests of an all inclusive approach to the solution of employee dissatisfaction. Selekman, for example, in challenging too much formalism in handling grievances has stated that "A grievance is never 'not a grievance.' "[31]

These nine characteristics of the grievance procedure in American industry may have elements in common with methods for handling discontents in other types of social organizations. It is believed, however, that the particular combination of all these elements found in the idustrial grievance procedure is unique to business organizations. American grievance procedures are a unique social invention for handling employee discontents in work organizations.

GRIEVANCE SUBJECTS

We now will examine the subject matter of grievances in terms of the institutional areas of discontent they represent. In general, grievances involve authority, power, and status relations. In addition, the technical behavior systems of work are a frequent source of discontent and grievances.

Grievances resulting from authority relations at work are those involving discipline. Typically, insubordination is met by prompt action of a supervisor to discipline the recalcitrant worker. As a consequence, the worker may file a grievance claiming that he was not in the wrong and should not have been disciplined, or that the amount of discipline meted out to him was too great.

A second general class of grievances has to do with the application of job classifications to particular kinds of work, or the assignment of individuals to particular kinds of jobs. These grievances are concerned with the distribution of functions and, therefore, with the distribution of power within the work organization.

Another common kind of grievance concerns the seniority standing of a worker. A worker's seniority may determine his opportunity for promotion, his chance of retention during layoffs, and the order in which he will be called back to work after a layoff. Seniority therefore, obviously affects the economic well-being of the individual worker insofar as it determines his opportunity to hold, or return to, his job. In addition, as we have earlier pointed out, seniority may entitle the worker to important status position in the organization. Therefore, seniority grievances often involve issues of status in the organization.

Job rates and wages are other frequent subjects of grievances. Here again, the income factor is important. Disputes over job rates and wages can also be viewed as problems of status. When an individual claims that the rate for his job is too low, he invariably compares himself and his job with like jobs in the plant. This is a status comparison. The differential may be only a matter of a few cents. Nevertheless, these few pennies per hour are exceedingly important to the individual seeking them as marks of status.

Job conditions, work loads, and production standards are additional subjects of common grievances. It will be noted that each of these subjects has to do with the technical behavior systems involved in getting work done, or conditions surrounding working operations. Thus, the technical behavior systems become an important subject around which discontent arises, and about which grievances are filed.

Grievances are not uniform for all industry. Grievance subjects vary greatly by industry, by individual establishment, and through time. In some industries having special working conditions, like the hotel and restaurant field, job factors like tipping, free meals, uniforms, and part time work, are frequent subjects of grievances. In mass production work, individual wage rate and job classification problems, and the application of seniority rules are likely to be important sources of grievances. During World War II tight labor market conditions in many industries resulted in a marked falling off of grievances involving such subjects as discipline, hiring control, and seniority. In the post war reconversion period, on the other hand, there was a heavy increase of seniority grievances in many industries.

INSTITUTIONALIZING DISCONTENT

From a closer examination of union-management relations we can discover how the grievance procedure is one way of institutionalizing discontent. The subject matter and the modes of handling discontent are standardized.

UNION-MANAGEMENT RELATIONS

After the union contract is signed, there is the ensuing period during which it is in effect. During this time the contract provisions, as well as the working rules of the company, become subjects of controversy. These controversies are handled through the grievance procedure.

The rule making and rule interpreting phases of union-management relations are distinctive, but nevertheless connected, stages in their relationship. There is a continuity between the bargaining of a contract and its subsequent interpretation through the grievance procedure.[32]

Should any disagreements arise over interpreting the union contract, or company working rules (and they usually do) the grievance procedure provides a means for handling them. Management may interpret a contract provision and act on its interpretation. A worker, group of workers, or the union as a whole, may dispute this interpretation, and file a grievance. The stage is then set, through the grievance decision, for making explicit an unclear aspect of working rules.

The kinds of discontent that get expressed in the grievance procedure have as their subject matter the interpretation of the union agreement and company working rules. The grievance procedure limits "grieving" to these subjects of discontent.

In an extreme case, where the union feels the contract is silent on an important point, it may file a whole series of grievances. Management may act negatively on all of them. Management position is based on the contention that the discontents fall outside the contract, and are not subject to its provisions. The union, however, may have purposely initiated the grievances in order to prepare a case for a new contract demand when the contract is reopened. The grievance procedure channels expression of discontent by preparing the grounds, through the filing of grievances, for future demands on management.[33]

A third phase of institutionalized discontent is revealed in the way in which grievance decisions extend the meaning or scope of rules and regulations. Decisions settle individual cases, and also become precedents for future cases of a similar sort. A single grievance decision may constitute a significant interpretation of a contract clause, or a working rule. This may be either a clarification or extension of existing ideas about contract provisions or working rules. In either instance, a favorable grievance decision becomes a modification of rules by interpretation.

The body of common law represented in grievance decisions becomes the governing precedent for future management action. The grievance process serves to institutionalize discontent by building a body of common law in terms of which the legitimacy of discontent is measured.

GRIEVANCES AND INDUSTRIAL CONFLICT

Existence of a grievance procedure standardizes conflict between management and union in non-violent ways. The existence of this judicial machinery provides an effective institutionalized alternative to constant violence and open use of force.

Whenever appeal is taken to higher levels of management in a decision on a grievance, there is the opportunity for more detached people to handle the dispute. Higher levels of management are usually less immersed in the emotions of the original incident. Higher levels of management may also know more about the union agreement, the relationship with the union, and be in a better position to command full information about a grievance. In the progressive movement to higher levels of grievance decision, there is a significant shift in the kinds of people involved in making decisions. Thus, there is genuine opportunity for a change in the original management grievance decision as appeal is taken to higher management levels. This makes it worthwhile for the union to undertake appeals of adverse decisions rather than resort to force or economic pressure.

The procedures of grievance handling standardize the expression of discontent by requiring some rationality in stating dissatisfaction. At higher steps of the grievance procedure the evidence is typically written down and carefully marshaled. The heat of emotion that may have surrounded the incident giving rise to the grievance is replaced by an atmosphere of reasoned judicial deliberation. The grievance is shifted away from its emotionally charged expression at its point of origin, into a reasoned case of discontent. This is still another factor in institutionalizing the ways of handling industrial discontent.

NON-FORMAL INSTITUTIONALIZING

Even at the most informal level of union-management relations, where union grievance committeeman and foreman bargain, there develops an institutionalization of their relationships with respect to grievances. Dalton has pointed out that in a large manufacturing plant, the most successful union grievance committeemen settle a large proportion of all grievances without formal processing.[34] What typically develops between union representative and foreman in this informal settlement process is a system of reciprocal favors. A foreman may do a favor in agreeing to rule affirmatively for an aggrieved employee. He does so, however, with the full expectation that in the future the grievance committeeman will reciprocate the favor.

This system of reciprocal favors in handling employee discontent becomes an important part of the whole grievance procedure. Davey has estimated that the settlement of grievances between foreman and union steward constitutes as much as 95 per cent of all grievance settlements in smoothly operating grievance procedures.[35] Karsh somewhat more conservatively than Davey estimated for an automobile plant during World War II that five times as many grievances were settled between foreman and shop steward as were sent to the higher stages of the grievance procedure.[36]

As Kennedy has facetiously pointed out, it is a general principle of lower levels of an organization that "what their supervisors do not know about deals made at the work level will not hurt them."[37] At what we have called in this book the non-formal levels of behavior a high percentage of worker discontent is handled through grievance negotiation. This illustrates the operation of one non-formal behavior system in the initial step of the grievance process.

GRIEVANCE RESULTS

In a recent study of who wins what in the grievance process, it was firmly established that the nature of the union-management relationship largely determines the decision on grievance discontents.[38]

This study contrasted the operation of the grievance procedure in three major companies, each characterized by a different type of union-management relationship ranging from general cooperation to continuous conflict. It was shown through a study of 200 grievances which had gone beyond the foreman-union committeeman in each company, that where conflict dominated the union-management relationship, management won 75 per cent of all grievances.[39] Where cooperation characterized the relationship the proportion was almost exactly reversed, with management winning only 31.5 per cent of all grievances. Where the relationship between management and union was one of accommodation the management won 60 per cent of all grievances.

When the types of grievances arising in each of the three union-management relations are examined, the following patterns emerge. In cooperation relationships there is a significantly higher percentage of all grievances involving the simple application of established contract provisions, or working conditions. On the other hand, in the conflict relationship, the union filed a significantly higher percentage of grievances designed to extend the union agreement through the grievance process. Finally, in both the conflict and accommodation relationship there was a significantly higher proportion of disputes involving supervisory discrimination towards workers than was true in the instance of union-management cooperation. These are only a few of the findings of the study.

The general point is that the nature of the union-management relationship provides a mold that fashions the kinds of grievances arising, and their disposition through the grievance procedure. The atmosphere of the union management relationship provides the norms by which the grievance procedure operates. Again, we can see how industrial discontents become institutionalized in terms of the normative patterns that govern the union-management relationship.

PERSONAL DISCONTENTS

No person is so capable of dividing up the segments of his life that he can keep his personal life completely isolated from his working life. Furthermore, the subjective aspects of his working life may constitute problems for the individual. It is necessary, then, to examine briefly the nature of personal discontents and some techniques for handling them.

TOTAL LIFE VS. WORKING LIFE

Personal discontents are the product of disparities between the individual's total life and his working life. This incompatibility takes two general forms.

The first category of personal discontents involves basic disparities between working and non-working segments of life. A nagging wife may demand that her husband get ahead, but he knows the reality of his job simply will not provide him advancement opportunities. A man with genuine religious-moral convictions finds that his work requires expediency and immorality for its accomplishment. A job may demand personality characteristics like decisiveness and drive that are simply foreign to the personality structure of the individual. These are a few examples of the kinds of basic disparities that can exist between working and non-working segments of life.

A second fundamental form of personal discontent derives from the differences between the organizational definition of the job, position, or office with its accompanying behavior systems, and the subjective personal view the individual has of them. Where these disparities become large and persistent enough, considerable discontent develops. The individual may be in a staff position where he must show respect and deference toward a boss he believes to be stupid. Great hostilities may arise in the situation. Another individual may try to fill a position calling for the exercise of considerable authority by becoming authoritarian and arbitrary to mask his sense of inadequacy. These are common examples of the disparities that can arise between a subjective view and the organization expectation in filling a job.

At the other end of the scale of employee dissatisfactions can be found a group of personal problems very transitory in character. It is commonplace to point out variations in everyone's daily demeanor. To "get up on the wrong side of the bed" may have a bearing on a person's relations with working associates for a matter of hours or even an entire day. Unless this is a continuing break in normal relationships, it is unnecessary to give such manifestations of temporary personal discontents any recognition in administering personnel policy. Such monetary gripes are of short duration, and not permanently associated with the work situation. For all practical purposes they are of a self-healing character, and require no action by management.

The fundamental characteristic of personal discontents from the organizational standpoint is this. To handle such discontents requires mechanisms for adjusting the person *to* his working environment. This is clearly the realm of psychotherapy, psychiatry, psychology, and counseling. It is the individual who needs to be changed, in some aspects of his inner life, to become better adjusted to his working environment.

Personal discontents can be distinguished from grievances on the following grounds. Personal discontents involve disparities between the person's view of his work and organization expectations; grievances test the logic and adequacy of organization expectations in given situations, leading to their modification, where necessary. Personal discontents are always subjective, in contrast with grievances which have meaning only when formulated according to the reality of the working situation which gives to them an objective form. Grievances are always expressed publicly through the grievance procedure; personal discontents may remain pent up within the individual, or expressed only indirectly in his behavior.

COUNSELING

The aims and purposes of psychotherapy are matters of more or less general agreement among professional practitioners of this field. Great variation exists, however, as to the techniques to be used in adjusting the individual with personal discontents *to* his environment.

Cost is one of the most important limitations on the use of psychotherapeutic methods. Where depth therapy is used, extending over long periods of time with each patient, companies usually feel justified in underwriting the consultations only for top level employees. A number of companies provide free psychiatric services for executives.

Much more common, because of its lower cost per patient in terms of immediate results, is the use of some sort of counseling program. Trained counselors are added to the staff of the personnel department where they are available to help employees with personal discontents.[40]

There is a considerable literature on counseling for industrial employees. It is not our purpose to review this literature here.[41] However, there is one phase of counseling deserving particular attention. This is the cathartic result of the counseling situation. Without the counselor intervening directly in the life of his patient, the counseling situation provides an opportunity for "blowing off steam" that is therapeutic in itself.

The studies of the Western Electric Company by Elton Mayo and his associates led to the establishment of a counseling program in the company.[42] The Western Electric studies have made a contribution to personnel administration in pointing out the importance of a management interviewing program. Interviews may afford relief to employees able to talk out feelings of dissatisfaction. Relief may come from the interview situation itself without expectation that what has been said will result in any action beneficial to the employee, or any change in the work situation that may have been the source of the complaint. Roethlisberger and Dickson reported that employees who had used the counseling services of the Hawthorne Plant were delighted with the results. These researchers found that employees had nursed discontents for years, finally being able to express them through the counseling services of the company. The researchers also suggested that psychological mechanisms operated to give relief to people who had an opportunity to talk out their discontents with neither the fear of punishment nor the anticipation of direct efforts to change them.[43]

The personnel counselor as a listener is very useful for handling ill-defined dissatisfactions that probably never get into the grievance channel because they are difficult to formulate realistically. Such personal discontents are not properly termed grievances. A skilled interviewing program is perhaps the best technique for handling them.

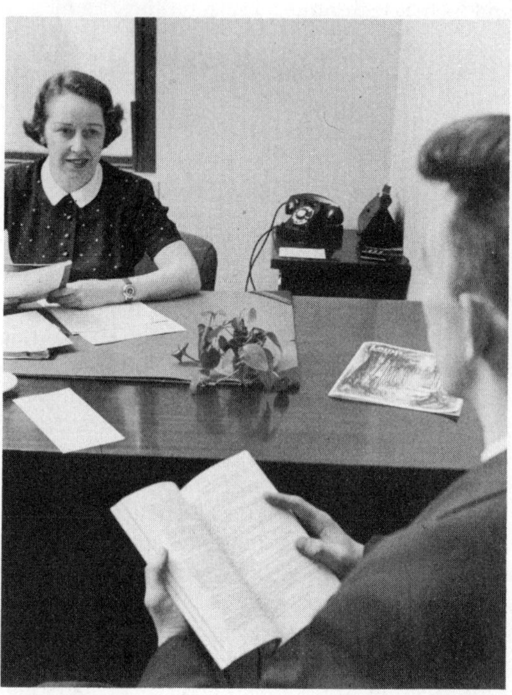

Sometimes full time people are added to the personnel department as counselors, helping employees with a variety of personal problems, some of which are only remotely related to work. This counselor is advising a young employee on possible college courses he can take at night. This kind of service may communicate to the employee that the company has an interest in him; or it may serve to drain off some personal discontent an employee may harbor.

Other types of counseling programs exist to help employees with specific problems in which direct guidance is needed. For younger employees, vocational guidance may be provided by the company. For people about to retire some firms have undertaken to supply guidance on the problems of leaving work. Help in education and recreation may also be afforded to employees through company counseling. Even personal financial problems may become the subject of company guidance and help. Health is another general area in which the company medical services provide help in counseling employees.[44]

EMPLOYEE SERVICES

Management often takes action through the personnel department to provide assistance to workers on problems not directly related to the work situation.[45] Certain simple problems of community living such as transportation, rationing, housing, small loans, and so on, are handled through special programs. While they may be important to employees, the non-existence of such services in a company's personnel program will seldom give rise to a grievance. However, many companies consider it important to provide such assistance as part of the regular personnel service.

The CIO officially adopted a union assistance program for members at its 1944 convention after observing the success of the UAW-CIO program established in January of that year in Detroit. "The immediate purpose of union counseling is to get help to CIO members on their community problems."[46] Thus, unions are beginning to show an increasing interest in activities that traditionally have been within the province of the company personnel department.

Recreational programs and in some cases even educational programs are generally conceived as personnel activities that contribute to developing favorable employee attitudes and are set up as part of a regular personnel program. These welfare programs are concerned with establishing attitudes of good will towards the company and promoting development of job-centered social relations by fostering off-the-job association of fellow workers.

Obvious interest and enjoyment is registered by these bowlers in a company bowling league. But they would enjoy the game just as much under other sponsorship. What companies gain in supporting such recreational programs is a possible growth of employee good will.

WORK AND HAPPINESS

For all the prescriptions about how to behave that are built into the work organization, there is still wide latitude for unhappiness about working. Two fundamental adjustments can be made to reduce the amount of unhappiness.

The individual can be adjusted *in* his job. The grievance procedure is the social invention for accomplishing this. It permits modifications of job and working conditions to bring them into accord with the systematic expectations of workers and the promises of management. The grievance procedure also provides the criteria by which the individual develops his expectations about the treatment he will receive as a worker. The grievance procedure is a two-way adjustment process through which job conditions can be changed, or the job holder's expectations can be modified to bring the two into closer accord.

The individual worker can also be adjusted *to* his work. Employee counseling and services for workers are the methods for doing this. It is assumed that unhappiness has its roots inside the person. Through counseling an attempt is made to change him to produce a better adjustment with his working environment. When employee services are provided, one goal is to divert inner discontents into satisfying activities.

Every possible effort is made in work organizations to design jobs, positions, and offices, and their accompanying behavior systems, so that minimal discontent will result among their occupants. Unhappiness may still occur. When it does, the grievance procedure, counseling, and employee services are used to reduce, if not eliminate, discontent.

NOTES FOR CHAPTER 17

1 B. M. Selekman, "Handling Shop Grievances," *Harvard Business Review,* 23:469-483 (Summer, 1945).

2 *Ibid.*, p. 474.

3 National War Labor Board, in the matter of *Pacific Telephone and Telegraph Co.*, No. 3407-D (July 26, 1943); *Reuben H. Donnelley Corporation,* No. 4207-DS-D (April 26, 1944); and *Underwood, Elliot, Fisher Co.*, No. 178 (October 2, 1942).

4 National War Labor Board, *Johns Manville Co., Inc.* (No. 2526-D, February 15, 1944).

5 National War Labor Board, *Hummer Manufacturing Co.,* No. 2842-D (August 26, 1942); and *McQuay-Norris Manufacturing Co.,* No. 697 (July 3, 1943).

6 National War Labor Board, *Gray Manufacturing Company,* No. 506 (April 5, 1943); and *Shower Bros. Co.,* Nos. 3996-A, and 3997-A (June 3, 1943).

7 National War Labor Board, *Wright Aeronautical Corp.,* No. 111-1375-D (October 3, 1943).

8 National War Labor Board, *Henry I. Siegel Co.,* No. 111-964-D (April 18, 1944).

9 F. J. Roethlisberger and W. J. Dickson, *Management and the Worker* (Cambridge: Harvard University Press, 1939); adapted from page 224.

10 National War Labor Board, No. 111-18 (November 27, 1943).

11 National War Labor Board, *Montgomery Ward & Co.,* No. 111-5353-D (August 21, 1944).

12 Roethlisberger and Dickson, *op. cit.*, pp. 257-258.

13 See, for example, the following, which deal with "imaginary" grievances: W. H. Davis, "Industrial Peace is a War 'Must'," *Mill and Factory,* 33:73-75 (August, 1943); Solomon Barkin, "Unions and Grievances," *Personnel Journal,* 22:38-48 (June, 1943); and J. A. Lapp, *How to Handle Labor Grievances* (Deep River, Connecticut: National Foremen's Institute, 1945), Chapter 3.

14 See Chapter 10 for detailed treatment of job specifications, and Chapter 19 for the analysis of rules and their enforcement.

15 This is illustrated, for example, in the analysis of the railroad industry by J. J. Kaufman, "Grievance Procedures under the Railway Labor Act," *Southern Economic Journal,* 19:66-78 (July, 1952).

16 Cf. B. B. Gardner, *Human Relations in Industry* (Chicago: R. D. Irwin, Inc., 1944), Chapter 7.

17 Lapp, *How to Handle Labor Grievances,* p. 24. In Robert Dubin, *Working Union-Management Relations* (Englewood Cliffs, N.J.: Prentice-Hall, Inc., 1958) collective bargaining is analyzed in detail, including the role of the grievance procedure in it. In this present volume the emphasis is on the grievance procedure's relations to getting work done and "handling" employee discontents. Here we are concerned with the consequences of the grievance procedure in minimizing disruptive consequences of discontent for production.

18 *Handling Shop Grievances* (Pittsburgh: Steel Workers Organizing Committee, n.d.), p. 23. It is interesting to note that this was the first publication of the SWOC, the union group out of which came the present United Steelworkers of America. This suggests the importance, to union functioning and growth, of grievance procedures.

19 *Ibid.*

20 Lapp, *op. cit.*, pp. 13-15, presents the historical materials summarized in this paragraph.

21 See: H. A. Millis and R. E. Montgomery, *Organized Labor* (New York: McGraw-Hill Book Co., 1945).

22 We will point out later that individuals and the union as a whole use the grievance procedure. The union may use the grievance machinery as a device to extend collective bargaining beyond the usual negotiating period. It is one of the latent functions of the grievance machinery to permit covert bargaining. At the same time, the union may have a general interest to protect in a given grievance. When it does and actually uses the grievance procedure rather than direct economic pressure, it is conserving its power for use during negotiations.

23 Often management plays the role of prosecutor as well. The prosecutor role is evident in discipline cases where management applies punishment against an employee, and supports the discipline by arguments through each step of the grievance procedure, if the worker appeals the punitive action against him. Management always judges the grievance except where a third party, an arbitrator or umpire, is designated the court of last appeal.

24 Cf. L. Hill and C. H. Hook, *Management at the Bargaining Table* (New York: McGraw-Hill Book Co., 1946), *passim.*

25 For a good discussion of this see W. E. Simkin and Van Dusen Kennedy, *Arbitration of Grievances,*

NOTES FOR CHAPTER 17 (CONT.)

Bulletin No. 82, U. S. Department of Labor, Division of Labor Standards (Washington: Government Printing Office, 1946).

26 For example, the 1946 agreement between the General Motors Corporation and the United Automobile Workers, providing for a permanent arbitrator (umpire), was printed in large page format and ran 112 pages. The agreement between the Studebaker Corporation and the same union, with no permanent arbitrator culminating the grievance procedure was printed in 36 pages, smaller in size than the GM agreement.

27 President's National Labor Management Conference, Committee on Management's Right to Manage, *Report of the Labor Members,* Doc. No. 120, November 28, 1945 (Washington: Government Printing Office, 1945), p. 1.

28 *Ibid., Report of the Management Members,* Doc. No. 125, November 25, 1945 (Washington: Government Printing Office, 1945), p. 1.

29 National War Labor Board, Wage Stabilization Division, "Grievance Procedure Problems," Research and Statistics Report, No. 26, mimeographed (1944), p. 6.

30 Selekman, "Handling Shop Grievances," especially p. 470.

31 *Ibid.,* p. 475.

32 Cf. N. W. Chamberlain, "Grievance Proceedings and Collective Bargaining," in R. A. Lester and Joseph Shister, *Insights into Labor Issues* (New York: The Macmillan Company, 1948), pp. 62-86.

33 See Sid Lens, "Meaning of the Grievance Procedure," *Harvard Business Review,* 26:713-722 (November, 1948).

34 Melville Dalton, "Unofficial Union-Management Relations," *American Sociological Review,* 15:611-619 (October, 1950).

35 Harold Davey, *Contemporary Collective Bargaining* (Englewood Cliffs, N.J.: Prentice-Hall, Inc., 1951), p. 283.

36 Bernard Karsh, "The Grievance Process in Union-Management Relations," Department of Sociology, University of Chicago, Masters Thesis (1950), pp. 134-138.

37 Van Dusen Kennedy, "Grievance Negotiation," in Arthur Kornhauser, Robert Dubin, and Arthur Ross (eds.), *Industrial Conflict* (New York: McGraw-Hill Book Co., 1954), Chapter 21.

38 Robert Dubin, "The Grievance Process—A Study of Union-Management Relations," Ph.D. Dissertation, Department of Sociology, University of Chicago (1947.)

39 Remembering that management is the judge in grievance decisions, this result accords with expectations.

40 A good description of such a program for civilian employees of the Navy Department is contained in E. B. Strong, "Individual Adjustment in Industrial Society," *American Sociological Review,* 14:335-346 (June, 1949).

41 An excellent summary of this field is contained in Nathaniel Cantor, *Employee Counseling* (New York: McGraw-Hill Book Co., 1945).

42 That the original intent of the counseling program at Western Electric was modified by unanticipated consequences is revealed in J. L. and H. L. Wilensky, "Personnel Counseling: The Hawthorne Case," *American Journal of Sociology,* 57:265-280 (November, 1951).

43 Roethlisberger and Dickson, *Management and the Worker,* pp. 227-228.

44 An interesting problem of health is that of alcoholism. Some companies have attempted rehabilitation of alcoholics among employees. A report of the efforts of the Consolidated Edison Company of New York is contained in S. C. Franco, "Problem Drinking and Industry: Policies and Procedure," *Quarterly Journal for the Study of Alcoholism,* 15:453-468 (September, 1954). For a general discussion of industrial health programs see M. C. Klem, M. F. McKiever, and W. J. Lear, *Industrial Health and Medical Programs,* United States Public Health Service, Publication No. 15 (Washington: Government Printing Office, 1950).

45 Cf. Harriet Herring, *Welfare Work in Mill Villages* (Chapel Hill: University of North Carolina Press, 1929). The "welfare capitalism" of the first three decades of this century centered on intervening in the lives of workers away from the plant on the asumption that management knew best how to manage the firm as well as the lives of its employees.

46 National CIO War Relief Committee, "Minutes of the Union Counseling Institute," July 27-29, mimeographed (1945), p. 19. Some unions, like the Amalgamated Clothing Workers and the United Mine Workers, have a long history of union-sponsored services for members. A crowning achievement of the long-time regime of John L. Lewis as President of the Mine Workers is the establishment of a chain of hospitals throughout the coal regions to serve miners and their families.

Part V

MANAGEMENT OF WORK ORGANIZATIONS

The telephones in use, the stacks of paper, and the moving lips tell at a glance the pervasive feature of communication in work organizations. This is a picture of a public relations department, whose very specialization gives emphasis to the communication networks tying a work organization to the world around it.

Chapter **18**

COMMUNICATION AND WORK

All cooperative human activity takes place within a matrix of communication. Where two or more people work together, communication serves to unify their behavior, and provides means for continuing cooperative activity. Communication is a fundamental process in all social groups and in all group behavior.[1]

Communication becomes a central process in work organizations for a number of reasons. The highly intricate nature of the cooperative processes of business requires extensive communication for orienting and indoctrinating new people into the firm. Communication is involved in giving direction to work activities, and for coordinating the diverse activities of the people involved. The business firm is constantly confronted with changes in its environment that necessitate corresponding changes in the organization and its operation.[2] In order that the changes may be carried out effectively, it is necessary that extensive communication take place among the people of the organization. Much of the management environment in a business firm consists of communications of some sort from points in the organization.[3]

In general, it can be suggested that communication is like the impulses that travel along the nervous system of an organism. These impulses carry the signals from one portion of the complex system to another and to a central coordinating agency through which the entire system is kept in balance and functioning.[4]

Communication is a process of exchanging significant symbols. What passes between two persons when they are in communication with each other is a set of significant symbols that are interpreted similarly by both. The significant symbols, when assembled together, are normally called a language. However, we have to interpret "language" broadly for it includes all forms of significant exchange of symbols, not merely verbal or written forms.[5]

It is important to know that significant symbols can be expressed in any form. A word, a gesture, even a look in the eye may constitute significant symbols that are appropriate to the circumstance of their expression. The hooker who attaches the crane hook to a load is in significant communication with the overhead crane operator through hand signals clearly indicating what the operator is to do in positioning the hook and manipulating the load. The boss who breezes through an office and deliberately avoids acknowledging the presence of one of his subordinates is significantly communicating his displeasure with that subordinate by the very act of ignoring him. This same boss may, at a later date, deal with the subordinate in quite other terms by calling him into his office and giving him a severe dressing down in choice and expressive language. Still another time the boss may communicate with his hapless subordinate through the medium of a long, involved, formal memorandum that has been dictated to a secretary and transmitted in writing.

The actual process of communication is unlimited with respect to its means. The only requirement that any means of interchange has to meet in order to be communication is that there be a meaningful exchange of symbols between the communicators.

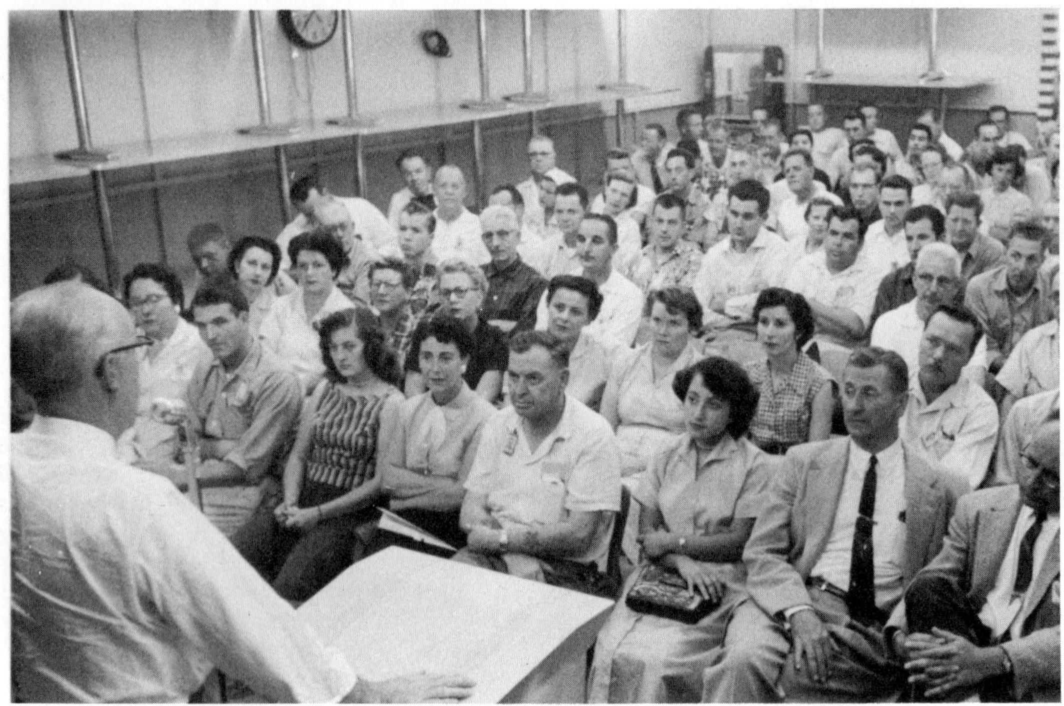

Orientation and indoctrination may be continuous in smaller organizations. In this company, periodic meetings are held at which top executives discuss company problems before the assembled employees.

FUNCTIONS OF COMMUNICATION

We will examine four broad functions of communication in work organizations: the functions of communication (A) in orienting and indoctrinating new members of an organization; (B) in directing and commanding members of the organization; (C) in coordinating diverse activities in the organization; and (D) in non-formal and informal interaction.

It will be noted that the first three functions of communication deal with aspects of the organization's operations. The last function of communication relates persons to each other at work.[6]

ORIENTATION AND INDOCTRINATION

The central purpose in orienting and indoctrinating the new member of the organization is one of communicating to him the expectations he faces in fulfilling his role as a member of the organization. Fundamental to this socializing process is communication of information to the new organization recruit.

Orientation and indoctrination of the new member are essentially processes of acculturation. He has to learn ways of behaving, a set of standards and expectations, and a point of view and outlook, largely foreign to him in their specific details, although he may be generally familiar with them in their broad outline. A great deal of the new employee's time may be spent during his early weeks and months of employment simply becoming adjusted to the organization.

The adjustment process first involves becoming familiar with the language and its significant symbols that are used in the organization. In order for the new individual to understand how the organization operates and his roles in it, he has to understand the language by which communication is carried out. Accordingly at the initial stage of orientation and indoctrination, a great deal of attention is paid, both by the new member and by those who are teaching him, to learning a vocabulary and a set of symbols that communicate significantly. In order to maximize understanding of what goes on, the new recruit has to become fairly familiar with the language of the organization.

At another level of behavior, as the individual becomes part of a work group, a whole new language may have to be learned in addition to the organizational language. The subtle and special meaning that individual words and phrases may take on in the work group is an important part of the orientation and indoctrination that the new individual faces in being incorporated in it. He becomes a full fledged member when he is able to talk the language of the group and to understand the meaning of the subtle phrases, words, and gestures used in the language of the group.

In general, orientation and indoctrination functions of communication serve to provide new individuals with a means of understanding the operating environment of the organization. They learn to know what working colleagues are saying when they are communicating with them.

Orientation and indoctrination may be spread over a long period of time. When the new individual comes into the organization, he may be confronted with only special situations and limited aspects of the organization until he has learned the tasks he is to perform. At some later time, and often only on very special occasions, is he likely to learn more about the unusual and infrequently used aspects of language. The period of learning, therefore, may be prolonged.

For the new member of the organization, there are a variety of ways in which the same instructions may be given. For example, a secretary might be instructed by her boss always to find out who is calling before putting the caller on the telephone line to the boss. In the absence of such instruction, the new secretary may answer the phone the first several times, buzzing her boss and telling him he has a phone call. If he first asks who is calling, the secretary soon learns that she is expected to inquire the caller's name. There is obviously quite a difference between telling the secretary to do this and indicating to her indirectly that it is expected, even though both approaches come to the same end.

It is contended by some who have studied this problem, that different modes of communication can produce varying results even though the functional goal of each type of communication is the same.[7] Thus, a great deal of attention has been paid to methods of indirection with subordinates that are designed to enhance their future cooperative response to command. The mere change in language and in symbols is often alleged to be the basis on which improved cooperation is achieved. From a functional standpoint, however, this assumes that subordinates are too stupid to recognize that the purpose of indirection is to secure the same behavior that the direct command sought. There is certainly no evidence to support the conclusion that the functional equivalence of direct and indirect approaches is not noted and observed by subordinates, and objected to on grounds that it is not legitimate for a supervisor to mask his purposes in relation to subordinates.

COMMAND AND DIRECTION

The circumstances for issuing commands are those in which traditional or established behavior is not automatically forthcoming. Thus, a command may be issued in order to initiate an activity or to change its direction. A command may also be issued in a situation in which subordinates are not sure about the appropriate course of action to follow. Commands may serve to train people in dealing with uncertain situations in which the present order may become precedent for future habitual behavior.[8]

The function of communication in command is, therefore, to specify expected behavior and its timing. There is an imperative quality about the command that in turn affects the language used. By and large, the the effective command is one that is unequivocal in its content. The language is likely to be direct; the symbols used in language are generally known, and the action or actions expected clearly defined.[9]

Direction and command are preeminently processes of the organization grounded in communication. Giving and receiving orders are an inevitable aspect of every organized activity involving the exercise of authority.

COORDINATION OF ACTIVITIES

Communication that relates to coordination of activities can be complicated by the fact that the activities may be diverse in character. Accordingly, those who are coordinated may think in special terms with special lingoes, and have great difficulty communicating across activity lines.

In order to make himself clear to all the people involved, the coordinator of diverse activities has to have knowledge of the special symbols and language of the activities he is coordinating, as well as of language that can bridge the differences and reach all people in uniform terms. A good deal of confusion often arises through the failure of the coordinator to use language that can produce the same results through uniform interpretation of the symbols involved.

NON-FORMAL AND INFORMAL INTERACTION

Every group situation has its purely social aspects. The circumstance of two people being thrown together is usually the occasion for small talk and communication about a variety of related and unrelated topics.

The function of this communication is to establish a basis for interaction between two persons. The interaction is meaningful because the two people can understand each other. The content of the interaction may be totally unrelated to the circumstances of their being together. Seat mates on a street car may talk about the weather, which is scarcely related to the fact that they are simultaneous occupants of the street car. Yet, as total strangers they prefer to talk to each other rather than to sit in uncomfortable silence side by side rubbing elbows. The sociability of man, everywhere evident, depends on communication.

Work organizations, as we have already seen, are composed of many people thrown together while working. Their sociable interaction requires communication through a commonly understood language. This common language makes sociable interaction possible and is often important in getting work done.

FORMS OF COMMUNICATION

We can readily distinguish three forms of communication: oral communication, written communication, and gestural communication. In general, we say that any kind of meaningful symbolism represents a form of communication. The wave of a hand or the look in the eye, just as much as the written or spoken word, can be a meaningful communication. Gestures often constitute a very important aspect of the spoken word. With the written word, "reading between the lines" is a meaningful aspect of the intended communication.

We can generally distinguish among these three forms of communication, not only in terms of their distinctive origin, but also in terms of the occasions for their use. Written communication is typically reserved for occasions where some degree of performance is desired in the communication. Written communication is also used where the communicator is separated at some distance from the object of his communication, and sends it in written form to insure its transmission.[10]

The use of a teletype as a form of business communication whereby a central office can send telegram-like messages directly to branch offices or scattered plants is an interesting case of written communication. It is obvious that the system of communication could be maintained by voice, through the telephone. Apparently, writing the message is more likely to insure its delivery and comprehension because it is a permanent record that can be retained as long as it is useful. Furthermore, messages are transmitted exactly as they were sent and, therefore, there can be no question that the words intended by the sender actually reached the receiver.

Oral communication takes place where speed is essential, where indeterminacy exists about the content of communication and it is necessary to "talk it over" before commitments are made, where trivia or non-essential content is exchanged, or where the "true" meaning depends on accompanying modes of expression and nuances of speech. Talking is the most common mode of communication. Unless there is good reason to substitute written communication for it, verbal communication is the central means for getting work done, and interacting with fellow men while doing it.

Gestural communication is perhaps the most limited form of communication. Its sometimes subtle character often means that the audience is limited, and has to be exceptionally alert even to catch the communication. Indeed, unless the communicator is carefully watched, the audience may not catch the wink which gives a special meaning to the words he is uttering. There is generally an immediacy about gestural communication.

CHANNELS OF COMMUNICATION

Official communication in the organization generally follows the flow of organization authority.[11] Command and coordination flow downward through channels of authority. Coordination also requires that there be considerable horizontal communication among the departments whose activities interlock. Formal control of organization behavior necessitates a two-way flow of standards and expectations downward, and reports of actual operations upward, through the authority structure.

UPWARD COMMUNICATION

Much has been made in the literature on organization communication about the need for channels upward from the rank-and-file. It is often vigorously argued that top management is isolated, because of poor upward communication, from what really goes on in the organization.[12] Solutions suggested include the "open door" policy of urging employees to "pop in any time," suggestion systems, and surveys of employee attitudes. These methods do serve to increase the flow of information to top management.[13]

What is not always entirely clear is why top management wants more information in the first place. There can be two general motives. Top management may be concerned with constant innovation looking toward improvement, and will want all relevant information that will make innovations most effective. Operating on this motive, management is justified in seeking the most imaginative ways for increasing the upward flow of information.[14]

The second motive for increasing upward communication is based on vanity. Some authority holders constantly seek approval of subordinates. Sometimes there is insufficient evidence that such approval exists. Efforts may be made to increase communication upward with the hope that the boss will be made to look good, or at least feel good. The boss wants yes men, and his subordinates obligingly polish the apple.

In a later section dealing with subordination we point out that the boss is very likely to hear what he wants to hear without formal action to increase upward communication. Where the desire to improve is the motive for enhancing the upward flow of communication, it is often difficult to separate the honest reaction of subordinates from their responses in terms of what they think top management wants to hear. For that reason it is desirable to gather information at points of critical behavior. For example, exit interviews with employees leaving the company can often be exceedingly enlightening about what is really going on, since the departing employee no longer cares about making an impression on the boss. A careful analysis of grievances often conveys important information to management about what is really happening.

THE GRAPEVINE

The chains of friendship and casual associations in work organizations are the communication channels through which flows the daily gossip. This is usually called the grapevine. The grapevine supplements formal channels of communication by carrying the information no one had thought to transmit formally, or which cannot really pass through formal channels.[15] The grapevine also carries the personal impressions and reactions of each gossip on the party line. The grapevine can be exceedingly fast in spreading information; it can also be inaccurate about what moves along its channels.[16]

The grapevine, like social groups at work, is a natural phenomenon of organization. It can never be eliminated. Seldom can it be controlled or systematically used. Sometimes official communications have to confront the grapevine in order to correct inaccuracies carried by it. Generally, however, informal communication is ephemeral and requires only time to lose its currency and interest.[17]

Some employees become central transmitters on the grapevine. They are the people consulted when it is desired to know "what is really going on." It is difficult to determine how much the reputation of grapevine "stars" is based on accuracy of their information, and how much on their imaginative style or on the sheer volume of their output.

LANGUAGE OF COMMUNICATION

The meanings attaching to symbols of communication are a consequence of social experience.[18] A particular word, phrase, or even an entire idea may have special meaning because of the particular interpretation given to it in a limited social setting.

LANGUAGE AND SOCIAL BACKGROUND

If the general social background of management men and the rank and file of an organization were more or less identical, there would be fewer barriers to communication between them. However, the social experience of these two classes of people tend to be quite distinct and different.[19] As a consequence, the kinds of symbols and language used by management may differ markedly from those used by the rank and file of the organization. Furthermore, the same symbols may have different meanings in the two classes of people. The use of a particular word or phrase by management with one intended interpretation may be accompanied by quite a different interpretation among employees.[20]

A great deal of effort management spends on training its younger talent is concerned with developing a language, a set of symbols, and a means of expression typically managerial in its style and content. Indeed, it can be suggested that when management talks about developing a "management outlook" on the part of its promising young men or its newly elevated supervisors, attention is being focused on the symbols to use, and the language to develop, in communicating management ideas, orders, and commands.[21]

Difficulties encountered in rising from the ranks into management are often difficulties of vocabulary and language. Men out of the ranks usually lack the vocabulary and general elegance of language, together with the symbolic meanings attached to words, that are ordinarily found among those in management. Where an individual rises from the ranks into a managerial position he may sense his language difficulties. The result is often a slavish imitation of someone in management, chosen as an example of the perfect management person.

The college graduate typically has a distinct advantage in entering management because of his larger vocabulary already oriented towards the symbolic meanings used by management. It is one function of college education to provide this vocabulary and to cast it into such forms as are most compatible with the symbols of management.

It has often been noted that differences in social background may constitute important barriers to effective communication within work organizations.[22] Management finds it difficult to talk in the language of the worker. The worker finds it equally difficult to convey his thoughts in such a way that they can be understood by management.

This has given rise to a number of attempts by communication specialists to convert management ideas into the language of the masses. These attempts invariably take the form of reducing ideas and language to their bare minimum, often presenting them in comic books, or other formats at a similar level. Whether these attempts at simplifying and reducing the level of language are effective remains to be seen. It is certainly true that the balance sheet in the annual statement of a company can be simplified. It is also true that many basic management notions can be presented in comic book form. The work of Rudolph Flesch and others in the same field has been important in pointing out the need for clarification in communication.[23] However, there is some real question as to whether or not comic books are really the natural medium of workers.[24]

It seems reasonably clear, then, that there is a correlation between the class structure of a society and the language used by the several classes.[25] Where the classes are mixed in staffing an organization, the differences in language that are represented by the mixture may constitute important obstacles to effective communication.[26]

The occupational argot of some experts can become exceedingly esoteric. Three development engineers discussing a technical problem.

OCCUPATIONAL ARGOTS

It is one of the characteristic features of distinctive occupations that they develop specialized languages peculiar to the occupations. Special words and phrases come into use in the occupation that are largely unknown to outsiders. We can see the occupational argot characteristically in the professions where the language is highly specialized, and the terms are entirely for communication among experts, not between experts and laymen.

Occupational argots have been noted in most of the traditional occupations in our society and have been catalogued for the professional thief, the railroader, and other occupations.[27]

An occupational argot serves to identify the member of the occupation and to distinguish him from those outside the occupation. Furthermore, it serves to protect the occupation from the intrusion of the outsider. An outsider readily betrays himself by his failure to use the right language at the right time. The occupational argot is an important protective device whereby the occupation is kept relatively free from invasion by outsiders.[28]

From the standpoint of the apprentice, an important part of learning his occupation is to learn its specialized language. He may accomplish this as a result of formal schooling. In many trades and professions, acquisition of a new vocabulary specialized to the occupation is a feature of on-the-job experience.

Occupational argots may constitute particular problems in the communication that goes on between occupations, and from management to specialized occupations within a work organization. It may often be necessary to translate management directives and orders into language that is more compatible with the particular occupational argot of special groups within the enterprise. Correspondingly, it may be necessary for the spokesman of specialists to be interpreters of their occupational language to management, and to those in other specialties.

STYLISTIC ASPECTS OF INDUSTRIAL LANGUAGE

Occupational argots serve to distinguish particular occupations and identify those within them as separate from those who are not. Stylistic aspects of industrial language tend to identify those who are part of an industry, and distinguish them from those who are outside that industry. Thus, the stylistic aspects of industrial language tend to cut across all of an industry and to serve as a bond that unites those who work in it. Identification with the industry is determined by the language used that is stylistically peculiar to that particular industry. Failure to use the language clearly identifies strangers to the industry.

Variations in industrial language style tend to be less extreme in language content than occupational argots. Occupational argots are typically full of invented words or highly specialized interpretations of old words. Stylistic aspects of the language of an industry are likely to be less distinctive in character.

COMMUNICATION AND LEARNING

There are a number of different theories of learning, basic to all of which is the communication process. It is not our purpose here to evaluate various learning theories, but we are concerned with understanding the role that communication plays in learning.

The thing to be learned is always symbolically meaningful to the learner. It would be impossible to learn something which did not have meaning in some way or other to the individual. This meaning may be deep and extensive or it may be superficial and more or less irrelevant to the learning process. Thus, learning to respond in a loving fashion to another human being may involve not only an intellectual comprehension of a love relationship but also an accompanying and fortifying emotional state. On the other hand, learning a set of nonsense syllables to be able to repeat them from memory, may entail only recognition of the fact that the nonsense syllables are composed of understandable letters put together in nonsensical combinations.

We can then see that symbols enter into the learning process either as stimuli or as content; they must always be meaningful and, hence, communicable, in order that learning may occur.

JOB TRAINING

All training programs of a formal or informal character, designed to prepare an individual better for a task, are based on communication. The training may be highly formalized in a classroom session, or contained in written material. It may be relatively informal, involving largely on-the-job participation and observation.

It should be noted that there are different kinds of learning that take place using different methods of communication. Written communication is likely to cover the most general and rigid portions of the material to be learned. This written material may apply generally to all learners and tends to cover a specific situation with little variation.

The kind of learning resulting from verbal communication is likely to be specialized to the individual. It may involve small details that do not warrant permanent recording in writing. Verbal communication may aid learning by transmitting attitudes and points of view, or by elaborating and interpreting specific points. Verbal communication may also be used to correct individual errors and instruct a new person about his particular skill needs.

The most subtle form of learning about industrial behavior takes place through gestural communication. Here the learner comes to observe minor variations in behavior of the trainer, who very often is not really aware of the extent to which he is influencing the learner by the cues that his physical behavior provides. By and large, gestural communication involves the semi-conscious or implicit attitudes and values that surround an area of learning.

In the typical learning situation, the three basic forms of communication are used. Since each form of communication has a somewhat different relationship to the learning process, it is not always certain that different forms of communication will be reinforcing. Indeed, they may tend to negate each other. For example, the gestures or the look in the eye of the instructor may make it clear that he does not believe the things he is attempting to teach. In such an instance, the cue that the instructor gives will obviously override the expectation that the spoken or written word attempts to achieve in the learner.

JOB ORIENTATION

Orientation and indoctrination are essentially concerned with achieving relative adjustment of the new individual to the organization. There is a minimum amount the new member must be told about his place in it and the kinds of expectations that play on him in filling this place. Furthermore, he has to be informed about the rewards he will receive for doing his job, and the limitations that surround appropriate behavior for him.

The content of orientation and indoctrination is relatively rigid and invariant. The individual learns about the organization and the general rules governing behavior in it. This can readily be incorporated in a manual or booklet.[29] With respect to a specific job, orientation takes place through the use of job descriptions and operating procedures, specifying in exact detail, and invariant order, the activities by which tasks are performed.

Indoctrination and orientation give the individual a fairly rigid framework within which he sees himself as an operating member of the organization. Consequently, the kind of communication in orientation and indoctrination tends to be rigid, invariant, specific, and stable. A great share of orientation can be accomplished through written communication. In some instances this may be supplemented by other visual forms of communication, such as slides and moving pictures.

DISCIPLINE

We can consider discipline as established learning. From this standpoint discipline represents a learned response that is made with little variation in the face of the appropriate stimulus. A great deal of communication in orientation and indoctrination is designed to condition the individual to invariant responses under appropriate circumstances. We can see this most obviously in military organizations where a great deal of the initial basic training involves establishing a disciplined series of responses to appropriate military situations.

Since the nature of discipline is to inculcate and establish a response that has a very narrow range of variation, the communication devices used are typically rigid and subject to little personal interpretation. Indeed, it might be argued that the effectiveness of discipline is partly a consequence of the rigidity of the communications that establish it. The catechism of the church, the close-order drill of the soldier, and the continuous performance of a repetitive task by an industrial worker all fortify the individual's discipline through a system of repetitive and invarying communication.

The kinds of communication that satisfy the functions of orientation and indoctrination tend to be fixed, objective, and rigid in character.

COMMUNICATION AND COMMAND

In order to analyze command communications, it is necessary to describe the circumstances in which command is displayed. Command is exercised in situations in which there is a question of changing operations, or in which there is a question of alternatives in operations. In both instances, a function of command is to keep an operation going in case it threatens to stop. Knowing this function of command, we can understand the special characteristics of communications used in commanding.[30]

A command exhibits the following characteristics: (A) it specifies the situation of action completely and unequivocally, (B) it describes the actions necessary in the particular situation, and (C) it designates the beginning and end of the required action, together with its timing.

DEFINING THE SITUATION

A command applying to a situation requires adequate definition of the situation. Accordingly, a command may be issued with a complete description of the situation to which it applies. Alternatively, a command may be issued under circumstances where the situation itself is obvious to all concerned. The command then may ignore the description of the situation because it is issued in the midst of it. Nevertheless, the description of the situation, or its acknowledgment, is a necessary part of every command.

A command always has an explicit and obvious reality orientation. It is oriented to some specific operating situation or reality in the life of the organization. The command, therefore, may not only have to specify the situation to which it applies, but it also may have to delineate the boundaries between that situation and others. Usually this separation of different situations of command is implicit. Under some circumstances it may have to be made explicit.

SPECIFYING BEHAVIOR

The second feature of a command is that it describes the response or behavior those commanded are to exhibit in the specified situation.[31] The command is specific and concrete as to expected behavior. There is typically no choice presented to the subordinate about his expected behavior.

A command is issued on the assumption that the behavior is known, and will be forthcoming without any question. Thus, the specification of behavior for subordinates has the particular characteristic that it is unitary and not a series of alternatives. Subordinates are not given an opportunity to choose among several possibilities. They are told to do something which is either set forth specifically, or so well known that it can be designated by a key descriptive word or phrase.

It is clear that commands, requiring fixed responses, depend on a high degree of discipline among subordinates. Thus, the effectiveness of command, or the effectiveness of authority, is dependent on inculcating discipline in the organization so that commands will be obeyed when issued. [32]

TIMING BEHAVIOR

The third feature of a command rests on the limited time span it covers. The command usually specifies a beginning and an end for the action, and often a timing of the action commanded, as well. These are important characteristics of every command. Failure to establish the limits within which the command is operative and, therefore, the time during which the commanded behavior will continue, leads to inappropriate behavior by subordinates who continue to carry out a command that is no longer applicable.

STANDING ORDERS

There are special kinds of commands that may be incorporated in standing orders. In the military context these may be designated as standing operating procedures, for which there are industrial counterparts.

Standing orders can be effective as commands in those situations in which there are relatively frequent recurrences of circumtances requiring direction. Furthermore, the situations are fairly standard and of uniform characteristics. Accordingly, it may be possible for the authority holder to establish a permanent order or directive covering such a situation and have it known well in advance to all those who would be affected by it. When that situation occurs, the standing order is automatically operative. At the end of the situation the standing order is automatically inoperative. It is one of the problems of executives to be able to distinguish the situations in which *ad hoc* commands are to be used from situations in which standing orders are applicable.

The language of command tends to be highly precise, relatively impersonal, and effectively descriptive. Furthermore, it tends to be concise in its expression, and the symbols in which it is couched tend to be uniquely appropriate to the organization.

LANGUAGE OF SUBORDINATION

There is an obvious language used by subordinates in communicating with their organization superiors. This language of subordination is one of the most visible aspects of authority and status relations in work organizations. "Sir" and "Mister" are common parts of subordinates' language. Equally common are the attitudes of "speaking only when spoken to," and posture of rapt attention to the boss' words. Still obvious, but at a gestural level, are head nodding in automatic agreement, tensed bodily positions indicating obeisance, rising from a seat when the boss enters, or ceremonially following him in walking.

All status relations and all authority relations involve two-way communication of status differences or differential authority level. The high status person reveals, in his mode of communication, his superior position when communicating with a lower status individual. At the same time, the status difference is reinforced by the lower status person confirming his lower position when responding to the person of higher status. Similarly, differences in authority level are sustained by the reciprocal confirmation of their relative positions through the languages of superior and subordinate.

A particular aspect of the language of subordination is the subordinate's anticipation of what is required or wanted by the superior. The superior has expectations for the organization and his subordinates; these may cover attitudes, behavior, the outcome of plans, or even the spirit and atmosphere of the organization. Subordinates, knowing these expectations, find ways to tell the boss they are being met. If the superior expects cooperation, he hears his subordinates talk to him in terms of cooperation; if harmony is one of his goals, reports and communications to him stress harmony; if working hard is a precept, then subordinates make sure to communicate their hard-working efforts to the boss.

The superior tends to be engulfed in communications that make him "look good," and give the impression that things are going according to expectations. This aspect of the language of subordination is an important part of the isolation of the executive.[33] The executive, so long as his effective operations depend on communications flowing to him, is a partial prisoner of the communication network. Subordinates can color information reaching the boss, or even keep things from him. They can give the boss a false impression about what is happening in the organization.

The executive can suffer in the effectiveness with which he does his job by isolation from the reality of his organization.

There is a subtle line distinguishing the language of subordination from the language of insubordination. A slight exaggeration in the language of subordination may be enough to make the communication an act of effective insubordination. Too many "Yes, Sir's" or too obvious obeisance may, in fact, be actually disrespectful in intent. Sarcasm is an effective weapon of insubordination.

At the other extreme, what appears to be insubordinate language may be intended as genuine expressions of subordination. "That S.O.B." or "Old Stinky" may actually be words of respect for the boss in some reaches of the industrial world.

The fine line in communicating, between the languages of subordination and insubordination, underscores again the subtlety of human interaction. Language is a medium of interaction. Its fine shades of meanings and significant symbolism are more than adequate to cover the full range of human sentiments. At work, as in all social relations, the attentive ear can find these subtle meanings that denote subordination and insubordination.

COMMUNICATION AND COORDINATION

Coordinating activities requires a special content to communication. There is generally involved in coordination a need for comprehending diverse languages, and then translating the coordinating activities into common language comprehensible to all the specialists involved.

The coordinator has to have considerable knowledge of the diverse occupational argots used by those whose activities he is coordinating. He may achieve this by having a specialist in each field as a translator from the special language to a more general language, or he may himself be the translator able to take the special languages and make general sense out of them.[34]

Out of this need for understanding special occupational argots arises the tendency for the coordinator to be particularly critical about communications coming to him from specialized areas. The coordinator raises questions about the meaning, intent, and purpose

A remarkable amount of coordination of activities is achieved in conferences and small working groups where talking is the major form of interaction. Here production men and engineers are conferring on a proposed production line layout. The lone man at the left almost seems to bend his ear to catch a word from either of the two groups conferring. Perhaps he is just lonesome and feels left out of things because nobody is talking to him.

of proposals, ideas, suggestions, and plans that come from specialized areas of the organization. The language of the coordinator in securing his information is, therefore, of a questioning, critical character. His questions are designed to maximize the amount of useful knowledge that can be secured from each specialized area of operations. There may be no limit on the range of questions asked to clarify information flowing to the coordinator.[35]

When the coordinator, in turn, issues his commands for coordination, his language tends to be universal enough to be understood by all specialists involved. This language may contain many stylistic aspects of the industry, but it is likely to have a minimum amount of the occupational argot of departments whose activities are being coordinated.

From the standpoint of content rather than language form, there is heavy emphasis in coordinating communications on the interrelations among separate activities. This may take the form of delegating responsibilities to special departments. It may take the form of commanding that certain kinds of joint activities be carried on, or that activities proceed in serial order. Coordinating commands usually include directions as to the flow of ideas, the flow of work, or the flow of responsibility.

COMMUNICATION AND INTERACTION

Both spoken and written communication automatically command attention. The spoken word has the privilege of being heard uninterrupted. The written word also draws attention insofar as it is read at all.

Informal relations fundamentally change the position of the communicator and his subject. The subject must now be attentive and seek out appropriate interpretations, rather than expect the speaker to make these interpretations clear and unequivocal. There may be very much more subtle communication taking place through gesture or through special meaning attached to words and phrases. It is the hearer's responsibility to pay attention to these subtle aspects of communication and try to fathom their meanings and implications.[36]

GROUP BELONGING

In the communication that takes place in social groups at work, responsibility rests with the newcomer to demonstrate language behavior appropriate to acceptance as a member. The group may not be at all concerned about whether the newcomer achieves membership in it. He has to prove his readiness to be accepted as a peer with the privileges of equal association in the group.[37]

The judgments made as to the readiness of an individual to be accepted in the group depend partly on the propriety of his own communications. The newcomer learns to use appropriate phrases, to pronounce words in special ways, and to avoid inappropriate words, phrases, and general language.

The level of sensitivity is raised on both sides in this game of fraternization. The newcomer is highly sensitive to nuances of the new situation about which he is learning. The old members of the group are equally sensitive to the failures of the newcomer to learn the style and proper forms of group communication. The phenomenon of hazing takes place as much at the verbal level and at the level of communication as it does at a physical level in the process of introducing a newcomer into an established social group.

FRATERNIZATION

When someone in a position of authority attempts to fraternize with his subordinates on an informal basis, the impropriety of the action is usually clearly evident to both parties.[38] To the subordinate, the executive may not ring true in his language usage, in the meanings that he attaches to his symbols, and in his interpretation of the language of the subordinates. The executive is probably equally aware of the inappropriateness of his discourse. Both undoubtedly become extremely uncomfortable in this artificial situation. It probably does little good for an executive to be "hail-fellow-well-met" with subordinates where there is no genuine social communication with them.[39]

This perhaps suggests why much fraternization with subordinates takes place in specific activities providing the necessary focus of attention, and also the basis for social communication. When the boss bowls with his subordinates, or plays golf with them, or engages in some other form of single-purpose behavior, the focus of attention becomes the game, or the activity on which they can center attention. Under these circumstances, fraternization may ring true, and there can well be a very effective social interaction between superior and subordinates.

SEMANTICS AND SOCIAL ACTION

It has been suggested in this chapter that the behavior of individuals and the requirements placed on them in fulfilling their positions in an organization, determine the kind of language they will use, and the content of the communications with which they will deal. In a broader sense, then, we can suggest that social action and language are interrelated.[40]

Some of the problems that arise in communication are a consequence of the failure to see the relationship between language and behavior. We suggested in this chapter that there is a distinct difference between the language used in orienting and indoctrinating new employees and the language that is typical when commands are given and coordination achieved.

We have furthermore indicated that the communication forms include behavior itself as an aspect of communication. It should be clear that the executive or commander is always in the position of telling, directing, ordering, or coordinating subordinates. His own behavior also becomes an effective form of communication. The old phrase, "Your actions speak so loud I can't hear what you say," is a significant folk description of the impact an executive can have on his subordinates.

NOTES FOR CHAPTER 18

[1] C. I. Barnard, *The Functions of the Executive* (Cambridge: Harvard University Press, 1938), has stated: "... the first executive function is to develop and maintain a system of communication," p. 226.

[2] See in this connection a fictionalized account of what happened in a company whose organization structure was inefficient, blocking effective communication John Perry and R. W. Straus, "A Story of Executive Relationships," *Harvard Business Review*, 30:53-72 (March-April, 1952).

[3] See Barnard, *op. cit.*, pp. 217-226; and Helen Baker, J. W. Ballantine, and J. M. True, *Transmitting Information Through Management and Union Channels* (Princeton: Princeton University Industrial Relations Section, 1949).

[4] It has been pointed out that communication in organizations does not require that all members be part of the main stream of communication flow. The linkage is maintained so long as each member is "... touched by some part of a network of communication which also touches each of the others at some point." H. J. Leavitt, "Some Effects of Certain Communication Patterns on Group Performance," in G. E. Swanson, Theodore Newcomb, and Eugene Hartley (eds.), *Readings in Social Psychology*, Revised Edition (New York: Henry Holt and Co., 1952), p. 445. Barnard, *op. cit.*, has made the point that the executive is the center of communication nets. See especially Chapter 15, "The Executive Functions."

[5] It has been suggested that the environment of the executive is largely that of communication, and particularly verbal communication. See F. J. Roethlisberger, *Management and Morale* (Cambridge: Harvard University Press, 1941), pp. 88-92.

[6] For a general treatment of organization communication that analyzes many more topics than those dealt with here, see R. W. Peters, *Communication within Industry* (New York: Harper & Brothers, 1949).

[7] In this conection, see especially C. I. Hovland, A. A. Lumsdaine, and F. D. Sheffield, *Experiments in Mass Communication;* Studies in Social Psychology in World War II, Vol. 3 (Princeton: Princeton University Press, 1950).

[8] An actual study of executive behavior reveals

NOTES FOR CHAPTER 18 (CONT.)

the tremendous amounts of time executives spend commanding and directing subordinates. The study is of a British factory, but the results are probably representative of most modern industrial organizations. See Tom Burns, "The Directions of Activity and Communication in a Departmental Executive Group: A Quantitative Study in a British Engineering Factory with a Self-Recorder Technique," *Human Relations,* 7:73-79 (February, 1954).

[9] Cf. M. L. Blum, *Industrial Psychology and Its Social Foundations* (New York: Harper & Brothers, 1956), pp. 206-207.

[10] There is, of course, a vast amount of communication that informs about the organization and what is happening in it. Much of this is in written form because it is the most effective and cheapest for widespread distribution. It also is meant to have relative permanence. See, for example, a discussion of company publications and magazines "How to Play the House Organ," *Fortune,* 46:144 ff (October, 1952).

[11] Cf. R. F. Bales, "Some Uniformities of Behavior in Small Social Systems," in Swanson, Newcomb, and Hartley, *Readings in Social Psychology,* Revised Edition, especially p. 155, where it is pointed out that a leadership role in a group is also a position of centrality in the communication network.

[12] Cf. S. D. Hoslett, "Barriers to Communication," *Personnel,* 28:108-114 (September, 1951).

[13] "Consultative management" is a technique for increasing the flow of information through active communication to and from subordinates or the union. See, in this connection G. S. Walpole, *Management and Men: A Study of the Theory and Practice of Joint Consultation at All Levels* (London: Jonathan Cape, 1944); H. H. Carey, "Consultative Supervision and Management," *Personnel,* 18:1-11 (January, 1942); and Robert Dubin, "Union-Management Cooperation and Productivity," *Industrial and Labor Relations Review,* 2:198-209 (January, 1949).

[14] The current management literature extols the virtues of "flattening" the hierarchy of authority in order to increase effective communication. At least one experimental study suggests, however, that some kinds of tasks require authority hierarchies and that these may not develop effectively without certain kinds of restrictions on communication. Thus, operating efficiency may actually be lost in attempting to maximize communication flow. See Harold Guetzkow and H. A. Simon, "The Impact of Certain Communication Nets upon Organization and Performance in Task-Oriented Groups," *Management Science,* 1:233-250 (April-July, 1955).

[15] Barnard, *The Functions of the Executive,* p. 225, points out that the grapevine among executives permits communication of "... intangible facts, opinions, suggestions, suspicions, that cannot pass through formal channels without raising issues calling for decisions, without dissipating dignity and objective authority . . . ."

[16] See H. A. Simon, *Administrative Behavior* (New York: The Macmillan Company, 1947), especially pp. 160-162.

[17] See Keith Davis, "Management Communication and the Grapevine," *Harvard Business Review* 31:43-49 (September-October, 1953), for a treatment of the grapevine based on a case study.

[18] An excellent treatment is contained in C. R. Rogers and F. J. Roethlisberger, "Barriers and Gateways to Communications," *Harvard Business Review,* 30:46-52 (July-August, 1952).

[19] See, in this connection, Chapters 9 and 15.

[20] This problem has been analyzed in the area of industrial relations in W. F. Whyte, "Semantics and Industrial Relations," *Human Organization,* 8:4-10 (Spring, 1949).

[21] The story of this is told with real zest and considerable irony in W. H. Whyte, Jr., *Is Anybody Listening?* (New York: Simon and Schuster, 1952).

[22] See, for example, W. W. Finlay, A. Q. Sartain, and W. M. Tate, *Human Behavior in Industry* (New York: McGraw-Hill Book Co., 1954), p. 94.

[23] Rudolph Flesch, *The Art of Plain Talk* (New York: Harper & Brothers, 1946); and *The Art of Readable Writing* (New York: Harper & Brothers, 1949).

[24] Cf. Bernard Rosenberg and D. M. White (eds.), *Mass Culture: The Popular Arts in America* (Glencoe: The Free Press, 1957), especially, pp. 187-224. In the article on "Comic Strips and Their Adult Readers," by Leo Bogart, it is suggested that they serve as a vehicle of entertainment rather than information (p. 191).

[25] Cf. Nahum Sabsay, "From the Workers' Point of View," *Harvard Business Review,* 25:339-347 (Spring, 1947).

[26] This issue is examined effectively in H. O. Ronken, "Communication in the Work Group," *Harvard Business Review,* 29:108-114 (July, 1951).

[27] See W. Fred Cottrell, *The Railroader* (Stanford: Stanford University Press, 1940).

[28] An excellent analysis of the strategems of experts to keep laymen in ignorance is contained in W. E. Moore and M. M. Tumin, "Some Social Functions of Ignorance," *American Sociological Review,* 14:787-795 (December, 1949).

[29] For example, this printed form can be used regarding the policies in industrial relations. See Helen Baker, *Company-wide Understanding of Industrial Relations Policies: A Study in Communications* (Princeton: Princeton University Industrial Relations Section, 1948).

[30] The significance of command functions in communication is illustrated with real insight in D. N. Ulrich, D. R. Booz, and P. R. Lawrence, *Management Behavior and Foreman Attitude: A Case Study* (Boston: Harvard Graduate School of Business Administration, 1950).

NOTES FOR CHAPTER 18 (CONT.)

[31] Cf. Simon, *Administrative Behavior*, pp. 71-73.

[32] This implication follows from the experimental study of communication and organization continued in Alex Bavelas and Dermot Barrett, "An Experimental Approach to Organizational Communication," *Personnel*, 27:366-371 (March, 1951).

[33] See, in this connection, "Problem for the Front Office," *Fortune*, 43:78 ff (May, 1951).

[34] This is discussed in detail in Roethlisberger, *Management and Morale*, pp. 62-63.

[35] In the special circumstance of asking how the scientist influences business decision makers to adopt technological innovations, this problem of translation from occupational argot to general language is dealt with in J. R. Gass, "The Human Element in the Application of Science," *Impact of Science on Society*, 5:93-112 (June, 1954).

[36] Barnard, The *Functions of the Executive*, p. 90, has coined a phrase, "observational feeling," to describe sensitivity to subtle communication in face-to-face relations.

[37] The process of acceptance in a voluntary social group is described with sensitivity in E. C. Hughes, "Dilemmas and Contradictions of Status," *American Journal of Sociology*, 50:353-356 (March, 1945).

[38] Cf. C. W. Lawshe, *Psychology of Industrial Relations* (New York: McGraw-Hill Book Co., 1953), p. 265.

[39] See in this connection a typical treatment of fraternization in "Getting to Know Your People," *Modern Industry*, 25:37-41 (April, 1953).

[40] It is interesting to note that with the recognition of the intimate connections between language and action, communication has become another management specialty with its own professional practitioners. It is reported that the General Electric Company has a communications department with seven staff consultants who counsel the various G.E. plant managements on their plant and community relations problems. The American Management Association has a course in executive communications that is given nine times a year. Lehigh University and the University of California give a degree course in communications for industry. See *Factory Management and Maintenance*, 62:136 (November, 1955).

The sign, permanently affixed to this 350 ton punch press used for stamping gasoline pump parts, reads: "Hazardous work—Do not talk to operator." This is one of the more obvious rules among the many found in industrial establishments.

Chapter **19**

WORK RULES AND THEIR ENFORCEMENT

In this chapter we will analyze rules governing work behavior and the methods of their enforcement. We will first examine rules and regulations governing behavior in work organizations, and then consider the enforcing devices employed in making sure that most members behave according to the rules most of the time.

WORK RULES AND REGULATIONS

The central function of rules and regulations is to provide a basis for predicting behavior. A rule supposes that a future situation will occur for which the proper responsive behavior can be established in advance. This established behavior, together with the circumstance of its occurrence is the content of the work rule.

The importance of rules as predictors of behavior cannot be overemphasized. In the industrial demands for high speed, repetitive operations, and consistency in result, regulations become all important in insuring continuity of production. Complex work can be planned in all its details if each operator's contributions to the work flow can be predicted with reasonable accuracy. When the operator has his work behavior limited by rules and regulations, he and those who direct him have a common basis for prediction of outcome.[1]

Preceding chapters of this book have laid great stress on the tremendous range and variety of constraints and restraints, of formal rules and regulations, of informal expectations and demands, that surround the performance of every work assignment.[2] A major generalization of this analysis is that these defining characteristics of work function to increase accurate predictions about work processes.

In this chapter we will analyze the features of rule-making in work organizations. Conforming to work rules is not always automatic. Rules and regulations have to be policed and enforced. We will, therefore, also turn attention to the analysis of methods for enforcing rules.

In the next two sections we will analyze functions of rules and regulations. It should be clearly recognized, however, that these are functions either secondary, or supplementary, to those of providing grounds for predicting working behavior.

AFFIRMATIVE RULES

The affirmative rules and regulations of a work organization are by far the most numerous. They cover many aspects of work behavior. They are designed to give new and old members of the organization a clear-cut statement of what is expected in their working behavior.[3]

The question might well be raised as to why it is necessary to have so many rules in an organization. It might be assumed that membership in the organization and habituation to tasks would be sufficient to teach each individual what is expected of him, and the proper methods of filling his job. Why then is it necessary to commit many of the affirmative procedures governing behavior to books of rules, or to incorporate them into directives, orders, or regulations?

We can see the need for objective rules and regulations in five developments that are typical of modern organizations. In the first place there is rather high personnel turnover in most work organizations. Consequently there are at any one time a fair number of individuals who are relatively new to the organization. Accordingly, it becomes most efficient to provide new people with written or explicit regulations governing their working behavior.

A second reason for developing regulations is the relatively high degree of internal mobility in most organizations.[4] An employee may move from one operation, or from one level of management, to another. There may be many aspects of the new job that cannot be learned in anticipation. In order to make the transition to higher, more important, or different kinds of jobs rapid and easy, it becomes desirable to make explicit the rules governing work assignments.

A third factor leading to rules and regulations is the impersonality of administration in modern work organizations. If each individual's performance is to be the basis for judging his success or failure, then it becomes necessary to provide each employee with a specific statement of organization expectations so that he may be able to conform most adequately. Consequently, to make impersonal administration effective, it is necessary to set down working expectations in concrete rules.[5]

A fourth organizational feature of regulations is that they permit managers to ignore extenuating circumstances favoring subordinates engaged in questionable or prohibited behavior. With an established set of rules, the supervisor determines whether the individual's behavior is covered by one or another class of regulations. Once having established the class of rules that applies, the supervisor then determines if its conditions have been satisfied. If the manager finds the rule broken, he may take appropriate action to secure future compliance. Thus from the standpoint of management an explicit body of rules and regulations makes the directing function more impersonal, more objective, and thereby more universally applicable.

The fifth characteristic of the "reign of rules" is that the individual worker has a sense of the generality of the work regime under which he operates. This derives from his recognition that the organization rules apply to whole classes of employees, and that authority is not exercised at the whim of a superior. The individual worker recognizes that what is expected of him is also expected of fellow workers; what he has to do, others must also. As a consequence the work regime is seen as non-discriminatory with respect to the individual.[6]

The rules and regulations of a work organization result from developments within the organization. Indeed, as we show elsewhere, much of the relationship between management and unions is concerned with elaborating systems of rules and regulations, and their objective statement and codification in a union contract.[7] Rules are characteristic features of all modern work organizations.

NEGATIVE RULES AND PROHIBITIONS

Negative rules and prohibitions governing behavior in the organization tend to be imperative and demanding. Certain kinds of behaviors are prohibited for reasons of safety and protection against physical hazards. There are other kinds of prohibitions having to do with protection of business secrets, or with honesty in handling valuable property of the organization.

Negative rules tend to be clear in establishing the standards beyond which lies prohibited activity. They are made as unequivocal as possible and are generally widely circulated and distributed throughout the organization. Furthermore, there is usually a clear statement of the consequences of failure to abide by the prohibitions.

Why is it necessary to specify for an employee both the things he should do, and the things he should not? The vast quantity of rules and regulations in any organization could lead the individual to assume that any area not covered by a regulation might be open to freely chosen action. We can perhaps liken the existence of both affirmative and negative rules to the more general moral precepts of our society. We have the golden rule, which represents an affirmative declaration of a fundamental relationship to one's fellows. But we also have the Ten Commandments, some of which are prefaced with "thou shalt not." These are the negative rules, the things that are prohibited to every moral individual.

Affirmative and negative rules are necessary in the society as a whole. They are equally necessary in work organizations. The analogy can be carried one step further. The golden rule specifies a general goal or objective but it does not set forth the procedures by which one establishes and maintains the love of his fellow men. Affirmative regulations are phrased in generalized terms. They are likely to emphasize objectives to be attained, rather than their method of attainment. On the other hand, prohibitions are specific and concrete. They say what cannot, should not, and must not be done. The Ten Commandments are unequivocal. The prohibitions that are written into the rules of an organization are equally unequivocal. A "no smoking" sign in a hazard area means no smoking for everybody, without exception, in the interest of safety.

TYPES OF RULES AND REGULATIONS

Rules and regulations govern different aspects of behavior in the organization. We will now examine these types and note the areas of behavior to which they apply.

PERSONAL CONDUCT

The most elementary and universal rules of a work organization are those governing personal conduct. These rules have their origin in the heterogeneous background of employees of modern organizations. As we have noted in Chapter 9, the American labor force is composed of people reared in widely different settings. Accordingly one expects that they bring to the organizations employing them differing standards of personal conduct. In

TABLE 19.1

NEGATIVE RULES ARE SPECIFIC, WITH CLEARLY STATED PENALTIES

Prohibited Activity	*Penalty*
Theft from fellow employees or Company	Discharge
Assault, brawling or fighting on Company property	Two weeks' layoff to discharge for men involved
Any act of threat	Two weeks' layoff to discharge
Disobedience to proper authority	One day's layoff to discharge
Working under assumed name	Subject to discharge
Possession of illegal weapons on Company property	Discharge
Malicious or careless destruction of Company property	Three days' layoff to discharge
Solicitation on Company property without permission	Reprimand to discharge
Habitual garnishments	Discharge
Careless making of unnecessary scrap (spoilage)	Reprimand to three days' layoff
Smoking where or when prohibited	Three days' layoff to discharge: reprimand to three days, first offense; two weeks, second offense; discharge, third offense
Influence of liquor	Three days' layoff to discharge
Leaving department or building during working hours without notifying foreman or reasonable excuse	Reprimand to three days' layoff
Clean-up or idling before proper time at quitting time	Reprimand to three days' layoff
Wilfully ringing clock card of another	One week's layoff to discharge
Gambling on Company property	Reprimand to two weeks' layoff, first offense; discharge, second offense
Drinking or possessing liquor on Company property	Two weeks' layoff to discharge
Engaging in carnal acts or relations with employees of opposite sex on Company property	Discharge
Constant breach of safety rules	Reprimand to discharge

This is a typical set of negative rules incorporated in a union contract in the automobile industry and reported in N. W. Chamberlain, *The Union Challenge to Management Control* (New York: Harper & Brothers, 1948), pp. 271-272. Used by permission.

order to establish some basic uniformity in the interpersonal relations among members of the organization, rules of personal conduct are set forth in its personnel policy. For example, personal tidiness varies widely. The habit of throwing refuse on the floor is common. Business firms constantly urge employees to use waste baskets, and to keep their work stations neat. Sometimes corners are painted white to discourage their use as refuse dumps, and signs posted to urge tidiness. There is a lowest common denominator of personal neatness necessary to give employees the feeling that their company is a good place to work.

There is usually little objection to rules governing personal conduct. It is seldom that a union, for example, will attempt to include these kinds of rules within the scope of collective bargaining.[8] There is recognition on the part of all concerned that some kind of code is necessary to govern interpersonal relations.

RELATIONS WITH THE WORK ORGANIZATION

The individual's relations with his employing organization is specified in a number of different categories of regulations. The most elementary of these rules sets forth the conditions of employment. When is a person an employee, and when does he cease to be an employee? The answers are, in part, a consequence of legal definitions, but are also a consequence of organizational definitions.

The general rules governing continuing membership are to be included in this area. Thus it may be necessary to establish rules for determining presence or absence from the job. Time clocks may be installed so that the ringing of the card in and out may be taken as *prima facie* evidence that the individual has been on the job for the period reported on the time card.

Health and safety rules of the organization are usually set forth in terms of affirmative and negative regulations governing individual behavior. In some industries where protection of the product is essential from a sanitary standpoint, regulations may be stringent regarding personal sanitation in handling protected products.

Still another type of regulation, dealing with the individual's relation to his work organization, concerns authority and its exercise by superiors.[9] Insubordination is usually defined. The requirement of obedience to direction by management officials is usually set forth. It is interesting to note that in this area there is a good deal of circumlocution. Ordinarily the employee is not openly directed to give complete obedience to his supervisor. Instead, certain acts are designated as acts for which severe penalties will be enforced. Rules dealing with authority are usually expressed in terms of penalties rather than affirmative descriptions of expected behavior when authority is exercised. Workers are not enjoined from punching the foreman in the nose, but physical violence is generally prohibited, on penalty of severe punishment.

Another set of rules relating individuals to their work organizations deals with rights.[10] A rule may be established covering vacations. It is declared to be a right of the individual to enjoy a vacation of a given length, after a specified number of months of service with the organization. Other rights of the individual may include his opportunity to use the company medical service, the company counseling service, the company credit union, the company recreational facilities, and the company eating facilities.

Generally, rules that express the rights of the individuals in the organization also establish limits to prevent the abuse of these rights. For example, where company medical service is provided, there may be rules specifying that the service is not available for non-work disabilities. The rules and regulations are designed to prevent exploitation of rights in an unjustified manner.

Another area of regulations and rules relating the individual to the organization deals with the individual's obligations.[11] Obligations are of a general character. However, it is interesting that many obligations set forth in regulations carry only a moral imperative for their fulfillment. There may be an implicit threat that failure to fulfill obligations can have repercussions in the individual's promotion, pay raise, or general opportunity in the organization. Usually, however, the statement of obligation does not carry with it penalties for failure to fulfill it. Thus, it may be an obligation to report, within a specified time, the nature of an absence from work. Such obligation may be honored more in the breach than the observance since failure to carry it out is seldom penalized.

Other kinds of rules specifying the general duties of each individual in the organization also have a moral imperative rather than the force of penalties behind them. There may be a regulation that employees are to report all cases of stealing. The intent is, of course, to discourage pilfering in the organization. However, there is very little opportunity to pressure people into reporting thefts. Consequently, the only force behind such a rule is the moral indignation of an individual, so outraged by the act of stealing that he will report it to the proper authority.

JOB TASKS

There are many kinds of regulations surrounding the performance of specific tasks. Often we do not recognize them as rules. They are sometimes called operating procedures, instructions, and methods. Nevertheless, it is clear that the actual task performance on the job is often clearly specified, and set forth in routine instructions. These instructions may apply to the job as it is usually performed. On the other hand, instructions may be specific to each job task. This is true for the man who works from a set of blueprints. The blueprints constitute, for him, specific instructions about what he is to do, and often how he is to do it.

It is one of the features of the specification of job tasks that we do not ordinarily think of these instructions as rules and regulations. However, they have exactly the same function as rules and are ordinarily stated in affirmative terms.

One of the sources of irritation to workers is to find that their job is so highly specified that the worker is assumed to have no initiative or skill in the performance of his tasks. Often workers react to over-specification of their tasks by finding more efficient or effective ways of using their time in performing their jobs. Rather than sharing this knowledge with management in the form of increased output, workers may often use it to their own benefit. Thus, an individual might be able to accomplish eight hours of work in six hours by virtue of short-cuts and more effective methods he has discovered. He will then use the extra two hours a day for his own purposes, either maintaining a watchful idleness or, as sometimes happens, even making things for his own use.

In general, over-specification of tasks where the workers are competent to determine many aspects of their own technical work behavior may result in turning energies of workers away from the goals of management.

FELLOW WORKERS

Organization rules deal indirectly with expected behavior towards fellow workers. Rules in this area often have a rather formal character, attempting to embody moral precepts in operating regulations. We have already noted how person-to-person relations are worked out in voluntary human associations.[12] Typically, it is not necessary for the formal organization to be either explicit or detailed in specifying relations among fellow workers. These relations are usually worked out through the social processes that take place in work groups.[13]

There are some kinds of regulations that grow up covering fellow worker relations. These are typically directed at prohibiting undesirable consequences of close associations. For example, there may be a prohibition against ringing the time card of another worker. This is intended to insure that the time card accurately reflects the actual working time of its owner. On the other hand, the conditions under which one would ring the time card of another are those of friendship, or a desire to perform a favor, or an attempt to protect the second worker from loss of time. The rule against ringing the time card of another worker operates against the social ties that grow up in a primary association. The objective of the rule is sound and equitable. It illustrates the indirect nature of the regulative process in worker-to-worker relations.

ORGANIZING AND APPLYING RULES AND REGULATIONS

It is accurate to assert that the moment a set of rules and regulations is set forth in public form it is already obsolete. This is another way of saying that modern organizations, particularly industrial and business firms, are in a state of continuous change and development; their regulations are rapidly outdated.[14]

CODIFYING RULES

It is necessary for the organization to have an established body of rules and regulations, set forth in a manner readily accessible to those affected by them. Accordingly, there is a proliferation of rule books, operating manuals, procedures manuals, directives, and instructions—all designed to make objective and concrete the rules governing behavior in the organization.

Military organization illustrates the extent to which this rule making process can be carried. Down to the company level in the Army, for example, the unit commander has available to him a printed set of major Army Regulations applying to his unit. Furthermore, he has a whole library of training manuals and operating manuals dealing with the use of equipment, and tactical and other procedures to be followed by his kind of unit. The military organization attempts to specify every possible situation, in some kind of regulatory fashion, so that even the most stupid, or the most incompetent, can be properly guided in the execution of his military tasks. Before assuming that military organizations alone emphasize rules and regulations, it should be pointed out that government bureaus, business firms, and industrial companies exhibit this same characteristic in various degrees. Today's five-foot book shelf for the typical industrial employee is a set of the company rules, regulations, operating manuals, procedures manuals, and technical data manuals —all of which have something to do with job performance, or behavior in the organization.

Dependence on explicitly stated rules and regulations creates demand for still more rules and regulations. That is, the individual supervisor and manager find that they can direct the affairs of their subordinates " by the book" rather than on the basis of their own good judgment. They increasingly turn to "the book" to seek out answers to all their supervising and managing problems.

To a central management group, the desire for uniformity in executing work may be a paralleling pressure towards establishing and codifying rules and regulations. Put another way, the control of behavior depends in part on explicit statement of expectations, and the ability then to determine whether an individual, be he a supervisor or an operator, is conforming to expectations.

Maintenance of the systems of rules and regulations requires considerable attention to the problems of duplication, currency of directives, and conflicts among rules. It is already possible to discern a specialization in management staffs dealing almost exclusively with writing rules and regulations, and maintaining them systematically as a more or less coordinate body of operating doctrine.[15]

A problem exists of retaining all the knowledge that is contained in the rules and regulations. There are many times that an individual can claim innocence in his failure to perform as expected because of his lack of knowledge of the proper rule or procedure. One of the ways in which success can be achieved in an organization is to become a "regulation virtuoso." In the Army such a character is often designated a "barracks lawyer" or "latrine lawyer." An individual with this special skill has a ready knowledge of the large and small regulations of the organization. He can find a justification for almost any kind of behavior, and can exploit fully, to his own benefit and for his own protection, the intricate systems of rules and regulations.

The late Harry Millis, an outstanding labor economist, often pointed out that one of the major weaknesses of management lay in the fact that it could be sabotaged by the conscientious pursuit of rules by workers.[16] In illustrating this point he called attention to a strike in the early 'twenties on a street railway system organized by the IWW. The strike was carried out by having each motorman and conductor conscientiously follow the safety rules for operating street cars. In the course of just several hours, the entire public transportation system was tied up in knots, incapable of operating. The strikers had simply looked into the rule books and found many obsolete requirements which they carried out, to the ultimate destruction of service.

Rules and regulations have important, positive functions of standardizing behavior in work organizations. Because of this standardization it is possible to make accurate predictions about individual and group behavior in the organization. In the broadest sense, therefore, the function of rules and regulations in an organization is to make possible accurate predictions about the course of events.

We have not yet invented other kinds of social structures or devices that will permit the same degree of precision in prediction achieved through systems of rules and regulations.[17] The real problem for management is to maintain an adequate balance between over-specification of behavior with its ultimate inefficiency, and under-specification of behavior with its loss in prediction.[18]

APPLYING RULES

There is no guarantee that the existence of directives will insure compliance. There may be ignorance of specific regulations, or the concrete rule or regulation may not precisely fit an actual situation. Non-compliance may result because of conflicts among rules and regulations applicable to a given situation. Finally, the actual practice that has grown up around a task may be different from that specified in the rules and regulations.[19] The actual practice has come to be accepted, with official procedures simply being out-of-date, having failed to keep pace with operating changes. Any and all of these factors may operate, therefore, to prevent compliance with regulations.

It is also important to note that particular styles of work are developed by individuals, work groups, and even whole departments. These are the habitual but non-official ways of carrying out work. The habitual procedures may differ from regulations. So long as there is general agreement by workers and supervisors that these habitual procedures can be followed, the work may be turned out at least as adequately as under applicable regulations.

In a sense, therefore, the application of rules and directives is never automatic. We are likely to consider this indeterminism in the application of a governing system of rules as the consequence of human softness, error, or lack of knowledge. We should also take into account, however, the fact that a production situation may achieve a system of stability and effectiveness resulting from its evolution at the hands of those involved in it.[20] The work group, for example, may develop its own special techniques for turning out a job. The equilibrium of on-going operating habits may be achieved on a basis somewhat different from formal requirements. The perceptive supervisor or the perceptive manager is clearly aware of this, and is willing to accept a stable, non-official behavior system as justified by virtue of its stability and efficiency, regardless of its compliance with the detailed regulations governing it.

There is likely to be a return to rule enforcement and rule application whenever a new supervisor or manager is brought in. His familiarity with operating realities is likely to be at a minimum and he is, therefore, constrained to judge the organization largely in terms of its formal requirements. The new manager is likely to be concerned with why his organization does not observe certain existing rules and regulations. If, for a variety of reasons, he was to exercise his authority, he might insist on rule compliance regardless of the effects of his insistence on established systems of equilibrium in the on-going activities of his organization. When the manager or supervisor gets "in the know," he is likely to recognize the divergence between expected and actual patterns of behavior, and to accept the latter as the reality with which he operates.[21]

In the operating situation, this may result in the knowing violation of regulations. Thus, the foreman may know that workers smoke in prohibited areas. He also knows that danger from this practice is relatively small. He is willing to secure workers' satisfaction in having the opportunity to smoke, at the expense of possible censure for permitting this rule violation.

Where there is this kind of tacit agreement between supervisor and men with respect to rule violation, there may grow up a consensus bringing the supervisor closer to his men. The men are restrained from taking advantage of their supervisor by the possibility that he may become more strict in applying rules, should they attempt to go too far. This is the typical situation encountered where supervisors claim that privileges have been accorded subordinates, and then find that some individuals have taken advantage of the privileges. The supervisor usually insists that if such behavior continues he will go back to a strict application of rules, and everyone will lose the privileges. This kind of behavior is observed over and over again; for example, with respect to rest periods and coffee breaks. The rules may specify fixed amounts of time available for such periods. As more and more time is taken, the supervisor is pushed to the breaking point. He then announces that unless the official, and only the official, period is used, he will do something about removing the entire privilege. The supervisor does not do this the minute there is a violation, let us say, of a fifteen-minute break period. It is not until a customary twenty or twenty-five minutes are taken that the supervisor begins to get uneasy and seeks to restrain the creeping encroachment on work time.

We can look at systems of rules and regulations as an ever-present set of standards that may be invoked under appropriate circumstances. However, their existence does not mean they will be invoked. One of the problems of developing the managerial skills of supervisors, administrators, and executives is to get them to realize the balance that must exist between strict adherence to rules, and a willingness to be flexible in their application. Either extreme may result in difficulties in the operating unit. Neither extreme is the most effective system of management. On the other hand, it is difficult to suggest, except in each specific operating situation, where the proper balance lies.

Divergence from expected patterns of behavior will be tolerated so long as the substitute behaviors are themselves successful in achieving the objectives of the organization, and in reaching the goals expected of the individual operator. However, should failure to reach the proper goals be serious enough, or should the failure occur too frequently, there may be recourse to the rules as a way of "putting things back on the track."

WORK RULE ENFORCEMENT

Up to this point we have considered the systems within which behavior tends to be routinized in the organization. Particular attention has been paid to the systems of rules and regulations that embody the expected behavior patterns to which the individual is presumed to respond in the desired direction.

Any system that prescribes a course of action or a sequence of behavior is typically accompanied by some means for enforcing or policing the observance of the expected behavior patterns. Accordingly we will next consider the kinds of penalties, deprivations, and sanctions that are used in enforcing working rules.

PENALTIES

The most direct form of rule enforcement is a code of penalties. Penalties for work rule violation are analogous to punitive features of laws in the society. It is customary for every law which sets up a standard of behavior to contain prescribed penalties for failure to observe its requirements. The penalty is generally established in accordance with the severity of the law violation. Thus, in traffic court, a speeding charge may be cause for a twenty-five dollar fine, but a reckless driving charge, considered more serious, may lead to a two hundred dollar fine or actual imprisonment.

Penalties are the balancing losses incurred when rules and regulations are violated. Penalties are assessed directly and in proportion to the seriousness of the rule violated. Furthermore, penalties are typically known in advance, being just as important bits of knowledge as the substantive requirements of the regulations themselves.

In an organization, penalties are of several kinds. The most severe penalty that can be meted out by the organization is immediate dismissal. In most governmental organizations, in all business organizations, and in many other kinds of organizations like schools, colleges, and churches, the most devasting of all penalties is removal from membership. In the military organization there are additional penalties that permit personnel to be imprisoned, and in extreme situations, put to death, for failure to comply with regulations.

In the typical industrial or commercial organization, the most feared penalty is dismissal from the job. This is a penalty which may be invoked in serious situations, or under circumstances that threaten the organization.[22] For example, dishonesty in handling a trust may subject one to immediate dismissal from the organization. Physical violence usually has associated with it the supreme penalty of dismissal. Moral turpitude is another area in which dismissal is the most frequent outcome. Somewhat lesser situations are sometimes enforced with the supreme penalty. It may be a rule of an organization that ringing the time card of another worker is followed by immediate dismissal. Misuse of equipment may require discharge.

We must recognize, however, that the supreme penalty of discharge is not the sole penalty, nor is it the one most frequently used. Other penalties include fines, disciplinary layoffs, demotions, and reprimands.[23] These are the most common kinds of penalties used in organizations.

It is a characteristic of penalties that they are an immediate and direct form of retribution. The individual who is penalized suffers some kind of direct and personal loss. He may lose his job permanently. He may be temporarily laid off in the interests of discipline. He may be fined. The central feature of penalties is that they are visible, personal, and tied directly to the rule violation. Penalties are typically applied immediately after the prohibited behavior has been detected.

A system of penalties has slate-clearing value to the people involved. A penalty is usually in proportion to the crime or rule violation. Once the penalty has been served, it is assumed that the rule violation has been wiped out. Thus, the penalty represents a kind of complete repayment to the organization for any difficulties caused by breaking rules. It is in this connection that the rapidity with which penalties are applied, the concreteness with which the penalties are stated, and the appropriateness of the penalties to the violation are all important. Once the penalty has been served, the individual is assumed to be cleansed of rule breaking.

Systems of penalties have a dual purpose. They police the rules and regulations of the organization. Penalties also provide a means by which, once a regulation is broken, the individual can be purged of his violations and returned to the status of full-fledged membership.

Penalties are always invoked after rule breaking. There has to be some kind of violation of organization standards before the penalty is operative. The individual may anticipate probable penalties in the event of being caught at the rule violation. There is, however, no anticipatory response by management in order to forestall the possible rule breaking. Any system of penalties in an organization is, therefore, a system of last resort in policing the regulations by which behavior is governed in the organization.

DEPRIVATIONS

Deprivations are also used to police behavior in organizations. They are different in their operation and purpose from penalties.

Deprivation is withholding an expected outcome. Work organizations are able to provide employees with desirable future rewards for faithful and worthwhile service. Granting these rewards, however, is based on an accumulation of credits in the individual's record for adequate work performance.

When the individual has failed to live up to expectations, he may not experience any immediate penalty. However, in the calculation of his long-range career in the organization, his small failures over a period of time may add up to a larger failure in being deprived of some rewarding outcome he expected.

Promotions and promotional opportunities are often used in connection with systems of deprivation. Salary increases and wage increases are sometimes used in the same manner. The individual is, in effect, told that failure to meet a minimum standard of performance is likely to have future consequences for his success in the organization. No single failure is considered serious enough to invoke penalties. However, the sum of all the failures, however small, tend to label the individual as unsuited for the expected rewards of faithful and desirable performance.

There are other kinds of deprivations that are of a more immediate and direct character. For example, a group may abuse a coffee break privilege. The management response may be to remove the privilege temporarily, or to limit the number of people who can go off on a coffee break at any one time. Management may also carefully schedule coffee breaks so that people are observed when they leave and return. Management may even change the location at which the break can be taken so as to bring under observation those who are on their break. This kind of action is designed to make clear the revocable character of the privileges that are being violated or abused. The deprivations in this instance consist of withholding or modifying what otherwise might be a pleasant outcome in the form of a relatively free coffee break period.

The deprivation may be a matter for the

immediate or the long term future. Effectiveness of deprivations depends on the uncertainty about the future among those who could suffer from the deprivation. For example, an individual may strive for a promotion so long as he thinks it is possible, always with the knowledge that he may be deprived of it for failure to meet the general expectations of the organization. In the case of a group, the same process operates. A group may be self limiting in its violation of regulations by the fear that a privilege being sought by the group may be withheld at some point in the future should rule violation become too flagrant and too serious.

We can see that systems of deprivation are part of the incentive systems of an organization. Incentives are the positive inducements to work. Deprivations are withheld inducements if there is failure to perform as expected.[24]

Penalties and deprivations found in work organizations are products of impersonal administrative processes. The applications of penalties or deprivations may be at the discretion of individual managers. However, the kinds of penalties they can invoke, or the extent of the deprivations they may order, are determined in the larger organization and are part of the general understandings that exist in it. It is usually not within the power of a single individual to exercise full discretion in withholding opportunities, or in invoking penalties against subordinates.

Impersonal systems for policing rules and regulations are another facet of organizational behavior that tend to focus loyalty of the membership on the organization rather than an individual executive, administrator, or supervisor. This is what Max Weber meant when he said that loyalty in the modern bureaucratic type of organization is directed towards an impersonal order rather than the personality of the leader.[25]

SANCTIONS

Sanctions are used in the interpersonal relations between boss and subordinate to enforce regulations. To sanction something is to approve it or at least permit it. To apply sanctions against someone is to withdraw approval. It is in this sense of withdrawal of approval that we can see sanctions as an organization device for policing behavior.[26]

Sanctions are the consequence of the personal relations between supervisors and subordinates. Sanctions operate by changing the personal relationships between manager and men. A manager or supervisor may make full use of the systems of penalties and deprivations that are available to him. He also has within his grasp the opportunity to manipulate his interpersonal relations with his subordinates. In the process of so doing, he may exercise sanctions that are just as effective, even though personally oriented, as penalties and deprivations in affecting the behavior of his subordinates.

Some examples of personal control by supervisors over subordinates will make clear the effectiveness of sanctions. A supervisor may refuse to talk to a subordinate because he has misbehaved. This break in the opportunity for social intercourse may be a serious blow to the subordinate, and may operate to bring him around to a more acceptable mode of behavior. The supervisor may extend his sanctions against an individual by upbraiding him publicly or privately, or otherwise indicating he knows that rules have been broken. Here again the direct exercise of sanctions by the supervisor constitutes an important threat to the subordinate. At the other extreme of the behavior spectrum the supervisor may withhold his direct approval of proper behavior for a period of time until he feels that the subordinate is fully aware that a preceding episode of his was improper. The supervisor may know that a man is now doing a good job, but waits some time before telling him, because of previous misbehavior. Withholding merited approval may be an important sanction to communicate to a subordinate the disapproval felt for his past misbehavior.

There are still other ways the supervisor may exhibit displeasure by temporarily withdrawing approval. The disapproved person may be given less desirable assignments and work to perform. He may be assigned to more difficult tasks, to more difficult machines, or to "cranky" operations. A supervisor can use "the dirty end of the stick" as an effective sanction, having some penalty characteristics. This can boomerang, of course, if the undesirable work is a permanent feature of the group task and there aren't enough misdemeanors to keep it going by this means alone. "Innocent" men given this work will suffer the more because it is sometimes punitive. This seems to have been the military experience with KP duty, for example.

The supervisor has opportunity to express his displeasure by withholding approval, displaying this in his behavior and attitude. He can also take the opportunity to express it in the normal course of assigning tasks and work to his subordinates.

Sanctions are applied by changing the personal relations between superior and subordinate. The force and effectiveness of the sanctions are therefore dependent on the extent to which the subordinate values the approval of his superior. If this approval is not valued, then sanctions become ineffective.

The effectiveness of any system of sanctions depends on the prior effectiveness of the system of supervision. If authority is disputed, if insubordination and disrespect for supervision are widespread, then systems of sanctions become ineffective in policing the rules, regulations, and standards of behavior of the organization.

PUNISHMENT, INCENTIVES, AND WORK

In Chapter 13 we analyzed incentives as the inducements placed along the course of an activity to keep people moving towards a desired goal. In this chapter we have seen that the opposite of the incentives for work is the punishment that can be administered for not working properly. Punishments define the boundaries of the course of activity. If these boundaries are crossed, penalties, deprivations, or sanctions may be invoked.

Work organizations try to make work in them attractive enough that their members will feel enthusiastic about working. The administrative problems, arising in making uniform rules and regulations operate to standardize working behavior, necessitate some kind of enforcement methods. Systems of penalties, deprivations, and sanctions police behavior to insure that it corresponds to acceptable standards.

NOTES FOR CHAPTER 19

[1] A point made with considerable clarity by J. L. Meij, "Some Fundamental Principles of a General Theory of Management," *Journal of Industrial Economics,* 4:16-32 (October, 1955).

[2] See especially Chapter 4, 5, 10, and 16.

[3] Cf. C. A. Myers, "Basic Employment Relations," Chapter 24 in A. Kornhauser, R. Dubin, and A. Ross (eds.), *Industrial Conflict* (New York: McGraw-Hill Book Company, 1954).

[4] See the evidence in Chapter 15.

[5] This point is made with respect to the relationships between control rules and decentralization of business management in Raymond Villers, "Control and Freedom in a Decentralized Company," *Harvard Business Review,* 32:89-96 (March, 1954).

[6] In Chapter 17 we saw that grievances arising from the authority relationship contain a central element of perceived discrimination.

[7] See Robert Dubin, *Working Union-Management Relations* (Englewood Cliffs, N. J.: Prentice-Hall, Inc., 1958), especially Chapter 6. The consequences of failure to agree to working rules through collective bargaining in an industry where these rules are largely subject to collective bargaining are revealed in J. J. Kaufman, "Working Rules in the Railroad Industry," *Labor Law Journal,* 5:819-827 (December, 1954).

[8] Some rules having to do with personal conduct also have other consequences. For example, in some kinds of work it is necessary as a safety measure to have employees take showers after completing their workday. This is to make sure that they are not contaminated by industrial poisons. A question then arises as to whose time the shower shall be on. This economic issue has generally been solved by considering washup a company requirement, to be paid for on company time. Issues like that of washup become collective bargaining controversies because of their economic consequences, and not because the rules invade personal privacy.

[9] A good study of the reaction of clerical workers to the location and amount of authority exercised is N. C. Morse, Everett Reimer, and A. S. Tannenbaum, "Regulations and Control in Hier-

NOTES FOR CHAPTER 19 (CONT.)

archical Organizations," *Journal of Social Issues,* 7:3:41-48 (1951).

[10] Rights are defined and analyzed in Chapter 5.

[11] Obligations are also defined and analyzed in Chapter 5.

[12] See especially Chapter 16 and the discussions of types of relationships in both voluntary and organized social groups.

[13] A recent study of a manufacturing firm and a radar airsite of the Air Defense Command suggests that among specialized workers, the conduct standards of the social groups supplement the formal controls of the organization. We have analyzed this in Chapter 16 in dealing with the conduct standards developed and enforced in social groups, and in the section analyzing social groups and cooperation. See Edward Gross, "Some Functional Consequences of Primary Controls in Formal Work Organizations," *American Sociological Review,* 18:368-373 (August, 1953).

[14] Merton's analysis of ritualism as a form of social deviancy is relevant here. Ritualistic behavior clings tenaciously to existing rules and regulations even though they may no longer be efficient in getting work done. See R. K. Merton, *Social Theory and Social Structure* (Glencoe: The Free Press, 1949), especially Chapter 4, "Social Structure and Anomie," especially pp. 140-142.

[15] These staff groups are standards departments.

[16] Lectures, University of Chicago.

[17] The extreme development of the "reign of rules" is in the Soviet system of industrial control. See Alexander Vucinich, "The Structure of Factory Control in the Soviet Union," *American Sociological Review,* 15:179-186 (April, 1950). In 1957, a significant move was made to develop some degree of local autonomy in Soviet industry by decentralizing some of the planning and control functions. Apparently, the point of diminishing returns had been so seriously passed in controlling industry through rigid rules and regulations, that official steps had to be taken.

[18] A beautiful illustration of the difficulty in reaching the balancing point between over- and under-specification of behavior is contained in Melville Dalton, "Industrial Controls and Personal Relations," *Social Forces,* 33:244-249 (March, 1955). Dalton points out the administrative changes and shifts in interpersonal relations that occurred as a company modified its system of repairing and maintaining equipment.

[19] The actual behavior that may deviate from official behavior is, of course, one of the unanticipated consequences of purposive social action. See, in this connection, the outstanding paper by R. K. Merton, "The Unanticipated Consequences of Purposive Social Action," *American Sociological Review,* 1:894-904 (December, 1936). Insofar as deviant behavior is systematically pursued we have called it non-official behavior. See especially Chapter 4.

[20] Illustrated in Orvis Collins, Melville Dalton, and Donald Roy, "Restriction of Output and Social Cleavage in Industry," *Applied Anthropology,* 5:1-14 (Summer, 1946).

[21] The difference between an executive who is "in the know" about how his organization actually works, and his successor who is not, is the central theme of a study of a gypsum plant. See A. W. Gouldner, *Patterns of Industrial Bureaucracy* (Glencoe: The Free Press, 1954). The original plant manager had what Gouldner called a "leniency pattern" of management, which permitted considerable deviation from rules and regulations. His successor was a "book" man who demanded observance of formal rules. Gouldner traces out the points of resistance to the new manager and the social processes involved.

[22] Cf. J. N. Brewer, "Cause of Discharge," *Personnel Journal,* 6:171-172 (August, 1927). Brewer's study shows that discharge is more frequent because of inability to get along with supervisors and fellow workers than because of work inefficiency. Such friction with supervisors or peers is, of course, threatening to the organization.

[23] In the General Motors Corporation, as in many large companies, a highly formalized system of written reprimands is used to discipline workers. Where there has been a rule infraction, the worker receives a written reprimand indicating what he has done wrong, and how he should correct such behavior in the future. A copy goes into his personnel file. If he continues to be "difficult," his personnel record shows previous warnings, thus providing a "case" for his discharge. An appeal of such discharge to the umpire, who rules on union contract disputes, then becomes more difficult since the record clearly shows the discharged employee to be a rule breaker, whose previous violations have been tolerated while management tried to "bring him into line" with warnings and attempts at rehabilitation.

[24] Chapter 13 is an extended analysis of incentives.

[25] This general point about the impersonality of bureaucratic administration is treated at length in the next chapter, "Management as Bureaucracy."

[26] This use of sanctions is comparable to what Radcliffe-Brown calls "diffuse social sanctions." See A. R. Radcliffe-Brown, "Sanctions, Social," *Encyclopaedia of the Social Sciences,* 13:531-534 (New York: The Macmillan Company, 1934).

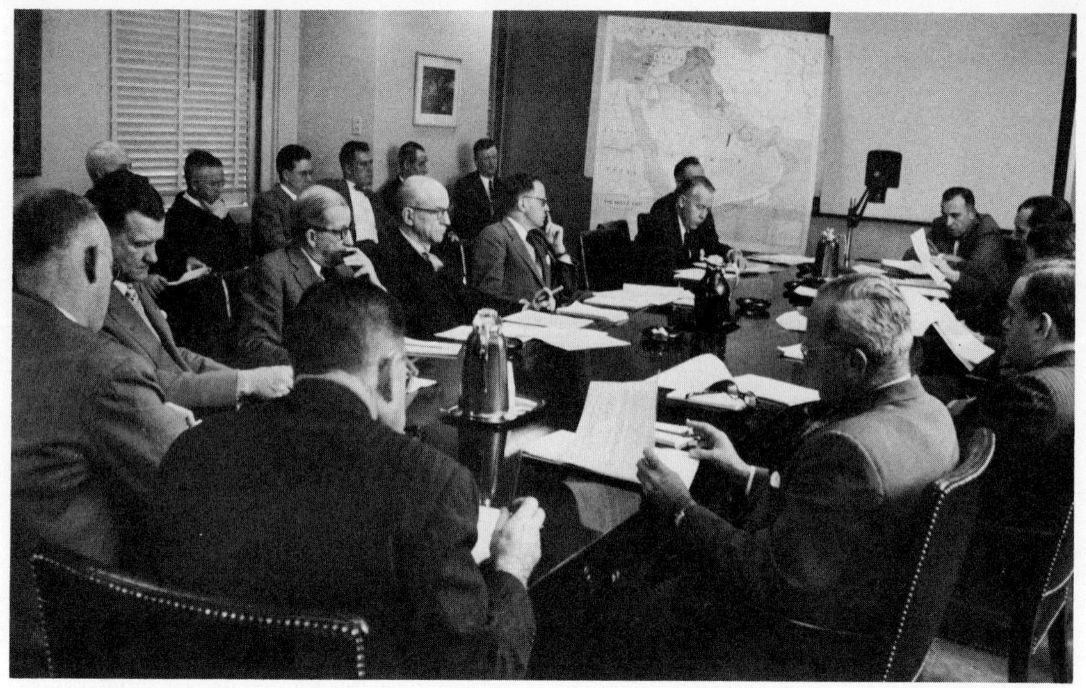

This is a meeting of the coordination committee of a large corporation. Its very existence recognizes the significance of command functions in management bureaucracies. Commanding involves directing, coordinating, and controlling activities. Note also the second level men from various departments who sit in on the meetings but figuratively and literally take back seats.

Chapter **20**

MANAGEMENT AS BUREAUCRACY

In our common language, "bureaucracy" means something "bad." When we use the term, we conjure up a mental picture of too many lazy people doing unnecessary work.

Bureaucracy has a technical meaning. The term is used to describe a method of work organization administration. In particular we use it to describe the middle reaches of administration. All sizeable work organizations have bureaucracies.

The particular organization significance of bureaucracies is the fact that bureaucrats are crucial in translating organization policies into operating directives. This translation starts with general purposes and puts them into the form of commands.

In analyzing management as bureaucracy, we will deal with the following problems: (A) the organizational causes of bureaucracy; (B) the nature of bureaucratic administration, and bureaucrats; (C) how bureaucratic functions are standardized; and (D) how bureaucrats can produce undesirable consequences for their organizations.

CAUSES OF BUREAUCRACY

Causes of bureaucratic administration can be found in four major developments characteristic of modern work organizations. Most important is the large size of these organizations. Direction of large-sized organizations requires intermediate links between decision makers and workers. This linkage is achieved through the administrative bureaucracy.

Another linkage problem between policy makers and those who get work done is created by organizational complexity. Complexity results from specialization of operating functions. In coordinating diverse operations, special administrative posts have to be created. These coordinating tasks are carried out by administrative bureaucrats.

Communication is complicated by both size and complexity of organization. Orders and commands have to flow through many communication links in going from policy makers to workers. Information used for controlling and changing operations has to flow upward through similar communication channels. Administrative bureaucrats play a central role in organization communication.

A fourth factor in the development of administrative bureaucracy is the need for organizing adequate chains of command. Command positions are created. These positions are occupied by bureaucrats. Every organization chart exhibits the chain of command, which is the structural picture of the administrative bureaucracy.

LARGE SIZE REQUIRES BUREAUCRACY

Industrial firms have grown very rapidly in size. If, for example, we examine the average number of workers employed, we discover that in the half century from 1899 to 1952 the typical American manufacturing establishment has grown three-fold in size.

Another way of seeing how large our work organizations have become is to examine the proportion of them employing more than 1,000 workers. In 1952, 8.1 per cent of all manufacturing firms hired more than 1,000 people. This contrasts with less than one per cent of manufacturing companies of that size in 1900. It is clear that American business firms have grown very rapidly in size over the past fifty years.

CHART 20.1

THE RISING TIDE OF MANAGEMENT

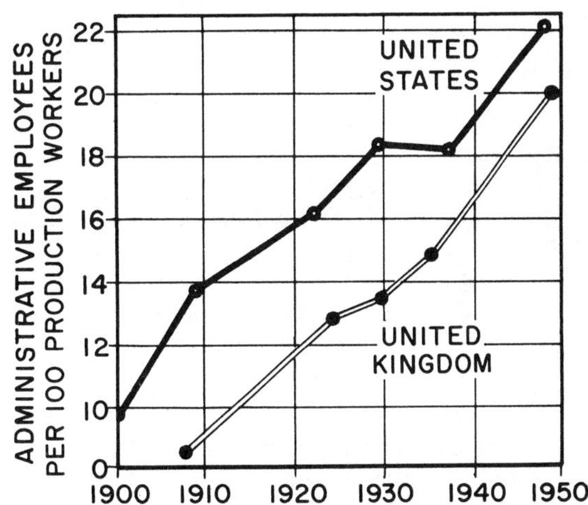

Reprinted with permission from Seymour Melman, "The Rising Cost of Management," *Manchester Guardian*, "Survey of Industry, Trade, and Finance, 1954," p. 31.

Our interest, of course, is in knowing what has happened to management with this increased size of work organizations. Does it take more people in management and administration to run larger size firms?

Professor Melman, in the most detailed studies yet available, has demonstrated that an increasing proportion of people in industry are concerned exclusively with management and administration.[1] The startling increase in the proportion of administrative personnel is revealed in Chart 20.1 where evidence is shown for the United States and the United Kingdom, two highly industrialized countries. Professor Bendix presents similar data showing identical trends for France, Germany, and Sweden, as well.[2] In 1900 in the United States, there were almost ten administrative workers for every 100 production workers in manufacturing firms. By 1947 it took more than 22 people in management to direct the affairs of 100 production workers. This is more than a 100 per cent increase in the proportion of administrative personnel. The facts for the United Kingdom are very much the same, except that the rise in proportion of people working at administration has been even more marked.

spend less of each sales dollar on administration costs. Profit advantage of larger firms derives, on the average, from their lower administration expenses.

The facts so far presented give us two trends. First, we have seen a marked increase in the proportion of people in industry who are in the ranks of management. This has accompanied the growth in size of the business organizations. Second, it seems clear that big firms have lower administrative costs for each dollar of sales.

Melman explains the increased relative size of management as resulting from adding new managerial functions. Industrial management has solved its problems partly through extension of formal managerial controls over ever-widening areas. Management has extended its controls over the work force, its

CHART 20.2

BIG BUSINESS DOES NOT MEAN MORE COSTLY MANAGEMENT

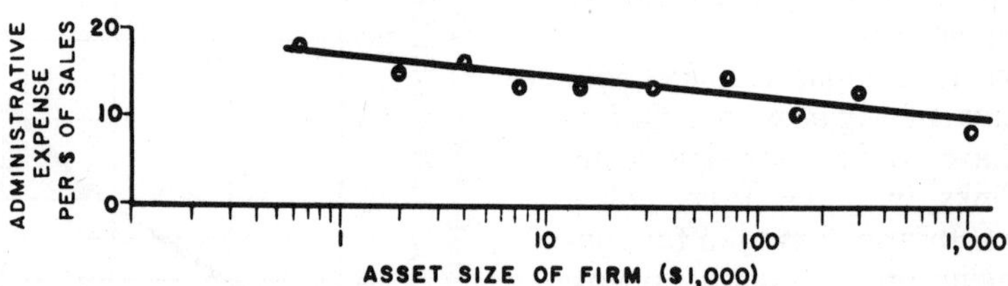

From Seymour Melman, "Production and Administration Cost in Relation to Size of Firm." *Applied Statistics*, 3:5, 1954.

Large-size firms apparently demand a lot of managing. For manufacturing industries as a whole in mid-century America, industry required more than two members of management for every five production workers. This contrasts sharply with the need for only one manager or administrator for every ten production workers in 1900.

In a succeeding study, Melman has shown that as the size of the firm increases, its administrative expense per dollar of sales decreases.[3] This study is based on over 1,000 manufacturing firms for the year 1937. At the same time, he demonstrates that production costs per dollar of sales are nearly constant regardless of the size of firm. Chart 20.2 shows the relationship between administrative costs and size of firm. Melman concludes that large firms

own administrative staff, and indirectly even over the buyers of its products.[4]

The ranks of management have grown relative to the growth of the productive work force. This multiplication of management results from larger size of work organizations. Bigger companies need proportionately more people to manage and administer their affairs. This growth has not necessarily meant more costly operations. Indeed, the evidence suggests that large firms have competitive advantages over smaller ones because of their significantly lower unit costs of administration for every dollar returned through sales. We can conclude that size of work organization is perhaps the most important single factor fostering the growth of bureaucratic administration.

COMPLEXITY REQUIRES BUREAUCRACY

Modern work organizations are more complex than their predecessors. The most important evidence of complexity is the increase in the kinds and varities of activities carried on by industrial managers and their staffs.

Increased size alone is one condition making for complexity. Large work organizations have problems of multiple locations, with branch plants and regional or area sales organizations. Large size leads to extension of the geographic area served. Indeed, the history of early capitalism has been largely written in terms of expansion of markets from small localities to regional, national, and international fields.[5]

Organizational complexity also results from the addition of new functions, and elaboration of old. This has made management more complex. The addition of new managerial functions is a logical outgrowth of the need for top management to keep its fingers on the pulse of the enterprise. With larger size, top management has limited opportunity for continuous and intimate contact with all work operations. A top executive of General Motors, for example, cannot simultaneously be in the Buick, Oldsmobile, Cadillac, Pontiac, and Chevrolet Divisions. Furthermore, he cannot work in Detroit headquarters and have immediate control over the more than 100 domestic plants of the Corporation lying outside Detroit.

Problems of changing the organization, its products, and its work methods have become highly technical. This has led to the establishment of staff innovating groups. These groups, like research departments, have the primary function of developing new ideas ultimately useful in the firm's operations. Innovating functions are typically located in middle management ranks. These innovating groups provide necessary links between operating problems of the work organization, and top policy makers whose decisions affect the ways in which the problems will be met.

In small and simple firms, top managers can personally perform the major managerial functions. As organizations get larger, these functions are delegated to middle management groups and individuals. Specialists are recruited and trained to perform these delegated functions.

We can illustrate the complexity of a modern organization by examining some of the departments of the Standard Oil Company (New Jersey). The parent organization, called Standard of New Jersey, has four principal divisions. These are each divided into departments or units as shown on Chart 20.3.

This simplified picture of the parent company only begins to set forth some of the complexity of this firm. Most of the departments are composed of small units. Furthermore, the chart pictures only the parent company, which, together with its affiliates, provides almost one-fifth of the liquid energy used in the world outside the Iron Curtain. If we simply count the principal affiliates of Standard of New Jersey, we find there are 12 such affiliated companies in the United States; 3 in Canada; 9 in Latin America; 19 in Europe and North Africa; and 7 in the Middle and Far East. This is a total of 50 principal subsidiaries located throughout the world. Many of these affiliated companies have internal structures even more complex than that of the parent company. Standard of New Jersey is one of the giants of American industry. The mere listing of the number of affiliated companies and a brief examination of the major subdivisions of the parent company provide a perfect example of organizational complexity.

It takes a lot of people to get work done in a highly industrialized society. In particular, it takes a lot of people in the ranks of management to provide necessary connecting links between workers and top decision makers.

COMMUNICATION NETWORKS REQUIRE BUREAUCRACY

Large and complex organizations need a high input of information to keep them going. Directing, coordinating, and innovating functions all involve continuous issuance of commands and orders. Management control functions require a constant flow of information about work operations upward to the decision makers.

Large size and complexity have aggravated the problems of communication within work

CHART 20.3

A MODERN CORPORATION IS A VERY COMPLEX ORGANIZATION

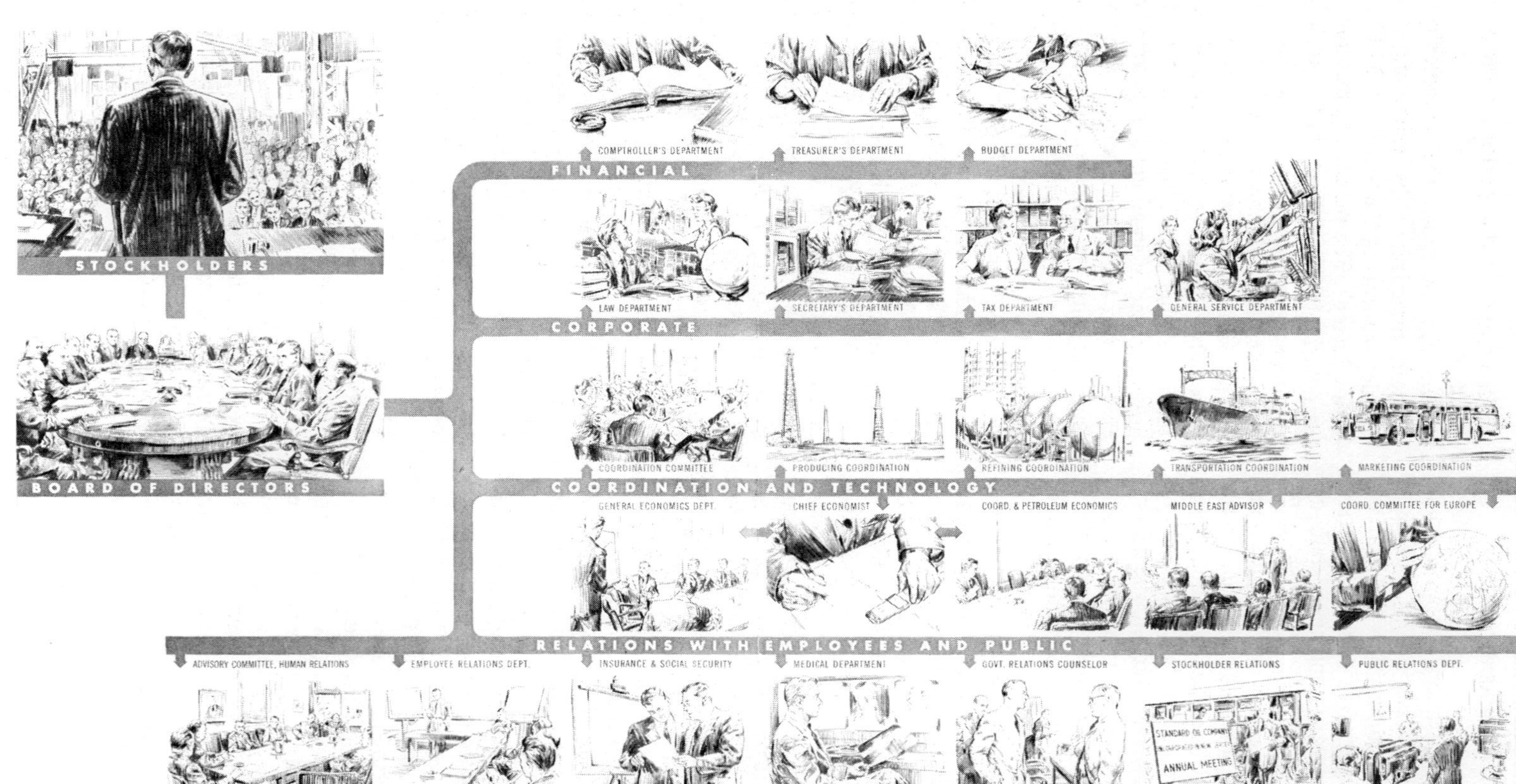

Horizontal division of labor in the Standard Oil Company (N.J.), 1955.
Only major departments and functions are shown.

organizations. This, in turn, has led to important developments and inventions designed to standardize communication. In the process management functions have themselves been standardized. Some in the ranks of management occupy positions whose major tasks is undistorted transmission of orders and commands downward from top decision makers. Other management specializations are concerned with a continuous flow upward of information about operations. In particular, control functions for production, budget, costs, scrap loss, and safety are specialized to secure standard information about particular kinds of operations for organization decision makers.

It is said that the size of the Roman legion was determined by the number of men over whom the commander could exercise direct voice control. In large and complex organizations, substitutes have to be found for direct face-to-face control by the commander. The invention of additional means of communication within the organization inevitably gives rise to new positions in the ranks of management. A growth of management in the form of bureaucratic administration is therefore also a product of the growth of internal communication networks in work organiaztions.

When direct voice control is replaced by commands removed from the point of execution, it is necessary to insure a minimum of distortion in the transmission process. To minimize distortion, communication becomes standardized. This means a common language is used and forms of permanent communication employed. Written orders and directives tend to replace verbal ones. A written document is permanent and can be retained in the records as long as necessary. Its interpretation is less variable because the same words can be transmitted to everyone affected by an order or command.

The middle ranks of management, who are the bureaucrats of modern work organizations, have an increasingly standardized communication function. What is communicated either downward as commands or upward as information, why it is communicated, and how it is communicated are all determined for the bureaucrat. His area of discretion is almost completely concerned with the timing of communication. Thus, the very content of communication is often no longer within the jurisdiction of the bureaucrat.

The complex communication networks of modern work organizations have a dual impact on bureaucratic administration. The bureaucrats are necessary links in extended communication networks. Bureaucrats serve as transmission and receiving stations in the flow of communications within work organizations. At the same time, the degree to which the bureaucrat can vary the information flowing through him is considerably limited. This has the consequence of standardizing the communication behavior of the bureaucrat himself.[6]

CHAIN OF COMMAND REQUIRES BUREAUCRACY

The central problem for bureaucratic administration is to establish and maintain chains of command. The usual meaning of chain of command is that there be proper links between policy-makers and workers so that policy may be carried out adequately.

In Chapter 5 we analyzed in some detail the nature of management chains of command. In particular it was emphasized that managerial functions changed from the top to the lowest level of administrative personnel. At top levels, innovating and coordinating functions predominate. At middle levels, coordinating and controlling functions are central. At the lowest levels, the dominant concern is directing other people.

In working out an organization chart, these differences in management functions are recognized in the duties assigned to each level of management. The chain of command of the work organization then becomes a distribution of the various management functions to succeeding levels of management. These functions are further distributed to the specialized departments of the organization and the managers responsible for them. The adequacy of any particular chain of command is determined by the degree to which overlaps in functions are minimized. A second test of chain command adequacy is whether the four principal functions of management are distributed reasonably among managerial personnel.

The chain of command can also be viewed as the person-to-person linkage among the members of management. This is typically displayed on an organization chart by drawing lines between positions showing who gives directions to whom, and who reports to whom. The lines connecting management positions are really lines of communications. The chain of command therefore also describes the formal channels of communication among management personnel.

There is a two-fold organization problem in developing chains of command. The first problem is to insure that the assigned fuctions will actually be carried out adequately by the position holder. The second problem is to make certain that the channels of communication will be observed in transmitting information upward and downward through the organization.

Assignment of functions usually requires fixing positions for the people who carry them out. Specialization of management functions then results in the designation of fixed positions in which the responsibilities are centered. These positions in turn are linked together by the lines of authority showing who directs whom. Down these lines of authority flows the information called commands of the organization. Up these lines of authority flows the information necessary for controlling operations.

We can now summarize the four principal organization causes of bureaucratic administration. As organizations grow larger in size, intermediate groups have to be developed to link the top decision makers with the workers. When organization activities become specialized and the total group of activities more complex, there arises need for coordinating diverse activities. Both size and complexity of the organization necessitate indirect communication from top to bottom. The middle positions of management become communication links in getting work done and in maintaining information about the progress of operations. When the middle reaches of management are formalized into chains of command the bureaucratic structure is established, composed of lower management executives and administrators. These bureaucratic positions are organized in systematic ways so that there is a minimum of confusion in the authority structure. The chain of command becomes the authority structure. At the same time the chain of command becomes the formal channel of communication for control information.

Bureaucratic administration is viewed as a social invention designed to provide a rational method for administering modern work organizations. Middle management positions are logically described and systematically interrelated so that commands can move through the whole range of the organization in ways that insure their execution. The same administrative structure is also used to transmit operating information from the working levels to the decision-making levels of the organization.

CHARACTERISTICS OF BUREAUCRATIC ADMINISTRATION

We can now turn to examine the characteristics of bureaucratic administration. Particular attention will be given to showing who the bureaucrats are, how they are recruited and selected, the nature of their attachment to the organization, and their characteristic working behavior.

WHO ARE THE BUREAUCRATS?

The inhabitants of the bureaucratic world are the members of management who stand between top policy makers and workers. This middle group is distinguished in our common language by being referred to as *members of* management. It should be noted that they are not called *the* management.

Max Weber has distinguished three basic types of organization administration.[7] The leader-oriented organization is one in which all members serve as loyal subjects of a leader. In such an organization every member holds his position or job by virtue of decisions of the leader. Dependence on the leader makes all followers exceptionally sensitive to the leader's whims and desires. No delegations of management functions are made that cannot be recalled by the leader. A leader-oriented organization has a clear-cut break between the leader as *the* management, and all followers regardless of their present position or job.

A second type of administrative structure suggested by Weber is one in which positions and jobs are assigned on the basis of tradition. Managerial positions may be handed down from generation to generation. The leader accepts the hereditary or traditional basis of division of labor in the organization. Schooling for jobs and positions is built into the education of each individual whose productive destiny is determined by traditional criteria. Certain classes of people, for example, may be traditionally designated the officer group of armies. In the case of the German Junkers, whose tradition destined their males for position as military officers, training and schooling were directed from childhood toward their future vocations. Who you are, rather than what you can do, becomes a primary criterion for work assignment in tradition-oriented organizations.

The third major type of administration suggested by Weber is the bureaucratic. Here the delegation of management responsibilities is based on reasonable judgments as to how best to design the organizational structure. Members of management are then recruited to fill established positions. Recruitment is based on the ability, either already demonstrated or promised by virtue of schooling and training, to fill the established positions. In bureaucratic administration the organizational structure exists prior to filling its positions with people. No one can claim a particular position because of exceptional and unwaivering loyalty to the leader. Nor can anyone claim a position because that position has been traditionally held by members of his family or class. People earn positions because they are presumed to be the best capable of filling them.

These three basic types of administrative organization show, in the contrast among them, the importance of bureaucratic administration. Bureaucratic administration breaks the absolute power of the leader to determine the fate of the organization and its members. Bureaucratic administration also breaks the hold that tradition and social custom have on assignment to positions of authority. In short, bureaucratic administration frees the organization from absolute rule by a single individual, and from the dead hand of the past.

Bureaucracy can be viewed as the logical extension of management, when it becomes impossible for one person to fulfill all managerial functions. The management organization becomes specialized, with specific responsibilities and functions delegated to positions created within the ranks of management. Once the management positions are established, recruitment is concerned with finding and securing the persons best able to carry out the requirements of each position.

The test of a bureaucracy is its ability to link up top policy makers with production workers. Where this linkage is adequate, the organization is capable of carrying out policy efficiently. If this linkage breaks down, then inefficiencies creep into the organization. In work organizations these inefficiencies eventually appear as excessive costs of operations. Thus even the criterion—cost—for bureaucratic success is objective.

The classic example of bureaucratic administration is government organization. Indeed, the very term, bureau, derives from the typical designation of a government administrative unit. When governmental bureaucracy is charged with inefficiency the cost criterion is invariably applied. The usual response of the bureaucrat is to allege that governmental costs are increasing because more services are being demanded by the citizenry of the government, not because of inefficiencies in administration.

There is one crucial difference between bureaucracy in government and bureaucracy in work organizations. Government bureaucracy is a special case of work organization bureaucracy. The difference lies in the fact that in government a bureaucracy is typically the connecting link between the executive and the citizens. That is, the group for which the bureaucracy exists to provide services and to control is not, in a formal sense, a part of the organization. The average citizen becomes involved with government bureaucracy only when he is in need of services or has violated rules, regulations, and laws of the society. Thus, government bureaucracy operates intermittently in linking government executives with the public. Many members of the public may seldom have occasion to encounter the bureaucrats. In production organizations the situation is quite different. Here the operating level is limited and known. Productive workers are in contact with management bureaucracy, constantly receiving direction from and being controlled by it. The productive work organization is closed in the sense that it has a limited and prescribed total membership. The linkage provided by the administrative bureaucracy between policy makers and productive workers operates within this closed system. Greater continuity in the linkage makes for more immediate and objective criteria for the bureaucrats' behaviors.

The bureaucrats of productive work organizations are the *members of* management, but not *the* management. This is a sizeable group, which in modern American manufacturing enterprises consists of one person for every five productive workers. A lot of money is spent on industrial bureaucracies, for they embody tremendous reservoirs of skills. Bureaucratic administration is indispensible in providing the long arm of management for our large-sized and complex work organizations.

Without the bureaucratic form of administration, business firms would have to depend on traditional or leader-oriented administration. In France the evidence seems to suggest that tradition-oriented business administration is not as efficient as bureaucratic administration.[8] The upheaval in Montgomery Ward and Company in recent years seems to suggest that leader-oriented administration is at least unstable; the company lost one president and ten vice-presidents in the course of several weeks after disagreements with Mr. Sewell Avery, the acknowledged leader.[9]

WHERE DO BUREAUCRATS COME FROM?

The bureaucrats of business have to be recruited from the general population. In a mass society such as that in the United States, recruitment to business bureaucracies is the major ladder up which people climb in achieving social esteem. The rapid increase in the absolute number of administrative personnel requires that the bases of recruitment be very broad in order to insure that adequate numbers will be available.

Studies of business leadership and the origins of business leaders give us only a partial clue about the origins of the bureaucrats of business. Most of these studies concentrate on top business leaders. Even for this group of people, who have reached the highest rungs of the management ladder, it is clear that education is important to their rise.[10]

It is hardly surprising that education provides the greatest assurance of positions in management. We already know that management functions and operations are highly technical in character. We also know that the technical training required to fill such positions is usually secured in formal schooling, principally at the college level. Thus, a very large proportion of the bureaucrats of business are people who have college training. For those who are unable to secure a college education, many companies provide internal schooling opportunities as a substitute. The central fact is that it takes knowledge and technical skills to perform administrative tasks. Either formal schooling, or supplementary on-the-job training, is required to learn these skills.

From an analytical standpoint, it is much more important for us to understand the consequences of recruitment for the behavior of bureaucrats. The impersonality of selection, and the objective criteria used, have important consequences for the outlook of those selected, and their behavior as management functionaries.

Typically a position is established for which a person is recruited. The position is described in considerable detail. The functions and work operations to be performed are objectively set forth, normally in writing. The power characteristics of the position, and its place in the authority structure are also set forth. Finally, there is usually a set of minimum criteria of schooling, education, background, and experience considered necessary to fill the position. These facts are usually incorporated in a job description.

Once the job description is established, a search is made among available people for likely candidates. Present employees of the organization may be considered. Outsiders may be sought through normal recruiting channels.

The central feature in this recruiting process is that the successful candidate is selected in terms of *what* he is rather than *who* he is. He is selected in terms of what he appears to be able to do, or what he has already successfully accomplished. In short, his qualifications are matched against the requirements of the position. The legendary story about references for a Boston blue blood is pertinent here. A Chicago firm wrote to a Boston businessman for references on a job applicant. In due course the reference letter came back full of praises for the applicant's family tree, relatives, and manners. A reply was sent by the Chicago firm giving thanks for the reference and noting that the man was being considered as a junior executive, and not for breeding purposes.[11]

On entering the position, the successful candidate is given considerable instruction regarding it. His job description is usually made known to him, and the operating instructions and policy manuals relevant to his position become part of the "book" by which he operates.

We now have a picture of a person recruited to a position, not to an organization, nor to a leader. His first responsibility is to adequate performance in his position. His most immediate tie to the organization is through his position. His future success depends on the adequacy with which he is judged to fill that position. Neither personal relations nor organizational loyalty is the primary bond uniting the bureaucrat with his employing organization. He is judged against the requirements of the position and his ability to meet them.

It would be naive to assume that the bureaucracies of work organizations are recruited solely on objective grounds. Favoritism, nepotism, and considerations of organizational loyalty may become highly relevant in particular situations. The idealist who suggests that every swinging door can be entered only by obeying the sign on it that reads, "PUSH," can always be brought down to earth by the thought that the sign on the other side of the door reads "PULL." Nevertheless, the operation of favoritism and prejudicial choices is minimized in bureaucratic administration, as contrasted with leader-oriented organizations, and those based on tradition.

What are the consequences of the bureaucrat's attachment first and foremost to his position? The consequences are two-fold: his objects of loyalty are determined by the method of his recruitment, and his normal behavior is also a product of the mode of his recruitment. We will turn to these two consequences immediately.

LOYALTY OF BUREAUCRATS

What kind of loyalty does a bureaucrat have, and to what does he direct it? His loyalties are first and foremost given to his technical, or professional specialization. The methods engineer wants to be the best possible man in his field and bends his efforts in that direction; the cost accountant wants to excel in that specialty; the production control man envisions his career unfolding rapidly as he gets better at his tasks.

The final chart in Chapter 5 pictures the working person as the product of his social roles and his work assignments. Both of these aspects of the working person are highlighted for the bureaucrat.

The social role of the bureaucrat is reinforced very strongly for him in his formal schooling, training, and experience. College students pointing toward careers in business generally know early in their schooling that they are going to be engineers, accountants, or junior executives. Much of their actual school work is concerned with building up their self-image as occupants of such positions. This is in addition to learning the technical knowledge necessary to perform the tasks associated with these positions. Furthermore, after becoming members of management, many specialists continue to fortify their role conceptions by joining professional and technical organizations that place frank emphasis on the special characteristics of their members. Admission to these technical organizations requires minimum levels of competence, and membership tends to confer the assurance that such competence is possessed by the member. From the standpoint of the bureaucrat's social role, he is strongly fortified by his schooling and training, as well as by his professional reference groups, with the belief that his specialization is central to his career.

When we turn to the bureaucrat's working assignments, we note, as has already been discussed, that he typically occupies an established position in the organization. That is to say, his power, authority, and status relationships in the organization are objectively set forth and generally understood, not only by himself, but all others with knowledge of the organization. Here again the position occupied, rather than its organizational context, is emphasized.

We can now see that the loyalties of the bureaucrat are reinforced from inside and outside the organization, in being focused on his position and its fulfillment. The bureaucrat gives his loyalties to his own position.

In a leader-oriented organization, every member of the organization has his fate determined by the leader. Accordingly, loyalty to the leader has to be genuinely, or at least publicly, expressed. In tradition-directed organizations, loyalty attaches to the social structures that maintain traditional divisions of labor. A member of management whose position is the consequence of being the son of the founder can be fiercely loyal to the custom that family membership confers the right of succession to leadership.

Max Weber suggested that a bureaucrat is loyal to the impersonal order surrounding the bureaucracy.[12] He meant by this that the bureaucrat is particularly concerned with maintaining the criteria by which his position in the organization is considered legitimate. Reisman's study of bureaucrats in public service makes clear their sense of attachment to their specialized positions, and the professional and technical reference groups that give legitimacy to these positions.[13]

BEHAVIOR OF BUREAUCRATS

The bureaucrat is first of all recognizable in his behavior by his preoccupation with the technical tasks of his position. Most of his time is devoted to performing these technical tasks.

Being an expert, as the bureaucrats of management generally are, has important advantages as well as disadvantages. The advantages are these. In the area of assigned organization responsibility the expert can operate with a high degree of self-confidence. He has personal resources that lend conviction to his belief that he knows better than non-experts how to fill his position. Furthermore, the very specialization of his position serves notice to himself and all other members of the organization that he alone is responsible for adequate fulfillment of his working tasks. The expert, then, has both an inner belief in his own competence, and an organizational legitimation of his competence by assigning special responsibility to him.

A meeting of department heads with the general manager. This is an important kind of meeting for a great deal of the coordination of departments is achieved through the decisions and agreements reached here. Note that the meeting takes place on neutral ground, in a conference room, rather than in the boss' office. This helps to neutralize authority and status differences among the participants while they are engaged in their deliberations.

The disadvantage of specialization and expertness is the limited point of view that it develops. Harold Laski has pointed out that the expert views the world as having its center in his special interest.[14] From the standpoint of his organization position, the expert tends to view his own working assignment as more important than any others. The design engineer, for example, is likely to claim that the success of a product depends on his designs. The production man, on the other hand, will assert that the product is only as good, or profitable to sell, as the ingenuity of its manufacture permits. The sales executive, in turn, is certain that the crucial element in successful marketing of the product is the diligence and cleverness with which it is presented to the consuming public. Each expert honestly believes that the destiny and prosperity of the firm depend on the adequacy with which he fulfills his position.

This concentration on doing a good job in his own position insulates each specialist from those around him. As a consequence he can lose battles, in the course of coordinating his specialty and others, without feeling defeated. If the sales executive does not succeed in having a particular gadget added to a product to make it more saleable, because the production people have won the argument on the cost of making the addition, the sales executive has no reason to believe his own idea was wrong. He has simply lost a battle in which other considerations than sales appeal have dominated the decision. On another product, or at another time, the sales executive may come back and "win" with exactly the same arguments. The bureaucrat is seldom forced to concede that his own decisions can be wrong, because the lost battle can be rationalized on grounds that external criteria have been used to decide it.

Coordinating the efforts of independent specialists who do not share a common framework is obviously difficult. Indeed, one of the tests of the extent to which management functions can be specialized, is the difficulty encountered in coordination. We have analyzed this issue in Chapter 18 as a problem in communication for the coordinating executive. We will analyze the same problem as an issue for the leader in the next chapter.

Another positive consequence of this form of administration is that bureaucratic functionaries are largely insulated from the impact of turnover in top management. Since the bureaucrat is devoted to his position and not to a particular leader, it is generally a matter of relative indifference who the leaders are. So long as the bureaucrat can operate in a stable position, he can be indifferent to leadership turnover. When a new leader, however, comes in and begins to shake up the organization, he may be bitterly opposed by the bureaucracy. This is not uncommon, particularly where the new leader is brought in to improve the operation of the organization. In making improvements he will inevitably attempt to reorganize the management and reassign managerial responsibility. It is because he is changing bureaucrats' functions that they oppose him; they are not otherwise predisposed against him.

Bureaucrats' indifference to leadership operates to stabilize the organization in the face of leadership turnover. It is particularly important in governmental organizations, where changes in the party in power may produce continuous shifts in leadership. A governmental bureaucracy remains stable and relatively capable of performance so long as its structure and distribution of functions remain relatively unchanged. Put more bluntly, the bureaucrat fights back if he feels his actual position is threatened with abolishment. He will fight equally vigorously if he feels that his present managerial functions are being transferred, modified, or reduced in number and importance.

Bendix has made the point that modern management places great emphasis on human relations skills.[15] Ability to be articulate in talking to others, and felicity in relations with them, are central features. Bendix concludes that this is an inevitable consequence of bureaucratic administration. If people are selected and recruited for their positions on the basis of merit and ability, then they need to be accorded personal recognition in the form of humane treatment. In a leader-oriented organization the leader's whim is law. In a tradition-oriented organization the social structure provided customary ways of interacting.

In bureaucratic administration neither leadership whim nor customary patterns of behavior are sufficient. An additional requirement is that the personality integrity of the functionary be preserved by respectful treatment of him.

There are two additional factors leading to the human relations approach. A good deal of discourse in carrying out business operations is either irrelevant to the business at hand, or concerned with preserving realms of specialization. A human relations approach provides an adequate rationale for non-business interaction. It becomes reasonable for an executive to inquire about the welfare of a subordinate's family because this is a humane thing to do.

In preventing others from encroaching on one's organizational responsibilities, the human relations approach provides an adequate substitute for open conflict. If the sales executive can firmly but politely assert that selling is his job, and not that of the production man, he can preserve his jurisdiction over this operation. Indeed, an important part of the vocabulary of bureaucrats and functionaries is concerned with "selling" ideas. In this process the functionary convinces his colleague specialists that he alone is competent to handle his own specialization, and that the others ought to keep out. Thus the human relations approach provides an important way in which specialists can fend off the encroachments of colleagues.

We can now summarize the behaviors of the bureaucrat as follows: he is a man who occupies a specialized management position. The establishment of his position is the organizational acknowledgment that special responsibilities are centered in him and that he is expected to have the competence to fulfill these responsibilities. A bureaucrat's training and prior experience give him the inner conviction of competence. He tends to see the world of work revolving around the special importance of his own work assignments. This permits him to be independent of pressures to conform to other standards of judgment, and criteria irrelevant to his own specialization. At the same time, this myopia prevents him from entering wholeheartedly into cooperation with other specialists.

The bureaucrat then becomes a man to whom responsibility can be assigned with a reasonable assurance that he can fulfill it. His efforts must be coordinated with those of other specialists, and in particular situations he may be overruled by higher decision. This does not destroy the bureaucrat's belief in the correctness of his decisions, granting his own special criteria. He can continue in the organization with relative comfort even in the face of leadership changes if his own position is not threatened by new leaders. In personal interaction with other members of management the new human relations approach gives the bureaucrat a mode of behavior that preserves his personality integrity, and that of his colleagues, while providing him with defenses that involve "selling" rather than conflict.

STANDARDIZING COMMAND FUNCTIONS

The problems of command are increased with the complexity and size of the management group. It will be recalled that we mean by command the translation of top policy into operating reality. It is therefore necessary to standardize command functions in order to insure that the intentions of top management will, in fact, be carried out by the working levels of the organization. This standardization of command function takes two general forms. (A) Innovating and controlling functions are typically specialized in management departments. (B) Directing and coordinating functions are typically made uniform through standing operating procedures.

STANDARDIZING THROUGH SPECIALIZATION

The nature of innovating and controlling functions makes them particularly adaptable to staff specialization. Innovation is concerned with changing the organization, or its products, in the future. Control is concerned with insuring that the organization is operating as planned. Both of these management functions lie outside the scope of day-to-day operations. Innovating functions examine daily operations for their improvement potential. Controlling management functions consider day-to-day operations for their adequacy in the light of present ways of getting work done.

Innovation and control are important in gaining perspectives on regular operations. However, neither innovation nor control is directly involved in the on-going work of the organization. For this reason it is possible, and desirable, to specialize innovating and control functions to keep them out of the main stream of day-to-day command decisions.

In the usual management literature innovating and control functions are described as the characteristic activity of staff departments.[16] In contrast, directing and coordinating management functions are viewed as the command activities of the line organization. The line organization is the body of the management bureaucracy concerned with maintaining day-to-day activities. Staff departments are set aside from the line organization in order to insure relative simplicity in the direct command functions of coordinating and directing work.

Specialized control departments operate on simple bases. A standard of performance is established—for example, the budget of an operating department is a figure of total expenditures for that department against which its actual expenditures may be checked; the sales or production bogies are figures of anticipated volume of sales, or output, against which individual operating departments can be checked. Once the standard is established, the control department then gathers enough information from operations to test whether they are meeting established standards. This collection of information, most often in statistical form, is the major activity of control departments. Once the necessary information is secured, then actual operations are checked against standards of performance. This information is typically forwarded as reports to top management. Where wide discrepancies exist between the expected standards and the actual performance, top management may take action. Should performance fall below expectation, the operating department may be called on for explanation. Should performance exceed expectation, the operating department may be in for praise and commendation. Staff control departments are the watchdogs of performance levels.

Innovating functions are specialized in departments whose titles indicate their responsibility for change. Typical innovating departments carry titles like: research and development, product design, consumer or market preference, product engineering, process engineering, training, and organizational development. Members of innovating departments are expected to be fault-finders. The reason such departments exist is the belief that things can be done better. Innovators are given the task of constructive criticism of present ways of doing things, with the anticipation that they will come up with better answers. This often strains relations between innovators and operating personnel. The operating or line organization is wedded to present ways of doing things. Any changes suggested by innovators explicitly criticize present methods, and implicitly threaten those now responsible for them.

In the relationship between bureaucrats responsible for innovating functions and others responsible for day-to-day operations we find the classic conflicts between staff and line organizations. Dalton has shown in his study of three steel companies that the operating officials bitterly oppose management innovators in the person of engineers.[17] Engineers are viewed as half-baked college boys whose ideas can't be valuable because they are not based on long operating experience. When an engineer introduces a useable idea, the line officials, according to the Dalton study, often attempt to appropriate the idea as their own. In the steel companies, the engineers felt threatened by the antagonism of line officials, particularly as to its effect on advancement. A number of the engineers reacted by trying to get into the line organization, giving up innovating for directing and coordinating functions.

Innovating and controlling management functions are standardized by specialization. These functions are set apart in staff departments. They are separated from the line organization in order to simplify directing and coordinating. Staff departments concerned with innovation and control feed their discoveries and information to the top executives and line commanders. Management decision makers may then adopt staff recommendations and, by their approval, give legitimacy to the proposed actions. In this way, policy and command decisions are affected by innovating and controlling staffs.

STANDARDIZING OPERATING COMMAND

Members of management concerned with operating departments make regular command decisions, but these decisions are always surrounded by important restrictions designed to standardize command functions in the managerial bureaucracy.

Command functions have to be standardized. Bureaucracy directly linking top decision makers with operating levels must be a reliable instrument for transmitting policies with relatively little distortion. If distortion in commands is minimized, then the anticipated outcome of policy decisions is more likely to be achieved. If intermediate commands distort or change the policy intent, or methods for its achievement, then outcome of the policy may be different from expectation. Standardizing command functions of directing and coordinating is based on the desire to maximize predictability of outcome for any policy decision.

The personnel policies and rules of the organization constitute the most important limitation on directing commands issued by management members. Next in importance in limiting command decisions is the structure of job assignments embedded in the normal division of labor.

A department head has called his section heads into his office for a conference. At this level of command the boss typically does a lot of talking, explaining, directing. It is even significant that the conference is held in the boss' office. This tends to fortify his authority by making subordinates meet him on his grounds, not theirs.

Personnel policy and rules determine what is included and what excluded in the decision area of commanders. They also determine the modes for enforcing commands. A foreman may not have the right to hire, fire, transfer, or promote his subordinates. He may make recommendations about these matters, but the actual commands governing them will be issued elsewhere, usually in the personnel department, or by a line superior. In Dale's study of the best practices of American industry, based on a sample of 100 American firms, he found that the personnel department conducts interviews and selects new employees, with the foreman having the final say in two-thirds of the companies, while in the remaining third the foreman had no control of hiring. Dale also found that in only 10 per cent of the companies could the foreman discharge employees without consulting superiors, or the personnel department. He also found that in every instance pay increases and promotions had to be approved by higher authorities.[18]

In enforcing commands, a supervisor may have other kinds of restrictions imposed on him. He may be required by personnel policy to warn a worker who fails to follow a legitimate command. Further failure by the worker may result in his supervisor's report recommending discipline—a report that goes to a superior or to the personnel department for action. A supervisor may be restricted from using abusive language or physical force to secure compliance with his commands. Dale's study showed that foremen had complete charge of discipline in only 10 per cent of the companies studies.[19] The foreman may even be restricted in the kinds of deprivations he can use in enforcing his commands. He may not be permitted, on his own initiative, to ban smoking, or insist on working up to the closing whistle, without seeking superior's approval for such actions.

In general, personnel policies are a statement of prerogatives conferred on workers by management action. Viewed from the standpoint of the supervisor as the commander, these same employee prerogatives constitute limitations on the areas over which he can exercize immediate direction, and the ways in which he can insure commands will be followed. When we see both sides of the coin of command, we learn why supervisory ranks of management generally oppose restrictive personnel policies that shift out of their hands directing decisions. Much of the dilemma of supervisors in industry centers on this continual restriction on their directing functions through the operation of personnel rules.[20]

Division of labor in the work organization also places important restrictions on supervisory command functions. When tasks are segregated into departmental units, each supervisor can exercise command only over his own department. A foreman does not have, for example, command functions throughout the plant. He can only issue directions to his own departmental crews. The division of labor therefore initially specifies who comes within the command range of each supervisor. It is only to this particular group that the supervisor can issue legitimate directions. When a supervisor moves out of his own area he can issue directions only through the supervisors of the other areas.

Workers are exceedingly sensitive to the areas of a supervisor's command. They may willingly obey directions of their own supervisor, and openly ignore orders coming from other members of management. Such behavior is not insubordination. It simply reflects the fact that in complex organizations not all members of management, having the same level of supervision, can issue directions to anyone at a lower level. The area of command is always restricted. Legitimate directions can be given only within the departmental jurisdiction of the supervisor.

Division of labor also determines what a supervisor can order a subordinate to do. Here the basic criterion of right or wrong orders is the work assignment of the subordinate. Workers may refuse to do work if they can claim that the work does not fall within their job assignment. A supervisor is then put on the defensive, either to prove that the work does fall within the job assignment, or to rescind his order. Machine operators or skilled craftsmen, for example, may refuse to sweep scrap off the floor, claiming it is the job of the janitor. The supervisor, directing the men to clean up their own work places, may be on shaky grounds because the specialization of tasks does make the clean-up job the janitor's work. In other instances, a supervisor may order a man to move from one kind of machine operation to another, in order to get work done. If the worker refuses, claiming it is not part of his work assignment, the supervisor is in the position of having to prove that the particular division of labor permits transfers of the sort he ordered.

The first line supervisor operates face-to-face with workers. A foreman's command functions are typically carried out at the working stations of the men, not in the shop office. It is characteristic that at the lowest level of supervision, the boss goes to the men, as this foreman of a blast furnace is doing to give his men a safety talk.

In the interest of standardizing repetitive operations, job assignments become specialized and subdivided. The technology makes this necessary. In the very process of specialization and subdivision, however, an important limitation is placed on a supervisor's direction of his work force. He must live with the established work assignments, and limit his orders to keeping people at their assigned tasks. In a number of unionized plants, this may even include a limitation preventing the supervisor from performing any productive labor. His own actual working behavior may be restricted to supervising, and any attempt to do actual work will be resisted by the workers.

A third aspect of the division of labor limiting supervisors' command functions is the determination of job assignments by staff departments rather than by the supervisor. Most typically, job descriptions and operating procedures are written in staff departments, though the supervisor may be consulted in preparing such directives. The supervisor may, therefore, even lose direct control of the work assignments of his own crews.

Directing functions of supervisors are standardized by personnel policies and the organizational division of labor. The supervisor loses personal control of decisions in these areas. He becomes the administrator of rules, policies, and practices originating above him in the line organization or in staff departments. A supervisor is a master of his own department only insofar as he operates within the restrictions established by the organization. He is constantly pressured to become an administrator of complex rules and policies, and has little initiative to change rules or introduce new policies. The supervisor retains control over the timing of his commands. Even on timing, however, the demands of production schedules and continuous operations often reduce the supervisor's area of discretion.

The bureaucrats primarily concerned with directing others operate under tight wraps imposed by the work organization. This tends to insure standardization in directing commands. It also leads to rigidity in supervisory behavior.

STANDARDIZING COORDINATING COMMANDS

Command functions involving coordination have their own modes of standardization. The coordinating executive is concerned with maintaining balance among the organization's operations. For this purpose the organization structures give him important guidepoints. When doubt exists as to the proper point of balance, representative committees may be established to advise.

The power structure of the organization tells the coordinating executive a good deal about stable balance points within it. A good coordinator tries to keep departments and functions of equal power in relative balance. He seeks to prevent one department from achieving more power at the expense of another. The sales department, for example, may become aggressive with respect to design of product, rate of output, or selling price, in the interest of greater sales. The design engineers may balk; the production departments may rebel against increasing levels of output; and the accounting department may claim that the proposed selling price has no relationship to costs of production. Each department argues from the standpoint of its specialized responsibility in the organization. A coordinating executive making the final balancing decision evaluates the factual arguments, as well as the effects of his decision on future distributions of power. If his decision supports the sales department against the others, it may strengthen the future impact of sales viewpoints on organization policy. This will strengthen the relative power position of the sales department.

In making such balancing decisions, the coordinating executive takes into account the established power structure. Usually the least disturbing decision he can make is to leave the power distribution unchanged among the departments in conflict. Whether this promotes profits or efficiency is another matter.

Coordinating executives may choose to establish a committee to study a problem before making decisions. Typically such committees are composed of representatives drawn from interested departments. Through such a committee arrangement, coordinating executives delegate the planning functions to representatives of the contesting departments.

When a plan is finally submitted by the committee, the coordinating executive can use it as a basis for his own decision, with some assurance that the departments whose representatives drew up the plan will be at least partially committed to it. The representative committee is one way of making the interested departments work out a mutually satisfactory point of balance among themselves.

It often happens that representative committees, established to advise executives on their coordinating functions, fail to produce acceptable plans. Committees can be the burial ground for coordination plans as well as their birth place. Even where the committee fails, its efforts may prove enlightening to the coordinating executive; he may at least learn some of the points at which irreconcilable differences exist in the organization.

Where operating plans are produced by representative committees, the coordinating executive has lost freedom of decision to the committee. Should he choose not to accept the committee plan, he may antagonize all the departments whose representatives compose the committee. Use of such advisory committees is thus another way of standardizing the coordinating command functions, by delegating the planning of coordination to representatives of the departments whose activities must be fitted together.

Commands concerned with coordinating diverse departments of an organization are standardized on two bases. These commands may follow from the existing power structure of the organization, and reconfirm it. Coordinating commands may also result from new balances in the power structures worked out by representative committees drawn from the departments whose individual power may be affected by the commands issued.

We have now examined some of the ways in which the command functions of bureaucracy are standardized. Standardization of directing commands is achieved in special ways. Coordinating commands are standardized on different grounds. Innovating commands and controlling commands have their own modes of standardization.

The managerial functions of bureaucracy can now be seen in perspective. Bureaucracy is the linkage between top policy makers and workers. This in-between body of management is concerned with turning policy into commands to make the work of the organization effective. To insure this linkage between policy and operations, the commands of the bureaucracy need to be standardized. Standardization of commands is achieved by different modes for directing, controlling, innovating, and coordinating management functions.

We have treated the four general managerial functions as though they were performed separately by different members of management. Referring back to Chapter 5, it should be clear that many members of management perform all of these managerial functions. It should then be apparent that fulfilling command functions as members of the managerial bureaucracy requires extensive talent, considerable training, and experience.

NON-RESPONSIBLE BUREAUCRATIC BEHAVIOR

Some bureaucrats fail to fufill their assigned responsibilities. There is no automatic way to guard bureaucratic administration from non-responsible bureaucrats, but it is instructive to examine some types of non-responsible bureaucratic behavior in order to discover how inefficiency can creep into bureaucratic administration.

There are two forms of deviant bureaucratic behavior with which we will deal. The first results in avoiding responsibility. The second results in hoarding it.

In the accompanying chart the four management functions are set forth. In the second column the typical situations in which there is a need for making command decisions are illustrated. The third column shows the basis on which bureaucrats who avoid their responsibilities make their decisions. The last column shows the kinds of responsibility avoidance displayed.

A supervisor concerned with directing workers when faced with an operating problem, may make his decision according to "the book." In so doing he is appealing to the authority of the rules and policies under which he operates. He ascribes the existence of the policies and rules to higher level authorities, whose ways may be mysterious, or whose reasoning is esoteric. Avoidance of responsibility for directing commands leads to assertion that the commands are issued because

CHART 20.4

NON-RESPONSIBLE BUREAUCRATIC BEHAVIOR LEADS TO AVOIDING RESPONSIBILITY

Management Functions	*Need for making Command Decisions*	*Bases of Decision*	*Ways of Avoiding Responsibility—* BUCK PASSING TO:
DIRECTING	EXISTING OPERATING PROBLEM	"THE BOOK"	HIGHER OR LOWER AUTHORITIES
COORDINATING	DEPARTMENTAL CONFLICT	EXISTING POWER STRUCTURE	PAST HISTORY: "It has always been done that way."
CONTROLLING	QUESTIONING OF CONTROL INFORMATION	RIGHT TO EXERCISE CONTROL FUNCTIONS	TOP DECISION MAKERS
INNOVATING	NEW IDEAS	CUSTOM	PAST HISTORY: "Past methods or designs work."

the supervisor cannot help himself—he has to do it. He may even privately declare that he thinks the commands he issues are wrong, inefficient, or inapplicable. "I have to limit your smoking breaks to ten minutes, because that's the rule, even though I know we can get the work done with longer break periods." "You've got to use this lousy material because the jerks in purchasing goofed off in buying it. You know how those guys operate." Sometimes the buck passing for middle level supervisors may be downward to lower level supervisors. A middle level supervisor may see himself as being forced to support his subordinate. "I wouldn't have made that decision myself, but I've got to back Joe up now that he did."

Making coordinating command decisions in departmental conflicts may lead to decisions whose necessity is justified by the existing power structure. The coordinating executive may pass the buck to past history by asserting that "It has always been done that way, and my decision is to keep doing it that way." Complete dependence on past history may lead to ignoring new facts, or new situations, that require a break with precedent. Responsbility for making new command decisions can be avoided by the appeal to history.

The usefulness of control information is often questioned by operating departments. This is particularly true when vast amounts of statistical information are required in fulfilling the controlling functions. Such attacks by operating departments place the control functionaries on the defensive. They are likely to appeal to their delegated right to exercise control functions and collect controlling information, passing the buck to top decision makers who have ordered the complex controls. No attempt is made to re-examine the usefulness of the controlling information collected, or their cost in relation to their use. The exercise of the control function is jealously guarded as an immutable delegation from top management. Reasonable criteria are rejected in evaluating present control activities.

Innovating command functions are usually stimulated by new ideas coming either from inside or outside the organization. An appeal to custom or habitual procedure may lead to rejection of new ideas. Past success becomes its own justification for refusing to make innovations. Specialized departments whose sole function is that of innovating may run into this kind of responsibility avoidance on the part of top executives who have to pass on new ideas and proposals.

It should be noted that the kind of bureaucratic behavior which leads to an avoidance of responsibility makes use of organization processes for its own justification. If you now re-examine the third column of the chart, you will note that the body of rules and regulations, the existing power structure, the present authority structure, and the customary procedures of the organization are used in rejecting responsibility.

The second kind of irresponsible behavior among bureaucrats is a hoarding of responsibility. A bureaucrat who hoards responsibility has a self-image as an infallible authority. He tends to refuse to delegate to, or consult, colleagues, subordinates, or superiors. He is exceedingly eager to prove his competence, either to himself, or to his superiors. He views the test of his competence as his ability, unassisted, to solve all his operating and command problems. The result is a grasping after responsibility through a misplaced or misguided sense of initiative. Such a functionary wants to do everything himself, because he thinks he can do it better than anyone else. He refuses to delegate to subordinates, or does so reluctantly and without admitting their ability to do as well as himself. The responsibility hoarder may pile increasing work loads on himself, so that he appears to be exceedingly devoted to his position. He may stay late at his work, and return early, simply because he needs the time to do the work he refuses to share. He may become a bottleneck in the organization. It is clear that the hoarding of responsibility may not be consistent with the effective performance of responsibility. It should be pointed out, incidentally, that responsibility hoarding through personal initiative may actually be encouraged by superiors in their desire to foster aggressive and original thinking on the part of management functionaries. A responsibility hoarder simply misconstrues the assumption of personal responsibility for a display of personal initiative.

We have examined briefly two major forms of non-responsible bureaucratic behavior. The purpose is to indicate that even the bureaucratic form of administration is not without its problems.

BUREAUCRATIC ADMINISTRATION

This chapter has focused on the form that administration takes in large scale organizations. We have examined the sources of bureaucratic administration. Following that, we analyzed the general characteristics of bureaucracy. Next, attention was turned to the standardization of command functions in the bureaucratic reaches of management. Finally, the breakdown of bureaucratic responsibility was considered.

The bureaucracy of a large scale organization is *of* management but it is not *the* management. It is the necessary link between top decision makers and the operating levels of the work organization. There is no organizational invention yet in sight that will replace bureaucratic administration as the efficient tool for making large and complex organizations operate effectively.

NOTES FOR CHAPTER 20

1 Seymour Melman, "The Rising Cost of Management," *Manchester Guardian,* Survey of Industry, Trade, and Finance, 1954, pp. 31-32.

2 Reinhard Bendix, *Work and Authority in Industry* (New York: John Wiley & Sons, 1956), pp. 214-220.

3 Seymour Melman, "Production and Administration Cost in Relation to Size of Firm," *Applied Statistics,* 3:1-10 (March, 1954).

4 Melman, *op. cit.,* p. 32.

5 See in this connection the classic study edited by John R. Commons, *Documentary History of American Industrial Society* (Cleveland: The A. H. Clark Co., 1910, 1911).

6 In Chapter 18 emphasis was placed on the influences of the bureaucrat on communication. We are now asserting that these influences have limits, setting forth the nature of the limitations.

7 Max Weber, *Theory of Social and Economic Organization,* translated and edited by A. M. Henderson and T. Parsons (New York: Oxford University Press, 1947), especially Part III. See also Robert Dubin, *Human Relations in Administration* (Englewood Cliffs, N. J.: Prentice-Hall, Inc., 1951), pp. 156-163; 195-198.

8 See the report by Frederick H. Harbison and Eugene W. Burgess, "Modern Management in Western Europe," *American Journal of Sociology,* 60: 15-23 (July, 1954).

NOTES FOR CHAPTER 20 (CONT.)

[9] For an interesting and sympathetic account of Mr. Avery's leadership behaviors, see "The Stewardship of Mr. Avery," *Fortune,* 33:111-113, 179-186 (May, 1946).

[10] Cf. Reinhard Bendix, S. M. Lipset, T. F. Malm, "Social Origins and Career Patterns," *Industrial and Labor Relations Review,* 7:246-251 (January, 1954); Richard Centers, "Occupational Mobility of Urban Occupational Strata," *American Sociological Review,* 13:197-203 (April, 1948); H. S. Parnes, *Research on Labor Mobility: An Appraisal of Research Findings in the United States,* Bulletin #65 (New York: Social Science Research Council, 1954); P. A. Sorokin, *Social Mobility* (New York: Harper & Brothers, 1927), especially Chapter 7, "The Channels of Vertical Mobility," Frank Taussig and C. S. Joslyn, *American Business Leaders: A Study in Social Origins and Social Stratification* (New York: The Macmillan Company, 1932); W. L. Warner and J. C. Abegglen, *Occupational Mobility in American Business and Industry* (Minneapolis: University of Minnesota Press, 1955); and by the same authors, *Big Business Leaders in America* (New York: Harper & Brothers, 1955).

[11] As retold in Cleveland Amory, *The Proper Bostonians* (New York: E. P. Dutton, 1947).

[12] Max Weber, *Theory of Social and Economic Organization,* especially pp. 328-329.

[13] Leonard Reisman, "A Study of Role Concepts in a Bureaucracy," *Social Forces,* 27:305-310.

[14] Harold Laski, "The Limitations of the Expert," *Harper's Magazine,* 162: 102-106 (December, 1930).

[15] Reinhard Bendix, *Work and Authority in Industry,* especially Chapter 5.

[16] Typical works are: A. S. Knowles and R. D. Thompson, *Industrial Management* (New York: The Macmillan Company, 1944); R. T. Livingston, *The Engineering of Organization and Management* (New York: McGraw-Hill Book Co., 1949); Paul Mayer, "Staff and Line," *Revue Internationale des Sciences Administratives,* 1:9-28 (1955); W. H. Newman, *Administrative Action: The Techniques of Organization and Management* (Englewood Cliffs, N. J.: Prentice-Hall, Inc., 1951).

[17] Melville Dalton, "Conflict Between Staff and Line Managerial Officers," *American Sociological Review,* 15:342-351 (June, 1950).

[18] Ernest Dale, *The Development of Foremen in Management,* Research Report No. 7 (New York: American Management Association, 1945), p. 9.

[19] Ibid.

[20] An incisive examination of this dilemma is made in Fritz J. Roethlisberger, "The Foreman: Master and Victim of Double Task," *Harvard Business Review,* 23:285-294 (Spring, 1945).

The board of directors room, with its literal and physical separation from the operating offices of the company, and its distinctive furnishings and decor symbolize the attempt to be above the daily fray in performing leadership functions. Even the telephones on the conference table imply isolation as much as they do contact with mundane daily affairs—it takes a real emergency to call a director's attention away from the board meeting. Meeting of the board of directors, Standard Oil Company of New Jersey.

Chapter 21

MANAGEMENT AS LEADERSHIP

Leadership and command are not the same. In this chapter we are concerned with the circumstances under which leadership is exercised in organizations, and the ways in which leaders behave.[1]

The two previous chapters established the fact that much of the behavior of organization officials involves giving commands and policing performance. This kind of behavior fulfills a prescribed position in the organization, and can be carried out independently of personal relationships between leader and followers, and of the personal characteristics of the commander.

When we turn our attention to leadership, however, we must take into account more than the official relationships between order givers and order receivers. Much of the business of any organization can be accomplished without leadership. We therefore need to explain the functions of leadership, indicating the effects leaders have on human behavior in work organizations.[2]

There are two primary functions of organization leadership: (A) building and sustaining morale, and (B) confronting and meeting change affecting the organization.[3] These are distinctive leadership functions requiring different skills and activities. However, these do not necessarily require personal specialization; the same leader may perform both functions.

LEADERSHIP AND MORALE

All levels of leadership are concerned with building and sustaining the morale of the led group.[4] Techniques for affecting morale will vary according to the kind of leader and the kind of group being led. The informal leader who has a small group and who is related to his group by special ties will affect group morale in ways distinct from those of a leader in the larger formal organization.

We can examine the relation between leadership and the functions that it satisfies in a general way. We must also be clear that the two major types of leaders, formal and informal, having distinctive features of their own. In a later section of this chapter we will examine these types of leaders and point out their specific ways of carrying out their functions.[5]

For purposes of organization analysis we use a specific definition of morale. Morale is a feeling of identification with a group, and acceptance of the goals and purposes common to the group. We have already examined morale in Chapter 12. There we identified morale as the zeal with which the person identifies with his group associates and their collective goals.

Morale is not a state of well being so much as it is a state of belonging, and an awareness of the conditions of group membership. Indeed, a person may very well feel great unhappiness, and yet have a strong sense of belonging. It would be hard to argue, for example, that soldiers in battle are particularly happy, either about their chances of living, or their way of life. Nevertheless, fighting units in battle can exhibit high morale because of soldiers' close identification with their combat unit, and willingness to make supreme personal sacrifices for the immediate goals of this group.

We are sometimes led astray in analyzing morale by the tendency to identify a state of well being, or satisfaction, as high morale and the opposite as low morale. It is obvious that people have states of satisfaction and dissatisfaction. Not nearly so obvious is the fact that there may *not* be a one-to-one correspondence between personal satisfaction and a high sense of group belonging, including identification with group behavior and goals.

There are five functions that a leader fills in building and sustaining morale. These are: (A) group symbolizer, (B) group goal selector, (C) group decision maker, (D) group arbiter, and (E) group example. We will examine each of these in turn.

SYMBOLIC ASPECTS OF LEADERSHIP

One way the leader affects the morale of a group is through his role as its symbolic leader. Any leader can play a symbolic role for his group by standing for it, or symbolizing it, in relation to its social environment.

Top executives of organizations, as their formal leaders, are always viewed as group spokesmen. The formal leaders proclaim the goals and policies of the organization to the public at large; they testify on its behalf in public gatherings; and "sell" its virtues whenever given the opportunity to reach an audience. It is one of the outstanding transformations of American business leadership that its principal figures have been made over from the image of the "robber baron," with a public-be-damned outlook, into the picture of industrial statesmen, with broad concerns for social welfare.[6] This has been almost wholly a shift in the position of business executives as the symbolic embodiments of their organizations.[7]

In the voluntary and organized social

groups of work there tends to be at least a minimum differentiation between a leader and followers. Such informal leaders may operate as group spokesmen, or symbols, in appropriate circumstances. The leader may be the one who publicly deals with attacks on the group. He may simply serve as the focal point by which the group is labelled "Joe's gang" or "Bill's clique." Insofar as the group is labelled, the leader may be the one who gives the designation to it, and the one who stands for the group in the eyes of outsiders.

The symbolic aspect of leadership has value to the group. It clarifies, for its members, who shall be the spokesman, and who shall represent the group in its dealings with outsiders. Similarly, for the outsiders ease in approaching and dealing with the group is facilitated by the role that the leader plays as its symbolic center.[8]

It is interesting to note that the formal leader of the organization always plays the symbolic role. The informal leader typically carries out this function if the informal group is recognized as such. If the informal group is genuinely subversive of the work organization, it may attempt to hide its identity and conceal its leadership. Under these circumstances the symbolic leadership role has only its intra-group functions, and does not serve to relate the group to its social environment.

LEADER AS GOAL SELECTOR

Another important function of a leader is defining group goals. Once the goals are determined, the leader may also influence the selection of means for their attainment.

Goal selection is one of the most characteristic functions of leadership. Indeed, the classic concept of leadership is that of leading a group toward a goal that is not determined by the group.[9]

In his position of defining group goals, or in specifying the means for reaching these goals, the leader is most obviously separated and distinguished from his followers. The leader comes to be isolated from his group most clearly in his goal-determining function. This isolation is grounded partly in the authority that the leader exercises as he sets the group's goals. The followers look on the leader as the one who is appropriate to choose the proper goals for the group and, in a sense, delegate this task to him.

When group goals are set by the leader there develops an additional bond connecting the leader and his followers. Followers not only identify themselves with the group, but also identify with group goals associated with the leader who determined them. Consequently, loyalty of members is given to the group, and to the leader, who is the source of some of the group goals. The leader comes to be personally identified as essential to the attainment of these goals.

Goal-determining behavior is not a universal leadership phenomenon. Indeed, there are leaders who fill some of the other functions of leadership, but clearly follow their followers, rather than lead by selecting goals. Some leaders seem to be highly sensitive to what they take to be the wishes, desires, or goals of their followers, and seek to satisfy these as nearly as possible. Where the group is a formal or informal electorate, the leader will often not function to set goals.[10] For example, an elected government official, insofar as he is a leader at all, may be highly responsive to his interpretation of the desires of his electorate.[11]

Goal-setting activities tend to isolate the leader. Failure to carry out such function on the part of a leader may throw him back into a more responsive relationship with his followers.

LEADER AND GROUP CHOICES

When the group is faced with choices, the leader often resolves them into a set of obvious alternatives. He may even choose the final alternative himself. Resolving group choices is a function related to that of providing goals and means for attaining them.

In resolving group choices the leader has the advantage that he sees them not only from inside the group, but also in the group's relation to its larger environment. Thus, the leader may well have a broader point of view that proves most valuable to the group in the choosing among alternate goals or objectives, as Rice has shown for an English factory.[12]

Where there is some discussion within the group about possible alternatives that the group faces, the leader may resolve the problem of choice by giving his support to a particular alternative. He is here entering into the group deliberations. He throws the prestige, importance, and authority of his position on one side or the other of a discussion.[13]

Resolution of group choices is often performed by the leader who is at the same time an expert in an area of knowledge. A person may combine the leadership position he holds with an acknowledged expertness in an area which together give his opinion and contribution to a discussion exceptionally heavy weight.

In this function of resolving the problems of choice in the group, the leader preserves group energies so that they are not dissipated in fruitless and over-extended concern with programs or courses of action. Put another way, the leader keeps the group from becoming merely a debating society. By resolving its choices, the leader turns it into an action group.

LEADER AND GROUP DIFFERENCES

Another major function of the leader is that of resolving internal group differences. These differences may have a variety of sources, ranging from personal rivalries between group members, to significant debate on major issues.

When the leader plays the role of arbiter of group differences, he does not enter into the group discussions as a participant in the same way that he would when he takes leadership in resolving the problems of group choice. When the leader deals with group differences, he approaches them more nearly in the spirit of a judge, and tends to behave in a judicial fashion. He may hear out all sides of an issue and then decide on a solution.

The leader may have these important judicial functions, particularly as he is required to coordinate diverse activities in the group, or to keep it welded together in the face of potential splitting because of severe personality differences among its members. The judicial role of leaders becomes complicated because it can involve standards of justice that are part of the values of the group.[14] It may also involve balancing political cliques and personal powers in the interests of group unity.

In filling the judicial role, it seems clear that the leader must have a fairly long-time experience in the group. This provides the leader with knowledge of group values and standards of justice. It also develops the leader's sensitivity to the more subtle distributions of group power so that he makes realistic evaluations in the power area in judging or refereeing internal group differences.[15]

LEADER AS EXAMPLE

There is another area of leadership behavior in which the leader becomes a model, or example, for the followers. This is generally based on a strong personal tie between leader and followers. The leader is viewed as the embodiment of the highest values of personal behavior and outlook.[16] Accordingly, followers attempt to pattern themselves after the leader in behavior, point of view, outlook, language, dress, and in all the ways in which it is possible to imitate a person.[17]

For the follower there are important limitations on his imitation of the leader's behavior. When the leader is behaving as a leader—that is, when his behavior is not personal but functional in his role as leader—the followers typically are in no position to imitate him. On the other hand, the characteristic personal behaviors of the leader are eagerly imitated. For example, the leader may exhibit decisiveness in his behavior, and his followers may attempt to take on this decisive characteristic in their own behavior. However, none of the followers would attempt to make decisions in areas of leadership.

The most imitated aspects of the leader are those of personal behavior, of dress, and of general demeanor. The function of this imitation is not to supplant the leader, nor is it to reduce the level of the leader to that of the followers. Imitation of leader behavior turns out to be a means for identifying followers with the leader and his cause through external marks that are readily visible to outsiders.

LEADER AND MORALE

In general, in the relation between leadership and group morale we have been emphasizing here the means by which the leader is able to enhance or maintain identification of members with the group. He may do this by making himself the symbolic center of the group, or by providing an example for personal behavior that is readily imitated. He may be the originator of significant ideas in the group, and determine the group goals and means for their achievement. He may act to throw the weight of his position in favor of a particular alternative among choices with which the group is concerned. Finally, he may act as the judge or arbiter of differences within the group. All these activities provide opportunities for the leader to weld the group together into a unified whole, and keep it unified over the period of his leadership.

A leader may often play a more general inspirational role for his followers. He may "lecture" them, exhort them, or use personal example. Inspirational efforts are usually unproductive, however, unless they fill one or more of the five functions of leadership. Put another way, attempts to use influence, whether straight propaganda or more subtle forms of persuasion, are valuable only to the extent that the leader in fact has influence over his followers. This influence will exist only if the leader is really performing one or more of the five functions of leadership.

LEADERSHIP AND ORGANIZATION CHANGE

Innovation is one of the important authority activities of management, as we discovered in Chapter 5. A particularly crucial kind of innovating behavior that may affect the future of the work organization is displayed by leaders in confronting change. A change in the internal or external environment of the organization may be unstabilizing.

A leader functions effectively when he devises ways of meeting changed conditions. This almost invariably means that he is innovating. A leader's innovations may be improvised or planned. His innovations are always designed to point the direction for organization evolution. Leaders' innovations may also point towards an anticipated state of future stability. In short, the long term future of a work organization may depend on the skill and imagination of its leaders in confronting change.[18]

In general, the relationship between leadership and morale is based on a direct or symbolic personal relationship between leader and followers. On the other hand, leadership exercised in handling changes confronting an organization may be of a relatively impersonal character. It represents leadership *in* the organization rather than leadership *of* people directly.[19]

By way of example we can think of the President of the General Motors Corporation as exercising important leadership in directing the affairs of that far-flung industrial empire. From the standpoint of the half million members of that organization, the President can be a highly impersonal and very remote individual. His role with respect to the morale of the group may be negligible. Nevertheless, in the organization as a whole, he is a crucial person because he is the primary officer concerned with internal and external conditions of change that the organization must meet successfully in order to continue in business.

LEADERSHIP AND TECHNICAL STAFFS

Leadership functions having to do with building and maintaining group morale can never be delegated by the leader to a staff or subordinate individual. On the other hand, many of the functions of leadership in organizational change are typically delegated and assigned to staff individuals. This fact serves to characterize one of the important differences between the leader as a morale builder, and the leader as controller of the organization's destiny.

In some position or office in every organization there has to be the responsibility for recognizing when the organization is in need of some kind of readjustment or realignment.

There also has to be an official who will determine when the environment of the organization needs to be considered in its operations.[20] Both of these functions often involve very technical considerations, and continuing systems of appraisal and evaluation of organizational conditions and external influences that bear on operations.

Controls necessary to keep an organization in balance or determine its operating condition may involve highly technical operations. These controls are often initiated and evaluated by special staffs. Similarly, the evaluation of the larger environment of the organization may involve complex market analyses, economic analyses of general trends in the economy, investment decisions, inventory decisions, and the like. Again it will be recognized that action in these areas may also involve highly technical operations.

For both these complex areas of operations the leader may not himself be completely competent to gather the required information, or to evaluate it. Furthermore, the leader's relation to these problems is one of relative impersonality as far as the members of the organization are concerned. The leader is not in a position of losing any influence, prestige, or authority to his followers by delegating to special experts the information gathering and evaluating tasks in these complex areas. Ultimate responsibility still resides in the leader to make necessary decisions guiding the organization in responding to internal or external influences.[21]

Whether the leader assumes responsibility for these decisions by accepting without change the recommendation of his staff experts, or whether he makes an independent decision that takes into account the recommendations of the staff experts, is not important. The real test of the leader in confronting the conditions of change on behalf of the organization is his ability to recognize the need for organizational adjustment. To put it another way, the executive either has to be smart enough to know when and how his organization needs to be shaken up and reoriented, or he has to be smart enough to employ the necessary staff experts who can make these discoveries for him. In either instance, he gets deserved credit for being a capable executive in exercising his leadership functions of confronting conditions of change.

PROGRAMING THE FUTURE

A second aspect of leadership behavior in the face of dynamic conditions affecting operations of an organization involves determining next steps in its development. A leader is expected not only to know when change is necessary in the organization, but to know in what direction the change should be made. In short, the leader is expected to provide some kind of program for the future of the organization.[22]

Sigurd F. Varian, developer of important advances in electronic tubes, found that the presidency of his company, Varian Associates, demanded entirely too much time in fulfilling command functions. He has recently moved to the position of vice-chairman of the board of directors, and chief engineer, in order to devote his full time to innovating new technical advances as well as broad company policies.

Programs for the future may take standardized forms like production schedules, sales programs, and regular style or model changes. Alternatively, the program developed by the executive leader may entail continuation of present plans, or even a cutback to former levels of output, and modes and methods of operation.

Whether the executive's plan is forward-looking or backward-looking, or tends to hold a stable present position, is less important than the fact that it is announced as a program and appears definitely to face up to the contingencies of the present. From the standpoint of subordinates, it is important that there be a definite program for meeting conditions of uncertainty or change facing the organization. The content of the program is much less important than the fact that a program exists and is being put into effect.

A distinction has to be drawn between programs that are the product of leadership in confronting organizational change, and programs that are a product of leadership affecting group morale. When the leader as morale builder is resolving problems of choice in the group, or selecting goals for the group, he is really providing a program of action. However, the group members identify themselves with this program of action through the leader. It is the leader's program, and group unity and morale are focused upon the leader as the source of these programs.[23]

The leader who is confronting organizational change may be personally unknown to the majority of the organization members. Their identification may be either with immediate supervisors, or with the organization in its larger, impersonal aspect. To these members, the function of a program of action is to insure some prospect of continued operations in the organization. It is a matter of little concern who originates the plan of action, or, by and large, what its content is. The primary fact of importance is that, in the face of some uncertainty challenging or threatening the organization, a plan of action does exist that has some prospect of proving successful in overcoming uncertainty.[24]

LEADERSHIP AND TIMING

In the regular on-going activities of most organizations it is recognized that there are going to be daily or seasonal shifts and adjustments in operations. These adjustments are expected. Leaders are attuned to this expectation, and have techniques for making necessary adjustments. These can be called the routine leadership decisions of the organization, although the routineness does not necessarily imply that these decisions are not critical. They are routine only in the sense that they are likely to be made repeatedly, over a relatively short period of time, and certainly will recur over a time period of at least a year.[25]

There are less frequently occurring situations in which basic reorganization may be required. This may involve fundamental changes in the goals and objectives of the organization; important technological innovations; the removal of plants and offices; or the personnel reorganization of major divisions and departments. It is one of the functions of leadership, in meeting change, to be aware of the needs for such major but infrequent reorganizations, and to be prepared to carry out the reorganizations as required.[26]

The reorganizing process itself may be very detailed and difficult. Once completed there is an immediate leadership problem of reestablishing stability in the organization. Major reorganizations require plans for the new organization. They also require careful working out of the administration of new plans so that they result ultimately in new stability.[27] While the crisis of reorganization may permit rapid change, the requirement of the organization is to return again to some level of relative stability.

The leader, therefore, has to be sensitive to the opportunities for change and to careful working out of programs for achieving it. Leaders must also be sensitive to the requirements of organization stability and the methods for achieving it.[28]

LEADERSHIP AND ORGANIZATION

In general, we have suggested that leadership functions in organization change are of an impersonal, organization-wide character. Leadership functions in building and maintaining morale are largely departmental or work-group oriented.

LOCATION OF LEADERSHIP

It is possible to sketch out the rough organizational locations of the various leadership functions that have been analyzed. Leadership as a morale building and sustaining function is to be found primarily among first-line leaders. Morale building leaders are individuals who have commands, and a group of subordinates responding to them as commanders.[29]

At a higher level, the general operating management of a firm can be considered the impersonal leadership group concerned with recognizing conditions creating the need for change in the organization and developing programs to carry it out.[30] At a still higher level, the board of directors of a typical firm can be viewed as the body making the fundamental policy decisions with respect to significant reorganizations of the entire firm's operations.[31]

This distinction among levels of leadership perhaps suggests why leaders at succeeding levels of the organization behave differently. The leader as morale builder is personally known to his followers, constantly in their view, and in contact with them.[32] The leader in handling change may seldom, if ever, be in contact with those affected by his leadership decisions, and their acceptance or rejection of his decisions does not depend on reactions to him as a person.[33]

WHEN DO LEADERS LEAD?

Those members of an organization who are in positions of leadership do not always behave as leaders. That is to say, there are many times and occasions when leaders do not lead. This paradox is worthy of examination.

As we have seen from the previous chapter, it is possible for management positions of an organization to be filled by officials capable of issuing commands, and technically competent to fill the requirements of their positions and offices. These same individuals, under special circumstances, may also display the qualities of leadership. In those periods when they are not behaving as leaders, they may be giving full attention to their activities as commanders.

If we look more closely at the functions of leadership, we will perhaps discover why leadership is not a continuous activity. In the morale building and sustaining functions of leadership, it is not necessary continually to build, repair, and maintain group identification. Indeed, the longer the same individuals operate together as a group, the less will be the need to reinforce their sense of group identification and the behaviors that sustain morale. The leader in fulfilling his morale functions will therefore operate only where he perceives the morale of the group to be threatened, or where it seems desirable to enhance the sense of group identification in the interest of meeting a particular crisis.[34] If the leader perceives that the group seems to be losing some of its unity, he may take action to restore its cohesiveness. If a special requirement is placed on the work group to give service above and beyond the normal demands made of it, the leader may also step in to use techniques for heightening morale in order that these special demands will be met.

Leadership behavior in handling change depends on the existence of unstabilizing influences.[35] There may be long periods in which the organization enjoys relative stability. During these periods the leadership function of confronting change lies in abeyance.

We can begin to see why the generalization that "the best executive is the one with a clear desk" can, in fact, be a fair description of an effective executive who is also a capable leader. Such an executive may have delegated large measures of the command functions of his position, and may recognize that his leadership functions are not called into constant play.[36] This analysis might also help us to understand why Barnard, for example, suggests that it is an important characteristic of a good leader to know when *not* to make a decision as well as when he ought to make decisions.[37]

The distinction between command functions and leadership functions may not always be easy to make. Nor, for the executive who is accustomed to operating at high speed and under considerable tension, is it always possible to stop exercising the leadership function when the circumstances for its exercise have ceased.[38]

It should be noted further that there may be command and leadership situations which, by the very nature of their recurrence, and the standard character of the problems dealt with, are susceptible to handling by standing orders. Standing orders are applicable to situations in which problems recur in substantially the same form and can be dealt with in standard ways.[39]

The need for exercising leadership or exhibiting command may be removed and replaced by the standing orders that have an automatic application in situations that are clearly defined and recognized.

Another aspect of the periodic character of leadership behavior deserves attention. There is a general potentiality for leadership, characteristics of all groups. Under circumstances where the official or accepted leader is absent, or where he is removed from the group for some reason, a temporary leader may arise.

A group abhors confusion, including the confusion resulting from being leaderless. Every organization has more people in it who can exercise leadership, at least temporarily, than there are positions of leadership to be filled. It is often in situations of crisis, where an individual, not previously known to possess such qualities, becomes a leader, that the officials of an organization learn where the potential leadership skills are to be found.

TYPES OF LEADERS

In the light of the preceding discussion of leadership functions, it is now possible to examine the types of leaders found in work organizations.[40]

INFORMAL LEADERS

An informal leader is an individual at the center of a face-to-face group providing necessary leadership that maintains the group in existence and gives direction to its activities. Such a leader is always recognized as being influential in the group and is invariably selected as its spokesman in relation to the world surrounding the group. He may not, however, bear any title, nor is it necessary that he be officially designated as leader by the group members. His pre-eminence in the group as its leader is typically a consequence of his personal qualities and their high evaluation by his followers.[41]

The informal leader may be viewed by his followers as being specially endowed with intelligence, forcefulness, exceptional skills, prowess in athletics or other activities, foresight, shrewdness, or cunning. Not all of these characteristics are ascribed to every informal leader, but at least some of them are usually believed to be possessed by each informal leader.[42]

The informal leader has a man-to-man relationship with all his followers. He is personally known to them, and they to him. The informal leader typically shares many characteristics with his followers. These shared characteristics may be of a personal nature. They may also be a common background and common outlook, or similar stations in life. In general, the informal leader can be characterized as one who is like his followers in all respects except those in which he is viewed by them as having special talents or abilities. The informal leader is at the same time like his following, and distinguished from it.[43] The grounds on which he is distinguished from the group he leads are fewer than the bases on which he is like his group.

Informal leaders may exercise influence over followers by manipulating the group sanctions that are within their control. Their primary function in the group is that of building and maintaining a sense of group identification and unity. Informal leaders are concerned with the morale of the group. Voluntary social groups at work do not have programs of action, nor are they particularly concerned with changes in their environment.[44] Consequently, leadership in such groups is not focused on meeting environmental changes.

In the relationships between a supervisor and his immediate subordinates, there can be an interesting mixture of both informal and formal leadership behavior patterns. This is particularly true for first line supervisors and foremen. The supervisor has all the weight of his position behind him to support his authority over subordinates.[45] In addition, as he displays informal leadership he may succeed in winning the respect, fondness, admiration, and willing support of his subordinates. Their bases of judgment about him fit the work situation so that they admire him for the things he can do as a foreman either for the department or for them. This leadership skill clearly resides in the supervisor, as Jackson has shown by experimentally shifting leaders among work groups.[46] Part of the informal

The conflicting demands of leadership and command are revealed in this picture of the plant manager of the automated Ford engine plant in Cleveland. The hat on in the office is the traditional badge of the production-minded executive, ready—at least symbolically—to rush out into the shop on a hot problem. The telephone calls attention to immediate command problems. But the folders and stacks of papers and even the magazine on the desk suggest the innovating functions of leadership.

leadership seems to develop if the supervisor interacts more frequently with his subordinates than the mere conduct of business would warrant, as Turner has shown.[47]

There may be important problems of transition when an informal leader is chosen for an official position of command in a work organization. This happens when an informal leader is promoted to a supervisory position. The informal leader who becomes an official of the formal organization must learn an entirely new set of behaviors. He must also divest himself of many of the relationships he enjoyed as an informal leader. This transition may be exceptionally hard to make if the informal leader is given an official position of command over those who formerly were his followers. It is often desirable to move such an informal leader and give him his command position in some other part of the work organization, where he is no longer thrown in contact with, and expected to command his former informal group associates.

FORMAL LEADERS

The formal leader has the initial advantage of his command functions on which to establish his leadership position. His authority is vested in his office or position without immediate need for him to confirm it personally.[48]

The exercise of formal leadership is often limited by organization features. In the area of morale, the formal leader may not have as many channels of behavior open to him as the informal leader. The formal leader may certainly operate as the symbolic center of the group, and as an example through his own behavior. He can also choose group goals. Unless he can get close to and in an informal relationship with his followers, he may have a great deal of difficulty in resolving the problems of choice in the group, or in acting as an arbiter of its differences. At least these two channels for building group unity and morale may be foreclosed to the formal leader.[49]

In a military situation we seen an interesting example of how the formal leader, when he moves out of garrison with his troops, is likely to emphasize informality with subordinates. On the basis of this informality, the formal commander can exercise the full range of morale-building leadership functions. The battlefield commander, at the platoon or company level, may often give up some of his command functions, or command authority, in the interest of building his leadership functions. This does not mean the officer destroys his authority as a commander. It simply means that he shifts the grounds on which the loyalty of the group is built and maintained. He substitutes for the formal authority of his position, the leadership functions he is able to carry out within the group. Foremen and supervisors can, in similar ways, weave together their command and leadership behaviors.

In his role as leader handling change affecting the organization, the formal leader builds on and makes use of the authority of his office. He has an official responsibility to carry out these functions. Therefore, he has no problem of confirming his right to these functions. Whether he accepts the responsibility and carries it out may be a matter of personal choice for him.[50]

LEADERSHIP AND CLIQUES

A special and interesting kind of leader is the individual who is a power seeker or "politician." Such individuals are relatively common and may, in fact, be encouraged by the very nature of the competition the organization fosters for its higher positions of command. The novel, *Executive Suite,* illustrates the classic struggle within a business firm to take over the position of president.[51]

One of the sure ways of discovering the officials of an organization who have leadership is to find those who have been able to mobilize a clique behind them. Such individuals give evidence of their skill and ability in developing and holding a following in the organization. It is certainly true that leadership of a clique may be used for purely personal and selfish purposes in gaining a higher office or position of command. But precisely because the clique is centered on a leader and not on an official command position, the clique leader is marked as an individual who possesses effective leadership qualities.[52]

In a contest for command positions within an organization, having a program plays an important role in the relative success of the contestants. Again referring to *Executive Suite,* the uncertainty of the hero's ultimate success is clearly revealed in the fact that he has no program with which to confront the treasurer's plans for the company. It is only in the dramatic scene at a board of directors meeting that the hero rises and, in a highly charged speech, lays out a clear-cut program for the company that is both the embodiment of his ideals and the operating basis for the product development of the company. With his program dramatically unfolded, the hero is elected to the presidency by acclaim.

Most clique-supported battles for higher positions of command are almost invariably disguised as contests between alternative programs for the organization. This turns out to be highly functional. When the contest over command positions is put in these terms, the evaluation of the principal contestants can focus on their programs, and not on the personal merits of the contestants. The clique leader who is ultimately defeated in his attempt to move up in the organization can remain within the organization, beaten but unbowed. The defeat rests on the program and not on the person of the unsuccessful bidder for the higher post.

In this way schism in the organization is avoided. The organization is not torn apart by the defeated leader moving off with a group of loyal followers, leaving the organization or attempting to subvert its future progress by refusing to give full cooperation to his successful rival.

In the circumstances where two men of genuine leadership ability struggle against each other, there is always a probability that a dark horse will be chosen as the occupant of the higher office for which the contest has been held. While the dark horse may face very sizeable problems in winning the allegiance and support of the unsuccessful contestants, the organization may benefit through the retention of the defeated clique leaders with their obvious leadership skills.

Ordinarily, clique struggles within an organization are viewed as undesirable, but insofar as they tend to reveal the real leaders in the organization, they may be functional for it. Furthermore, insofar as the contest for command positions are carried on in terms of programs, the organization may also benefit by a very serious consideration of the merits of competing programs, and the opportunity to choose among them.

In some respects, clique conflicts within modern large-scale organizations are inevitable. A large number of capable individuals compete for a diminishing number of jobs, the higher they go in the organization. This may make the need for amassing clique support in order to move upward almost an imperative for driving and highly motivated executives.

LEADERS AND COMMANDERS

It should now be clear that there is a significant difference between a leader and a commander. In this chapter we have analyzed characteristic features of leadership, and types of leadership behavior. In our analysis of "Management as Bureaucracy" (Chapter 20), emphasis was placed on the command functions of management behavior. When attention was focused on rules and their enforcement (Chapter 19), the specific functions of managers in policing organization behavior were analyzed.

We have filled out the range of functions and behaviors of management men. Any commander must, at some time, act to enforce rules and regulations; these functions go together. Leadership may be an asset to a commander, but its absence may not disqualify him. Some leaders command and enforce regulations. Some leaders just lead.

The behavior of the informal leader is independent of any formal command functions. Indeed, it is one of the characteristics of the informal leader that he is not in a position of command, does not hold an organization position, and that he has an intimate, personal relationship with his followers.

Every official who fills an organization position or office has some command functions. It is not always certain that each official will display leadership. It is relatively easy to train persons to carry out management command functions.[53] It is much more difficult to select persons to be leaders in management, or to train managers in leadership behavior.[54]

The qualities of leadership seem to be rarer than the qualities of command. Command behavior can be learned more readily than leadership can be inculcated. Consequently the search for executives of organizations lays great stress on discovering and nurturing leadership abilities.[55]

NOTES FOR CHAPTER 21

1 Consistent with the whole orientation of this book, we will not deal with materials on the personality characteristics of leaders, or the psychodynamics of leadership roles. An analysis compatible with the one used in this volume will be found in Philip Selznick, *Leadership in Administration* (Evanston: Row, Peterson and Company, 1957).

2 An excellent set of empirical studies of leaders in various organization settings will be found in A. W. Gouldner (ed.), *Studies in Leadership* (New York: Harper & Brothers, 1950). T. N. Whitehead, *Leadership in a Free Society* (Cambridge: Harvard University Press, 1936), analyzes leadership in industrial firms and emphasizes the dependence of social well being on broad gage industrial leadership.

3 Cf. T. N. Whitehead, "Human Relations Within Industrial Groups," *Harvard Business Review* 14:1-13 (Autumn, 1935), in which the two-fold responsibility of industrial leadership is declared to be: attainment of firm's economic objectives (our confronting of change), and maintenance of satisfactory human relations (our morale building).

4 One of the best general sources of studies and approaches to the morale building functions of leadership is Harold Guetzkow (ed.), *Groups, Leadership, and Men* (Pittsburgh: Carnegie Institute of Technology Press, 1951).

5 A general analysis of a case in which the behavior of a business executive and subordinate's responses to him provide materials for generalization about leadership functions is Chris Argyris, *Executive Leadership* (New York: Harper & Brothers, 1953). C. L. Shartle, "Leadership and Executive Performance," *Personnel,* 25:370-380 (March, 1949), suggests some of the relationships between leadership types and leader functions.

6 See: T. C. Cochran and William Miller, *The Age of Enterprise* (New York: The Macmillan Company, 1942); William Miller (ed.), *Men in Business* (Cambridge: Harvard University Press, 1952); and Reinhard Bendix, *Work and Authority in Industry* (New York: John Wiley & Sons, 1956), especially Chapter 5, for a general discussion of this transformation.

7 There is by no means general agreement that such transformation in the symbolic position of business leaders has really taken place. Mills argues that the "power elite" has been strengthened by coalescence of business elites with military and other elites. *The* power elite is now more coherent, and organized around a program which is nonresponsible and immoral measured by social values according to Mills. C. W. Mills, *The Power Elite* (New York: Oxford University Press, 1956), especially Chapter 15, "The Higher Immorality."

8 One of the interesting mechanisms by which symbolic leadership is developed and sustained is through organization fictions. See Robert Dubin, *Human Relations in Administration* (Englewood Cliffs, N. J.: Prentice-Hall, Inc., 1951), pp. 341-345.

9 Max Weber chose to see the goal selecting behavior of the leader as resulting from ascription of extraordinary abilities to him. He considered charismatic leaders as having essentially unrestricted opportunity to determine group goals. Max Weber, *The Theory of Social and Economic Organization,* translated and edited by A. M. Henderson and T. Parsons (New York: Oxford University Press, 1947), pp. 358-363.

10 This has been particularly well analyzed in Philip Selznick, "An Approach to a Theory of Bureaucracy," *American Sociological Review,* 8:51-54 (February, 1943).

11 C. I. Barnard has made an excellent analysis of this point in: Chapter 2, "Dilemmas of Leadership in the Democratic Process," of his volume of essays, *Organization and Management* (Cambridge:

NOTES FOR CHAPTER 21 (CONT.)

Harvard University Press, 1948), especially pp. 39-42.

[12] A group of workers in an expanding company were constantly seeking adaptive mechanisms to overcome their feelings of insecurity in the face of changing conditions in their company. Leadership helped to formulate and guide group choices in uncertain situations. A. K. Rice, "The Use of Unrecognized Cultural Mechanisms in an Expanding Machine-Shop; With a Contribution to the Theory of Leadership (The Glacier Project)—III," *Human Relations,* 4:143-160 (1951).

[13] Cf. Donald Pelz, "Influence: A Key to Effective Leadership in the First Line Supervisor," *Personnel,* 29:3-11 (November, 1952).

[14] Barnard also points out that the leader creates moral codes, besides administering those already a part of the group ethos. C. I. Barnard, *The Functions of the Executive* (Cambridge: Harnard University Press, 1938), pp. 272-284, and especially p. 279.

[15] A literature has grown up concerned with social perception of others as a variable determining behavior. Leader perception of followers as it affects leadership is examined in: F. E. Fiedler, "The Influence of Leader-Keyman Relations on Combat Crew Effectiveness," Technical Report No. 9, Project on Social Perception and Group Effectiveness, Group Effectiveness Research Laboratory, University of Illinois, n.d., Mimeographed.

[16] Weber, *op. cit.,* pp. 358-359.

[17] It is somewhat old-fashioned to talk about a leader as an example, but this does not obviate the relevance of example in leadership. Cf. W. D. Scott, *Increasing Human Efficiency in Business* (New York: The Macmillan Company, 1914), in which stress is put on the leader's example.

[18] A very interesting analysis of the consequences for organization of different kinds of leadership in confronting change is the comparison made of government *vs.* private entrepreneurs in the development of industry in under-developed areas. Brozen concludes that the latter is more functional. See: Yale Brozen, "Business Leadership and Technological Change," *American Journal of Economics and Sociology,* 14:13-30 (October, 1954).

[19] This distinction is particularly highlighted in the role of consultant to management of an organization. The consultant is not even an organization member and certainly does not lead its members. See *Journal of Social Issues,* 4:1-53 (Summer, 1948), entire issue, and especially Alex Bavelas, "Some Problems of Organizational Change."

[20] This is substantially the point made by Barnard when he emphasizes that the organization "is the instrumentality of action so far as leaders are concerned . . . ." C. I. Barnard, *Organization and Management,* p. 89.

[21] In one of the early and still important studies of business leadership, Gordon stressed the fact that the "real" decisions had different points in the management structure at which they were made, depending on the subject of decision. R. A. Gordon, *Business Leadership in the Large Corporation* (Washington: The Brookings Institution, 1945).

[22] This is illustrated in the field of labor relations in the plea by Slichter that businessmen must adopt new strategies to regain social influence in the face of labor dominance of the economy. Slichter proposes a program for a new business outlook. S. H. Slichter, "The Businessman in a Laboristic Economy," *Fortune* 42:108 ff. (September, 1949).

[23] A study of management succession illustrates this identification of program with leader. C. R. Christensen, *Management Succession in Small and Growing Enterprises* (Boston: Harvard Graduate School of Business Administration, Division of Research, 1953).

[24] A case history of railroad leaders during the golden age of transcontinental expansion makes this clear. T. C. Cochran, "The Executive Mind: The Role of Railroad Leaders, 1845-1890," *Bulletin of the Business Historical Society,* 25:230-241 (December, 1951).

[25] Illustrative of the distribution of time in executive behavior that points up the episodic character of certain kinds of decisions is: Sune Carlson, *Executive Behavior: A Study of the Work Load and the Working Methods of Managing Directors* (Stockholm: Stromborgs, 1951).

[26] A fascinating analysis of the role of leadership in destroying present operating arrangements in order to replace them with improvements emphasizes creative destruction in Schumpeter's sense. The author suggests labeling such leaders who may be called on specially to carry out the destructive role as demonic figures. See: Fritz Redlich, "Business Leader as a 'Daimonic' Figure," *American Journal of Economics and Sociology* 12:163-177 (January, 1953).

[27] It has been observed that stability in employer-employee relations as measured by a reduction in conflict occurs where some agreement develops on the firm's objectives. Douglas McGregor, "Conditions of Effective Leadership in the Industrial Organization," *Journal of Consulting Psychology,* 8: 55-63 (March-April, 1944).

[28] One of the best studies of leadership problems in confronting change is the analysis of management of one of the wartime relocation camps for West Coast residents of Japanese ancestry who were removed from the coastal area by government directive. The author was part of the camp administration and describes in detail the continuous equilibrium problems faced. A. H. Leighton, *The Governing of Men* (Princeton: Princeton University Press, 1945).

[29] See Donald Pelz, "Leadership within a Hierarchical Organization," *Journal of Social Issues,* 7:49-55 (1951).

NOTES FOR CHAPTER 21 (CONT.)

[30] Cf. R. C. Davis, *The Fundamentals of Top Management* (New York: Harper & Brothers, 1951).

[31] In this connection see L. R. Boulware, "The Business Leader's Larger Job," pp. 46-69 in Marvin Bower (ed.), *The Development of Executive Leadership* (Cambridge: Harvard University Press, 1949). In the small work organization the three general levels of leadership functions may be combined into two or one.

[32] It is from this standpoint that the literature on supervision is oriented. See, for example, G. D. Halsey, *Supervising People* (New York: Harper & Brothers, 1946).

[33] A sense of this progression from one level of leadership to the next highest, with its attendant problems, is conveyed in "The Nine Hundred," *Fortune,* 46:132 ff. (November, 1952).

[34] The chain-like character of the morale functions of leadership is revealed in a study of a motor truck plant where the foremen's morale functions are shown to be partly the consequence of the way in which their own morale was built and sustained by superiors. E. A. Fleishman, *"Leadership Climate" and Supervisory Behavior: A Study of the Leadership Role of the Foreman in an Industrial Situation* (Columbus: Ohio State University Personnel Research Board, 1951).

[35] This is well illustrated in an analysis of the advent of a new executive installing new policies and programs. E. P. Learned, "Problems of a New Executive," *Harvard Business Review,* 27:362-372 (May, 1949).

[36] An illuminating discussion of this point is contained in Melville Dalton, "Managing the Managers," *Human Organization,* 14:4-10 (Fall, 1955).

[37] C. I. Barnard, *The Functions of the Executive,* p. 194.

[38] This is related to the hoarding of responsibility discussed in the previous chapter.

[39] See Chapter 19 for a further discussion of standing orders.

[40] A study of the imagery of successful business leaders suggests certain value orientations held in common. This is typology based on outlook quite different from our typology using organization position as its differentiating criterion. W. E. Henry, "The Business Executive: The Psycho-Dynamics of a Social Role," *American Journal of Sociology,* 54:286-291 (January, 1949).

[41] A detailed examination of the functions of a leader in primary associations will be found in George C. Homans, *The Human Group* (New York: Harcourt, Brace, and Co., 1950), Chapter 16, "The Job of the Leader."

[42] See an analysis of the basis of leadership in primary associations in R. L. Pellegrin, "The Achievement of High Statuses and Leadership in the Small Group," *Social Forces,* 32:10-16 (October, 1953).

[43] This is the central point made in C. K. Warriner, "Leadership in the Small Group," *American Journal of Sociology,* 60:361-369 (January, 1955).

[44] See Chapter 16.

[45] Cf. C. I. Barnard, *Organization and Management,* pp. 42-43.

[46] See J. M. Jackson, "The Effect of Changing the Leadership of Small Works Groups," *Human Relations,* 6:25-44 (1953).

[47] Reported in A. N. Turner, "Interaction and Sentiment in the Foreman-Worker Relationship," *Human Organization,* 14:10-16 (Spring, 1955).

[48] This is suggested in the study of the top executives of a tire and rubber company. See C. G. Browne, "Study of Executive Leadership in Business," *Journal of Applied Psychology,* 33:521-526 (December, 1949). Three additional parts of this study are reported in the same journal: 34:12-15 (February, 1950) 34:82-87 (April, 1950) and 35: 34-37 (February, 1951).

[49] Perhaps one important reason that paternalism of industrial managers toward their employees fails is to be found in this point. Paternalists try to resolve group choices and act as group arbiters.

[50] This is what is usually implied when managers are accused of being willful or blind to their real opportunities for exercising leadership. Cf. B. M. Selekman, "Wanted: Mature Managers," *Harvard Business Review,* 24:288-244 (Winter, 1946).

[51] Cameron Hawley, *Executive Suite* (New York: Ballantine Books).

[52] Selznick points out that the organization often protects itself from the opposition of dissident groups by "coopting" their leaders into the structure of management. We are here pointing out that leaders who are coopted are clique leaders. See Philip Selznick, "Foundation of the Theory of Organization," *American Sociological Review,* 13:34-35 (February, 1948).

[53] See an interesting description of the goals of foreman training for command in T. V. Purcell, "Observing People," *Harvard Business Reviek,* 33: 90-100 (March-April, 1955).

[54] This point is set forth with real feeling in "Bringing Up the Boss," *Fortune,* 43:118ff (June, 1951).

[55] Barnard makes this point in examining the ideal education for executives. C. I. Barnard, "Education for Executives," *Journal of Business of the University of Chicago,* 18:175-182 (October, 1945). An operating businessman stresses this point in: J. L. McCaffrey, "What Corporation Presidents Think about at Night," *Fortune,* 48:129ff (September, 1953).

SUPPLEMENTARY BIBLIOGRAPHY

This bibliography supplements but does not duplicate the works cited in the chapter notes. Students using this book will find the bibliography invaluable in their further study, and in carrying out written classroom assignments. For practitioners and scholars to whom this volume is a reference, this bibliography provides extended coverage of the literature.

In general, each work is listed in only one place. In the case of books covering many subjects, the listing is under the chapter to which the book has greatest relevance.

CHAPTER 1. WORLD OF WORK

THEORY AND FRAME OF REFERENCE

Anthony, Arthur B., *Economic and Social Problems of the Machine Age,* University of Southern California Social Series, No. 3, Los Angeles: University of Southern California Press, 1930.

Arensberg, Conrad M., "Industry and Community," *American Journal of Sociology,* 48 (July 1942).

———, "Toward a 'Control' System for Industrial Relations," *Applied Anthropology,* 1 (October-December 1941).

Argyris, Chris, "The Present State of Research in Human Relations in Industry," Mimeographed, New Haven: Yale Labor and Management Center, 1954.

Bain, Robert K., "The Researcher's Role: A Case Study," *Human Organization,* 9 (Spring 1950).

Bakke, E. Wight, "Need for Scientific Study of Human Relations in Industry," *Advanced Management,* 12 (June 1947).

Blumer, Herbert, "Sociological Theory in Industrial Relations," *American Sociological Review,* 12, No. 3 (1947).

Cabot, Hugh, and Joseph A. Kahl, *Human Relations: Concepts and Cases in Concrete Social Science,* 2 Vols., Cambridge: Harvard University Press, 1953.

Caplow, Theodore, *The Sociology of Work,* Minneapolis: University of Minnesota Press, 1954.

Chapple, Eliot D., with the collaboration of Conrad M. Arensberg, "Measuring Human Relations: An Introduction to the Study of the Interaction of Individuals," *Genetic Psychology Monographs,* 22, No. 1 (1940).

Chase, Stuart, "Social Science: Friend of Management," *Personnel,* 27 (January 1951).

Committee on Labor Market Research of the Social Science Research Council, *Memorandum on University Research Programs in the Field of Labor,* Washington: Social Science Research Council, 1949.

De Grazia, Alfred, *Human Relations in Public Administration,* Chicago: Public Administration Service, 1949.

Dunlop, John, and William F. Whyte, "Framework for Analysis of Industrial Relations: Two Views," *Industrial and Labor Relations Review,* 3 (April 1950).

Elmer, G. A., "Maintaining Rapport Necessary for Reliability in Industrial Research," *American Sociological Review,* 16 (1951).

Friedmann, Georges, *La Crise du Progrès, Esquisse d'Histoire des Idées (1895–1935),* Paris: 1936, revised 1954.

———, *Industrial Society,* trans. Harold Sheppard, Glencoe, Ill.: The Free Press, 1956.

———, *Où Va le Travail Humain,* Paris: Librairie Gallimard, 1950.

From Max Weber, ed. and trans. H. H. Gerth and C. W. Mills, New York: Oxford University Press, 1946.

Gardner, Burleigh B., and David G. Moore, *Human Relations in Industry,* revised edition, Chicago: Richard D. Irwin, 1950.

———, and William F. Whyte, "Methods for the Study of Human Relations in Industry," *American Sociological Review,* 11 (October 1946).

Glaister, A. Elmer, "Maintaining Rapport Necessary for Reliability in Industrial Research," *American Sociological Review,* 16 (February 1951).

Gross, Edward, "Some Suggestions for the Legitimation of Industrial Studies in Sociology," *Social Forces,* 33, No. 3 (1955).

Gullahorn, John, and George Strauss, "The Field Worker in Union Research," *Human Organization,* 13, No. 3 (1954).

Hart, C. W. M., "Industrial Relations Research and Social Theory," *Canadian Journal of Economics and Political Science,* 15 (February 1949).

Homans, George C., "The Strategy of Industrial Sociology," *American Journal of Sociology,* 54 (January 1949).

Hughes, Everett C., "The Sociological Study of Work: An Editorial Foreword," *American Journal of Sociology,* 57, No. 5 (1952).

Illinois, University of, Institute of Labor and Industrial Relations, *Industrial Sociology: An Annotated Bibliography,* Bibliographic Contributions No. 3, Champaign, Ill.: The Institute, 1953.

Jacobson, E., R. Kahn, F. Mann, and, N. Morse, eds., "Human Relations Research in Large Organizations," *Journal of Social Issues,* 7, No. 3 (1951).

Knox, John, "Sociological Theory and Industrial Sociology," *Social Forces,* 33, No. 3 (1955).

———, *The Sociology of Industrial Relations,* New York: Random House, 1955.

Koivisto, W. A., "Value, Theory, and Fact in Industrial Sociology," *The American Journal of Sociology,* 58 (1953).

McConnell, John W., "Problems of Method in the Study of Human Relations," *Industrial and Labor Relations Review,* 3 (July 1950).

McGregor, Douglas, "Changing Patterns in Human Relations," *National Industrial Conference Board, Management Record,* 12 (September 1950).

Marx, Karl, *Capital,* 3 Vols., Chicago: Charles H. Kerr and Company, 1906–1909.

Massarik, Fred, and Paula Brown, "Social Research Faces Industry," *Personnel,* (May 1954).

Meadows, Paul, *The Culture of Industrial Man,* Lincoln: University of Nebraska Press, 1950.

———, "Culture Theory and Industrial Analysis," *Annals, American Academy of Political and Social Science,* 274 (March 1951).

Miller, Delbert C., "The Future Development of Industrial Sociology," *Proceedings of the Pacific Sociological Society,* (April 1947).

———, "Industrial Sociology," *American Sociological Review,* 16 (February 1951).

———, and William H. Form, *Industrial Sociology,* New York: Harper and Brothers, 1951.

Miller, S. M., "The Rise of Industrial Sociology," *Sociology and Social Research,* 36 (November 1951).

Mills, C. Wright, "The Contributions of Sociology to Studies of Industrial Relations," *Industrial Relations Research Association, Proceedings 1948,* Milton Derber, ed., Publication No. 1, Urbana, Ill.: The Association, 1949.

Moore, Wilbert E., "Current Issues in Industrial Sociology," *American Sociological Review,* 12 (December 1947).

———, *Industrial Relations and the Social Order,* revised edition, New York: The Macmillan Company, 1951.

———, "Industrial Sociology; Status and Prospects," *American Sociological Review,* 13 (August 1948).

Parsons, Talcott, *The Structure of Social Action,* New York: McGraw-Hill Book Company, 1937.

Renard, G., *Life and Work in Prehistoric Times,* trans. R. T. Clark, New York: Alfred A. Knopf, 1929.

———, and G. Weulersse, *Life and Work in Modern Europe,* New York: Alfred A. Knopf, 1926.

Rogers, Maria, "Problems of Human Relations within Industry," *Sociometry,* 9 (November 1946).

Schneider, Eugene V., "Limitation on Observation in Industrial Sociology," *Social Forces,* 28 (March 1950).

Schneider, Louis, "An Industrial Sociology: For What Ends?" *Antioch Review,* 10 (Fall 1950).

Schumpeter, Joseph A., *Capitalism, Socialism, and Democracy,* revised edition, New York: Harper and Brothers, 1947.

Sée, Henri Eugène, *Modern Capitalism, Its Origin and Evolution,* trans. Homer V. Vanderblue and Georges F. Doriot, London: N. Douglas, 1928.

Social Process in Hawaii, "Industrial Sociology in Hawaii," 15 (1951); entire issue.

Sombart, Werner, "Capitalism," *Encyclopaedia of the Social Sciences,* New York: The Macmillan Company, 1930–1934.

Sombart, Werner, *The Quintessence of Capitalism; A Study of the History and Psychology of the Modern Business Man,* trans. and ed. M. Epstein, London: Unwin, 1915.

Todd, Arthur James, *Industry and Society; A Sociological Appraisal of Modern Industrialism,* New York: Henry Holt and Company, 1933.

Viteles, Morris S., *The Science of Work,* New York: W. W. Norton and Company, 1934.

Van Kleeck, Mary, "Towards an Industrial Sociology," *American Sociological Review,* 11 (October 1946).

Weber, Max, *The Theory of Social and Economic Organization,* trans. A. M. Henderson and Talcott Parsons, New York: Oxford University Press, 1947.

Weiss, Hilda, "Human Relations in Industry; From Ernest Abbe to Karl Mannheim," *American Journal of Economics and Sociology,* 8 (April 1949).

WORKING AND SOCIETY

American Business Leaders, *Human Relations in Modern Business,* Englewood Cliffs, N. J.: Prentice-Hall, Inc., 1949.

Anderson, C. Arnold, and Mary Jean Bowman, "The Vanishing Servant and the Contemporary Status System of the American South," *American Journal of Sociology,* 59, No. 3 (1953).

Bakke, E. Wight, *Citizens without Work,* New Haven: Yale University Press for the Institute of Human Relations, 1940.

———, *Organization and the Individual,* New Haven: Yale University Labor and Management Center, 1952.

———, *The Unemployed Man: A Social Study,* London: Nisbet, 1934.

———, *The Unemployed Worker: A Study of the Task of Making a Living Without a Job,* New Haven: Yale University Press, 1940.

———, and Ewan Clague, *After the Shutdown,* New Haven: Yale University Institute of Human Relations, 1934.

Balandier, G., "The Problem of the African Worker in the Gaboon and the Congo," *International Social Science Bulletin,* 6, No. 3 (1954).

Beard, Charles A. and Mary R., *The Rise of American Civilization,* New York: The Macmillan Company, 1930.

Bell, Daniel, "Work in the Life of an American," William Haber, *et. al.,* eds., *Manpower in the United States: Problems and Policies,* New York: Harper and Brothers, 1954.

Bellin, Seymour, and Frank Riessman, Jr., "Education, Culture, and the Anarchic Worker," *The Journal of Social Issues,* 5 (Winter 1949).

Bennett, John W., "Social Aspects of Japanese Forestry Economy: Two Case Studies," Interim Technical Report No. 5, The Ohio State University Research Foundation, Columbus, Ohio, April 1953.

Bestor, A. E., Jr., *Backwoods Utopias,* Philadelphia: University of Pennsylvania, 1950.

Birjay, R. M., "Textile Labor in Bombay City: Its Evolution and Composition 1934–1949," *Indian Journal of Social Work,* 14, No. 2 (1953).

Bowden, Witt, *Industrial Society in England Towards the End of the Eighteenth Century,* New York: The Macmillan Company, 1925.

Brennan, Niall, *The Making of a Moron,* New York: Sheed and Ward, 1953.

Briefs, G. A., *The Proletariat,* New York: McGraw-Hill Book Company, 1937.

Bushnell, Charles, "Some Social Aspects of the Chicago Stock Yards," *American Journal of Sociology,* 7, No. 2-5 (1901–1902).

Buxton, L. H. Dudley, *Primitive Labor,* London: Methuen and Company, 1924.

Carr-Saunders, A. M., and D. Caradog Jones, *A Survey of the Social Structure of England and Wales: as Illustrated by Statistics,* 2nd edition, Oxford: The Clarendon Press, 1937.

Centers, Richard, "The American Class Structure: A Psychological Analysis," Theodore M. Newcomb and Eugene L. Hartley, eds.,

Readings in Social Psychology, New York: Henry Holt and Company, 1947.

———, *The Psychology of Social Classes,* Princeton: Princeton University Press, 1949.

Clark, Alice, *Working Life of Women in the Seventeenth Century,* New York: Harcourt, Brace and Company, 1920.

Corey, Lewis, "The Middle Class," *Antioch Review,* (Spring 1945).

Cottrell, W. Fred, *The Railroader,* Stanford: Stanford University Press, 1940.

Curle, Adam, "Incentive to Work," *Human Relations,* 2 (1949).

Desenberg, Bernard N., "Occupational Attitudes of Taxi Dancers," *Sociology and Social Research,* 25, No. 3 (1941).

Donovan, Frances R., *The Saleslady,* Chicago: University of Chicago Press, 1929.

———, *The Schoolma'am,* New York: Frederick A. Stokes Company, 1938.

———, *The Woman Who Waits,* Boston: Richard G. Badger, 1920.

Doucy, A., "The Unsettled Attitude of Negro Workers in the Belgian Congo," *International Social Science Bulletin,* 6, No. 3 (1954).

Drucker, Peter F., *The Future of Industrial Man: A Conservative Approach,* New York: John Day, 1942.

———, *The New Society: The Anatomy of the Industrial Order,* New York: Harper and Brothers, 1950.

Duncan, Beverly, "Factors in Work-Residence Separation," *American Sociological Review,* 21, No. 1 (1956).

Engels, Frederick, *The Condition of the Working Class in England in 1844,* trans. F. K. Wischnewestzky, London: George Allen and Unwin, 1892.

Fay, C. R., *Life and Labor in the Nineteenth Century,* Cambridge: Cambridge University Press, 1947.

Firth, Raymond, *Primitive Economics of the New Zealand Maori,* New York: E. P. Dutton and Company, 1929.

———, *Primitive Polynesian Economy,* London: George Routledge and Sons, 1939.

———, *We, the Tikopia,* London: George Allen and Unwin, 1936.

Fitch, John A., *The Steel Workers,* part of the Pittsburgh Survey, Paul Underwood Kellog, ed., for the Russell Sage Foundation, New York: Charities Publication Committee, 1910.

Fite, Emerson D., *Social and Industrial Conditions in the North During the Civil War,* New York: Peter Smith, 1930.

Ford, H., *My Life and Work,* Garden City, New York: Doubleday and Company, 1922.

Frazier, Franklin, "Occupational Classes among Negroes in Cities," *American Journal of Sociology,* 35, No. 4 (1930).

Friedmann, E. A., and R. J. Havighurst, eds., *The Meaning of Work and Retirement,* Chicago: The University of Chicago Press, 1954.

Gillen, Paul Bates, *The Distribution of Occupations as a City Yardstick,* New York: King's Crown Press, 1951.

Glotz, Gustave, *Le Travail dans la Grece ancienne,* Paris: 1920.

Gras, N. S. B., *An Introduction to Economic History,* New York: Harper and Brothers, 1922.

Green, Constance M., *Holyoke, Massachusetts: A Case History of the Industrial Revolution in America,* New Haven: Yale University Press, 1939.

Hammond, J. L., and Barbara Hammond, *The Rise of Modern Industry,* New York: Harcourt, Brace and Company, 1926.

———, *The Town Labourer, 1760-1832: The New Civilisation,* New York: Longmans, Green, 1932.

Hannay, Agnes, *A Chronicle of Industry on the Mill River,* Smith College Studies in History, 21, Nos. 1-4 (October 1935-July 1936), Northampton, Mass.: Smith College.

Hayner, Norman, "Taming the Lumberjack," *American Sociological Review,* 10, No. 2 (1945).

Healey, James C., *Foc's'le and Glory-Hole: A Study of the Merchant Seaman and His Occupation,* New York: Merchant Marine Publishers' Association, 1936.

Heberle, Rudolph, "Social Consequences of the Industrialization of Southern Cities," *Social Forces,* 27 (October 1948).

Herring, Harriet L., "The Outside Employer in the Southern Industrial Pattern," *Social Forces,* 18 (October 1939).

Herskovitz, Melville J., *Economic Anthropology,* New York: Alfred A. Knopf, 1952.

Hobhouse, L. T., G. C. Wheeler, and M. Ginsberg, *The Material Culture and Social Institutions of the Simpler Peoples: An Essay in Correlation,* London: Chapman and Hall, 1930.

Hormann, Bernard L., "Hawaii's Industrial Revolution," *Social Process in Hawaii,* 15 (1951).

Hsu, F. L. K., and J. H. Hu, "Guild and Kinship Among the Butchers in West Town," *American Sociological Review,* 10 (1945).

Hughes, Everett C., "Industry and the Rural System in Quebec," *Canadian Journal of Economics and Political Science,* 4, No. 3 (1938).

———, "Position and Status in a Quebec Industrial Town," *American Sociological Review,* 3 (October 1938).

Ishino, Iwao, and John W. Bennett, "The Japanese Labor Boss System: A Description and a Preliminary Sociological Analysis," Mimeograph, Columbus: Ohio State University Research Foundation and Department of Sociology, April 1953.

James, E. J., "Street Railway Employees in Paris," *The American Journal of Sociology,* 5 (1899-1900).

Josephson, Hannah, *The Golden Threads,* New York: Duell, Sloan and Pearce, 1949.

Keller, Albert G., "The Working Boy," *American Journal of Sociology,* 2, No. 3 (1896).

Kerr, Clark, Frederick H. Harbison, John T. Dunlop, and Charles A. Myers, "The Labour Problem in Economic Development: A Framework for a Reappraisal," *International Labour Review,* 71, No. 3 (1955).

———, and Abraham Siegel, "The Structuring of the Labor Force in Industrial Society: New Dimensions and New Questions," *Industrial and Labor Relations Review,* 8, No. 2 (1955).

Komarovsky, Mirra, *The Unemployed Man and His Family,* New York: Dryden Press, 1940.

Kornhauser, Arthur W., *Detroit as the People See It: A Survey of Attitudes in an Industrial City,* Detroit: Wayne University Press, 1952.

———, "The Study of Work Feelings," *Personnel Journal,* 1930.

Lahne, Herbert J., *The Cotton Mill Worker,* New York: Farrar and Rinehart, 1944.

Landis, Paul H., "The Life Cycle of the Iron Mining Town," *Social Forces,* 13 (December 1934).

———, and Katherine H. Day, *Farm and Small Town Workers in Metropolitan War Industry: A Sociological Study of War Migrants in Spokane, Washington,* Experiment Station Bulletin No. 460, Pullman: State College of Washington, 1945.

Lee, Rose Hum, "Occupational Invasion, Succession, and Accommodation of the Chinese of Butte, Montana," *American Journal of Sociology,* 55, No. 1 (1949).

Lewis, Oscar, "Plow Culture and Hoe Culture—A Study in Contrasts," *Rural Sociology,* 14, No. 2 (1949).

Liepmann, Kate K., *The Journey to Work: Its Significance for Industrial and Community Life,* New York: Oxford University Press, 1944.

Lyman, Elizabeth L., "Occupational Differences in the Value Attached to Work," *American Journal of Sociology,* 61, No. 2 (1955).

McConnell, John W., *The Evolution of Social Classes,* Washington: American Council on Public Affairs, 1942.

MacDonald, Lois, *Southern Mill Hills,* New York: Alex L. Hillman, 1928.

Malinowski, Bronislaw, *Argonauts of the Western Pacific: An Account of Native Enterprise and Adventures in the Archipelagoes of Melanesian New Guinea,* London: George Routledge and Sons, 1932.

Manis, Jerome G., and Bernard N. Meltzer, "Attitude of Textile Workers to Class Structure," *American Journal of Sociology,* 60, No. 1 (1954).

Mannheim, Karl, *Ideology and Utopia,* trans. Louis Wirth and Edward Shils, London: Kegan Paul, 1936.

———, *Man and Society in an Age of Reconstruction,* New York: Harcourt, Brace and Company, 1940.

Marshall, Leon Carroll, ed., *Readings in Industrial Society,* Chicago: University of Chicago Press, 1918.

Mills, C. Wright, "The Middle Classes in Middle-Sized Cities; The Stratification and Political Position of Small Business and White Collar Strata," *American Sociological Review,* 11 (October 1946).

———, and Melville J. Ulmer, *Small Business and Civic Welfare,* Report of the Smaller War Plants Corporation to the Special Committee to Study Problems of American

Small Business, United States Senate, 79th Congress, 2nd Session, Document No. 135, Washington: Government Printing Office, 1946.

Mitchell, Broadus, and Sinclair Mitchell, *Industrial Development in the South*, Baltimore: Johns Hopkins Press, 1930.

Moore, Wilbert E., "Primitives and Peasants in Industry," *Social Research*, 15, No. 1 (1948).

Murphy, Gardner, Lois Barclay Murphy, and Theodore M. Newcomb, *Experimental Social Psychology: An Interpretation of Research upon the Socialization of the Individual*, revised edition, New York: Harper and Brothers, 1937.

Nimkoff, Meyer, "Occupational Factors and Marriage," *American Journal of Sociology*, 49, No. 3 (1943).

Odaka, Kunio, "An Iron Workers' Community in Japan: A Study in the Sociology of Industrial Groups," *American Sociological Review*, 15, No. 2 (1950).

Oliver, Douglas L., "Personnel Management in Overseas Business Enterprises," *Applied Anthropology*, 7 (Winter 1948).

Page, Charles Hunt, *Class and American Sociology*, New York: The Dial Press, 1940.

Parker, Margaret Terrell, *Lowell: A Study of Industrial Development*, New York: The Macmillan Company, 1940.

Parsons, Talcott, *The Social System*, Glencoe, Ill.: The Free Press, 1951.

Paterson, Donald G., and C. Harold Stone, "Dissatisfaction with Life Work Among Adult Workers," *Occupations*, 21, No. 3 (1942).

Pellegrin, Roland J., and Charles H. Coates, "Absentee-owned Corporations and Community Power Structure," *American Journal of Sociology*, 61, No. 5 (1956).

Richards, Audrey, *Hunger and Work in a Savage Community*, Glencoe, Ill.: The Free Press, 1948.

Rosten, Leo C., *Hollywood: The Movie Colony, the Movie Makers*, New York: Harcourt, Brace and Company, 1941.

Shih, Kuo-Heng, *China Enters the Machine Age: A Study of Labor in Chinese War Industry*, ed. and trans. Hsiao-Tung Fe and Francis L. K. Hsu, Cambridge: Harvard University Press, 1944.

Shlakman, Vera, *Economic History of a Factory Town: A Study of Chicopee, Massachusetts*, Smith College Studies in History, Vol. 20, Nos. 1–4 (October 1934-July 1935), Northampton, Mass.: Smith College.

Singer, Hans W., "Problems of Industrialization of Underdeveloped Countries," *International Social Science Bulletin*, 6, No. 2 (1954).

Staley, Eugene, ed., *Creating an Industrial Civilization*, New York: Harper and Brothers, 1952.

Sumner, William Graham, *What Social Classes Owe to Each Other*, New Haven: Yale University Press, 1934.

Taylor, Walter F., *The Economic Novel in America*, Chapel Hill: University of North Carolina Press, 1942.

Tawney, Richard H., *The Acquisitive Society*, New York: Harcourt, Brace and Company, 1920.

Theodorson, George A., "Acceptance of Industrialization and Its Attendant Consequences for the Social Patterns of Non-Western Societies," *American Sociological Review*, 18, No. 5 (1953).

Thurnwald, Richard, *Economics in Primitive Communities*, London: Oxford University Press, 1932.

Tilgher, Adriano, *Work: What It has Meant to Men through the Ages*, trans. Dorothy Canfield Fisher (from *Homo Faber*), New York: Harcourt, Brace and Company, 1930.

Timasheff, N. S., "Business and the Professions in Liberal Fascist and Communist Society," *American Journal of Sociology*, 45, No. 6 (1940).

Viljoen, Stephen, *The Economics of Primitive People*, London: P. S. King and Son, 1936.

Vucinich, Alexander, "The Kolkhoz: Its Social Structure and Development," *The American Slavic and East European Review*, 8 (February 1949).

Warne, Colston, "The Workers' Approach to the Labor Problem," Emanuel Stein and Jerome Davis, eds., *Labor Problems in America*, Book 3, New York: Farrar Rinehart, 1940.

Warner, W. Lloyd, and Paul S. Lunt, *The Social Life of a Modern Community*, first volume of the "Yankee City" series, New Haven: Yale University Press, 1941.

Warner, W. Lloyd, *et al.*, *Democracy in Jonesville*, New York: Harper and Brothers, 1949.

———, *Social Class in America*, Chicago: Science Research Associates, 1949.

Weber, Max, *General Economic History,* trans. Frank H. Knight, New York: Greenberg Publisher, 1927.

Weil, Simone, "Factory Work," *Politics,* (December 1946).

Welcker, John W., "The Community Relations Problems of Industrial Companies," *Harvard Business Review,* 27 (November 1949).

Whyte, William H., Jr., "The Wives of Management," *Fortune,* (October 1951).

Wolfbein, Seymour Louis, *The Decline of a Cotton Textile City: A Study of New Bedford,* New York: Columbia University Press, 1944.

Yang, Martin C., *A Chinese Village: Taitou, Shantung Province,* London: International Library of Sociology and Social Reconstruction, 1947.

Zimmerman, Carle C., *The Changing Community,* New York: Harper and Brothers, 1938.

CHAPTER 2. HUMAN RELATIONS

Alford, L. P., *Principles of Industrial Management,* New York: The Ronald Press Company, 1940.

Alchian, Armen A., Stephen Enke, and Edith T. Penrose, "Biological Analogies in the Theory of the Firm," comments and rejoinder, *American Economic Review,* 43 (September 1953).

Argyris, Chris, "Organization of a Bank: A Study of the Nature of Organization and the Fusion Process," *Studies in Organizational Behavior No. 1,* New Haven: Yale University, 1954.

Atteslander, Peter M., "The Interactio-Gram," *Human Organization,* 13, No. 1, (1954).

Bakke E. Wight, *Bonds of Organization; An Appraisal of Corporate Human Relations,* Yale Labor and Management Center Series, New York: Harper and Brothers, 1950.

———, *The Fusion Process,* An Interim Report, New Haven: Yale University Labor and Management Center, 1946.

———, *Principles of Adaptive Human Behavior,* Mimeograph, 2nd edition, New Haven: Yale University Labor and Management Center, 1946.

———, and Chris Argyris, *Organizational Structure and Dynamics: A Framework for Theory,* An Interim Report, New Haven: Yale University Labor and Management Center, 1954.

Baur, E. Jackson, "The Function of Ceremony in the Advertising Business," *Social Forces,* 27, No. 4 (1949).

Beckerath, Herbert von, *Modern Industrial Organization,* New York: McGraw-Hill Book Company, 1939.

Brech, Edward F. L., *Management: Its Nature and Significance,* London: Isaac Pitman and Sons, 1948.

Brown, Alvin, *Organization: A Formulation of Principle,* New York: Hibbert Printing Company, 1945.

———, *Organization of Industry,* Englewood Cliffs, N. J.: Prentice-Hall, Inc., 1947.

Carney, Marie L., *Etiquette in Business,* New York: McGraw-Hill Book Company, 1948.

Clark, Burton R., *Adult Education in Transition: A Study of Institutional Insecurity.* Berkeley and Los Angeles: University of California Press, 1956.

Cole, G. D. H., "Industrialism," *Encyclopaedia of the Social Sciences,* New York: The Macmillan Company, 1930-1934.

Cooke, Taylor, and R. Whately, *The Modern Factory System,* London: Kegan Paul, Trench, Trubner and Company, 1891.

Davis, Kingsley, and Wilbert Moore, "Some Principles of Stratification," *American Sociological Review.* 10, No. 2 (1945).

Drucker, Peter F., *Concept of the Corporation,* New York: The John Day Company, 1946.

———, *The Practice of Management,* New York: Harper and Brothers, 1954.

Fayol, Henri, *Industrial and General Administration,* London: Sir Isaac Pitman and Sons, for International Management Institute, n.d.

Florence, P. Sargant, *The Logic of British and American Industry,* London: Routledge and Kegan Paul, 1953.

Ginsberg, Morris, "Class Consciousness," *Encyclopaedia of the Social Sciences,* New York: The Macmillan Company, 1930-1934.

Graicunas, V. A., "Relationship in Organization," Luther Gulick and L. Urwick, eds., *Papers on the Science of Administration,* New York: Institute of Public Administration, Columbia University, 1937.

Gulick, Luther, "Notes on the Theory of Organization," Luther Gulick and L. Urwick, eds., *Papers on the Science of Administration,* New York: Institute of Public Administration, Columbia University, 1937.

Haire, Mason, "Size, Shape, and Function in Industrial Organizations," *Human Organization,* 14 (Spring 1955).

Hamilton, Walton H., "Organization, Economic," *Encyclopaedia of the Social Sciences,* New York: The Macmillan Company, 1930-1934.

Hammond, John L., "Factory System," *Encyclopaedia of the Social Sciences,* New York: The Macmillan Company, 1930-1934.

Hertz, David B., and Robert T. Livingston, "Contemporary Organizational Theory: A Review of Current Concepts and Methods," *Human Relations,* 3 (1950).

———, "Organization and Management at the Cross-Roads," *Personnel,* 27 (July 1950).

Hiller, E. T., *Social Relations and Structures: A Study in Principles of Sociology,* New York: Harper and Brothers, 1947.

Hollingshead, August B., "Behavior Systems as a Field for Research," *American Sociological Review,* 4, No. 6 (1939).

Hoslett, Schuyler D., ed., *Human Factors in Management,* revised edition, New York: Harper and Brothers, 1951.

Hurff, George B., *Social Aspects of Enterprise in the Large Corporation,* Philadelphia: University of Pennsylvania Press, 1950.

Linton, Ralph, "Age and Sex Categories," *American Sociological Review,* 7 (1942).

———, *The Study of Man,* New York: D. Appleton-Century Company, 1936.

Litchfield, Edward H., "Notes on a General Theory of Administration," *Administrative Science Quarterly,* 1, No. 1 (1956).

Metcalf, Henry C., and Lyndall Urwick, eds., *Dynamic Administration: The Collected Papers of Mary Parker Follett,* New York: Harper and Brothers, 1942.

Pareto, Vilfredo, *The Mind and Society,* Arthur Livingston, ed., 4 vols., New York: Harcourt, Brace and Company, 1935.

Parsons, Talcott, "Sociological Approach to the Theory of Organizations—I," *Administrative Science Quarterly,* 1, No. 1 (1956).

Pfiffner, John M., "The 'Third Dimension' of Organization," *Personnel,* 28 (March 1952).

Roethlisberger, Fritz J., "Human Relations: Rare, Medium, or Well Done?" *Harvard Business Review,* 26 (January 1948).

———, "Social Behavior in Industry," *Harvard Business Review,* 16 (Summer 1938).

Urwick, L., "Organization as a Technical Problem," *Papers on the Science of Administration,* Luther Gulick and L. Urwick, eds., New York: Institute of Public Administration, Columbia University, 1937.

Weiss, R., "Processes of Organization," Ph.D. thesis, Ann Arbor: University of Michigan, 1954.

CHAPTER 3. STRUCTURES OF ORGANIZATIONS

Anderson, Arthur G., *Industrial Engineering and Factory Management,* New York: The Ronald Press Company, 1928.

———, Merten Joseph Mandeville, and John Mueller Anderson, *Industrial Management,* New York: The Ronald Press Company, 1942.

Anderson, W. A., "Family Social Participation and Social Status Self-ratings," *American Sociological Review,* 11, No. 3 (1946).

Baudler, Lucille, and Donald G. Paterson, "Social Status of Women's Occupations," *Occupations,* 26, No. 7 (1948).

Beckman, R. O., "A New Scale for Gauging Occupational Rank," *Personnel Journal,* 13 (September 1934).

Bogardus, Emory, "Occupational Distance," *Sociology and Social Research,* 13, No. 1 (1928).

Centers, Richard, 'Social Class, Occupation, and Imputed Belief," *American Journal of Sociology*, 58, No. 6 (1953).

Counts, George S., "The Social Status of Occupations: A Problem in Vocational Guidance," *School Review*, 33 (January 1925).

Crum, William L., *The Age Structure of the Corporate System*, Berkeley: University of California Press, 1953.

Deeg, Maethel E., and Donald G. Paterson, "Changes in Social Status of Occupations," *Occupations*, 25, No. 4 (1947).

Devereux, George, and Florence R. Weiner, "The Occupational Status of Nurses," *American Sociological Review*, 15, No. 4 (1950).

Evans, Kenneth, Vernon Hughes, and Logan Wilson, "A Comparison of Occupational Attitudes," *Sociology and Social Research*, 21, No. 2 (1936).

Hatt, Paul K., "Stratification in the Mass Society," *American Sociological Review*, 15 (April 1950).

Hawley, Cameron, *Executive Suite*, Boston: Houghton Mifflin Company, 1952; and New York: Ballantine Books.

Hyman, Herbert H., "The Values of Different Classes: A Social Psychological Contribution to the Analysis of Stratification," Reinhard Bendix and Seymour Martin Lipset, eds., *Class, Status and Power: A Reader in Social Stratification*, Glencoe, Ill.: The Free Press, 1953.

Jacobson, E., "An Analysis of Foreman-Steward Power Relationships," Mimeograph, Ann Arbor: Institute for Social Research, University of Michigan, 1949.

Janowitz, Morris, and Neil Wright, "The Prestige of Public Employment: 1929 and 1954," *Public Administration Review*, 16, No. 1 (1956).

Kingsbury, Susan M., "The Relations of Women to Industry," *Publications of the American Sociological Society*, 15, (1920).

Lehman, Harvey C., and P. A. Witty, "Further Study of the Social Status of Occupations," *Journal of Educational Sociology*, 5 (1931).

Manis, Jerome G., and Bernard N. Meltzer, "Attitudes of Textile Workers to Class Structure," *American Journal of Sociology*, 60, No. 1 (1954).

Mason, W. S., and N. Gross, "Intra-Occupational Prestige Differentiation: The School Superintendency," *American Sociological Review*, 20 (1955).

Menger, C., "The Social Status of Occupations for Women," *Teachers College Record*, 33 (1932).

Meyer, Julie, "Hierarchy and Stratification of the Shop," *Social Research*, 14 (June 1947).

Mombert, Paul, "Class," *Encyclopaedia of the Social Sciences*, New York: The Macmillan Company, 1930-1934.

Monk, M., and T. M. Newcomb, "Perceived Consensus and Occupational Classes," *American Sociological Review*, 21, No. 1 (1956).

National Opinion Research Center, "Jobs and Occupations: A Popular Evaluation," Reinhard Bendix and Seymour Martin Lipset, eds., *Class, Status and Power: A Reader in Social Stratification*, Glencoe, Ill.: The Free Press, 1953.

Nimkoff, Meyer F., "Opportunities for Prestige in Six Professions," *American Sociological Review*, 8 (1943).

North, Cecil Clare, *Social Differentiation*, Chapel Hill: The University of North Carolina Press, 1926.

Organizational Behavior Project, Princeton University, *Organizational Behavior: Report on a Research Program*, Mimeograph, 1953.

Parsons, Talcott, "Age and Sex in the Social Structure of the United States," *American Sociological Review*, 7, No. 5 (1942).

Pfautz, Harold W., and Otis Dudley Duncan, "A Critical Evaluation of Warner's Work in Community Stratification," *American Sociological Review*, 15 (April 1950).

Schulte, K. O., "Grading of Labor Occupations," *Seventh International Management Congress*, Production Papers, Washington: 1938.

Shartle, Carroll L., "Organization Structure," *Current Trends in Industrial Psychology*, Wayne Davis, *et al.*, eds., Pittsburgh: University of Pittsburgh Press, 1949.

Simon, Herbert A., "Comments on the Theory of Organizations," *The American Political Science Review*, 46, No. 4 (1952).

———, "A Comparison of Organization Theories," *Review of Economic Studies*, 20 (1952).

Smith, Mapheus, "An Empirical Scale of Prestige Status of Occupations," *American Sociological Review*, 8, No. 2 (1943).

———, "Proposals for Making a Scale of Status of Occupations," *Sociology and Social Research*, 20, No. 1 (1935).

Thomas, Brinley, "The Problem of Bridges and Barriers," T. H. Marshall, ed., *Class Sonflict and Social Stratification*, London: LePlay House Press, 1938.

Turner, Ralph H., "Occupational Patterns of Inequality," *American Journal of Sociology*, 59, No. 5 (1954).

———, "Role-Taking, Role Standpoint, and Reference-Group Behavior," *American Journal of Sociology,* 61, No. 4 (1956).

Vucinich, Alexander, *Soviet Economic Institutions: The Social Structure of Production Units*, Stanford, Calif.: Stanford University Press, 1952.

Warner, W. Lloyd, and Paul S. Lunt, *The Status System of a Modern Community*, second volume of the "Yankee City" series, New Haven: Yale University Press, 1942.

Welch, Maryon K., "The Ranking of Occupations on the Basis of Social Status," *Occupations*, 26, No. 4 (1949).

CHAPTER 5. JOBS, POSITIONS, OFFICES

Alpert, Harry, *Emile Durkheim and His Sociology*, Studies in History, Economics, and Public Law, No. 445, New York: Columbia University Press, 1939.

Bavelas, Alex, "Role Playing and Management Training," *Sociatry*, 1, No. 2 (1947).

Charters, W., "A Study of Role Conflict among Foremen in a Heavy Industry," Ph.D. thesis, University of Michigan, 1952.

Davis, Edwin W., "Aids to Occupational Research," *Occupations,* 3, No. 6 (1935).

Durkheim, Emile, *Emile Durkheim on the Division of Labor in Society*, trans. George Simpson, New York: The Macmillan Company, 1933.

Farquar, Henry H., "The Anomaly of Functional Authority at the Top," *Advanced Management*, 7 (April-June 1942).

Form, William H., "Toward an Occupational Social Psychology," *Journal of Social Psychology*, 24, (1946).

Gist, Noel P., "Occupational Differentiation in South India," *Social Forces*, 33, No. 2 (1954).

Gold, Ray, "Janitors versus Tenants: A Status-Income Dilemma," *American Journal of Sociology*, 57, No. 5 (1952).

Knight, Melvin M., "Handicraft," *Encyclopaedia of the Social Sciences*, New York: The Macmillan Company, 1930-1934.

Papandreou, Andreas G., "The Location and Scope of the Entrepreneurial Function," Ph.D. dissertation, Harvard University, 1943.

Roethlisberger, Fritz J., "The Territory and Skill of the Administrator," *Michigan Business Review,* 6 (November 1954).

Salz, Arthur, "Occupation," *Encyclopaedia of the Social Sciences*, New York: The Macmillan Company, 1930-1934.

———, "Specialization," *Encyclopaedia of the Social Sciences*, New York: The Macmillan Company, 1930-1934.

Sheldon, Oliver, "Management," *Encyclopaedia of the Social Sciences*, New York: The Macmillan Company, 1930-1934.

Simon, Herbert A., "Birth of an Organization: The Economic Cooperation Administration," *Public Administration Review*, 13, No. 4 (1953).

———, Donald W. Smithburg, and Victor A. Thompson, *Public Administration*, New York: Alfred A. Knopf, 1950.

Smigel, E. O., "Trends in Occupational Sociology in the United States: A Survey of Postwar Research," *American Sociological Review*, 19 (1954).

Smith, Adam, *An Inquiry into the Nature and Causes of the Wealth of Nations*, Everyman's Library edition, London and Toronto: J. M. Dent and Sons; New York: E. P. Dutton & Company, 1910.

Stauss, James H., "The Entrepreneur: The Firm," *Journal of Political Economy*, 52 (June 1944).

Taylor, Frederick W., *The Principles of Scientific Management*, New York: Harper and Brothers, 1911.

CHAPTER 6. GROUP LIFE OF ORGANIZATIONS

Auten, Nellie, "Sweating System in the Garment Trades of Chicago," *American Journal of Sociology*, 6, No. 5 (1901).

Barkin, Solomon, "A Pattern for the Study of Human Relations in Industry," *Industrial and Labor Relations Review*, 9, No. 1 (1955).

Berliner, Joseph S., "The Informal Organization of the Soviet Firm," *Quarterly Journal of Economics*, 66 (August 1952).

Burgess, E. W., "Social Relations, Activities, and Personal Adjustment," *The American Journal of Sociology*, 59 (January 1954).

Caplow, Theodore, "The Definition and Measurement of Ambiences," *Social Forces*, 34 (October 1955).

Chapple, Eliot D., "Natural Groups in Industry," *Journal of Educational Sociology*, 19 (May 1946).

Cook, P. H., and A. J. Wyndham, "Patterns of Eating Behavior: A Study of Industrial Workers," *Human Relations*, 6 (1953).

Firey, Walter, "Informal Organization and the Theory of Schism," *American Sociological Review*, 13 (February 1948).

French, John R. R., Jr., and Alvin Zander, "The Group Dynamics Approach," Arthur Kornhauser, ed., *Psychology of Labor-Management Relations*, Champaign, Ill.: Industrial Relations Research Association, 1949.

Gay, Edwin F., "Putting Out System," *Encyclopaedia of the Social Sciences*, New York: The Macmillan Company, 1930-1934.

Gillespie, James J., *Free Expression in Industry, a Social-psychlogical Study of Work and Leisure*, London: Pilot Press, 1948.

Hope, John, "Industrial Integration of Negroes: The Upgrading Process," *Human Organization*, 11, No. 4 (1952).

Hughes, Everett C., "The Knitting of Racial Groups in Industry," *American Sociological Review*, 11 (October 1946).

McLean, A. M., "Sweat Shop in Summer," *American Journal of Sociology*, 9 (1903).

———, "Two Weeks in Department Stores," *American Journal of Sociology*, 4, No. 6 (1899).

———, "With Oregon Hop Pickers," *American Journal of Sociology*, 15, No. 1 (1909).

Marschak, Jacob, "Elements for a Theory of Teams," *Management Science*, 1 (January 1955).

Merton, Robert K., "Social Structure and Anomie," R. N. Anshen, ed., *The Family: Its Function and Destiny*, New York: Harper and Brothers, 1949.

Nieto, Bernardino H., "Introduccion al Estudio de la Sociologia Industrial. (An Introduction to the Study of Industrial Sociology), *Revue Internationale de Sociologie*, 11, No. 4 (1953).

Seiniger, W. B., "Charting the Informal Organization," *Advanced Management*, 16, No. 11 (1951).

Sheppard, Harold L., "The Social and Historical Philosophy of Elton Mayo," *Antioch Review* (Fall 1950).

Simmel, Georg, "The Sociology of Sociability," trans. Everett C. Hughes, *American Journal of Sociology*, 55, No. 3 (1949).

———, *The Web of Group-Affiliations*, trans. Reinhard Bendix, Glencoe, Ill.: The Free Press, 1955.

Spykman, Nicholas J., *The Social Theory of Georg Simmel*, Chicago: University of Chicago Press, 1925.

Toennies, Ferdinand, *Fundamental Concepts of Sociology*, trans. and suppl. C. P. Loomis, New York: The American Book Company, 1940.

Weschler, Irving R., Robert Tannenbaum, and Eugene Talbot, "A New Management Tool: The Multi-Relation Sociometric Survey," *Personnel*, 29 (July 1952).

Whyte, William Foote, *Street Corner Society: The Social Structure of an Italian Slum*, Chicago: University of Chicago Press, 1943.

Willerman, G., "Group Identification in Industry," Ph.D. thesis, Massachusetts Institute of Technology, 1949.

CHAPTER 7. INSTITUTIONAL BASES OF DECISIONS

Adelman, M. A., "Is Big Business Getting Bigger?" *Fortune*, 45, No. 1 (1952).

———, "The Measurement of Industrial Concentration," *The Review of Economics and Statistics*, 34 (1951).

Appley, Lawrence A., "Emergence of a New Management Era," *Personnel*, 25 (May 1949).

Arnold, Thurman W., *Democracy and Free Enterprise*, Norman, Okla.: University of Oklahoma Press, 1942.

———, *The Folklore of Capitalism*, New Haven: Yale University Press, 1937.

Ayres, C. E., *The Theory of Economic Progress*, Chapel Hill: University of North Carolina Press, 1944.

Bendix, Reinhard, "The Self-legitimation of an Entrepreneurial Class: The Case of England," *Zeitschrift fur die Gesamte Statts-wissenschaft*, 111, No. 1 (1954).

———, "A Study of Managerial Ideologies, as It Bears on Drucker's Thesis," paper read before the American Sociological Society, Atlantic City, N. J., September 3, 1952.

Berle, Adolf A., Jr., and Gardiner C. Means, "Corporation," in *Encyclopaedia of the Social Sciences*, New York: The Macmillan Company, 1930-1934.

———, *The Modern Corporation and Private Property*, New York: The Macmillan Company, 1933.

Bernheim, A. L., ed., *Big Business, Its Growth and Its Place*, New York: Twentieth Century Fund, 1937.

Black, Duncan, "On the Rationale of Group Decision-Making," *Journal of Political Economy*, 56 (February 1948).

Bogart, Ernest L., and Charles E. Landon, *Modern Industry*, New York: Longmans, Green and Company, 1927.

Brookings, Robert S., *Industrial Ownership*, New York: The Macmillan Company, 1925.

Bross, Irvin D. J., *Design for Decision*, New York: The Macmillan Company, 1953.

Bunting, J. Whitney, ed., *Ethics for Modern Business Practice*, Englewood Cliffs, N. J.: Prentice-Hall, Inc., 1953.

Chamberlain, Neil W., "The Organized Business in America," *Journal of Political Economy*, 52 (June 1944).

Cochran, Thomas C., "A Plan for the Study of Business Thinking," *Political Science Quarterly*, 62 (March 1947).

Commons, John R., *Legal Foundations of Capitalism*, New York: The Macmillan Company, 1924.

Cowles Commission for Research in Economics, *Rational Decision-making and Economic Behavior*, 19th Annual Report, 1950-1951, Chicago: University of Chicago, 1951.

Dale, Earnest, "New Perspectives in Managerial Decision-making," *Journal of Business of the University of Chicago*, 26 (January 1953).

Davis, Jerome, *Capitalism and Its Culture*, New York: Farrar and Rinehart, 1935.

Diamond, Sigmund, *The Reputation of the American Businessman*, Cambridge: Harvard University Press, 1955.

Drucker, Peter F., "Management Must Manage," *Harvard Business Review*, 28 (March 1950).

Fairchild, Henry P., "Business as an Institution," *American Sociological Review*, 2 (February 1937).

Filipetti, George, *Industrial Management in Transition*, Chicago: Richard D. Irwin, 1946.

Evans, George Heberton, Jr., "A Sketch of American Business Organization 1832-1900," *Journal of Political Economy*, 60 (December 1952).

Frank, Glenn, *The Politics of Industry: A Footnote to the Social Unrest*, New York: The Twentieth Century Fund, 1919.

Goldsmith, Raymond W., Rexford C. Parmelee, *et al.*, "The Distribution of Ownership in the 200 Largest Nonfinancial Corporations," *Investigation of Concentration of Economic Power, Monograph No. 29*, United States Congress, Temporary National Economic Committee, Washington: Government Printing Office 1940.

Graham, Frank D., *Social Goals and Economic Institutions*, Princeton: Princeton University Press, 1942.

Granby, Helene, "Survey of Shareholdings in 1,710 Corporations with Securities Listed on a National Securities Exchange," *Investigation of Concentration of Economic Power, Monograph No. 30*, United States Congress, Temporary National Economic Committee, Washington: Government Printing Office, 1941.

Gras, Norman S. B., and Henrietta M. Larson, *Casebook in American Business History*, New York: F. S. Crofts and Company, 1939.

Heaton, Herbert, "Industrial Revolution," *Encyclopaedia of the Social Sciences*, New York: The Macmillan Company, 1930-1934.

Hilgard, Ernest R., "Business Policy and Social Science: Past, Present, and Future," *Social Science for Industry: Proceedings of a Seminar Arranged by Stanford Research Institute*, Stanford, Calif., 1953.

Kaplan, Abrams D. H., *Big Enterprise in a Competitive System*, Washington: Brookings Institution, 1954.

Knauth, Oswald W., *Managerial Enterprise*, New York: W. W. Norton and Company, 1948.

———, "Group Interest and Managerial Enterprise," *Journal of Industrial Economics*, 1 (April 1953).

Knight, Frank H., *Risk, Uncertainty, and Profit*, Boston: Houghton Mifflin Company, 1921.

Lindgren, Gunnar, "How Long Does a Company Live?" *Oxford Economic Papers, N. S.* 5 (October 1953).

Lynch, David, *The Concentration of Economic Power*, New York: Columbia University Press, 1946.

Marshall, Alfred, "The Social Possibilities of Economic Chivalry," *Economic Journal*, 17 (March 1907).

Meadows, Paul, "The Industrial Future and the Conflict of Ideologies," *American Journal of Economics and Sociology*, 7 (October 1947).

Moore, Wilbert E., "The Emergence of New Property Conceptions in America," *Journal of Legal and Political Sociology*, 1 (April 1943).

National Association of Manufacturers, Economic Principles Commission, *The American Individual Enterprise System: Its Nature, Evolution, and Future*, 2 Vols., New York: McGraw-Hill Book Company, 1946.

Newman, William H., "Basic Objectives Which Shape the Character of a Company," *Journal of Business of the University of Chicago*, 26 (October 1953).

O'Donnell, Cyril, "The Source of Managerial Authority," *Political Science Quarterly*, 67 (December 1952).

Schroeder, G. G., *The Growth of Major Steel Companies, 1900-1950*, Baltimore: Johns Hopkins Press, 1953.

Stauss, James H., "The Entrepreneur: The Firm," *Journal of Political Economy*, 52 (June 1944).

Sweezy, Paul M., "The Illusion of the 'Managerial Revolution,'" *Science and Society*, 6 (Winter 1942).

Tawney, Richard H., *Religion and the Rise of Capitalism*, New York: Penguin Books, 1926; and New American Library.

Taylor, Horace, and Harold Barger, *The American Economy in Operation*, New York: Harcourt, Brace and Company, 1949.

"The Transformation of American Capitalism," *Fortune*, 43, No. 2 (1951).

Truman, David, *The Governmental Process*, New York: Alfred A. Knopf, 1951.

United Nations Technical Assistance Administration, *Some Problems in the Organization and Administration of Public Enterprises in the Industrial Field*, New York: Columbia University Press, 1954.

United States Congress Temporary National Economic Committee, *Investigation of Concentration of Economic Power*, Hearings . . . , Washington: Government Printing Office, 1941.

Veblen, Thorstein, *Absentee Ownership and Business Enterprise in Recent Times: The Case of America*, New York: B. W. Huebsch, 1923.

———, *Imperial Germany and the Industrial Revolution*, New York: The Viking Press, 1939.

———, *The Vested Interests and the State of the Industrial Arts*, New York: B. W. Huebsch, 1919.

Weber, Max, *The Protestant Ethic and the Spirit of Capitalism*, trans. Talcott Parsons, London: George Allen and Unwin, 1930.

Weiss, R., "Factors Determining the Adoption of Decision-making as a Role Behavior: A Study of Scientists in a Government Organization," Mimeograph, Ann Arbor: Institute for Social Research, University of Michigan, September 1954.

CHAPTER 8. LABOR FORCE

Amidon, Beulah, "Manpower for Industry," *Survey Graphic*, 29 (December 1940).

Anderson, H. Dewey, and Percy E. Davidson, *Occupational Trends in the United States*, Stanford: Stanford University Press, 1940.

Bancroft, Gertrude, "Trends in the Labor Force," William Haber, *et al.*, eds., *Manpower in the United States: Problems and Policies*, New York: Harper and Brothers, 1954.

Bickham, Martin H., "The American Labor Market," *American Journal of Sociology*, 43, No. 4 (1938).

Biddle, Erle H., *Manpower, a Summary of British Experience, Publication* No. 84, Chicago: Public Administration Service, 1942.

Brown, J. Douglas, "Meeting Requirements for Scientific, Engineering, and Managerial Manpower," William Haber, *et al.*, eds., *Manpower in the United States: Problems and Policies,* New York: Harper and Brothers, 1954.

Bureau of Labor Statistics, *Handbook of Labor Statistics,* Washington: Government Printing Office, 1950.

Clark, Colin, *The Conditions of Economic Progress,* London: Macmillan and Company, 1940.

Clark, Harold R., *Economic Theory and Correct Occupational Distribution*, New York: Bureau of Publication, Teachers College, Columbia University, 1931.

Corson, John J., "The Labor Force: Its Recruitment and Training," *Law and Contemporary Problems*, 9 (Summer 1942).

Dorfman, Robert, "The Labor Force Status of Persons Aged Sixty-Five and Over," *American Economic Review*, 44, No. 2 (1954).

Edwards, Alba M., *Comparative Occupation Statistics for the United States, 1870-1940*, Washington: Government Printing Office, 1943.

Gill, Corrington, *Wasted Manpower*, New York: W. W. Norton and Company, 1939.

Ginzberg, Eli, *Conservation of Human Resources*, Progress Report, New York: Conservation of Human Resources Project, Graduate School of Business, Columbia University, Summer 1953.

Greenberg, Walter, "A Bibliography of Occupational Monographs Available through the Federal Government," *Occupations,* 25, No. 7 (1947).

Hauser, Philip M., "Changes in the Labor Force Participation of the Older Worker," *American Journal of Sociology*, 49 (January 1954).

———, "Mobility in Labor Force Participation," *Labor Mobility and Economic Opportunity*, Cambridge: The Technology Press of M. I. T.; New York: John Wiley and Sons, 1954.

Hurlin, Ralph G., and Meredith B. Givens, "Shifting Occupational Patterns," *Recent Social Trends in the United States*, New York: McGraw-Hill Book Company, 1934.

Kerr, Clark, "Balkanization of Labor Markets," *Labor Mobility and Economic Opportunity*, Cambridge: The Technology Press of M. I. T.; New York: John Wiley and Sons, 1954.

———, "Labor Markets: Their Character and Consequences," Milton Derber, ed., *Proceedings of the Second Annual Meeting, Industrial Relations Research Association*, Champaign, Ill.: 1950.

Kitson, Harry D., "Distribution of Workers in Selected Occupations," *Occupations*, 25, No. 3 (1946).

Knox, John B., "Employment of Handicapped Persons," *The Conference Board Management Record*, December 1941.

Landis, Paul H., *Population Problems: A Cultural Interpretation*, New York: American Book Company, 1943.

Lastrucci, Carlo L., "The Status and Significance of Occupational Research," *American Sociological Review*, 11, No. 1 (1946).

Levine, Louis, "Problems in Labor Market Organization and Administration," William Haber, *et al.*, eds., *Manpower in the United States: Problems and Policies,* New York: Harper and Brothers, 1954.

Likert, Rensis, and Stanley E. Seashore, "Increasing Utilization through Better Management of Human Resources," William Haber, *et al.*, eds., *Manpower in the United States: Problems and Policies,* New York: Harper and Brothers, 1954.

Malm, F. Theodore, "Recruiting Patterns and the Functioning of Labor Markets," *Industrial and Labor Relations Review,* 7, No. 4 (1954).

Moore, Wilbert E., "Utilization of Human Resources through Industrialization," *The Mil-Bank Memorial Fund Quarterly,* 28, No. 1 (1950).

———, "Urbanization and Industrialization of the Labor Force in a Developing Economy. Labor Attitudes Toward Industrialization in Underdeveloped Countries," *Journal of the American Economic Association,* 45, No. 2 (1955).

Myers, Howard B., "Dynamics of Labor Supply," *Journal of the American Statistical Association,* 36 (June 1941).

National Manpower Council, *A Policy for Skilled Manpower,* New York: Columbia University Press, 1954.

Noland, E. William, and E. Wight Bakke, *Workers Wanted: A Study of Employers' Hiring Policies, Preferences, and Practices in New Haven and Charlotte,* New York: Harper and Brothers, 1949.

Ogburn, William, and Clark Tibbitts, "Occupations," *American Journal of Sociology,* 34, No. 6 (1929).

Orzack, Louis H., "Aspects of Employment in a Changing Rural Social Structure," *Indiana Magazine of History,* 46, No. 4 (1950).

Palmer, Gladys L., and Ann R. Miller, "The Occupational and Industrial Distribution of Employment, 1910-50," William Haber, *et al.,* eds., *Manpower in the United States: Problems and Policies,* New York: Harper and Brothers, 1954.

Parrish, John B., "Women in the Nation's Labor Market," *Quarterly Journal of Economics,* 54 (1940).

Ravenstein, E. G., "The Laws of Migration," *Journal of the Royal Statistical Society,* 52 (June 1889).

Rogoff, Natalie, "Recent Trends in Occupational Mobility," unpublished Ph.D. thesis, Chicago: University of Chicago Libraries, 1950.

———, "Recent Trends in Urban Occupational Mobility," *Class, Status and Power: A Reader in Social Stratification,* eds. Reinhard Bendix and Seymour Martin Lipset, Glencoe, Ill.: The Free Press, 1953.

Science Research Associates, *Occupational Briefs on America's Major Job Fields,* Chicago: Science Research Associates, 1946.

Shister, Joseph, "Labor Mobility: Some Institutional Aspects," *Proceedings of the Third Annual Meeting, Industrial Relations Research Association,* Champaign, Ill.: 1950.

Shock, N. W., "Older People and Their Potentialities for Gainful Employment," *Journal of Gerontology,* 2 (April 1947).

Shryock, Henry, Jr., and Hope Tisdale Eldridge, "Internal Migration in Peace and War," *American Sociological Review,* 12, No. 1 (1947).

Smith, T. Lynn, *Population Analysis,* New York: McGraw-Hill Book Company, 1948.

Spengler, Joseph J., "Some Effects of Changes in the Age Composition of the Labor Force," *The Southern Economic Journal,* 8, No. 11 (1941).

Stouffer, Samuel A., "Intervening Opportunities: A Theory relating Mobility and Distance," *American Sociological Review,* 5, No. 6 (1940).

Thomas, R. E., "Vocational Rehabilitation," *Monthly Labor Review,* 53 (July 1941).

Thompson, Warren S., *Population Problems,* New York: McGraw-Hill Book Company, 1953.

Trabue, Marion R., "Functional Classification of Occupations," *Occupations,* 15, No. 2 (1936).

United States Department of Labor, Division of Labor Standards, *Safeguarding Manpower for Greater Production,* Special Bulletin No. 1, Washington: Government Printing Office, 1940.

United States Department of Labor, Bureau of Labor Statistics, "Employment and Production in Manufacturing Industries, 1919-1936," *Monthly Labor Review,* 49 (December 1939).

United States House of Representatives, Select Committee Investigating National Defense Migration, *Hearings,* Washington: Government Printing Office, 1942.

United States Senate, Committee on Education and Labor, *Investigation of Manpower Resources, Hearings before a Subcommittee,* Washington: Government Printing Office, 1942.

Vance, Rupert B., and Nadia Danilevski, "Population and the Pattern of Unemployment, 1930-1937," *Milbank Memorial Fund Quarterly*, 18 (January 1940).

Weiss, Samuel, and A. J. Jaffe, "Puerto Rico: The Labor Force and Level of Living," *Monthly Labor Review*, 78, No. 12 (1955).

Wilcock, Richard C., "New Firms and the Labor Supply in Small Communities," *Current Economic Comment*, November 1954.

———, and Irvin Sobel, "Secondary Labor Force Mobility in Four Midwestern Shoe Towns," *Industrial and Labor Relations Review*, 8, No. 4 (1955).

Wolfbein, Seymour L., "The Geographic Distribution of Nonfarm Employment," William Haber, *et al.*, eds., *Manpower in the United States: Problems and Policies*, New York: Harper and Brothers, 1954.

———, and A. J. Jaffe, "Demographic Factors in Labor Force Growth," *American Sociological Review*, 11, No. 4(1946).

Wolfle, Dael, "Intellectual Resources," *Scientific American*, 185, No. 3 (1951).

Wolman, Leo, and Gustav Peck, "Labor Groups in the Social Structure," *Recent Social Trends in the United States*, New York: McGraw-Hill Book Company, 1934.

Woofter, T. J., Jr., "The Future Working Population," *Rural Sociology*, 4 (September 1939).

Woytinsky, W. S., *Additional Workers and the Volume of Unemployment in the Depression*, Pamphlet Series No. 1, Washington: Committee on Social Security, Social Science Research Council, 1940.

———, *Labor in the United States: Basic Statistics for Social Security*, Washington: Committee on Social Security, Social Science Research Council, 1938.

———, *The Labor Supply in the United States*, revised edition, Committee on Social Security, Social Science Research Council, 1937.

Yoder, Dale, *Manpower Economics and Labor Problems*, New York: McGraw-Hill Book Company, 1939.

———, "Manpower Mobility: Two Studies," *Labor Mobility and Economic Opportunity*, Cambridge: The Technology Press of M. I. T.; New York: John Wiley and Sons, 1954.

———, Donald G. Paterson, Herbert G. Heneman, Jr., and others, *Local Labor Market Research*, Minneapolis: Industrial Relations Center, University of Minnesota, 1948.

Zimand, Gertrude Folks, "The Changing Picture of Child Labor," *Annals*, The American Academy of Political and Social Science, 236 (November 1944).

CHAPTER 9. BACKGROUNDS OF WORKERS

Amidon, Beaulah, "Negroes and Defense," *Survey Graphic*, 30 (June 1941).

Anderson, Nels, *Men on the Move*, Chicago: University of Chicago Press, 1940.

Beard, Mary R., *Woman as a Force in History: A Study in Traditions and Realities*, New York: The Macmillan Company, 1946.

Collins, Henry Hill, Jr., *America's Own Refugees*, Princeton: Princeton University Press, 1941.

Johnson, Charles S., *Into the Main Stream*, Chapel Hill: University of North Carolina Press, 1947.

Leevy, J. R., "The Modern Industrial Working Woman," *American Sociological Review*, 8 (1943).

Schlesinger, A. M., *Political and Social History of the United States, 1829-1925*, New York: The Macmillan Company, 1926.

Schneider, Joseph, "Social Origins and Fame: The United States and England," *American Sociological Review*, 10, No. 1 (1945).

Smith, M., "The Differential Impact of Selective Service Inductions on Occupations in the United States," *American Sociological Review*, 11 (1946).

United States Department of Labor, Bureau of Labor Statistics, "Young and Old at the Employment Office," *Monthly Labor Review*, 46 (January 1938).

Vreeland, F. M., and E. J. Fitzgerald, *Farm-City Migration and Industry's Labor Reserve*,

Report No. L-7, Works Project Administration, National Research Project, Philadelphia: 1939.

Williams, Robin M., Jr., *American Society: A Sociological Interpretation*, New York: Alfred A. Knopf, 1952.

"The Workers," *Fortune*, 21, No. 2 (1940).

Zimmerman, C. C., and J. J. Corson, "The Migrations to Towns and Cities," *Social Forces*, 8, No. 3 (1930).

CHAPTER 10. TECHNOLOGY AND PRODUCTION

Armand, Louis, "Machines, Technology and the Life of the Mind," *Impact of Science on Society*, 3 (1952).

Barkin, Solomon, "Human and Social Impact of Technical Changes," *Proceedings of the Third Annual Meeting of the Industrial Relations Research Association*, Champaign, Ill.: 1950.

———, "The Technical Engineering Service of an American Trade Union," *International Labour Review*, 61 (June 1950).

———, "Trade-Union Attitudes and Their Effect Upon Productivity," Solomon Barkin, *et al.*, eds., *Industrial Productivity*, Champaign, Ill.: Industrial Relations Research Association, December 1951.

Bernal, J. D., *The Social Function of Science*, New York: The Macmillan Company, 1939.

Blair, John M., "Technology and Size," *American Economic Review*, 38 (May 1948).

Brooks, R. S., A. B. B. Eyre, E. Farmer, and B. Muscio, "An Investigation into the Packing of Chocolates," *Journal of the National Institute of Industrial Psychology*, 1 (January-April 1922).

Chase, Stuart, *Men and Machines*, New York: The Macmillan Company, 1937.

Cogen, A., and A. Zander, "The Effects of Clarity of the Job and Confidence in One's Self on the Reactions of Telephone Operators," Spirit-duplicated, Ann Arbor: Institute of Social Research, University of Michigan, May 1953.

"The Coming Boom: Preview of 1960," *Nation's Business*, 43, No. 5 (1955).

Cottrell, W. Fred, "Death by Dieselization: A Case Study in the Reaction to Technological Change," *American Sociological Review*, 16 (June 1951).

———, *Energy and Society: The Relation Between Energy, Social Change and Economic Development*, New York: McGraw-Hill Book Company, 1955.

———, "Of Time and the Railroader," *American Sociological Review*, 4 (1939).

Dahmén, Erik, "Technology, Innovation and International Industrial Transformation," *International Social Science Bulletin*, 6, No. 2 (1954).

Davis, Hiram S., "The Meaning and Measurement of Productivity," Solomon Barkin, *et al.*, eds., *Industrial Productivity*, Champaign, Ill.: Industrial Relations Research Association, December 1951.

Davis, John C., "Productivity Trends and Some Economic Implications," Solomon Barkin, *et al.*, eds., *Industrial Productivity*, Champaign, Ill.: Industrial Relations Research Association, December 1951.

Dewhurst, J. Frederic, and associates, *America's Needs and Resources*, revised edition, New York: The Twentieth Century Fund, 1955.

Engel-Frisch, G., "A Study of the Effects of Odd-Shifts Upon the Food Habits of War Workers," *American Sociological Review*, 8 (1943).

Farmer, E., "Time and Motion Study," Report 14, *Industrial Fatigue Research Board Reports*, London: His Majesty's Stationery Office, 1923.

Flinn, Frederick Bonner, "Industrial Aspects of Human Fatigue," *Journal of Personnel Research*, 2 (November 1923).

Gilbreth, Frank B., *Bricklaying System*, New York: M. C. Clark, 1909.

———, and Lillian Gilbreth, *Applied Motion Study*, New York: Sturgis and Walton, 1917.

———, *Fatigue Study*, New York: 1916.

Gillespie, James J., "Work Psychology and Time and Motion Study," *Advanced Management*, 16 (April 1951).

Gitlow, Abraham L., "An Economic Evaluation

of the Gains and Costs of Technological Change," Solomon Barkin, *et al.*, eds., *Industrial Productivity*, Champaign, Ill.: Industrial Relations Research Association, December 1951.

Gompers, S., "The Effect of Industrial Combinations on Labor Conditions," *Annals*. The American Academy of Political and Social Science, (July 1912).

Kornhauser, Arthur W., "The Effect of Noise on Office Output," *Industrial Psychology*, 1927.

Lahy, J. M., *Le Systeme Taylor et la Physiologie du Travail Professional*, Paris: 1921.

Laird, D. A., "Experiments on the Physiological Cost of Noise," *Journal of the National Institute of Industrial Psychology*, 5 (January 1929).

Legros, L. A., and H. C. Weston, "On the Design of Machinery in Relation to the Operator," Report 36, *Industrial Fatigue Research Board Reports*, London: His Majesty's Stationery Office, n.d.

Lipmann, O., "The German Industrial Inquiry: Some Findings with Reference to the Psychology of Labor," *Personnel Journal*, 9 (1930).

Lonigan, E., "Effect of Modern Technological Conditions upon the Employment of Labor," *American Economic Review*, 29 (June 1939).

Lumpkin, Katharine Du Pre, and Mabel V. Combs, *Shutdowns in the Connecticut Valley: A Study of Worker Displacement in the Small Industrial Community*, Smith College Studies in History, Vol. 19 (April-July 1934), Northampton, Mass.: Smith College.

Marx, Walter John, *Mechanization and Culture*, St. Louis: Herder Book Company, 1941.

Mayo, Elton, "The Human Effect of Mechanization," *Papers and Proceedings of the 42nd Annual Meeting of the American Economic Association*, 20, No. 1 (1930).

Merton, Robert K., *Science, Technology and Society in Seventeenth Century England*, in the series *Osiris*, Vol. 4, Bruges, Belgium: The Saint Catherine Press, 1938.

Miller, Spencer, Jr., "Labor's Attitude toward Time and Motion Study," *Mechanical Engineering*, 60 (April 1938).

Moore, Wilbert E., "Theoretical Aspects of Industrialization," *Social Research*, 15, No. 3 (1948).

Myers, C. S., *Industrial Psychology in Great Britain*, London: 1925.

———, "The National Institute of Industrial Psychology at London," *Scientific Review of Labor*, (June 1929).

———, "The Study of Fatigue," *Journal of Personnel Research*, 3 (January 1925).

Neel, R., "Nervous Stress in the Industrial Situation," Mimeograph, Ann Arbor: Institute for Social Research, University of Michigan, September 1954.

Nourse, Edwin C., and associates, *America's Capacity to Produce*, Washington: The Brookings Institution, 1934.

Ogburn, William Fielding, "Technology and the Standard of Living in the United States," *American Journal of Sociology*, 60, No. 4 (1955).

Potter, David M., *People of Plenty: Economic Abundance and the American Character*, Chicago: University of Chicago Press, 1954.

Rosen, S. McKee, and Laura Rosen, *Technology and Society: The Influence of Machines in the United States*, New York: The Macmillan Company, 1941.

Scott, Howard, *et al.*, *Introduction to Technocracy*, New York: John Day Company, 1933.

Siegel, Irving H., "Labor Productivity in the Soviet Union," *Journal of the American Statistical Association*, 48 (1953).

The Social Aspects of Rationalization, Geneva: International Labor Office, 1931.

Sottonin, K., "The Problem of Industrial Fatigue," *Problems of the Psychology, Physiology, Reflexes and Hygiene of Labor*, 3 (April 1928).

Spicer, Edward H., ed., *Human Problems in Technological Change: A Casebook*, New York: Russell Sage Foundation, 1952.

Thompson, Samuel, "Factors Affecting Inter-Plant Differences in Productivity," Solomon Barkin, *et al.*, eds., *Industrial Productivity*, Champaign, Ill.: Industrial Relations Research Association, December 1951.

United States Congress, Temporary National Economic Committee, *Investigation of Concentration of Economic Power, Hearings . . .* Part 30, "Technology and Concentration of Economic Power," Washington: Government Printing Office, 1940.

United States Department of Labor, Bureau of Labor Statistics, "Hours, Fatigue, and Health in British Munition Factories," *Bulletin No. 221*, Washington: Government Printing Office, 1917.

———, "Industrial Efficiency and Fatigue in British Munition Factories," *Bulletin No. 230,* Washington: Government Printing Office, 1917.

United States Navy, *Handbook of Human Engineering Data for Design Engineers,* Medford, Mass.: Tufts College, 1951.

Vernon, H. M., "On Certain Effects of Long Spells of Repetitive Work," *British Journal of Psychology,* 16 (1926).

———, "Fatigue in Industry," *Human Factor,* (January 1937).

———, *The Health and Efficiency of Munition Workers,* London: Oxford University Press, 1940.

———, and S. Wyatt, "Two Studies on Rest Pauses in Industry," Report 25, *Industrial Fatigue Research Board Reports,* London: His Majesty's Stationery Office, n.d.

———, and T. Bedford, "Rest Pauses in Heavy and Moderately Heavy Industrial Work," Report 41, *Industrial Fatigue Research Board Reports,* London: His Majesty's Stationery Office, 1927.

Weintraub, David, "Increased Productivity and Unemployment," *Personnel Journal,* 16 (November 1937).

———, "Unemployment and Increasing Productivity," *Technological Trends and National Policy,* National Resources Committee, Washington: Government Printing Office, 1937.

Weston, H. C., and A. K. Taylor, "The Relation between Illumination and Efficiency in Fine Work," Joint Report of the Industrial Fatigue Research Board, British Medical Research Council, and the Illumination Research Committee, 1926.

Weston, H. C., and S. Adams, "The Performance of Weavers under Varying Conditions of Noise," Report 70, *Industrial Health Research Board Reports,* British Medical Research Council, 1935.

Wubnig, Arthur, "The Measurement of the Technological Factor in Labor Productivity," *Journal of the American Statistical Association,* 34 (June 1939).

Wyatt, S., "Machine Speeds and Output," *Journal of the National Institute of Industrial Psychology,* 3 (October 1927).

———, "Studies in Repetitive Work," Report 32, *Industrial Fatigue Research Board Reports,* London: His Majesty's Stationery Office, 1925.

———, and J. A. Fraser, "The Effects of Monotony in Work, A Preliminary Inquiry," Report 56, *Industrial Fatigue Research Board Reports, London*: His Majesty's Stationery Office, 1929.

———, "The Machine and the Worker," Report 82, *Industrial Research Board Reports,* London: His Majesty's Stationery Office, 1938.

Zobel, Sigmund P., "On the Measurement of the Productivity of Labor," *Journal of the American Statistical Association,* 45 (June 1950).

Ure, Andrew, *Philosophy of Manufactures,* London: 1835.

CHAPTER 11. AUTOMATION AND HUMAN RELATIONS

"Automation," *Tomorrow's Job,* 17, No. 6 (1955).

Couffignal, L., *L'Homme, la Technique et la Nature,* Paris: 1938.

———, *Sur l 'analyse Mécanique: Application aux Machines à Calculer et aux Calculs de la Mécanique Céleste,* Paris: 1938.

Friedmann, Georges, "Automatisme et Travail Industriel," *Cahiers Internationaux de Sociologie,* 1 (1946).

———, "Automatism and Industrial Work," *Applied Anthropology,* 7 (Summer 1948).

Larsen, Douglas, "Labor Matches Wits with Automation: Second Industrial Revolution," Last of three newspaper articles released by National Education Association during February, 1956.

Lasswell, Harold D., "Current Studies of the Decision Process: Automation versus Creativity," *The Western Political Quarterly,* 8 (September 1955).

Maurer, P., *Machinisme et Automatiques, Mecaniques et Electriques,* Paris: 1934.

"Reuther Streamlines an Old Spook," *Nation's Business,* 43, No. 3 (1955).

CHAPTER 12. MOTIVATION AND MORALE
AND
CHAPTER 13. INCENTIVES

Attitudes and Opinions of Hourly Employees, University of Michigan, Survey Research Center Report, August 1950.

Baker, John C., *Executive Salaries and Bonus Plans,* New York: McGraw-Hill Book Company, 1938.

Baldamus, W., "Type of Work and Motivation," *Journal of Sociology*, 2 (March 1951).

Baumgartel, H., and F. Mann, "Research on Productivity and Motivation of Civilian and Military Personnel at Air Material Command Installations," *Technical Research Report*, Mimeograph, Ann Arbor: Institute for Social Research, University of Michigan, April 1954.

Berrien, E. K., *Comments and Cases on Human Relations,* New York: Harper and Brothers, 1951.

Brayfield, Arthur H., and Walter H. Crockett, "Employee Attitudes and Employee Performance," *Psychological Bulletin*, 52, No. 5 (1955).

Brown, J. Douglas, and Helen Baker, *Optimum Hours of Work in War Production*, Princeton: Industrial Relations Section, Princeton University, 1942.

Burns, Robert K., "Employee Morale—Its Meaning and Measurement," *Proceedings of the Fourth Annual Meeting*, Champaign, Ill.: Industrial Releations Research Association.

Carlsson, G., "An Analysis of Morale Dimensions (Preliminary)," Mimeograph, Ann Arbor: Institute for Social Research, University of Michigan, 1951.

Cleeton, Glen U., "The Human Factor in Industry," *Annals,* American Academy of Political and Social Sciences, 274 (March 1951).

Cole, G. D. H., "Owen and Owenism," *Encyclopaedia of the Social Sciences*, New York: The Macmillan Company, 1930-1934.

Drucker, Peter, "The Human Being in Industrial Production," *Proceedings, Fifth Annual Time Study and Methods Conference*, Sponsored by Society for Advancement of Management and American Society of Mechanical Engineers, Management Division, New York, April 20-21, 1950.

Duggins, G. H., and F. R. Eastwood, *Planning Industrial Recreation*, Lafayette, Ind.: Purdue University, 1941.

"Effective Morale," *Fortune Magazine*, (August 1950).

Foerster, R. F., "Employee Stock Ownership," *Encyclopaedia of the Social Sciences*, New York: The Macmillan Company, 1930-34.

Gangrade, K. D., "Employee Morale," *Indian Journal of Social Work*, 15, No. 3 (1954).

Hickman, C. Addison, "Managerial Motivation and the Theory of the Firm," *American Economic Review*, 45 (May 1955).

Howerth, I. W., "Profit-sharing at Ivorydale," *American Journal of Sociology*, 2 (1896).

"Human Relations: A New Art Brings a Revolution to Industry," *Time*, (April 20, 1952).

Jacobson, E., "Morale and Motivation in a Changing Economy," Spirit-duplicated, Ann Arbor: Institute for Social Research, University of Michigan, 1952.

Kahn, R., "The Human Factors Underlying Industrial Productivity," *Michigan Business Review* (November 1952).

———, and N. Morse, "The Relation of Productivity to Morale," *Proceedings of the Fourth Annual Meeting, Industrial Relations Research Association,* adapted from an article in *Journal of Social Issues*, 7, No. 3 (1951).

Katz, Daniel, "The Attitude Survey Approach," Arthur Kornhauser, ed., *Psychology of Labor-Management Relations*, Champaign, Ill.: Industrial Relations Research Association, 1949.

———, and Herbert Hyman, "Industrial Morale and Public Opinion Methods," *International Journal of Opinion and Attitude Research*, 1 (September 1947).

———, *et al., Productivity, Supervision, and Morale among Railroad Workers,* Ann Arbor: University of Michigan, Institute for Social Research, 1951.

Kerr, Clark, "Social and Economic Implications of Private Pension Plans," *The Commercial and Financial Chronicle*, December 1, 1949.

Kornhauser, Arthur, and A. A. Sharp, "Employees' Attitudes," *Personnel Journal,* 1932.

Likert, R., and S. Seashore, "Employee Attitudes and Output," *Monthly Labor Review*, 77, No. 6 (1954).

Livernash, Edward R., "Wage Administration and Production Standards," Arthur Kornhauser, Robert Dubin, and Arthur Ross, *eds.*, *Industrial Conflict*, New York: McGraw-Hill Book Company, 1954.

Maccoby, N., "The Relationship of Supervisory Behavior and Attitudes to Group Productivity in Two Widely Different Industrial Settings," Mimeograph, Ann Arbor: Institute for Social Research, University of Michigan, 1949.

McGregor, Douglas, "Toward a Theory of Organized Human Effort in Industry," Arthur Kornhauser, *ed.*, *Psychology of Labor-Management Relations*, Champaign, Ill.: Industrial Relations Research Association, 1949.

Mahoney, Gerald, "Supervisory and Administrative Practices Associated with Employee Attitudes toward an Incentive System," Mimeograph, Ann Arbor: Institute for Social Research, University of Michigan, 1953.

———, "Unidimensional Scales for the Measurement of Morale in an Industrial Situation," *Human Relations*, 9, No. 1 (1956).

Marquand, John P., *Point of No Return*, New York: Bantam Books, 1952.

Medalia, Nahum Z., *Morale, Efficiency, and Human Relations Leadership*, Mimeograph, Seattle: Department of Sociology Air Site Project, University of Washington.

"Motivating Workers for Productivity," *Modern Industry*, (April 1952).

Northcote, C. H., "The Bedaux System," *Unity, The Journal of the National Industrial Alliance*, Bedaux Number, May 1932.

Peterson, Robert L., "Work Incentives for Your Personnel," University of Illinois, *Business Management Service Bulletin*, 49, No. 1 (1951).

Rahdert, Karl G., "What You Should Know About Profit Sharing," Business Information Bulletin No. 5, Bloomington, Ind.: Bureau of Business Research, School of Business, Indiana University, May 30, 1949.

Redmon, Edward J., "Social Processes Motivating Employee Behavior in the Factory Workshop," *Sociometry*, 9 (November 1946).

———, "The Human Element in Industry," *Sociology and Social Research*, 31 (July-August 1947).

Roy, Donald, "Work Satisfaction and Social Reward in Quota Achievement: An Analysis of Piecework Incentive," *American Sociological Review*, 18, No. 5 (1953).

Ryan, T. A., *Work and Effort*, New York: The Ronald Press Company, 1947.

Shlakman, Vera, "Business and the Salaried Worker," *Science and Society*, 15 (Spring 1951).

———, "Status and Ideology of Office Workers," *Science and Society*, 16, (Winter 1951-52).

Smith, Henry C., *Music in Relation to Employee Attitudes, Piece-Work Production, and Industrial Accidents*, Stanford: Stanford University Press, 1947.

Stein, Emanuel, "Financial Incentives and Profit Sharing," Emanual Stein and Jerome Davis, *eds.*, *Labor Problems in America*, New York: Farrar and Rinehart, 1940.

Tipper, Harry, *Human Factors in Industry*, New York: The Ronald Press Company, 1922.

Tripp, L. Reed, ed., *Industrial Productivity*, Publication No. 7, Madison, Wis.: Industrial Relations Research Association, 1951.

Walker, Charles R., *Steel: The Diary of a Furnace Worker*, Boston: Atlantic Monthly Press, 1922.

Waring, A. B., *First Report on the Joint Committee on Human Relations in Industry*, London: Her Majesty's Stationery Office, 1954.

Whyte, William F., "Incentives for Productivity: The Bundy Tubing Company Case," *Applied Anthropology*, 7 (Spring 1948).

Wolf, Robert B., "Making Men Like Their Jobs," *System: Magazine of Business* (January-February 1919).

"Worker Attitude on Incentives," *Dun's Review and Modern Industry*, 1953.

Wyatt, S., "Incentives in Repetitive Work," Report 77, *Industrial Fatigue Research Board Reports*, London: His Majesty's Stationery Office, 1937.

———, L. Frost, and F. G. L. Stock, "Incentives in Repetitive Work, A Practical Experiment in a Factory," Report 69, *Industrial Health Research Board Reports*, British Medical Research Council, 1934.

Zander, A., and J. Gyr, "Training Telephone Operators to Improve their Tone: A Study of the Conditions Related to their Willingness to Change," Detroit: Michigan Bell Telephone Company, 1952.

CHAPTER 14. THE INDIVIDUAL WORKER

Bellows, Roger M., *Psychology of Personnel in Business and Industry*, second edition, Englewood Cliffs, N. J.: Prentice-Hall, Inc., 1949.

Bingham, Walter Van Dyke, *Aptitudes and Aptitude Testing*, 12th edition, New York: Published for the National Occupational Conference by Harper and Brothers, 1937.

Boggs, T. H., "Certain Social Effects of Individualistic Industry," *American Journal of Sociology*, 21 (1915).

Cartwright, Dorwin, "Psychological Economics," James G. Miller, ed., *Experiments in Social Process*, New York: McGraw-Hill Book Company, 1950.

Cathcart, E. P., *The Human Factor in Industry*, London: Oxford University Press, 1928.

Dana, Richard T., *The Human Machine in Industry*, New York: Codex Book Company, 1927.

Dennis, Wayne, *et al.*, *Current Trends in Industrial Psychology*, Pittsburgh: University of Pittsburgh Press, 1949.

Farmer, E., and E. G. Chambers, "A Psychological Study of Individual Differences in the Accident Rates," Report 38, *Industrial Fatigue Research Board Reports*, London: His Majesty's Stationery Office, 1926.

———, "A Study of Personal Qualities in Accident Proneness and Proficiency," Report 55, *Industrial Fatigue Research Board Reports*, London: His Majesty's Stationery Office, 1929.

Findings from the Employee Questionnaire, Ann Arbor: Survey Research Center Report, University of Michigan, 1949.

Fraser, Russell, "The Incidence of Neurosis among Factory Workers," Report 90, *Industrial Health Research Board Reports*, British Medical Research Council, 1947.

Gerth, Hans, and C. Wright Mills, *Character and Social Structure*, London: Routledge and Kegan Paul, 1954.

Ginzberg, Eli, "The Occupational Adjustment of 1000 Selectees," *American Sociological Review*, 8 (1943).

Haire, Mason, and Willa Freeman Grunes, "Perceptual Defenses: Processes Protecting and Organized Perception of Another Personality," *Human Relations*, 3, No. 4 (1950).

Harrell, T. W., *Industrial Psychology*, New York: Rinehart, 1949.

Hickman, C. Addison, and Manford H. Kuhn, *Individuals, Groups, and Economic Behavior*, New York: The Dryden Press, 1956.

Katona, George, *Psychological Analysis of Economic Behavior*, New York: McGraw-Hill Book Company, 1951.

Kavanaugh, Nelson, "New Terms for Occupational Roles," *Occupations*, 20, No. 4 (1942).

Kornhauser, Arthur, "The Contribution of Psychology to Industrial Relations Research," *Proceedings of the First Annual Meeting, Industrial Relations Research Association*, ed. Milton Derber, Champaign, Ill.: 1949.

———, "Human Motivations Underlying Industrial Conflict," Arthur Kornhauser, Robert Dubin, and Arthur Ross, eds., *Industrial Conflict*, New York: McGraw-Hill Book Company, 1954.

———, ed., *Psychology of Labor Management Relations*, Industrial Relations Research Associations, 1949.

Lieberman, S., "An Analysis of Role Change in a Factory Situation," Mimeograph, Ann Arbor: Institute for Social Research, University of Michigan, 1951.

Ling, Thomas Mortimer, ed., *Mental Health and Human Relations in Industry*, London: H. K. Lewis, 1954.

R. N. McMurry, "The Clinical Psychology Approach," Arthur Kornhauser, ed., *Psychology of Labor-Management Relations*, Champaign, Ill.: Industrial Relations Research Association, 1949.

Mann, F., "A Study of Work Satisfactions as a Function of the Discrepancy between Inferred Aspirations and Achievements," Ph.D. thesis, University of Michigan, 1953.

———, "Work Satisfactions as Related to Aspirations and Achievements," Mimeograph, Ann Arbor: Institute for Social Research, University of Michigan, 1953.

Marot, H., *The Creative Impulse in Industry*, New York: Dutton, 1918.

Mayo, Elton, "Basis of Industrial Psychology," *Bulletin of the Taylor Society*, 9 (1924).

———, "Day Dreaming and Output in a Spinning Mill," *Journal of the National Institute of Industrial Psychology*, 1925.

———, "Psychopathologic Aspects of Industry," *Transactions of the American Neurological Association*, 1931.

———, "Revery and Industrial Fatigue," *Journal of Personnel Research*, 3 (December 1924).

Menninger, W. C., *Social Change and Scientific Progress*, Cambridge: Massachusetts Institute of Technology, 1951.

Moore, Herbert, *Psychology for Business and Industry*, New York: McGraw-Hill Book Company, 1939.

Morse, N. C., "What Workers Want," *Michigan Business Review*, 6, No. 3 (1954).

Munsterberg, H., *Psychology and Industrial Efficiency*, Cambridge: The Houghton Mifflin Company, 1913.

Murray, H. M. L., "Bases of Worker Efficiency," *Personnel Journal*, 21 (October 1942).

Myers, Charles S., *Industrial Psychology*, New York: The People's Institute Publishing Company, 1925.

Pangburn, Weaver, "The Worker's Leisure and His Individuality," *American Journal of Sociology*, 27, No. 4 (1922).

Robbins, H., "The Man with a Job," *American Journal of Sociology*, 20 (1914).

Speroff, B. J., "Job Satisfaction and Interpersonal Desirability Values," *Sociometry*, 18, No. 1 (1955).

Stagner, Ross, J. N. Rich, and R. H. Britten, Jr., "Job Attitudes, I. Defense Workers," *Personnel Journal*, 20 (September 1941).

Stephenson, A., "Accidents in Industry," *Journal of the National Institute of Industrial Psychology*, 3, No. 4.

Tipper, Harry, "Personal Aspirations More Important to Worker than Economic Laws," *Automotive Industries*, 47 (October 5, 1922).

Tredgold, R. F., *Human Relations in Modern Industry*, London: Duckworth, 1949.

Walker, Kenneth F., "The Application of the J-Curve Hypothesis of Conforming Behavior to Industrial Absenteeism," *Journal of Social Psychology*, 25 (May 1947).

Williams, Whiting, *What's on the Worker's Mind?* New York: Charles Scribner and Sons, 1920.

CHAPTER 15. INDIVIDUAL MOBILITY

Amidon, Beulah, "Jobs after Forty," *Public Affairs Pamphlets No. 35*, New York: Public Affairs Committee, 1939.

Anderson, W. A., "The Occupational Attitudes of College Men," *Journal of Social Psychology*, 5 (1934).

Bell, Howard M., *Youth Tell Their Story*, Washington: American Council on Education, 1938.

Bingham, Walter V., "Abilities and Opportunities," *Occupations*, 12, No. 6 (1934).

Bogue, Donald J., "Residential Mobility and Migration of Workers," William Haber, *et al.*, eds., *Manpower in the United States: Problems and Policies*, New York: Harper and Brothers, 1954.

Brewer, J. N., "Report by Robert N. McMurry and Company of Chicago," *Business Week*, (November 27, 1948).

Burns, Robert K., and Leonard B. Brown, "The Older Worker in Industry," Albert I. Lansing, ed., *Cowdry's Problems of Ageing*, 3rd edition, Baltimore: The Williams and Wilkins Company, 1952.

Clark, Carroll D., and Noel P. Gist, "Intelligence as a Factor in Occupational Choice," *American Sociological Review*, 3, No. 5 (1938).

Crawford, Albert Beecher, and Stuart Holmes Clement, eds., *The Choice of an Occupation*, New Haven: Department of Personnel Study, Yale University, 1932.

"Employability of the Older Person," *Personnel*, (March 1950).

Form, William H., and Delbert C. Miller, "Occupational Career Pattern as a Sociological Instrument," *American Journal of Sociology*, 54, No. 4 (1949).

Freedman, Ronald, and Amos Hawley, "Migration and Occupational Mobility in the Depression," *American Journal of Sociology*, 55, No. 2 (1949).

Goodrich, Carter, *et al.*, *Migration and Economic Opportunity*, Philadelphia: University of Pennsylvania Press, 1936.

Hollingshead, August B., *Elmtown's Youth: The Impact of Social Classes on Adolescents*, New York: John Wiley and Sons, 1949.

Kahler, Alfred, and Ernest Hamburger, *Education for an Industrial Age*, Ithaca: Cornell University Press, 1948.

Kaplan, Oscar J., ed., *Encyclopedia of Vocational Guidance*, New York: Philosophical Library, 1948.

Kerr, Clark, J. Douglas Brown, and Edwin E. Witte, eds., *The Aged and Society*, Champaign, Ill.: Industrial Relations Research Association, 1950.

Knox, John B., "Occupation and Education in a Democracy," *Social Forces*, 20 (1941).

Lawshe, C. H., Jr., *Principles of Personnel Testing*, New York: McGraw-Hill Book Company, 1948.

Lester, Richard A., *Hiring Practices and Labor Competition*, Princeton: Princeton University Press, 1954.

Malm, F. Theodore, "Hiring Procedures and Selection Standards in the San Francisco Bay Area," *Industrial and Labor Relations Review*, 8, No. 2 (1955).

Manson, Grace E., *Occupational Interests and Personality Requirements of Women in Business and the Professions*, Vol. 3, Ann Arbor: Bureau of Business Research, University of Michigan, 1931.

Merton, Robert K., and Alice S. Kitt, "Reference Group Theory and Social Mobility," Reinhard Bendix and Seymour Martin Lipset, eds., *Class, Status and Power: A Reader in Social Stratification*, Glencoe, Ill.: The Free Press, 1953.

Michigan State College, Social Research Service, *Youth and the World of Work*, East Lansing, Mich.: 1949.

Miller, Delbert C., and William H. Form, "Measuring Patterns of Occupational Security," *Sociometry*, 10 (November 1947).

Myers, Charles A., "Labor Mobility in Two Communities," *Labor Mobility and Economic Opportunity*, Cambridge: The Technology Press of M. I. T.; New York: John Wiley and Sons, 1954.

———, "Patterns of Labor Mobility," William Haber, *et al.*, eds., *Manpower in the United States: Problems and Policies*, New York: Harper and Brothers, 1954.

———, and W. Rupert MacLaurin, *The Movement of Factory Workers: A Study of a New England Industrial Community, 1937-1939 and 1942*, New York: John Wiley and Sons, 1943.

Nickerson, J. W., "Work Assignment," *Annals*, American Academy of Political and Social Science, 184 (March 1936).

Nosow, Sigmund, "Toward a Theory of the Labor Market," *Social Forces*, 33, No. 3 (1955).

OSS Assessment Staff, *Assessment of Men*, New York: Rinehart, 1943.

Palmer, Gladys L., "Epilogue: Social Values in Labor Mobility," *Labor Mobility and Economic Opportunity*, Cambridge: The Technology Press of M. I. T.; New York: John Wiley and Sons, 1954.

———, "Interpreting Patterns of Labor Mobility," *Labor Mobility and Economic Opportunity*, Cambridge: The Technology Press of M. I. T.; New York: John Wiley and Sons, 1954.

Park, R. E., "Introduction," Frances R. Donovan, *The Saleslady*, Chicago: University of Chicago Press, 1929.

Political and Economic Planning, *The Entrance to Industry*, London: Political and Economic Planning, 1935.

Pollack, Otto, "Discrimination against Older Workers in Industry," *American Journal of Sociology*, 50 (September 1944).

Raney, Edward T., "Recognition and Utilization of Employees' Abilities," Arthur Kornhauser, Robert Dubin, and Arthur Ross, eds., *Industrial Conflict*, New York: McGraw-Hill Book Company, 1954.

Reder, Melvin W., "Age and Income," *American Economic Review*, 44, No. 2 (1954).

Reeves, Floyd W., *Frontier Thinking in Guidance*, Chicago: Science Research Associates, 1945.

Reissman, Leonard, "Life Careers, Power and the Professions," *American Sociological Review*, 21, No. 2 (1956).

Stead, William H., Carroll L. Shartle, *et al.*, *Occupational Counseling Techniques, Their Development and Application*, New York: American Book Company, 1940.

Stevens, R. B., "The Attitudes of College Women toward Women's Vocations," *Journal of Applied Psychology*, 24 (1940).

Terman, Lewis M., *et al.*, *The Gifted Child Grows Up*, Genetic Studies of Genius, Vol.

4, Stanford: Stanford University Press, 1947.

Thorndike, Edward L., *et al.*, *Prediction of Vocational Success*, New York: The Commonwealth Fund, 1934.

Thorner, I., "Nursing: The Functional Significance of an Institutional Pattern," *American Sociological Review*, 20 (1955).

Tibbitts, Clark, "Retirement Problems in American Society," *American Journal of Sociology*, 49 (January 1954).

United States Department of Labor, Bureau of Labor Statistics, "Standard Procedure for Computing Labor Turnover," *Monthly Labor Review*, 41 (December 1935); 43 (December 1936).

United States War Manpower Commission, Bureau of Training, Training within Industry Service, *The Training within Industry Report, 1940-1945*, Washington: Government Printing Office, 1945.

Veblen, Thorstein, *The Theory of the Leisure Class*, New York: B. W. Huebsch, 1918; and New American Library.

Visher, Stephen S., "Environmental Backgrounds of Leading American Scientists," *American Sociological Review*, 13, No. 1 (1948).

Webb, John N., and Albert Westfield, "Industrial Aspects of Labor Mobility," *Monthly Labor Review*, 48 (April 1939).

Wohl, R. Richard, "The 'Rages to Riches Story': An Episode of Secular Idealism," Reinhard Bendix and Seymour Martin Lipset, eds., *Class, Status and Power: A Reader in Social Stratification*, Glencoe, Ill.: The Free Press, 1953.

Wood, Helen, "Trends in the Specialization of Occupational Requirements," William Haber, *et al.*, eds., *Manpower in the United States: Problems and Policies*, New York: Harper and Brothers, 1954.

· CHAPTER 16. WORK GROUPS AND WORK

Bendix, Reinhard, and L. H. Fisher, "The Perspectives of Elton Mayo," *Review of Economics and Statistics*, 31 (November 1949).

Benne, Kenneth D., and Dozidar Muntyan, *Human Relations in Curriculum Change: Selected Readings with Special Emphasis on Group Development*, Bulletin No. 7, Illinois Secondary School Curriculum Program (June 1949).

Campbell, A., "Working Together," Mimeograph, paper read March 24, 1955 at Sixth Annual Valley-Wide Cooperative Conference of the TVA, Fontana Dam, N. C., Ann Arbor: Institute for Social Research, University of Michigan.

Darley, John G., Neal Gross, and William E. Martin, "Studies of Group Behavior: Stability, Change, and Interrelations of Psychometric and Sociometric Variables," *Journal of Abnormal and Social Psychology*, 46, No. 4 (1951).

Darley, John G., Neal Gross, and William E. Martin, "Studies of Group Behavior: Factors Associated with the Productivity of Groups," *Journal of Applied Psychology*, 36, No. 6 (1952).

Daya, E., "Human Relations in Industry," *International Labour Review*, 65 (May 1952).

Fiedler, Fred E., "The Influence of Leader-Keyman Relations on Combat Crew Effectiveness," Mimeograph, Technical Report No. 9, Urbana, Ill.: Group Effectiveness Research Laboratory, Department of Psychology, University of Illinois.

French, J. R. P., Jr., "Field Experiments: Changing Group Productivity," J. G. Miller, ed., *Experiments in Social Process*, New York: McGraw-Hill Book Company, 1950.

Friedman, Georges, "Philosophy Underlying the Hawthorne Investigation," *Social Forces*, 28 (December 1949).

Ghiselli, E. E., and C. W. Brown, *Personnel and Industrial Psychology*, New York: McGraw-Hill Book Company, 1948.

Gross, Neal, and William E. Martin, "On Group Cohesiveness," *American Journal of Sociology*, 57, No. 6 (1952).

Hall, Oswald, "The Informal Organization of the Medical Profession," *Canadian Journal of Economics and Political Science*, 12, No. 1 (1946).

Jackson, Jay M., "The Effect of Changing the Leadership of Small Work Groups," *Human Relations*, 6 (1953).

Jacobson, E., "Foreman-Steward Participation Practices and Worker Attitudes in a Unionized Factory," Ph.D. thesis, Ann Arbor: University of Michigan, 1951.

James, John, "An Experimental Study of Tensions in Work Behavior," Berkeley: University of California Publications in Culture and Society, 2, No. 4 (1951).

Kahn, R., and D. Katz, "Some Relationships between Organizational Characteristics and Productivity," Spirit-duplicated, Ann Arbor: Institute for Social Research, University of Michigan, September 1951.

Kaye, C., "The Effects on Organizational Goal Achievement of a Change in the Structure of Roles," Mimeograph, Ann Arbor: Institute for Social Research, University of Michigan, 1954.

Lamb, Robert K., "Productivity and Social Structure," Solomon Barkin, *et al.*, eds., *Industrial Productivity*, Champaign, Ill.: Industrial Relations Research Association, 1951.

Lippitt, R., "Employee Success in Work Groups," *Personnel Administrator*, 4 (1945).

Mann, F., "Studies of Processes and Determinants of Social Change in Complex Organizations," Mimeograph, Ann Arbor: Institute for Social Research, University of Michigan, 1952.

Martin, William E., Neal Gross, and John G. Darley, "Studies of Group Behavior: Leaders, Followers, and Isolates in Small Organized Groups," *Journal of Abnormal and Social Psychology*, 47, No. 4 (1952).

———, "Studies of Group Behavior: II. Methodological Problems in the Study of Interrelationships of Group Members," *Educational and Psychological Measurement*, 12, No. 4 (1952).

Marvin, Donald M., "Occupational Propinquity as a Factor in Marriage Selection," *Publications of the American Statistical Association*, 16 (1918-19).

Miller, Delbert C., "The Social Factors of the Work Situation," *American Sociological Review*, 11 (June 1946).

Parker, Willard E., and Robert W. Kleemeier, *Human Relations in Supervision*, New York: McGraw-Hill Book Company, 1951.

Patterson, S. Howard, *Social Aspects of Industry*, 3rd edition, New York: McGraw-Hill Book Company, 1943.

Pellegrin, R. J., "The Achievement of High Statuses and Leadership in the Small Group," *Social Forces*, 32 (1953).

Pigors, Paul, and Charles A. Myers, *Personnel Administration: A Point of View and a Method*, New York: McGraw-Hill Book Company, 1947.

Recknagel, Kenneth H., "Teamwork in Industry," *Journal of Educational Sociology*, 26, No. 6 (1953).

Roethlisberger, Fritz J., *Training for Human Relations: An Interim Report*, Boston: Harvard University Graduate School of Business Administration, 1954.

Schachter, Stanley, Norris Ellertson, Dorothy McBride, and Doris Gregory, "An Experimental Study of Cohesiveness and Productivity," *Human Relations*, 4, No. 3 (1951).

Schachter, Stanley, and Robert Hall, "Briefer Studies and Annotations: Group-Derived Restraints and Audience Persuasion," *Human Relations*, 5, No. 4 (1952).

Seashore, S., *Group Cohesiveness in the Industrial Work Group*, SRC Monograph Series No. 14, Ann Arbor: Publications Distribution Service, University of Michigan.

———, "A Modified Sociometric Technique for the Study of Functioning Organizations," Mimeograph, Ann Arbor: Institute for Social Research, University of Michigan, September 1951.

———, "Teamwork: Key to Production?" *Adult Leadership*, 3, No. 8 (1955).

Shils, Edward A., "Primary Groups in the American Army," Robert K. Merton and Paul F. Lazarsfeld, eds., *Continuities in Social Research: Studies in the Scope and Method of "The American Soldier,"* Glencoe, Ill.: The Free Press, 1950.

Sorokin, P. A., *et al.*, "An Experimental Study of the Efficiency of Work under Various Specified Conditions," *American Journal of Sociology*, 36 (March 1930).

Troxell, John P., "Employee Understanding and Teamwork for Greater Productivity," abstract made available by the National Association of Manufacturers of the United States of America, 1954.

Valentine, R. G., "The Human Element in Production," *American Journal of Sociology*, 22 (1916).

Whyte, William F., "The Social Structure of the Restaurant," *American Journal of Sociology*, 54, No. 4 (1949).

CHAPTER 17. DISCONTENTS AND GRIEVANCES

Arbous, A. G., and H. S. Sichel, "New Techniques for the Analysis of Absenteeism Data," *Biometrika*, 41 (1954).

Archbald, Hugh, *The Four Hour Day in Coal: A Study of the Relation between the Engineering of the Organization of Work and the Discontent among Workers in the Coal Mines*, New York: Wilson, 1952.

Buzzard, R. B., "Attendance and Absence in Industry: The Nature of the Evidence," *British Journal of Sociology*, 5, No. 3 (1954).

Committee on Labor and Public Welfare, "Welfare of Coal Miners," 82d Congress, 2d Session, Senate Report No. 1223, February 27, 1952.

De Man, Henri, "Reaction to Subordination," *Joy in Work*, trans. Eden and Cedar Paul, London: George Allen and Unwin, 1929.

Eaton, Walter, "Hypotheses Relating to Worker Frustrations," *Journal of Social Psychology*, 35 (February 1952).

French, J. R. P., Jr., A. Kornhauser, and A. Marrow, "Conflict and Cooperation in Industry," *Journal of Social Issues*, 2 (1946).

Giles, W. A., "Social Discontent and the Labor Troubles," *American Journal of Sociology*, 9 (1903).

Great Britain, Medical Research Council, Industrial Health Research Board, *Hours of Work, Lost Time and Labour Wastage*, Emergency Report No. 2, London: His Majesty's Stationery Office, 1942.

Kuhn, James W., "Grievance Machinery and Strikes in Australia," *Industrial and Labor Relations Review*, 8, No. 2 (1955).

Lapping, Douglas, "Social Health Aspects of Industrial Absenteeism," *Journal of Social Research*, 4, No. 2 (1953).

Liddell, F. D. K., "Attendance in the Coal-Mining Industry," *British Journal of Sociology*, 5, No. 1 (1954).

Mann, Floyd, and Howard Baumgartel, "Absences and Employee Attitudes in an Electric Power Company," Report from the Survey Research Center, University of Michigan, Human Relations Program, Series 1, Report 2, Ann Arbor: Institute for Social Research, December 1952.

Monthly Labor Review, "Grievance Procedures in Union Agreements, 1950-1951," 73 (July 1951).

Murthy, S. A. S., "Absenteeism in Industry," *Indian Journal of Social Work*, 14, No. 2 (1953).

Noland, E. William, "An Application of Scaling to an Industrial Problem," *American Sociological Review*, 10 (October 1945).

———, "Worker Attitudes and Industrial Absenteeism: A Statistical Appraisal," *American Sociological Review*, 10 (August 1945).

Pound, A., *The Iron Man in Industry*, Boston: Atlantic Monthly Press, 1922.

Roper, Elmo, "Discrimination in Industry: Extravagant Injustice," *Industrial and Labor Relations Review*, 5 (July 1952).

Strauss, George, "The Set-up Man: A Case Study of Organizational Change," *Human Organization*, 13, No. 2.

United States Department of Labor, Division of Labor Standards, *Settling Plant Grievances*, Bulletin No. 640, Washington: Government Printing Office, 1943.

———, Bureau of Labor Statistics, "Grievance Procedure under Collective Bargaining," Mimeograph, August 1946.

CHAPTER 18. COMMUNICATION AND WORK

Baker, Helen, *Company-wide Understanding of Industrial Relations Policies: A Study in Communications*, Research Report Series No. 78, Princeton: Princeton University, Industrial Relations Section, 1948.

Baumgartel, H., "The Survey Feedback Experiment: A Study Program for the Use of Attitude Survey Data in a Large Organization," Mimeograph, Ann Arbor: Institute for Social Research, U. of Mich., 1953.

Davis, R., G. Mellinger, D. Pelz, and H. Baumgartel, *Interpersonal Factors in Research, Studies in Selected Aspects of Performance, Communication and Attitudes, Part I,* Mimeograph, Ann Arbor: Institute for Social Research, University of Michigan, 1954.

French, J., and A. Marrow, "Changing a Stereotype in Industry," *Journal of Social Issues,* 1 (1945).

"Getting to Know Your People," *Modern Industry,* (April 15, 1953).

Guetzkow, Harold, and Herbert A. Simon, "The Impact of Certain Communication Nets upon Organization and Performance in Task-Oriented Groups," *Management Science,* 1 (April-July 1955).

Jacobson, E., "Communication Structure and Attitudes in Large Organizations, Spirit-duplicated, Ann Arbor: Institute for Social Research, University of Michigan, 1951.

Jaques, E., "Interpretative Group Discussion as a Method of Facilitating Social Change," *Human Relations,* 1, No. 4 (1948).

Perry, John, and Robert W. Straus, "A Story of Executive Relationships," *Harvard Business Review,* 30 (March-April 1952).

"Problem for the Front Office," *Fortune,* 43 (May 1954).

Thomas, Merlin, "Sexual Symbolism in Industry," *International Journal of Psychoanalysis,* 32 (1951).

CHAPTER 19. WORK RULES AND THEIR ENFORCEMENT

Blumberg, Mark S., and James C. Coffin, "A Syllabus on Work Absence," *A. M. A. Archives of Industrial Health,* 13 (January 1956).

Department of Social Science, University of Liverpool, *The Dock Worker: An Analysis of Conditions of Employment in the Port of Manchester,* Liverpool: University Press of Liverpool, 1954.

Jaques, Elliott, A. K. Rice, and J. M. M. Hill, "The Social and Psychological Impact of a Change in Method of Wage Payment (The Glacier Project)—V," *Human Relations,* 4 (1951).

Magdoff, Harry, "The Purpose and Method of Measuring Productivity," *Journal of the American Statistical Association,* 34 (June 1939).

Morse, N. C., Everett Reimer, and Arnold S. Tannenbaum, "Regulation and Control in Hierarchical Organizations," *Journal of Social Issues,* 7, No. 3 (1951).

Sofer, Cyril, "Reaction to Administrative Change: A Study of Staff Relations in Three British Hospitals," *Human Relations,* 8 (1955).

"What Makes People Absent?" *Modern Industry,* (June 15, 1953).

CHAPTER 20. MANAGEMENT AS BUREAUCRACY

Alderson, Wroe, "Social Adjustment in Business Management," *Explorations in Entrepreneurial History,* 6 (October 1953).

American Management Association, *Planning Supervisory Development,* New York: The Association, 1945.

Anderson, E. H., "The Meaning of Scientific Management," *Harvard Business Review,* 27 (November 1949).

Arakelian, A., *Industrial Management in the USSR,* trans. Ellsworth L. Raymond, Washington: Public Affairs Press, 1950.

Baker, Alton W., and Ralph C. Davis, *Ratios of Staff and Line Employees and States of Differentiation of Staff Functions: A Study of Ohio Manufacturing Companies,* Research Monograph No. 72, Columbus: Bureau of Business Research, College of Commerce and Administration, Ohio State University, 1954.

Baker, Helen, and Robert R. France, *Centralization and Decentralization in Industrial Relations,* Princeton: Princeton University Press, 1954.

Bendix, Reinhard, "Bureaucracy and the Problem of Power," *Public Administration Review*, 5 (1945).

———, "Bureaucracy: The Problem and Its Setting," *American Sociological Review*, 12 (October 1947).

———, "Bureaucratization in Industry," Arthur Kornhauser, Robert Dubin, and Arthur Ross, eds., *Industrial Conflict*, New York: McGraw-Hill Book Company, 1954.

———, *Higher Civil Servants in American Society*, Boulder: University of Colorado Studies, 1949.

Berliner, Joseph S., "A Problem in Soviet Business Administration," *Administrative Science Quarterly*, 1, No. 1 (1956).

Bienstock, Gregory, Solomon M. Schwarz, and Aaron Yogow, *Management in Russian Industry and Agriculture*, London: Oxford University Press, 1944.

Blau, Peter M., *Bureaucracy in Modern Society*, New York: Random House, 1956.

———, "Co-operation and Competition in a Bureaucracy," *American Journal of Sociology*, 59, No. 6 (1954).

———, *The Dynamics of Bureaucracy: A Study of Interpersonal Relations in Two Government Agencies*, Chicago: The University of Chicago Press, 1955.

Brady, Robert A., "Bureaucracy in Business," *Journal of Social Issues*, 1 (December 1945).

Brown, Paula, "Bureaucracy in a Government Laboratory," *Social Forces*, 32, No. 3 (1954).

Cantor, Nathaniel, "A Sociologist Looks at Personnel Administration," *Personnel*, 28 (September 1951).

Caplow, Theodore, "The Criteria of Organizational Success," *Social Forces*, 32, No. 1 (1953).

"The Changing Position of Foremen in American Industry," *Advanced Management*, 10 (December 1945).

Comfrey, A. L., J. M. Pfifner, and H. P. Beem, *Studies in Organizational Effectiveness, I. The U. S. Forest Survey*, Technical Report No. 3, The Office of Naval Research, University of Southern California, 1951.

Cooper, Alfred M., *How to Supervise People*, New York and London: McGraw-Hill Book Company, 1941.

Copley, F. B., *Frederick W. Taylor, Father of Scientific Management*, Vol. 1, New York: Harper and Brothers, 1923.

Dalton, Melville, "The Role of Supervision," Arthur Kornhauser, Robert Dubin, and Arthur Ross, eds., *Industrial Conflict*, New York: McGraw-Hill Book Company, 1954.

Davis, Arthur K., "Bureaucratic Patterns in the Navy Officer Corps," *Social Forces*, 27 (December 1948).

Davis, Ralph Currier, *Shop Management for the Shop Supervisor*, New York: Harper and Brothers, 1941.

Dimock, Marshall E., and Howard K. Hyde, "Bureaucracy and Trusteeship in Large Corporations," *Investigation of Concentration of Economic Power, Monograph No. 11*, United States Congress, Temporary National Economic Committee, Washington: Government Printing Office, 1940.

Donham, Wallace B., "The Professional Side of Business Training," Henry C. Metcalf, ed., *Business Management as a Profession*, Chicago: A. W. Shaw Company, 1927.

Drake, Frances S., and Charles A., *A Human Relations Casebook for Executives and Supervisors*, New York: McGraw-Hill Book Company, 1947.

Drucker, Peter F., "Management and the Professional Employee," *Harvard Business Review*, 30 (May-June 1952).

———, "Success Won't Save Your Business," *Nation's Business*, 43, No. 10 (1955).

Drury, H. B., *Scientific Management, A History and Criticism*, New York: Columbia University Press, 1918.

Edwards, J., "The Fetishism of Scientific Management," *Journal of the American Society of Naval Engineers*, May 1912.

Follett, M. P., "How Must Business Management Develop in Order to Become a Profession?" Henry C. Metcalf, ed., *Business Management as a Profession*, Chicago: A. W. Shaw Company, 1927.

Gillespie, James J., *The Principles of Rational Industrial Management*, New York: Pitman, 1938.

Glick, Philip M., "The Role of the Lawyer in Management," *Advanced Management*, 5 (April-June 1940).

Glover, John G., and Coleman L. Maze, *Managerial Control*, New York: The Ronald Press Company, 1937.

Granick, David, *Management of the Industrial Firm in the USSR*, New York: Columbia University Press, 1954.

"How Foremen Get That Way," *Dun's Review*, (January 1955).

Jacobson, Eugene, W. W. Charters, Jr., and Seymour Lieberman, "The Use of the Role Concept in the Study of Complex Organizations," *Journal of Social Issues*, 7, No. 3 (1951).

Kimball, Dexter S. and Dexter S., Jr., *Principles of Industrial Organization*, New York: McGraw-Hill Book Company, 1947.

Knauth, Oswald W., *Managerial Enterprise: Its Growth and Methods of Operation*, New York: Norton, 1948.

Knowles, W. M., "Supervision in the British West Indies: Source of Labor Unrest," *Industrial and Labor Relations Review*, 8, No. 4 (1955).

———, "Techniques and Philosophy in Industrial Relations," *American Journal of Economics and Sociology*, 11 (October 1951).

———, "What Personnel Men Face in a South American Jungle," *The Personnel Journal*, 33, No. 10 (1955).

Langerock, Hubert, "Professionalism: A Study in Professional Deformation," *American Journal of Sociology*, 21, No. 1 (1915).

Lansburgh, Richard H., and William R. Spriegel, *Industrial Management*, New York: John Wiley and Sons, 1940.

Laski, Harold J., "Bureaucracy," *Encyclopaedia of the Social Sciences*, New York: The Macmillan Company, 1930-34.

Learned, Edmund P., David N. Ulrich, and Donald R. Booz, *Executive Action*, Boston: Harvard University, Graduate School of Business Administration, 1951.

Leiter, Robert David, *The Foreman in Industrial Relations*, New York: Columbia University Press, 1948.

Lystad, M. H., and R. C. Stone, "Bureaucratic Mass Media: A Study in Role Definitions," *Social Forces*, 34 (May 1956).

Mace, Myles L., *The Growth and Development of Executives*, Boston: Harvard University, Graduate School of Business Administration, 1950.

Maier, Norman R. F., "Improving Supervision Through Training," Arthur Kornhauser, ed., *Psychology of Labor-Management Relations*, Champaign, Ill.: Industrial Relations Research Association, 1949.

"The Management Consultant," *Modern Industry*, 20, No. 6 (December 15, 1950).

Mann, Floyd, "Changing Superior-Subordinate Relations," Mimeograph, Ann Arbor: Institute for Social Research, University of Michigan, 1952.

———, and H. Baumgartel, *The Supervisor's Concern with Costs in an Electric Power Company*, Ann Arbor: Institute for Social Research, University of Michigan, 1953.

———, "Supervisors' Views on Costs," *Office Management Series*, American Management Association, 138 (November 1954).

———, and J. Dent, *Appraisals of Supervisors and Attitudes of Their Employees in an Electric Power Company*, Ann Arbor: Institute for Social Research, University of Michigan, 1954.

———, "The Supervisor: Member of Two Organization Families," *Harvard Business Review*, 32, No. 6 (1954).

Marvick, D., *Career Perspectives in a Bureaucratic Setting*, Ann Arbor: Institute of Public Administration, University of Michigan, 1954.

Maynard, Harold B., ed., *Effective Foremanship*, New York: McGraw-Hill Book Company, 1941.

Mee, J. F., ed., *Personnel Handbook*, New York: The Ronald Press Company, 1951.

Melman, Seymour, "The Rise of Administrative Overhead in the Manufacturing Industries of the United States, 1899-1947," *Oxford Economic Papers, New Series*, 3, No. 1 (1951).

Merton, Robert K., "Role of the Intellectual in Public Bureaucracy," *Social Forces*, 23, No. 4 (1945).

———, *et al.*, *Reader in Bureaucracy*, Glencoe, Ill.: The Free Press, 1952.

Metcalf, Henry C., ed., *Business Management as a Profession*, Chicago: A. W. Shaw Company, 1927.

Meyer, Paul, "Staff and Line," *Revue Internationale des Sciences Administratives, 1955*, No. 1, Brussels, Belgium: Institut International des Sciences Administratives.

Michels, Robert, *Political Parties*, Glencoe, Ill.: The Free Press, 1949.

Mitchell, Wiliam N., *Production Management*, Chicago: University of Chicago Press, 1931.

Moley, Raymond, "Presidential Isolation," from the syndicated newspaper column published in May 1951, Bell Syndicate, Inc.

Moore, David G., and Richard Renck, "The Professional Employee in Industry: The Unhappy Engineers," *Journal of Business*, (January 1955).

Mullan, Hugh, M. D., "The Regular Service Myth," *American Journal of Sociology*, 53, No. 4 (1948).

National Institute of Industrial Psychology, *The Foreman: A Study of Supervision in British Industry*, London: Staples, 1951.

Neumann, Franz, *Behemoth*, New York: Oxford University Press, 1942.

Newman, William H., and James P. Logan, *Management of Expanding Enterprises: Report of Round Table Discussions of Leading Business and Professional Men*, New York: Columbia University Press, 1955.

Niles, Mary Cushing, *Middle Management, The Job of the Junior Executive*, New York: Harper and Brothers, 1941.

Northrup, Herbert, "Unionization of Foremen," *Harvard Business Review*, 21 (Summer 1943).

Osborn, Richards C., "Effects of Corporate Size on Efficiency and Profitability," *Bulletin*, 48, No. 7, University of Illinois, Bureau of Economic and Business Research.

Page, Charles H., "Bureaucracy and Higher Education," *Journal of General Education*, 5, No. 2 (1951).

———, "Bureaucracy's Other Face," *Social Forces*, 25 (1946).

Passer, Harold C., "Development of Large-Scale Organization: Electrical Manufacturing around 1900," *Journal of Economic History*, (Fall 1952).

Pearson, Norman M., "Fayolism as the Necessary Complement of Taylorism," *American Political Science Review*, 39 (February 1945).

Person, H. S., ed., for the Taylor Society, *Scientific Management in American Industry*, New York: Harper and Brothers, 1929.

Petersen, Elmore, and E. Grosvenor Plowman, *Business Organization and Management*, revised edition, Chicago: Richard D. Irwin, 1948.

Popiel, Gerald, "Bureaucracy in the Mass Industrial Union," *American Journal of Economics and Sociology*, 15, No. 1 (1955).

Reck, Dickson, "National Standards in Industrial Administration: Part I and Part II," *Advanced Management*, (November and December 1954).

———, "The Role of Company Standards in Industrial Administration," *Advanced Management*, (April 1954).

Roll, Erich, *An Early Experiment in Industrial Organization, Being a History of the Firm of Boulton and Watt*, 1775-1805, New York: Longmans, Green, 1930.

Ross, Thurston H., "The Engineer's Responsibility in Management," *Mechanical Engineering*, 63, (July 1941).

Schell, Erwin Haskell, *The Technique of Executive Control,* New York: McGraw-Hill Book Company, 1946.

Schroder, M., "Bedrijfsgrootte en Moreel," (The Relationship of Size and Morale), *Mens Onder.*, 9, No. 5 (1955).

Scott, Walter D., Robert C. Clothier, Stanley B. Mathewson, and William R. Spriegel, *Personnel Management: Principles, Practices, and Point of View,* New York: McGraw-Hill Book Company, 1941.

Selznick, Philip, *TVA and the Grass Roots,* Berkeley and Los Angeles: University of California Press, 1949.

Sharp, Walter R., *The French Civil Service: Bureaucracy in Transition,* New York: The Macmillan Company, 1931.

Smith, Charles Copeland, *The Foreman's Place in Management,* New York: Harper and Brothers, 1946.

Stryker, Perrin, "The Ambitious Consultants," *Fortune,* 49 (May 1954).

———, and the editors of *Fortune, A Guide to Modern Management Methods,* New York: McGraw-Hill Book Company, 1954.

Tannenbaum, Robert, "Managerial Decision-Making," *Journal of Business of the University of Chicago,* 23 (January 1950).

———, and Fred Massarik, "Participation by Subordinates in the Managerial Decision-making Process," *Canadian Journal of Economics and Political Science,* 16 (August 1950).

Thompson, Claude E., *Personnel Management for Supervisors,* Englewood Cliffs, N. J., Prentice-Hall, Inc., 1948.

Thorp, Willard L., "The Changing Structure of Industry," *Recent Economic Changes in the United States,* New York: McGraw-Hill Book Company, 1929.

———, Walter F. Crowder, *et al.,* "The Structure of Industry," *Investigation of Concentration of Economic Power, Monograph No. 27,* United States Congress, Temporary

National Economic Committee, Washington: Government Printing office, 1941.

Tolman, W. H., *Social Engineering,* New York: McGraw-Hill Book Company, 1909.

Turner, Ralph H., "The Navy Disbursing Officer as a Bureaucrat," *American Sociological Review,* 12, No. 3 (1947).

United States Department of Labor, Division of Labor Standards, *The Foreman's Guide to Labor Relations,* Bulletin No. 66, Washington: Government Printing office, 1943.

Urwick, L., "Executive Decentralization with Functional Coordination," *Management Review,* 24 (December 1935).

———, "The Function of Administration, with Special Reference to the Work of Henri Fayol," Luther Gulick and L. Urwick, eds., *Papers on the Science of Administration,* New York: Institute of Public Administration, Columbia University, 1937.

Veblen, Thorstein, *Absentee Ownership and Business Enterprise in Recent Times,* New York: B. W. Huebsch, 1923.

———, *The Engineers of the Price System,* New York: The Viking Press, 1933.

———, *The Theory of Business Enterprise,* New York: Charles Scribner's Sons, 1936.

Warren, Roland L., "The Naval Reserve Officer: A Study in Assimilation," *American Sociological Review,* 11, No. 2 (1946).

Whyte, William F., "Organization and Motivation of Management," Solomon Barkin, *et al.* eds., *Industrial Productivity,* Champaign, Ill.: Industrial Relations Research Association, December 1951.

———, "Pity the Personnel Men," *Advanced Management* 9 (October-December 1944).

———, "Social Science and Industrial Relations: How Management Can Use the Human Relations Specialist," *Personnel,* 27, No. 4 (1951).

———, and Burleigh B. Gardner, "The Man in the Middle: Position and Problems of the Foreman," *Applied Anthropology,* 4 (Spring 1945).

Worthy, James C., "Organizational Structure and Employee Morale," *American Sociological Review,* 15 (April 1950).

Yoder, Dale, *Personnel Principles and Policies: Modern Manpower Management,* Englewood Cliffs, N. J.: Prentice-Hall, Inc., 1952.

CHAPTER 21. MANAGEMENT AS LEADERSHIP

Adams, Stuart, "Trends in Occupational Origins of Business Leaders," *American Sociological Review,* 19 (October 1954).

Axtelle, George E., "The Management of Men," *Journal of Educational Sociology,* 21 (April 1948).

Baker, John Calhoun, *Directors and Their Functions: A Preliminary Study,* Boston: Harvard University Graduate School of Business Administration, 1945.

Barnard, Chester C., "Comments on the Job of the Executive," *Harvard Business Review,* 18 (Spring 1940).

———, "The Nature of Leadership," S. D. Hoslett, ed., *Human Factors in Management,* Parksville, Mo.: Park College Press, 1946.

Beard, Miriam, *A History of the Businessman,* New York: The Macmillan Company, 1938.

Brown, C. C., "Toward a New Business Philosophy," *Saturday Review,* 36, No. 38 (1953).

Chamberlain, John, "The Businessman in Fiction," *Fortune,* 38 (November 1948).

Cherne, Leo, "The Writer and the Entrepreneur," *Saturday Review,* 35 (January 19, 1952).

Coffin, T. E., "A Three-Component Theory of Leadership," *Journal of Abnormal and Social Psychology,* 39 (1944).

Copeland, Melvin T., "The Job of an Executive," *Harvard Business Review,* 18 (Winter 1940).

Courtney, Douglas, F. Loyal Greer, and Joseph Masling, "Leadership Identification and Acceptance," Mimeograph, Institute for Research in Human Relations, Series 1952, Institute Report No. 1, February 1952.

Craig, D., and R. Charters, *Personnel Leadership in Industry,* New York: McGraw-Hill Book Company, 1925.

Dent, A. G. H., "The Era of Management," *Fortnightly,* 150 (September 1938).

Diamond, Sigmund, *The Reputation of the American Businessman,* Cambridge: Harvard University Press, 1955.

Dimock, Marshall E., *The Executive in Action,* New York: Harper and Brothers, 1945.

"Foremen by Popular Acclaim," *Business Week* (March 26, 1955).

Franklin, B. A., *The Industrial Executive,* New York: The Ronald Press Company, 1926.

French, J. R. P., Jr., "Retraining an Autocratic Leader," *Journal of Abnormal and Social Psychology,* 39 (1944).

Gambatese, Joseph M., "Training Method Tests Executive Judgement," *Nation's Business* 43, No. 6 (1955).

Gibb, C. A., "The Principles and Traits of Leadership," *Journal of Abnormal and Social Psychology,* 42 (1947).

Ginsberg, E., ed., *What Makes an Executive?* New York: Columbia University Press, 1955.

Hemphill, John K., "Group Factors in Leadership: I. Relations Between the Size of the Group and the Behavior of 'Superior Leaders,' " Mimeograph, n.d.

Hencke, Paul, "What Makes an Executive?" *Nation's Business,* 43, No. 6 (1955).

Holbrook, Stewart H., *The Age of the Moguls,* New York: Doubleday and Company, 1953.

Holden, Paul E., Launsbury S. Fish, and Hubert L. Smith, *Top-Management Organization and Control,* Stanford: Stanford University Press, 1941.

———, "Top-Management, Organization and Control," *Personnel Journal,* 20 (January 1942).

Janney, J. E., "Pick Your Manager: Let Him Manage," *Nation's Business,* 43, No. 6.

Jenkins, W. O., "A Review of Leadership Studies with Particular References to Military Problems," *Psychological Bulletin,* 44 (1947).

Juran, Joseph M., "Management Techniques for Stimulating Productivity," Solomon Barkin, *et al.,* eds., *Industrial Productivity,* Champaign, Ill.: Industrial Relations Research Association, 1951.

Kahn, R., "Leadership Patterns and Organizational Effectiveness," Mimeograph, Ann Arbor: Institute for Social Research, University of Michigan, January 1955.

———, and D. Katz, "Leadership Practices in Relation to Productivity and Morale," D. Cartwright and A. Zander, eds., *Group Dynamics: Research and Theory,* Evanston, Ill.: Row, Peterson, 1953.

Landes, David S., "French Business and the Business Man: A Social and Cultural Analysis," Edward M. Earle, ed., *Modern France,* Princeton: Princeton University Press, 1951.

Lehman, Harvey C., "The Age of Eminent Leaders: Then and Now," *American Journal of Sociology,* 52, No. 4 (1947).

Lewis, Ben W., "The Corporate Enterpreneur," *Quarterly Journal of Economics,* 51 (May 1937).

Lewisohn, Sam A., *Human Leadership in Industry: The Challenge of Tomorrow,* New York: Harper and Brothers, 1945.

Likert, R., "Findings of Research on Management and Leadership," *Proceedings,* Pacific Coast Gas Association, 43 (1953).

McGregor, Douglas, I. Knickerbocker, M. Haire, and A. Bavelas, "The Consultant Role and Organizational Leadership: Improving Human Relationships in Industry," *The Journal of Social Issues,* 4, No. 3 (1948).

McNair, M. P., and H. J. Lewis, eds., *Business and Modern Society,* Cambridge: Harvard University Press, 1938.

Maurer, Herrymon, "Boards of Directors," *Fortune,* 41, No. 5 (1950).

Metcalf, Henry, ed., *The Psychological Foundations of Management,* Chicago: A. W. Shaw Company, 1927.

Miller, William, "American Historians and the Business Elite," *Journal of Economic History,* 9 (November 1949).

———, "The Recruitment of the American Business Elite," *Quarterly Journal of Economics,* 64 (May 1950).

Mills, C. Wright, "The American Business Elite: A Collective Portrait," *The Tasks of Economic History,* Supplement 5 to *The Journal of Economic History,* (December 1945).

Moreno, J. L., and Edgar F. Borgatta, "An Experiment with Sociodrama in Industry," *Sociometry,* 14 (February 1951).

Newcomer, Mabel, *The Big Business Executive —The Factors That Made Him, 1900-1950,* New York: Columbia University Press, 1955.

Oates, James F., Jr., "Management Responsibility for Human Relations," Mimeograph,

Industrial Relations Association of Chicago, October 1951.

Pelz, Donald, "The Influence of the Supervisor within His Department as a Conditioner of the Way Supervisory Practices Affect Employee Attitudes," Ph. D. thesis, University of Michigan, 1951.

Redlich, Fritz L., *History of American Business Leaders,* Vol. 1, Ann Arbor: Edwards Brothers, 1940; Vol. 2, New York: Hafner Publishing Company, 1947, 1951.

Robinson, A., "Problem of Management and the Size of Firms," *Economic Journal,* 44 (June 1934).

Shannon, J. R., and M. Shaw, "Education of Business and Professional Leaders," *American Sociological Review,* 5 (1940).

Sheldon, Oliver, *The Philosophy of Management,* London: Sir Isaac Pitman and Sons, 1924.

Slichter, Summer H., "The Problems of Business Leadership in a Laboristic Economy," Marvin Bower, ed., *The Development of Executive Leadership,* Cambridge: Harvard University Press, 1949.

Stanbery, J. N., "Some Modern Aspects of Management Development," Mimeograph, Industrial Relations Association of Chicago, November 1954.

Stogdill, R. M., "Personal Factors Associated with Leadership: A Survey of the Literature," *Journal of Psychology,* 25 (1948).

Sward, Keith, *The Legend of Henry Ford,* New York: Rinehart and Company, 1948.

Tannenbaum, Robert, Verne Kallejian, and Irving R. Weschler, "Training Managers for Leadership," *Personnel,* (January 1954).

Villalon, Luis J. A., ed., *Management Men and Their Methods,* New York: Funk and Wagnalls Company, 1949.

Wald, Robert M., and Roy A. Doty, "The Top Executive—A Firsthand Profile," *Harvard Business Review,* 32 (July-August 1954).

Warner, W. Lloyd, and James C. Abegglen, *Big Business Leaders in America,* New York: Harper and Brothers, 1955.

Wecter, Dixon, *The Saga of American Society,* New York: Charles Scribner's Sons, 1937.

Whitehead, Thomas N., "The Engineer as a Servant of Society," *Journal of Engineering Education,* 28 (October 1937).

———, "Leadership within Industrial Organizations," *Harvard Business Review,* 14 (Winter 1936).

Worthy, James C., "A Working Philosophy of Personnel Management," Mimeograph, Industrial Relations Association of Chicago, June 11, 1951.

NAME INDEX

SUBJECT INDEX